TRI-AXIUM WRITINGS 2

TRI-AXIUM WRITINGS 2

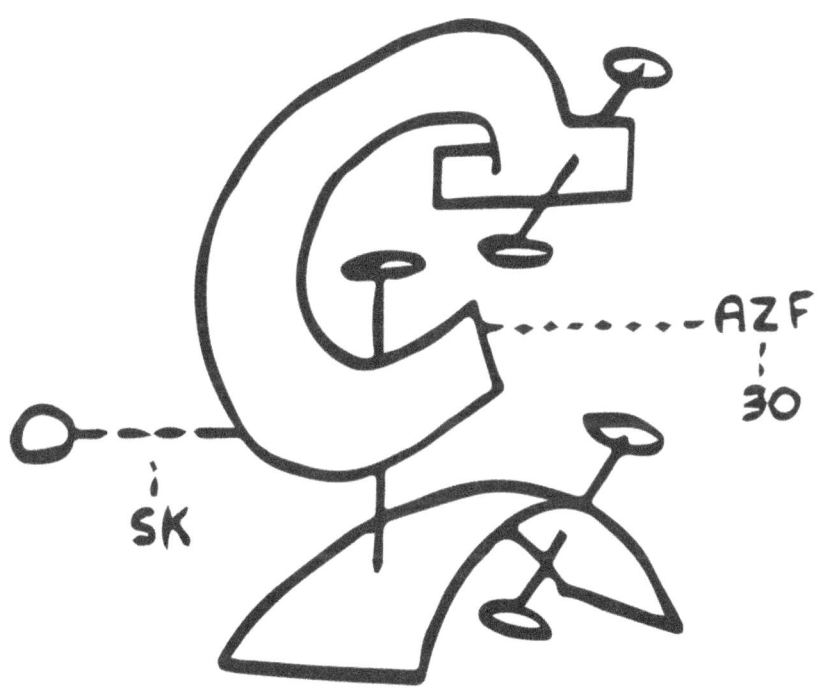

ANTHONY BRAXTON

TRI-AXIUM WRITINGS 2

1985 first edition: Synthesis Music

1985–2023 distributed by Frog Peak Music

2024 second edition: Frog Peak Music

Paperback ISBN 978-0-945996-25-5

Tri-Axium Writings 2

Contents

1	Preface & Acknowledgements (second edition)	
3	Introduction	
15	Glossary Integration	
		chapter prefix
I. Social Reality and Trans-Information		SR(TRS)
	A. Level One	
25	1. The Spectacle-Diversion Syndrome	SD(SY)
73	2. Affinity Dynamics	AF(D)
113	3. Aspect Essence (Perception Dynamics)	AE(PD)
145	B. Level Two	SR(TRS)II
189	C. Level Three: Questions & Answers	SR(TRS)III
II. Creative Music Outside of America		CMOA
	A. Level One	
207	1. Britain, Germany, Holland	CMOA (I)
243	2. France, Italy, Northern Europe, Japan	CMOA (II)
	B. Level Two (no Level Two)	
299	C. Level Three: Questions & Answers	CMOA (III)
III. Reality Aspect of Creative Music		R(AS) CM
317	A. Level One	R(AS) CM(I)
357	B. Level Two	R(AS) CM(II)
409	C. Level Three: Questions & Answers	R(AS) CM(III)
III. Music and Politics		MP
427	A. Level One	MP(I)
483	B. Level Two	MP(II)
529	C. Level Three: Questions & Answers	MP(III)
549	Glossary	

PREFACE & ACKNOWLEDGEMENTS

The *Tri-Axium Writings* were approached as the beginning of a re-philosophic system that could map out fresh options and choices for the friendly experiencer on the tri-plane. This is not a system of thought that tells the individual what to think or do, but rather a set of choices that can be interpreted by a friendly experiencer based on one's individual experiences and individual value systems. This system is not a forming religion, but rather an attempt to create a model that is trans-idiomatic with flex options to suit the needs of the individual in real time. The word here is "agency."

    I thank the creator of the universe that the Tri-Centric community has come into my life. What we have here is a movement of positive spirits who believe in the power of creativity and the wonder of radiant hope—and these artists are activists who are not simply waiting for public acknowledgment and/or faux celebrity status. The key word here is "action," with old-time serious groundwork and planning. The men and women of the Tri-Centric Foundation are foot soldiers for third millennial evolution and reconstruction—based on a love of composite humanity and world unification. I have no doubt that the good work of the Tri-Centric Foundation will inspire the creation of new artistic models all over the country and will continue the tradition of exposing our citizens to the challenge of composite creativity as a separate subject from marketplace focus and/or popular music—which I also love, but there's no lack of support for this community and we do not have to worry about its survival. Even so, let it be said that there is creativity all over: in America—from sea to shining sea—and in the world beyond. We have the people and the energy to evolve fresh visions to explore every focused discipline and strata.

    I want to thank the Tri-Centric Foundation for the profound help this organization has given me—both in initiating the re-publication of

Tri-Axium Writings, and for the effort to literally save my creative work from the last sixty years and some. Because of their dedication I can now hope to have my music and writings documented safely into the future so that anyone interested in my effort can assess the material in the classic sense of research and discovery. In thanking my colleagues I am referring to Taylor Ho Bynum, James Fei, Kyoko Kitamura, Carl Testa, Zach Rowden, Jean Cook, Jonathan Piper, Jeanette Vuocolo, Rachael Bernsen, Tyler Rai, Chris Jonas, Chris McIntyre, and Andrew Raffo Dewar.

I would also like to thank Frog Peak Music (a composers' collective) for the support they have given me since the first publication of the Tri-Axium Writings in 1985. A special thank you to Jody Diamond and Larry Polansky for the great courage and dedication they have shown in the nearly forty years since Frog Peak Music began.

For this new edition, I am especially grateful to John McGhee for copyediting and proofreading all three books, to Carl Testa for making new schematics, and to Jody Diamond for designing both the print and digital versions. Proofreaders for Book One included Scott Campbell, Andrew Dewar, Michael Heller, Forrest Larson, and Carl Testa.

There is a difference between talk and action. All of these people can be viewed as real champions of global values and free expression—they are all artists in their own right and deserve more support as we move forward through the vibrational challenges of the recent time period.

We seem to be coming to a new era of vibrational realignment and sub-specialization. There is now a struggle to redefine reality and fantasy from a two-dimensional perspective that might not be in our best interest. More than ever, we need the input of the artist community to balance the spectrum of possibilities in a given political moment. This is a challenge that must be defended. Together, we have the creativity and the talent to succeed in every vibrational space.

Anthony Braxton
Hamden, Connecticut
2021

INTRODUCTION

WRITINGS TWO IS THE SECOND BOOK IN A SET OF THREE on creative music and its related information continuum. Hopefully, this series of books will be viewed as a positive contribution to the reality of information surrounding creativity. More than ever before, there is a need for alternative viewpoints on this most important subject, and unless efforts are made to restore a more practical—and positive—basis for viewing creativity in this time period, serious repercussions will await us in the near future. The release of this book is the end result of seven years of struggling—and involved more than four complete rewrites (and more on given sections). Needless to say, I am extremely grateful to have completed this project, and I hope that the thrust of this work will be viewed as worth the effort. I believe the future will see more musicians become involved in writing about creative music, for the present reality of this subject—and especially creative music from the black aesthetic—has never been more in disarray. We have now entered what can only be called a very serious period in the progressional continuum of world creativity, and the challenge of redefinitions can no longer only be left to the so-called experts. I have written this book—and this series of books—as a response to the present state of things, with the hope that my viewpoint will inspire other efforts—this is what is needed. The writings which have helped motivate my interest in this area have all come from people who were (and are) involved in the dynamics of creativity, and I feel the special insight that creative people must have—by virtue of their involvement with creativity—can be beneficial to restoring a more correct and just viewpoint about this most important subject. I believe if more people were exposed to the writings of creative people, many of the present distortions surrounding creative music would not have materialized. To read the works of thinking musicians like Rex Stewart, Harry Partch, and Leo Smith is to gain a viewpoint from people whose lives are not separate from what they wrote about. The inspiration I have received from their work gave me the strength to complete this project, and hopefully this work will serve as a positive source to others.

I originally began this series of writings in response to the reality of information surrounding creative music in the early seventies—especially the misinformation that characterized creative music writings in monthly periodicals and newspapers. It seemed to me at the time that the level of accurate commentary had gone from bad to worse, and it also seemed as if the smearing of post-Ayler creativity was more than a series of unrelated coincidences, but instead a co-ordinated attack. My first efforts on this book took place in Paris in September 1973, as a means to challenge what I felt to be deliberate misinformation about black creativity and black creative dynamics, and the thrust of this first effort would take over a year before completion. For if my original efforts had been directed towards combating the manipulation of post-Ayler creativity, by the end of 1974 the act of writing and researching had totally changed my own perspective of the music as well as the reality of information that supported my understanding of music. For the most basic assumption that dictated my early attempts to respond to creative music commentary was the mistaken belief that western journalists had some fundamental understanding of black creativity—or even western creativity—but this assumption was seriously in error. Rather, I now believe that the reality of African and trans-African continuance is being undermined by interpretations that seek to destroy both the dynamic implications of its information nature and the particulars of its affinity dictates. As such, the whole of my first draft had nothing to do with the real reality of western commentary, because the actualness of this phenomenon is much greater than the focus on a given argument—or opinion.

It is important to understand that the reality of a given interpretation cannot be outside of the affinity nature it purports to comment on. As such, one cannot comment on the reality specifics of non-western focuses without making serious adjustments in the vibrational nature of one's use of language, as well as the particulars underlying how a given conceptual focus is viewed. In actual fact, many of the distortions that have come to permeate black music journalism are directly related to the use of western inquiry terms that have no relevance to the reality nature of black creativity, or not in the way presently understood. Nor have I meant to imply that only black creativity has suffered from the misuse of western definitions, because the whole of world creativity has been profoundly misdocumented in this same manner. The challenge of erecting a positive basis for understanding creative music must necessarily involve a complete examination of every area of creative music—regardless of form or style. We must move to seek out a more human understanding of this subject that is free of petty accusations or racist doctrine, and the time to do it is now—not later. The act of writing this book has helped me to see how deeply I disagree with the present reality of commentary about creativity—and its related information continuum. Because the dynamic misinformation that has been generated in music commentary is not separate from what has transpired in the composite quilt of our society; that is, the misinformation presently attempting to solidify our relationship with creative invention also affects our composite relationship with fundamental information (or as this period of time would have it, "alternative fundamental information")—and this is what worries me.

By 1976—and after two more drafts—the essence of the book began to form, and I have attempted in this series of works to develop another approach for writing about creative music. That being: an approach that attempts to vibrationally and systematically view the whole of earth creativity and its related information continuums as a basis to resolidify a transformational viewpoint about this subject. Yet by no means does this book accomplish the whole of this challenge, nor have I meant to imply that my understanding of the universe is such that I have the necessary insight for such a task—because this is not what I mean. Instead the realness of this challenge will involve every sector of humanity. For to really attempt understanding of the reality of creativity is to transcend the particulars of a given focus, and instead reinvestigate the dynamics of composite earth information.

As such, the thrust of these writings is as concerned about the vibrational and philosophical implications of a given information focus (interpretation) as the particulars of its related music. Because the reality of creativity is not limited to only how a given phenomenon works but also involves the meta-reality context from which that phenomenon takes its laws. This is what concerns me, and this is what my writing is directed towards examining.

I believe the thrust of the eighties and nineties will see many more individual efforts of this sort—involving attempts to redefine every area of information and information dynamics. Nothing less than this will do—because the composite realness of present-day information is profoundly distorted—and I do not view this distortion as the result of a grand accident, but instead the end product of deliberate policies and intentions. The spectrum of this misinformation seems to encompass every area of dynamic focus—our understanding of science, music, spiritualism and functionalism. No area has been untouched—and if we are to ever shape the future then we must first correct the present: that is, we must first correct the reality of information that influences how we have come to either approach living, or approach understanding information about living. Certainly I have not meant to imply my writings will clarify all of these dynamic questions—because to imply such would be nonsense. But I do feel that the challenge of attempting to change a given state begins with the first step, and I also feel that the success of a given change indirectly relates to how many people are involved. In this series of books I have tried to the best of my ability to contribute a viewpoint that could be of relevance towards re-examining the realness of creativity. The dynamic implications of this book should hopefully stimulate the commentary scan of creative music if nothing else. This is my hope anyway. I have also deliberately not included scholastic-type footnotes in this series of books because (1) the thrust of this book is only an affirmation of what I have been learning and feeling—which is to say a snapshot of what I have been thinking from a period of September 1973 to March 1980, and (2) the thrust of this book is also conceived with respect to what I believe—which is to say I offer nothing in this book as definitively "true" (because for too long we have been deluged by so-called experts with interpretations that are presented as fact—but aren't—and this misuse of interpretation has moved to damage the whole of this time period). I have also tried in this series of books to refrain from attacking any individuals—even when I felt a given attack would clarify the nature of a particular viewpoint—because there can be no room for petty accusations if the basic focus of this book is concerned about what is really true (not to mention, the present state of things is not about any one or two given individuals).

Finally, it is important to state that none of the viewpoints written in this book are viewed as complete in any real sense. Instead I have made the decision to release this material because the completion of the entire project is dependent on what I am able to totally realize in my life—and hopefully I will have another ten, twenty, or thirty years (and some) on this planet to continue my learning, and work. After rewriting these sections for seven years, I felt this material was good enough to publish and, moreover, holding it any longer actually made no sense. But it is important to emphasize that all of these concepts are only one aspect of a much greater viewpoint—and this is really what is important. I believe the reality of commentary about creativity should give insight on more than just the surface specifics of the music but also its conceptual and philosophical implications—and this is what I have attempted in this series of writings. There are so many aspects of creative music that have been ignored in the last three hundred years that something must be done to review our present reality and vibrational position with composite information and composite information dynamics. Like most musicians, I have always thought the job of attempting to secure cultural awareness about creativity was the responsibility of so-called music journalism—and to some extent the music journalist has functioned as a positive generator for real understanding. But for the most part few, if any, of these functioning journalists have worked in the area of creative music or black creativity. As such, the thrust of journalism in the past fifty years has developed much dynamic information about western art music but very little on black creativity—or improvised music. I believe the present reality of black creativity is directly related to what information has not been developed—as opposed to what has—and this is indeed a tragedy for anyone concerned about world creativity. Rather than wait for a change of attitude by jazz journalists, I have instead made the decision to become involved in writing—and now I understand that this decision should have been made fifteen years ago. We can no longer wait for black music journalism to rise to the challenge of what it implies nor can we afford to wait on the so-called liberal white documentalists to straighten out the present state of things—for that matter, we can no longer hope for the emergence of black writers who are not afraid to speak out. We can no longer wait, because time is running out. The challenge is to solidify the correct and positive definitions that are needed now—in this time period. At present, the reality of creative music commentary has very little to do with supplying transformational viewpoints—let alone transformational solutions. As such—if you want something done—you must do it yourself. I offer this book—and this series of books—as an attempt to begin re-examining the composite reality of creative music. These writings are offered as only the beginning of what I hope will be a massive body of alternative literature on creative music.

Construction

Each of the books in this series of writings is constructed so as to insure maximum idea interchange. This has been done in accordance with my belief that given viewpoints must now be examined not only on more than one level or focus—but on as many levels as possible. Moreover, the thrust of this effort is conceived as a composite attempt to examine the whole of earth creativity—and as such, the reality of a given definition must necessarily "be presented in its broadest terms," because I am not concerned with only some aspect of what seems to be true—I am interested in what seems to be really true. Since the complexity of creative music commentary involves so many different areas of inquiry, I believe the challenge of transformational journalism is to find creative ways to interpret information. It is because of this belief that I have solidified this approach to my writings. For the great thrust of creative music writings in this time period is in extremely uncreative attempts at journalism, and this is especially interesting when one considers the position jazz critics have put themselves in—that being attempting to evaluate the worth of other people's creativity. As such, the basic construction of these books contains several approaches for both reading and interconnecting concepts. I have tried to construct a systematic approach that gives the greatest focus reference possible, because the seriousness of creativity demands something more than a one-dimensional viewpoint.

The dictates of these books are constructed so that the reader must read through the material in at least six different ways, and the interconnections of concepts are set up so as to give maximum diversity. In other words, the reader will be able to view a given concept from as many different standpoints as possible. The thrust of these writings is not about any one concept but instead involves the reality of cross-information, as a means to solidify the broadest possible inquiry terms. It is my hope that an approach of this nature might prove useful for establishing a more realistic look at creative music, for much of the literature I have seen on this subject seems either too simplistic or too academic. Yet, by the same token, I have not solidified this approach as a joke, nor have I included anything in these books which was not necessary. I have tried, in this effort, to view a given concept to the farthest point of my ability with the hope that either real understanding can come from an approach of this type, or that real intellectual stimulation about world creativity can be developed. I view either objective as positive.

The construction of this book is as follows:

Within each principal section or chapter (which is designated by the use of capital letters) there are what I call levels of inquiry—or simply levels. The whole of these series of writings is constructed around the dynamics of this approach. There are three inquiry sections that can be used in a given chapter, and every idea is expressed throughout each aspect of what this division means. The explanation of each level designation is as follows:

1. Level One has to do with focusing on some particular aspect of its principal chapter, and this region of inquiry can number from one to four approaches (depending on how many "particulars" are focused on in a given section). Each of these areas of focus is separated into different colors for convenience.

The code is as follows:
> brown for approach one;
> green for approach two;
> orange for approach three;
> purple for approach four.

2. Level Two investigation is a summary of the given approaches focused on in Level One. In other words, this area of inquiry can only be utilized if there are two or more approaches examined in Level One. The thrust of a given focus in this context is geared towards the composite context of what a given viewpoint might mean in a broader context (or with respect to the whole of this book and this series of books). The color of this section is blue.

3. Level Three investigation involves the use of questions and answers in a one-dimensional context as a means to include shorter viewpoints that can be integrated throughout the whole of this book. This is necessary because the basic structure of the book is systematic to the degree that "grounded definitions" can provide a healthy pivotal factor for clarification. By including this section, the range of a given focus is all-encompassing—that is, the dynamics of this total approach run from open interpretation possibilities (i.e., understanding something in your own way—with respect to one's own affinity dynamics) to closed exact definitions. The color for this section is red.

I have tried to accent many of the important concepts in bold type as a means for the reader to have easy referral to a given viewpoint more readily.

Thus, to really utilize this book in the way I have intended, the reader is expected to read this book:

(1) completely from the beginning to the end;

(2) with respect to the arguments of only one level region at a time (i.e., read only Level One sections in each chapter, later read only Level Two chapters, etc.);

(3) read the whole book interconnected with the other books in this series through what I call the integration code—which is in every section of every focus;

(4) read only the isolated concepts that have been marked by bold type;

(5) study the isolated terminology chart—or glossary of terms (at the back of the book)—to understand the systemic interconnection (as well as application) of these concepts throughout the total integration complex of all three books, as a means to better understand both my extended viewpoint as well as the logic dynamics of its total application; and

(6) the reader is asked to translate my terminology—from the glossary and throughout the whole book—as a means to view each focus in one's own terms: in other words, I am saying, "this is my viewpoint in this context, and these are my terms, but what do you think?"—with respect to your own personal viewpoint and/or perception dynamics (in the context of my terminology—as well as your own terminology) about this same information. Only after all of the approaches have been tried can the reader have some idea as to what I am trying to communicate—yet on this comment it is important to explain my intentions. I have not meant to imply that my understanding of phenomena is such that one must necessarily reach for my so-called level, because to believe this has nothing to do with reality. Instead, I have constructed these writings in this manner because the realness of what I am really trying to communicate is not about "only one point of view"—or one level of transference. I believe the traditional use of so-called deductive logic has been greatly violated in this time period. What we now need is the use of every kind of information transference affinity position—whether or not it corresponds to what is now called logic. It is for this reason that *Tri-Axium Writings* is constructed in the manner you have before you. I have also included a code for all of the signs and symbols used in this book—and series of books.

CODE

1. A straight line under a paragraph means that the focus of that particular subject has been completed; after which the next paragraph will move to another area of relevant focus.

2. A dotted line under a paragraph means that the next paragraph is an insert that is separate from the basic flow of what is being written on. As such, the end of the insert is also marked with a dotted line—and

the reader is back on the same subject material. It is possible to simply skip the material that is presented between the dotted line sections and come back to it later.

3. All of the concepts are abbreviated as a means to trace an information line in the integration charts.

The bracketed abbreviations are:

(R) = the reality of
(C) = the concept of
(IN)DE = inquiry degree
(CT) = the criterion of
(P) = point of idea completion for a given interpretation (or schematic)
(PFC) = point for future calibration
(PO) = point of
(L) = level
(P-AT) = point of activation (a physical universe term to point out where a given idea or the effects of a given idea—can take shape or become real)
(D) = the dynamics of = when viewed in the context of
 = can be viewed
 = as it involves
 = viewed with respect to
 = particulars of a given
 = (dotted line) amplifies some aspect of the main concept it is connected to
 = is connected to on the physical universe level
(P-IN) = its position in
(D-T) = determines the _____ of its _____

The name of this system of thought is "TRI-AXIUM," which is my term for gathering axiom tenets from the past and present—to get to the future. The reality of this inquiry is perceived and offered as a bridge for re-information designation (for possible transformational observation—tenets—and/or use). For the most part, this series of writings is based on present-time affinity postulation (or affinity observation). But the whole of the completed effort—in the next ten, twenty years—or whatever time I have to work on this project—will deal with:

1. Affinity postulation:
(a) establishing basis (through physical universe observation—and research);
(b) challenging present time definitions;
(c) establishing affinity redesignation systems (that also allow for individual interpretation).

2. Axiom correlation:
(a) researching world culture information tenets for resolidification;
(b) re-establishing transformational functionalism particulars;
(c) establishing a platform for alternative investigation.

3. Reality imposition:
(a) isolating particulars with respect for respiritual participation;
(b) resecuring the significance of ritualism and symbolic participation;
(c) re-investigating spiritual dynamics as a basis to establish transformational spiritualism.

To use the integration schematics one must first become familiar with the abbreviation of terms. The basic idea of this system is that all of the concepts in this book—and this series of books—must be viewed in more than one context. The reality of a given schematic is not isolated to only what it poses for a given focus; rather, I have designed this approach as a means to keep an extended information platform—which is to say each given schematic should be viewed as axiom tenets. To read a given schematic the reader must first view it in terms of its basic designation—which has an arrow to denote its starting point. In actual fact the term (or abbreviation) with the arrow pointing to it is the subject of the schematic. In the figure below this paragraph the subject then is "vibrational dynamics" (and since there is also an [R] in brackets, the subject is "the reality of vibrational dynamics" as this concept relates

13

to the concept of "postulation"). Whenever there is no prefix or bracket before a given abbreviation it means to view the terms as a concept—or as the concept (in this case) of "postulation."

This is then the schematic:

(R)VT. DY.------ POST.

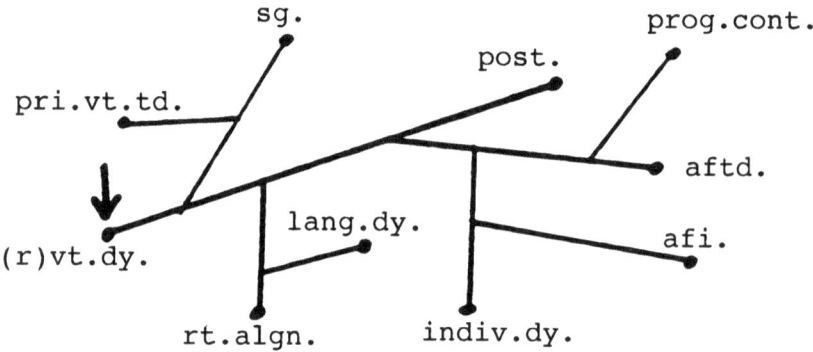

To read (or see) this schematic in words would go like this:

The reality of vibrational dynamics as this term relates to the concept of "postulation"—in three different contexts, those being: in the context of (1) SG, source initiation (involving PRI-VT-TD, primary vibrational tendencies); or in the context of (2) RT-ALGN, reality alignment (involving LANG-DY, language dynamics); or in the context of (3) AFTD, affinity tendencies (involving INDIV-DY, individual dynamics as related to AFI, affinity insight—or involving PROG-CONT, progressional continuance).

The reader is expected to probe the dynamics of this axiom as a means to better understand these terms (i.e., what is being posed in a given information complex), as well as what all of this information means when calibrated into a composite philosophy (my philosophy at first, after which the reader is expected to view this same material—and terms—[with substitutions when needed] for his or her own philosophy).

All of the various symbols that are attached to particular schematics can be found in this CODE section.

GLOSSARY INTEGRATION
See the Glossary at the back of the book for definitions of terms.

A-PR	all-purpose
ACC-DY	accelerated dynamics
ACC-FT	accelerated functionalism
ACT	activism
ACT-T	actual terms
ACT-TR	actual transformation
AF-COMP	affinity compression
AF-CON	affinity convergence
AF-NT	affinity nature
AF-POST	affinity postulation
AFI	affinity insight
AFI(1)	affinity insight—first degree
AFI(2)	affinity insight—second degree
AFL	affinity alignment
AFL-DT	affinity dictates
AFL-DY	affinity dynamics
AFN	affinity negation
AFTD	affinity tendencies
AFTF	affinity transfer
AGT	agreement
ALT-ACT	alternative activism
ALT-C-PG	alternative composite progressionalism
ALT-D	alternative definitions
ALT-F	alternative functionalism
APL-DT	application dictates
APP-RDEF	applied redefinitions
ASP-ES	aspect essence
ATT	attitude
ATTC	attachment
ATTN	attraction

BIA	bi-aitional (or bi-aitionalism)
BSCF	basic science (or basic scientific functionalism)
C-ACT	composite activism
C-AF-ALGN	composite affinity alignment
C-CONT	composite continuance
C-CULT-AT	composite culture attitude
C-FO-ACT	composite focused activism
C-HM	composite humanity
C-INFO	composite information
C-RH	composite research
CN-INFO	controlled information
COLC-FR-WC	collected forces of western culture
COS-AGN	cosmic assignment
COS-D	cosmic dictates
COS-P	cosmic particulars
CR-INFO-DY	circular information dynamics
CRT	criticism
CRTF-D	cross-transfer definitions
CRTF-PROG	cross-transfer progressionalism
CUL-TF-S	cultural transfer shift(s)
CULT-AF-BS	culture affinity basis
CULT-INFO-B	culture information basis
CULT-INFO-DY	culture information dynamics
CULT-INFO-F	culture information focus
CULT-O	culture order
CULT-SOLD	culture solidification
DE-SPTL	despiritualization (or despiritualism)
DEC	decentralization
DEF	definition
DIS-C-CT	disintegration of a culture's center
DOC	documentation
DYM-F	dynamic functionalism

DYM-SEP	dynamic separation
DYM-SPT	dynamic spiritualism
ECO-DYM	economic dynamics
EXB-H-OR	establishing high order
EXP-CONT	expansion condition (the concept of)
EXP-CONT(1)	expansion condition (composite focus)
EXP-CONT(2)	expansion condition (isolated focus)
EXP-DT	expansion dictates
EXP-DYM	expansion dynamics
EXP-INFO-B	expansion information basis
EXPM	expansionism
EXT-DYM	extended dynamics
EXT-FT	extended functionalism
EXTN	existentialism
EXTN-D	existential definition
EXTN-OB	existential observation
EXTS	extension (or nature of extension)
F	form
FUND-DYN	fundamental dynamics
FUND-P	fundamental particulars
GRAD	gradualism
HI-P	high purpose
IF-SPT	infra-spirituality
IF-ST-DY	infra-structure dynamics
IMPOV	improvisation (the concept of)
INDIV-DY	individual dynamics
INDIV-DY-RT	individual dynamic reality
INDIV-TD (or INDIV-DY-TD)	individual tendencies (the reality of or concept of)

INFO-AF-B	information affinity basis
INFO-ALGN	information alignment
INFO-COMP	information compression
INFO-CON	information convergence
INFO-DE(B)	information degrees (or information degree basis)
INFO-DOC	information documentation
INFO-DS	information dissemination
INFO-F	information focus
INFO-F-D	information focus distortion
INFO-FM (or FR)	information forum
INFO-INTG	information integration
INFO-INTR	information interpretation
INFO-OR	information order
INFO-PROJ	information projection
INFO-RT	information reality
INFO-SOLD	information solidification
INFO-TRNS	information transference
INT	intention (the reality of)
INTL	intellectualism
INTR	interpretation
INVT-DT	investigation dictates
IST-ACT	isolated activism
IST-F	isolated focus
IST-F-AT	isolated focus activism
IST-F-DT	isolated focus dictates
IST-PT	isolated particulars
IST-S-ALGN	isolated systematic alignment
JR-DYM	journalism dynamics
LANG	language
LANG-DY	language dynamics
LG-DISA	logical dissolution
LG-DY	logical dynamics

LG-EXT	logical extension
LK-IMP	linkage implications
MD-DY	media dynamics
MDT-DY	motivation dynamics
MN-DI	mono-dimensional
MPT	manipulation (the reality of)
MT-DEVF	multiple diversification
MT-DI	multi-dimensional (or ISM)
MT-IF-DB	multi-informational degree basis
MT-IMP	multi-implications
MT-INFO	multi-information
MT-INTR	multiple interpretation
MT-TFS-AT	multi-transfer shift activity
MTA-IMP	meta-implications
MTA-RT	meta-reality
MTA-RT-SIGN	meta-reality significance
MTH	methodology
OBS	observation (or reality of)
OP-SPD	option spread
P-FC	particular focus
P-PROG	particular progressionalism
PART	participation
PER-DY	perception dynamics
PER-PHY-U-FUND	perceived physical universe fundamental
PER-TR	perceived transformation
PER-TRS	perceived transition
PER-VT-U-FUND	perceived vibrational universe fundamental
PHY-U-C	physical universe context
PHY-U-FUND	physical universe fundamental
PHY-U-P	physical universe particular
POL-CON	political consciousness

POL-DYM	political dynamics
POL-OR	political order
POL-P	political policies (or execution of)
POL-SIGN	political significance
POL-ST	political state
POST	postulation
PR-INT	primary intention
PRI-AF-TO	primary affinity tendencies
PRI-INFO	principle information
PRI-VT-TD	principle vibrational tendencies
PROG-CONT	progressional continuance
PROG-EXT-FT	progressional extended functionalism
PROG-SIGN	progressional significance
PROG-TF-C	progressional transfer cycles
PROJ	projection
PROJ-CONT	projectional continuance
PROJ-DY	projectional dynamics
RC	race
RE-CONT	recontinuance
RE-DIF	redefinitions
RE-DOC	redocumentation
RE-ST	restructuralism
REL-APC	relevant application
REL-TECH	relevant technology
RES-RT	responsibility ratio
RET-AF-TD	retrograde affinity tendencies
RIT-DY	ritual dynamics
ROTP	responsibility of the position (the concept of)
RT-ALGN	reality alignment
RT-DY	reality dynamics
RT-IMP	reality implications
RT-INT-TR	reality initiative traits

RT-OP	reality options
RTD-PRD	related procedure
S-PROJ	source projection
S-ST	source shift (progressionalism) manipulation
SCI-DYM	scientific dynamics
SF-RZ	self-realization
SI	source initiation
SOC-PR	social programs
SOC-RT	social reality
SOC-RT-DEVF	social reality diversification
SOC-RT-DT	social reality dictates
SOC-RT-DY	social reality dynamics
SOC-RT-INT	social reality interpretation
SOC-RT-P	social reality particular(s)
SPT-AW	spiritual awareness
SPT-DY	spiritual dynamics
SPT-GH	spiritual growth
SPT-UNF	spiritual unification
SPTC-D	spectacle diversion
STF	source transfer
STY	style (or the concept of)
T-C-IMP	time continuum implications
T-L	time lag
T-P	time presence
T-SC	theoretical science
TECH-DY	technological (or technology) dynamics
TF-SH	transfer shift(s)
TH-AF-ALGN	thrust affinity alignment
TH-CONT	thrust continuance
TH-CONT-DY	thrust continuance dynamics
TM	terminology—or terms of a definition

TR	transformation
TR-DEF	trans-definition
TR-INFO	trans-information
TRS	transition
UNF-PI	unification (positively intended)/world unification
UPB	underlying philosophical basis
UTZ	utilization
V-SY	value system
VT-AF/ATT	vibrational affinity and/or attitude
VT-ATT	vibrational attitude
VT-DY	vibrational dynamics
VT-IMP	vibrational implications
VT-PLT	vibrational platform
VT-POST	vibrational postulation
VT-S	vibrational science
VT-TD	vibrational tendencies
VT-U-PT	vibrational universe particulars
WO-CH	world change
WO-EXP-PRI	world expansion principle
WO-MTH	world methodology
WO-UNF	world unification

SOCIAL REALITY AND TRANS-INFORMATION

(Level One) THE SPECTACLE-DIVERSION SYNDROME

The challenge of solidifying a transformational understanding of world creativity implies that some attempt must first be made to provide a more realistic context for information examination—regardless of focus. Because creativity is not limited to only the reality particulars of a given encounter or person, but is instead a subject connected to the composite spread of information dynamics. The realness of creativity can thus be viewed as "postulation in accordance to the dynamics of vibrational dictates as well as physical universe specifics." In other words, the physical universe particulars of a given postulation are necessarily connected to the life of that postulation—and the thrust of this chapter is concerned with understanding what that relationship is—in both physical universe and vibrational terms (with respect for creativity and the creative person). The importance of establishing a composite approach about this most relevant subject can better be understood if we take into account the present "state of things"—because many of us have come to view creativity only with respect to the specifics of a given focus. We have progressively come to perceive this subject as separate from the composite realness of earth life, and in doing so, have moved further away from solidifying a unified basis for re-functionalism. But creativity is not only about how one acquires a given technique for music or painting—nor is this subject limited to only one level of "experiencing." Instead, the dynamic realness of creativity is related to the composite fabric of existence—whether we are commenting on the chemical or vibrational universe, or the physical and spiritual universe. In other words, creativity, in its most real context, moves to give insight as to the "state of things" (and in functional terms moves to give insight into "how to approach living").

Before the possibility of establishing a transformational viewpoint on creativity can be brought about, we must first understand what has transpired to bring us into this time period. This is so because the present "reality of events" did not simply spring from nowhere but was instead a natural by-product related to even greater considerations (having to do with the multi-implications of earth dynamic change). In other words, the relationship western culture has solidified with creativity in this time cycle has not only to do with creativity as such, but also comments on the total reality fabric of its progressionalism. Thus, if we are to view the realness of creativity as a positive tool for world change, then it is important that some effort is made to view this subject with respect to as many contexts as possible—and this is especially true if we desire some understanding of what has happened to creativity in the west (because western culture has already entered into what promises to be an important change cycle). The seriousness of even the next twenty years demands that some effort is put forth to examine what has happened to bring us into this time period. The reality implications of creativity in this context must be viewed as necessarily intertwined with the composite culture, including social reality—regardless of sector. Because the events shaping reality dynamics for the greater culture are not separate from the events which influence cultural vibrational dynamics—including how given focuses of creativity are perceived. Creativity is directly related to the social reality particulars of its basis.

The basic focus of this section is concerned with the dynamic reality position of western culture—and in particular America—as a means to understand what factors have contributed to shaping the present "state of things" we now live in—and how. A focus of this type could possibly be useful in helping to bring about some understanding of composite creativity in the west. At the heart of this inquiry is my belief that western culture's present relationship to creativity has necessitated the implementation of certain decisions—concerning the regulation of its information lines—as a means to secure a pre-conceived vibrational state. In other words, the collective manipulation of western culture's information dynamics involving both the necessary suppression and distortion of creativity and/or composite information—has not come about by accident, but is related to the composite nature of the route western culture has taken. Thus, if we are to view the present reality position of America as a means to begin understanding the progressional implications of alternative functionalism, then we cannot afford to limit the scope of our investigation to only one area of information focus (or relevant focus). Because creativity cannot be isolated from social reality and/or social dynamics.

My point is this: it is possible to view the vibrational path American culture has taken in the past two hundred years as a means to understand the present vibrationaltory state of creativity in this time zone. For the collective decisions which have shaped western continuance in the past are not very different from those factors that dictate information and decision-making in this time period. The fact is, it is possible to view the early solidification of American culture with respect to both the vibrational and actual positions that were taken in that time period as well as the consequences of what those decisions pose for the present. This is not to imply that everything about America's path is negative—because it isn't, nor by singling out America have I meant to imply that somehow the nature of progressionalism in this one country is different from the rest of the planet—because it isn't. Rather, I have chosen to focus on American "culture" because it is my place of birth and also because it is directly related to the particulars of composite western social reality (which is to say, because of its present political and economic position, America has long had a dynamic influence on composite western continuance—regardless of whether one is referring to Europe, Australia, or Canada). Moreover, the progressional dynamics of American "culture" in this cycle have moved to permeate the composite identity imprint of all western culture—which is to say, a given information-affinity position solidified in America will, in many cases, eventually be manifested throughout the whole of western culture. As such, to examine the vibrational particulars of American "culture," as a means to view the greater arena of world culture, can be a useful approach if approached carefully (although it is also clear that no single affinity position in itself characterizes the composite reality platform of world culture) because America's present relationship with creativity does signal more than just an isolated phenomenon when viewed on a composite level. It is important that some attempts are made to begin understanding what has and is happening to the greater reality implications of vibrational alignment—and what this phenomenon poses to living (especially if the accelerated momentum of the last fifty years is taken into account). Never before has information dynamics been subjected to the rate of exchange we now take for granted in this time period. What is new today will be viewed as antique in five to ten years even—which is to say, contemporary living is constantly being subjected to more factors than most of us are aware of (and more factors than anyone can keep up with). Add to this dynamic acceleration the nature of present-day affinity manipulation and information control, and one can begin understanding the complexities underlying life in the twentieth century. If creativity is to serve as a positive tool for functional and vibrational change, then it is important that the physical universe and social reality implications of this subject are understood and dealt with. This is not to say that the reality position of composite creativity in the west is necessarily in danger, nor have I meant to imply that nothing of value has taken place in the west either, because in fact much of value has solidified in this and every time zone. My point, however, is that the reality implications of creativity in the west, and in particular, for this section—America—can be viewed as related to particular decisions and attitudes that give insight into the total progressional implications of recent history. The challenge of the next ten to twenty years will most certainly involve whether or not we are able to understand what has happened to solidify our present vibrational and reality life position. The seriousness of this understanding will not be separate from what vibrational alignments will dictate the greater "culture's" affinity position with future creative and dynamic information postulations—and this is true whether we are focusing on the realness of music or science interpretation, medicine or alternative functionalism in general. The past will not simply go away—nor should we really want this anyway—because it is part of us. Instead, we must move to use what is "most" about the past as a means to gain the insight to not repeat the same mistakes over and over again. This is not to write that everything in the past is a mistake, nor have I meant to paint a grim picture of western and/or American reality. But the present reality position of the west in this time zone cannot simply be ignored. The fact is "there seems to be something strange happening"—and it will not simply go away. Certainly the realness of this something transcends any one subject or focus, but my point is that it can be sensed in many different areas—including creativity (which is supposed to be the primary focus of this book). To really view the reality dynamics of creativity in this time zone is to be made even more aware that "something is not quite right," which is to say, to be concerned about the greater implications of creativity is to be forced to examine the greater reality implications of this most important subject. While I have no illusions that my one viewpoint in itself can change anything, it is also clear that the vibrational solidification of alternative viewpoints will not simply materialize from nowhere. Instead, the realness of world change will come together slowly from the thoughts of many people. My point is that the present reality position of information and creative dynamics is important enough to be examined on as many levels as possible. There is a need to view creativity in a more extended (and real) context, if we are to solidify positive transformational functionalism in the next time or vibrational cycle. The question then is, "what has determined the reality of our (American culture) position with creativity" and "what role has creativity played with respect to progressional continuity (and what role should it play)." It is important that these questions are dealt with, for the reality position of creativity involves how we as a people actually live with vibrational dynamics and/or information (and information dynamics). The weight of these questions can move to clarify the significance of both past and present initiations—because, as I have stated before, the reality implication of our present alignment with creativity has remained consistent with the whole of progressionalism—and this can clearly be understood by viewing composite American history.

SD(SY)-8

CULT.INFO.F. ------AF.DY.

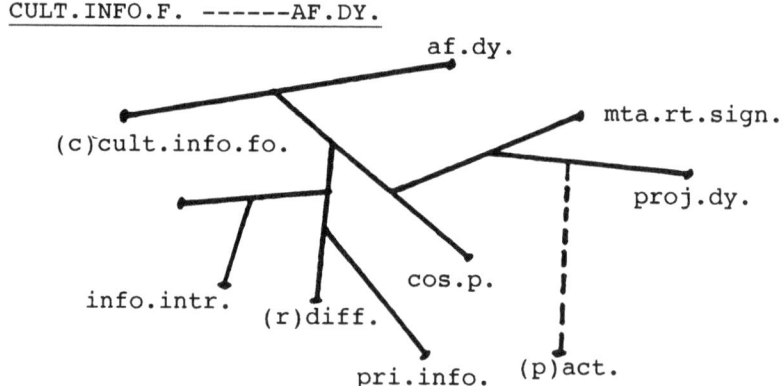

(R)DIFF.------AFL.

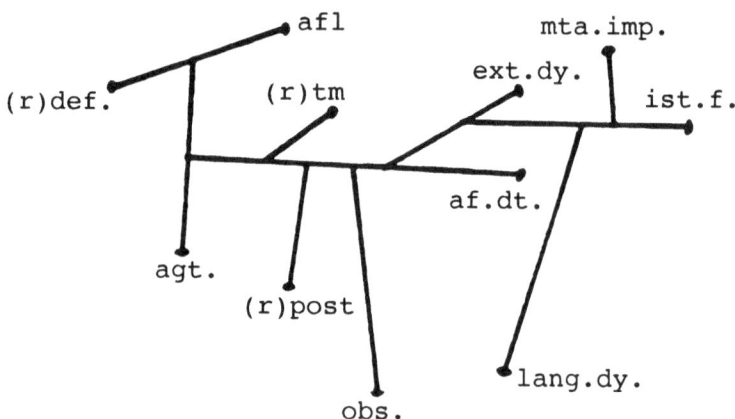

America's relationship with creativity in this time period is related to the composite vibrational state of its reality identity as a whole—which is to say, the peculiar relationship that creativity now has in America is not separate from the general peculiarities of vibrational life in American culture—and this is important to understand. This is not to say that creativity in itself is responsible for the "present state of things" nor can any one factor account for the composite solidification of the "present reality focus" of any one region or country, but the present affinity alignment of creativity and information dynamics in American society does in fact mean something if one wants to view the reality imprint of present-day

American "culture." It is also important to understand that the nature of America's relationship with creativity is not separate from the overall vibrational lining of its "life participation"—which is to say, the reality position of creativity in this context is related to the overall vibrational arena that people live and function in (as such, to comment on the vibrational lining of a given space is not only isolated commentary about theory but also matters that pertain to actual "living"). There are several things about America's relationship with creativity that are directly connected with the overall vibrational position of composite America—having to do with vibrational attitude and information scan—that sheds insight into the very nature underlying how "things are perceived" in general. More important, the realness of the peculiar position creativity has in American culture has also produced very real consequences—having to do with what "forces" are redirected back into the composite lining of the general culture. In other words, the peculiar relationship creativity has in America has produced a peculiar response that is manifested throughout the entire "culture." The dynamic implications of this response move to shed light on the progressional nature of post-existential America as we move into the eighties. It is important that some attempt is made to understand what this difference means.

The nature of America's relationship with creativity can better be understood by examining the composite imprint of its path—which in this context is American history. For the peculiar relationship I have written of has to do with a progressional attitude that dictates what areas of information focus are "made real" for cultural dissemination. I write of America in this section because the relatively short history of this country can make it easy to see what has really happened in the last two hundred years. For the solidification of America in its most positive context seemed to imply the solidification of "new" information continuums—having to do with the information brought from Europe, as well as the information of the American Indians, the various divisions of Europeans, and later the coming (or taking) of black and Asian people. The realness of all of these different people—with their collective experiences—seemed to forecast another level of information dynamics, and in fact, this resolidification did represent a new beginning. But to only lightly view American history is to see the suppression of composite information dynamics, and in its place the elevation of western information and affinity dynamics as an exclusive thrust or continuum. This is true for the realness of western information and this is also true for what happened with western creativity (as an extended alternative projection of its related affinity nature). This is not to ignore the source-transfer implications of progressionalism, for surely the routes of all information in American culture intersected at many points, on many different levels; rather, the state of composite interpretation in America has never involved a cross-section of multi-cultural participation, but instead had only to do with America's white community (which in itself is not new, for certainly the political and economic factors which control a country also control its information dynamics)—but what does all of this mean with respect to progressionalism?

The progressional disenfranchisement of world creativity and composite affinity dynamics is directly related to the present physical universe situation we now find ourselves in during this time zone. This is true whether we are focusing on the dynamic implications of alternative creativity, or composite alternative functionalism. Moreover, if the implications of creativity are really understood—that being, creativity as a main factor related to the establishment and securing of its culture's vibrational state—then the seriousness of what this distance implies cannot continue to be ignored if we desire real positive change. In short, any attempt to deal with creativity would also imply that the sociological physical universe decisions responsible for creating the present vibrational "state of things" be understood. Because by isolating and suppressing the realness of alternative composite creativity—and multi-information—America has put herself on a particular course that is not conducive to positive transformation—either with respect to its whole culture, or with respect to its particular specifics (i.e., individuals).

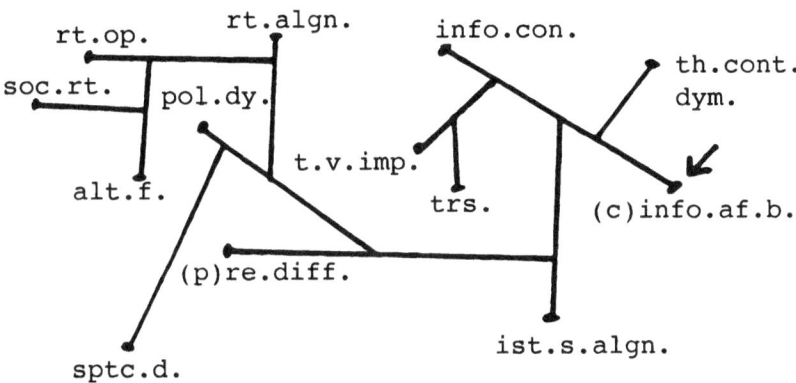

The reality and vibrational implications of American progressionalism in the past two hundred years cannot be viewed in narrow terms, for the dynamics of this subject defy any one context. One thing is clear: the present "reality of events" does indeed tell us something about the affinity nature of "what factors didn't take place" in America's historical solidification. In other words, the historical realness of early progressionalism does indeed give insight into the real intentions that would solidify the vibrational lining of American "reality"—and today those intentions have yet to be really dealt with (or changed—except on the surface). In actual terms, dealing with what has transpired in American history as to the collective mistreatment of the American Indian, and the dynamic utilization of slavery, has produced a profound vibrational karma for American society even though it might not appear to be so on the surface. This is not to say that only one or two factors are historically responsible for our present relationship with affinity dynamics, but when added to the long list of unresolved "participations," the seriousness of what these events compositely signify are most certainly not diminished. Certainly I have not meant to single out America as necessarily different from any of the other sectors of this planet—either in this time zone or any other, because history does not seem to show any time periods or focuses that are "godly or without shame"—but this information still does not help change the progressional implications of western culture's route (because in the end, all crimes—especially when accelerated—have historically signaled the decline of that culture's greatness—or potential greatness). America's reality position must be viewed if we are concerned about her longevity as well as for the contributions she is capable of making to humanity (and world transformation) in the future.

Quite possibly the first signals of America's present vibrational position could be seen in viewing the relationship this country developed with the American Indians. I focus on this relationship not as a means to extract some form of useless guilt (not to mention, no one seems to even be concerned about this subject anyway), but only as a means to focus on the early solidification of a particular "attitude" that has permeated American progressionalism. My point is this: the early settlement of America, and the early solidification of America as separate from Europe had to do with a desire to establish a more "just society" that glorified the concept of humanity and spiritual values. Thus the very beginning of America necessitated that fabrication would have to play an important role in its "reality perception" from the signing of the Constitution to the present. Because the crimes perpetrated against the American Indians were quite real, and also quite separate from the essence ideals that the country was founded under—and the dichotomy between the ideals of American culture and its actual reality has maintained a peculiar distance ever since, and has on occasion only been reinforced by the progressional focus of dynamic expansion. It is also possible to view the solidification of slavery in this same context—that being, another reality decision that widened the gap between actual reality and ideals—and so on and so on. But this is not a history lesson, I am looking for something else.

To write that various crimes have been perpetuated by America is in itself nothing new, nor have I meant, in citing the examples of the American Indian or slavery, that any one person or sector should be blamed—since this means nothing anyway. Instead by viewing the dynamics of American progressionalism I have tried to comment on the uniqueness surrounding how these particulars were perceived. In other words, the nature underlying how America's vibrational reality continuance has reordered its philosophic and spiritual arena, as a means to not deal with its past, is what interests me.

Because, unlike Europe, America's past is still happening—which is to say, the two hundred years that Americans view as their past, is nothing when viewed in the composite context of continuance. As such, to not deal with the reality dynamics of progressionalism is to not be in a good position to really understand and positively correct what is happening in the present. Moreover, by not moving to deal with composite progressionalism, the dynamic implications of future expansion cannot learn from its collective experiences—which is to say, by not learning from the past you must repeat the past. Yet I do not mean to over-simplify this most serious subject, because I am not commenting on something separated from "actual life" in America (or earth). My point here is only that "the past does mean something—and this is true on several levels."

If we can say that black people in America are still recovering from the effects of slavery—and this can be seen very clearly; one does not need to be a philosopher to look at the situation black people are dealing with in America to understand that is not a normal situation, that black people are still trying to recover from the collective effects of slavery—then we can also say that white Americans are still suffering from the vibrational and philosophical consequences of the attitudes and intentions that allowed this phenomenon to happen. I am saying the seriousness of the dichotomy that solidified when slavery was embraced—having to do with the so-called image foundation of American idealism; reflecting on the very reason white people left Europe (as a means to build a new society of equal rights and justice); yet at the same time employing slavery with a cruelty and inhumanity that was unprecedented (while moving to practically annihilate the American Indian)—is what white people are dealing with today. I am not stating that white Americans are walking around thinking about how wrong they have been to non-white people, but I am stating that the vibrational and meta-vibrational implications of this phenomenon are very much in the basic cosmic lining of American (and western) culture. Moreover, the reality implications of this phenomenon seem to also shed insight into the nature of both American and western culture's destiny option—for clearly the very future of American culture is not separate from whether or not some real effort is made to deal with (not correct,

SD(SY)-14

because none of this can be corrected) what those decisions pose for future continuance. But it is important to not lose the basic point of this essay, because obviously the present reality of social progressionalism cannot exclude its composite nature—my point however is this: The reordering of one's meta-physics to employ the type of misdeeds America practiced in her forming cycle is directly related to the peculiar vibrational alignment that American culture has developed as an essence continuum. In other words, the implementation of these misdeeds has dictated not only the social reality dynamics of present day continuance, but the vibrational consequences of this phenomenon have affected the composite reality of American culture—affecting everyone. This is true whether we are focusing on the reality position of American culture, or the vibrational spiritual position of American (western) culture.

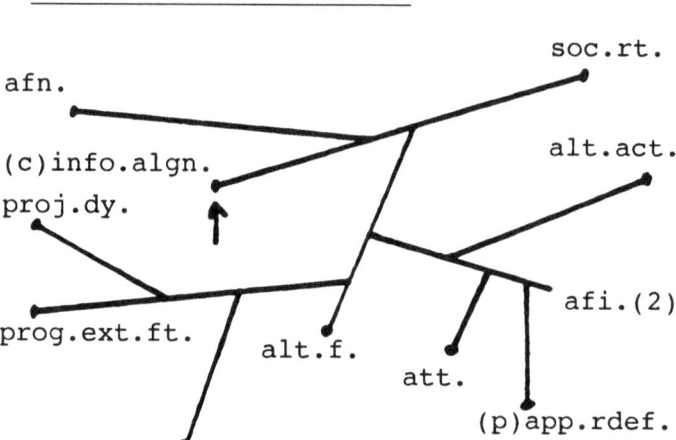

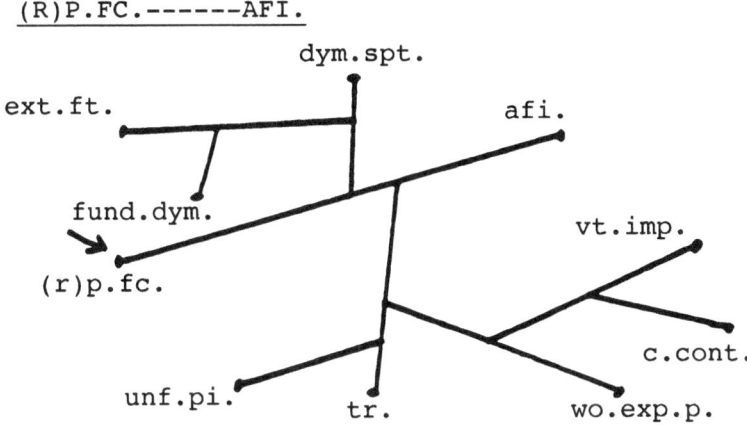

I have not meant to imply that the progressional implications of American culture are unique with respect to what its decisions have posed for social reality—because they aren't. Nor have I meant to focus on—what I have chosen to call—the "misdeeds" of American progressionalism as a means to comment on something unique—because every culture can be viewed with respect to these same considerations. Certainly the progressional continuance of American culture is no different from European expansionalism and/or Indian and African expansionalism. The sad truth is, humanity has never really been able to deal with the dichotomy between what it poses, as a vibrational postulate, and what it desires, as a physical universe focus. But if we are to understand the reality dynamics of this time zone—as an alternative means to possibly function for positive transformation—then it is important that the specifics of this time period be examined. There are only two positions we can take: either the reality implications of a given progressionalism can be shaped—and as such there is a reason to function to bring about ideals—or it cannot (and as such, the nature of a given progressionalism has to do with only cosmic matters and we are doomed to relive the past and present). My position is that we, as human beings, have the opportunity to shape the nature of a given progressionalism (although I also believe that after a given progressionalism actualizes, it could not have gone any other way). As such, to examine the vibrational implications of progressionalism is to hopefully gain insight into the nature of what factors are supporting the present "reality" of things, and hopefully this information can be of positive value in seeking alternatives for the next cycle. This is especially true if we are to understand what has happened to creativity in this time period, and what this could mean for the future. For that reason, the focus of this essay will be directed towards social reality implications in American culture as a means to view the composite nature of this phenomenon—in its expanded context. I start with America because the focus of this book has been on the reality of extended functionalism and what this concept poses for alternative creativity. In its early state, America was also viewed as a positive alternative from the existing situation that solidified Europe (or at least that is what we are taught in classrooms throughout America—even though the first wave of settlers are really documented as "outcasts"—who were not among the "more desirables" of European culture).

By refusing to deal with the dynamic implications of composite information lines, America has instead created a special progressionalism with its own vibrational dictates. If we are to ever solidify a positive composite reality position for transformation, then some effort must be made to understand the particulars of this most special phenomenon (or at least, some effort must be made if we desire real change in this time zone). The realness of America's special route can be viewed as a kind of diversionary progressionalism; and in its deeper implications this phenomenon also moves to give some understanding about the peculiar nature of present-day western information dynamics. Yet I have not meant to imply that the nature of this special route is based on only one aspect of composite information distortion—because it isn't. It is possible to view the nature of American continuance with respect to several areas of information regulation—having to do with the misinterpretation of world information as well as the manipulation of black creativity, and all of these contexts are important. The basic focus of this section will attempt to view the whole of this phenomenon with respect to its composite implications—regardless of focus—yet at the same time with particular emphasis on what progressionalism poses for creativity—and especially black creativity and affinity dynamics—

as a means to integrate information throughout the whole of this series of writings (this approach is necessary since the basic focus of this series of books has been on the reality implications of world creativity). The thrust of this section will thus attempt to elaborate on the reality implications of what I have come to call "the spectacle-diversion sequence" of American progressionalism—involving what this phenomenon has posed for western affinity dynamics and expansion as well as creativity. An investigation of this type can hopefully establish a wider context for viewing present-day progressionalism, and "doing" this most certainly is needed.

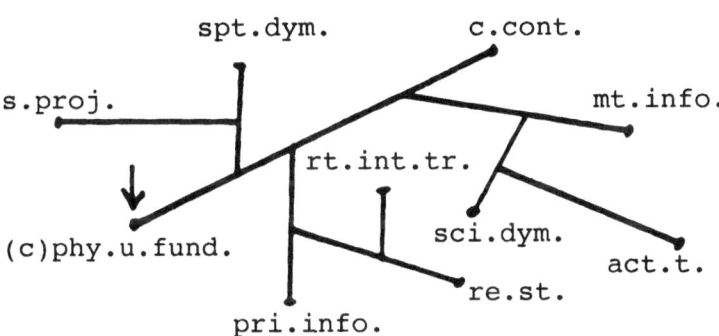

PHY.U.FUND.------C.CONT.

It is important to elaborate on the term "spectacle diversion," and also define each aspect of its focus. The concept of "spectacle" in this context can be understood as "events happening on the physical plane that, while having no substantial validity as far as affirming the general reality of its culture, nevertheless, 'are interesting.'" In other words, events that are initiated because they are "interesting" rather than "of substance" to the essence continuum of the culture. To really view the realness of this concept, it might be necessary to give an example on the physical universe level—because the concept of spectacle diversion is not simply a theoretical exercise, but a phenomenon that comments on the particulars of America's peculiar progressionalism. An example that illustrates the dynamics of spectacle diversion can be found in the present concept western culture has of "entertainment" as opposed to creativity. For if the highest understanding of creativity in world culture terms has to do with activity that affirms the vibrational alignment of its culture group (as a means to establish both how to live and the composite dynamics of its spiritual intent); what we have instead in America when we talk of entertainment is activity that moves to take our minds off of reality. The realness of this difference sheds light on the affinity position of western culture—yet I do not mean to over-simplify this most complex example, because obviously there is much more to western culture than any one focus. My point is only that America's bizarre understanding of entertainment without either spiritual or functional (living) intent is what I refer to when I use the word "spectacle." Yet I have not meant to imply that every time one goes to see a given play or movie "nothing" of substance can be experienced, nor have I meant to lump every creative outlet in one zone—because this would not only grossly distort the concept of spectacle diversion (as well as real life) but the whole intent of this book. I have instead tried to comment on the actual situation of creativity with regards to the vibrational position it occupies in western culture. Nor have I meant to imply that television doesn't give some real idea of American culture—even "Mighty Mouse" and "Johnny Carson" represent some aspect of what is happening in America, and to that extent, it does mirror something real. My point, though, is that by substantiating, I am referring to activity which affirms who we are (and what we could be), as it relates to the essences we profess to be about, and that we live in. "Mighty Mouse" can only be talked of, then, as a phenomenon that is interesting—or not interesting—but certainly not in accordance with the primary considerations we vibrate to. Another way of explaining the idea of spectacle would be: activity which confirms the present reality of events—in this case new events—without offering any insight towards strengthening the vibrational lining underlying what that given culture professes to be about. Thus, the end result of exposure to a given spectacle can only be evaluated by how effective that exposure was for a given moment (as opposed to an exposure which dictates a way for people to proceed—with their lives—in accordance to what that particular culture "is about"). Something which means something—if I can write it in that way.

```
PRI.VT.TD.------AF.DY.
```

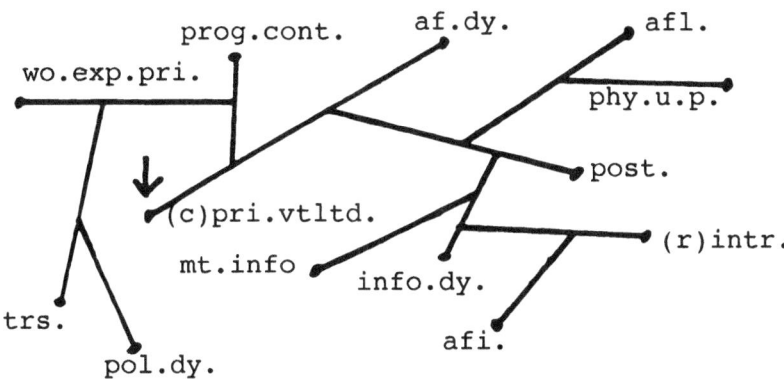

The diversion sequence in America can be talked of as patterns that occur within a given time cycle which invariably determine how a given group of people see themselves—both conceptually and vibrationally. The extended realness of this concept also involves the construction of alternative realities as a basis to program the dynamics of "particulars" (whether it involves behavior and/or attitude). Nor should the actualness of this phenomenon be viewed as the inevitable result of natural progressionalism but rather the logical effect of, what can only be called, extremely sophisticated manipulation. As such, to examine the reality implications of spectacle diversion is to not limit the information scan of a given focus, because depending on what level one is interested in viewing, there is no vibrational and/or conceptual area not affected by this phenomenon. This concept is not to be confused with natural (or legitimate) physical universe progressions that are a fact of existence, for it is understood that, on the planet level—because of the way life seems to be—we are always forced to deal with new "particulars" (whether its reality dynamics are empirically or vibrationally manifested). Instead, by spectacle diversion I am commenting on something not indigenous to the basic "reality basis" that people move with, nor is this concept related to something engrained in the philosophical and functional affinity relationship of American culture (in terms of what American culture professes to be about—and this distinction is important).

In actual terms, it is possible to view the realness of spectacle-diversion dynamics by focusing on the reality particulars of given periods of progressionalism in American culture. The basic focus of this section will be restricted to given developments that occurred after 1950 as a means to deal with current material—and as a means to have material that can be transformed throughout the whole of this book for integration, and refocus. The first example of spectacle diversion that can be focused on from the fifties would be the concept of the "fad" as an extracurricular manipulation tool. This phenomenon (the fad) seems to move from initiations that occur in six to ten year cycles, and is directly related to the rotation of present-day information particulars. The nature, or focus, of a given diversion has to do with the composite factors that are "operative" to make a given "fad" real—which is to say, the solidification of a "fad" in this context is not simply about a natural "coming together" of particulars. The collective solidification of the "beatnik" period is an example that can be viewed as one manifestation of the spectacle-diversion syndrome that occurred in the fifties (although I do not mean to imply that any particular period has only one "fad" or spectacle focus—because this is not necessarily true; in fact, a given time zone usually experiences a multitude of spectacles—and spectacle-diversion syndromes as well).

The beatnik period could best be understood as a vibrational response to the First and Second World War vibrational continuum as well as a vibrational postulate of the post-existential vacuum that had become real to "those individuals in that zone." The reality of this phenomenon would have to do with either the vibrational desire for alternative functionalism as well as dropping out of the so-called status quo—with the understanding being, that this vibrational and actual response would signify something of meaning in a positive (or real) context. Moreover, many of the participants in the beatnik period were so-called educated or "inclined to be educated" people—which is to say, the beatnik movement was not really about Mr. John Doe reacting to the composite vibrational lining of American culture, but was instead a vibrational indication of what America's intellectuals were postulating. The dynamics of this phenomenon were definitely related to the vibrational solidification of what would later come to be called the "counter-culture," or so-called underground culture, and in many ways this description was true—but only part true. For in the final analysis, the beatnik period really only solidified the nature of post-existential source-transfer continuance as an attitude rather than a reality (or as a style rather than "life purpose"). The progressional dynamics of this movement would, in the final analysis, only be significant for how it supplied fuel for the composite culture to provide diversion. And as such, the beatnik period would be "something to talk about," or "something to write on." This phenomenon would thus define the surface dynamics necessary to establish cross-transfer information progressionalism—and in doing so, helped establish the next generation of writers and "things." This phenomenon would also dictate what areas of information and/or dynamic particulars could be successfully co-opted from the non-white community as a transfer stimulant (like having a new dress). By the middle fifties, everybody wondered what had happened to "beatniks"—but by then hula hoops had come down (in).

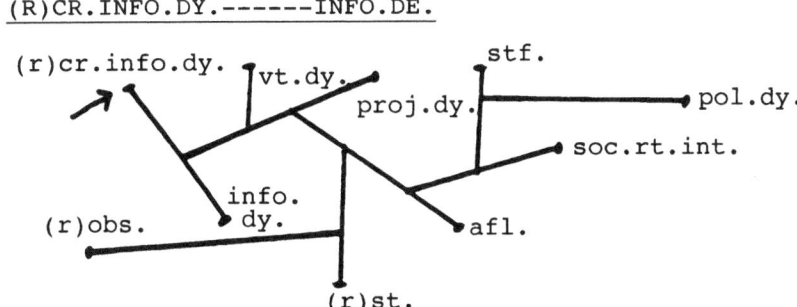

SD(SY)–22

ASP.ES. ----- AF.DY.

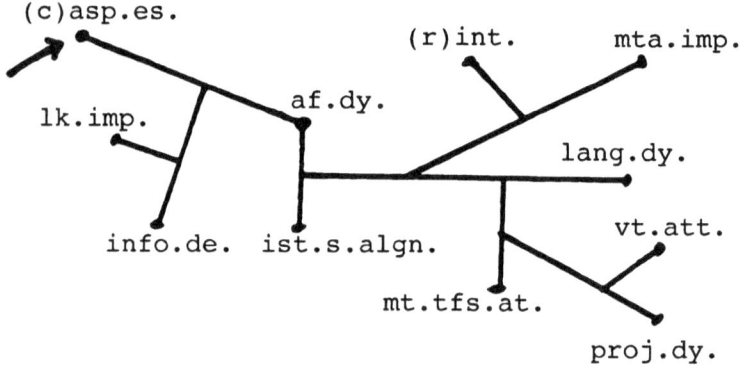

To view the reality of the diversion sequence phenomenon it is important to understand that the activity (or focus of the diversion—how it is manifested, or what form it takes) is usually associated with events that are "of substance." Which is to say the spectacle-diversion syndrome is not separate from the composite lining of its culture group in terms of observation—for the factors that generate a given spectacle diversion can be viewed throughout the total culture. But while this phenomenon is related to actual culture reality—it is not in itself "culture reality" (or the vibrational reality position of its composite culture) but rather a "symptom" of events. Yet the dynamic implications of this phenomenon transcend any one context, for its position in a given culture is only the beginning. My point is this: the significance of a given spectacle diversion lies in its ability to progressionally re-dictate the reality dynamics of its time zone—or focus. In other words, the solidification of a given spectacle-diversion syndrome moves to determine how its composite culture will view a given aspect of its reality—even at the expense of "actual reality" (that being what people are doing, and how life in that given culture actually proceeds). Moreover, the uniqueness of this phenomenon (and the reason I have gone through such lengths to explain the idea) is that while the spectacle-diversion syndrome seems connected to the "actual reality of events" in its given culture group (in terms of being a legitimate manifestation of relevant focuses in its information scan), in fact, the spectacle-diversion syndrome is actually without substance.

In other words, real events—that being, activity that is constantly being manifested on the physical plane, which in its natural "isness" affects life on every level—not only become a catalyst for the spectacle-diversion syndrome, but also the very nature of this phenomenon moves to distort the essence that its diversion is based on. This phenomenon can only be understood through what it poses to the concept of "interesting"—or "something to do." In other words, the diversion syndrome that takes place every six to ten years moves on the proposition that "isolated-interesting" itself can be a cultural and actual basis for dealing with life. It is this understanding of "isolated-interesting" that motivates the nature underlying how information dynamics are manipulated in this time zone—and this phenomenon is not without consequence for what it poses to the composite culture. For in the final analysis, the spectacle-diversion syndrome—which in its most real "isness" is nothing—moves to solidify nothing as a cultural vibrational attitude. To clarify: the spectacle-diversion syndrome seems to progress towards each new cycle—it doesn't matter what that cycle is attached to (certainly this concept is related to the solidification of the "fad" or "style")—until it finally arrives at the "nothing" it started with. It is this understanding—the movement of nothing to nothing—that underlies the reality of this phenomenon. My point is that the realness of this concept sheds light on the nature underlying how progressionalism is utilized in American culture—both with regards to information dynamics as well as information and reality-focus. For the realness of this concept must be viewed on several levels—(1) with respect to the rotation of vibrational physical universe events as a means to provide backdrop for motivation and/or source-transfer information stimulation, and (2) with respect to what this concept poses for sophisticated manipulation. The spectacle-diversion syndrome is related to all of these concepts, and more.

If the beatnik generation was one example of the form a given diversion takes (and what that usage posed to the progressionalism of the early fifties), then quite possibly by focusing on the dynamics of the sixties, it might be possible to clarify the nature of this phenomenon as a "working concept."

SD(SY)–24

Without doubt, the best example of the spectacle-diversion syndrome in the sixties would be the nature of the progressionalism that solidified what we now refer to as the "love generation." More specifically, the reality particulars of the so-called hippie movement which came into prominence from the greater west coast movement in the same period. Just as the "beat" period was directly related to events in the fifties (and in the same peculiar position to spectacle as an added ingredient), the same holds true for the hippie movement of the sixties. Which is to say the hippie movement has all of the necessary requirements to give one insight into the progressional significance of spectacle-diversion manipulation—and what this subject means as a relevant phenomenon preceding this time period (with the implications being that the reality position of this time period—the late seventies—was prepared and solidified in the sixties). Moreover, the hippie movement is also a perfect example to view the dynamic realness of spectacle-diversion dynamics as a means to gain insight on contemporary perspectives (or "non-perspectives") and what this means for affinity dynamics. For the realness of this phenomenon (the hippie movement) would establish a basis for viewing not only the nature of progressionalism in this time zone, but also the greater forces surrounding how information and information dynamics are brought forward (or backward, which is closer to the truth). The realness of this concept (spectacle-diversion progressionalism) can be viewed for how it has underlined the whole of American history if approached correctly—for it must be understood; my most basic position in this section is that "nothing" in America—as far as vibrational reality of intent—has changed since its inception. Instead, we are dealing with the dynamics—or sophistication—that surrounds how controlled progressionalism is practiced. To really view the seriousness of spectacle-diversion progressionalism is to begin viewing how reality extension is practiced in America—and this information is important. It should also be emphasized that when I write of spectacle-diversion progressionalism, I am not commenting on an isolated phenomenon, but instead a pattern which has developed since America's inception. This is a phenomenon that maintains a distinct vibrational alignment—although somewhat peculiar—regardless of the time zone it appears in. The nature underlying how this sequence is utilized by American society—and the American people—tells us something about how this culture really sees life. It is this relationship—the principles which manifest themselves in each spectacle-diversion sequence, and how people relate to what this sequence is supposed to mean—that clarifies the real fabric of American "culture."

```
SOC.RT.DY.------PHY.U.P.
```

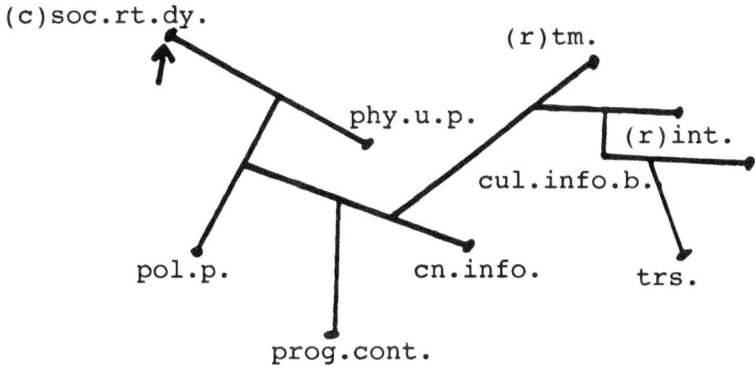

The phenomenon which occurred in the sixties that was labeled the "hippie" movement had something to do with very real events signaling the coming transformation of American culture. Whatever the ultimate effect of that movement (as seen from a later vantage point), we have to realize that the hippie movement was only possible because of the conditions in the air at that time (the "actual" atmosphere and the vibrational particulars of the sixties). We cannot under-estimate the events that took place in the sixties in terms of their effect on both the country and the vibrational transformations which were later to supply a basis for other alternatives. The realness of the war in Vietnam was certainly a divisive factor in the vibrational reality of the sixties, and even today we can only speculate about the implications this one vibrational schism created. In fact, any attempt to understand the factors which led to the "ising" of the "hippie" spectacle-diversion sequence will only document the complexities of social reality and vibrational dynamics in the sixties. For, like the "beat" period, the hippie movement was the direct result of a growing awareness by young white people of what was really happening in America—(in regards to both the political reality of the day, or the realness of social reality, etc.). The solidification of the hippie movement could be understood as an attempt to create alternative lifestyles—that is, this movement represented a rejection of the basic vibrational principles in the air during that time zone—or at least that was how it was perceived in its early period. There were, of course, other reasons for the hippie movement, for it is clear that objections to the war in Vietnam were not always based on moral considerations: many of the young men simply did not want to fight in the military. But I believe the basic thrust that personified the time zone of the middle sixties was a concern about the vibrational consequences happening—or not happening—in American society. This was the period which saw many demonstrations objecting to American political policies, as well as collective efforts to make known deep-seated injustices (e.g., the March on Washington). And, of course, it is understood that the hippie movement was only one group among many in that time zone (nor have I intended to make this movement any more important than it was), but the vibrational factors which made it possible for this group to come together were in fact the same factors that dictated all of the previously mentioned movements as well—no matter how each movement was labeled. I have only chosen to focus on the hippie movement because it is convenient.

The hippie-yippie period is generally talked of as a movement which was formed in reaction to both the social and political situation in America at that time. To some degree this perception was accurate, in the sense that young white people suddenly found themselves becoming conscious of what was happening in their country. What they did with their awareness, and what they finally wound up with, is what concerns this essay. Because as the time zone of the sixties progressed, what emerged was a movement large enough to take on the appearance of an actual counter-culture. That is, the magnitude of the changes in that period—the variation in language style, the change in dress, etc.—transcended the boundaries of isolated reaction. Yet we must also understand that if the reactionary forces which emerged in the sixties were really based upon some amount of cognition in regards to the basic vibrationary thrust of American culture, then we would have something to show for this renewed awareness today. It is in looking at the hippie-yippie cycle that we can most clearly see the dilemma of American culture, for, as in the example of the "beatnik" period, nothing was established by this movement that has any relevance to actual life—let alone the future. My point is that the hippie-yippie syndrome was no more than another spectacle which fed off of real events, at the expense of those events. Nor do I mean to make a distinction between this movement, or the beatnik movement—the spectacle-movement hula hoops—baseball—the ecological movement or "the bump"—because in the final analysis all of these factors are perceived in the same vibrational context. I am saying that the spectacle-diversion syndrome is what America has rather than culture.

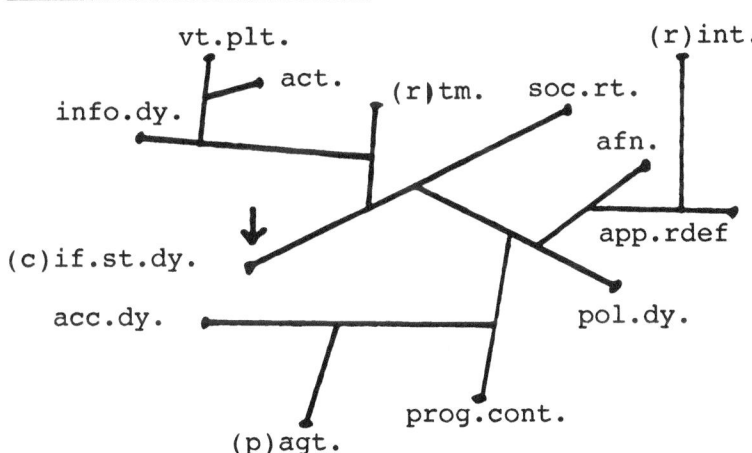

There are, of course, many factors that determine how a given vibrational focus is manifested (and solidified as a spectacle-diversion initiation) and it is important to not over-generalize the concept. Because I am not commenting on a given phenomenon that only functions from a limited dynamic range—or physical universe property mix, but rather a vibrational phenomenon that encompasses both affinity dynamics and multi-intentions—that are manifested in a variety of ways. The specifics of a given focus in this context have to do with the form (physical universe appearance) a given movement takes, as well as the nature of its vibrational postulates. In actual terms, the option dynamics of this phenomenon is wide enough to encompass both the emergence of the "disco"—as a new craze for social reality—and the traditional continuance of our present political system: involving in this case the concept of the Democratic and Republican parties (as an idea that is supposed to be about two separate political ideologies whose ultimate decisions will affirm—or actualize—the greater intentions of the voting public). My point—in this context—is this: the most basic factor that determines the particulars of spectacle-diversion initiations has to do with the "style" of a given movement—rather than its intention. This is so because the concept of spectacle-diversion cycles is really not about a "real" postulation—in terms of something in accordance to the dictates of relevant information (in composite world culture calibration terms), but instead a phenomenon that is practiced because of what illusion it provides—in terms of spectacle.

In other words, it is possible to look back at the time zone of the sixties and see very clearly that there was no real difference between the people who were protesting (i.e., the hippie-yippies) and the people they were protesting against. All of the activity which took place in the sixties could best be understood as "games for a particular time cycle," rather than a period that gave birth to a new commitment for either social or political change. The basic "stuff" which defined this period (the sixties) had to do with the adaptation of "style" as a basis for new diversion, nothing more. The time zone of the sixties could be understood as a period that exploited the surface fundamental "shifts" in American society with patterns which have long been established as a means to successful procedural devices. The realness of the war in Vietnam, the realness of the position of non-white and poor people in America, and the realness of the ecological dilemma we are all moving towards, were only factors ripe for exploitation, rather than something real in a multidimensional sense. Nor do I mean to imply that any particular group consciously utilized some aspect of what was happening in the sixties as a move to create intended artificial diversion, because this is not necessarily true either: in fact, I believe the great majority of activists in that period really believed in what they were doing or at least really thought they were doing what they were doing. However, the factors which really determined the vibrational reality of the country revealed that the dominant affinity that dictated individual and/or group activism in that period was directly in accordance with the spectacle-diversion affinity phenomenon, rather than a renewed or reawakened fundamental commitment. It is now possible to see that there was no difference between the so-called status quo and the many protesting individuals and factors which had developed throughout the sixties.

It is in looking at the hippie-yippie syndrome where we can see most clearly that not only did this movement not understand the actual physical universe situation in America—let alone how to deal with it, but moreover, what we finally have is young people playing games, and in the final analysis "ising" the very phenomena that they were reacting to. Reaction in America during this period became only a "fad" at the expense of the real situation: young people thus found the substance to create new games and hence continue the normal life flow of American progressionalism. We can also say that these same young people found new games at the expense of the real situation. To clarify this further: they found a valid dilemma, but rather than deal with it, they instead became part of it. This is so because the sixties activists never really understood what they were dealing with, nor did they attempt to understand the "affinity relationships" that underline how events are perceived in America. It is the irony of American "culture" that all of the events which took place in the sixties can now be viewed and shown to have had practically no effect on the dynamics of this time period. Which is to say, however one chooses to understand the social activism in the sixties, it is now clear that the extent of that phenomenon (and the scope underlying how that commitment was understood) did not extend into the seventies.

SD(SY)–30

(R)INFO.DS.------AF.DY.

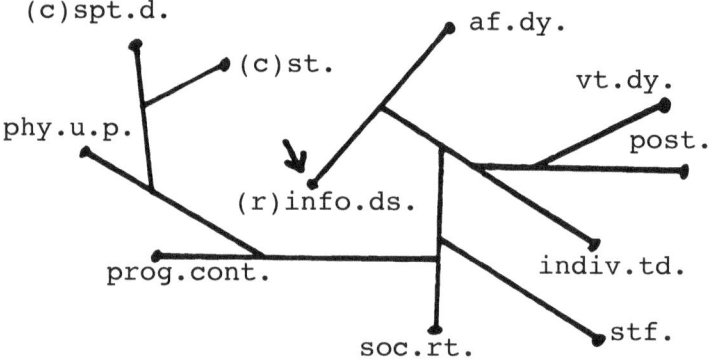

The concept of spectacle diversion also extends to other equally significant levels. For it must be understood that, on the physical universe level, spectacle diversion is also the juncture which most lends itself to "source transfer." In other words, the actual realness of spectacle diversion functions as the phenomenon which allows for style transference as the most apparent tool for diversion. This "adaptation of style" is always directly related to a synthesis between western and non-western vibrational factors: where the surface aspects of a given alternative group (e.g., black people, Indian or Asian) are adopted by western forces as a means for synthesizing. In the case of the sixties, it is clear that many of the activist groups were indebted to "world group" influences on style (e.g., the dress of the hippies, the borrowing of Indian religion, etc.) as well as its related functionalism (e.g., the women's movement use of black functionalism as a means to redefine how to proceed). I realize that cultures have always influenced one another, and that cultural trading is a fact of life, but to merely accept this phenomenon as a natural factor in present-day information dynamics would be to ignore the particular nature of American information transference. My point is that the concept of "transfer shift" in this context cannot be divorced from the sociological and philosophical considerations which dictated its use. In other words, the fact that there has long been a relationship between the spectacle-diversion sequence of western information transference to black initiations, or non-western initiations, means something—especially if we are made aware of the obvious low regard that Americans have long had for these same groups. How is it that the "swing period"—"jazz period," the "ragtime period" (and practically every vibrational period that I can think of)—draws from the aesthetic lining of a non-western source for the basis for forming its diversion?

It is common knowledge that white Americans see themselves separately from non-white Americans. Usually the level of that separateness doesn't matter, and any attempt to understand what was raised in the time zone of the sixties—the political rhetoric and the change in style—would only shed light on what has always been a most peculiar phenomenon: that being the incredible influence of the black sensibility on American culture. Another way of understanding my point in this context would be to focus on the implementation of the black sensibility as a basis to sustain the concept of style (dynamics) and as a factor to also lay basis for diversion—which in this case would imply "lifeblood." It is not simply the realness that the black aesthetic has cast the profoundest influencing sensibility in creative American music that I am addressing when I write about the usurpation of the black vibrational sensibility by western civilization; instead, it is the fact that the strongest underlying alternative sensibility to influence the whole of America's relationship to vibrational cycles actually depends upon "vibrational-transfer focus input." If this is understood then it is possible to also understand what the spectacle-diversion sequence really means. Because the spectacle-diversion sequence is the name I have given to the nature underlying how America utilizes "source transfer" as a factor to sustain the "lifeblood" of her culture. Yet I have not meant to imply that alternative sensibilities are adopted to be utilized for "actual change," nor have I meant to imply that the concept of spectacled diversion has to do with actual "vibrationaltory realignment," but rather—spectacle diversion as a phenomenon that can be utilized to sustain "original intentions" (which, in this case, is information and information focus in accordance to the exclusive flow of the western sensibility). In other words, the time zone which "ised" the hippie-yippie movement only provided what factors would be utilized for this phenomenon and nothing more. All of the movements that functioned in this time zone merely participated in the surface vibrational-alignment particulars of that period as a means to be involved or not involved—with how each person saw his own life. Obviously this is so, for by the time the middle seventies arrived, all of the activity that took place in the sixties had passed, and more than that: nothing had changed anyway.

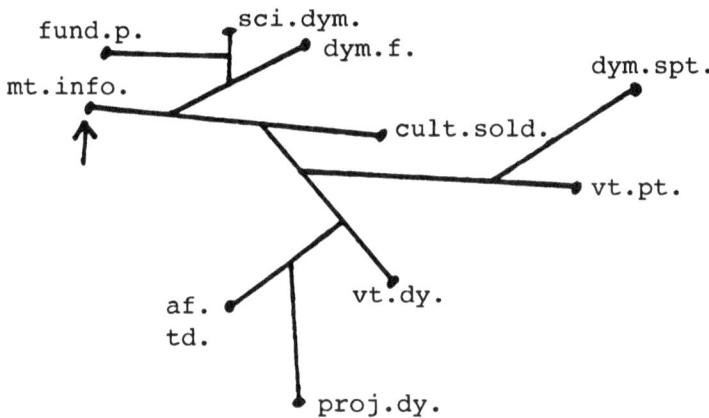

I mention these variables—the attempts to move towards the third world, rock music, politics—as a means for giving the full vibrational atmosphere of this time cycle so that we may look at these movements—the hippies and yippies—to understand not only what they were dealing with, but also what they weren't able to deal with. Because in the final analysis it is clear that these people were no more equipped to deal with the transition which took place in the sixties than their parents were.

The difference between the alternative activist groups and the status quo in the sixties was so slight that together they only moved to reinforce the chain of events which keeps America in its present position. It is in viewing the events of the sixties and seventies that we can better understand this phenomenon. For neither the activist's movement nor the status quo has given us any real change, in terms of functional meta-physics, or for that matter a more realistic alignment towards "essence." What we have in this time period instead is the same situation that has always existed in America, with one difference. That difference is in style manifested through its ability to incorporate new language (always a mutation of black language), new fashion, and a pseudo new sensibility.

The particular functionalism which took place in the sixties could be talked of in terms of its class groups: because each movement had its own style and value systems (on the surface). All of these class groups could basically be labeled "anti-establishment" and/or "establishment"—which is to say one group was directly vibrating to the surface particulars which defined the diversion for that time zone (this was the sector that adopted long hair—beads, mysticism, civil rights—rock music) while the other group was characterized by its relationship to function with respect to the established reality continuum or the so-called establishment (usually referred to as the status quo). As the time zone of the sixties moved to the seventies, it was interesting to note that the alternative culture's sensibilities—as manifested in "style"—became integrated with the total reality of the country. Thus, not only was there no difference between how both groups perceive of phenomenon—in the realest sense of what "affinity-alignment" means; but there was also a clear interdependency between the alternative activist groups and the status quo—as they both exist in America (and the west). In this context, the spectacle diversion sequence functioned as a basis to "infuse life-blood" into composite western culture; which is to say—the spectacle diversion sequence is a phenomenon which moves to "sustain" a given predicament (culture) rather than dynamically aid world transformation.

I have already stated that in order to understand the concept of spectacle diversion one must first have some understanding of the nature underlying how a given diversion is perceived. We must also understand that this phenomenon is indicative of the progressive aspects inherent in the total fabric of western information dynamics. The extent to which a spectacle-diversion sequence can be utilized then is a result of the fact that its particulars are a reaction to real events—real in the sense that given events are physical and meta-physical actualities that occur in particular time slots. It follows then that whatever the problems of

SD(SY)–34

the diversion sequence syndrome, it does in fact affirm an alternative vibration—or vibrational intention—and we are forced to look at how given considerations can be incorporated into the general reality of the society without actually changing the "essence factor" of the culture.

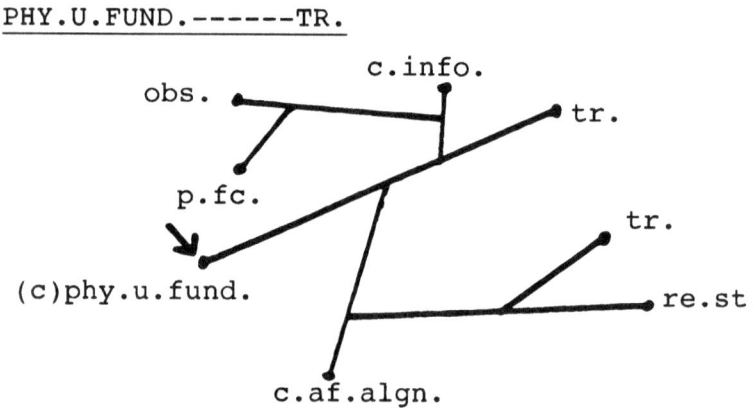

To the degree that the sixties thrust movement flowed as an effect (or so-called reaction) of the basic vibrationaltory lining of American culture, it must also be emphasized that there were other factors that did function with regards with the forces defining the "agreed" reality of composite America and her information dynamics. Those factors were the vibrational groups representing the agreement of the status quo, or whatever we now choose to call the establishment. It is this sector of culture functionalism which best represents the "stuff" that defines the "actual" reality of a given country—how events are compositely understood and defined throughout its given culture. There can be no possibility of changing a given reality unless the established culture's information realities are both understood and prepared for—this is so because of the enormous advantages any established group has by nature of its political position. The ensuing relationship between the activist movements and the establishment movement in the sixties also clarified the actual position of the spectacle-diversion sequence phenomenon. For whatever the activist movements lacked in their functional know-how, it was more than made up in the establishment's understanding of how to absorb alternative considerations—into the greater culture. Because the sophistication of America's technological know-how has always been her forte. This technological functionalism is manifested in the culture's philosophical position as well as through its ability to control and manipulate all events in its information lines (as well as how those events are interpreted). One should never underestimate the sophistication which surrounds the controlling and defining factors in American culture, for the whole of this subject must be understood in any attempt to deal with the established vibrational reality of a given country. It is a credit to western civilization that she has developed a sophistication—whether it's empirical structuralism or meta-physics—whose ultimate meaning can be twisted by the clever use of one or two words.

The most basic point that this essay hopes to make would be that there is a major difference between the natural progression of events (on the physical and vibrational plane) as it is "ised" in a given culture, and the spectacle diversion sequence cycle that we have instead in America. The most basic difference between these two considerations would pertain to the origin of given phenomenon, and the ultimate effect that each "vibrational transfer shift" has on its culture. I am also aware that there are many similarities between both "transfer conditions" as well—the most obvious being that both phenomenons represent time continuums whose dynamic tendencies move toward information realignment. For this reason, many of us have come to accept the particulars surrounding our existence in the west as something normal (because this is simply "how life is"). When the McCarthy period was at its greatest vibrational height during the fifties, the basic understanding that permeated the greater culture was that no matter how frantic things had become "this kind of 'participation' was still normal in regards to what life is." This was also true for the cold-war period in the fifties. The rock period—especially in the sixties—showed still another mass vibrational-alignment adaptation of this phenomenon, and the particulars of spectacle-diversion manipulation has been the basis of quite a few sociological studies. It is my opinion, however, that there are major differences between the underlying factors which determine vibrational periods in American culture, and the underlying factors which have always been an integral part of world vibrational and physical universe continuance. Without doubt, the most basic difference is that one condition is "natural" (in the sense that however the concept of transfer-cycles is understood, it was and is connected to the spiritual and vibrationaltory factors that interconnect with how progressional information as a phenomenon is understood—and practiced on—or utilized on—a universal level: that is, how information is perceived in its composite relationship concerning what has been observed in vibrational and physical universe change) and the other condition is manufactured (both as the result of actual planning as well as the end result of a peculiar vibrational alignment—that is, "manufactured" as a direct result of the flaws in the western philosophical and vibrational position—or "manufactured" as a consequence of the western aesthetic and vibrational position).

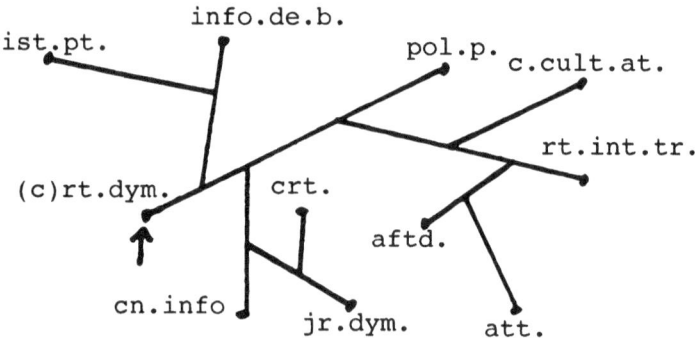

There are other major differences between normal "transfer cycles" and the spectacle-diversion sequence. For the concept of "transfer cycle" progressionalism (which is the phrase I use to denote physical and vibrational information change in a given culture) has to do with a phenomenon which in its natural state serves as a factor to initiate "actual" change. But this is not the case with the spectacle-diversion cycle, for one of the most basic features of this phenomenon is the realness that its utilization changes nothing—or nothing was meant to change. In other words, whatever the physical universe appearance—in a given time cycle, the spectacle-diversion sequence phenomenon functions as a mask to obscure any possibilities of real change, and in its place gives diversion as a basis to perpetuate the illusion of "life activity" ("something to do"). The spectacle-diversion cycle is a vibrational time zone phenomenon that blends itself into whatever "stuff" is being adopted, as a means to solidify that adaptation in accordance with the accepted vibrational alignment and hence interpretations of its base culture. This blending is done as a safety valve to guard against "real" change, or at least the end results of this phenomenon serve as a substitute for real culture change.

The spectacle-diversion sequence phenomenon is determined by (1) the time cycle of a given situation, (2) the vibrational cycle (and how this consideration is manifested in a given physical universe situation), (3) the social reality cycle of a given culture, and finally (4) the political particulars of a given culture.

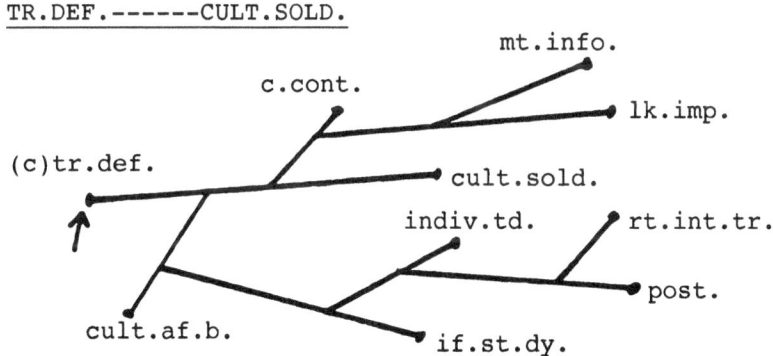

By the phrase "time cycle" in this context, I am referring to the realness that a given event begins and finally ends—or at least the particulars which defined how a given situation is understood can be perceived as starting from a given point and later ending—or ceasing to correspond to the afforded definition. The realness of the consideration of time is an important factor in any attempt to understand the depth of a particular spectacle-diversion sequence, for it is clear that the intensity which characterizes a given affinity change will have moments which are more "real" than other moments. For example, the March on Washington in the middle sixties was a period where the diversion cycle which "ised" civil rights moved into its peak, but in the middle seventies, only ten years later, there was hardly any concern at all for human rights. It is thus the consideration of time which determines whether or not a given variable can be introduced or dealt with—either on an individual level or a cultural level.

It is somewhat difficult to write about the significance of a given vibrational postulate with regards to spectacle diversion because there is no way one can determine what is really happening with questions of this type without some insight about "actual" cosmic information which I don't have. However this area of information is understood, it would undoubtedly have to touch on "what is really happening" as opposed to "what is happening" on the planet (or off the planet). I believe that the vibrational factor or factors which determine actual "isness" permeates every level of everything and as such is a subject that transcends the scope of what I can now deal with.

Whatever, the social and political implications of this phenomenon can be understood on many different levels, for both of these factors directly shape how a given time zone is perceived. The social factors in this context would have to do with both the realness of different vibrational groups mixing—or coming into contact—with each other and the end result of what that contact means in actual terms. I have long believed that every so-called race represents a particular vibrationaltory state as well, and if this is true then the social implications of spectacle diversion (as a multi-convergence phenomenon) would relate to the nature underlying how a given vibration group flows with regards to a given physical or vibrationaltory universe situation, or how a given multi-vibrational mixture would result when two or more vibrational groups are in contact with each other. This multi-vibrational phenomenon is especially true in areas where the composite cultural reality imprint is comprised of many different so-called ethnic groups. The spread and dissemination of black culture in this period is directly related to this phenomenon as well. For the spectacle-diversion sequence also functions as a deterrent to prevent the forming of a real "composite" reality, and in its place what we instead have is the exploitation of non-so-called-caucasian races as a means to sustain the exclusive political position of Europeans and/or trans-Europeans. This phenomenon can be substantiated by looking at how the collective controlling forces of western culture have learned to utilize redocumentation as a means to distort the composite reality of its total space—on the physical universe plane. The present state of the western position has been secured by the political implications which surround how spectacle-diversion manipulation is initiated.

The related political implications that substantiate spectacle diversion as a basic factor in daily life progressions in the west operate on as many levels as one can imagine. It is this factor which safeguards both the status quo as well as the basic "vibrational alignment" which personifies how western culture works. For however much one would like to view the last two hundred years as a time period that has moved towards greater opportunities for all people (i.e., "things are getting better"), the fact is, it is clear that the distance between the "haves" and "have nots" has actually progressively increased. Moreso, the expansion of the western position on the composite planet in the last two hundred years has increased—not decreased. As such, one would have to be quite naive not to realize that this expansion has been at the expense of the world community. It is not a question of simply casting the achievements "ised" through the western position as something inherently negative, instead I am only commenting on what these achievements have implied on a world level. Needless to say, many other factors have also been employed to create the present state of this planet, and it would not be in the interest of truth to over-simplify this one subject. My reason for mentioning the position of western civilization in this time zone is only to state that among the factors that help support how this predicament is maintained is the phenomenon I now call the spectacle-diversion sequence—having to do with how "source transfer" progressionalism is both perceived and utilized in western culture (and what its related information transference really means). In other words, this concept relates to the way we have been taught to participate in life, as well as how we have been programmed to perceive of alternative information inputs.

SD(SY)–40

Certainly the best example of the information manipulation employed in the sixties would be the technological sophistication that developed to accelerate the position of present-day western media control. There is no one in this time zone who is not affected—in one way or another—by the sophistication that surrounds the dissemination of information as it is now utilized today through media (as an option is made real through the western information interpretation position). I am not merely commenting about the fact that everybody in this time period watches television or reads the newspaper when I comment on the profound impact of media either, for the implications of this subject are much more profound than any one factor. I am commenting on the multi-dimensional consequences of this medium as a factor not separate from the reality of "vibrational transfer" in language affinity (as a juncture which promotes a particular affinity alignment to the western vibration) as well as a tool for disconnecting from any sensibility related to the world group. For while the sophistication of contemporary media is a factor that has the potential to transform our awareness on many different levels, it is important to remember that this same medium can also do more harm than one might imagine. There are many facets in present-day media which are not necessarily conceived to be conducive to what is most positive for culture responsibility. The use of present-day information dissemination is symptomatic of what is really happening in western culture.

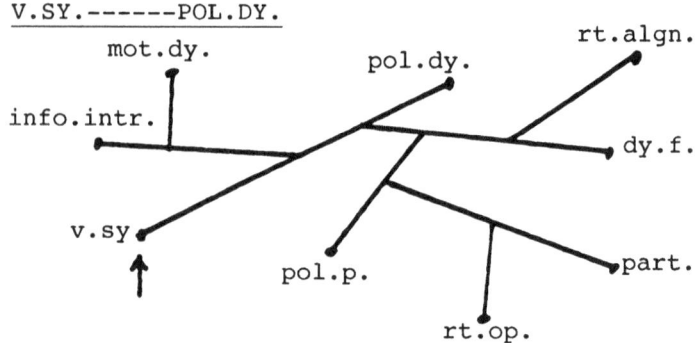

I have previously stated that the difference between the so-called radical groups and the status quo are practically nil. I have also stated that the difference between the people who control and the people who are the effects of that control is not as great as some of us would like to believe, but there is one difference. That difference is the position of the definer. For the control group, by its very nature, has the power and the sophistication to make the affected group deal with its initiations. This is a very serious difference. Any alternative consideration that emerges in the west is continually subjected to spectacle-diversion information manipulation until the potential of that consideration—as a meaning alternative factor—is redefined in accordance to the vibrational fabric of western culture. As such, the first condition that any alternative initiation must pass is the condition posed by media. As long as western culture can give the illusion that western information principles are valid when applied to any offering from the world group aesthetic, this practice will continue.

VT.U.PT.-----INFO.DE.B.

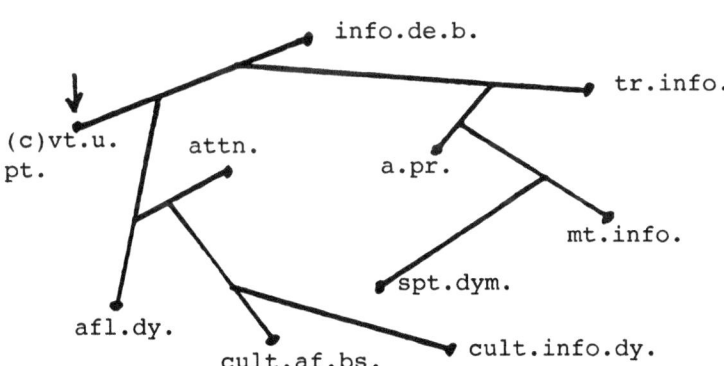

In the beginning of this essay I wrote that the emergence of the black aesthetic and its affinity alignment has served as the most significant alternative sensibility to have emerged in the west during this time period. I have also in this section attempted to write on what the realness of this aesthetic poses on the physical universe level. Yet it would be ridiculous to state that all of the cycles which govern events in the west are created solely because of its rejection of the black aesthetic, nor do I intend to make this mistake. But there is a relationship between the peculiarities that surround the vibrational-affinity arena in American culture and the distortions which surround the black aesthetic, and I have tried to point out some of these connections. If I am correct, the real problem which dictates perception in this time zone has to do with the flaws underlining how western culture perceives of its own center factor. In short, the physical universe reality that we exist in—in the west—is perceived directly in accordance to the philosophical and vibrational arena which defined it. "What you see is what you get."

Progressionalism

The dynamic continuum of accelerated progressionalism has had a profound effect on our lives on every level, and the seriousness of the changes taking place in this time zone promises to totally reshape our lives in the coming period. Moreover, the social reality implications of rapid change must be viewed for their effects on both actual and vibrational living; for while we have constantly been told about the virtues of contemporary living, in actual fact only in this period have we (as a collective people) begun to view the consequences of what these changes have brought about. In other words, the dynamics of contemporary living cannot always be viewed only with respect to its so-called advantages, because this subject has many unknown considerations (some of which are not necessarily positive). This is true not only for creativity but extends to every area of expanded functionalism, and it is important to understand what this means. The realness of dynamic extension in accelerated technology must be carefully viewed for its role in progressionalism—and this is especially true if the lessons of the last twenty years are to be grasped. For the solidification of dynamic technology has greatly determined the nature of living in this period—and this is true regardless of focus. That being, the emergence of atomic energy, computer technology, extended electronics, etc., has totally altered the basic state of things—and this has been both positive and negative. But if the accident at Three Mile Island in the late seventies means anything—and surely it must—then quite possibly it is now time to reflect on the nature of present-day progressionalism as a means to understand both what is happening in this period and what it poses for tomorrow. Either we ask these questions now or run the risk of not having the chance later.

The nature of present-day functionalism has altered the dynamics of spectacle-diversion manipulation on several levels, for the solidification of this phenomenon carries with it many new ways of "being effective." The realness of this effectiveness should not be lightly viewed for the sophistication of present-day manipulation exceeds all expectations. In short, we now live in one of the most highly controlled cultures on the planet—only it doesn't look that way on the surface. But to view the collective vibrational imprint of "American culture" is to see a reality focus quite removed from actual physical universe reality. This is not to say that America has no relationship to "living," because obviously we are alive—on one or two levels anyway, but rather, the nature of the composite forces shaping information in composite America has moved to create a "very particular vibrational state"—and this creation has not been done as an accident. If we are to really understand social reality dynamics as we move into the eighties (and nineties) then some effort must be made to come to terms with this "very special state."

There is a reason why the collective consciousness that emerged in the sixties suddenly vanished in the seventies (even though, as I have stated before, the dynamics of this new consciousness was not necessarily "all consciousness" but "game time in the Rockies") and there is also a reason for the state of information dynamics in this time zone—whether one is commenting on the relationship Americans have to "art" or world consciousness and/or spiritualism. For to view the nature of progressionalism in the sixties on through to the seventies is to deal with the dynamic manipulation of contemporary collective media—and this is also true of our educational institutions. In short, the dynamic de-acceleration of alternative functionalism is not separate from the success of contemporary manipulation, and the success of new functionalism will be directly linked to how well these areas of extended information control are dealt with. For positive change is directly related to whether

SD(SY)–44

or not people are able to deal with the composite "nature of things"—that being, the state of the whole planet, as opposed to only that of America.

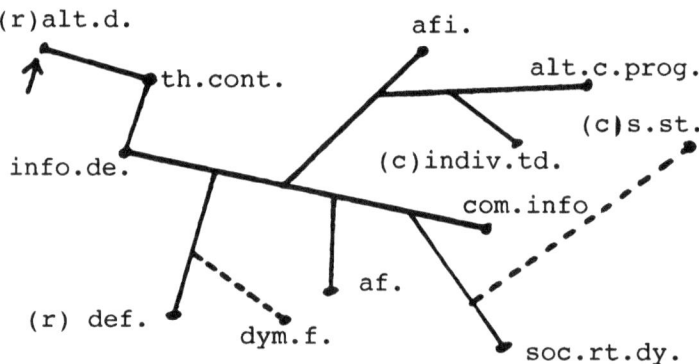

Many of us assumed that the reality of education would invariably be better for our children than what it was for us—and this is especially true for the grammar to high school experience. But in actual fact, it is possible now to view the present reality of public school education and see that not only in many cases has nothing improved but in many instances the situation has gotten worse. To understand what this means is to begin to view the composite factors that are shaping the next cycle of American progressionalism (understand, too, that this phenomenon is not universally manifested, which is to say western education is not necessarily declining in Europe, nor is education in Japan on the wane). The realness of a decreased information scan can tell us not only what has happened to composite dynamics (composite culture dynamics) but also what this means when viewed with respect to individual dynamic options. Unless some effort is made to change the deterioration of education in America there will be even more serious consequences for the greater culture.

The basic focus of this section has been directed towards understanding how artificially produced information dynamics are implanted as a means to control the "nature of things" in western continuity. It is important to understand what this concept means in dynamic terms, for the nature of spectacle-diversion progressionalism in the sixties represents only one aspect of this most complex phenomenon. The realness of this concept permeates every level of American culture—and what's more—this phenomenon has been extremely successful in vibrationally shaping "participation" and "remotivation." Nor by applying this concept on the nature of progressionalism in the sixties (on young white youth) have I meant to imply that black people are outside of the "effect spread" of this phenomenon—because if anything, non-white people are even more susceptible to this "chain of events." As such, it is important that some effort is made by the composite society to deal with this phenomenon, because I am not discussing a concept that only affects certain segments of the public and not others. The dynamics of spectacle-diversion progressionalism affect the composite culture—regardless of what so-called class or race one sees him- or herself in.

By the middle of the seventies, America began to manifest accelerated traits that, if not changed, threaten to cast a "particular" vibrational shadow over all of her citizens (and these traits will be difficult to ever remove if not checked soon). This is not to say that before the seventies everything was perfect—obviously it wasn't. Moreover, I have already commented on the progressional realness of spectacle diversion as an ingrained phenomenon that is related to how America was formed in her inception—which is to say, to view how this phenomenon is manifested today only shows the particulars of its path. Nevertheless, the dynamics of accelerated functionalism have brought America to a particular point in time that seems to carry serious implications for future extension. It will be important to understand the nature of what options we stand to deal with in further pursuing the course this country has chosen. In short, the dynamic implications of extended functionalism have helped to produce a situation where an unintended mistake might be difficult to correct if carried too far—and in fact, this is exactly what seems to be happening.

Cartoon Time

The accelerated traits I wrote of involve the nature of the forces that are presently shaping the composite vibrational reality of American culture. At present, the accelerated progressionalism of this phenomenon has moved to solidify a particular "view" of things, and "way of living" that characterizes a special way of "being" that is extremely detrimental to real understanding. My point is that America seems to be slowly evolving into a giant "cartoon"—or at least its reality dynamics—involving the way people are being taught to live—seem to be more related to a "cartoon" than actual life. By "cartoon culture" I am commenting on the nature underlying how information is dealt with in this period as well as how information is "not dealt" with. Life in America seems to kind of hum along without any real spiritual direction and/or purpose—nor do I mean this on one level. The dynamics of spectacle diversion can be viewed for its role in shaping new particulars (disco music and/or the craze for roller skates) as well as the concept of success (the exclusive focus on money or super-stardom). In practically every area, living in America seems to necessarily imply a separation between "progressional information" (that being, in this context, information about living that corresponds to the historical realness of what this experience could be about if understood—involving the role of creativity, the role of positive functionalism, the role of politics, the dynamics of ritual, etc.) and "concept living" (that being, existence only with respect to what is presumed to be new, or "the next focus"). In place of real life, America has moved to cast a shadow over understanding and in its place solidify a kind of "apple pie" philosophical base. I write this not to knock America, because I have feeling for this country—not to mention the phenomenon I am commenting on can be viewed throughout composite western culture (nor do I mean to imply that non-western countries are without their own special problems)—but only to comment on what seems to be happening. The fact is, existence in America has begun to take the form of some kind of game—this is true if one views the reality of music manipulating television (with all of the new programs of no social or redeeming value at all), fashion (every three months, if one believes these people, it's time to buy a whole new wardrobe), and cultural productivity (and everyone knows that while it's currently fashionable to comment about the lack of quality that seems to be drifting into production output in America—the fact is, the level of quality in American productivity does seem to be worse than it's ever been).

This is not to say that everything is wrong in the west or in America—because it isn't, but it is clear that all of the signs for "real change" have solidified and the question now is "which way will events take us" (since we no longer seem to be in charge of anything—if ever anyone was ever in charge). But the dynamic implications of alternative functionalism (i.e., alternative activism for positive change) are not separate from the nature of one's information scan. Which is to say, the most basic factor to induce the need for positive change is the awareness of extended information. This is not to say that a given information line will necessarily promote a particular path of activity—and/or viewpoint, because this does not seem to be the case either. Rather, some effort must be made to combat the reality focus that permeates American and western culture. For the progressional weight of contemporary information manipulation is currently isolating the dynamics of composite perception. Our actual lives are beginning to resemble the television commercials that saturate the composite tone of the culture—when in fact "we do deserve a break today!" Unless something is done, the collective manipulation of present-day information lines will move to solidify a vibrational state that will be practically impossible to simply shake off—and the consequences of this phenomenon can already be viewed.

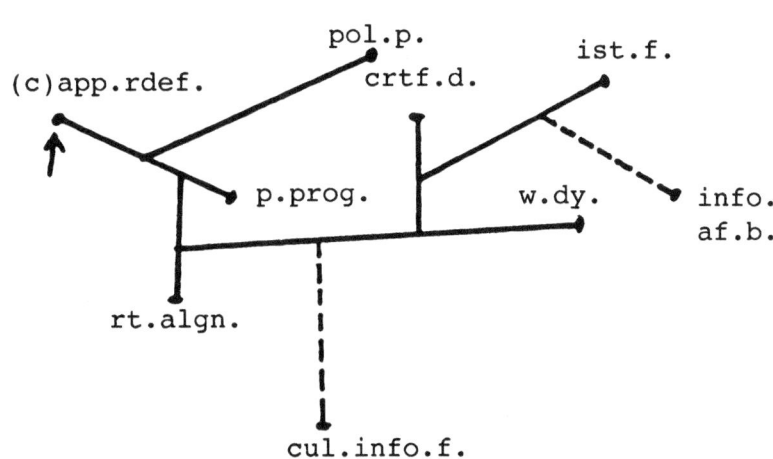

SD(SY)–48

The nature of "circular information dynamics" in western culture is directly related to the "return of the good ole days" phenomenon that American culture is presently dealing with. But the realness of this phenomenon has much greater vibrational and actual implications than what is generally recognized. For the net effect of this manipulation—or latest fad—is directly related to both spectacle-diversion regulation as well as reformation and dis-unification. To understand this is to really understand just what the "good ole days" really were—because either we have forgotten or somehow we have preferred not to remember. Moreover, the "return to the good ole days" syndrome is manifested throughout the composite information dynamics of present-day American culture—which is to say, we are entering the eighties with our minds in the fifties. On the surface, this could possibly be very interesting, but on the "not surface" the seriousness of this vibrational position could be devastating.

The greater thrust of the late seventies can be viewed as extremely interesting for what it poses for the next cycle (on through to the year 2000). At present, the progressional manipulation of composite information has moved to totally distort the composite reality implications of alternative ideas and/or focuses. The "return to the good ole days" syndrome has even moved to redirect how the progressional reality of creative music is viewed—and in doing so runs the risk of profoundly altering the affinity significance of "alternative participation." This is not to say that nothing good can come from the past, because obviously there is much to be learned from progressionalism—but the reality alignment of this period in time does not seem to be about really "learning" as much as "holding" (a time pattern). It would be different if western culture was going "forward into the past" rather than backward into some aspect of what is now being mis-documented as the past. Unless some insight is utilized, the realness of this phenomenon will play an important role in establishing (or dis-establishing) the solidification of the next cycle. This is true for both social reality as well as creative postulation. For inherent in the manipulation surrounding what we are told is the "good ole days" is the dis-unification which underlies the very nature of this time period. Even now, one can begin to view the rise of racism and fascism—directed not only at black people but towards practically every area of information and/or physical universe focus. The dynamics of this period have now seen the emergence of the Ku Klux Klan mentality, the rise of Nazism, and the acceleration of "gang resurgence." My point is that the nature of social reality is too important to be left in the hands of the present collective forces of western culture. It is now time for those who profess some love of humanity and world information to begin to function for "real" change. Either responsible people will act now or the future of the planet will be "up for grabs" (which it is anyway).

There is now the need for a real vision of the future or at least a cultural composite viewpoint concerning relevant functionalism—if the positive implications of progressionalism are to be secured (or advanced). I believe the most important factor that must be addressed is the challenge of supplying broader viewpoints (based on respect for all humanity and spiritual values). For this reason, it is important that efforts are made to examine the nature of spectacle-diversion progressionalism as a basis to restore relevant information alternatives. My understanding being that exposure to real information will serve to bring humanity together, and also provide some insight into what actual "living" is or could be about. I have not meant to imply that the concept of spectacle diversion is all-consuming (and as such answers every aspect of contemporary western progressionalism)—because no one viewpoint carries this much weight (or at least no viewpoint of mine carries that much weight), but I do believe this concept has some relevance with respect to what it does comment on. One thing is certain, America as a country is slowly coming to what I believe will be an important juncture in her existence and this juncture is not separate from the greater theatre of events reshaping composite world culture. The realness of social and vibrational reality will be an important factor related to what decisions are made in the not-so-distant future—and as such, it is important that efforts are made in this time zone to better understand what "options" we are dealing with. One thing is certain: nothing remains the same—which is to say, particulars will either be corrected or not (with the consequences being what we would call positive or negative). In short, "something is going to happen."

(Level One) AFFINITY DYNAMICS

To understand and view the realness of creativity, one must first have some awareness of progressional dynamics and multi-information (as well as what these terms signify about composite earth creativity). It would not be in the interest of "what really is" to limit a subject as serious as creativity to only one strata or focus. The fact is, when I wrote there are many intersecting junctures in earth creativity—as a basis to view the composite underlying philosophical realness of this subject—it is important that this diversity is understood and included in any real attempt to forge a universal world perspective. Because to view this area of information is to focus on the reality of transfer cycles as a "natural" or normal progressional phenomenon in earth developments—and the inevitable result of this knowledge should move to bring people together, not apart. Moreover, the acknowledgement of transfer cycles does not imply any disrespect for particular projections (creative routes)—I have already in this series of works expressed my respect for the composite thrust of earth creativity (regardless of projection, and in this regard I will continue to do so)—but rather, the realness of transfer cycles is a phenomenon that contains its own challenges and insight. If we are to view the progressional continuity of earth creativity then we are forced to deal with the significance underlying how given projections actualize. This information will better help us view the projectional spread of given creative routes in both vibrational and actual terms—and this is important. For if the concept of information-transfer shift does indeed have relevance—as a viewpoint that gives insight into the meta-reality content of a given projection—then to ignore this subject would risk misinterpreting the nature of particular projections (creative routes)—and, of course, that is exactly what has happened in this time period. The end result of this neglect is that the progressional transfer implication of earth creativity has moved towards distortion, and there are many reasons for this.

(AF)D-2

The fact is, the natural tendency of every cultural group (vibrational group) in the last three hundred years has been to promote its own individual dynamic tendencies as a means to proclaim vibrational (although most groups in this time period perceive themselves under the ill-conceived notion of "separate race") superiority—or political and/or cultural superiority. This tendency is only possible when the progressional information which solidified how that group achieved its culture eminence is distorted—or suppressed. The end result of this "vibrational position" (cultural perceived separateness) is that it promotes isolation (thus retarding the possibility of earth unification). I do not mean, however, to imply that there are no differences between culture groups, nor have I meant to give the impression that particular nations have not brought forth "particular" knowledge—because this is not true either. My point, however, is that the progressional thrust of earth information is multi-complexual and related to the composite realness of all earth knowledge (or principle information routes), and as such cannot be claimed as actualized exclusively from any one sector or section of the planet. Moreover, as we move towards the next transformation cycle, the composite significance of affinity transfer information will take on an added meaning, for if my observations are correct and if we as a people—with the emergence of technology (and the possibility to bring forth positive alternative technology as well as the advent of rapid communication)—are moving towards the resolidification of humanity (not as an end but as a cycle—after which undoubtedly there will be other cycles), then quite possibly the realness of affinity transfer can better prepare us for this move.

Thus the significance of affinity-transfer progressionalism is important—especially in this section of the book—for how it can help provide some backdrop for understanding the physical universe (social) progressions taking place in this period—and this concept will also give some insight into the meta-realness of earth creativity. For if the concept of spectacle diversion does indeed comment on the progressional use of information manipulation in western culture today, it would be to our advantage to understand what affinity position has resulted from this use—both with respect to how we now perceive of phenomenon (concepts and actualities) as well as how we function (postulation). My point is simple: **I believe that the collected forces of western culture have deliberately designed a reality perspective that retards the function of any affinity slant other than what it perceives as its own.** The consequences of this phenomenon are that only a selected area of information is made available to the public (and that information only moves—or at least is designed—to affirm the perceived affinity position of white people—with the consequence being the distortion and rejection—and redocumenting—of any "alignments" thought to be relevant to the basic world community—including white people). The seriousness of this phenomenon cannot be overstated, and the realness of what it signifies about the nature of western continuance cannot be simply overlooked. I am writing of something of monumental importance.

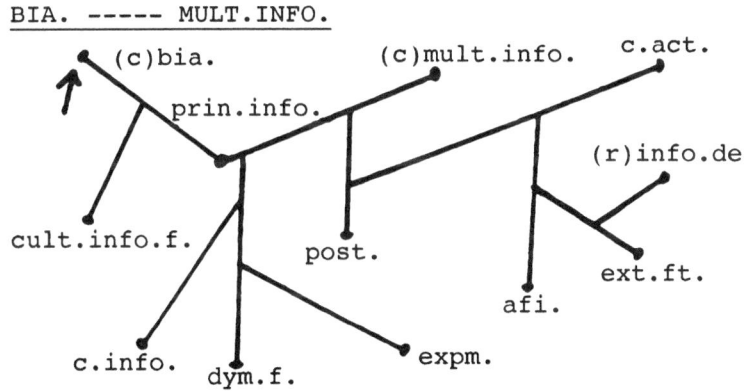

The net effect of the suppression (or negation) of affinity-transfer progressionalism is manifested in the inability of western culture to deal with the multi-dynamic implications of "information"—and as such, nine-tenths of the information disseminated in this time zone can be viewed with respect to the dynamics that are not understood—rather than what is understood. This suppression extends to all of the information focuses—pertaining to the nature underlying how discipline is perceived—whether we are discussing philosophy, medicine, art, or magic, etc. The composite realness of this suppression is also directly related to the present "vibrational position" of western culture—which is to say, the actuality of world culture information (in its correct affinity position) could well serve as the strongest transformation factor (or at least the availability of composite information interpretation in all of its dynamic affinity degrees could well serve as the strongest base for realigning how present-day information is understood—in this time zone). This is so because the present situation we are now in can be viewed as the direct result of the inability of nations to deal with the composite realness of our position on this planet. The realness of transfer cycles is directly related to how transition has been achieved (in this last cycle—say, the last four hundred years), and this phenomenon cannot be taken lightly—especially if we are to ever understand the significance of what has been raised in the composite spectrum of earth creativity. The fact is, all information will be relevant as the greater forces move towards actualizing the next cycle of our existence on earth (and indeed, quite possibly this move has already begun—or at least there is already some evidence to suggest that the nature of this time period has already moved towards real change). Before I can elaborate on the implications of particular transfer cycles—or what this phenomenon seems to pose (in both its vibrational and physical universe sense)—it is first necessary to provide a base context for investigation. What exactly is the concept of transfer shifts, and what does this concept have to do with creativity or solidifying culture? Without this information, none of these concepts can necessarily be viewed in any productive sense.

To understand the concept of information affinity transfer is to have some awareness that the basis which has substantiated three-fourths of the information this culture (western culture) now utilizes has its roots in world culture. This is not to say that western culture—or any other culture for that matter—has not contributed (and abundantly) to the wellspring of world information, because obviously it has. My point, however, is that many of us have not been made aware of the progressional spread of information from world culture—and how given routes of that information have served as the foundation for much of the knowledge we now function from today. To better understand the contribution of world culture is to have some awareness of the progressional rise and fall of various culture groups—regardless of planet region—as well as the nature underlying how transitions (and transformations) have occurred—on the physical universe plane. My point is that before we can deal with the realness of affinity transfer, it is first necessary to understand the nature of how information is perceived—or at least it is necessary to understand that the route a given information thrust travels is not regulated by any one country or culture. Long before the present concept we have of "race" was established, history tells us of many periods where various so-called culture groups participated in collectively interchanging and shaping information. The very idea of "high" culture is related to the position of that culture's information—and the relationship of that information to both the vibrational functional and political realness of its living dictates. What this means is that even though the surface dynamics of a given projection can be perceived as being uniquely western, eastern, etc., in fact the "source initiation" realness of practically every projectional thrust is connected to the progressional route of composite world culture—and as such, the reality of this phenomenon has to do with the composite whole of humanity. The very basis of source initiation rests on this very concept—that being, **all of the principle areas of information (knowledge) that we are now dealing with in this time zone can be researched back into the progressional rise and fall of various cultures in the world community—and as such, the surface differences of a given route of information only tell of the progressional path that information has traveled.**

INFO.ALGN. ------PROG.CONT.

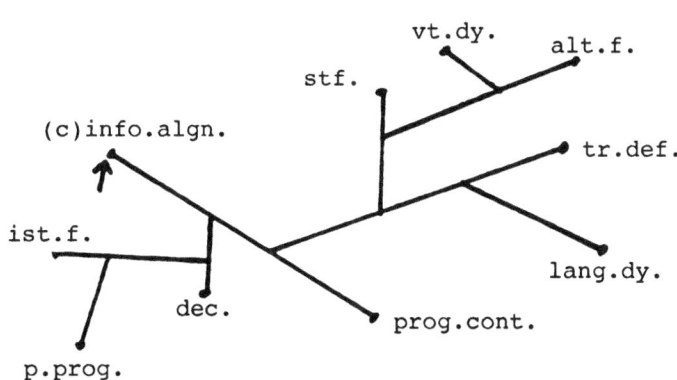

(AF)D–6

Thus, the source-initiation projection of a given affinity thrust (knowledge) can be viewed as the essence foundation that solidifies the principle state (route) of a given area of information with regards to its essence. The reality of this phenomenon has to do with how a given information route affirms both its spiritual and functional position. Because of this, it is possible to trace the progressional continuity particulars that tell how a given route of information actualized as well as how it was viewed (within its principle meta-reality). It is from this point that we can view the transfer-shift implications of information—for before any projectional route can be traced (with respect to how given aspects of its dictates are perceived as different), it is first necessary to have some idea of what source initiation is. Moreover, the implications of transfer shift are directly related to the particulars underlying how events are perceived in this time period as well—which is to say, the seriousness of this phenomenon has multi-dimensional consequences— or at least it has had multi-dimensional consequences (because we are presently living in the consequences of this position—and this position has lasted for over four hundred years). Whatever, at the heart of this idea is the realness that given information routes have been de-utilized and redocumented. Thus, the investigation of source initiation remains one of the greatest needs in this time zone—for this information can help bring the clarity that we will need in the next cycle. That is, the realness of source initiation can provide the proper context for understanding world culture and reviewing present-day "information" as a means to extract what is most relevant about that information for future transformation.

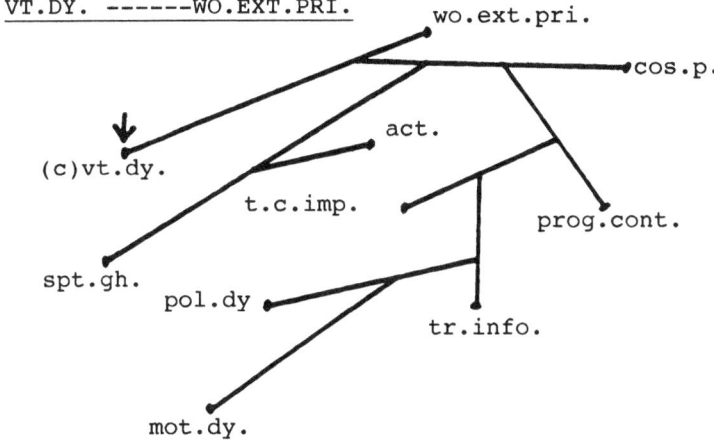

The concept of transfer shifts can be viewed with respect to the "natural" (or unnatural) dynamics which are manifested on this planet—those being: (1) the seemingly realness that there are different types of beings in a given society and as such—given routes of information subjectively and objectively (bi-jectively) are perceived by given groups of people in different terms; (2) the realness that given physical universe areas on the planet seem to also color the affinity nature underlying how information is perceived; and (3) the progressional spread of information can also be viewed in mystical terms—that is, certain aspects of information seem not to actualize unless the tone level of the society reaches a certain point. To understand these contexts is to have some awareness of the complexity of what has and is happening on earth in this period of time, for if the focus of this chapter was perceived to deal with the physical universe factors shaping progressional creativity—(and from that point, to also include the political and sociological factors that have existed in the total position we are now in as a people)—as of yet I have only begun to lay basis for dealing with this subject. The concept of transfer-shift information is important to the whole of this series of writings.

When I wrote that affinity-transfer information is related to the dynamics surrounding different people—in a given culture group or

(AF)D–8

whatever—it is necessary to elaborate on what this means. For it must be noted that in earlier cultures there was no concept of race as such (yet I have not meant to imply that, say, people in Egypt were not aware of the surface differences surrounding how people looked—obviously they were), but rather, this concept did not have the same position in Egypt that it has in western culture during this time zone. Many of us in this period have come to view the term race as the most basic notion that distinguishes what is happening with human beings—at least as far as projectional-affinity thrust (and/or classification) is concerned—and while this concept is certainly meaningful on some levels, this has not been the progressional view brought forth through world culture information. Yet obviously there have always been different groups—and cultures—of people throughout recorded history. My point in mentioning the concept of race—and how this concept was viewed throughout different time periods on earth—is that there are other factors related to this subject which are equally important if we are to understand information dynamics. One view is this: **it is possible to view the dynamic spectrum of people in a single culture as representing and manifesting the realness of affinity dynamics in the same context as we now ascribe to race. In other words, if the concept of race is related to how the cross-sectional spread of information is viewed, then this focus can only be viewed as one factor among many related to information dynamics.** In other words, the significance of affinity projection would have to do with an expanded understanding of ourselves as human beings (as well as how that new understanding can help us deal with the progressional thrust of world information).

(AF)D-9

AF.POST. ------TR.

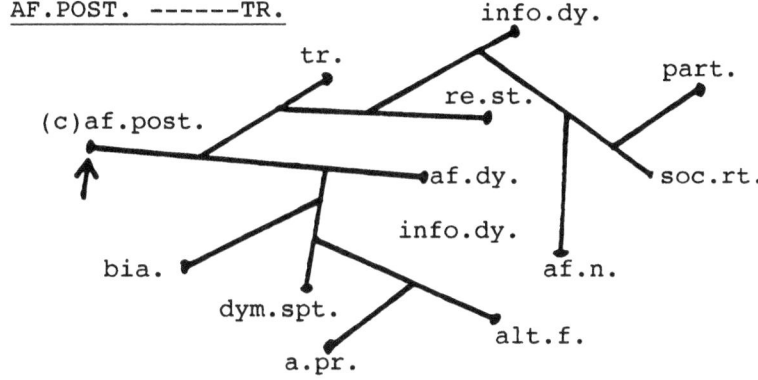

INFO.DY.------C.CONT.

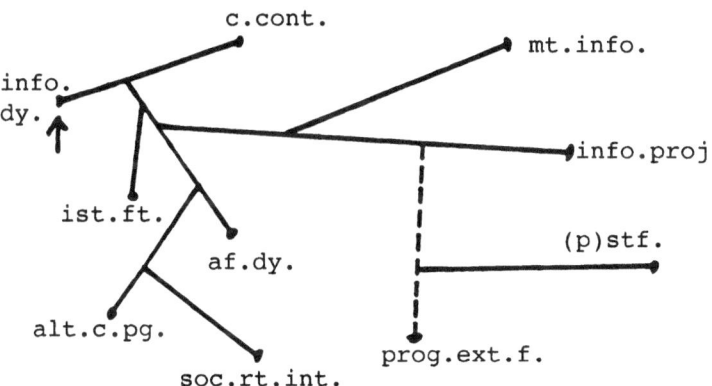

By citing the vibrational diversity of people—in a given culture—as an example of affinity dynamics, I am only commenting on the most basic physical universe information. Obviously people are different from one another, but my point is that all of this means something. The fact is, by only lightly examining different areas of information—say (in world culture), the study of astrology—it is possible to view how this difference was perceived in progressional history (and the methodology which resulted from that understanding) and this information can better help us to understand the present. The concept of affinity dynamics is directly related to what this means as well. **To say that different individuals can**

be viewed with respect for the concept of affinity dynamics is to say that, given a principle exposure to a particular information projection (knowledge), different people will vibrate to particular regions of that information. And inherent in this phenomenon is the realness that information cannot be viewed in mono-dimensional terms—but rather, every projectional thrust of knowledge must take into account its affinity dynamics. For any given route of information carries with it a much wider meta and functional consequence than we have usually come to recognize. The realness of this expanded understanding of information projection must also be viewed with respect to both what it implies about the meta-reality actualness of this time period and the social (functional) questions it raises. I am not writing of an isolated concept—the irregularities concerning how we as a people deal with ideas—but rather, a phenomenon intrinsically related to the present particulars underlying this experience (living, and the laws related to how the all-cosmic realness of living is—or seems to be—maintained).

Thus, the solidification of "information projection" and/or "information-affinity basis" can be viewed within several contexts, and each of these categories reflect on how phenomenon can be viewed. There is the information-affinity realness of the individual, as a dynamic force in his or her own right (and the actualness that people are born into certain vibrationaltory zones with the ability to perceive of events in accordance to that zone)—there is the "information affinity" nature of the group, as a center factor which substantiates the nature underlying how a given projection is to be actualized (viewed or utilized)—and finally, there is the "information affinity" influence of the cosmic and/or spiritual arena (which seemingly can be viewed in several contexts—the realness that different areas of the planet seem to affect viewpoints—and projectional motivation—in particular ways, and the effect of what forces are utilized in religious practices). The solidification of a given information route can be viewed in one of these contexts (if we are talking about tracing the progressional thrust underlying how a given projection solidified, or if we are interested in viewing how a given projection manifested some aspect of a particular sector—in a particular

(AF)D–11

culture structure). To understand this is to have some awareness of what the solidification of "principle" information is, and as such, all of these conditions should be viewed in any given culture situation. Because every culture situation can be viewed with respect to the composite layers of activity which are taking place (concerning its information), and this is true on a number of levels. Moreover, it is important to understand that none of the three contexts mentioned (individual information affinity—group informational affinity—cosmic informational affinity) need to be viewed in separate terms. In other words, the realness of a living and breathing culture has the spectrum of its affinity-dynamics particulars in constant multi-function. To view a given culture group—regardless of time period—is to view a situation where all of the "information affinity natures" I have previously mentioned are functioning at the same time—and finally (what is even more amazing) is the realness that permeates the total fabric of every culture group is the vibrational imprint of the sum of its composite activity. In other words, a culture can be viewed with respect to both its individual brilliance (and as such, in this context viewing the nature underlying how information projections were actualized) and its collective vibrational identity. All of which brings us to the real position of transfer cycles—what it means (and the relationship of this viewpoint to the progressional spread of creativity in both a vibrational and physical universe context)—and also what it tells us about the present cycle we are now living through. Because by focusing on the nature underlying how information routes are actualized, we can hopefully begin to expand our basis for perceiving what information really is.

(AF)D–12

ASP.ES.------SPT.D.

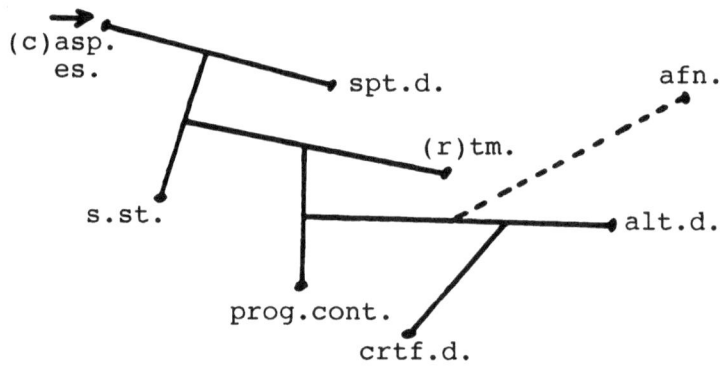

C.INFO.------PROG.CONT.

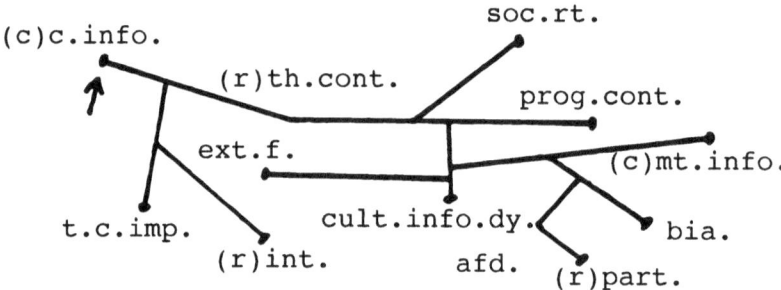

Thus, the concept of transfer cycles can be viewed with respect to the nature underlying how information is passed through various time zones and culture groups. That is, the concept of transfer cycles can be viewed with respect to differences of composite affinity (having to do with what a culture group is) as well as the time-presence implications that dictated how a given information projection solidified. It then is important to view the many culture groups which have been on the planet as a means to understand the route of a given information thrust (and for this reason alone, the study of history and historical progressions takes on added importance), because it is understood that every cultural group has, on one level or another, utilized some (or every) aspect of "principle information." In other words, the progressional shifting of information can be viewed as just that. Because the projectional realness of principle-information lines (avenues of knowledge) can be viewed in every cultural center regardless of planet region. Moreover, the surface difference of a given information route can be viewed with respect to the concept of affinity dynamics (rather than to applied empiricism). In other words, the individual brilliance that has underlined how given culture groups attain "high culture" (or awareness and/or ability to function from that awareness) has more to do with the realness of affinity dynamics than any notion of superiority or "misplaced notion of advanced." As such, we can all learn from the composite information offered to us from world culture (which we have also helped to actualize as well) in all of its dynamic forms.

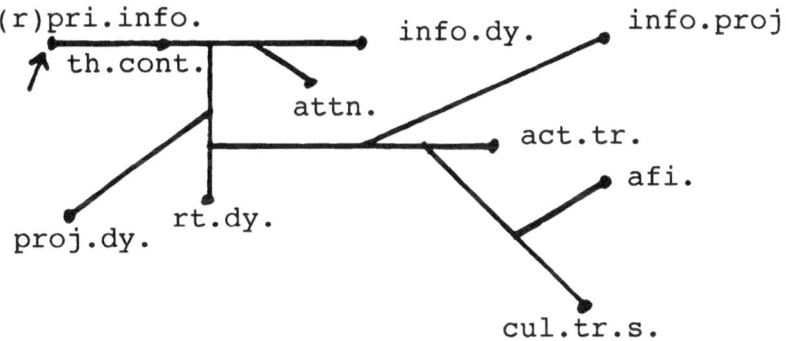

The nature underlying how cultural transfer shifts are established on the physical universe level can tell us much about progressional development. Certainly every high culture has utilized great centers of learning—and many of these centers were open to all people—in the same context as our university system today. Many people, for instance, came into Egypt to study information (and the information spectrum that would later solidify the Greek and Roman high-culture cycle can be viewed as directly related to what was learned in this period). Yet if institutionalized education can be viewed as the best example of cultural responsibility (and as such, a tool to make information available for all people—and cultures—with the hope that constructive activity can result from its availability), it cannot be said that this context was the predominant mode of information transfer. The fact is, the great predominance of information spread (or transfer) has been brought about through the destruction of nation against nation—what we call war, and the realness of this fact can be viewed throughout the pages of history. The savagery that human beings have committed against each other can be viewed as a factor that has greatly affected the progressional spread of all earth information—and the seriousness of this tendency must be understood on several levels. For the end results of this phenomenon—on the physical universe plane—has brought forth special problems with respect to the reality underlying how information is viewed—throughout recorded history—and any attempt to understand the dynamics of information transfer would imply that these "problems" are acknowledged, and examined.

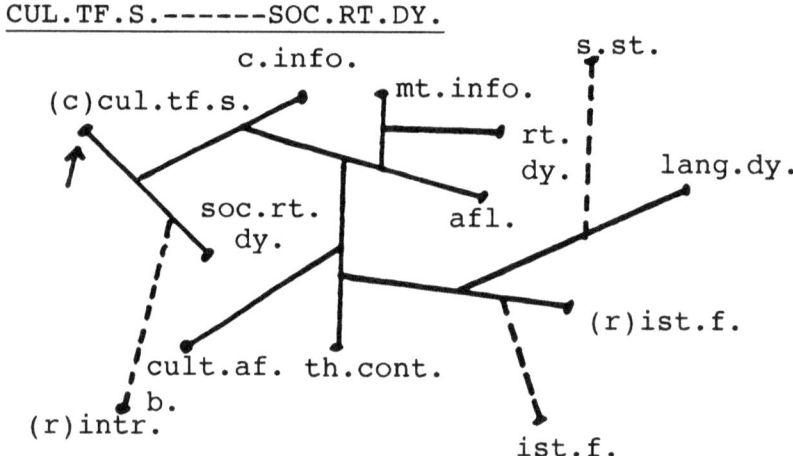

In other words, to examine the progressional spread of information—on the physical universe plane—is to deal with both the realness of redocumentation as an integral (and cyclical) factor attached to practically every strain of information presently available, as well as gradualism as a transfer shift factor related to how affinity shift is secured—nor do I mean this on one level. For the projectional thrust of any informational continuum cannot be viewed as being separate from the physical universe factors from which it was extracted—and from which it derives its significance. The realness of what this means (i.e., the inability of given groups to acknowledge the dynamic offerings of another group—or the seriousness of time change, as a factor that promotes memory gaps) can better help us to understand what has happened to make this cycle as it is. Add to this phenomenon the rise and fall of given culture groups within the "natural" cosmic order (or what I will call order) that seems to be happening on the physical universe level, and one can begin to view the complexual realness of thrust continuance (or the concept of information and time changes).

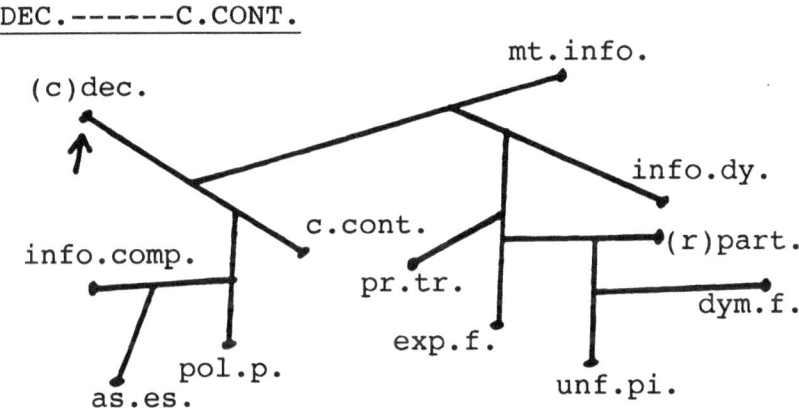

By redocumentation I am commenting on how certain areas of information are portrayed in a given time cycle (and culture). Moreover, when I wrote in the beginning of this section on what seemed to be the natural tendencies of culture groups to accent their dynamic culture information at the expense of the world group, I was commenting on how this focus usually leads to some type of unbalance. Again, I have not meant to give the impression that I recognize no particular cultural achievement, because obviously various culture groups have contributed particular information thrusts—nor am I unaware of the nature of the spread of humanity over this planet (that being, the realness that in earlier times it was not always possible to be informed about the activities of another culture group because of time and space)—and the actualness of redocumentation cannot be over-simplified. At the same time, the realness of principle information routes can be seen in the progressional continuity of every so-called cultural group, and it is also possible to view the probable nature underlying how a given information route extended on the physical universe level. **The fact is, the history of this planet seems to reveal that the nature of information transfer can be viewed (and to some degree understood)—as related to what happened (or at least "how" it happened) on the physical universe level.** Moreover, this same history also documents that after certain information routes are secured (and after a given time zone has passed), the culture's transition always involves some level of redocumentation—to the extent that the "source initiation" of a principle-information thrust is no longer recognized (or embraced—or talked about). Yet I have not meant to make an unfair charge, or state that redocumentation in itself is wrong—because certainly there is the realness that the reality of information transfer must also involve affinity dynamics (and as such, alternative information projections as well)—and any real attempt to understand the realness of this subject would imply that all of these considerations are taken into account. Because by affinity dynamics in this context, I am commenting on the realness that everyone or every group (in this case, culture group) functions with respect to his or her own affinity dynamics—including the nature of how borrowed (or learned) information is perceived (in other words—all of us have something of value to add to a given projectional thrust of information—knowledge)—and as such, it would not be correct to merely state that given culture groups cannot also reshape aspects of learned information. Yet by the same token, the realness of redocumentation has been utilized on a scale that moves to completely distort the progressional thrust of a given information route. For by not dealing with the composite reality of a given information route, there is the realness of losing the meta-reality dynamics which solidified how a thrust (information route) got to be what it is—or was. The resultant information would have to be viewed as "less than what it is" in its own progressional realness—and as such, this use of information transference is not the optimum position for understanding. For this reason, it is important to re-understand the progressional continuum of composite world information—with the awareness that the composite solidification of a given thrust projection can better give insight into the dynamic reality of its information route. In the final analysis, every culture suffers if relevant information is not understood (and when possible, practiced—with respect to what is most positive about all of us). The restoring of information dynamics remains one of the most important challenges for transformation.

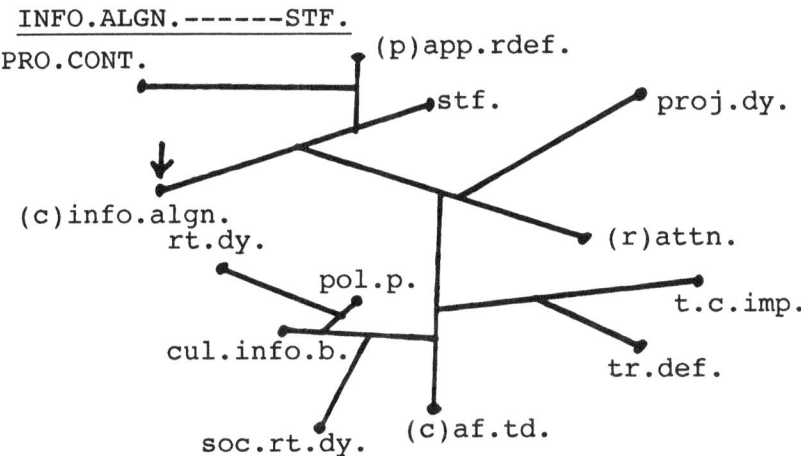

The most basic point I have been trying to make in this section is that the concept of transfer shifts is an integral factor coupled to how the spread of information has come about. Hopefully an awareness of transferred composite information (from culture to culture) can better help us to deal with the affinity-dynamic implications surrounding principle-information routes. It is important to understand that the projectional realness of information is directly related to how all of us have come to view our lives—either on an individual or cultural (collective) level. Which is to say, I am not simply writing of theoretical information that has nothing to do with actual life. The seriousness of this subject cannot be over-emphasized—especially if we are concerned with what form the next transformation will take. Our ability to shape the next cycle is directly related to what we are able to understand in this cycle (about the past and present). And while it has been necessary to invent separate terms to convey my thoughts on the reality of "information transfer," I have not done this as an intellectual exercise—rather, this subject is directly related to what is happening on the social physical universe level in this period—and as such, there is an urgency surrounding my decision to introduce this material. To view the progressional developments taking place in earth culture in this time zone is to have some idea about the complexity that has resulted from the use—or misuse (or controlled use)—of information, and this is what concerns this essay. The question then is what does alternative investigation mean to these developments—and how does this information translate into physical universe terms? Because in the final analysis, whether or not the concept of affinity transfer is valid is irrelevant unless it helps us to better view the present situation we are now in on this planet. For this reason, the implication of transferred information must be viewed with respect to the factors which have (and are) shaping the present cycle that we are now living in. But it should be stated that the realness of this subject means different things to different segments of the human community and cannot be lightly applied —because the dynamics of information-transfer are manifested in different forms and/or people. For this reason, I have found it necessary to write of the physical universe relevance of this concept in separate terms—or particular terms. It is my hope that a proper focus and application of this viewpoint can help clarify the reality of information transference (as a relevant and meaningful concept). The implications of any particular focus can help us better view the universal realness of being, and while doing so, also increase our perspective (which is to say, the concept of isolated focus can have universal applications if used correctly).

Without doubt, the realness of information transfer is related to the present situation that black people are dealing with in western culture in this cycle. By that I mean the present situation that black people are dealing with is directly related to the realness of information transfer and distortion. Moreover, this phenomenon is manifested on many different levels. **For the collective forces of western culture have moved to create a complex and highly dangerous situation surrounding several vibrational (and actual) positions that are detrimental to the realness of black people—**

and in particular, black people in western culture. Those positions are: (1) that black culture has never contributed to the progressional spread of "high culture" (and the information that is related to high culture), (2) the understanding that the dynamic affinity thrust of black people can be viewed as narrower than that of the caucasians, and (3) the idea that the composite solidification of western culture can be viewed as separate (and superior) to that of the world group (with the understanding being that western culture owes nothing to the progressional spread of world culture). All of these ideas must be dealt with on some level, and all of these ideas must be viewed with respect to what it has brought about on the physical universe level. For the seriousness of these "vibrational positions" is directly related to the social and vibrational reality that all non-white people are dealing with (understand too, that when I write of black people I do not simply mean African-American black people or African-Caribbean people—for the realness of the distortions we are dealing with in this period have totally affected the realities of all non-white people). The principle focus of this series of books has been on black culture because I am black (and as such my research has been shaped by my own immediate interest), but the realness of true information extends isolated viewpoints. The fact is, the magnification of western culture—and the informational affinity stance which has come as a result of that magnification—has produced a situation that moves to distort the total realness of world culture (including western culture) and as such, the effect of that magnification is not only manifested in black culture (and people) but includes the composite realness of world culture as well. Yet without focusing on one manifestation (and example) of this phenomenon, it would be difficult to clarify this section.

Possibly the best way for one to deal with my charge that the collected forces of western culture have moved to suppress the vibrational dynamics of black culture is to examine the information surrounding how black creativity is viewed in this period. Even in this context the realness of my viewpoint can be understood. **Because the most basic notion that western culture has perpetrated in this time zone is the idea that black creativity can be viewed only with respect to certain areas of creativity**

(AF)D–20

(as opposed to the normal idea that human beings—and groups—have participated and contributed to the spectrum of creativity regardless of medium). It is currently popular to view black creativity only with regards to the progressional particulars of black people's social and political existence in the Americas—having only to do with the projections most of us have come to know as blues or ragtime (on up to what is now called jazz). Moreover, the picture that has slowly formed from our mis-awareness of black culture has to do with "the happy slave," or creativity that only addresses itself to a narrow vibrational spectrum (and that this spectrum is only relevant to black people—as opposed to the world community). From that viewpoint, the information that surrounds black creativity can be viewed as both stagnating and distorted. But the distortions I have just mentioned are obviously not true, and my reasons for restating these notions are not just to restate the obvious—because I am looking for something else here. The fact is, while most people would—if questioned—deny that their viewpoint of black creativity is as I have stated, it is possible to view the collected manipulation of western education as a prime example of this attitude (and viewpoint)—and even worse, it is also possible to view the composite thrust of black education (and journalism) in this same light. Obviously this is true, but my point is that the realness of these misconceptions have multi-dimensional implications—concerning both the vibrational and actual position of black people in this period.

It must be understood that the styles we refer to as blues, ragtime, etc. are of course projections that have actualized through the vibrational dynamics of black people, and all of us can be thankful for the emergence of these forms—of course this is true. My point, however, is that the solidification of these forms are only one aspect of the composite dynamics of black creativity—furthermore, my point is that the information related to those forms are only one aspect of the composite information actualized from the affinity dynamics of black culture. The present-day isolation of black culture affinity dynamics and multi-information has profoundly affected the reality options of black people. For the progressional spread of false notions about black creativity has moved to create a situation where few black people can perceive of themselves in an extended context without feeling as if they have violated the proper vibrational reality of black culture (the distortions surrounding the participation of white musicians in improvised music are also related to the false identity—and vibrational—roles that have been created to justify how this manipulation works). But my point is that all of these notions have been fabricated as a means to narrow—and finally, suppress to oblivion—the realness of vibrational dynamics. The end result of this manipulation is that the solidification of alternative viewpoints cannot affect the basic lining of western culture—and because of this, positive transformation is negated (or stopped). The consequences of this manipulation have also moved to create a situation where the only affinity option that can affect the progressional development of this planet will be from the caucasian western culture position exclusively—and this cannot be viewed as positive on any level. For while it is clear that the composite affinity stance of western culture has indeed contributed to the solidification of this planet's well-being, the truth is that no one projectional thrust constitutes in itself what is most positive (or negative). The suppression of the spectrum of affinity dynamics in this period is important for what it signifies for the next cycle.

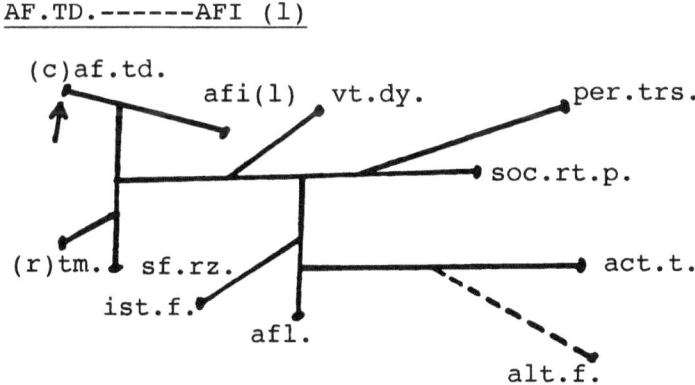

In the beginning of this section I wrote about the implications of affinity dynamics as a factor that gives insight into the projectional realness of information routes. The realness of what this means is also related to the composite aesthetic solidification of creativity as well. In other words, the emergence of a given projection (style) can be viewed with respect to what that projection signifies in both its actual solidification and vibrational solidification (i.e., what it sounds like and what it means vibrationally). To understand this is to understand that a given projection (style) derives its significance not only from how it sounds on a surface level but also from what it signifies about the vibrational and cosmic information of its affinity nature. Because of this relationship, the realness of affinity dynamic takes on added importance. For if the projectional significance of a given style does indeed have relevance on a cosmic plane, then the concept of affinity dynamics has to do with how given projections solidify, as well as what those projections mean (in vibrational terms). My point is that the phenomenon of affinity dynamics is related to the affinity insight principle in the sense that this "state of being" is directly connected with how given individuals (and cultures for that matter) move towards knowingness (or simply move "towards"). **Affinity dynamics, then, is my phrase to comment on the vibrational attraction mechanism which determines how a given individual or person moves towards defining—and interpreting.** Moreover, my point is also that the "natural" (in the sense that people and cultures seem to be born with this "state of being") affinity attraction is significant for what it signifies about its particular information route. To understand this is to understand that all information routes are of value to a given segment of "what is" (or at least to understand this is to understand that people are not born "wrong" as such, but rather directly "involved"—if I can write it that way). The significance, then, of a given area of information is directly related to what affinity interpretation is dealt with—and this is important. For if my observations are correct—and there is a collective attempt to suppress the realness of affinity dynamics—then this time zone must be looked at very carefully for what it tells us about the progressional continuity. The fact is, the move to suppress the affinity options of alternative alignments (which is how the composite realness of non-western "state of being" can be viewed—although on some levels this is not true [because to imply that there is a natural superiority of non-western "states of beings" to western affinities is equally ridiculous]) must also be viewed as a move to suppress what areas of information are related to those alignments ("interpretations") as well. This is so because

(AF)D-23

I am not simply writing of an isolated alignment that means nothing in itself. The significance of the concept of affinity alignment is that it in fact does mean something. The attempts to suppress this most important phenomenon must not be taken lightly.

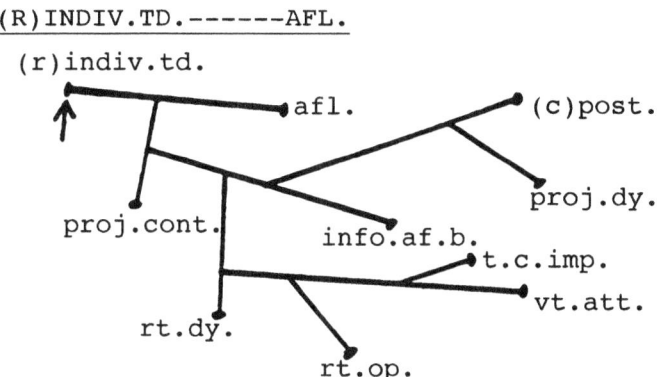

The situation we are living in during this cycle can be viewed with respect to the seriousness of affinity compression—on both a physical universe and vibrational level. For the realness of this phenomenon has created a situation ripe for exploitation—and of course that is exactly what has happened. The end result of this exploitation is that the composite realness of black culture has moved towards separation on many different levels. The realness of this split became quite clear in the sixties and is still with us now (end of the seventies). The shame of it is that the breakdown in the composite solidification of alternative culture has helped to strengthen the over-balance of the western stronghold responsible for putting the world group in the very situation we are now in. In actual terms, even the black community can be viewed with respect to the many artificial separations that have emerged in this period concerning: what is black and what is hip; what route politically to take; the split between those who see themselves as nationalists and those who do not—the divisions between the middle class and the poor, etc. So real have these separations become that the composite potential of the black community has yet to be tapped. Moreover, the end result of these many separations is that black people are in an even weaker position to change the existing power structure than we were in the fifties. The progressional realness of this phenomenon is directly related to how the suppression of black culture is maintained. Because if the world group themselves cannot deal with the dynamic spectrum of their own "information lines," how can they expect anyone else to. In other words, the realness of the separations that have taken place in the black (and world—for all practical purposes this phenomenon is directly related to the reality options of women, the Middle East and India, etc.) community has moved to create a situation that is detrimental for positive transformation—but this is only the beginning. Because to view the seriousness of the separations existing in this cycle is to understand how far we are—as earth people—from understanding the meta-reality significance of alternative culture (whether we are talking about knowingness through the African projection and/or through the feminine projection or world group). In other words, the present physical universe situation is detrimental to uncovering the composite realness of multi-information.

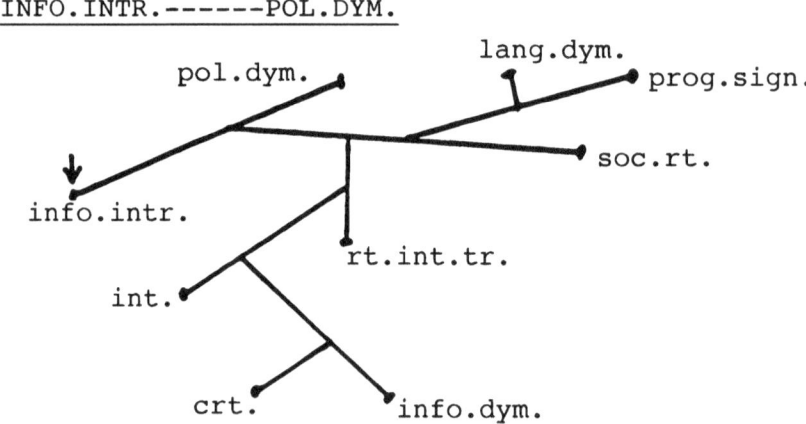

Quite possibly the most basic tool that has been used to stop the move towards "all investigation" has been the use of affinity negation (that is, the move to negate how a person or persons perceive of themselves). Without doubt, the educational system and media are the best examples of this phenomenon—for our most basic relationship to a given area of information is affected by how well it holds up against institutionalized prodding ("how well a given route of knowledge can hold up against four thousand books—or how well one can pursue a given route of information even if it doesn't affirm the reality of twelve thousand experts"). This is so because the most basic idea that is communicated by the established information lines is the notion that "you are less than you are"—and this is especially true for non-white people (if there is such a thing). The end result of this vibrational (and actual) position is that the nature of being is suppressed—which is to say, both creative and functional information routes are perceived in accordance to the established power structure dictates. The net effect of this manipulation is that the nature of inquiry (or investigation) is suppressed—which is to say, many important information lines are not dealt with.

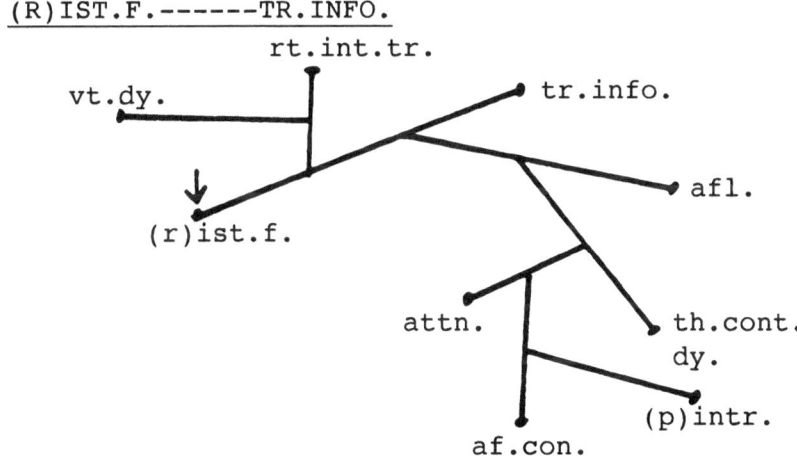

To better understand the realness of affinity dynamics, one can look at how the solidification of western culture was achieved. For the historical records clearly show that the progressional forces of western culture are outgrowths of the transformation cycle between the dissolution of the Egyptian high culture continuum and the later forming of the Greek and Roman culture continuum. This is not to say that every aspect of information from the Egyptian cycle was taken by western culture (nor is this my point—not to mention much information was simply lost or destroyed)—but rather, a significant amount of information was in fact transferred and utilized within its transfer shift context. What this means is that much of the information we are now working from in this cycle can be viewed with respect to its world linkage implications as well as its present affinity dynamics. In other words, because of the state of this planet (in this time period), it is possible to view a given information projection with regards to its projectional (in this context meaning through route traveled—or world group spread) significance as well as its "present-time" significance (and it is important to understand that the significance of a given information is multi-dimensional). Because of this, the reality of western culture must be dealt with, for the information—positive and negative—which has solidified in this time juncture does have precedence, and does vibrationally signify something important for all of us. My most basic point is that the progressional spread and solidification of present-day multi-information can be viewed with respect to how given information lines are re-integrated into the vibrational essence of its greater center—and that this phenomenon is related to the actuality of information transfer (in accordance to the dictates of affinity dynamics). This seems to be the natural (unnatural) cycle that surrounds the forming and dissolution of various culture groups. My point, however, is that the transfer-shift junction of western civilization was possible because given areas of information were made available (or taken) for its use. What we have in this cycle is quite the opposite (unless one happens to live in Yale University's library).

The move to limit the vibrational options of non-white people must be viewed as a functionary move designed to narrow the affinity dynamics of both black culture and world culture. The net result of the manipulation which has surrounded our "education" is that more and more non-white people are unable to tap their own affinity dynamics—and as such, are moved to perceive of themselves in terms of sanctioned definitions that are deemed real by the controlling forces that determine how present-day reality is to be viewed. On the physical universe level, one can view the effect of this phenomenon and begin understanding what has happened. This is not to write that people should avoid all the information that comes from western institutions, nor am I advocating that one should not read the newspapers (or look at TV)—obviously it is practically impossible to avoid dealing with the spectrum of present-day controlled information lines (not to mention, I am not against any area of information as such—because there is something to learn from everything), but my point is that without alternative considerations, the progressional and dynamic realness of "sanctioned information" in western culture moves to create a separation between non-western vibrational alignments and its own center foundation. The magnification of the western vibrational affinity pull in this period can be viewed with respect to what information compression really implies—that is, the over-balance of information from the western "perceived" affinity alignment (taught without regard for its progressional significance—source initiation) must be viewed as a negative factor for positive transformation.

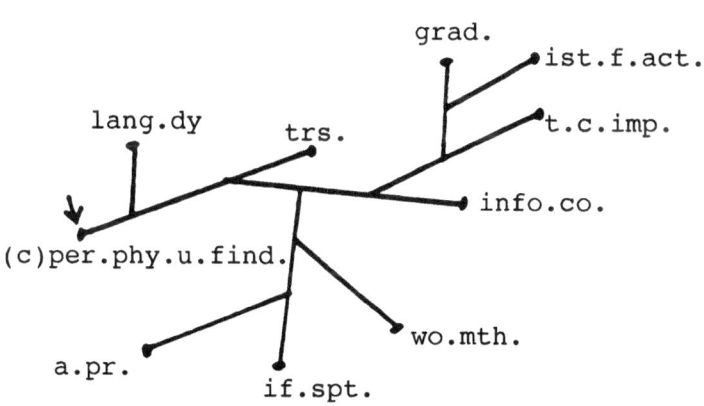

The suppression of affinity dynamics in world culture is not only related to the narrowing of the present-day reality focus (in terms of how given groups perceive of themselves), but the realness of this manipulation has also affected what options are available for functional change. In other words, the realness of what has transpired in the last two hundred years (and some) in education—and later communications—has narrowed our understanding of information options. The net effect of this phenomenon is that certain areas of relevant information are not sought out (or if sought out, not dealt with). Because in the final analysis, I am writing of the progressional effect of culture programming as a tool that functions to suppress alternative affinity dynamics (which of course is related to alternative information). Many of the developments which have occurred in this time zone (the late seventies) can be understood if this manipulation is kept in mind, for to view the emergence of the transition cycle which opened up universities and centers of higher learning to non-white people (and see very little constructive activity) only underscores the significance of affinity compression. **The fact is, if the sixties can be viewed as the time cycle which showed the most promise for lending itself to alternative activism, the seventies (and especially the late seventies) can be viewed as "sleep time in the Rockies"—that is, very little of value has come about towards alternative functionalism.** Yet there are many reasons for this. My point, however, is that the suppression of affinity dynamics can also be viewed as an important factor related to what information lines were (and are) perceived as relevant, and as such, this suppression is significant. Moreover, the realness of this suppression sheds light on the actual position of our educational institutions in this time zone as well—for it must be understood that the actualness of affinity dynamics can be molded (or taught)—even though we are all born with our own natural alignments. In other words, the realness of affinity dynamics can be viewed as something directly related to what we experience on the physical universe level as well as the progressional summation underlying how we move through events on the physical (and vibrational) plane. In this context, obviously the educational centers affect how the dynamics of our alignment are to expand (or contract), for this is the purpose of the education system. But the fact that dynamic options are viewed as only relevant for particular "zones" (or alignments) cannot be overlooked. The magnification of—what is perceived as—the composite western affinity alignment (which isn't the western affinity alignment) functions as a factor to distort the total overview of information options in this cycle. The net effect of this magnification is that all of us are "less than we are," and the implications of this reduction are that the dynamic options of world information have yet to be dealt with. It is my opinion that the restoration of world information is the single most important factor related to the positive shaping of the next transformation. Without an expanded information option context, we will be forced to deal with the effect of multi-suppression on many different levels.

RC------AFL.

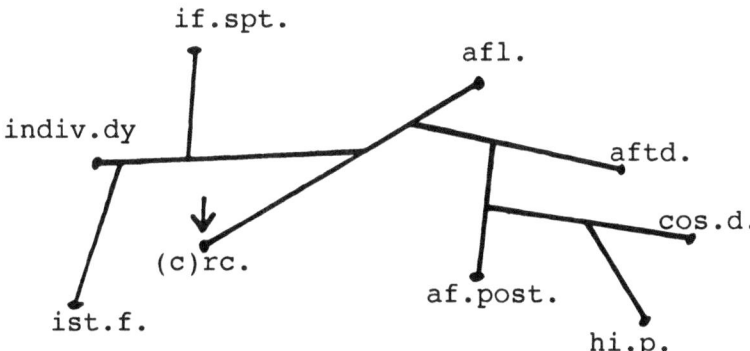

When I wrote that the perceived composite western affinity alignment is not the composite western affinity alignment I was not trying to make light of something that is serious. For it must be understood that—as I have stated earlier—if the present concepts concerning people were taken away, there would still be the realness of affinity dynamics as well as the dynamic uniqueness of given planet areas and/or vibrational groups. Which is to say, the information projections we are dealing with in this period should have meaning to all of us—or at least, the present information lines can have meaning for all of the people it has meaning to (and of course, those people would transcend the present notions we entertain about groups of people). I mention this (for the thousandth time) because it is necessary to maintain a balanced view about this most sensitive subject. I have not meant to imply any disrespect for the composite western affinity alignment as such—for this would serve no real purpose (not to mention, to negate any aspect of what "is" would discredit the basic purpose of this book). My purpose in examining the perceived composite western affinity alignment is to better view what has happened in this cycle as a means to prepare for the next cycle. The fact that the composite western affinity alignment is magnified in this cycle to the point where it functions as a distortion factor for composite world information is what I have tried to focus on in this chapter. The consequences of this magnification are directly related to the present position of world culture—and this is important to understand. Moreover the magnification of the composite western affinity alignment cannot be viewed as beneficial to even western culture. For in the final analysis, all of us are affected by an unbalanced vibrational position. The fact that the composite western identity vibration cannot properly absorb the dynamic spectrum of its own citizens must be viewed as a serious flaw—for the seriousness of this non-absorption is that many people are vibrationally repressed (or at least "dynamically less" than what they should or could be). Nor is this repression limited to one area. When I wrote that the perceived composite western affinity alignment does not function as an all-inclusive thrust (which no one alignment can), it must be understood that many white people also suffer the effects of what this means as well. The earlier example of the white improvisor should not be taken lightly, because at the heart of the concept of affinity dynamics is the actuality of the composite affinity insight principle. It is for this reason that everyone is entitled to vibrate towards the "zone" of their choice. To simply write that the white improvisor has no right to function in improvised music contradicts the dynamic cosmic order (or what I call order)—of what seems to be. Not only does everyone have a right to move towards what he perceives as attractive, but each of us has a responsibility to align ourselves with what is most real to our reality. The present cycle we are dealing with concerning women's liberation (which is really human being liberation) can be viewed as directly related to affinity dynamic suppression. It is also possible to view the transitions reshaping spirituality in this period as being directly related to the realness of affinity dynamics (and there are many other factors related to this phenomenon). In short, it would be wrong to merely assume that the restoration (or instigation) of world affinity dynamics only moves to affect particular groups of people—rather than the world group. The fact is, everyone could benefit from an expanded affinity (and information) alignment.

(AF)D–31

`(R)AFI.DY.------MT.INFO.`

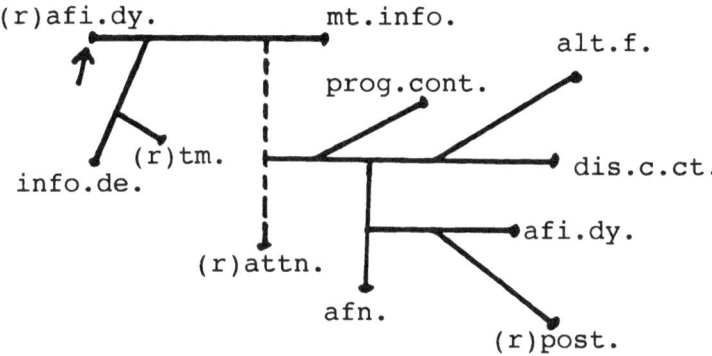

The significance of a composite affinity alignment would directly affect the vibrationaltory lining of western culture in the spectrum of information possibilities that it could utilize. It is not simply a question of adding a given information line while dropping something else—which is to say, I am not advocating that any strain of information be dropped or discarded. The significance of a composite affinity alignment would have to do with an expanded basis for viewing information—and that is what is important. Many of the problems we are dealing with in this time zone are the direct result of narrow information alignments. The solidification of an expanded affinity stance would move to realign every segment of western and world culture—affecting the progressional development of both the arts as well as the science that determines how given cultural expansions can be actualized. Not to mention, this "state of being" would not necessarily interfere with existing information lines (I say necessarily because, in fact, an expanded information basis would of course affect every projectional thrust of information, but this does not necessarily have to inhibit individuals who prefer to deal with particulars—any person should have the right to not deal with a given thrust of information as well). This additional information could be viewed as "optional." I believe a composite affinity stance is necessary if we are to respect—and include—the dynamic spectrum of all earth people. What this means is that every culture must become responsible for the dynamic spectrum of its information lines. The significance of a composite affinity alignment must

(AF)D–32

be viewed in these terms—because it is not just a question of developing only a positive and meaningful physical universe situation. Because the net effect of this phenomenon can be viewed with respect to the concept of "high culture" (which is the optimum state of being that people can exist in on the physical universe level).

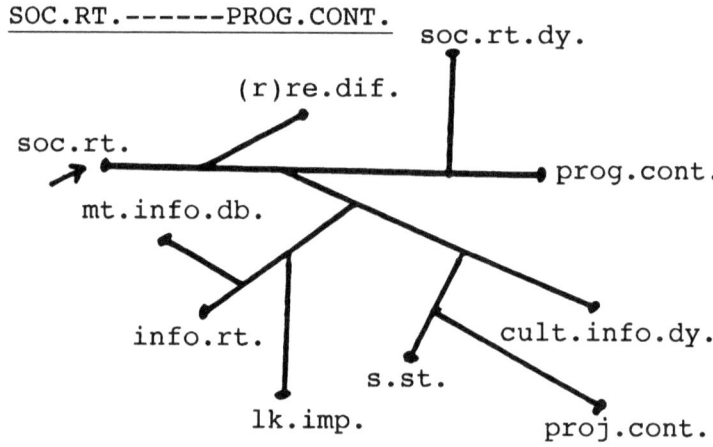

The dissolution of the composite-affinity-alignment aspect of source transfer can also be viewed with respect to the political developments which have taken place in the progressional rise and fall of world culture groups, as well as the implication of "scattered information" (related to this same phenomenon). For the most basic effect of a narrow information line has to exclude a large segment of people. In other words, it is possible to view the progressional rise and fall of particular world culture groups as an example of affinity isolation. With this viewpoint one can examine the nature underlying how given transfer shifts developed—and what it meant (on some level). My point is that the manipulation of affinity dynamics is not separate from manipulation on the physical universe level; that being, the realness that only certain areas of information are made "really" available (and that information is only relevant for a particular segment of society) and this phenomenon has multi-complexual implications. In other words, the isolation of information (and information affinity implications) must be viewed as political—because the effects of this phenomenon most certainly are political (I write it this way as opposed to saying that information isolation in itself is political, because I see manipulation on this level as a cosmic violation rather than a social violation); to view the progressional solidification and decline of given world culture groups is to see what information isolation really means in actual terms.

On the physical universe level, the most apparent signals of information compression can be viewed with respect to the dynamics of cultural dis-unification. The present vibrationaltory factors affecting black (and American Indian) communities throughout America in this period are perfect examples of what results from controlled information (yet I am not saying that dis-unification is manifested only in the black or Indian communities in America, because obviously to some extent every sector —and so-called racial group—is experiencing this same phenomenon—I mention the black community in particular because this phenomenon directly sheds light on the concept of affinity dynamics), and this is true on many levels. Moreover, the dynamics of this suppression directly shed light on the reality options surrounding non-western—so-called—people in western culture during this time period. That being—the realness that information relevant to the affinity dynamics of non-caucasian people is only utilized in a controlled way (having nothing to do with positively promoting the welfare of the people, but used to enforce the present state of western culture). The end result of controlled information lines is that the present reality of black culture can be viewed as dispersed on several levels, and the realness of that dispersal has brought about an even weaker political and functional stance. This is not to say that there is no awareness of what is happening on a dynamic global or vibrational level by given individuals, nor have I meant to imply that as of this time zone (late seventies) there are no sophisticated groups (organizations) functioning from a political and practical consciousness—obviously there are many such groups. But the realness of affinity and information suppression does mean something, and there is no way to view the present social and physical universe situation in non-caucasian communities in western culture without also viewing what controlled manipulation has helped create. That is, it is possible to view the realness of affinity and information suppression as the

(AF)D–34

most basic factor related to the "spread" of the center factor in the black community (but do not misunderstand my point, for the "spread" of a given cultural projection can also be commented on with respect to the positive attributes of its spectacle diversification—or its dynamic spectrum—in other words, I am not using "spread" in this sense, but rather "spread" as a word to comment on the fact that the affinity tenets which determine how multi-information is to be viewed in the black community is itself not understood). This is exactly the situation that black and white people are dealing with today, but there is a difference, for while every given sector of people in the west are basically confronting the same controlling forces, the fact that the social and political reality of composite western culture is designed with respect for what "white people are supposed to be" is the most basic difference. In other words, the concept and realness of racism distinguished how affinity compression is utilized, and as such, it is possible to write of the resulting effect of this compression in the same context—in fact, to not make this distinction would be ridiculous. My reasons for commenting on this aspect of information compression is that the manipulation of affinity dynamics is not separate from the social and political factors dictating the present period we are now living in. Moreover, the effect of that manipulation is not separate from the social reality realness of politics, and, as such, this phenomenon must be viewed in a relevant context. Above all, I am writing of a phenomenon that has involved people—and actual lives—and the realness of what this means cannot be avoided if this section of the book is to be relevant (or more important, if what I am writing about is relevant).

VT.U.PT.------C.CONT.

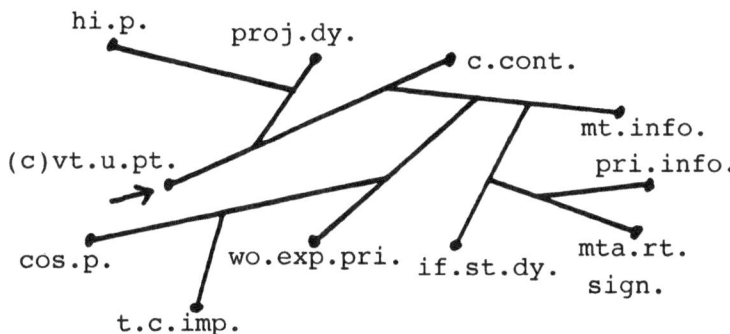

The most basic resultant that has developed through information compression has been the multi-levels of dis-unification between people (regardless of nationality or affinity nature)—and as a result, non-functionalism. The realness of this dis-unification must be viewed with respect for what it implies on a total level, for I am not only commenting on the dissolution of the American Asian community or black community—but rather the composite whole of western—and world—culture. To view the realness of the present social and political factors controlling our lives is to understand that only a selected segment of forces have benefited from the present situation of humanity. Which is to say, the most basic resultant that has emerged from the present-day use of information and affinity compression is the entrenchment of the forces which are controlling this time sector—or what is commonly called the western power structure—and it is important to understand that there is a big difference between the controlling forces which are manipulating events on the physical universe level and the concept we have today of "white people" per se (I say this because most non-white people tend to view white people as "all white people," with the understanding being that only non-white people are in the "effects" position of the western power structure—but the truth is that only a handful of so-called white or black people have any idea about what is really happening in western power politics, and in this respect their position is no different from that of composite non-white people—in the sense of not being able to really affect the culture—with, say, alternative ideas). The present breakdown of information alternatives in this time cycle has moved to create a situation ripe for sustaining the present power alignment. This is so because the dynamics of information are directly related to the realness of vibrational-center factors (which is actually what different physical universe regions—and, as such, people—really are). In other words, if we would view a given segment of people as the vibrational resultant of the composite beings of that group and also the physical universe coordinates of the region that group existed in, then it would be possible to also view the high culture solidification of that group as an affirmation of the composite particulars underlying what these dynamic factors cosmically meant—I call that resultant "center" (or cultural center), and from that basis I have come to refer to a given sector with respect to its "vibrational-center factor." In the final analysis—with these terms—it is possible to view the use of affinity-information compression as the most basic factor that has dictated how the distortion of a given vibrational-center factor has come about, and as such, this distortion must also be viewed in both its social and political sense. The realness of this manipulation cannot be taken lightly, nor have I advanced this term to only conceptualize an irrelevant phenomenon. Because in basic terms, the use of affinity information compression can be viewed as directly instrumental in channeling the events which transpired the progressional development of this vibrational cycle (which is to say, the present position we are in as a people could not have been possible without the gradual manipulation of essential composite information). What this means is that the present cycle we are living in cannot be viewed as the sole time period responsible for how this manipulation came about—only for how it advances given tendencies in its own isolated time cycle.

Without doubt, the most basic problem that surrounds dis-unification is what it implies for functionalism. For if the compression of world affinity dynamics (and its resultant information lines) moves to create an unbalanced physical universe situation—and what that means with respect to social reality—then the first manifestation of this phenomenon can be viewed by its effect on social and political organization. It is with these operatives at play where individuals begin to perceive of themselves with respect to what they think is "different" about their reality as compared to their compatriots (as opposed to what a collective movement might have in common). In this type of situation, the compression of information moves to create an inability to unify and, as such, positive functional activity is thwarted. It must also be understood that the realness of cultural and dynamic suppression is not simply a primitive attempt to dis-unify people—rather I am commenting on what I perceive to be a very sophisticated move towards manipulation. In other words, I am not just writing that a given power structure naively moves towards separating people on, say, either the concept of race, politics or social options—rather, I am writing of a dynamic and complex move to secure both how a given group sees themselves throughout their progressional (and immediate) history as well as how that same group relates to given areas of information (knowledge)—not to mention that in many cases, the progressional use of mis-history is used to turn given groups against each other (in other words, the manipulation I am commenting on is extremely sophisticated). The end result of this phenomenon is that social and functional unification is very difficult—and sensitive. And the net resultant of this phenomenon has allowed for few (if any) collective moves to restore order on the physical universe level. For the best basic force that could possibly reshape the present situation we are in during this cycle would have to be a composite force—having to do with a dynamic cross-section of earth people. This is so because of the enormity of the problems facing the planet in this cycle, and this is so because only the dynamic force of composite humanity would have the best possibility to deal with transformation.

Because of the success "the powers that be" have had in separating humanity (either in a given country or separation between nations), the move towards world unification can be viewed in isolated sectors. In this context, one can better view the reality dynamics related to how, say, the black community has had to function. That being, the realness that there are many groups (and potential groups) who in themselves have the desire to reshape given aspects of their "total" situation but are ineffective because of no united force to consolidate into. The end result of this phenomenon is that the success ratio for any one organization is less than what it could be—and what it has to be. What is worse is that given physical universe cycles move to create complexities that allow for perceived animosities to develop between given functional groups (for both real and imagined reasons) and the vibrationaltory effect of this dilemma is that unification becomes even more difficult. To understand this phenomenon is to accept that there will always be surface differences between how given groups perceive of themselves—especially since the information related to those perceptions is distorted. As long as the affinity dynamic implications of information is not dealt with, we will undoubtedly continue to view ourselves with respect to what we feel is most unique to our own particular group (and may the cosmics help the one who claims no group). Whatever, the manipulation that has helped to create this situation cannot be viewed without understanding its political implications as well. Because in the final analysis, all of these concepts do translate on the physical universe level—which is to say, our actual lives are related to what has happened from the distortion of true information.

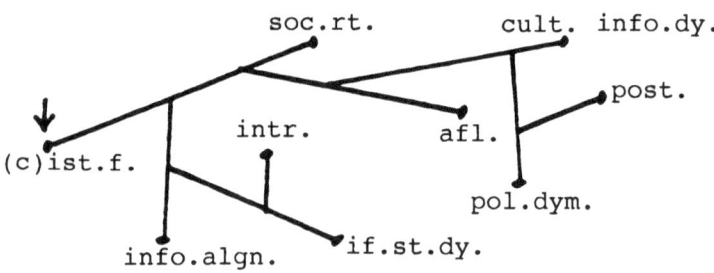

Certainly the dis-unification that permeates isolated functionalism (in this time cycle) has helped to sustain the physical universe situation we are now dealing with, and it is also clear that without some effort to solidify, the present reality of earth life will continue unabated. But as difficult as this problem seems to be, there are still other factors which must also be dealt with. For while it is understood that isolated functionalism by its nature moves towards general confusion and separation, there is still the realness that the resultant physical universe situation we are left with (from separation) is ripe for alien definition. In other words, the present physical universe situation is perfect for the collective forces of western culture in the sense that separation is conducive for continued control. Because while all of the various functional groups are struggling against one another, the overall vibrational tone of the culture is still being defined and controlled by special elite groups. It is important, however, to understand that I have not meant to imply the only way positive transformation can come about is for everyone and every group to agree on everything—obviously this will never happen. Nor have I meant to imply that any given group sacrifice what it believes to be real (with respect to information that reflects positively on what that group is about—or would like to be about), for to do this would in itself be death. My point, however, is that the solidification (or even awareness) of world information can give the necessary backdrop that could allow for positive composite functionalism. Because without the involvement of a cross-section of humanity, real change will be impossible, and until this transition comes about, the progressional continuance of this culture (and world culture) will continue to evolve along separate (real separate, as opposed to natural separate) lines, and the net effect of this phenomenon will promote mis-information. I have not meant to imply that separation only induces distortions in the conceptual intellectual and/or vibrational aspects of culture, but rather this factor can be observed in the total lining of this plane of existence: affecting the vibrational as well as the physical universe level.

The implications of affinity dynamics and multi-information should not be viewed lightly, for awareness of this subject can directly shed light on the realness of progressional continuance. For if the problems we are dealing with in this time zone were really viewed in all of their dynamic ramifications, we might be able to change the basic flaws connected to present-day surface transition. In other words, the progressional spread of humanity (and principal information) can be viewed in the same context that has characterized documented human problems throughout recorded history—those problems being mis-information, separation, war, hunger, and insensitivity. It is possible to view practically every cultural progression with respect to these conditions (of course, it is also possible

(AF)D–40

to view anything with anything), and hopefully the solidification of world information will have positive multi-implications. This is what I believe. One thing is certain: without some attempt to correct the problems we are now having in this time cycle (the last two thousand and some years), nothing will "really" change. Real change can only come about when culture groups (and individuals) are dealing with real information, and the interesting thing about real information is its ability to show us how much we are alike, and how much our destinies are intertwined as a human family.

(Level One) ASPECT ESSENCE (Perception Dynamics)

I HAVE ALREADY WRITTEN ABOUT HOW PROGRESSIONALISM IS PRACTICED in American culture—and what this phenomenon poses for information dynamics—and I have also tried to view this subject with respect to its social reality implications. Unless some effort is made to change the reality dynamics of progressionalism—in this time zone—there can be no serious hope of positive transformation (or at least positive intended transformation). This is not to imply that only one factor is related to transformation, because obviously there are many factors connected to this most important consideration, but this is to state that the seriousness of progressionalism should not be viewed lightly. Nor by commenting on the particulars of sixties functionalism have I meant to discredit the higher intentions of many of the functioning (activist) groups, because this would serve no positive or constructive purpose either. It is important to understand that much of the functionalism that characterized the time zone of the sixties was in fact born out of an honest desire to participate in social and political change. Many of the groups that functioned in this period were trying to correct the vibrational and actual state of American (and western) culture—and this must be respected. The work which took place in the black community and the collective developments that brought forth the movement for women's liberation were an outgrowth of very real physical universe challenges. In other words, it would be a great distortion of the sixties to merely focus on the dynamics of spectacle diversion progressionalism—and what it implied for focuses like the hippie-yippie syndrome—at the expense of the composite events characterizing this time zone. For the collective realness of this period would underlie the very nature of America's (and as such, western culture's) vibrational state—up until the present (late seventies on into the eighties). Which is to say, the realness of the sixties must be viewed on every possible level, because this one period has dictated the nature of America's progressionalism for the last decade—and some (and shows no indication of letting up).

The dynamic implications of this time period must be viewed from every possible context before we, as a nation, can move into the next time cycle—and I am not alone in this viewpoint (for the last five years even have seen an explosion of new literature on this most important period). Quite possibly, we have now come to a point in time where it might be possible to begin understanding the sixties. So much happened in this one time period that no one viewpoint could encompass the dynamic spectrum of this subject—which is to say, hopefully there will continue to be more literature on this most decisive period in American history. I consider the realness of the sixties to be important for what it signified about future progressionalism for both America and western culture (with the dynamics of this consideration also affecting world culture).

While the surface perceived objectives of a given activist movement can be viewed with respect to its separate vibrational and actual focuses, there were profound similarities that united all of the various functioning movements in the sixties. Because the vibrational nature underlining how functionalism was viewed and practiced in that period also gave insight into the reality platform of sixties functionalism. The similarities between the spectrum of functioning movements really characterized what the time zone of the sixties would mean in actual and vibrational terms. For the composite affinity position inherent in all of these movements would necessarily adopt the same most basic vibrational traits (and foundation). That being: (1) the goals with which each reality initiative chose to define itself; and (2) the perspective underlying how its adopted functionalism was practiced. What was common to all of the activist groups in this period was that the meta-reality of their information affinity position reflected the same flaws responsible for what they were fighting against. In other words, not only did the composite reality of sixties functionalism come to view itself in western information degree terms (of a post-Aristotelian nature—that being information isolation and existential evaluation), but the alternatives they were looking for were based on the conceptual-affinity alignment that created the very situation they were trying to change. The resulting factors that determined the political and social direction in the seventies can be reduced to the inability of sixties activists to understand or foresee the consequences of conceptual decisions as well as vibrational decisions. Yet I have not meant to imply that no important work was done in this time zone—obviously the realness of the sixties saw much important work done, and this must be respected. But if we are to view the sixties as a means to better understand the composite dynamics of progressional continuance (that being, the path America, among others, has taken), and if we are to view the sixties as a means to understand the seventies, eighties, and nineties, then it is important that the nature of sixties functionalism is thoroughly examined. In other words, there is a need to focus on which areas of functionalism were not realized as a means to understand what happened—and why.

Before this essay can move to focus on the particulars of sixties functionalism (or activism), it is necessary to first define the objectives of this inquiry, as well as what terms are to be employed. This is necessary because I have not simply decided to write on the sixties as a means to have something to comment on, but instead as a relevant focus for the whole of this book. My understanding is that the particulars of physical universe progressionalism are not separate from the greater vibrational nature concerning how a given culture, or group, perceives of participation. In other words, the reality underlying how information is viewed in a given culture is not isolated to only one focus, but is instead compositely manifested throughout the whole of that culture's affinity dynamics. As such, to view the nature of a given progressionalism is to have a basis for viewing a given vibrational position clearly—or at least to have a basis for better understanding a given culture's meta-reality position. For this reason, it is important that physical universe progressionalism is viewed, and this is especially true of the time zone of the sixties. For, as I have already stated, the seriousness of this time period has dictated the nature of events until this period (the late seventies) and seems to also be relevant for the eighties. As such, to focus on the nature of progressionalism in the sixties can be valuable as a means to begin gaining insight as to the whole of this time cycle. This is true with respect to creativity and this is also true for social reality (or social/vibrational reality—since there is no such thing as social separate from its vibrational context). The thrust of this section is perceived to hopefully not violate what this relationship signifies—what we need now, more than ever, are viewpoints that attempt to look beneath the "surface of things"—with respect to a given focus's dynamic and spiritual significance.

The concept of aspect essence has to do with the reality of both perception implications and decision dynamics (or consequences). The understanding being "that the nature determining how a given focus is perceived is directly related to what vibrational zone it affirms"—or another way of writing this is "that the nature of a given participation has multi-cosmic implications" and as such, every "participation" must be viewed as necessarily relevant to what it implies about the individual as well as the idea and/or ideals that individual or movement professes to desire. Yet, by focusing on the multi-implications of "participation," I have not meant to focus only on what this concept poses for one aspect of existence—because in fact, the realness of this concept transcends any one context. The fact is, the reality of a given "participation" is not separate from its greater cosmic and vibrational implications, but this does not rule out an examination of "what a given decision means in itself." In conceptual terms, the reality focus of aspect essence information dynamics can be viewed as follows: "to solve an aspect or the understanding of an aspect, and not deal with the essence that defined the nature of that aspect, will, by the very nature of this progression, not only not change the (or a) given physical universe situation, but also enforce it; because the realness of this phenomenon employs the same information affinity position that "ised" the vibrational reality it purports to reshape (or change). As such, the nature of a given aspect essence focus can be viewed with respect to its relationship to both meta-physical vibrational decisions and physical universe functionalism, and the thrust of this section will move to elaborate on what this phenomenon has meant to the present nature of progressionalism. For all practical purposes, the aspect essence information focus can be applied to the spectrum of events that solidified the sixties, whether we are commenting on the dynamics of functionalism in black power activism—concerning the reality surrounding what approach or route a given movement utilized as a means to function—as well as that of women's liberation, gay rights, and nuclear activism. This examination is important for understanding the nature of present-day progressionalism.

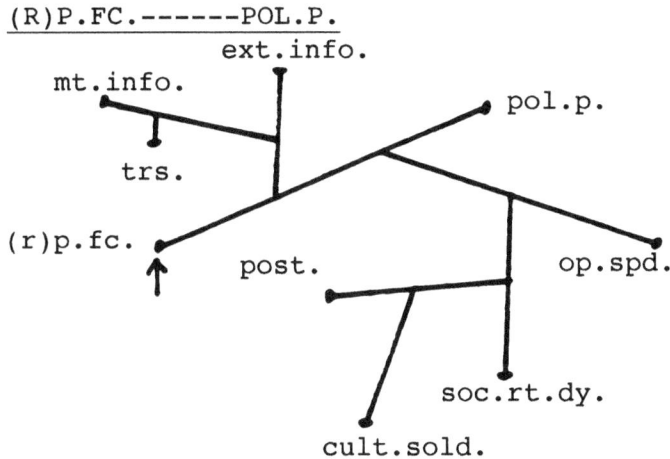

In actual terms, to view the realness of aspect essence is to deal with the multi-implications surrounding a given vibrational position (or decision and its subsequent participation) with respect to what that position posed in its greater cosmic sense or its relationship to "doing." This can better be understood by examining the progressionalism of the sixties—or at least the nature of sixties activism. As early as 1964, the move towards serious activism could be viewed in many different areas of social reality—which is to say, the dynamic solidification of composite activism in the sixties provides an excellent platform to begin focusing on this phenomenon. My point is this—the vibrational platform that solidified in the sixties would establish the first real move towards alternative functionalism for the post–World War Two generation (from the middle forties to the middle fifties). This generation would, in the sixties, solidify the composite vibrational perspective that we are still dealing with in this time zone. The realness of this alternative activism would thus focus on the particulars of Vietnam and civil rights in its early development, and later expand to include sexism and ageism. It is important that some attempt is made to understand how events solidified in the early sixties because, for all of the work that took place in that cycle, very little has been carried forward into the eighties—which is to say, somewhere along the way, the composite vibrational forces which solidified the move towards activism (or participation and involvement) somehow became distorted. This is true because the reality position of American culture was not elevated in the sixties—which is to say, the problems that underlined activism in the sixties have not been solved, by any stretch of the imagination. Nor can this phenomenon—the succession of dedicated activism—be simply explained by the fact that many of those who were functioning in the sixties are now in their thirties, with more responsibilities, because while this is true, it still does not deal with the dynamic implications of real activism. For not only are there different young people who, in a conscious transitional situation, would reoccupy the roles of the previous generation, but there is also the realness that activism (functionalism) does not only imply one state (or context) anyway. In other words, there is no reason why concerned people cannot actively function for change regardless of their particular situation. I believe that the move towards non-functionalism in the seventies is directly related to the realness of both spectacle diversion progressionalism (and what this phenomenon has posed for information dynamics) as well as the aspect-essence distortions which came to permeate composite information dissemination—but what does this mean?

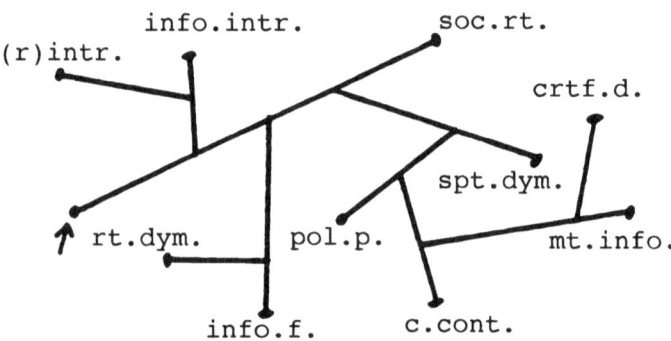

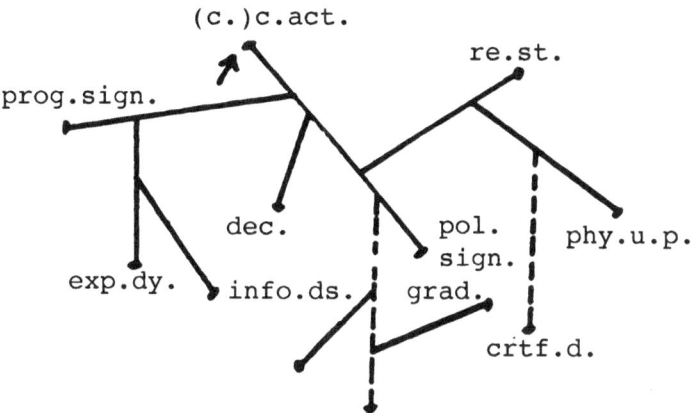

As early as 1964 one could view the solidification of dynamic functionalism in American social reality, and this was especially true for the emergence of alternative functionalism—as related to the reality position of poor and disenfranchised Americans. Groups like the Congress of Racial Equality (CORE) would advance the realness of alternative functionalism (activism) to new heights—and in doing so also increase its focus. The basic concentration of their functionalism in the early sixties helped to develop awareness about the nature of inequalities that existed for black people in the south, and this work directly led to the subsequent media focus that established civil rights as a major national concern. CORE also worked for alternative functionalism in the north of America as well, and in cities like Chicago, developed consciousness about the reality of slum landlords. The realness of this work brought about serious changes in the laws giving protection to slum landlords. There of course is much more, for CORE was only one group among many—and by not focusing on, say, the Southern Christian Leadership Conference, or any of the other relevant organizations in that same time period, I have not meant to slight their activity. My reason for mentioning the functionalism of this period is only to lay a basis for examining what happened in the seventies. It is important that the time zone of the sixties is reviewed as a means to understand the dynamics of progressionalism in America, because the nature of participation in that period—especially in the early sixties—is directly related to the dictates of aspect essence as a "real" phenomenon. This is so because the vibrational arena that solidified alternative activism in the early sixties would attract individuals who were really concerned about changing social reality. Many of those individuals were also highly motivated and dedicated people. The dynamics of sixties participation would see people from every section of the country come to work for real change—and more important, this participation transcended ethnic and/or racial lines; that is, of the small group that emerged in the sixties as dedicated activists, there was no one type of participation, and there was no one group of individuals whose participation dominated the total theatre of events. Rather, the realness of sixties activism—in its early period—was distinguished by its composite affinity base, as a means to deal with the greater reality implications of dynamic social change and alternative functionalism.

By 1966 the focus of functional activism in the civil rights movement had expanded into many other areas of social reform, and in doing so had become even more all-inclusive. For by the second half of the sixties, the dynamics of alternative functionalism had begun to constitute a new power base in itself. The realness of this phenomenon would thus become a significant political force in composite American social dynamics—affecting the nature of civil rights litigation as well as assisting the particulars of political campaigning (e.g., the gains of so-called alternative candidates like Eugene McCarthy). As the intensity of this phenomenon gained momentum, the collective forces of alternative activism would begin to make even greater inroads to the social reality particulars of northern and northeastern America, necessitating the use of new strategies. The thrust of these movements would clarify the social dilemma surrounding education for poor people, as well as unfair laws directed at housing for minorities. And by exposing the dynamics of racism in American culture, the composite activism that took place in the sixties also helped to establish a basis for bringing about real change—and this was important. When the dynamic March on Washington actualized in the sixties, it was clear that the collective participation of the civil rights movement had established the possibility of real change in America's social reality. In short, the functionalism which led to the March on Washington and the later rise to prominence of Dr. Martin Luther King was a significant period in American progressionalism—and this should never be forgotten. The realness of this period would see many people give their lives for the possibility of positive social and vibrational change—which is to say, the dynamics of sixties activism was not about "games" but was instead a matter as serious as life or death. When one refers to the realness of the sixties, it is important that all of these considerations are remembered, because while not everyone was involved in functioning at the forefront of social change (since "everyone" is not involved in anything), there was a significant amount of composite involvement and dedication (to the realness of "uplifting existence") from a great sector of the American people—and this does say something about the vibrational reality tone of America's culture potential.

I have chosen to comment briefly on the particulars of sixties functionalism because of what this phenomenon poses to dynamic progressionalism. Certainly the struggle for civil rights did not start in the sixties, but is instead connected to the greater activism that has characterized American history; and by focusing on the sixties I have not meant to ignore the composite realness of this subject. But my reasons for focusing on the physical universe factors which shaped alternative functionalism in that period have to do with the nature underlying how its related progressionalism has transpired—as well as what finally resulted in the seventies. Yet, by only briefly commenting on the particulars of sixties progressionalism I have not meant to over-generalize this most important subject, for obviously there is much more to discuss if we are to view the sixties in a total context. The nature of my inquiry into this time period is intended to be relevant for the overall dictates of this book. Because the reality of events that took place in the sixties does indeed give insight about the composite "nature" of American progressionalism, and moreso, the dynamics of this same period have totally altered present-day functionalism (not essence but "route of")—as well as the particulars of "given approaches." To view the realness of this period is to understand the dynamic implications of alternative functionalism, and this is necessary if we are to gain some understanding of the vibrational nature of America's cosmic identity (and earth's vibrational alignment). For I believe the civil rights functionalism that solidified in the early sixties was based on honest desires and concern for humanity in its most "real" sense, and I also believe that the spiritual vibrational alignment which "ised" the solidification of alternative activism in this same period had to do with the composite affinity position of a cross-section of concerned people throughout the nation—the realness of which conjured up concepts like unification and brother- and sisterhood; having to do with the desire to uplift consciousness and also having to do with the desire to uplift consciousness and spirituality.

I believe that the spirit factor of alternative functionalism in the sixties had to do with hopes for a better life (and world)—and as such was seeded in high spirituality. This is not to say every aspect of sixties functionalism was noble, because it wasn't, nor by having high ideals was this movement "necessarily realistic." But the intensity of activism in the middle sixties did help to actualize real programs of change—which is to say, the realness of alternative functionalism in the early sixties was "effective" and not simply "something to do."

By commenting on the dynamics of sixties functionalism I have not meant to give the impression that no ideological differences existed between various organizations and/or individuals (i.e., how a given movement perceived of its function, or what objectives a given individual desired from that function). Because in fact there were many differences, as there always are when many individuals come together—whatever the overall objective. Nor have I meant to write of sixties activism in totally utopian terms by over-accenting concepts like unification and/or spiritualism—because the most sophisticated of these movements had no illusions about the hardships of their struggles, and no one in his or her right mind really believed that years of suppression could be rectified overnight. Instead, the dynamic reality of sixties activism is commented on in this section as a means to begin viewing the nature of sixties progressionalism. It is important to focus on the collective dynamics of this period if we are to view the primary umbrella that dictated how its alternative functionalism was solidified (as a meaningful and effective force for change). Because my point is that the vibrational factors which helped to solidify alternative functionalism in the sixties did have a relevant affinity basis that was similar for all of the people who made the decision to function; which is to say, the affinity lining of sixties functionalism was significant in that by being all-inclusive it was able to attract many different people from many different sectors of society. I believe this "affinity lining" is directly related to the success of sixties activism—especially in the early stages of the movement. In other words, however different the people who functioned in sixties activism saw themselves—with respect to either their background or purpose—there were vibrational areas (feelings) that all of these people shared which transcended isolated reality positions, and these vibrational areas were crucial to the success of their composite activism—as a "real" factor in America's social reality scheme. The progressional realness of this expanded affinity basis for alternative functionalism would lead to the success of the March on Washington—having to do with a renewed commitment to work towards uplifting the reality of humanity and world consciousness. The famous speech of Dr. Martin Luther King only accented what was felt by most of the people who had been instrumental in shaping new activism. This was the beginning of a drive for new consciousness and social responsibility.

To really understand the dynamic implications of sixties activism is to focus on the nature of its affinity alignment—with respect to what an expanded affinity posed for participation. My point is that the foundation underlying sixties activism had to do with an expanded affinity base that was relevant for anyone concerned about active participation for change (understanding too that there are only a select group of people, regardless of time zone or belief, who will move towards active involvement—or who can move towards active involvement). It was this expanded affinity base that helped to attract people from such diversified backgrounds, and it was this same affinity base that helped to establish the vibrational nature of "greater motivation." The realness of this phenomenon—as a factor that influenced the participation of composite humanity—can be viewed as related to the essence of what alternative functionalism is all about. In other words—rather than focusing on the particulars of a given physical universe situation as the primary factor that motivated composite functionalism, I am saying instead that the real motivating factor that determines the multi-dimensional consequences of a given participation has to do with what position a focus has to its greater information implications. I write this because a given participation is not about words, nor does it necessarily have anything to do with the particulars of a given focus (because while one person might "see it this way," another person might "see it *this* way," etc., etc.). My point is that the real factor that served to transcend the narrowness of a given focus is the relationship of what that focus stimulates with respect to its primary essence—because this consideration dictates what any zone of information is all about (and this is also true of response as well). As such, the basic motivating factor which underlined the solidification of alternative functionalism in the sixties had not so much to do with the dynamics of any one focus, but rather had to do with a greater cosmic awareness (and concern) for human rights. In other words, however different each person's physical universe slant—in terms of so-called race or ideology—the basic affinity that solidified the resurgence of alternative functionalism in the sixties could be reduced to how people related to the concept of human rights.

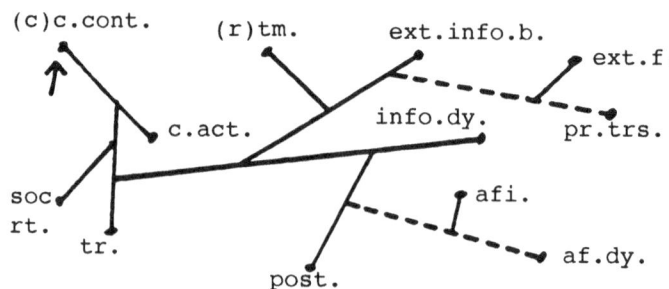

The dynamics of sixties activism would move towards a total reshaping of American culture, and for a span of four to six years seemed to plant the seeds for a new reordering of social priorities and consciousness throughout the whole of the culture. The thrust of this movement would also bring with it a new sense of hope for America. There was suddenly the feeling that anything could be accomplished, and for a brief period one could sense the possibility of a composite concern for positive social and vibrational change. Yet at the same time, the extended implications of alternative functionalism would dictate several areas of natural separation as well. For the extended functionalism that surrounded activism in the black community would be different from what was being posed in women's liberation, and both of these movements had necessarily different functional approaches than, say, the activism surrounding ecology. In other words, the spread of alternative functionalism in the sixties would be directly related to the nature of how isolation came to be practiced in the seventies. The difference between what composite activism posed, as a dynamic strategy and vibrational state, to the emergence of isolated activism would reshape the total reality position of sixties progressionalism. It is important that some attempt is made to understand what happened.

There are two most basic expansion conditions—(1) with respect to the composite focus of a given objective, and (2) with respect to the particulars of a given route. Both of these conditions are important if a given transition is to be achieved. In other words, without an overview of a given reality base, there can be no greater understanding of what a given participation means, and without an understanding of the particulars of a given route, no change can be accomplished either. The dilemma of the sixties activism had to do with the inability of the various areas of concern to understand the balance between both of these expansion conditions. By the beginning of the seventies, the dynamic functionalism that had emerged in the sixties had moved into the "everyone for him (her) self" zone—and this vibrational posture would move to totally change the reality position (and potential) of alternative functionalism. My reasons for commenting on this phenomenon is that it is directly related to the concept of aspect-essence information manipulation—which is to say, the seeds underlying how alternative functionalism was sapped in the seventies is not inconsistent with the total reality position western culture has developed with information dynamics and/or progressionalism.

I have previously commented on the first condition of dynamic expansion—that being, motivation with respect to what a given focus poses for its composite implications, but it is also important that some attempt is made to view the particulars of isolated focus as well, because this route of involvement is just as essential for bringing or creating change. In actual terms, the significance of isolated functionalism could be understood by examining the collected activism which has long characterized alternative functionalism. Black people have long understood that the commitment to change social reality in America has been shallow to say the least—this has been true for the nature of change in the sixties as well as the last two hundred years. There have been many other time junctions in American history which have corresponded to a kind of social sentiment resembling the sixties, in that surface focus was given to the conditions of black Americans and later abandoned (the period of Reconstruction is a perfect example of this phenomenon). In other words, the seriousness of isolated functionalism must also be based on what the historical arena has shown to be true—that being, "if you want something done then you must do it yourself." But the significance of isolated functionalism is not limited to any one context, because the dynamics of motivation transcend one-dimensional interest. There was also the honest desire—and need—for black people to isolate and concentrate their functionalism, with respect to the separate developments in the black community, as a means to deal with the special situation that surrounded bringing about change—involving change with respect to social reality and change as a part of the renewed focus on black culture. The enormity of these challenges alone dictated that some type of separation was necessary as a means to reconsider the total reality position of black people—as well as all non-caucasians in the weight of the over-accented position of western culture. Nor was the nature of isolated progressionalism only manifested in functionalism in the black community, because by the beginning of the seventies, the route women's liberation would take could also be viewed in the same context—which is to say, one route functioned with respect for what liberation meant in its composite context, and one route functioned with respect to the specifics of women's liberation as a total focus in itself.

By the middle to late sixties, the intensity of social reality particulars in American culture would move to provide a split between various areas of functionalism, and this is true for progressional dynamics as well as composite alternative functionalism. To understand the reality nature of the seventies is to deal with what transpired from this split, for the gradual dissolution of effective activism is directly related to the various levels of separation which solidified in the sixties. From a time period that saw both social and political involvement on every level—involving every sector of the culture—to a time period where no activism could be viewed in any context, the difference between the sixties and seventies could not have been much greater had it been planned (and it was). By the end of the sixties, the greater thrust of alternative activism was focused on disagreements with each other—this was true of the black power movement, this was true of the anarchist movement, and later the women's liberation movement would also be affected by this same phenomenon (although not to the same degree). The resulting ineffectiveness of alternative activism in the sixties can better be understood by viewing the present dilemma we now face in the eighties. For the problems that stimulated activism in the sixties are still with us today—that is, nothing has really changed, unless in many cases for the worse. If the next cycle of concerned activists (that being, concerned people making the decision to actively participate in attempting to change the reality particulars of their culture) is to be more successful than before, then it is important that some attempt is made to deal with the reality dynamics of expansion—with respect to what this consideration poses to actual people. Either some attempt must be made now or we run the risk of repeating the mistakes of the sixties.

C.FO.ACT. ------ PRI.INFO.

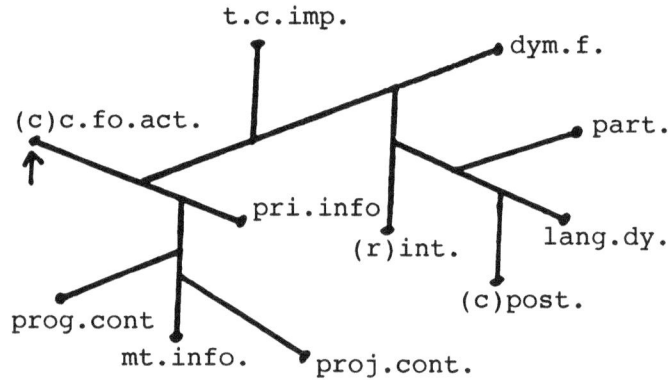

GRAD. ------ INFO.DY.

P.FC.------PHY.U.P.

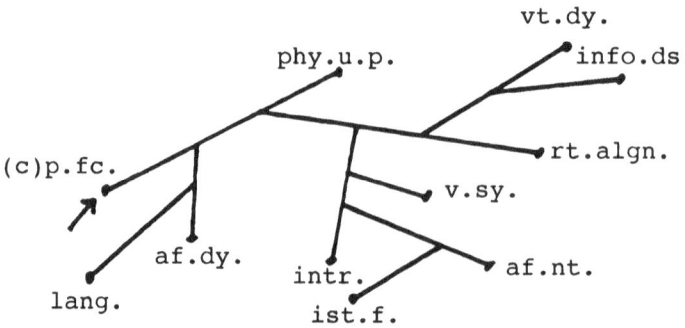

The fact is, the reality dynamics of a given expansion route are not separate from the implications of both attraction (affinity dynamics) and information alignment. In other words, the attractiveness of a given type of participation reflects on the total vibrational position of the person doing the perceiving—and this has nothing in itself to do with the concept of positive or negative, but instead gives insight into the tendency dynamics of human beings. In actual terms, the vibrational reality of a given individual directly shapes what area of participation that individual will effectively vibrate to—which is to say, what area is "real" for that person. In the sixties, however, the natural dynamics of a given information focus were not taken into account (and as such utilized positively), but instead became an issue into itself. Individuals who were united in the same cause but saw different approaches to the same problem would turn on each other because of a difference in functional perspective rather than focus. The net result of these disagreements moved to undermine the whole of sixties functionalism—and even today this schism has yet to be corrected.

The "expansion with respect to isolated particulars movement" has long viewed any focus outside their own as less committed or (in the black community) what is now called a "Tom." This is understandable on one level when one considers the intensity of what this movement has traditionally had to deal with. For the greater thrust of "isolated particular activism" has had to confront in many cases "the enemy" on the most basic level—either in actual combat (with the loss of life that this situation carries with it) or the vibrational state related to intensive activism. To this movement, any functionalism that doesn't move to emotionally focus on the "nature of the problem" in the spirit of "its given focus" does not meet the requirements for "comradery"—and in many ways, this position is understandable. For it must be understood that the "isolated functionalism" sector of dynamic activism in most cases is the primary factor responsible for establishing focus on the reality position of a given "problem" or "injustice"—which is to say, if left to the "composite activists," the route of a given change cycle would take much longer. An example of this can be viewed in the reality factors which shaped black activism in the sixties between the younger, more intense activists (the movements which utilized "isolated focus") as opposed to the composite-focus movement. For the acceleration of civil rights awareness can be credited to the intensity of the isolated focused movement moreso than from the composite group—and there are many reasons for this. One, the dynamic implications of "isolated activism" moves to incite the intensity of "its given situation" by its need to apply direct solutions (which in many cases calls for the use of physicality and/or the possibility of real harm), and also the nature of its focus moves to directly create opposition lines (that being "them" against "us"). The significance of this type of functionalism can then be viewed with respect to its effect on quick solutions. For, on one hand, the effectiveness of a given confrontation could, in its extended context, eradicate a given problem by simply destroying all of the factors that are in opposition to the "nature of its focus"; on the other hand, the threat of a given isolated focus policy could also serve as a stimulant for "one's opposition" to begin either understanding new alternatives for change or understand new alternatives to prevent change (but nevertheless changing the "nature" of the given physical or vibrational universe situation). The realness of "isolated focus activism" is directly related to all of these possibilities and more—nor does this relationship necessarily have to be viewed as negative, because it isn't. For the reality of alternative functionalism has to do with changing the nature of a given participation—which is to say, the use of dynamic activism in the sixties solidified because of a real need for social change. The particulars of change in the sixties have obviously not been all-continuing—which is to say, many of the focuses which were changed were only in fact altered for a short time period—but the dynamics of "isolated focused activism" established the "realness" of vibrational momentum, which is to say, the nature of this progressional phenomenon is not without its positive attributes.

Thus it is no wonder that the nature of difference between "isolated focused activism" and "composite focused activism" moves to create negative static. For while one area of functionalism is fighting and dying as a means to change the composite state of things, the other area of activism (which in many cases is also benefiting from the work of the "isolated focused movement") is working towards re-establishing a situation that, on the surface, seems to move towards "keeping things as they were." Thus while one movement will design a philosophy that portrays "white people as the villain of social reality"—and as such, creates a philosophy that can make an immediate kind of functionalism (that being, "if they are the villain then we must move to stop the villain")—the composite focus activist movements try to shape change by working, in many cases, with the very people who have been labeled the villains. The complexities of these differences obviously have been the site of profound disagreements—and even today are not resolved. Before any real functionalism can be solidified as we move towards the next cycle, there must be some move to resolve the vibrational schism between these two areas of functionalism.

The reality position of "composite focused activism," in its most separate context, has to do with how the progressionalism of a given time period can be advanced with respect to both the composite participants of that time period as well as the underlying cosmic implications of participation. In other words, the thrust of this area of activism is directed towards trying to involve the greater sector of its culture community in bringing about dynamic change. The basic vibration underlying this functionalism is that all of humanity stands to be less unless we begin to collectively move to correct what is most unjust about this planet. The basic reality tone position of this movement tends to accent the spiritual implications of social reality as a means to solidify an awareness and concern about the greater cosmic implications of "unconstructive actions." Moreover, the thrust of this viewpoint, when effective, has the best potential for dynamically altering the greater society because the nature of its focus is all-inclusive as opposed to "decidedly pointed." Yet there are disadvantages related to this area of functionalism that cannot be ignored. Because by attempting to solidify a composite functional position, the progressional implications of activism in this context are necessarily slow—and in some cases, the effectiveness of a given rate of change is everything (which is to say, there are cases where "the time" of a given change is crucial to whether or not a given "state" can survive). Nevertheless, the dynamics of "composite activism" are important for what they signify about the implications of cultural identity—in that the effectiveness of a given intention can permeate the total lining of its culture and culture imprint. The seeds underlying a given composite activist participation can move to redirect an entire culture, and in doing so, serve as a positive factor for reunification—and hopefully, later, even cultural greatness.

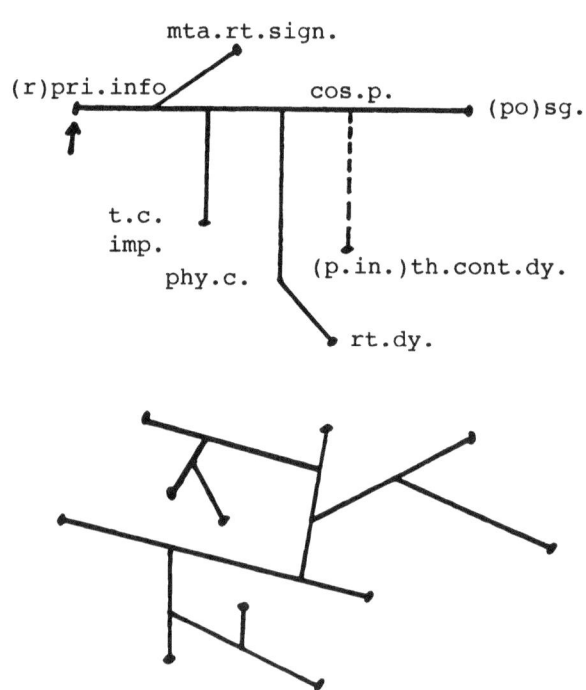

Yet by focusing on the particulars of dynamic activism, I have not meant to imply that there is no relationship between any given area of progressionalism. For the dynamics of both isolated and composite activism have many factors in common, and even more important, these "persuasions" can also complement each other if alternative functionalism is to be effective in any real sense. In short, it is important for given sectors of a culture to understand the dynamic inter-relationship of its composite activism to the total reality position of its culture. For the particulars of a given focus do not necessarily imply the suppression of someone else's focus—it is a question of how one chooses to view the greater culture. In the final analysis, the dynamics of social reality will move to have us decide whether the dictates of the next time zone will be perceived with respect to individual interest, or cultural (or even greater—the planet) interest. This is so because the reality position of earth itself seems to be changing. That is, the present-day dynamics of earth information transcend any one context—we can now look at the reality of a given action with respect to what that action will pose for the greater world group. In the coming cycle we will be forced to decide the nature of the next continuum of applied progressionalism—that being, will we move to perceive of progressionalism only by what this consideration implies for our isolated national interest, or will we view this consideration with respect for its composite implications—understanding too that everything affects everything (which is to say, whatever decisions solidify the next time cycle, it is important to understand the nature underlying what response a given position activates, because to each progressional route there is also what I will call "national consequences" as well).

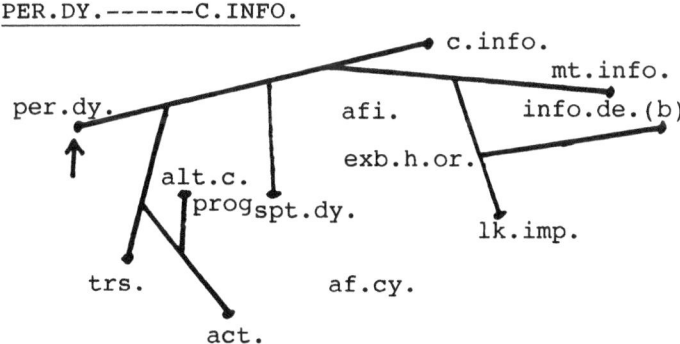

To better understand the dynamic implications of progressionalism, it is important to view what transpired in the sixties. For the reality of events in that time period has established the vibrational tone level of this period—and there are many unresolved considerations which must be dealt with—concerning: the route western culture has since taken in the seventies and the implications of what that direction has posed to the reality of information dynamics—that being, what this phenomenon has posed to the greater realness of alternative functionalism—and, finally, what this phenomenon means when viewed in the context of aspect-essence interpretation. This is what I am interested in.

By the late sixties, the dynamics of disunification had moved to slowly bring the realness of alternative functionalism to a halt. The nature of this disunification would involve practically every sector of the activist community—from the functionalism which solidified through isolated or composite participation, as well as the spectrum of self-interest activism. This time period would see many movements work against each other—and in doing so, virtually bringing any possibility for change to a standstill. Moreover, at the same time, the collective forces of western culture would move to dismantle most of the surface gains that had been won from the collective struggles in the sixties—and this dismantling is still being done today (although there is not much more to dismantle). It would be impossible to comment on the total reality of "particulars" related to the decline of sixties dynamic activism—for the realness of this subject involves many different factors. As such, the basis of my viewpoint on this period has to do with the role of information distortion and/or information compression. For at the heart of the many levels of disagreement that finally thwarted dynamic activism was a profound inability of the functioning movements to agree on what constituted the "essence" basis of composite functionalism. Which is to say, the move towards isolated activism in the end served as a disintegrating factor for the composite platform of dynamic activism—resulting finally in "activism with respect to the dictates of self-interest," rather than composite change. The thrust of this section of the book is concerned with reviewing the nature of sixties disunification as a means to understand what this phenomenon really meant with respect to the reality of western culture's information focus. For the decline of effective activism gives insight about the very nature of western perception, and unless changed, this same phenomenon has grave implications for the next cycle. The realness of sixties functionalism seems to make several factors clear—(1) that there are flaws underlying our very relationship with "source vibrational intentions" which, unless changed (or re-understood), promises to have multi-implicational consequences for the next time cycle, and (2) that the resolidification of composite activism is directly related to the nature of the next transformation (that being, the realness that the coming transformation can only be shaped—not stopped). The nature of the meta-reality position of western information dynamics must be re-examined now—for the "particulars" of its dynamic misinterpretations permeate the whole of western culture, from our relationship to creativity as well as our understanding of functionalism.

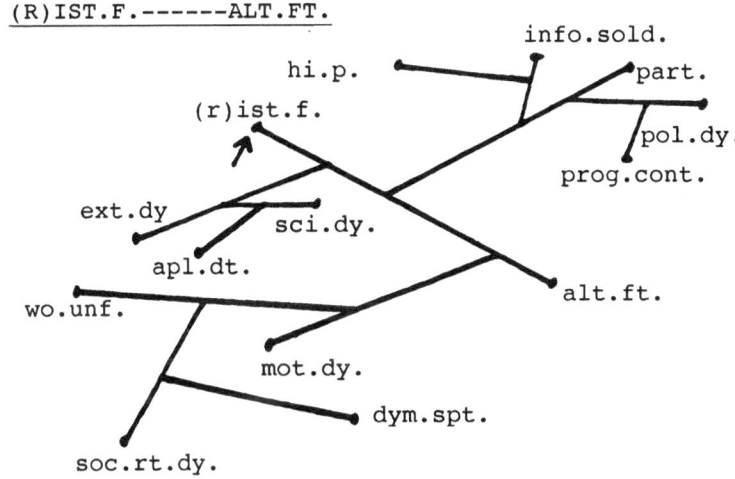

The dynamic particulars of isolated functionalism can be viewed as directly related to how disunification gained momentum in the sixties—and it is important that efforts are made to restore a composite basis for dynamic activism. In progressional terms, it is important that some attempt is made to detail what transpired to create the "haze of the seventies." Because where the injustices to black people or women had, in its original focus, come to be viewed as one of the many problems to be changed in dynamic activism—by the middle sixties, many of these same activist groups had come to see these injustices as the major problem (in some cases the only problem) of the west. Which is to say, the basis which defined the early period in civil rights had more to do with what these injustices posed to the whole of planet reality—even though the early activism was directed only towards particular aspects of that problem (both since there was a shortage of people and because the focus of a given activism cannot begin by taking the composite platform of world change at one stroke). Thus, where America's racial problem in the beginning could be viewed as an *aspect* of what was wrong with the culture, later the physical universe situation would transport this problem to the position of *essence*. In viewing the nature of this refocus, we can begin to understand the dynamics of western progressionalism (or at least how progressionalism is utilized as a factor to manipulate information dynamics). Because the particulars of information transfer (or the refocusing of information reality specifics) give insight into the very nature of western information dynamics (or western thinking).

    To clarify further: the goal in the sixties became to uplift the position of black people as a means to begin correcting the greater dynamics of western culture, later the goal became to uplift the position of black people exclusively, and even later the goal became just about being "black." In other words, what had been interpreted as an *aspect* symptomatic of what was wrong with this planet later became the sole absolute of what was wrong with the planet (and in becoming so, moved to either distort or not focus on the dynamic magnitude of composite planet problems—problems that if left unsolved would move to re-create the same dilemma we now find ourselves facing in this time zone). This is not to undermine the reality situation of black activism, nor by commenting on what sixties activism has posed to "isolated focus" have I meant to cast alternative functionalism from the black community in a negative light. Obviously there was and is a need for separate activism in the black community—and it is also clear that the forces which must be challenged are the collective forces of western culture—which is a platform for European and/or Euro-American caucasians. This is true for black activism and this is also true for trans-feminism—which is to say, there can be no disagreement as to the realness of what these struggles are, in this period as well as the past. But my point is that to separate these struggles from the composite realness of dynamic change is to in fact lose the necessary overview that can inspire real change. Because there can be no real change unless the composite dynamics of planet injustices are corrected—and this involves the particular reality dynamics of black people, women's liberation, the American Indian, human rights all over the planet, ecology, new politics, new spiritualism, etc., etc. The significance of any particular focus of activism has not only to do with what it poses for its isolated reality base but must also include what it poses for the greater dynamics of composite change (this is true even though "one must start at one place at a time"). The dissolution of dynamic activism in the sixties was brought about because the collective forces of western culture created a situation which moved to have people perceive of their activism as "starting at the place"—which is to say, the collected forces of western culture created a situation which moved to have given activists perceive the composite dynamics of world change in isolated terms. It must also be understood that the concept of aspect essence is not separate from the dynamics of "composite manifestation" (or circular manifestation) in that the realness of what it signifies is reflected on several different levels—its vibrational manifestation and its physical universe effect. Which is to say, the reality dynamics of progressionalism—especially as it applies to activism—can also be viewed as a factor which influences the success or failure of a given physical universe objective (or completion).

My understanding is as follows:

THE SOLVING OF AN ASPECT MERELY CHANGES THE DIVERSION BECAUSE THERE CAN BE NO SIGNIFICANT (REAL) CHANGE—OR ENLIGHTENMENT—UNLESS ONE DEALS WITH THE ESSENCE THAT DICTATES WHAT THAT GIVEN ASPECT REALLY MEANS.

I do not mean to negate the realness that people—in their own development—usually progress vibrationally and/or conceptually from their immediate physical universe reality to a universal position in their later development, because I am not writing on individual consciousness and how it develops. The concept of aspect essence has to do with the development and growth of functional movements and ideologies, as well as the sophistication of the collected forces of western culture and its ability to "transfer intentions"—and as such determine the nature of a given progressionalism (or determine the end result of a given postulation). I am also saying that the methods and principles we are taught concerning what constitutes ideas have a peculiar relationship to essence at best— and once more, this relationship lends itself very easily to aspect essence information perception (or mis-perception). If we are to deal with the challenges of the next time cycle then it is imperative that some effort is made in this period to investigate the realness of information dynamics. Because the discontinuance of civil rights activism is only one example of what has happened to western perception since the sixties. The composite nature of existence in the seventies can be viewed with respect to this same phenomenon—or at least this is true in the west anyway. The dynamics of spectacle diversion information perception have come to permeate the total lining of western culture and are manifested in everything from progressionalism to creativity (e.g., the relationship between how given techniques are viewed with respect to what the "music" is of that technique).

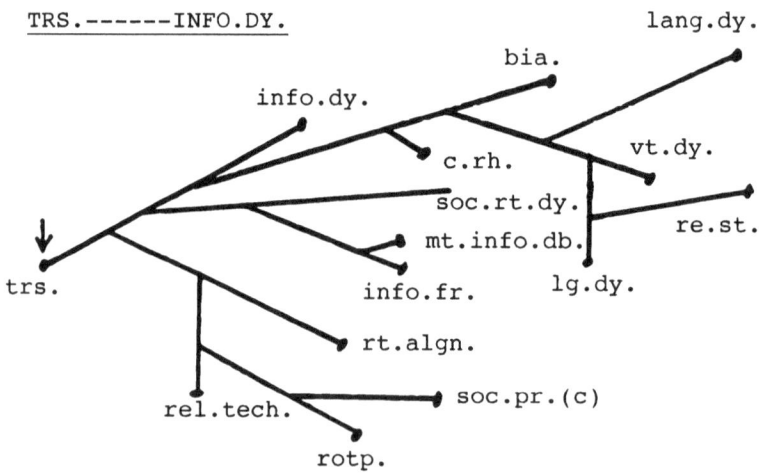

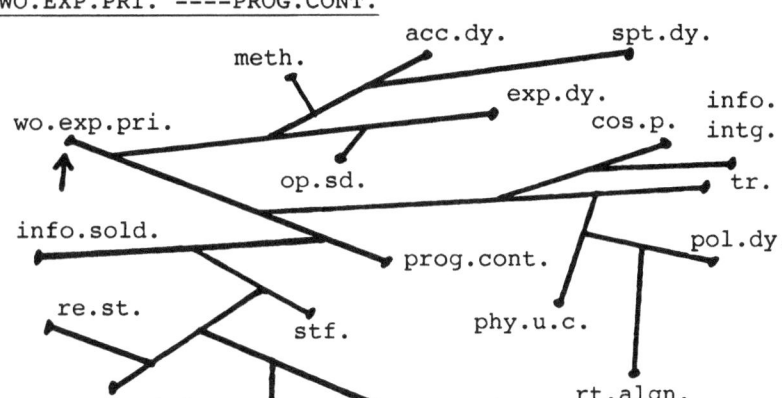

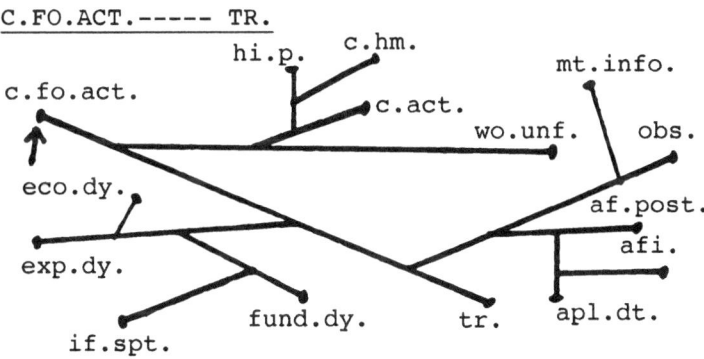

If the spectacle-diversion syndrome is the progressional platform underlying how events on the physical universe level are manipulated and perceived—as a controlling factor that moves to affect one's ability to participate in actual life or relevant change—then the aspect-essence information focus would have to do with what this manipulation has actualized with respect to the dynamic implication of information perception and interpretation. Yet I have not advanced this idea as a concept that is only interesting to look at. It is important to understand what this phenomenon has posed to progressionalism as well as creativity and/or attitude. It is my belief that the present "state of things" in western culture (in the late seventies) can be viewed as the direct result of the inability of concerned activists to foresee the consequences of transfer cycles. The reality position of poor people in America and the greater world community has changed very little since the sixties. In practically every case, the dynamics of social reality have gotten worse—not better. Moreover, the vibrational factors which have helped to dictate the particulars of social reality have not changed very much either. Thus if positive transformational activism is to ever again surface as a real consideration, some attempt must be made to re-investigate both what went wrong and how.

It is not enough to merely state that the flaws permeating progressionalism in the sixties can be understood by the concept of transfer cycles without some attempt to clarify what this means in actual terms. For if I have stated that the vibrational-affinity concept of world unification is the desired objective of any real attempt to better life on this planet, it is important to elaborate on what this really means or run the risk of simply extolling platitudes. By unification, I have not meant to paint a "pie in the sky" image of life in a Walt Disney picture, nor have I meant to comment on a state impossible to attain. I am only referring to the realness that the planet earth consists of many different (on the surface) kinds of people and that everyone on the planet should have a right to live. By unification in this context, I have only tried to translate the realness of this phenomenon into words, as well as what this subject poses to the greater cosmic and vibrational overtones related to existence. Moreover, I have also tried to state that any philosophy or thrust motivation that does not vibrate to the affinity and spiritual pull of "essence with respect to composite humanity" cannot be viewed as moving towards (and being of) positive transformation. As such the "realness" of a given route of functionalism has to do with whether or not that functionalism proceeds with respect to what its purpose will imply for collected humanity and world unification. We as a people in the future will have to understand that, in fact, unification is in the "self-interest" of everyone—if we are to survive—but I do not mean this in one-dimensional terms. Unification does not only imply one affinity attitude or worldview—nor does this concept imply any loss of respect for one's particular viewpoint. Rather, the concept of unification has to do with an expanded awareness of what is happening on this planet—in this experience (life)—during this particular time period (which is also other time periods).

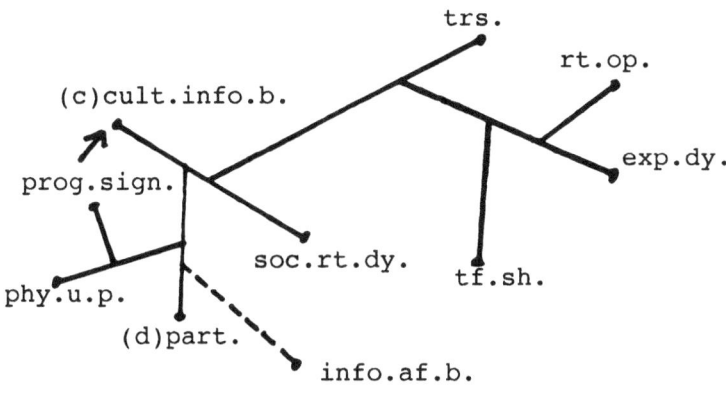

CULT.INFO.B.------SOC.RT.DY.

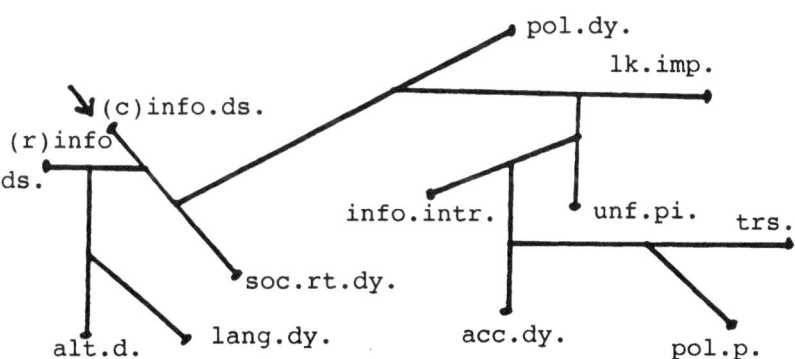

INFO.DS.------SOC.RT.DY.

The consideration of unification can be used to understand how the fragmentation which occurred in the sixties brought about stagnation on the part of some activist groups and limited success by other groups. It is important that the dynamics of this phenomenon are viewed and corrected, for while given surface focuses were necessarily perceived as separate from the greater arena of composite alternative functionalism, this difference does not necessarily imply a separate meta-reality (or physical universe reality) objective. As long as composite activism functions only with respect to the object of its separate focus—without respect for what a given object implies for the whole of alternative functionalism—there can be no hope of solidifying a composite stance for new functionalism. This is not to ignore the particulars of a given focus—because obviously the reality objective of a given functionalism carries its own challenge—but to instead widen the dynamic basis from which it is viewed. In the final analysis, we must understand that there is nothing separate in the universe—or at least separate in the way we have come to use the word. Rather, the significance of transformational functionalism will have to do with its ability to view the dynamic inter-relationship between the spectrum of its forces, as a means to work towards rebuilding the composite dynamics of its total forces. This is directly related to the concept of aspect-essence information focus. The particular of seventies functionalism has shown what happens when an aspect of social reality is focused on without respect for its greater reality implications. In the future, positive functionalism must have an expanded understanding of "self-interest"—that being, with respect to the composite planet. There can be no positive interest in the long run unless that interest takes the world position into account—yet I have not meant to imply that nothing is of value in "isolated focus" functionalism, because this would not be true either. Certainly there are situations that only "isolated focus" functionalism can best deal with—the realness of critical physical universe suffering in many cases cannot wait for composite awareness if its people are to survive. But in the long run, a given function can have longevity only if the dictates of its reality position are seeded with respect to the composite realness of greater humanity.

In the final analysis, the concept of unification must be viewed as a necessary objective having not only to do with the expansion of one's perceptional focus, but also as the first building block for transformation. The realness of this concept must be based on agreement rather than differences—because underlying the particulars of social and vibrational change (no matter what particular is focused on) is the realness that every real objective seeks the same basic state. That being, the reality of every desired intention can usually be underlined as a desire to have a positive and meaningful life on the planet—the desire to have the opportunity to make a living, to have a family, and to participate in one's relationship with his or her religion (with respect to what is perceived or felt to be one's identity alignment and/or vibrational alignment). Yet I do not mean to imply that every person in particular terms desires these objectives (because to do so would be to violate the dynamic spectrum of forces—people—that we have on this planet). There are many people (forces) whose vibrational alignments and life purpose have nothing to do with what I have written as "general life positions," and these people must also be respected. But the concept of "general life intentions" does have meaning when viewed with respect to the higher motivations that dictate (or that should dictate) the functionalism surrounding how cultures are created—and maintained. My point is that the dynamics of life intentions—with respect to what this consideration means when applied to social reality—have more in common with composite humanity than what we generally have come to believe. Which is to say, we are all very much alike as a human family, and the success of future progressionalism will be directly related to whether or not some attempt can be solidified that "proceeds with respect to the whole of humanity."

Finally, the move to focus on "essence"—as a means to perceive with respect to the widest information position possible—can help to focus on the spirituality of what a given information signifies. In other words, the thrust or a given information line is not relegated to only one function, nor is it limited to one vibrational position—instead, the essence reality position of a given viewpoint or information line moves to give insight into its region of spirituality. If we can learn to "view" with respect to the dynamic implications of a given information line then we can also come to experience the vibrational insight that is related to what a given information line really means. As such, the seriousness of world unification is not only about the particulars of a given functionalism but includes the dynamics of new spirituality—and this is what is needed. The significance of aspect-essence investigation can then be utilized as a positive tool rather than a divisive focus for self-interest. Before real change can be brought about, we must first move to recognize all of the many different levels of divisive interpretation and "over-extended isolations." This is not to say that the removal of false information interpretation can in itself change the reality tone of earth existence—because it won't; nor by correcting information perceptions will we necessarily have an "Alice in Wonderland" type of life on earth (which I doubt anyone would really want anyway), for the dynamics of earth life transcend any one criterion. But one thing is certain: if the present relationship western culture has now developed with information is not corrected, positive world change will be difficult, if not impossible, to achieve. The concept of aspect essence is directly related to the nature of sixties progressionalism in that the reality of its perception dynamics have helped to shape the definitions and redefinitions that have characterized events in this cycle. Not only that, but the implications of aspect-essence perception have also helped to create the vibrational attitude that surrounds our relationship with given areas of information. The spectrum of information distortion which has resulted from this phenomenon has permeated the composite reality of information focus from creativity to science to astronomy to politics. The aspect-essence information focus has moved to separate various sectors of humanity under the ill-conceived notion of self-interest, and has also moved to distort the relationship between a given functional methodology and its reality. The challenge of the next cycle is to restore a composite and meaningful world position to information and information dynamics. In other words, there is now a need "to begin seeing ourselves anew."

(Level Two)

I HAVE TRIED IN THIS SECTION OF THE BOOK to stress the world culture implications of both affinity dynamics and multi-information as a means to better understand the realness of creativity on a multi-dimensional level. It is important that the composite world implications of creativity are dealt with because too often the collected forces surrounding education would have us believe that creativity exists in a vacuum—having nothing to do with the dynamics of social reality. To really view this subject is to have real concern about the physical and vibrational factors which are the basis from which something is actualized. In other words, both the vibrational and scientific implications of a given projection—style—derives its realness from the total beingness of its culture group. For that reason, I have attempted to include this aspect of creativity (the physical universe implications in Writings 2)—with the hope that extended subject material can provide a healthier and more realistic approach to this subject. I believe we are moving to a cycle that will necessitate having the widest possible overview—with respect to both creativity as well as "actual" life (and living). For the vibrational realness of the physical universe is changing more than many of us would like to admit. Moreover, if the concept of transformation is valid, then the nature of a given change cycle can also be viewed with respect to composite planet consciousness. That is, the dynamics of a given transformation are not limited to only particular culture groups or planet regions. It is more than conceivable that the spectrum of planet options in the next cycle will bring about a situation where many of us might find ourselves in a completely different culture (or vibrational alignment)—which is to say, the composite awareness of creativity (and planet reality dynamics) could be essential information if we are to be prepared to change (life). Moreover, in the final analysis, if we are to deal with the social reality implications of creativity, then we are forced to deal with—social reality.

SR(TRS)II–2

The social reality realness of creativity is connected to many factors. For by social reality in this context, I am commenting on the state of the physical universe in a given time period and what that state posed for the understanding of creative postulation. Moreover, if the major thrust of this section has had to do with the progressional continuance of world culture in the time zone of the sixties to the end of the seventies, then the social reality implications of this subject must be viewed within this same context. Hopefully a probe of this type could be most useful in providing some basis for understanding the vibrational factors that are in the air in this period (the late seventies). For I believe that the time cycle of the sixties on through to the seventies was an important period in planet developments—and this is especially true for western culture. This cycle was also an incredible period for creativity as well, for the realness of this period would see the emergence of a spectrum of projections covering the total reality of information lines. Moreso, this same period would also provide the vibrational platform which solidified how the eighties time continuum views creativity (and how that viewpoint has affected the projectional spread or repression of creativity as well). In other words, the dynamic realness of this time cycle (the sixties) is too significant to be lightly viewed, especially if we desire insight into the projectional implications of creativity—regardless of strain (style).

Since the major focus of this book was conceived with respect for what has transpired through the progressional thrust of creative music in America, then quite possibly this would be the best focus to begin examining the physical universe factors related to what that phenomenon has posed. For the present physical universe cycle that America is in must be viewed as necessarily relevant to the total social dynamics surrounding how we have come to view creativity. To view the physical universe realness of this time cycle can better give us insight into what the coming cycle will be about—for it is understood that given physical and social universe "reality positions" are not separate from what is transpiring in the natural tendencies of the culture. This is especially true if we are to take into account the difference between "natural" (or at least not consciously designed) transitions, as opposed to progressional cycles that are "designed." To view the time cycle of the middle to late seventies in America is to deal with both types of progressional cycles—which is to say, the progressional factors surrounding creative music in America are extremely complex and interesting. For it is understood that creativity is not separate from the people who are creating, and if we are talking about viewing the progressional implications of creative music from the black aesthetic, then we cannot afford to not view the reality surrounding what has and is happening to black people as something not relevant (or important). The social reality dynamics of this area of information must be viewed as essential—that is, the reality implications which dictate what is happening on the physical universe level to black people can directly give one real insight as to the option spread (and/or affinity and dynamic implications) of black creativity, both as an alternative creative thrust which functions as a means to secure (and clarify) "source initiation" and also as the essence foundation from which the world community could be aligned. The question then is, "what is the physical universe reality that surrounds the composite realness of black creativity, and what does it mean?" Moreover, the seriousness of this question must also shed real light on the multi-complexual factors related to forming a total overview of planet events—for the reality options (and implications) of black culture in America are not separate from the composite realness of world culture. The reality implications surrounding the physical universe situation of black culture can tell us something about what vibrational factors are in the air, either with regards to actual functionalism (i.e., the ever-changing social decisions or real motivation) or vibrational change (i.e., the ever-changing social and/or spiritual arena—and what this implies for "new" or "unusual" viewpoints), and the seriousness of this information can better prepare all of us for the forces that will accompany what these changes will mean. For it is understood that the vibrational lining of a given cultural region (sector) is an integral factor that signals both the cosmic and physical universe consequences of what a given affinity intention really means. As such, the study of social reality is directly related to the projectional realness of creativity—in all of its given manifestations. As we move into the eighties, this area of information will assume ever greater importance, for the vibrational factors which are solidifying what the future will be about are in fact happening in this time zone—in other words, we are creating the future now.

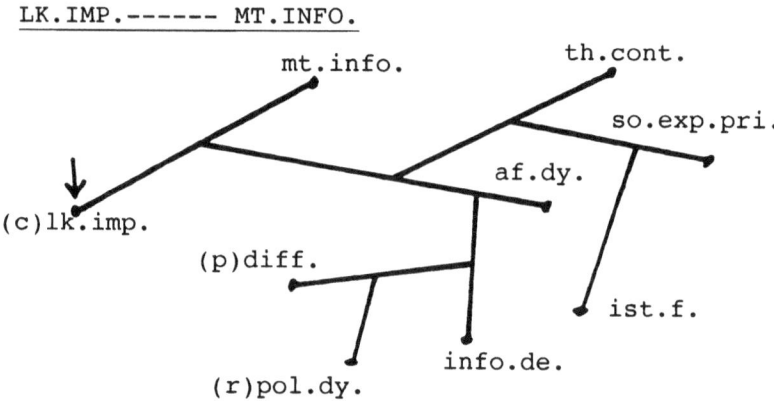

Without doubt, one of the more interesting concepts to have emerged in the late seventies is the idea that black people in western culture have finally arrived into the mainstream. In other words, there is at present in western culture the feeling that most of the injustices which have been committed against black people have now come to a stop, and now, at last, America can be viewed as a multi-racial culture—of equal opportunity. This feeling has been echoed on many levels. I recall listening to a poll result conducted by NBC that stated the most oppressed group of individuals in western culture are homosexuals (not the American Indians or Asians, mind you). This feeling can also be viewed with respect to how the collective functionalism of women's liberation is now seen—that being, the basic forces which are manipulating (and oppressing) western culture in this cycle have somehow accepted black people—and as such, the primary focus for alternative functionalism can now be directed towards other segments of the culture. Presently, one can read many articles on the emergence of the black middle class, and of course much has been made of the potential voting strength of the black community (with the understanding being that "now that you can vote there should be nothing to complain about"). In fact, the great majority of Americans in this time cycle (the late seventies)

view the reality of black culture as a subject that was solved in the sixties and as such can now be left alone—and it must be understood that this sentiment is not limited to any given thrust but instead signals the greater sentiment of the culture (not limited to any one area). It is also possible to view how given sectors of the country have helped to solidify this sentiment, for it must be understood that I am commenting on the developments reshaping the media as well—whether we are referring to newspapers, television, etc. So overwhelming is the feeling that black people have had enough "special treatment" that the next progressional expansion (or cycle) in western culture must be viewed with this in mind.

Of course I have not meant to imply that the only area worth dealing with—as far as social reality is concerned—is that of black American culture, because obviously it isn't. Nor have I meant to downrate the social reality struggle of any segment of American culture. There can be no question as to the validity of the struggle homosexuals are dealing with in this period, and I have not meant to imply that their struggle is not real, and important, because it is. And obviously the realness of women's liberation has to be dealt with as a major problem of planet consciousness as well (for the realness of this subject permeates the vibrationaltory lining of this time cycle). And of course there are other struggles which have nothing to do with developments in the black community that must also be dealt with (for if the subject is western culture and social reality, one could write twelve hundred books and still not properly cover everything). I write this out of respect for the dynamic realness of both world and western culture—and also I write this because it is true. Yet the complexities underlying what is happening in black culture also mean something and should not be ignored. For the composite sentiment that seems to be forming can be viewed as a direct result of the special position that non-white people are in during this cycle. Moreover, the implications of that position seem to forecast a particular vibrational thrust—especially with regards to social reality. For to understand that the collective reality of western culture has now come to believe the injustices which have been perpetrated against black people have been corrected is to see the beginning of something of profound importance—and it is my opinion that the functionalism related to this sentiment has already started to make itself felt. If this is true then the next cycle in western culture promises to be very ... "interesting."

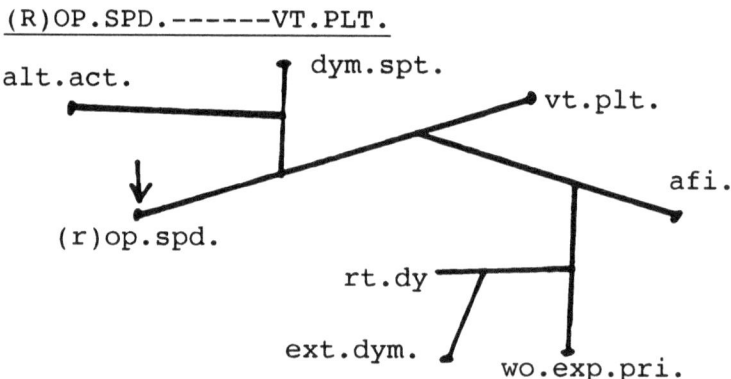

To deal with a given composite culture attitude as a means to understand the vibrational dynamics surrounding creativity is in itself nothing new. Yet if we are to understand the nature of the forces which are forming in this period, it is important to deal with the composite solidification of what these attitudes mean on a global level. For, quite possibly, this time zone can be viewed as an important cycle on many different levels. Not only does the physical universe and social reality of, say, American culture affect the vibrational continuance of western creativity—as it has always done (and of course this is the natural or so-called natural interrelationship of cross-sectional activity—that being, events in the culture and its vibrational manifestation in the creativity), but the realness of where western culture has developed in this time zone has world implications as well. Because of this, we are in a cycle which has brought the composite interrelationship of world culture together in a way that was impossible before. What this means is that to view the physical and social universe reality dynamics of American culture is to also understand the resultant (and/or consequences) of what those dynamics imply for world culture. And if this is understood, then the current vibrational sentiment that is solidifying in American culture cannot only be viewed with respect to the American people. With the advent of what Richard Teitelbaum called "rapid communication" and "high-speed travel," a given event can be—and usually is—experienced almost simultaneously all over the planet. Yet I do not mean to imply that world culture is necessarily even interested in every phase of American or western culture—because this is not my point either. Rather, the social realness of this time period must be viewed with regards to its most dynamic interpretation. In that light, there is a wealth of information that does affect the composite world group—and it is this information that concerns me. Moreover, I have mentioned the reality position of American black people because of my belief that the forces related to the present factors reshaping events in this area are directly connected to the composite world group. This is not to state that, in particular terms, world culture will view the social and vibrational situation of black Americans as necessarily relevant to their own special situation—because this is not necessarily true either. But I do believe the universal implications surrounding what is happening in the black community (in America) does have many informational aspects that are of relevance to the world community—and moreover, I also believe that the reality of composite non-white people on the planet is not as separate as might appear on the surface (yet I do not mean to over-generalize this most important point). My point is that the interrelationship of physical universe events transcends both national and cultural lines to the degree that given particular developments have global implications—and my point is that these implications come especially into play if the developments in question concern events in the black (non-white) community.

To view the present reality cycle of American black people, it is necessary to view the composite factors affecting the total society—which is to say, it is not necessary to single out black culture as representing a zone not related to the composite reality of American culture. For the reality options black people are dealing with in this time cycle are manifested throughout the composite spectrum of American culture. Yet by the same token, what has actualized from the composite particulars of American culture has not brought a universal end result. Nevertheless, the most basic way to examine what has and is happening in the black community is to deal with the universal particulars which affect everyone (for it is through a universal perspective that one can better understand what social reality is). It is important that this subject is viewed with respect for its composite implications because I am not commenting on the progressional reality cycles of the black community as a means to simply make a special case for black people—or special treatment. The fact is, the composite factors which determine how events are actualized in American culture must be dealt with and understood on some level if we are to understand the realness of present-day social reality, not to mention what this phenomenon means to creativity.

Without doubt, the most basic factor that determines how a given individual or group is to exist is the reality position of contraction or economics—that being, in this time zone anyway, the realness of money (and the systems constructed to support financial transactions). The universal dynamics of economics is a subject that transcends racial or regional boundaries—and in doing so, this area of information moves instead to give a more accurate interpretation of both culture participation and social dynamics. Economics, then, is a subject not separate from the reality of participation—on an individual or collective level—as well as composite postulation (e.g., jobs, goals, desire). Thus a subject of this magnitude can help clarify not only what has happened in American social reality—regardless of period—but the universality of this subject can also provide a more realistic context for viewing—and hopefully understanding—the broader implications of composite progressionalism. For in the final analysis, this book is not directed towards those events which have shaped social or vibrational reality for only western culture exclusively—instead, I am interested in what this subject poses for composite humanity. It is important to not forget that the policies dictating present-day social reality in America also affects—and indeed are directed with an even greater intensity to—the world group. Which is to say, the decisions that have shaped America's economic reality are not limited to what happens to any one sector of her shores, but instead these policies have multi-implications to the total reality of earth transactions. By the same token, it is possible to focus on the particulars of applied functionalism—which in this case is the reality systems of America's economic policies—as a means to establish some basis for understanding the larger context concerning how a given intention (i.e., policy) is "made real," or practiced. To view the economic reality particulars surrounding the black community in America can help to establish some understanding of what is really happening in present-day applied economics—and this is what I am interested in. All of this information is directly related to the underlying purposes of this book. Because creativity does not exist separate from actual life, and/or life and death decisions. On the contrary, the reality position of a given culture is directly related to its life support systems—whether that system is its creativity or economics. As such, to probe the particulars of present-day economics is directly relevant for better understanding creativity and what is happening in our society.

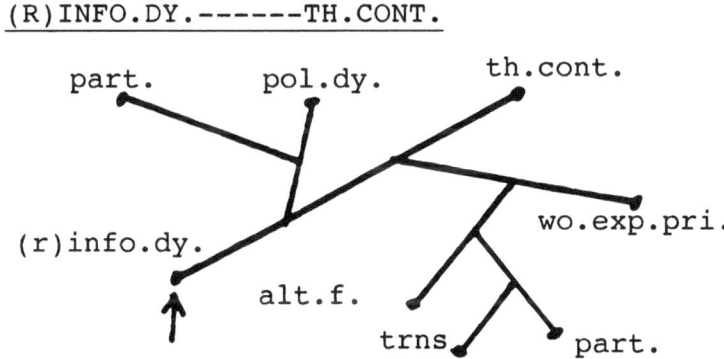

The actual reality that surrounds the black community in America in this cycle can be viewed as not very different than what it was before the sixties. In other words, the earlier statements I mentioned—concerning the emergence of the black middle class—doesn't really give a clear picture of what is happening in this cycle. The fact is—if the economic consideration is our first point of extension (observation)—unemployment figures for black people in the late seventies seem to suggest that the reality options for black people have decreased rather than increased. The seriousness of what this means cannot be avoided. For if the most basic understanding this culture has of black people is that the time zone of the sixties eliminated many of the inequalities created by racism, then what does this viewpoint mean. Moreover, it must be understood that when I wrote that black unemployment has increased I did not mean that this increase has taken place on only one level. The fact is, by black unemployment I am commenting on the total cross-sectional spread of black culture—encompassing both young and old people, men and women (I cite this fact from the government's own figures—which, based on my own individual observation, is much less than what actually is). To understand what this means is to have some idea of the situation black people are dealing with in this time cycle. Because in citing the unemployment situation that black people are dealing with, I am not writing of something so abstractly conceptual as to have no meaning on a practical physical universe level. If we are to understand the realness of social dynamics, then the realness of what this phenomenon means must be dealt with. Because I believe that the progressional forces dictating social reality in western culture (in this case, America) have now moved to another change cycle—and this should not be lightly viewed. The unemployment that is so rampant in the black community is symptomatic of what this change will mean in actual terms—yet I do not mean to over-emphasize this point and run the risk of obscuring this section.

Obviously there has been much talk in this time zone (the seventies) about the ills of inflation and the coming depression, and I have not meant to neglect this information. Moreover, I have also not meant to ignore the realness that many people are out of jobs in this time zone—which is to say, not only black people are under-employed. But the dynamics of this time zone are related to many other factors as well, and it is possible to view several progressional developments that are relevant to how this time zone solidified. In other words, there is a definite pattern that can be observed. For while black and non-white people should not be viewed as a special group—in the cosmic sense of what people are—there are other factors which must be dealt with if we are to understand this period. It is not just a question of me citing unemployment as a sign that the reality options of black people are under suppression—because in itself unemployment can be interpreted on many other levels (some of which might not have the same negative implications)—rather, it is a question of focusing on the composite factors which have characterized this time cycle. Because if the unemployment happening in this time zone does not in itself have multi-dimensional implications, then the vibrational climate of American culture is indeed interesting. To understand this is to understand that in the beginning of this chapter I mentioned a growing sentiment that seems to be moving towards a functional position concerning how Americans view black people and black culture—but, by definition, the fact that something has been growing implies a longer time span—that is, the present sentiment we are dealing with in this time zone is the result of a sustained time cycle. But what does this mean?

The most relevant overview that could supply the necessary perspective for understanding this cycle (late seventies) would be the progressional developments surrounding what transpired politically from the middle fifties to the present. This is true because the unemployment situation black people are dealing with in this cycle is a response to several factors. To understand what is happening to black Americans, one must trace the developments activated by the Brown decision in 1954. All of the social reality changes that moved to superficially change the position of black people in this cycle are related to the significance of that court case—and what it posed with respect to the Constitution, and—more importantly—to the spectacle diversion affinity nature of American culture. The progressional and vibrational continuum of the Brown decision would provide the platform for political diversion in the sixties, and this would be the time cycle where programs were supposedly developed to reshape the inequalities of the American system. The realness of this cycle would be magnified by the programs of Lyndon Johnson—having to do with the half-acknowledgement that indeed there were many areas of both discrimination and segregation— and the basic thrust of the sixties would see the introduction of legislative programs that were designed to correct this dilemma. For many black people, this acknowledgement was viewed as an end of the past and proof that a new era had come (it would be in this time zone that suddenly black people would even appear on television—"as if they really existed" like the rest of America's citizens). The dynamics of the surface changes that characterized the sixties actually made more of an impact than the functionalism it created, nevertheless the ten year cycle of the sixties would forecast the nature of events to come. This is so because if the sixties was the time zone which superficially gave hint of social change, the seventies was the time cycle which systematically reversed practically every legislative and conceptual move to establish a democratic society of integrity. (Yet I do not mean to imply that any of the functional programs created in the sixties actually were significant enough to have had a possibility to really change American society—for the great majority of these programs were not designed to really reshape the composite society, but rather were designed to give the illusion of change.) The totalness of the sixties can be viewed as a cycle that corresponded to the spectacle diversion factors of its time period having to do with the dissolution of the composite spirit of the country because of the loss of the war in Vietnam and the vibrations that accompanied the three assassinations. As the seventies solidified and the spectacle diversion cycle moved to its next focus, so too did any commitment to human rights—or at least the solidification of the seventies would see a completely different attitude—and completely different responses in actual terms as well. Of course there is more and I have not meant to give the impression that the rate of intention shift was sharp (rather than gradual)—and yet I do not mean to give the impression that what happened in this cycle can be viewed as some kind of accident either. The actual fact is, there has never been a real effort to deal with the reality implications of racism and discrimination in America—but this is only the beginning of my real point.

To really understand the reality implications of American society is to deal with the actualness of what economics really means. For when I wrote that the physical universe situation in this time zone has moved to create a jobless society that hurts those who need work the most, it is important to understand what this means in actual terms. The fact is, there are many people existing in America who can only be described as poor—that being, without jobs (or jobs that pay any relevant money) and without food. Nor do I mean to imply that this situation is only manifested in the black community—because it isn't. Americans of every race, regardless of sector, are affected by poverty and there are more of these people than many of us would like to admit. To really view the dynamics of social reality is to be forced to deal with this fact—because it must be understood that many of the so-called problems this culture is experiencing (e.g., breakdown in ethics, rise of crime, and in general loss of national pride) are related to the composite effect of the "real" social reality existing in this time period. All of these considerations cannot be divorced from the reality dynamics of this cycle. Moreover, if the subject of reality dynamics in the black community can be viewed as depressing, it is nothing compared with what this country (America) has and is doing to the American Indian—which is to say, the economic implications of this time period are not limited to any one factor—but instead must be viewed in its composite realness.

The dynamics of social reality must be viewed for what this concept poses for world consciousness. Because social reality is not the property of any one culture, but includes instead the whole of events on the planet. Moreover, if the basic point of departure for this section had to do with the position of economics as a factor which affects social reality, then to omit the world group would make no sense. Because when I wrote that there are many poor people in America as a means to convey the seriousness of what economics is (and what this consideration poses with respect to actual life), then to view the composite realness of this subject on a planet level should be even more unnerving. For if the composite realness of western culture can be viewed with respect for how its economics have functioned—and how given groups of people are starving as a result of that functioning—then the realness of what is happening in many of non-western and developing countries as a result of these same decisions might frighten many of us. The truth is, the progressional expansion of western culture is directly related to the progressional decline of world culture—which is to say, there are many cultures on the planet in this time zone that can be viewed as living in poverty because of America's foreign policies. Certainly I do not mean to imply that each and every one of us are directly connected to how this phenomenon has come about, nor have I meant to generalize about how this state of being has developed (without doubt, this is a complex subject) and I am not interested in trying to cultivate guilt either (especially since guilt really means nothing anyway). But to view the present physical universe cycle we are now in is to be confronted with what is really happening, and the only decision that can be immediately made concerns whether or not one is really honest about what seems to be true. Nor am I commenting on the dynamics of interpretation either. The fact is, there are many people on the planet who are barely existing, and as such the realness of social reality implies that this is understood on some level.

I have not introduced the subject of economics and poverty as a means to have something only to write on, rather it is from this position that we can begin moving towards really understanding present-day social dynamics (and consequences). Many of us have come to view the universe with respect to only particular corners of the planet, and the end result of this viewpoint is that only the so-called western countries are "real" in our minds. This viewpoint is enforced by the collective forces that control how we perceive information in western culture (not to mention the collective forces which determine how we have come to perceive what information is). The end result of this phenomenon is planet isolation, which is to say, there is no growth or real unification under this viewpoint. What we need in this time zone more than ever is a composite world consciousness—having to do with real concern for what is happening on the vibrational and physical universe level of our planet. From this awareness we can move to understand that isolated developments in any sector of the planet have universal consequences, and this is true on many levels. For if in the affinity dynamics section of this chapter I commented on the interrelationship of information lines as a means to show the universality of information, it is important to not view the cross-sectional implication of multi-information in light terms. The fact is, the cross-sectional implication of multi-information is not relegated to only one sector of the planet—which is to say, not only ideas and specific information routes are subjected to dynamic spread, but rather, the vibrational and dynamic wholeness of "actual information" (or composite information) moves to affect the composite physical universe. If this is true then the realness of what this implies must also be understood. Because when I wrote that the physical universe situation in many of the developing countries can be viewed as substandard (with respect to the consideration economics and/or poverty) and as a result, many people are barely able to exist, it is important for us to understand the vibrational implications of this phenomenon. For I have not meant to imply that because a given sector of the planet is experiencing starvation that social reality and justice implies we must necessarily attempt to starve in the same context, nor have I tried to blanket the realness of this subject by simply throwing meaningless accusations on western culture (and in doing so, move to create a viewpoint that seeks to make western culture totally responsible for everything happening in this time zone). To do so would completely distort both credibility and common sense, but I have tried to comment on the realness of trans-events: that being, the vibrational realness of given events is not limited to any one sector of the planet, and as such what transpired on the physical universe level does have meaning for what it signals about the whole of the planet. The reality dynamics of planet earth involves all of us—or at least should involve all of us. To understand the composite implications of this subject is to recognize that the challenge of the next cycle is directly related to a more realistic approach to education—education in the sense that hopefully real information can supply the necessary overview to deal with understanding what life on a planet is supposed to be about.

The significance of education must be viewed in several contexts—for the realness of this subject has different meanings depending on its application. The fact is, I believe the challenge of education is the single most important factor affecting the progressional spread of earth developments in this cycle. For it is understood that by education I am commenting on "real information" as opposed to spectacle diversion images. Yet to view the seriousness of what this subject poses for planet change is to also recognize that there are several different aspects to this challenge. For when I write of the significance of education as a transformational tool, there must also be the awareness that this information will mean different things to different groups—that is, education and the need to investigate will not be perceived in the world community as necessarily dealing with the same information lines as western culture—and this must be understood. For while the importance of world information is a universal necessity, the seriousness of the physical universe position of the world group (non-western cultures) implies an immediacy that is pronounced. In other words, the intensity of the present physical universe situation implies that given information lines be of a particular nature—with respect to both its vibrational and functional significance. It is not a question of negating any area of information but rather understanding that the present physical universe situation the world group is now dealing with is the direct result of the suppression and distortion of its information lines by western culture. Thus the progressional spread of the next cycle must be viewed with respect to what that information loss has signified, and if the consideration of education is to be relevant as a transformation tool, then the realness of this subject must be focused on accordingly—yet I have not meant to limit the dynamics of education. My point is only that the world community cannot afford the luxury of wasting time—or at least to not use this cycle as productively as possible, because there are many factors in the air which must be recognized. One being that the progressional expansion of events in this cycle seem to forecast even more oppression to those groups who are outside the basic thrust pool of contemporary information (and historically focused relevant information) dissemination. What this means is that the composite world group is in a very important cycle—nor by world group am I excluding non-white people in western culture. In other words, my point is that the progressional continuance of this cycle seems to hint that unless certain extensions are understood (and as such controlled), the very existence of non-white people can be viewed as . . . "interesting indeed." Everything seems to point to the realness that several transformations seem to be available for the next cycle—one of which undoubtedly has to do with the "natural" annihilation of given sectors of the planet community (in the drive towards perceived expansion). This is not to imply that there is a conscious move towards destroying given segments of humanity, but rather, to view the collected forces of western culture is to see a particular vibrational continuum that flows in a particular way—having to do with many factors. The particular aspects of this continuum can be viewed from many different viewpoints (for by "particular" in this context, I am writing of the diversification of life dynamics), but it is important for every non-caucasian to understand that the composite solidification of this phenomenon moves as an annihilation factor for world culture—and I do not mean this as a generalization but as an implicit warning. So real is this potential that the consideration of preparation cannot be lightly viewed. As such, the realness of education is not separate from what this challenge implies, for a given sector's ability to react to given physical and vibrational universe developments is directly related to what information options are understood. Yet I have not meant to imply that the need for education is only applicable to non-western people (or non-caucasian people) because this consideration—education—is important for all of the people on this planet. Certainly a composite approach to information could help everyone, including white Americans and/or Europeans (because real information serves as the strongest positive tool for world transformation). Moreover, I have not meant to racistly exclude white people by only accenting the needs of black people (for while the seriousness of this cycle is important, there is still the realness that the vibrational dynamics of human beings transcend the narrow categories we now have for people). In other words, to move to exclude a given sector of the community merely because that sector is white also violates the realness of what is really happening on the physical universe level. The complex fact is, "one never knows who a given person is"—which is to say, in the rush to move to positive transformation, it is important to not create a vibrational situation which will later create the same situation we hope to change.

SR(TRS)II–18

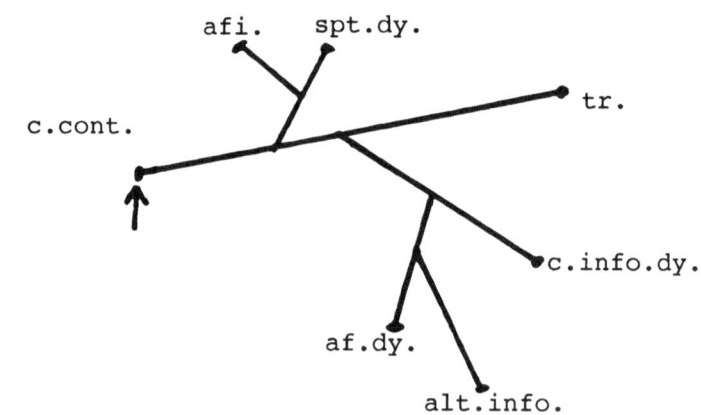

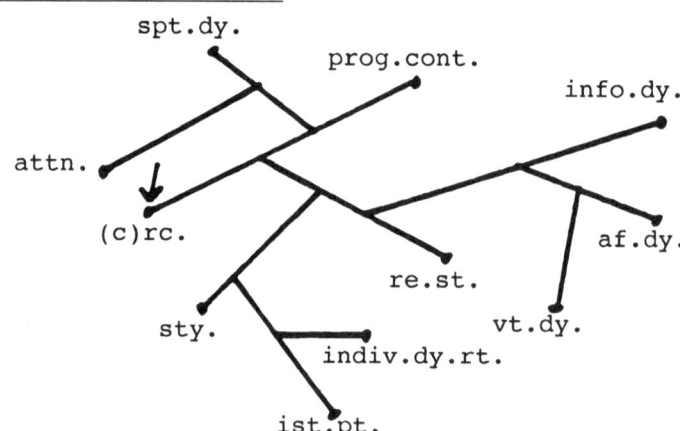

The importance of education for transformation cannot be overemphasized, because the present physical universe situation is directly sustained by narrow information lines. The truth is, most of us have come to view the physical universe—and for that matter, social reality—in non-transformational terms—which is to say, with respect to the forces which have shaped this cycle. The end result of this affinity viewpoint is that many of us have come to view individual initiation—or alternative group initiation—as something of little significance—and this viewpoint is understandable. For the realness of this time zone can, on many levels, appear to be too real—as if nothing can ever really change. Sometimes it seems as if the present situation has always been as it is, but this is not true. Only exposure to composite information lines can better give one a total perspective of what this time period really is, and only by dealing with this information can one move to begin reshaping his (or her) own personal life, and from that point composite social reality. Without exposure to real information, alternative functionalism is extremely difficult if not impossible. For it is not simply a question of how one reacts or functions in this time zone—certainly any person can desire to simply not function in the so-called standard mode or "order" of western culture, and as such merely drop out or create alternative lifestyles and/or movements—rather, it is a question of understanding the total factors shaping how this cycle came into being as a means to gain "relevant" perspectives. Without a composite understanding of earth developments, alternative activity can only be real on certain levels, because the progressional information related to the rise and fall of transitional and transformational earth is not separate from what alternative activity poses as a meaningful concept about this experience—regardless of time and focus. It is for this reason that I have stressed the significance of progressional information. For to view the realness of composite information is to know (1) that this time cycle is not necessarily unique or unchangeable, (2) that non-white people have not always been in the physical universe position they are now in, (3) that people who would like to change this period are not alone as such (for this viewpoint is related to desires which have been manifested throughout the whole of history), and (4) that the progressional cycles surrounding the transition of various culture groups do show alternative viewpoints with respect to how people and societies can exist—and as such, the move towards alternative functionalism can be based on something real.

SR(TRS)II–20

```
(R)INFO.DS.------SOC.RT.P.
            (r)info.ds.
                  ←
              ist.act.
soc.rt.p.              af.dy.        dym.f.

      (r)cult.info.fo.         alt.c.prog.
                                pr.tr.
              info.doc.
```

To understand that the present time cycle is not unique and that the forces which dictate physical universe events in this cycle have not always seen non-white people in the positions they are in now might be quite a revelation to many people. But to view the progressional development of earth activity is to learn about the dynamics of many different cultural cycles. It is because of this information that I have come to view history as an extremely important subject. Not only can this subject be of relevance for viewing this cycle, but the realness of history is important for providing the necessary backdrop to develop the character and confidence of young people. To understand this is to understand that even by the late sixties the only great figures black people could study in grammar and high school were George Washington Carver and Booker T. Washington (who were of course great men—but only two great men). The study of real history would provide the dynamics underlining what has really happened to world culture as well. For it is important to understand what took place in far away areas of the planet—like Egypt (as a means to objectively view the transformation which took place in what was principally a great black culture) or India (and what happened to suspend one of the greatest nations of this time sector)—and I won't even mention composite Africa in this section (because this subject is better examined in section one, book one). The fact is, all of this information is relevant for this time zone, and all of this information can also provide the proper composite context to begin examining what is now taking place on the planet. For the realness of social reality is not separate from the progressional factors which dictated how given transformations were actualized—in other words, there is a reason why the collective forces of western culture have moved to suppress the truth and realness about composite world history (in this period, these distortions are referred to as "interpretations"). Of course, I do not mean to imply that the study of history and progressional continuity can in itself solve everything, because this is only one aspect of a much greater puzzle—and if I have heavily emphasized this one area of information, it should not be viewed as an endorsement of history over everything else—rather, this subject is one area among several—but it is no less important than any other area of information (everything depends on each individual's own time cycle—or what a given group is dealing with on the physical universe level).

When I wrote that the second aspect of composite information gives insight into the position white people are now in during this cycle, I have not meant this in negative terms. Rather, the progressional continuance of this cycle has moved to affect non-white people with a somewhat distorted sense of reality consciousness—and this is particularly true of black people. For the most basic viewpoint that has solidified as a result of the collective forces of western culture is the idea that somehow the present position of white people can be viewed as proof of racial superiority, and that the present physical universe situation justly reflects the real dynamics that people are born in. What is worse is that without alternative information, many black people have either come to accept this viewpoint (although it must be understood that I am not simply writing of a viewpoint per se but rather an attitude and affinity posture that is the result of this given sensitivity persuasion) as being true on some level—although not many people would admit this (not to mention that this feeling isn't always a conscious feeling). The end result of this phenomenon is that a certain numbness to physical universe dynamics can be discerned in the black community—with the understanding being that the forces substantiating western culture are too great to be shaped (or affected) by individuals (or small groups of black people)—and this feeling is understandable. But to view the progressional realness of earth culture is to learn about the many dynamic cultures which have helped bring us to the juncture we are now in at present. Moreover, to investigate the realness of this subject is to also learn about the position of black culture (especially what we call today Africa—including Egypt) as one of the most basic if not the most basic (and my research has not, to this point, revealed any information that indicates otherwise) factors related to the high culture realness of present-day western culture. My point is that this information can better help one to perceive of the present physical universe situation with "necessary balance." For it is not my purpose to imply that black people are greater than white people, or Indians are greater than black people, etc., because this means nothing (not to mention this kind of thinking is responsible for how the present reality has solidified)—rather, the achievements in world culture can provide some basis for viewing this cycle as a cycle—which is to say, a point in time and nothing more.

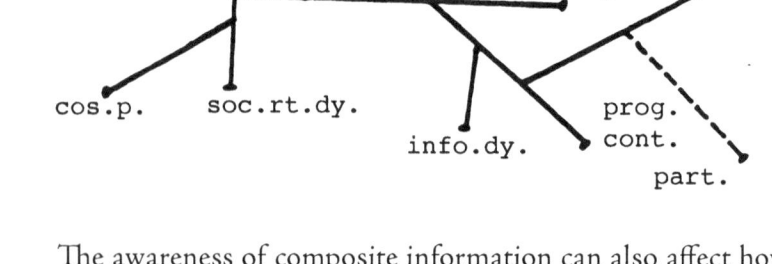

The awareness of composite information can also affect how one views the physical universe options we are now faced with in this cycle. That is, the move to reshape this cycle must be undertaken with respect to what is most sophisticated. Without doubt, one of the most glaring factors that contributed to the non-functionalism of the sixties was the narrow way in which information was perceived and utilized. To deal with the realness of the forces controlling the physical universe situation of western culture is to understand the sophistication that surrounds how events are controlled by those same forces. It is not just a question of desiring change but rather understanding how to go about creating that change. To deal with the composite information of progressional continuity is to have some basis for understanding transformation (and transition) on a composite and dynamic level—moreover, to deal with composite information is to also understand that the feelings and thoughts we are now experiencing—as a composite people—in this cycle are not so unique as to be outside of the realness of progressional continuity. I believe that this aspect of information is important. The awareness of progressional continuity can provide the most relevant overview for considering options to the present physical universe situation we are now in. This is important because the factors which support western culture in this time cycle are not unique—or separate from progressional continuity. The realness of physical universe change must be viewed with respect to composite progressional continuity, with the understanding being that real change can be viewed as a cosmic cyclical factor as well as a physical universe scientific factor. In other words, the realness of bringing about change is a discipline (and what this really means is not separate from what we can learn in composite progressional continuity). To understand this viewpoint is to understand what we are now dealing with in this time zone, for the solidification of western civilization is not just the acquisition of land and/or the erection of buildings, but to that is added the programming of "particular information" and the suppression of affinity dynamics. To change the realness of this time cycle is to become aware of what this phenomenon really means—on many different levels. For the extent that one is able to understand this cycle, for what is actually happening—is directly related to the success ratio that will determine whether or not a given physical universe participation can be of constructive value (or successful) in the future. It is for this reason that composite progressional information can be of relevance for positive functional change. Exposure to real information can help one to see that many of the feelings we are now dealing with—as a result of the present time cycle—are not separate from what others have felt throughout history, and that we can be viewed as part of an alternative order which extends at least three thousand years and some. For the solidification of this time cycle is not without its natural adversities. Nor is the dissolution of the composite realness of black culture separate from its own implications as well. In other words, while on one hand this dissolution can be viewed for what it has posed for the establishment of western culture, on the other hand this same dissolution also forecasts the projectional implications of "what must and can be done" by world culture. It is with this understanding that I view the next transformation cycle as a period that holds even greater promises for composite humanity (that being, "if certain things are understood from the experiences now taking place in this cycle"). Yet I do not mean to imply a "pie in the sky" approach to this book. The fact is, I view western culture—and the world situation in general—as "what seems to be happening in this cycle." There are of course positive aspects and negative aspects (especially negative aspects) to this subject if the focus is on social reality. The challenge of the next transformation is not separate from whether or not this cycle is viewed properly as a means to not repeat either this cycle or what happened to lead to this cycle. Nor am I simply engaging in wishful thinking (unless of course one chooses to view this as such … which is really OK), for the most basic factor that seems to be universally constant (at least with respect to what seems to be in accordance to the dictates of what composite information implies) is the realness of change—either with respect to particular aspects or extending to dynamic aspects. Within this context, change can be viewed as seeming to be a universal law. Nor am I simply basing my viewpoint on a word either. The fact is, there is much evidence that transitions and transformations are already forming in this cycle—not tomorrow, but in this time sector—and my viewpoint is based on what I perceive these changes to mean (in real terms). I believe the awareness of composite information is directly related to what this phenomenon ultimately means—which is to say, the awareness of composite information is not separate from the dynamics of alternative functionalism. For the realness of physical universe change cannot be viewed in isolated terms—or viewed in mono-dimensional terms. It is not just a question of viewing, say, the composite solidification of western civilization as the most basic factor that calls for transformation, nor is it a question of blaming any given sector of the human community for the present situation both the world group and planet are in—for this means nothing. Rather, the realness of composite progressional information can better help us to understand the dynamics which surround how all of this has come into being (and how all of this can and will come out of being), and this information will be relevant if we—as a human family—desire to not "come this way again."

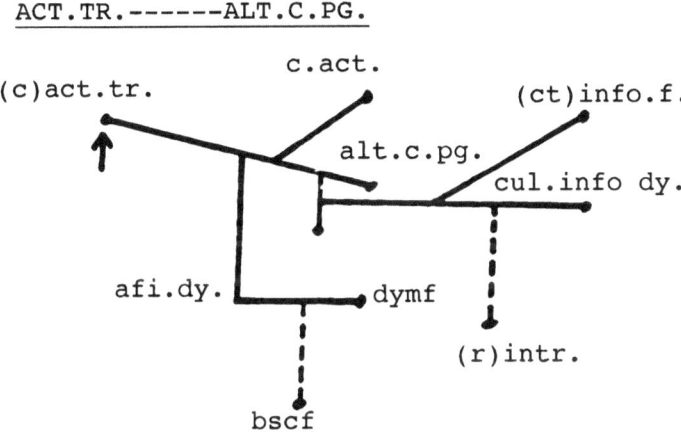

Nor is the significance of composite progressional information limited to only historical information separation from actual functionalism. For to view the progressional continuance of earth activity is to confront the realness of what "actual" information has brought forth from many sectors. In other words, the awareness of progressional continuity really is in "actual terms." What this means is that the realness of alternative functionalism is not separate from what progressional continuance poses—with respect to both ideology and conceptual information. By viewing the thrust continuance of world information, one can come to understand that there is no projectional aspect of information that has not been viewed (on some important level) in world culture. The dynamic spread of this information can be viewed for what it means with respect for its conceptual/mystical and cosmic implications, as well as its practical—particular—and functional realness. There is relevant information concerning the option position (and solidification) of human society—what this subject means and how it is most justly sustained—there is information concerning the foundation of what we now call "the art of masonry" have to do with both the science of construction as well as the significance underlying what a given structure posed (or poses) in "actual and cosmic" terms—there is insight into the total dynamics of what we now call art, etc., etc. To view this information is to begin to understand the realness of high culture as a living and breathing spiritual actuality. This is not to negatively comment on western culture—and what is happening in this time slot—because obviously, no matter how many problems we see in this cycle—we are living in some aspect of an advanced culture (quite possibly this culture can even be viewed as being in its high culture state—certainly there are many areas [mostly in technology] that are advanced. . .or is it?) and as such, my magnification of world culture should not be viewed as a backslap to this cycle. Not to mention, the dynamics of western culture are taught to us daily—both on the television and in the classroom. Which is to say, my emphasis on world culture is not a reaction to this time zone, but rather an attempt to comment on information that many of us may not have had a chance to become acquainted with. It is my belief that this information is important for the insight it can give for understanding the present. For however we choose to view the present time zone, it must be understood that the special situation of non-white (so-called) people—as well as white people—necessitates a move towards alternative information lines if we are to survive. Because the natural thrust continuum of western culture moves to destroy what is most real to world culture—and world culture people—either with respect to how we see ourselves or whether we are to stay on the planet or not.

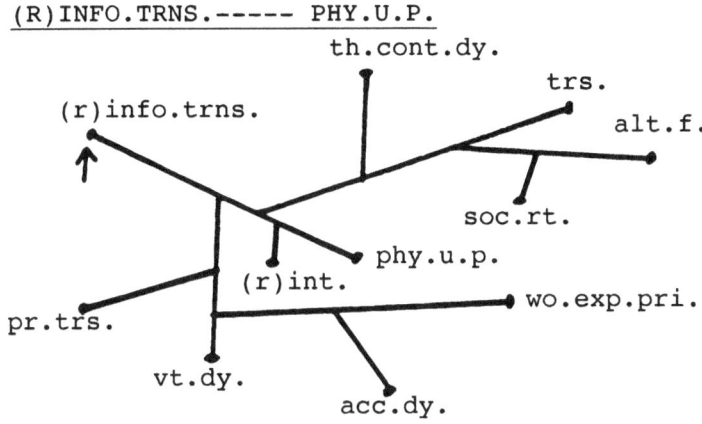

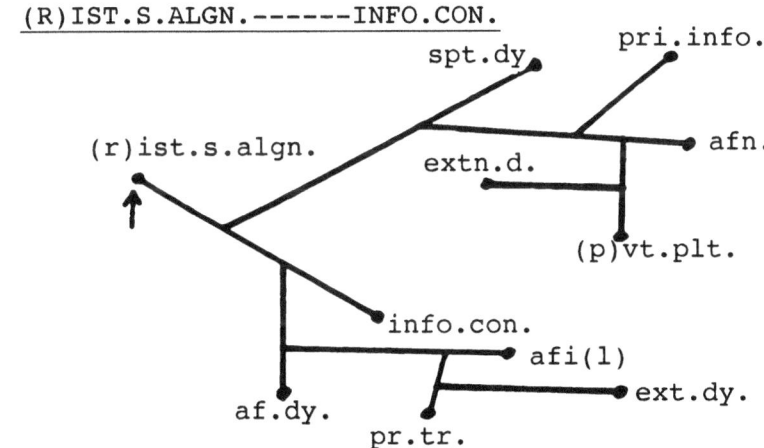

The significance of real information must be viewed on several levels if we are to effectively deal with the realness of social reality, for the dynamics of this subject cannot be over-generalized. To view the realness of world culture in this time zone is to be aware of the particulars which surround actual life—and what that means.

It is not just a question of viewing composite world information, but rather, the significance of world culture must be understood with respect to what progressional continuance implies about procedure. The fact is, there are many cultures on the planet which have felt the effect from western expansion policies on a level where the actual physical universe reality of that culture has necessitated particular application. Which is to say, when I wrote that the study of progressional continuance is relevant to this time cycle, I was taking into consideration the realness that the discipline implications of change are not manifested in narrow terms. There are many sectors of the planet at present that must be viewed with respect to what western culture calls "underdeveloped," and the particulars related to this condition cannot be ignored—with respect to what alternative functionalism poses as a concept. To understand the realness of these so-called "underdeveloped" countries is to understand that in certain planet sectors many people are starving and without the necessary tools to sustain their life—much less their high culture dynamics. The seriousness of this phenomenon cannot be ignored, for while the present interpretations in western culture would have us believe that many of these cultures only have themselves to blame for their present shape, the fact is only a little research would show that too many cross-factors are involved in this phenomenon to make such a one-dimensional assertion. Certainly I do not mean to oversimplify the dilemma many of these sectors (countries) are dealing with, for the reality actualness of earth in this time cycle cannot sustain any simplistic view. For while there is the realness that the progressional expansion of western culture has directly participated in shaping the composite world situation, there is also the realness that many other factors have also influenced the progressional spread of world developments. For the reality of world culture—especially the so-called underdeveloped countries—can be viewed with respect to the physical universe events which dictate particular actualities (e.g., the realness of soil suddenly becoming unconducive for growing food, the realness of physical universe change cycles—like hurricanes, floods—the realness that people are not completely unresponsible for their fates regardless of the given situation) as well as the implications of what has come about because of the western culture position in this cycle. To understand the realness of these viewpoints is to understand that the most basic assistance that could be of relevance to this subject is not necessarily the study of progressional-continuance—in the same sense as, say, for western people—but the giving of actual assistance (i.e., actual tools) for rebuilding. It must be understood that the study of world culture—and the progressional flow of events related to world culture—in itself means nothing if the people learning are in fact suffering from hunger, or affected by the present dynamics of their own immediate reality (not to mention, it would not necessarily be correct for us to assume that the progressional continuance of world culture—and its resultant information—is not known in many of these cultures anyway—for the fact is, many sectors of the world community are much better informed about the composite factors sustaining this cycle than we are). The physical universe reality situation of a given people or culture dictates what aspect of their information is to be relevant or utilized—which is to say, it would be counter-productive to over-generalize this most important subject.

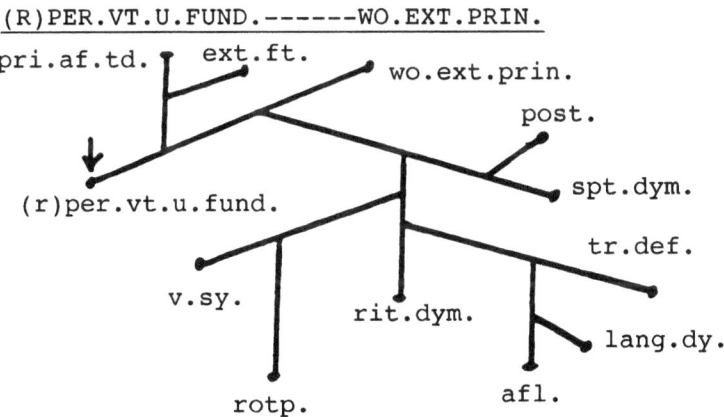

At the same time it would be impossible to view the realness of social reality without understanding what this concept poses to world culture. The fact that there are many countries presently existing in "intense" terms cannot be lightly viewed. Because if the concept of transformation is meaningful then we cannot isolate what this concept means for the composite community of the planet. It is for this reason that I have stressed the realness of world culture—as a concept that calls for an increased perspective about what is really happening in this cycle. It is important for people to understand that we are not separate from one another, and it is also important that one's viewpoint is not limited to only the dynamics of one given sector of the planet. This is necessary because the realness of the next transformation cycle will necessitate an awareness of cross-informational lines (and the significance of transfer cycles) as well as cross-vibrational affinity. The realness of what this expanded awareness implies dictates that the world community discard the many isolationist viewpoints which are so prevalent in this cycle. One can never know from what sector of the world community will come the information best suited for positive growth (and change) for a particular region. The fact that many culture groups are now living in crisis situations cannot be overlooked, nor can its implications. The present situation on this planet does not seem to be getting better—which is to say, unless something is done and done quickly, the present gap between the so-called developed countries and underdeveloped countries will increase rather than decrease. The social reality implications of this dilemma cannot be avoided if we are to deal with the realness of what this phenomenon means—in both human terms and vibrational terms. Nor is the problem only a question of insufficient tools for reshaping the world community—for the actual reality of many sectors of the planet is the realness that there is not enough food to survive the immediate present. In other words, the cultivation of land as a means to grow food is one thing, and the fact that there is a shortage of food in this cycle is another thing. This problem is not only limited to the so-called underdeveloped countries but can also be viewed in regions in India at present (not to mention, the realness of food shortages can also be viewed in the Americas—including America—as well). Before any given group can move to restore their culture, the realness of malnutrition must first be dealt with—which is to say, "present time order" must be restored. It is only when this position is secured that the composite implications of world information can be of relevance.

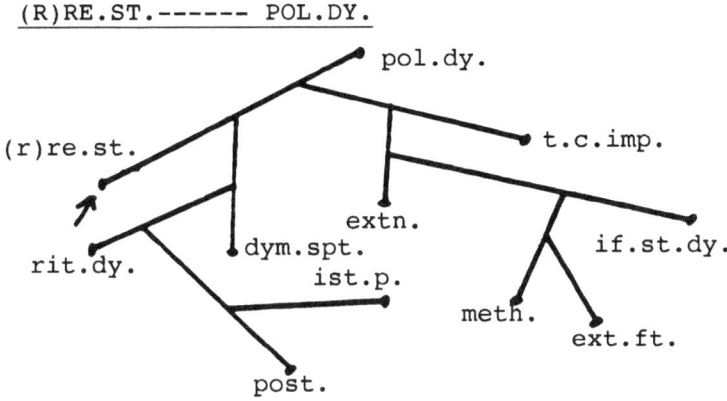

The meta-implications of world information must be viewed as the first cycle in a series of progressions which are related to the establishment of "reorder." It is important to understand that the dynamics of social reality are not simply a factor that can be reinstated in a single move—or that the realness of high culture represents a single vibrational position. The fact is, the route to transformation—positive transformation—will be as progressional as the developments which have produced this cycle, having to do with the gradual acquisition of information and composite functionalism as a means to move towards reinstatement. The time zone implications of transformation can be understood by viewing the present situation we are now in with respect to the distance—vibrational distance—that exists between people, yet I do not mean to imply that the closing of this distance has to take place in one single stroke, because it does not seem as if this can be the case. But the present cycle we are in on the physical universe level can be viewed with respect to how much further we have to come as a united people (I do not mean to imply "united" in the sense that there will be no difference at all between people, or that everyone has to look alike, etc.). The challenge of transformation is directly related to what the concept of composite reality implies (which is to say that if this kind of transformation doesn't occur, there will be another kind of transformation—and it is important to understand that the cosmic and physical universe seems to go on about its business whether we are prepared to positively assist or not). The significance of a composite transformation would have to do with what this concept poses for the idea of world culture and unification—yet I have not meant to imply that the route to this unification must be on my terms either (which is to say, this same resultant—if that is the resultant—can come about in ways other than what I am writing of as well).

The concept of social reality is important for what it signifies about the vibrational and physical universe factors which substantiate particular physical universe realities—or perceived reality. To view the situation that American black, Asian and Indian people are now in is to understand the uniqueness of what can only be called an "interesting situation." For many of us have come to view America with respect to what the collective forces of western culture would have us believe—the concept of the grand "melting pot" or the concept of "liberty, justice and the American way." The fact is, any non-caucasian who perceives of him or herself as somehow really connected with the composite reality of western culture is in bad shape . . . indeed. In other words, while there are of course many levels of a given culture, and while there are many factors related to how a given cultural thrust is "ised," at the same time there can be no debate as to what the reality dynamics of western culture seek to affirm. For to write of America and/or western civilization is to write of the solidification of a position which is designed for (and affirms) the dynamic initiations—and reality position—of the people who have come to perceive of themselves as European caucasians and/or its continuance—Euro-American caucasians (what we now call "white people"). In other words, the west is about white people, and the progressional realness of western culture is about the solidification and expansion of that which is most relevant for white people (no matter the many other layers of relevant factors that are connected with this viewpoint—and of course there are many other factors—my point is that in the final analysis, it does boil down to the realness of how "race" is perceived in this time zone, and how racism is viewed as a result of that viewpoint). Nor have I meant to overlook the dynamics of this cycle by reducing western culture to the question of race, for obviously there are individuals who are not white who have benefited from particular aspects of western culture (e.g., a person might have a good job and wind up thinking life is beautiful and everything is fine) and I have not meant to negate that factor. But to view the realness of western culture is to understand what factors are "really" at work, and what those factors seem to mean. Either that is the case or we must assume that the present situation which has developed in the last two thousand years—that being, the fact that at present white people control (with the exception of China) the whole of the planet—has been just a coincidence ("what a stroke of luck—huh")—and this does not seem to be the case. I am not writing this as a means to downgrade western culture, because this serves no productive purpose; nor by citing these developments have I meant to view the present time zone in only racial terms—because this type of attitude would not help us understand the seriousness of the next cycle (not to mention, there is no need to falsify the present situation because it is bad enough already). The fact is, western culture is about western caucasians, and the reality of western culture is about how events are integrated through the composite affinity dynamics of the collected forces which maintain western culture. This is not to say that given individuals are consciously functioning to maintain what this culture is in affinity terms, because the realness of culture—and controlled culture—transcends the particular effects of a particular aspect (or region or individual). Rather, what we have in the west is a situation designed to channel and control the nature of both affinity dynamics and composite functionalism to correspond to the functional and affinity reality of what is perceived (rightly or wrongly) as caucasian—or "of caucasian." To view this phenomenon—in western culture, and in particular America—is to see how various areas and people of a given sector of the country are allowed to participate—and how it works. The end result of the social mechanisms sustaining the center factor of western culture is that the lives and affinity realness of outside initiations are isolated from the mainstream (the mainstream being white people and their lives and their social, intellectual and functional reality). The actual resultant of this situation is that only the reality alignment of white people can be viewed as relevant to the composite realness of western culture. But I do not mean to not elaborate on this phenomenon—because the reality procedure of western culture is not without its complexities as well.

SR(TRS) II-34

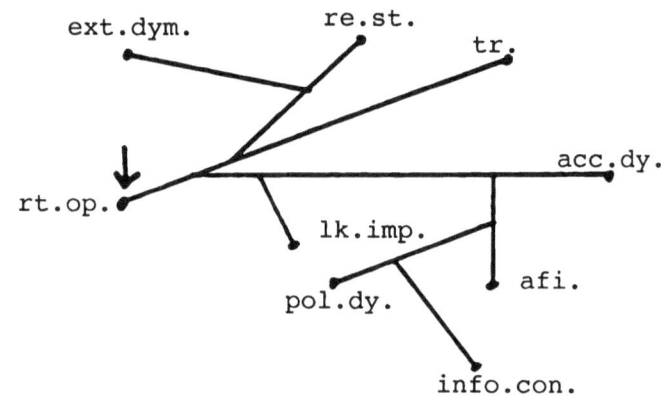

When I stated that only the reality alignment of white people is perceived to be relevant in western culture, I did not mean this in light terms—which is to say, I was not playing games. To view the realness of how western culture functions is to understand the real information reality that determines its cultural focus. The fact is, there are many different sectors in America and there are many different kinds of people in those sectors—I am commenting on the lives (and actual life activity) of Mexican Americans, Asian Americans, Hispanic Americans, black Americans, American Indians, Americans, etc. To understand that these so-called racial groups do exist and are functioning is to understand that none of these groups—no matter any given individual's so-called economic state—really have the power to affect the basic information interpretation lines of western culture. All of these groups can be viewed in the sense of "bit players"—that is, background antics, whose collective identity resides in what light they are able to cast on the "principle" subject. Moreover, I am not writing this viewpoint as a means to ignore the realness of non-white people and the fact that many people have contributed to this (western) culture, but rather as a basis to really view the actualness now taking place in this cycle—as far as cultural identity focus is concerned. For certainly many individuals of every so-called racial and vibrational persuasion have helped to make this culture what it is. But to view the vibrational and actual realness of western culture is to view non-white people as only supporting players—whose contributions, no matter how vast, do not really figure in the defining and controlling scheme that determines how events are to be culturally perceived. This viewpoint can better be understood by viewing what factors are really in operation when the political and economic policies—which determine practically every aspect of the culture's life—are determined. This viewpoint can also be better understood by viewing the historical progressions (and resultant decisions) that determined how the collective forces of western culture dealt with non-white people as compared to the present situation (which is supposed to be better . . . but is it really?).

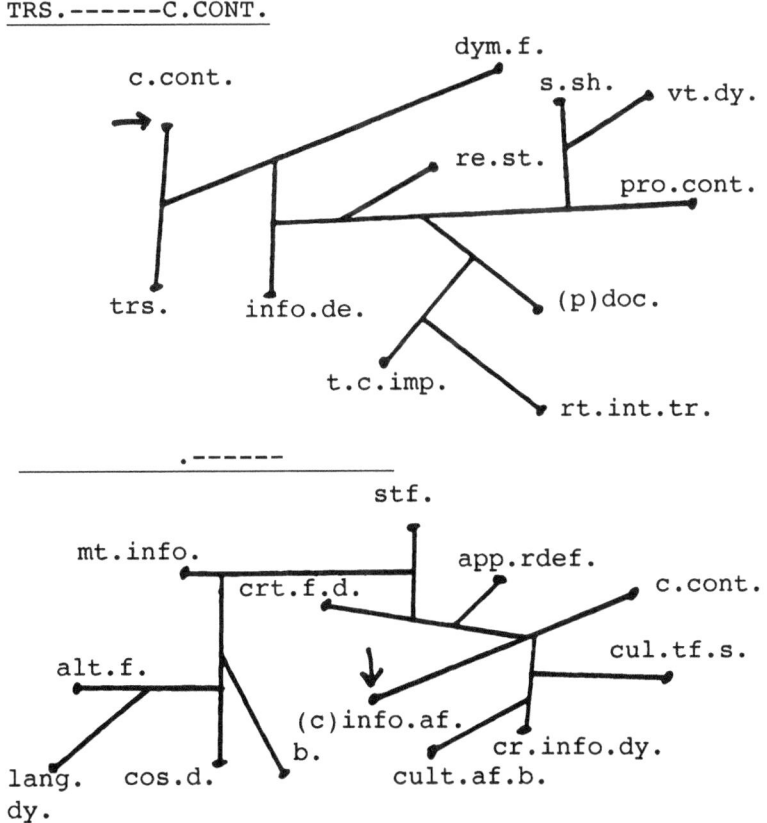

SR(TRS)II–36

    Certainly I am aware of the surface aspects related to how human rights are manifested in this time zone, and for that matter, it is clear that the theoretical position of black people can be perceived as "looking different" than the 1880's (yet everything in this time cycle looks different from 1880). Moreso, I am also aware that there are many non-white people who would disagree with my viewpoint in this regard as well. For the progressional developments which occurred in the sixties have been interpreted by many segments of the society as proof of a new cycle—and a move from the policies of the past. In this period it is possible to view black people on television—even TV commercials—and of course much attention has been focused on the emergence of the black middle class. It is now even possible to see black people in "established" magazines, and of course all of these developments cannot be separated from the realness of what social reality implies. For even the surface aspect of change has to be recognized as a positive sign—not to mention that the progressional development of any given change cycle takes time. And of course the social reality implications of western culture should be viewed in this light as well. Yet the interpretations that we are now being handed in this period—the late seventies—cannot go unchallenged—that being, that the emergence of the black middle class and the gains non-whites have made in certain employment sectors can be viewed as a sign that real equality is an actuality in American culture—because in itself this is not true.

    To deal with the present position of non-white people in America—and western culture in general—is to deal with the realness that information interpretation is supplied by white society exclusively. In other words, however one chooses to perceive of the present reality of non-white people in America, it is important to understand that the basic information focuses of this time period are not jointly regulated by the so-called multi-racial spectrum of the culture. Moreover, to view the realness of this cycle is to become aware of the inability of non-white people to supply their own reality (and conceptual) definitions, concerning both who they are and how they are, and what they are thinking, as well as what they postulate with respect to their own affinity dynamics. To understand what this means is to understand the true position that non-white people are dealing with. For while surface physical universe change cannot be completely ignored—as a factor that does comment on some aspect of social reality particulars or cultural life—at the same time, if a given culture group can't have its affinity dynamics affect the composite center of its own culture, then that group cannot be viewed in a positive context. This, then, is the true position that non-white people are in during this cycle, and the inability to sustain both information focus and alternative definitions must be viewed as directly related to what this position poses with respect to social reality—and transformation. The net effect of this phenomenon has produced a situation where the "particular reality cycle" of non-white people is subjected to the same spectacle diversion alignments which the composite culture maintains, and imposed definitions of the controlling culture group are utilized as a factor to suppress the possibility of both alternative ideas and alternative functionalism. The end result of this phenomenon is not separate from the composite world situation—with the exception of certain Asian countries and a limited amount of liberated territories in Africa—that being, the reality of white people of a certain class influences the progressional spread of composite information dynamics. The progressional development of this phenomenon is not separate from the physical universe particulars that we are now dealing with in this time cycle. Which is to say, the present power structures responsible for both the economic and political reality of earth are not separate from the sophistication surrounding how given information focuses and imposed definitions are utilized—in other words, these considerations are both social and political.

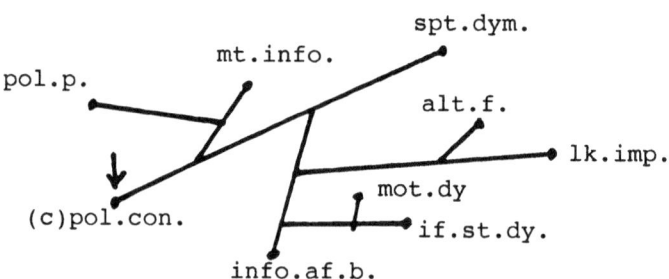

By "culture-information focus," I am commenting on the collective forces which dictate how given information lines are interpreted to either the composite spectrum (people) of a given culture, or to the composite whole of its effective parameter (which in this case is planet Earth). In actual terms, this phenomenon can be observed by dealing with the actualness of affinity dynamics—and the fact that every group has these dynamics as a factor which colors how a given aspect of information is perceived (and also as a factor related to what affinity lines are opened—or drawn—from cosmic sources—which is where I see all "information" coming from)—and as a factor which is necessary to have operable if its culture group—or sector—is to be "real." The present situation that is taking place in this cycle has to do with the suppression of composite information lines and the implication of "particular" information lines—(in this case "particular" information lines—and its related affinity positions—which are perceived to be in accordance to what is "real" about western culture)—as a means to maintain the present social reality of western culture. When I wrote that to view America in this cycle is to view a spectrum of separate culture groups, I was attempting to point out that the resultant informational complex related to what this spectrum should mean has not taken place. It is not a question of me writing that everyone is thinking alike—or that this is the optimum state of culture—because it isn't, and obviously the realness of so-called different culture groups implies different information affinities. Nor by citing this development am I implying that the composite community of white people in America has no right to vibrate to what is perceived as real for them. My point is only that the composite center of western culture does not really deal with or accept non-European (or non-Euro-American—or simply non-caucasian) information interpretations—as a consideration worthy of being relevant to its information complex lining—those being, definitions and/or policies relevant for the composite culture. To understand how this phenomenon is brought about is to view the concept of information focus. Because obviously every particular sector of America (and the planet) has something to say of relevance about what "is"—with respect to either the meta-vibrational spectrum of information or actual physical universe particulars. "Information focus" is my term to comment on how given viewpoints are either ignored or subjected to source-transfer manipulation before being made "known" to the general society. To understand this use of manipulation is to view the realness of media and/or the use of gradualism. Because in the final analysis, the policies and functional positions—as well as the vibrational and intellectual position—that affect how western culture deals with reality are actualized from only a segment of its people. The end result of this practice clarifies the real position of non-white people in western culture. For the emergence of the black middle class means nothing if the information related to that emergence is not recognized as such. Without the possibility to affect the composite lining of one's culture group, there is no such thing as freedom (or real participation).

Yet the realness of information focus is only one aspect of a much more complex question. For if the use of this consideration is directly related to how the suppression of non-white people is maintained, it also cannot be separated from what it poses about the realness of a given definition placement. The fact is, information focus is only one aspect of manipulation and is related to the more important question of defining terms—as well as the seriousness of definition placement. For the composite community of non-white people in America—and western culture—can be viewed as existing in a state of suppressed definitions. In other words, the progressional realness of western culture has moved to create a situation that functions to thwart the realness of alternative definitions—and in doing so, the dynamics of world culture have been stunted (as such)—or perceived as stunted. The importance of "defining terms" cannot be overemphasized if we are to view social reality.

LANG.DY.------POL.DY.

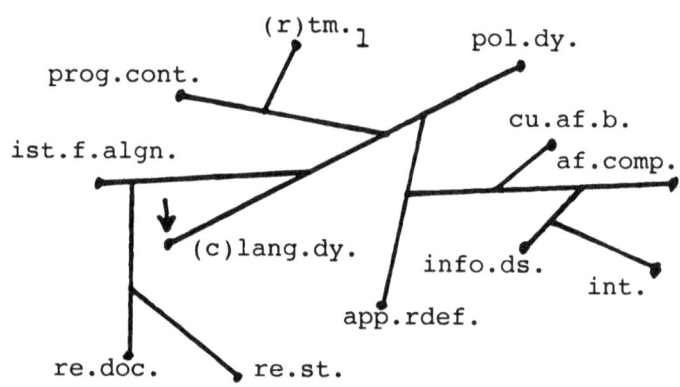

(R)DEF.------ AF.DY.

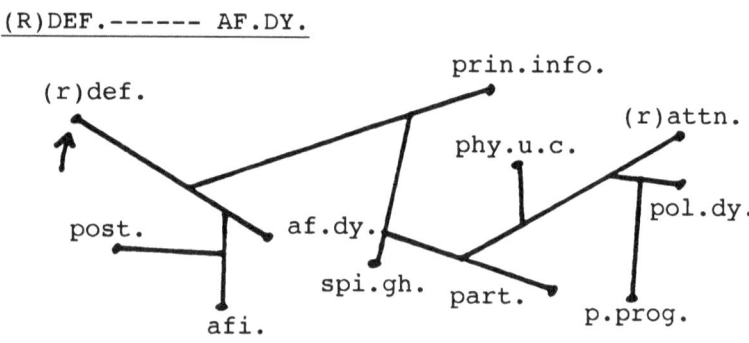

The significance of "definition" is directly related to the total concept of positive transformation. For the reality options of a given group are not separate from how that group perceives of itself. Moreover, the realness of composite definitions must be viewed as the sum of what a given culture is—that is, the realness of a given culture group consists of the spectrum of people in its territories. The move to suppress alternative definitions—or definitions which are perceived as being not in accordance to the principle vibrationaltory lining of a given state—must be understood as an attempt to negate the reality thrust related to what that information signifies. Thus, to view the present cycle of western culture is to view to what extent definition compression has affected the reality and affinity dynamics of both non-white people and western culture. Because the success of this suppression has moved to create the impression that there is no difference between the information affinity thrust of western culture and non-white people—and of course there is—there must be. Moreover, the realness of this suppression has profoundly affected all non-white people in this time period (regardless of region)—on every level. To view the educational system in this cycle is to understand the nature of this phenomenon—because very few people are able to survive western education and be mentally sane—or even balanced (let alone able to perceive of phenomena in multi-dynamic terms). The effect of this suppression is not separate from the dis-unification that can be seen in this time zone concerning functionalism, and the realness of definition suppression has also affected how non-white people view their own dynamics. The net effect of this phenomenon moves to enforce the controlling factors which dictate the vibrationaltory and actual lining of western culture. The social reality implications of this predicament can be viewed as "an inability to deal with the greater spectrum of 'composite information' and 'composite information dynamics.'" That is—the present situation makes it practically impossible to view what is really happening on the physical universe level with respect to alternative viewpoints. This is not to say that given individuals aren't able to move outside of definition compression, nor have I meant to imply that the present situation is hopeless. Rather, the composite suppression of alternative definitions is a factor that has crippled the great majority of non-white—and white—people with respect to what information lines are utilized, and what aren't. Because of the sophistication of this manipulation, the world community is left with many wrong interpretations—on matters of critical importance.

To imply that only non-white people are suppressed as a result of the collective forces of western culture would only be half true. For while it is clear world culture is in a state of intensity because of the forces of western culture, it is also clear that white people are also affected adversely by this same phenomenon. In other words, the progressional spread of western manipulation cannot be viewed as positive from any angle. Most non-white people have come to view this cycle as directly beneficial to all white people—but this is only true on given levels. The fact is, the collective forces of western culture can be viewed on one level, and the controlling forces of western culture can be viewed on another level. The end result of this situation is that the reality options of the individual must be perceived in limited terms. This is not to state that a given white person cannot enjoy the fruits of western culture, or that the influence ratio of white people is the same as that of non-white people, rather the dynamics of present-day social reality is constructed so as to admit only that sector of people who have completed certain information routes and/or social routes. The end result of this development is that the controlling forces of western culture do not necessarily function with respect to the desires of its composite white community either.

To understand the reality of white people in western culture is to view the realness of power—both political power and institutionalized power. What this means is that only those individuals connected to power can be viewed with respect to the ultimate reality position of western culture. The difference between the concept of collective forces as opposed to controlling forces would have to do with the option spread that is available to white people. The average white person in western culture—by heritage of his (or her—yet the "her" implications are most certainly not on the same level) skin—has the option spread potential to move into the upper echelon of western participatory culture—having to do with greater job opportunities and of course more money—and in this position that individual can also participate in the vibrationaltory lining of western culture (having the possibility to affect the information reality concerning how events are to be either understood or dealt with)—thus, having an opportunity to function inside of what I call the collective forces of western culture. But the real controlling factors which really determine American—and western—policy are quite separate from this option spread. The fact is, the individuals who form this inner circle are separated from the collective community of everybody. The decisions which have resulted from this level have more to do with power dynamics—related to the realness of money and dynamic control. To view this echelon is to become aware of the real factors which dictate cultural continuity: having to do with super rich people and giant multi-national corporations. It of course is possible for a given white person to move into this reality sector—but it is not really a probable postulation juncture. This is not a club that one can seriously aspire to—at least using the "work ethic" mentality, but rather calls for creative social moves (e.g., marrying into a situation that has what is called "promise"). The greater population of white people cannot be viewed with respect to what this sector poses—which is why I have deemed it necessary to make distinctions on the concept of "levels of control" (not to mention, the greater population of white people cannot be viewed as necessarily wanting to enter or vibrate towards anything on a composite level—because people are simply not alike).

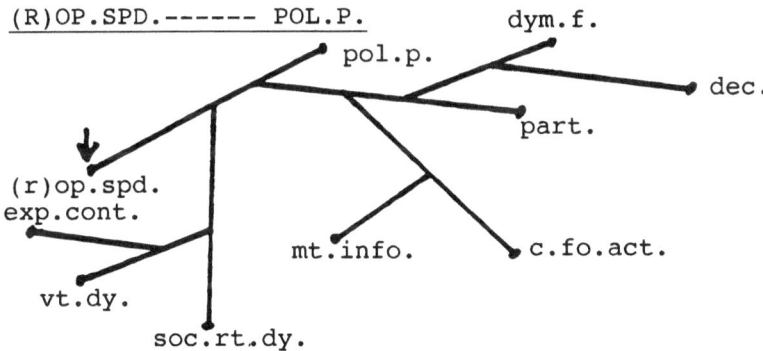

There is still another distinction which must be acknowledged concerning the dynamic of cultural manipulation. For if the dynamics of control that surround the world community can be viewed in its separateness—from that of the composite white community—then it is important to understand that there is still another level of social reality manipulation that affects the progressional reality of potential transformation. Which is to say, the present situation of earth women can be viewed both with respect to the particular implication of both one's race or one's planet sector—as well as the composite suppression of what feminism poses as a serious information (and mystical) line. Nor by commenting on this subject am I simply focusing on the present physical universe situation that western culture is dealing with—concerning what we now call women's liberation—rather, I am focusing on the suppressed dynamics of the feminine vibration and what this phenomenon implies with respect to alternative definitions. In other words, all projectional information has relevance to transformational insight (and composite information)—the implications of feminism are not separate from what it poses to re-understanding spiritualism, functionalism, humanism, conceptualism, etc. Until the social reality suppression that surrounds women is removed, we can never hope to deal with the concept of positive transformation. For the composite realness of alternative information is not separate from what this challenge poses.

By separating the concept of social reality implications from the present concepts we now have of women's liberation, I have not meant to imply a lack of respect for this time cycle—rather, I have taken this approach as a basis to view the realness of feminism in its own dynamic context. For while the physical universe is not separate from the affinity insight principles which determine how given tendencies are to flow, there is a difference between physical universe functionalism and the implications of feminism—(as a mystical and vibrational factor)—or at least the focus dynamics of this subject are distinct enough to necessitate its own separate focus. The realness of information dynamics with respect to feminism is rarely dealt with in this time cycle, yet if we are to uncover the many distortions which have solidified in the last four thousand years (and some), then it will be necessary to correct this neglect. The projectional brilliance of feminism is directly related to the challenge of the next cycle. For if the realness of vibrational postulation is related to what alternatives we can solidify in the next cycle, then what this implies is not separate from the potential of composite humanity—regardless of focus or region. The concept of social reality and trans-information has to do with what this subject means in actual and vibrational terms, and the challenge of the next cycle is directly related to whether or not its "particulars" are understood, and utilized. At the heart of transformation is the realness of both social dynamics and cosmic justice.

(Level Three)

1. Why is there a need for a section on social reality in a book about creative music?

There is a need to comment on social reality in a book primarily concerned about creativity because creativity is not separate from the dynamics of composite life in the physical universe. This is especially true if we are to better understand the special situation surrounding black creativity and/or world creativity. Because the misinformation that has long permeated black creativity is directly related to what has transpired on the physical universe level—in social reality. Moreover, the progressional application of western education has somehow transported creativity above real life, and the inclusion of a section on social reality is my attempt to review the composite dynamics of this most important subject. This is not to say I have necessarily touched on even one-eighth of what must be dealt with on this subject—certainly there are many areas I haven't even begun to understand, and on this I am not ashamed, nor do I apologize—for I have done my best . . . and this book represents only the beginning of what I hope will be a life's investigation into understanding (or trying to understand). This is what I am interested in. I have included the realness of social reality in this book as a means to provide a more realistic backdrop for dealing with this most important subject. Creativity is not only not separate from social reality, but the realness of life (being) is necessarily connected to how and why given projections have solidified. Creativity is about the experience of living.

2. Have the black student unions, which solidified in the sixties on college and university campuses throughout America, had any commitment to black creativity or world creativity?

I believe that the emergence of the black student union has had a profound effect on the reality of college organizations and creative curriculums. This is especially true in the area of budgeting and diversity, and the significance of this phenomenon has also been an important factor in helping the continuance—and hence, success—of many of the popular groups in black commercial music. Groups like Sly and the Family Stone and the Ohio Players were able to break in on the college circuit with the help of the black student unions. However, the music attraction of most of the black student unions does not include the composite spectrum of black creativity, nor have these groups really moved to affect composite decisions concerning either what groups or individuals are to be brought to lecture on "whatever" for the composite university. Instead, the thrust of the black student unions from the sixties has only been directed towards "having a good time"—which in itself is positive, but in itself will not alter the "present state of life in western culture." Hopefully the eighties will see this sector bring in people like Yosef Ben-Jochannan, or other great people whose viewpoints can help to stimulate dynamic motivation and ideals. This is necessary, because the most basic cycle of university lectureships are not normally made available to black people or women "of a certain creative persuasion." The challenge of the eighties implies that something must be done to change this situation. A musician like Ornette Coleman at present would do better to contact the white student unions for a possible performance than the black student unions—and this is unfortunate.

3. Why is the separation of extended black creativity and the black community so pronounced?

The reality position of extended black creativity has to do with many different things, because in discussing this consideration we are commenting on the nature of progressional continuance as well as vibrational dynamics. The realness of transitional black creativity—that being, the form we now call bebop—is basically the point of departure for extended invention, towards the dynamics of transitional change in the meta-position of both black people in America and black culture as a whole. The resulting separation that has developed between the music and black community has to do with the interpretations of the western defining and controlling media (not only on music but on everything) and the progressional manipulation of western economics. Both of these considerations (interpretations and economics) have moved to totally distort how black creativity is viewed—not only in the black community but in every community. The isolation of black creativity is related to the composite isolation of all musics not perceived as commercial. The particular situation of the black community must also be viewed with this in mind. Because the collective forces of western culture have moved to suppress the exposure of creative music as well as its perceived worth. It should come as no surprise to anyone that bebop is not received in the black community as compared with what is now called popular music.

4. What can be done to close the gap between the black community and the music?

There are many things that can be done to change the situation of creative music in both the black community and America as a whole. But first it is important to understand what this question really means, because there can be no changing of anything unless the vibrational realness of the culture is changed. In other words, it is not really possible to simply change the reality of the creativity as separate from the people who are producing that creativity. To really deal with this subject is to approach the total culture: that is, to approach re-examining what has happened and how, so that a basis can be laid to stimulate positive interest in all information. I would say that organizations like the AACM represents a start: that being, some kind of community approach to teaching about creativity. Secondly, efforts should be directed to create a forum for the performances of creative music (and it is important to not only utilize national talent—emphasis must also be directed towards regional creative people). In other words, anything that can be used to stimulate positive involvement with both one's community and creativity should be approached and/or attempted. I especially believe efforts must be directed towards helping children learn about and participate in creativity. If the next generation of black, white, and Asian people find themselves in the same position we are now in, then we will only have ourselves to blame. We need more involvement—on whatever level.

5. What is the significance of black language with regards to transformation?

I believe the disintegration of western culture in this time zone is directly related to the decomposition of its information reality. As such, the use of slang must be viewed for how it has helped to reshape the English language and revitalize it as well. It is important to understand that the present dissolution of American society has not come about because of one or two isolated factors, but rather this phenomenon is related to the realness that the old order did not satisfy the dictates of "what living is about" in this time period. In other words, by commenting on slang I am not commenting on something without basis. The changes brought about through black language are as important as the changes occurring in the music because in the final analysis we are really discussing creativity and affinity dynamics—regardless of focus. The importance of establishing transformational language is directly related to alternative functionalism. Non-white people especially have long experienced many extra problems in information transference because of their relationship to western traditional language. The establishment of a new language continuum will be important for what it will pose for alternative interpretations—and this will be beneficial for correcting many of the misconceptions we currently have concerning black people, black creativity, and black culture (or world people, etc.).

6. In this period (the beginning eighties) is there any one factor that you would single out as most responsible for the inability of black people to support composite black creativity?

I would say the inability to hear the music on the radio or see it on television, or read about it in the school system, or experience it live in one's community is "one" factor I can single out that is related to the present reality position of black creativity—in both the black community and the white community. I would also say the inability of American society to implant a real concern for culture and creativity is also related to this phenomenon. In other words, it is difficult to pin down any one factor and make it most responsible for the inability of black people to support their own composite creativity. Certainly the consideration of racism might be added to this growing list of "one" as well—not to mention the role of economics to information dynamics. There is no one factor responsible for the "present reality of events," but instead there are many different factors related to this most important subject. It is for this reason that I have approached this book with the broadest possible information scan.

7. What is your viewpoint on the emergence of black studies departments in many of the universities in the sixties?

I feel the emergence of this phenomenon represents one of the first really significant steps that the university has taken in re-aligning its dictates to include world information. The thrust of this area of education will be important for how it can provide alternative stimulants for both black and white students—as well as professors. This is true for the particular interpretation implications of alternative functionalism as well as for what black studies will pose to the existing state of western ideas. I see this phenomenon as positive in every way, unless its implementation amounts to only token gestures not adequately funded or attended. The realness of African and African-American studies should be a required course for all students—not to mention, there should also be special classes and departments for all sectors of society that normally are ignored and misdocumented. Classes on feminism, Asian studies, the real dynamics and significance of the American Indian, are courses that should be mandatory before any student is allowed to graduate.

8. Within the hierarchy of education, how do you view the black studies departments?

I consider the institution of black studies to be as important as reading, writing, and arithmetic, because in the final analysis, one's spirit relationship to information is not separate from one's spirit relationship to him- or herself. The reality of spirit alignment is necessarily connected to how far a given individual will be able to advance, with respect to both learning ability and personality dynamics. The study of information interpretation through black studies—which must be followed by the institution of feminist and Asian and American Indian studies—is really the establishment of an expanded basis for learning, and this is what is needed. I especially feel some attempt must be made to correctly teach young people about world history—as this subject concerns every sector of the planet. Somehow the realness of history helps to bring greater understanding about what is now happening—in both social reality and economic/political reality. Certainly I realize there can be no substitution for teaching young people particular trades—and this is especially true for non-white people—and by accenting black studies I have not meant to ignore the demands of this time period. It is clear that young people must be taught to read more, and obviously the realness of mathematics and science are profoundly important. But unless some attempt is made to help young people to develop an overview about living, the process of education can never be utilized to its potential. I view the solidification of black studies as a signal for change in the curriculum reality of western education. I believe that this phenomenon is positive, and hopefully represents only the beginning of a much greater signal about western education.

9. My friend Cloe Smith once compared the new black movies as a phenomenon akin to the race records of the thirties. What is your opinion?

I believe the so-called race records of the thirties had far more relevance in a positive way to black people than the new movies today. The race record cycle in American history was a period which saw the emergence of many dynamic creative people—involving the composite spectrum of black creativity, from blues to Vaudeville. The fact that those artists were assigned to what was called race records had to do with the nature of America's ostracization rather than the level of their (the artists') ability. But this is not the case at all with the new so-called black movies. I have yet to experience any movie from this sector that poses an alternative to the reality dynamics already happening in composite American cinema—not to mention world cinema. Rather, the thrust of the so-called new black movie moves to parody both black people and black culture—while at the same time functioning as a negative agent for down-aligning expectations and affinity dynamics. In the end, the new black movies celebrate the all-too-consuming need for "hipness," without supplying any real positive role models or areas of motivation to help people—especially young people—approach life and living. This cannot be said of the activity documented on the race records of the thirties—because, in the final analysis, much of that activity was dynamic creativity, dynamic positive creativity, and finally creativity of substance.

10. Is creativity stimulated by conflict?

It depends on the context. For the reality position of creativity depends on its position in the composite meta-lining of its culture's information. In other words, in a real culture, there is no reason to necessarily assume that in a situation of conflict, creativity will be stimulated. To assume that position would be to ignore the real precepts governing art as viewed through world culture terms. Because art, in this context, is not about conflict, or accelerated vibrational momentum, as much as about the composite dynamics of its solidified culture—when that culture is "most" as it is. This is not to say the consideration of conflict or transition will not affect the nature of a given creative projection, because everything that happens serves as a stimulant, on some level—rather, the extent of a given affect will probably not be accented to the degree that its stimulation moves to alter its principal creative reality. But the reality implications of creativity in an existential culture do have a different relationship to stimulation. For the reality of conflict in this context serves to advance the nature of spectacle diversion—in both individual and/or culture terms. This is so because when the precepts of a culture are intellectually based—as opposed to spiritually based—then "one word is as good as another"—or "one idea is as interesting, and as valid, as another." Thus the nature of a given stimulant can be viewed as "real" as long as it provides the necessary ingredients for "something interesting." In this context, the weight of a given conflict can possibly determine the composite reality position of creativity for as long as that conflict is operative—until the next stimulator comes along.

11. A large percentage of the people who listen to creative music from the black aesthetic are white. How does this phenomenon affect the blackness of the music?

I believe most musicians would agree that the optimum performance consideration is for a given concert to be attended by as many people as possible. This viewpoint would probably have meaning to musicians from every time zone or so-called style—including musicians in black creativity. The idea that the ethnic make-up of the audience affects the music is real, but the nature of that effect is so different from audience to audience, that it is impossible to formulate what it really means (if indeed there is meaning in this context). This is not to imply that every audience responds to the music in the same way, because they don't; nor have I meant to imply that the vibrational tone of the audience doesn't affect the music (that takes place)—because it does. But I do not believe the ethnic make-up of an audience dilutes either the realness of the music or the vibrational weight of its (the music's) intention. If performing to a multi-ethnic audience does have an effect on the vibrational nature—or blackness, in this case—of the music, that effect would not so much have to do with the musicians performing as much as the people experiencing the music. In other words, the people who support a given postulation will in the end inherit that postulation. Involvement is the second degree of participation (awareness must be the first degree). Which is to say, the projectional continuance of any consideration is directly related to the nature of its attraction as well as who is there to be attracted. For this reason, it is important to expose everyone to multi-information, and multi-information dynamics, because the future implications of a given phenomenon are not separate from who supports (or participates in) that phenomenon. Thus to answer this question correctly—if only white people listened to so-called black music (how could white people listen and enjoy black music unless the music has something of everyone—them—in it?) then that music would one day be white music. It is as simple as that.

12. Ultimately, what reality context is most conducive for transformational creativity?

I believe the ultimate reality context for creativity is activity that comments on the dynamics of spiritualism and cultural spiritualization. For me, everything else is about "interesting" as opposed to "what is really real." It is my hope that the next cycle will see the beginning of a composite multi-dimensional world consciousness and spiritualism—yet probably this will not take place tomorrow. The highest position of creativity—that I am able to understand anyway—has to do with the celebration of life and spiritual being through "doing," and in its most dynamic context, creativity as an affirmation of the laws governing the nature underlying how our universe breathes. As such, the optimum reality context for creativity is the same as the optimum reality context for living—because creativity is only a reflection of who and what we are. The present reality of this subject can also be viewed with respect to how we have come to view each other—that being, dynamic separation and misunderstanding. I believe creativity is a discipline that helps to accent the wonder of living.

13. How would you assess the significance of Muzak in western culture?

The basic concept of Muzak I find very attractive—that being, music throughout the culture—and if this were the only consideration related to this phenomenon I could completely endorse its use. The basic problem I have with this area of music is that in most cases there is no music—at least music as I understand the concept. This is not to imply that there is only one kind of Muzak because even in this area there are different variables. I recall hearing the music of Charlie Parker in a shopping store in Tokyo, and it is not unusual to hear even Beethoven now and then while waiting for the dentist—or elevator. There is, however, a special area of this phenomenon—that being, the music (or so-called music) created especially for the medium—that I find almost unbearable, yet maybe this is only my problem. I believe there is such a thing as sound pollution and I also believe the greater thrust of music created for Muzak corresponds to that concept. Muzak, and its various derivatives, can be viewed as the second degree of vibrational—or more like emotional—

manipulation (the first degree being the meta-reality of law dynamics). The thrust of this phenomenon is conceived to help people "have a good day" on one hand, while aligning their sensibilities to anti-music (or dynamic distortions through principle information) on the other hand. Because in most cases, to comment on Muzak is to comment on a thrust composed only with respect to the "surface of what creativity is"—just as western culture is solidified with respect to "what a culture is supposed to be"—on the surface, that is.

14. What factor is most responsible for the fact that in this time period more white people are able to embrace black creativity than black people?

The reality participation of the white person in western culture is directly related to the option possibilities each white individual has from birth, as well as each individual's potential information scan and attraction. This is not to say every individual white person must necessarily be happy, or benefit from western culture—because life is not like that. Rather, the fact that western culture is "about white people"—with respect to the images it perpetrates, its information affinity alignment, its documentation, its social reality, its advancement system and politics—puts the white person in a better position to possibly fulfill some aspect of whatever he or she desires than the person who is not supported by the system in like manner. This is not to say there are no problems for white people—because of course there are always problems—but cultural affirmation and support is not one of those problems. From this context the white young man or woman is able to grow up with a particular advantage for possibly receiving phenomena. That is, the sounder the cultural experience, the more natural it is to experience phenomena—on some level. This is not to say that any person who has graduated from Harvard will necessarily appreciate the blues—and I would be surprised if most Harvard grads are into the blues—but this is to say that most of these individuals are in a better position to be responsible for how they choose to deal with composite information than someone who has not had the benefits of their experience (there of course is much more to this argument—because obviously both of my points are not necessarily true either—nothing is either this way or that way—but hopefully the general point here has been communicated). However, to view the present reality of black people in America is to not only see a people who are disenfranchised by the composite culture, but also to view a progressional struggle to both recover from racism (not only America's racism, but the racism which has been leveled against African people for more than two thousand years) and poverty. I believe the fact that any black people are able to support the music at all is a testament to the strength and recoverability of all black people—and/or black culture—and a hint as to the realness of what lies ahead.

15. *What do the jazz polls really signify?*

On this I am not sure, because it is obvious that the ranking of creative people and creativity has nothing to do with actual life or accurate commentary. Certainly the polls are indicative of what focuses have penetrated the information scan of those who have done the voting, and it is also clear that in some way this phenomenon does give insight into how creativity—and perception in general—is viewed in the West. For the dictates of western culture have long been concerned about "who is first" and "who is best"—still, I have yet to see a poll on western art music or on which composer is the best—and we must understand that this omission means something as well. In the end, probably the poll signals another triumph for the dynamics of the American businessman—because the use of this phenomenon represents another tool that can be used for marketing. Somehow the reality of the poll and/or poll mentality helps to separate the culture even further from its creativity. Because the use of this tool helps to create a spectacle of creativity and to progressively distort its real reality position at the same time. As such, I view the realness of this concept as necessarily negative in the long run (and not much better in the short run).

16. *Why are there so few black writers involved with black creativity?*

At this point in my life I have not been able to understand the reality of this question myself. I am sure that my observations are probably wrong as well, because certainly there must be more black writers concerned about black creativity than those of whom I am aware . . . (huh?) . . . I think. Without doubt, the fact that so few outlets are available for the music journalist certainly must be considered—this is true for any writer, white or black. Add to this the realness of racism and one can imagine the special situation of the black writer. But even this doesn't excuse the lack of independent efforts. For with the exception of the magazine *The Grackle*, there are practically no outlets for one to experience viewpoints from the black writer and/or intellectual, and this is a shame. It does seem that either the black writer is not interested in composite black creativity, or that that interest has not been sufficient enough to stimulate the creation of alternative information outlets. This is not to say there are no outlets at all—nor have I meant to imply that *The Grackle* is the only source where black writers' viewpoints can be read on and talked about. For the Perspectives on Black Music book series has been around for many years—even though this source is not really well known or distributed. But one would have hoped that by the eighties there would now be several sources—relevant sources—for dealing with the information reality of the black writer. Certainly it is clear that my perception of this subject is necessarily limited to only those areas and focuses which have come under my attention—which is to say, there are probably many other sources that I am not aware of . . . I hope this is true.

17. Do you see more black journalists in the future writing on composite black creativity?

Yes. I believe more and more black journalists will find entry points to expose their viewpoints to the greater public. It is important that they are successful—for all of us. Because the challenge of positive transformation is directly tied to a re-examination of world information dynamics. The reality interpretation of creativity is important because phenomena are directly related to the forming of composite culture information. In other words, to really comment on the dynamic implications of a given creative projection is to begin interpreting the infra-information related to both a culture's reality and its nature. The interpretations of the black journalist must be viewed from this context, because the thrust of his or her work can help establish a more expanded basis for perceiving information—regardless of focus. As the realness of this challenge becomes clearer, there will be more black journalists willing to take the sacrifices necessary for dynamic change—and transformation. Now, more than ever before, we need their viewpoints.

18. What is the highest state of observation (that you can understand anyway)?

To me the highest state of observation would be an opinion that moves in accordance to the nature of real progressionalism: that being—insight with respect to the actualness of a given phenomenon—pertaining not only to its isolated particulars but including the composite implications of its being and route. As such, the significance of alternative journalism has to do with its ability to comment on the nature of world (or information) change without obstructing the path it purports to view. In short, there is now a need for definitions that have the same expansion capacity as the reality they purport to define.

19. What is the significance of elastic definitions with respect to the present particulars of alternative functionalism? What does this phenomenon mean with respect to black people in particular?

One of the most basic challenges that black people and/or culture must secure is a more flexible stance with regards to how we see ourselves. It is important that we not define ourselves in a limited context, because the reality objective of our composite struggle is to re-secure what was lost and taken during the dissolution of African culture. The need for elastic definitions is important because at this point in time there has been no composite philosophical and spiritual reality context from which to properly evaluate a given particular—in terms other than western terms. If the thrust interpretations of the white writer are to be taken as truth, then the future of all black people must be viewed as in serious danger, for the definitions and interpretations of the white writer are necessarily connected to the composite dictates of western culture. It is for this reason—among others—that black people can no longer afford to blindly accept the present reality of music criticism—or for that matter even general news interpretation. Because all of the present information lines are conceived with respect to the exclusive interests of western culture—and these interests are not the same as black culture, world culture, and composite humanity as a whole.

20. What is the most basic idea that western culture seeks to perpetuate about black people—in terms of progressional continuance and trans-information?

The most basic idea that western culture has continually sought to perpetuate is the notion that black people have never contributed to the progressional continuum of high culture or "high information." Black people, under this viewpoint, are somehow viewed as perennial background figures throughout the whole of earth history—a people who have never given anything to the solidification of either great cultures or relevant insight. The whole of western documentation and education has been used to solidify this mis-viewpoint, and real change will not be achieved overnight. For example, the study of world history in the western educational system has somehow come to trace the beginning of high civilization back to the early period of Greece—and as such, western historians would have us believe that all of the information related to how western culture has developed can be traced to only this sector of the world community. But in fact this viewpoint does not even remotely correspond with reality, because practically every source of historical documentation seems to indicate that much of the information that solidified in Greece can be traced to cultures which preceded it—notably Egypt and Samaria (both of which were inhabited by people we now refer to as black people).

21. What effect has western mis-documentation—and indoctrination—had on the life participation of black people, in the last two thousand years?

This, of course, is a very complex question that cannot be answered with one or two sentences. For the effects of racism and suppression have profoundly affected the reality of black people—whether in Africa, Europe, or America. Certainly one of the most serious outgrowths of this phenomenon is the helplessness that mis-information promotes. Because in this time cycle, very few black people grow up with the feeling that "they can change the world" and this is a tragedy which must be changed. The present state of life "and things" has moved to produce a feeling of resignation in many African and trans-African people, and in this state, there is no real hope of dynamically restoring order. For myself, I am particularly concerned that these resigned feelings of frustrations will not continually be transferred from generation to generation. It is important that the children of tomorrow are made to feel free of the burdens we now carry today—especially mental burdens concerning whether or not we can achieve what we desire. The challenge of tomorrow is directly related to whether all of the children on this planet can realize their potential—and this cannot happen unless each child is able to dream "those great dreams" that motivate dynamic participation. There of course is much more to be said about this question, but I do believe nothing is more serious than what this question poses for the reality of children.

CREATIVE MUSIC OUTSIDE AMERICA

(Level One) Britain, Germany, Holland

THE REALITY IMPLICATIONS SURROUNDING EUROPE'S RELATIONSHIP to black creativity and alternative functionalism cannot be understood by only viewing the present state of events, but must instead be viewed with respect to its greater progressional dynamics. For the accelerated dynamics that black creativity would activate in the post-Parker continuum cannot be separated from the overall historical pattern that has solidified through the dissolution of black Africa and the later emergence of European dominance—all of these considerations are interrelated. My point is this—to view the transfer-shift implications of information dynamics is to begin understanding the vibrational particulars that would underlie the "point of exposure" between how Europe perceived Africa and her treasures and what this viewpoint would necessitate in the transfer adaptation of African methodology and creative dynamics. In other words, the phenomenon of trans-African creativity is nothing new in Europe, for the historical progressions related to this most basic subject have seen many so-called forms come and go throughout the last two thousand years—and Europe has always listened because, unlike America, this continent is still aware of the nature of progressional continuance and African history—not to mention that the thrust continuum implications of given projections from Africa and Asia have played a role in the motivation and dynamic implications of European postulation and acceleration.

It is not the purpose of this book to document the state of every source-transfer adoption between Europe and Africa (i.e., black creativity) because this is a task for musicologists—and I am looking for something else anyway. The most basic point that concerns this essay is that the affinity relationship of Europe's perception of so-called jazz is very much connected to Europe's total affinity relationship with African dynamics—and/or its related functionalism. This interest has remained constant since the dissolution of black high composite culture and can be traced from the early treasures taken from Egypt (which can now be seen throughout

Europe, in museums or in the streets [the obelisks in Rome, for instance]) to the musical instruments that were brought to Europe—on through to the later tours in the thirties that would affect European creative dynamics (i.e., the emergence of ragtime, etc., etc.). Thus, the nature of progressional continuance in the forties was not new but, instead, a phenomenon related to a much longer progressional pattern.

I have not mentioned the progressional inter-reality of Europe's relationship to black creativity as a means to negatively comment about the whole of this phenomenon, because not only does this not mean anything, but the composite realness of this phenomenon has many different levels—many of which have nothing to do with being negative. For the realness of this phenomenon really sheds light on the nature of progressional significance and source-transfer information dynamics—and this information is not about being negative, but rather, how given states of being are interrelated (regardless of region, for African creativity itself can even be separated with respect to the routes of its various initiations—everything comes from everything). As such, the affinity relationship between Europe and African creativity must be viewed with respect to what this phenomenon means in extended terms—because the dynamic implication of this subject transcends the "finger-pointing stage" and moves to give some understanding of "what forces are in the air in a given time period" and the "nature of information continuance"—this is what I am interested in. To really understand the progressional reality of creative music outside of America we must first solidify a practical viewpoint for necessary postulation.

DOC. ------PROG.CONT.

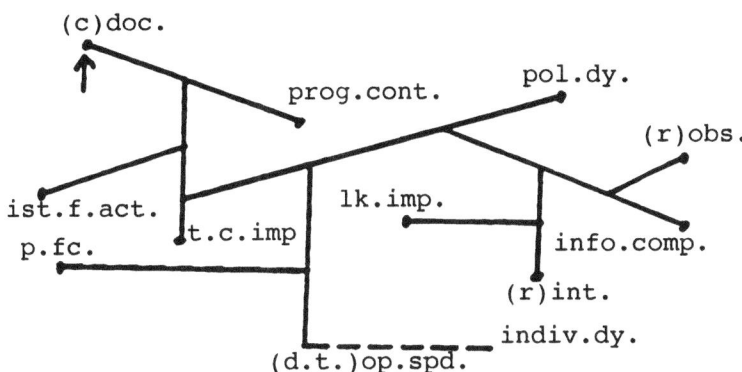

If the dynamic realness of pre-Parker creativity provided a balance to the progressional path western information and particulars would travel before the forties, then it is important to understand what the accelerated continuum of post-Parker creativity would imply from the late forties until the present. For the reality of black creativity before the emergence of bebop was perceived as a thrust alignment that simply balanced the intellectualism and complications of the post-Beethoven projectional European thrust continuum, and the realness of this balance would move many Europeans to view black creativity as a very exotic and primal continuance. This sentiment is important to understand because it underlies how black creativity has long been viewed—even in this period (the eighties). But Europe's relationship with black creativity is much more complex than only one vibrational attitude, because while the composite affinity underlying its perception of black creativity can be viewed as patronizing in the same sense as in America, on the other hand Europe realized the seriousness of the music on a level that escaped Americans (both then and now). Europe has always viewed the composite continuity of black creativity as a signal related to the progressional greater dynamics of black culture and world change—because not only does Europe remember Africa, she also remembers the nature of the transformation that put her in power. As such, the reality actualness of world change is not as abstract in Europe as it is in America because Europe has never forgotten her history—because she is her history.

The dynamic implications of post-Parker creativity would move to clarify the reality position of European extended functionalism in that the particulars of western information dynamics (i.e., its philosophy and technology) had moved into what is now referred to as "its crisis" period. By crisis, I mean that the meta-reality dictates underlying western functionalism—and postulation—had, by the late thirties, moved to function—and perceive—in strict intellectual terms, without spiritual tenets. The establishment of this vibrational position would affect the composite lining and identity of European culture—for, unlike America, which would arrive at this same position without knowing it (because there is no real understanding of philosophy in composite America to speak of—hence, how could this country understand a crisis of identity—let alone "essence foundation"), Europe is all too aware of the significance of affinity dynamics (and cultural postulation). The realness of bebop would include dynamic individual postulation—and as such, affinity dynamics (as opposed to the progressional limitations in western art music that instead moved to suppress individual dynamics) as well as real alternative functionalism (that being, the emergence of a route that hinted of both new alignments—or relevant alignments—and transformational change). It is from this point that one can begin understanding the nature of the progressional continuance that has shaped this time cycle. For the seeds underlying bebop would establish the basic attitude—as well as affinity relationship—that determined how black creativity has been viewed and utilized in Europe from the forties to the present, and it is important that this is understood. But this is only the beginning.

The emergence of the post-Coleman/Coltrane/Taylor junction of black creativity would have a profound effect on the composite nature of earth creativity—and this is no less true for what it would imply in Europe. For the thrust of this continuum would accelerate the restoration of a transformational attitude throughout Europe through what it posed to the affinity insight expansion principle. The dynamic implications of this phenomenon would serve as one of the most important factors for Europeans to begin re-establishing the composite continuation of European extended functionalism, as well as alternative functionalism that interconnects with the forming transformational world position (i.e., the makings of a world music and affinity position). Thus, if we are to understand the "particulars" related to this phenomenon, then it is important to understand the nature of its solidification as well as what this subject has posed in individual creative terms.

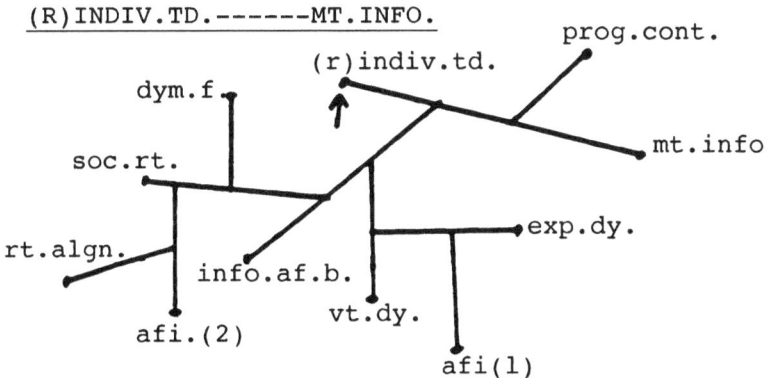

The nature of the impact post-Coleman creativity had in Europe must be viewed with respect to the reality position of European information dissemination—in other words, the effectiveness of the music is directly related to the fact that in Europe, black creativity has long been both available to the greater public and focused on.

But then, there has always been a marked difference between how black creativity is treated in Europe as compared to America. This is not to say black creativity in Europe is treated on the same level of European art music—because most certainly it isn't—but there can be no comparing the option spread possibilities for so-called jazz in Europe to the situation that exists in America. It is possible to find intelligent articles—directed towards really trying to understand the music—on every aspect of post-Coleman continuance, from the early sixties until now. The end result of this attention was that by 1965 there was an audience in Europe with a real understanding of the transition dictating the next period of creative music from America. While in America, it has only been in this time zone (middle seventies) where attempts are finally being made to expose this thrust of creative music. I do not mean, however, to imply that every

European who listened to this music necessarily liked the music—the fact is, the music was at least exposed.

In this type of atmosphere it was only natural that musicians would want to come and perform throughout the continent. By the middle sixties, the majority of creative musicians involved in the transition of the creative music in America could be found performing regularly in Europe. Because it is clear that the development of any creative thrust is directly related to the amount of exposure that thrust is able to generate. Not to mention, the very core of creative music feeds off of the affinity interchange between the "actual" music and the response of the people listening to that music. In short, Europe provided a platform where the music could continue to develop, and Europe also gave assurance to a movement desperately in need of an appreciative outlet—there was an audience for this music. There are many other considerations related to the exodus of American musicians to Europe—for the economic aspect of this situation cannot be dismissed either. That is to say, the realness of Europe as an economic source was also an important reason why many Americans visited regularly. Many musicians were starving in America because there were simply no performing outlets for their music. The question eventually became—either travel and hopefully find outlets for performance, or stay in America and starve to death—it was as simple as that.

Musicians like Cecil Taylor and Albert Ayler had a strong impact in the early sixties in places like Copenhagen, and to this day, many people have related to me their experience of listening to the music and dealing with its freshness, as the invention evolved in front of them. I have no doubt that the reception Taylor's Unit received in Copenhagen also served as a positive stimulating consideration to the musicians themselves (and this phenomenon probably greatly assisted the changes Taylor's activity was to later take). Archie Shepp's appearances in France and Germany certainly helped to spread the music as well. His performances in this time period helped to accelerate interest in alternative creativity throughout the whole of Europe. By the end of the sixties, the migration of American musicians to Europe was in full swing, and this period can now be looked at as one of the most dynamic time zones in improvised music from the post-Coleman cycle. This is so because of the many opportunities that solidified from the various projects which happened in Europe.

The rush of American musicians to Europe did not begin in the sixties. This phenomenon has been the trend in creative music—classical or improvisational—throughout the history of America. In the fifties, musicians like Dexter Gordon resided in Copenhagen for a period of ten years and some. The list of American musicians now residing in Europe, either permanently or semi-permanently would be too long to list. This phenomenon was the result of a more favorable environment—a chance to perform one's music and hence develop—and the opportunity to present music and have people experience it.

But the reality of creative music in Europe is not only about the particulars of the geo-migrations that occurred in the First and Second World Wars. Nor can this subject be understood by only focusing on the particulars of given American musicians. Instead, it is necessary that the dynamic implications of this subject are compositely considered. It is important to understand that the profound implications of creative music are not limited to only those who are playing that music, but instead must also include those "experiencing" that music as well. Because the implications related to what has been raised by creative musicians from the black aesthetic performing in such numbers in Europe have rarely been dealt with by most Americans. Even now, we find in America that most attitudes have not changed concerning how most Americans see themselves, and it is clear that few Americans are aware of the changes now taking place in creative music in this time zone—changes that include the European musician as well (but more on this later). Practically every American if asked about improvised music would reply that "JAZZ" is America's original art form, etc., etc. (even though only a handful of people support the music), and most Americans would also agree that the only important statements being made in creative music (jazz) are coming from American musicians. And while these notions float hazily in the air, and are continually drawn upon (the American black versus the American white, the American versus the European, the American white versus the European, etc.), there is now what seems to be the stirring of significant activity happening in Europe which hints at a potential very few Americans realize. It would be easy for me as an American to write that the musical activity in Europe is nothing more than a mutation of American improvised music to the degree that it can only be talked of as a stylistic variation, but this might not shed light on the real situation—not to mention, it does not seem to be true either. For the activity that has been growing in Europe for the past ten years seems to, among other things, manifest itself, in a sense, as a reaction to the position that European musicians have been in—and, now, in the early eighties, there are many concrete developments in European creativity that can be viewed as an alternative creative continuum with regards to its relationship to American improvised music. Alternative in the sense that much of the music I have been hearing is not just an imitation of American creative music. However, I do not mean to imply that there is no relationship between improvised music in Europe and improvised music in America, because that is not true either. I do believe, however, that the nature of that relationship is changing—much more than is generally understood. There, of course, must be a relationship between improvised music in Europe and America—if for no other reason that the basis which actualized the vibrational and spiritual hierarchy of improvised music in Europe was dictated in the lining of American creative music (or creative music from the black aesthetic)—this includes the actual aesthetic as well as the functional arena which dictates the science of the actual music. Yet if I have defined creative music from the black aesthetic as an aesthetic which moves to help solidify the world group, then it must also imply that the initiations of every group (vibrational thrust) must also be viewed as a factor that reshapes the "composite arena" of world music. In short, an aesthetic is affected by whoever participates in that aesthetic. As creative music moves towards the composite center, it will be less important where it came from (not to mention that the actual origin of the music did not start in America either) than where it's going and how it plans to get there.

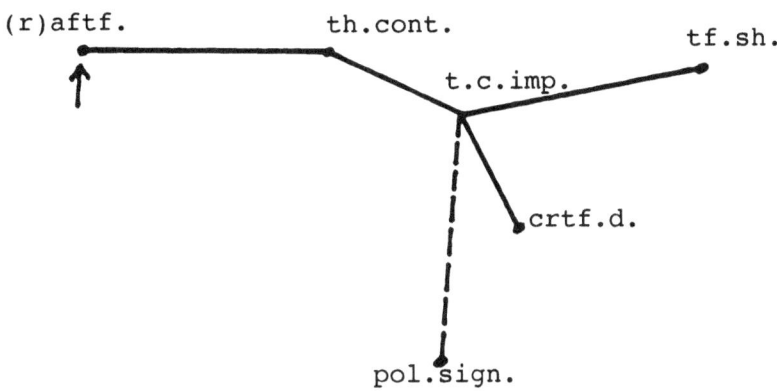

We must also understand that any discussion of new improvised music in Europe would have to take into account that the music differs from country to country. That is to say, it might not be useful to talk of recent developments in London with the activity happening in France, for instance, although in several cases there are parallels. The clearest instance of parallel development in European activity could be the interrelationship of the English and German music groups (this is especially true in the middle sixties as opposed to the present period)—nevertheless those similarities should not be overemphasized or we run the risk of not understanding the real situation that has been developing in Europe.

The emergence of new improvised music in Europe can also be looked at in accordance with the socio-economic developments which have occurred in western culture during the last forty years—especially the physical universe reality of Europe in this time zone (the sixties and seventies) as manifested by the relationship between various western European countries to each other, and also the situation of Europe as a whole unto itself. Many Americans prefer to believe that Europe is dead and entrenched in the annals of the western position—a post-existential culture feeding on the lifeblood of America. This viewpoint reflects the post–World War II type of mentality which was very prevalent in America: that being, America savior of the planet, and America as the lifeblood of the new frontier. Certainly it is true that Europe was in bad shape after the Second World War (who wouldn't be), and it is also true that improvisation—as an integral part of European art music—was practically non-existent. But there are many reasons for this. It is also true that the post-Webern movement which materialized at the end of the Second World War did not begin to really address the dynamics of improvisation—no matter what word or variation they eventually settled on—until the early fifties. The activity emerging in Europe during this time period is especially important because it signifies that basis is now being laid for a distinct and necessary creative thrust towards improvisation. Moreso, the creativity which I have been experiencing in the last ten years can clearly be looked at as a separate creative thrust that is distinctly European in its vibrational identity and directly coupled to the challenge of world music. The forming of the Common Market and the move towards unification in Europe are factors that are directly related to the progressions of this phenomenon. For however one looks at this present-day geopolitics, it was extremely important and in fact inevitable that the political and economic arena of Europe would come together, both as a means to dictate their own destinies as a composite defining community and also as the first move in the struggle to participate in the vibrationaltory consequences of transformation (on both the vibrational and physical universe sense). Europe in many ways has been caught between two defining communities—the Soviet Union and America—and the consequences of this position leave little choice but unification as a tool for survival. It is the insecurity manifested in this position that Europe has been dealing with since the Second World War—whether in the political arena or the creative arena—and the activity taking place in this time zone can be better understood by it being the period in which the first level of composite responses is secured. That is: the creativity taking place in this time zone cannot be separated from the total arena of events shaping the next cycle for the European and planet vibrational change.

Of course, as an American, I do not pretend to have the qualifications to write about the situation in Europe and the struggles that are taking place at present with any authority. But I make my observations with the realness that Europe's destiny is directly connected to America's. Not only that, but it must also be remembered that "established" America bases her tradition from Europe—even though there are obvious differences. I write of the vibrational and political reality of Europe because the same factors which have determined the European essence factor are still present in America. In other words, what really distinguishes America from Europe is not the general vibrational tone of the political defining community but instead the actual environment (the realness and dynamics of all the many different ethnic groups in America) on the physical universe level. The fact that America is not Europe is part of her dilemma and even today casts a shadow over her meta-reality and philosophy—and her historical misdocumentation (how things are put together and how events are understood). This can be understood merely by looking at the traditions which are handed down to Americans that have nothing to do with American culture. I mention the connection between America and Europe, then, as a means to hold a universal perspective, because however we look at the present situation in Europe today, we are all governed by the same basic forces—which is to say, there is no certainty America will never have to experience the same type of transition Europe has and is seeing; and also I write of this situation to lay basis for showing that the creative arena of the European musician has not simply stood still, but rather has changed—like everything else, and it would be to our advantage to better understand what this change really means. Yet, by the same token, the emergence of creative music from the black aesthetic has served as the most important stimulating factor in Europe, and has dictated the re-awareness of improvisation, and its use towards an alternative thrust functionalism. In this context, Europe and America are again similar—because improvised music in both countries has the position of an alternative re-generative factor.

It is important that the reality dynamics of non-American creativity are not viewed in one-dimensional terms. For the particulars of this most important subject defy easy generalizations. For instance, while most musicologists—and so-called jazz journalists—would have us believe that the consideration of improvisation represents what is most unique to black creativity (and this viewpoint is not correct), it is important to understand that the history of European art music also shows a use of improvisation as well. As such, the reality particulars of the last one hundred years cannot be singled out as the only context (basis) to view this subject. Creative music from the black aesthetic can most certainly be viewed as a major regenerative factor in present day European creative functionalism, but regenerative in the real sense of the word—starting something which has stopped. European improvised music is now in a period where many musicians are searching to find their own solutions to be creative. Some attempts are successful, some aren't (just as in America), and the musical references now being utilized in Europe are no longer based solely on black music solutions in improvised music. We now see European musicians emerging with a total awareness of their culture. Moreover, I believe we are now in a period of transition where European creative musicians are realigning their roots in improvised music from the black tradition as well as creative music from the European tradition. It should be understood that I am not saying improvised music in America and improvised music in Europe are the only considerations that European musicians are drawing from. To state that would be a gross distortion, for in reality, the situation for all creative musicians in this time period is not as separate as we might think. There are parallels and, in this instance, I agree with Buckminster Fuller's understanding concerning how the planet itself has diminished to the degree that within the western world people are basically dealing with the same things. Of course there are cultural and historical differences on the surface between every so-called group, but the basic underlying factors that determine how people move in their lives in the west are essentially the same. The uniqueness of the European musician's position would have to do with his/her being in that particular part of the planet as opposed to musicians who are occupying another part of the planet. Certainly there are different factors that each physical universe space poses for creative musicians, and, therefore, there must be differences in the creativity on some level, but the basic conditions that human beings live in are the same (for the dynamics of a planet can only be so much).

It becomes more a question of musicians celebrating their creativity in accordance with the vibrational dictates of their environment as well as their own cultural and vibrational pull.

MT.INFO.------ TRS.

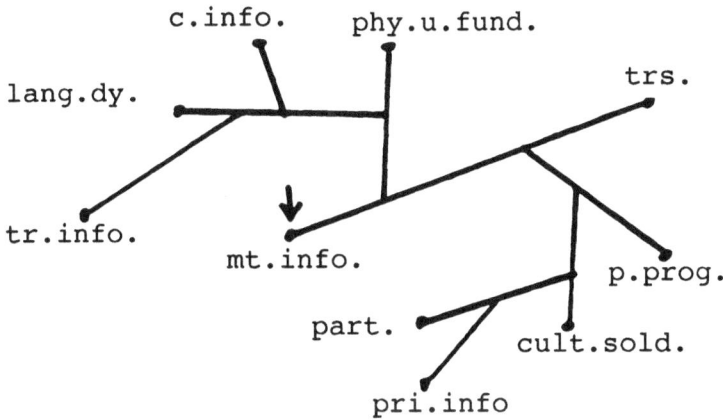

PRI.AF.TD. ------ TR.

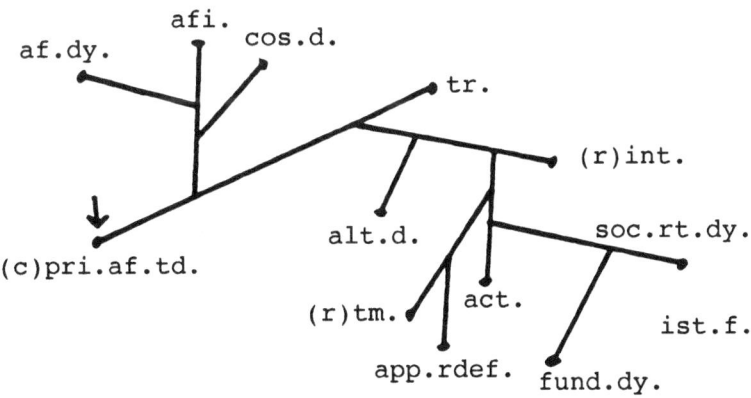

Of the articles I have read on European improvised music in which the musicians themselves have had the chance to talk about their music, there are many disagreements as to what constitutes the conceptual and meta-reality implications of new European music. In this regard, again,

European musicians are in the same situation that exists everywhere. In one camp of musicians there is a conscious attempt to create an alternative European improvised music, and in other camps there are efforts to establish a more nationalistic creativity even separate from the European composite aesthetic concept, and, finally, there is a movement which shares a natural affinity with the creativity taking place in America. If there is one discernible rallying point that I have been able to perceive about new European creativity, it would undoubtedly be the European musicians' insistence that their activity must now be taken seriously as an addition to the creative music scene, rather than merely an imitation of American creative music. For to understand the scene in Europe is to also understand that while the exodus of American musicians from the states to Europe in the forties, fifties, and sixties presented a chance to experience and learn about the activity from America, this same phenomenon also represented a chance to not work—in other words, even though the presence of American musicians in such large numbers (especially after the Second World War) represented a chance for European musicians to learn about the developments which had occurred in American music, the end result of this knowledge was that the work situation for European musicians would become extremely difficult. As I write this book, the situation between Britain and America is very interesting with regards to the work situation concerning creative improvised music. For any classical musician can enter and play in London (or America) without a work permit, and there are no laws prohibiting this. It is only for so-called jazz and rock forms of improvised music that there are basic restrictions. Moreover, by the late fifties we find in Europe a growing resentment to the position of the American presence in Europe. This resentment was rooted in both the economic and racial dynamics of present-day sentiment—for European musicians eventually began to see American musicians (in such force) as a threat to their abilities to make a living (their argument was that it was impossible for an English jazz musician to come to America and repeat what had taken place in Europe—for America represented and produced the music). Yet this argument doesn't deal with the fact that as music continuums go, only a handful of black musicians have been allowed to even participate in European art music—both in Europe and America (this is true even though black musicians and composers are historically documented as helping to solidify western art music). By the late fifties, there developed what can only be called a deep-seated resentment of American musicians as well as how their music was perceived as opposed to European music (and later the concept of "black power" would serve as yet another alienating factor for these musicians). All of these developments—the aesthetic interpretation of creative music in this time period and the economic factor—have contributed to how the European musicians now see themselves (as a separate group with their own identity). Moreover, the advances which have been made in European creativity during the last fifteen years (and some) have helped to change the relationship between these two movements of musicians. The rapid advances which have been made in creative European improvised music are slowly being recognized for their own value.

The most significant factor to shape the emergence of new creative European music in the sixties has been the forming of collective groups—much like the attempts in America by groups like the Jazz Composer's Orchestra or the AACM. In Europe I found several groups that have functioned as "center factors" for given creative-thrust continuums. Some of these collectives will provide the basis for my attempts to write about present-day developments in European creative music. In all probability (in every probability) there are many other groups I know nothing about, and in no way have I meant to imply that the organizations appearing in this book represent the composite picture of present-day creative music in Europe. Instead, these are the only groups I actually know about at present and therefore the only ones I can write on.

The situation of new music in Europe cannot be attributed solely to the fact that the music is more available in the media than it is in America. The encouragement the countries themselves have given their artists, in the use of facilities and the activity directed towards positive stimulation, has been enormously important. One example of this activity would be the workshop in Baden-Baden, Germany, where, for one week, musicians are able to come together and work in groups ranging from small to large ensembles. The results from these meetings, in most cases, are quite successful. There are also schools like the one in Vallekilde, Denmark, where attempts to encourage the spirit of the music—embracing the dynamics of styles—are undertaken. In many respects, the academic dynamics of European music curriculums (having to do with every aspect of the teaching of creative music) are much more in accordance with the music than many of the institutions I have seen in America. Vallekilde gives its students the opportunity to learn about the complete spectrum of creative music, from the very early forms to the present era.

The Baden-Baden workshops are also very important. Joachim Berendt has created a situation which promotes many different creative possibilities, and every year the Baden-Baden workshops are responsible for creating some of the most interesting approaches in creative music. After experiencing the music that had been created in Baden-Baden (in 1968), there could be no denying that not only was the music original and creative—in the sense it had its own vibrational flow—but I was very much aware that I had experienced some of the most interesting creative music in that time period. In short, the music I experienced in Baden-Baden was significant in any context.

With the exception of scattered ensembles like those of Sun Ra and Sam Rivers, there are very few creative music orchestras in America at present. The situation in Europe, however, is somewhat better—although it is clear that the economic complications of holding a large ensemble together is still no easy matter. It is for this reason that the work done in Baden-Baden was so necessary for this time zone. This workshop context helped to outline how differently Europe perceives of creative music as opposed to America. For the Baden-Baden workshops represented an attempt—in cooperation with the West German Radio Network—to develop (and hear) the large ensemble implications of creative music. In short, the workshops in the early seventies provided a platform for both working in and developing the big-band dynamics of creative music. In my first visit to the Baden-Baden workshops, I was made aware that the participation of musicians from all over Europe (as well as America) was an integral factor in every meeting. It was in this period when I began to focus on the different approaches developing in Europe—both as a means to learn what they were doing and also as a means to better understand the differences between the various schools of European thought. What I heard at Baden-Baden in a sense was a summation of all of the different conceptual paths that had developed in both Europe and America—since there were also American musicians—and the dynamic spectrum of the music was unbelievable. Moreover, the Baden-Baden workshop atmosphere is not unique in Europe. There are several other outlets for projects of this kind throughout the continent. In fact, the workshop situation seems to be a reality in Europe. Musicians have been able to participate in this context several times a year in various places throughout Europe. The gains which have been made from meetings of this type have been invaluable for what it has given to the music.

While I will attempt to write on various groups in European creative music, it should be made clear that I am greatly hampered in this particular section. For I have based this section of the book on what music I have heard myself (for the most part) and my real knowledge of this subject is somewhat superficial. My reasons for attempting to write on the various progressions taking place outside of so-called American creativity is that any real understanding of the present arena of creative music must deal with the multi-dimensional consequences of the subject as it involves composite earth. Moreover, if this book was conceived as a vehicle to hopefully provide some real information about creative music today, then to not write on the developments taking place outside of America would be unforgivable. Since I have not had the time to research—and live—in each of the countries I am about to write on, this section of the book must be approached in a general way—rather than absolute observations on my part. I offer these general notes only as a factor to shed some light on creative improvised music outside of America, and, in doing so, to possibly stimulate more interest and appreciation of non-American creativity. Since very little has been written on this subject in America, I figure that someone should at least make an attempt.

CMOA(I)–18
Britain
The creative music I have chosen to write about from Britain can be divided into three separate movements—or schools (I do this for convenience sake, to better deal with the individual solutions of each school), and each of these movements emerged as an alternative creative thrust from the post-Ayler period of creative music. The three movements could be broken down into the following: (1) the musicians who were associated with the percussionist John Stevens; (2) the activity of those musicians who had come to London from South Africa; and (3) the movement which centered around musicians like John Surman. I must take great care in making this type of breakdown, lest I give the wrong impression—so it is necessary to qualify these movements further. First, when I say "the movement which centered around John Stevens," I do not mean to imply that Stevens was the head of the actual movement, for actually I have no idea about this, nor am I really concerned about this question. I am only using Stevens' name as a rallying point (actually I discovered most of these musicians on Stevens' early record—thus it would be more appropriate to use John's name as opposed to, say, Trevor Watts); likewise, this is also the case in my use of John Surman's name—he was simply the first musician of this movement who I was to become familiar with. To my knowledge, all three of these movements solidified towards the late fifties and early sixties. Nor do I mean to imply that only three movements of creative music were taking place in London either, for that does not seem to be the case. Ensembles like AMM were certainly important for the work they contributed during the late fifties on to the present, but it would be impossible for me to write about this ensemble since I know very little about their "actual" work (not to mention, I have found it extremely difficult to obtain most of their recordings). There are other movements as well (e.g., Mike Gibbs or Mike Westbrook—that I know very little about) which are not represented in this book.

John Stevens as a Center Factor

The music that evolved from this movement seemed to have solidified around the middle sixties—coming into real focus after the dynamic implications of the post-Coleman era. The actual center of this movement would later come to be called the Music Improvisation Company, for the basic thrust of this movement's invention had never depended on the work of any one person. Instead, like the collectives that had sprung up in America, the actualness of the Music Improvisation Company would establish a particular "vibrational way of doing things" that breathed with its own identity. The functional dynamics of this continuum would move to focus on the dynamic implications of open-ended improvisation as its most basic point of extension for alternative investigation, and this interest would become a major factor in establishing the identity lining of their work. In other words, the most basic thrust of this movement would function completely separate from compositional or imposed organization, and would instead move to create a music that dynamically participated in open dialogue information exchange. This then would be a movement whose activity focus had no use for either the concept of thematic development, or the reality of ensemble time co-ordinates (as a programmed consideration). Instead, in the working theater of given performances, each musician would be able to collectively shape the "moment nature" of a given postulation. The end result of this approach would move to shape one of the most dynamic offerings of creative music in this cycle—and in doing so—open up another area for composite creative investigation. This is not to say that the Music Improvisation Company had innovated the concept of open-ended improvisation—because they hadn't—but rather, the reality and dynamic particulars (i.e., the actual music) that would move to solidify the work of this continuum did represent a new point of departure. The realness of this movement would more than simply challenge the nationalist (and racist) beliefs in America that only black people (or only "Americans") can successfully extend the thrust of creative music, for the dynamic realness of this thrust would also comment on the reality position of progressional continuance—as this concept applies to the composite realness of information extension.

CMOA(I)–20

To really understand the realness of what has been offered through this thrust, and any thrust for that matter, one must of course experience the actual music—both in its collective and solo brilliance. Many of the musicians who have come from this continuum have moved to establish themselves as among the vanguard in creative earth music, and any attempt to view the future of creative progressionalism must involve some understanding of their work. Among the musicians from this movement are: Derek Bailey, Evan Parker, Trevor Watts, and Paul Rutherford, to mention a few. Each of these musicians has helped to both collectively and individually advance the reality of alternative functionalism—as it applies to the composite music and as it applies to the dynamics of their chosen instruments. It is important that this is understood.

In recent years the thrust of musicians from this movement have come apart and back together, and apart (following the dynamics of all collective groups in this and every cycle)—and as such, the nature of this collective today is outside of my knowledge. Certainly the last seven years have seen many changes in this continuum, for the gains from the sector have attracted and interacted with many musicians from other parts of the country—and world. From what I am able to understand, the collected realness of this movement has continued to expand and diversify—and in doing so, continues to be a relevant continuance for the next cycle. By the late sixties, an alternative record company was formed to properly document and distribute the music from this continuum, and the solidification of this move is something we can all be grateful for. As such, the progressional spread and advancement of this continuum as we enter the eighties can be experienced on those musicians' own alternative record company (that being Incus Records).

Chris McGregor as a Center Factor

There is another group of musicians whose work is really important, for whom Chris McGregor serves as a center factor. The musicians from this movement, whatever their differences, have all come from South Africa, and it is at this point that one can immediately sense a different sensibility to their music. Many of these musicians have worked and played together in South Africa during their formative period—long before the move to London. In fact, the emergence of this group as a movement (or creative thrust) occurred around the late fifties (or early sixties)—in short, this was a music whose vibrational and functional factors were shaped before the musicians came to London. The actual creativity that has come from this movement could not be more different from the John Stevens movement of collective improvisation—for the dynamics of this continuum produced a more emotional, rhythmic and percussive music from the African tradition. The music from this group also distinguished itself from the other movements taking place in London by the distinctness of its sensibility and vibrational-source pull. It is in experiencing the Chris McGregor Brotherhood of Breath and/or the small ensemble Spear that one can begin to experience what I am trying to describe. Soloists like Mongezi Feza (who died in 1975), if known, would have had a considerable effect on the contemporary brass scene, because he was a brilliant trumpet soloist. Yet his work was never experienced outside of Europe. It is in listening to the creativity from this dynamic thrust where one can experience beautiful African melodies as well as forms which have adopted similar structural mannerisms of a composer like Duke Ellington (in fact there is a strong functional and vibrational relationship between McGregor's use of structure and harmony to Duke Ellington). It is with this movement that we can see an improvised music somewhat similar to that of America in its use of structure and composition but with a difference in sensibility—an African sensibility, and the actual music is very exciting and different.

Although the make-up of this group has changed in the past ten years, many of the original members of this movement are still functioning together. Some of the musicians who have emerged from this thrust are Louis Moholo, Dudu Pukwana, Harry Miller, and on occasion Johnny Dyani. The activity of Chris McGregor thus functioned as a center factor for keeping all of the musicians of this movement together, for in many ways (in every way) this group is like a family. Moreover, since it is difficult to keep a large ensemble like the Brotherhood of Breath constantly working, many of the musicians from this group have functioned in other areas of the music as well. Musicians like Mongezi Feza and Louis Moholo can be heard in many different capacities if one would experience the spectrum of their work. There is still another aspect of the activity from this movement that is important and must be mentioned. That aspect is the spirituality which naturally illuminates from this creative thrust. It is through the vibrational-spiritual pull of their creativity where one can experience the realness of their music and the relationship of their activity to the complete music scene—not only in Britain—but on the planet. To my knowledge there are only several recordings of their work available in this time zone. Unless this can be corrected, this will be very unfortunate for us.

John Surman as a Center Factor

The third movement I have chosen to write on is the group for which John Surman's activity serves as center—or best example. This is also the movement whose creative thrust is directly related to the activity inspired from America. In other words, the activity of this movement was directly inspired from what we now call American Jazz (of course I do not mean to imply that the other movements were not also influenced by the creativity in America, because they were—I stress the influence of American music with the Surman movement, however, because the actual creativity that came from this thrust was a direct utilization of established functional and language tools developed in America). In short, the activity which emerged from this movement was directly related to the solutions that many American groups adopted in the sixties, and for the same reasons—that being: the Surman movement functioned as a part of the post-Coltrane and -Coleman creative thrust. It would be a mistake, however, to underestimate their achievements in this avenue, for if their activity adopted the reality-essence factor of creative music from the black aesthetic, they also inherited the challenge that the form demands of its players. Some of the most dynamic music from the post-Coltrane period was to emerge from this movement.

In this movement one can find many creative and strong soloists with their own solutions and approaches to the music. Musicians like Alan

Skidmore and Mike Osborne are good examples of this thrust—and both musicians have carved out their own individual approaches to the music. Many extremely interesting soloists as well as strong technicians have come from this movement. Another factor associated with this school of music is the realness of a strong traditional foundation and good musicianship. Many Americans are probably aware of the activity of John Surman because several of his records are available in this country. In fact, Surman has won the *Down Beat* poll for new baritone saxophonist several times. There are only a few baritone players in his class on the planet, and his music is constantly developing. The reality and vibrational direction that this movement has taken could be talked of in terms of the absorption of Coltrane concepts in the early sixties and the eventual digesting of Albert Ayler and the so-called Free-Jazz period. But unlike many of the musicians from the John Stevens movement, the Surman movement did not change its vibrational or functional reality dictates. Instead, this movement seemed to naturally grow and expand through the conceptual reality of post-bebop creativity—eventually making it unique in their own terms. By the end of the sixties, this movement functioned with as strong an identity as the musicians from the John Stevens movement. Moreover, in the same period of growth (basically the period of the sixties), they developed a creative extension that was just as distinct in its own way as the musicians who functioned from the Chris McGregor group, or any creative thrust for that example (America included).

By the middle seventies, it was possible to experience the activity from the Surman movement and see quite a dynamic spectrum. The investigation of jazz-rock, the trio saxophone concerts of Skidmore, Osborne, and Surman, the utilization of the duo situation (Mike Osborne with Stan Tracey) and the adoption of electronic music possibilities (the trio of Surman, Barre Phillips, and Stu Martin), etc. These advances have no doubt affected the future direction of creative music—in London, Europe, and America. It would be impossible to comment on the dynamics of all of the creative musicians who have surfaced in Europe during the last fifteen years—and some. For the spectrum of relevant individuals would necessitate another book and some—and this is outside of what I could effectively accomplish. There is also the realness that many of the new musicians who have surfaced in Europe during the sixties cannot be easily fitted into any of the conventional categories of musical designation—because their work transcends any one context. Musicians like Kenny Wheeler or Gunter Hampel have long established themselves as important musicians—regardless of context. Both of these musicians must be viewed in extended world terms because the dynamics of their offerings are multi-significant. The realness of the next cycle will require that these musicians' offerings are experienced and digested—on every level. Because both Wheeler and Hampel are world musicians of the highest order.

While I have attempted to separate various musicians and groups as a way to write on some of the events I have experienced in London, it would be a gross distortion of the total scene if I did not make it clear that none of these movements are so distinct that they function separately from the basic creative community. By that, I am saying that most of the musicians I have mentioned have functioned in many contexts—both within and outside of the categories I have imposed for the purposes of this book. In short, it was possible to experience Mike Osborne and Louis Moholo performing in quartet or quintet for a period—it was also possible to hear a musician like Evan Parker performing with the Chris McGregor Big Band. I have not introduced the sectioning off of musicians as an absolute, but only as a clarification factor to write on given developments and/or focuses.

The historical progressions of European creative postulation have also determined the course of creativity as it now exists in London. There have long been creative music movements in this area, and the present situation in British creative music should come as no surprise if only the last twenty years are taken into account. It was in the sixties where I first became aware of the activity of altoist Joe Harriott, for example, and it is unfortunate that I never had the chance of experiencing his music live. But the stories I have heard about his activity seem to suggest that his activity expanded in the same principal vibrationaltory direction as Ornette Coleman—at the same time. There are other groups as well—the most significant probably being AMM (which was an improvisational ensemble that drew from both creative black music and contemporary western art music). In fact, AMM is somewhat legendary in London for the advances they made in creative music during the fifties and sixties—but I am hampered in my knowledge of this ensemble, for I have only heard a couple of examples of their work on record, and I have never heard them live. At present, I believe this group is still together—possibly only in duo form (the percussionist and saxophonist of the original group), but even on this information I am not sure. During a period of AMM's development, I have been told that collaborations were even done with the composer Cornelius Cardew. The basic idea I have lately begun to formulate is that this ensemble probably functioned as an important source-transfer factor between creative improvisational technique coming from the creative music from the black aesthetic and new compositional technique from the post-Cage movement—yet I have no basis for making this claim as fact.

Holland

The music which emerged in Holland towards the end of the sixties was very different from what solidified in London. Holland developed a movement that has moved towards the re-integration of its folk music coupled with alternative language factors as a means to lay basis for a distinct national creative music. By the middle sixties, the realness of their approach as a separate entity had become clear to the whole of the European community. The Holland creative movement has performed regularly throughout Europe, and their activity has been welcome as both an alternative thrust (something recognizably different from many of the other progressive movements) and a movement which understood the sophistication of live performance dynamics. This is a movement which utilizes a broad spectrum of compositional and theoretical approaches as well; and to experience their activity in many ways can be likened to going to a play.

The forces which have most shaped the present music scene in Holland are Han Bennink, Misha Mengelberg, and Willem Breuker. I believe it would be correct to say that every change that has reshaped the creativity in Holland can be reduced to the activity of one of these musicians. Together they have helped to mold a music that clearly relates to their own environment and has the potential to reshape the functional arena of composite creative music. If there is one aspect of Holland music that is consistent—no matter which group one experiences—that aspect would be the use of humor and theatre as a factor to draw both visual attention to their work and also theatre as a means to inject Dutch tradition into their work. In the past five years, this approach has completely changed the music scene in Holland, and the activity of Bennink, Mengelberg, and Breuker has now moved into public acceptance in Holland. In other words, the changes which were introduced into Dutch creative music have helped to create a national audience for the music. This was done by creating a functionally attractive music that people could relate to. If we can say that the period of the early seventies represented the time zone where many musicians felt the need to re-examine their roots (source-initiation) and integrate their activity with those roots—it is possible that the Dutch creative movement has made the most dynamic use of this re-evaluation in Europe.

The factors underlying the creative music arena in Holland can be traced to the early sixties. It was in this time zone where the activity of Coltrane and Ayler made their strongest impact on the continent. The end of the post-Coleman period was the beginning of a new era in contemporary Dutch creativity. In the early sixties, musicians like Bennink and Mengelberg worked with musicians like Eric Dolphy, for example, (and are in fact on Dolphy's last live recording in Europe). Later in this same decade, Holland would experience the same reaction towards American creativity that took place throughout the continent, and for several years Dutch musicians consciously strove to develop a music that was indigenous to their own culture and lifestyle. It was in this period where many Dutch musicians began to form cooperative groups (in Holland, the first organization of this type was the Instant Composers Pool) and later with other European movements. The two most influential allies with these cooperatives were the British and German movements, and by the middle to late seventies, all three groups interchanged activity on many different levels. Musicians like Han Bennink would function with

Derek Bailey and later Peter Brötzmann—Willem Breuker worked for a period with Gunter Hampel, etc. This time cycle was undoubtedly the final molding period for the activity that was to solidify in Holland, for by the early seventies, the Dutch music had profoundly changed. I have not meant to imply that no interaction took place between European and Dutch musicians after the seventies. Rather, the time zone of the seventies saw the actuality of independent conceptual development as a factor dictating natural affinities and separations.

Fortunately, the move towards unification that took place in the early sixties in Holland provided an outlet for recording and documenting the changes taking place in Dutch creativity. By 1970, it was possible to experience the emergence of Dutch creativity as a separate entity from both European and American creative music. Each of the individuals I have spoken of can be traced back into this period as a means to see the focal point involving how their activity began to take shape. The period of the middle sixties was the time zone that Han Bennink began to function as a multi-dimensional percussionist (or at least this was the period I have been able to trace—but I could be wrong). The basic progression which surrounded Holland's creativity was very much like the progressions both Europe and America went through: that is, the creativity of the early and late sixties was more an emotional breakthrough. The science which actually determined the next stage of the creativity emerged in the time zone of the late sixties or early seventies. This was the case for most European countries and America, and this was also the case for the Dutch musicians.

The early period of Dutch creative music produced an improvised music that functioned very similarly to the activity in London, in the sense that it contained no use of structure and basically only utilized "open-ended" improvisation techniques. It was in this period where many of the musicians began to embrace the concept of multi-instrumentalism as a factor to broaden sound possibilities for their music (there is a connection between this move towards multi-instrumentation and that of the AACM, but many musicians have stated both of these moves were arrived at independently—somehow I doubt this, but, then again, I have no basis in fact to really know), and by the late sixties, multi-instrumentalism in

Dutch creativity became apparent. The first recordings which signaled to me that the activity in Holland had moved into transition were done by Willem Breuker in the late sixties. Quite possibly, Breuker's activity is the strongest single factor that has shaped many of the characteristics of Dutch music today—but this is just my opinion. I have long singled out the activity of Breuker because the emergence of alternative composition dynamics is the most distinguishing factor underlying Dutch music in this period (the middle seventies), and Breuker functions as the most effective composer in Holland for this type of music.

There was a period in the development of present-day Dutch creative music in the middle seventies where the use of improvisation was completely discarded—this is especially true of Breuker—and in its place was a structural music which employed the use of traditional popular music devices and theatre. It was in this time zone where the early attempts at choreography were integrated into the music. As this phenomenon began to spread, musicians like Han Bennink helped to create the final elements to solidify a movement. Bennink's use of "spectacle" is as effective as any that I have experienced, and this is also true of Mengelberg. The general dynamics of the new Dutch music have not only moved to stimulate the composite creative scene in Holland, but while doing so also attracted a national audience. Moreover, this movement has long enjoyed governmental assistance—in the form of grants and loans—that have never been available to musicians in other countries. For that reason, musicians like Breuker and Mengelberg have been able to function with both small and large ensembles on a more regular basis than most musicians of the post-Coleman juncture. The end result of this situation has, undoubtedly, positively assisted their ability to develop and expand the full dynamics of their music (familiarity aided utilization). I have also been extremely impressed by the general level of musicianship I have experienced in Holland. This is true for individual musicians as well as the ensembles. The basic craftsmanship I have experienced in Holland is among the most sophisticated I have heard in creative music. I believe the composite continuum of Dutch creative music promises to be an important factor for creative music as we move into the new cycle.

Germany

Quite possibly, the situation in Germany seems to be the most conducive to creative music in this time zone. Not only are there more performing outlets for the musicians scattered throughout the country, but there is also an audience generally concerned about the music. Germany is one of the few countries with enough work where a musician can sustain himself from his craft, without having to resort to either popular forms of music or a regular day job. This is not to say everything in Germany with regard to creative music is perfect—because it isn't, but to comment on the actual reality of present day Germany as compared to the rest of Europe or America is to be made aware of the many extra possibilities this one country has. Nor have I meant to imply that the situation of the creative improvising musician in Germany is on the same level as that of the popular or classical musician—this has never been the case for any country. Nevertheless, it is possible to look at the developments in creative music from the middle sixties until now and see that much positive work has been done to create both outlets and a general appreciation of creative music in Germany—obviously this must be true, for the scene in Germany has attracted musicians from all over the world.

As far as the creativity from this environment is concerned, I find Germany to be somewhat like America in the sense that there is more than one or two major creative thrusts functioning on various levels. In short, the actual creativity of Germany is broadly manifested—regardless of focus. It is in Germany where one can find musicians of the magnitude of Albert Mangelsdorff, for instance. His ability to function in so many areas of creative music makes it difficult to catalog his work. A survey of contemporary German music would include a Mangelsdorff on one end and a musician like Peter Brötzmann on the other (yet these types of analogies are dangerous, for they tend to suggest that these musicians operate as separate thrusts when, in fact, Mangelsdorff and Brötzmann often play together). Yet it is possible to impose certain separations on the movements that emerged in Germany in the last ten years—as a means to comment on the overall developments affecting the music since 1960. The most significant of these developments would probably be the post-

CMOA(I)–30

Ayler movement that emerged in the early sixties to become a catalyst for the developments shaping present-day creative music in Germany. This movement has functioned as the most important factor for establishing the transformation of both present established political factors (the people who have controlled the music outlets and power since the initiation of bebop and the post-Webern movement since the early fifties) and the functional arena that surrounds creative music as it applies to creating alternative outlets for performance. Rather than attempt cataloging the whole spectrum of creativity in Germany, and run the risk of making mistakes—since I am not really aware of all the developments taking place in that country—I would prefer to concentrate instead on the activity of the post-Ayler movement and, in particular, the Globe Unity Orchestra and its members.

The Globe Unity Orchestra is a collective European ensemble that consists of musicians from all over Europe. This ensemble makes its home in Germany and as of this period is celebrating ten years of creative music as a unit. The Globe Unity Orchestra is an ensemble that has directed its interests to the challenge of post-Ayler concepts for the open-ended improvisation creative arena. The music director of Globe Unity is Alexander Von Schlippenbach, and under his guidance, the orchestra has pursued many different approaches to creative music. Whatever the difficulties that this group has had—and it has been difficult in many periods—the ten year existence of the Globe Unity Orchestra shows a degree of unification that is absent in America. The gains which have been made through this orchestra are directly related to the struggles of the last decade. This perseverance is especially important if one realizes that the orchestral implications of American creative music has suffered enormously in the last ten years because of the lack of existing outlets for rehearsal, practice, and performing. There have been many sporadic ensembles in America participating in creative music, but most of these have been short-lived.

The Experimental Band of the AACM was important to the developments which came out of Chicago, but even this ensemble did not fulfill the potential of its position (the potential being, a truly democratic ensemble that would work to fashion the various ideas of all AACM composers). In short, while creative ensembles in America formed and dissolved, the activity of the Globe Unity Orchestra continued, and it would be in the interest of the music if the end product that has come from this longevity were taken seriously.

The music that the Globe Unity Orchestra creates in this time zone is an actualization of the composite-vibrationaltory approach of its membership—and this, of course, is the desired relationship of any large ensemble. The basic focus of the orchestra is open improvisation and because of this, the orchestra tries to provide as much open space (or lack of composition) as possible. In many regards this area of Globe Unity approach can be looked at as a direct extension of post-Coltrane concepts. It was in the early sixties that Coltrane recorded his composition "Ascension," and the functional devices of that music would become the basis of many of the extensions I have heard in the music of the Globe Unity Orchestra. The characteristics of a normal given performance in that context by the Globe Unity (in the middle seventies) would reveal a very dense conceptual approach like "Ascension" and this is also true for its utilization of sound (timbre) and rhythmic-pulse factor (and mass density). This, then, is the first post-Coltrane orchestral thrust in that regard—and the members of the Globe Unity consider this structural setting to be an extremely important area of their work. I do not, however, mean to simply reduce the activity of the Globe Unity Orchestra to one viewpoint—because this is not the case. The "Ascension" type of functional arena is only the basis that these musicians have adopted—the actual music is very different from Coltrane's music.

The Globe Unity Orchestra also functions from a compositional framework as well, and in Alexander Von Schlippenbach, the orchestra has one of the strongest new composers to have emerged in the sixties. Schlippenbach has shown himself to be a composer with a dynamic range to draw from. In his position as music director, he has helped to broaden the compositional implications of creative music in Germany. Schlippenbach is a composer who has utilized many different compositional techniques—from graft music to fragmentary processes. Under his guidance, the orchestra has acquired quite a broad range of possibilities for a given performance. Nor is Schlippenbach the only composer who has molded the direction of Globe Unity, for the composer-trombonist Paul Rutherford and bassist Peter Kowald have shown themselves to be gifted and important composers (and many other members of Globe Unity have also contributed important works as well). The Globe Unity Orchestra has even recorded a piece of Jelly Roll Morton's, as well as an impressive arrangement of Thelonious Monk's "Ruby, My Dear" by Schlippenbach. Basically, in the last ten years the orchestra has tried to keep compositions at a minimum and, instead, concentrate on open music. Whether or not this policy will continue to be the rule for the next period of the orchestra's development is for us to wait and see (for there is no way to know). But the emphasis on open structure rather than composition is a factor that permeates creative German music in this period (late seventies). Practically three-fourths of the ensembles involved in new approaches to creative music in Germany have shown little interest in composition. Many of the musicians are instead interested in shaping the sound arena of their creativity through elementation, or through sequence planning (i.e., determining the order of solos or combination of players in a given context).

In the last five or six years, other factors have begun to move into the Globe Unity's approach to orchestral ensemble music. One of these factors has been compositions with more melodic-type lead arrangements—most of these are single or double line unisons that are used as propulsion devices for the soloist. This approach has been found to be extremely satisfying to many members of the orchestra, and several effective compositions have come from this technique. The most commonly used performance tool of the Globe Unity is the fast-pulse situation for soloists within a dense sound arena. In every case, the pulse functions as a rhythmic generating factor, yet to my knowledge, the Globe Unity has no use for tempo either as a compositional factor, or as a possible soloist-support possibility. The orchestra functions as an outlet for advancements which have been made in post-Cageian and post-Ayler new creative techniques, and addresses its attention on what these advancements imply for the needs of individual musicians inside the orchestra (in other words, there is no tempo consideration in this ensemble because everybody likes it that way).

Because most of the membership of the Globe Unity Orchestra is spread throughout the continent and work situations are difficult to create, the actual group probably comes together en masse maybe three or four times a year. It is a testament to the individual musicians that a group this large has been able to survive a decade with no sign of stopping. In various time zones, the orchestra has also invited guests to come and work with them—I have had the honor to receive one of these invitations—and for a period of two weeks and some, toured with the ensemble playing creative music. The time these musicians have put into this orchestra has been important for the composite music—and the Globe Unity Orchestra is slowly emerging to the greater public's awareness during this period. In the last year, the ensemble has performed throughout Europe and plans are being made to extend their borders even further. Some of the developments helping to change the situation of the orchestra are coming from the present power structure in Germany—it is only in this period where efforts have been made to change the neglect of this most important group. The orchestra has now found itself invited to many outlets that had previously refused to accept their activity—and this change is undoubtedly a sign that things are now beginning to change.

The work of the Free Music Production (FMP)—which is an organization of musicians in Germany—has been an important factor reshaping the political arena surrounding the German creative musicians' reality. This group has functioned on a number of levels related to the music and music business. Without doubt, the most important work of this organization has been the forming of alternative recording outlets. In the last five years (and some), the FMP has properly documented the developments reshaping creative German music. The documentation from this organization represented one of the first collective attempts of its kind, and the response to this phenomenon has necessitated a growing respect for the integrity of their membership (by the power structure in Germany). It will perhaps be some time before the records of FMP are properly distributed and available throughout the whole of Europe and

America (this is true for alternative record companies everywhere), but the forming of FMP represented an important move towards the establishment of alternative outlets for composite German creative music. The last ten years have shown that these musicians were right in moving toward unification. The next ten years will show the effect of that unification on many different levels.

The activity of FMP did not simply stop at recording the music either, but instead expanded to deal with other avenues of concern for the creative improvisor. The FMP was the main force behind the forming of an alternative festival in Berlin—the Total Music Meeting—and for five years and some, this festival has competed with the Berlin Jazz Festival very successfully. So real were the successes of the alternative festival by the FMP that in 1976, the established festival practically used all of the musicians from the alternate festival for their own festival. It is this type of activity which is helping to change the present situation in Germany. For even though Germany has emerged to be the best country for contemporary improvised music in this time cycle, there are still many challenges which must be met.

The festival situation is particularly interesting in Germany for many reasons. This was among the first countries to establish festivals for alternative creative music. (Today, some of these festivals are trying to broaden and present every aspect of the music—but even in this regard they are innovative. In other words, instead of the usual progression of starting only with earlier forms and gradually using new music, the festivals in Germany have started with contemporary music and are gradually attempting to broaden their spectrum for both presentation and programming purposes—yet the emphasis is still on the newer forms.) The forming of the Total Music Meeting and the Moers International Festival of New Music was both a response to the existing situation in Germany and a desire to change it. Both of these festivals have been enormously successful, and have served as an example to other outlets in Europe. The Hamburg Festival and Willisau Festival (in Willisau, Switzerland) are only two of the outlets which have emerged in the wake of Berlin and Moers. All of these changes have only increased the dynamics of

European creative postulation, and the future of European creativity is not separate from what this multi-phenomenon means as well. I have only lightly touched this subject in my writings—which is to say, all of my observations are necessarily limited. The real documentation about this subject will, hopefully, materialize in the coming decade.

(Level One) France, Italy, Northern Europe, Japan

To really understand the significance of creative music from the black aesthetic is to view the dynamics of its progressional spread throughout the planet. For the arrival of black creativity has changed the composite nature of every environment exposed to its dynamics. Nor is this phenomenon a recent development, for to examine the historical realness of expansion dynamics is to see similar developments in the world community. The progressional spread of black creativity is not limited to any one time zone but encompasses the whole of this time cycle. The realness of this phenomenon is not separate from the dissolution of black civilization and the later plundering of African culture. It is possible to view given aspects of African culture in practically every museum in Europe as an example of what transpired in composite progressionalism. Nor should the progressional spread of this phenomenon be viewed in narrow terms. For while a great portion of black culture was "taken" ("stolen" would actually be a better word) and brought to Europe, there was also the activity that came into Europe with the various settlements of black people throughout the continent, involving several different time periods. As such, it is important not to over-accent this phenomenon (for the reality particulars underlining composite progressionalism seem to indicate that the plundering of given culture groups is a cyclic factor). But to understand the realness of what has transpired in black culture, the transfer-shift implications underlying what has taken place on the physical universe level must be examined on some level. It is not just a question of viewing the composite world-transfer implications of creativity—for this phenomenon can be viewed between every cultural thrust (having to do with the dynamics of transition and the fact that every culture has incorporated and appreciated the creativity of other cultures)—rather, it is a question of understanding the special position black creativity has (and black culture—even though it is now dispersed in this time cycle). The fact is, the progressional spread of black creativity must be viewed for what it tells us about the composite reality of affinity dynamics. For the most basic factor that has necessitated this chapter is the present information and reality order underlining how black culture and black people are now exploited and suppressed. In other words, to view the progressional continuance of black creativity is to view the nature of present-day expansion dynamics, and this information is important.

The dynamic spread of black creativity is directly connected to the multi-dimensional implications of transition and transformation. Historically, the effects of this spread can be viewed and understood by focusing on the particulars of physical universe progressionalism. This is not to say creativity from the black aesthetic is responsible for all of the activity of the composite world group—because it isn't—but rather, the cross-sectional implications of black creativity are profoundly intertwined with the composite arena of dynamic functionalism and vibrational expansion. This can be understood by viewing the progressional spread of creative black music in the last thirty years, even. Yet the dynamic effect of black creativity is usually perceived in one light, and the musicians and realness of black culture is perceived in another light. In actual terms, the progressional spread of creative black music must be viewed for how it has dynamically affected the world community (and in particular western culture) and also for how (after a given time cycle) the actual musicians and black people in general are penalized as a result of that effect. Because the cross-sectional implication of black creativity is always accompanied by a move to "make both the music and the musicians 'less' than what they are." Another way of saying this is that after the thrust of a given projection of black creativity is perceived as "understood," it is always accompanied by a rejection of black musicians and culture—with the understanding being that "black music has not brought us anything we didn't already have"—or that "what we have made of what you have given us is better." This phenomenon is essential to understand if one is to view the progressional spread of black creativity—on whatever level. The effects of this sentiment are profoundly related to present-day expansionalism.

POL.DY.------PROG.CONT.

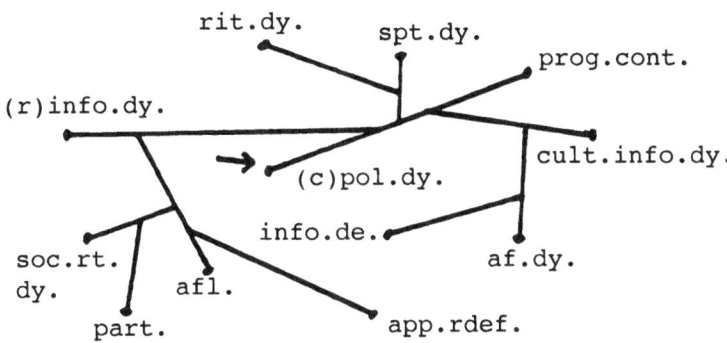

(R)GRAD.------SOC.RT.

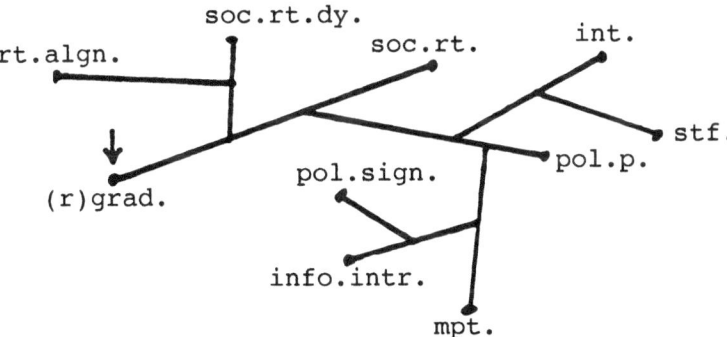

The planet expansion of post-Parker creativity can be viewed as related to the social-reality implications of the Second World War—and the subsequent interest (focus) on creative black music that solidified in that period profoundly affected the vibrational creative arena of both western Europe and Japan. This would be the period which would see the resolidification and rebuilding that took place after the Second World War. The resulting affinity focus on (attraction to) creative black music that emerged in that same period must be viewed as not separate from the composite nature of European continuance. This is not to say that creative black music per se supplied the alternative center factor for post-war Europe and Japan, rather that the (affinity focus) attraction to creative black music which took place in that time cycle would be a vibrational factor related to the spirit of composite alternative dynamics. To view creative developments (particulars) since the middle forties in Europe and/or Japan might surprise many Americans, for the last thirty years (and some) have seen the progressional lineage of many competent and creative musicians—which is to say, the European creative musicians I have previously focused on as representing this time cycle are not unique in the sense that their activity represents something without precedent—and it is important to keep this in mind. There have been many significant individuals participating in creative music from the black aesthetic from both Europe and Japan, and this is true regardless of sector. It is possible to look at countries like Sweden and see the dynamic activity of musicians like Lars Gullin as an example of the progressional realness of projectional spread—and in this respect, Gullin was not unique either. For if the awareness of the music was directly related to the end of the Second World War cycle, the dynamics of this awareness were not separate from whatever region the music visited. Which is to say, the dynamic spread of post-Parker creativity can be viewed by understanding the option-spread particulars related to what areas given musicians were in. In this regard, both the consideration of tour arrangements as well as the service (e.g., the Army in particular) installations would have multi-dynamic implications. For the progressional effect of these considerations would provide some basis for the transfer-shift solidification of trans-African, trans-Western, trans-American, and extended bebop functionalism.

LK.IMP.------TRS.

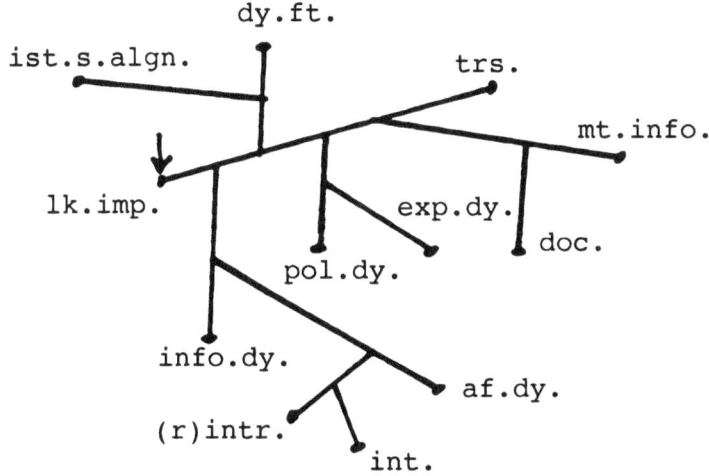

(R)C.INFO.------TH.CONT.

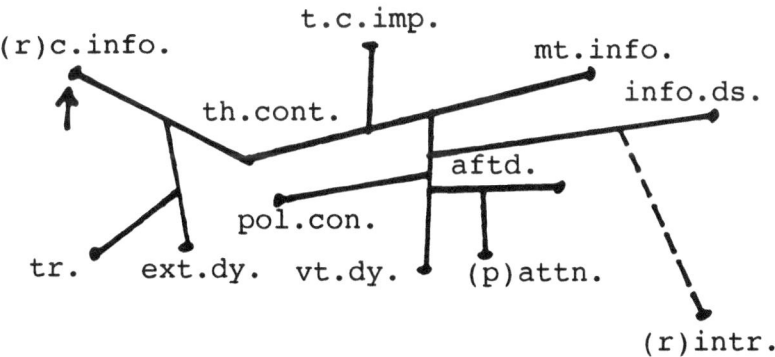

The influence (and impact) of given touring ensembles should not be viewed in narrow terms, for the exposure and effect generated through live performance is directly related to how the composite music was perceived (experienced). Yet the realness of this phenomenon should not be overgeneralized either, for the actual particulars of a given culture (country) profoundly affect the political and economic factors related to its attraction motivation. For example, the exposure of live creative music in Britain was different from that of France—in terms of its surrounding political and controlling factors—yet the ensuing interest that developed in Britain was not different from what transpired in France. To view the time cycle of the middle forties to the middle fifties is to see how the composite focus of bebop was actualized on a dynamic level.

This would be the cycle that determined the progressional resolidification of both Europe and Japan—and this phenomenon is not separate from its composite vibrational implications (including its creativity and attraction mechanisms). To understand how this spread has happened (as a positive factor for world culture) is to deal with the end result of what has been brought about in the actual creativity. Not to mention that the European affinity focus on bebop is not separate from its affinity adaptation of composite black creativity—regardless of projections. That is, the progressional adaptation of post-Parker creativity in Europe (and Japan) is related to the principal interest in black postulation dynamics. This interest developed as a result of the composite projectional spread of black creative invention in the last three thousand years. The dynamic realness of this phenomenon would be of profound importance to the resolidification of post-war Europe and Japan. To understand how black creativity has assumed this position is to have some basis for viewing the present world situation—that being, the dynamic implications of trans-affinity dynamics (creativity) as a composite world consideration.

AFI.------(R)PART.OR.POST.

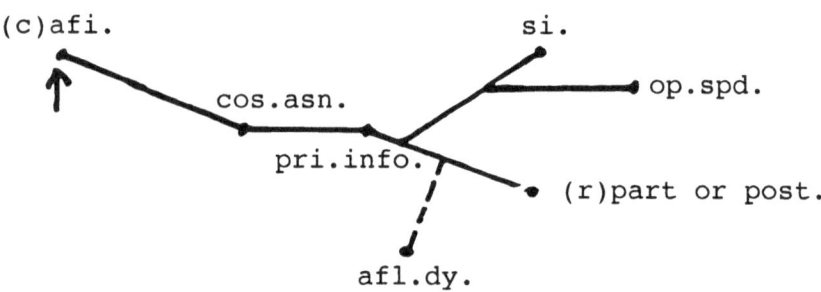

The progressional expansion of creative black music must be viewed on many levels. For the spread of black creativity is not related to only particular projections, but rather includes the total realness of the music. One cannot underestimate the dynamic effect of musicians like James Reece Europe, whose ensembles performed throughout Europe—giving an example of the brilliance of black marching music—as well as the many performances of black church music that took place throughout the continent. All of these factors are related to the progressional spread of black creativity—whether we are focusing on the time zone of the forties or whatever. For it must be understood that the projectional dynamics of black creativity are viewed for their composite realness in Europe (and Japan), as opposed to what is happening in America. Moreover, because of this perception, Europe in many ways can be viewed as more aware about black creativity than most Americans, for the social reality that dictates how events are perceived in America moves to discard and isolate information—including the composite continuity of creativity—making a total viewpoint extremely difficult (especially for the greater public, as opposed to given specialists). The emergence of bebop in Europe was perceived within the composite continuity of black creativity, and the dynamic of bebop would gain its significance for what it signaled and implied about the changing reality dynamics of post-war Europe and Japan. The truth of this viewpoint can even be seen in this cycle, for the affinity focus towards black creativity in Europe has consistently tried to deal with the composite spectrum of the music.

It has only been in the last decade—the sixties—where the composite interpretations of European culture have moved to isolate particular projections of black creativity—and this isolation really has more to do with the changing social and political factors that are presently reshaping Europe (especially concerning the emancipation of the next cycle of European creative musicians) rather than with the music.

APP.RDEF. -----STF. ------SOC.RT.

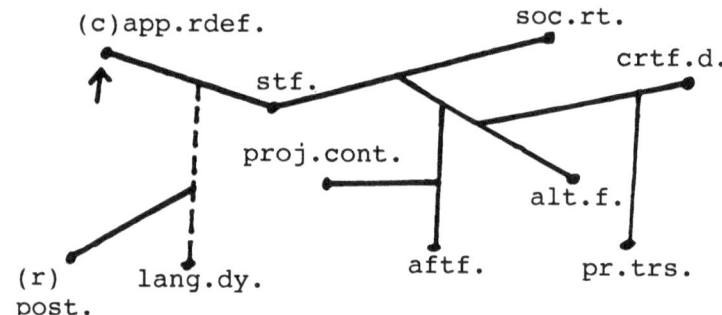

(R)CRTF.D.----POL.DY.

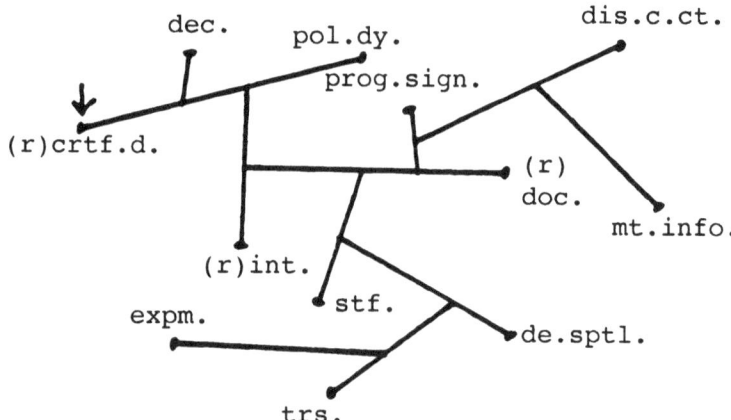

(R)INFO.DOC. ------CULT.SOLD.

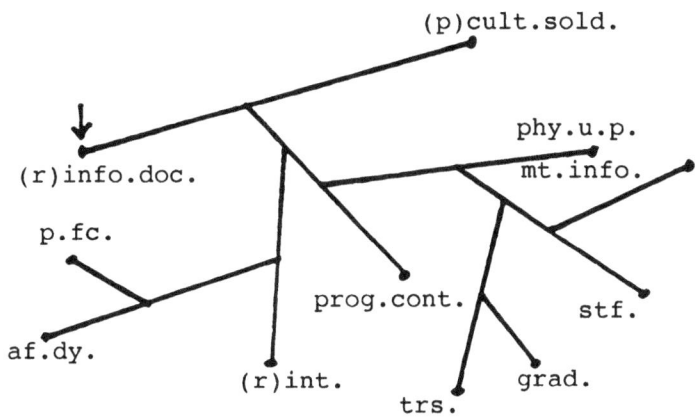

France

The projectional realness of black creativity in France can be viewed with respect to the composite factors I spoke of concerning the post–World War period—and even before the First World War. The fact is, black creativity has long enjoyed the support of the French public on many different levels. It is possible to see practically all of the musicians whom we have now come to respect as major contributors to the music on French television—at any given time. The exposure given to the music and the information related to that exposure would surprise many Americans. There are, and have always been, radio programs devoted to the music, and (unlike America) these programs broadcast the total spectrum of the music. Nor is the influence of creative black music simply felt on television or radio, because throughout the entire country one can see many examples of live music. Practically every small town has its own "maison de la culture" that exists for bringing in live music. What is interesting, however, is that practically all of the concert schedules of a given season have the inclusion of creative black music as well as western art music, etc. The end result of this development is that most people in France have some level of awareness about creative black music—which is not to say that every given person must necessarily like every aspect—or projection—of the music, but only that the chance to experience the music does exist. The realness of creativity can also be viewed as an important factor in the intellectual and cultural sectors of France, and the spirit of the music is not separate from the vibrational nature underlying how French culture views "alternativism." For this reason, many musicians have come to play and live in France. It is not just a question of having the possibility to perform one's music, rather, the lure of France represents, for many musicians, a chance to exist in a society that is really concerned about creativity.

Probably the single factor most responsible for the fact that musicians seem to naturally gravitate to France is the vibrational reality of the country itself—and this is particularly true of Paris. The vibrational dynamics of Paris have always been attractive to creative people because of the uniqueness of its social reality and the beauty of the city. In many ways, Paris can be viewed as representing the same position as New York City in America, for the composite vibration of this city is not only indicative of its principal culture but is also international. The resultant vibration of the city reflects the composite spectrum of many different people and influences, and as such, represents an attractive space to function from and/or perform in. Many musicians from America have lived in this city at one time or another, and musicians like Sidney Bechet were quite influential in the total culture. (France was one of the first—if not the first—countries to erect a statue of a creative musician as a gesture of respect for the music and respect for the accomplishments of the particular musician—who in this case was Sidney Bechet.) The attractiveness of Paris as a center for creative arts was not only for musicians, but artists from every medium. Practically every area of creativity is dealt with in Paris, and the resultant vibration that surrounds the city has helped to create an attractive aura around the city. In the time zone of a given year, practically all of the artists who are perceived as being significant on some level can be experienced performing in this one city. The end result of all of this activity has shaped the public's awareness of creativity, and the significance of Paris is related to what this awareness has brought about in actual terms.

Yet I have not meant to imply that the composite time realness of Paris can be viewed as constant with respect to the intensity of its relationship to any given medium or projection (of creativity)—because this is never the case. There are always particular cycles which are more intense than other cycles, and the progressional dynamics related to creativity must be viewed in this same context (i.e., performances and/or composite public's awareness level). But the basic tone level of Paris can be viewed as being conducive to creativity—and this has proven to be the case with every projection—from creative black music to creative world music. The intensity level of a given period in Paris is usually related directly to what individuals—or groups—are on the scene, or what so-called movement is perceived to be of interest. In many ways, the collective forces of European culture—including Paris—must also be viewed with respect to the spectacle-diversion implications of information focus. This is so because composite Europe has always been somewhat preoccupied with what is deemed "new"—and the intensity realness of a given cycle in Paris can be viewed for how that attitude has affected perception dynamics. But the progressional realness of this region usually moves with respect to the composite spectrum of the music—which is to say, even though the information focus that surrounds the perception of the music can sometimes move to overly isolate particular projections as a means to bring about its awareness on a composite (public) level, or for pseudo-intellectual commentary, for the most part there is a balanced awareness of the total music. To understand Paris's relationship with creative music is to view the historical and particular dynamics of this relationship from the early forms of black creative music to the present. The realness of this relationship can also clarify the reality position of French creative musicians and their role in extended functionalism. This is especially true if one wants to understand the present reality of creative music in France. For the realness of Paris and its historical dynamics (concerning its relationship to the music) are not separate from what is now happening in this time cycle. The historical significance of Paris's relationship with creative black music is important for what insight it sheds on the present situation that surrounds cross-sectional progressionalism.

 Perhaps the factor that most distinguishes France—and its French musicians' community—is that, unlike in northern Europe, there have been no attempts to nationally unify its functionalism on a composite level. There are no alternative musicians' collectives, at least not in the same sense as in Germany or Amsterdam. To my knowledge, there are not even small pockets of isolated small groups functioning from one given viewpoint (and if this situation has changed, then it is a recent development). The realness of this dis-unification is probably related to the internationalism of Paris as a cross-vibrational platform for many different kinds of musicians—and people. Yet even in places like New York City and Berlin there are effective collectives of creative musicians—which is to say, it would not necessarily be correct to simply reduce Paris' dis-unification to any one factor. I have cited the international realness of Paris as contributing to the fact that no collectives have emerged because many French musicians of note can usually be heard performing with either American or other European groups—and undoubtedly the internationalism of Paris has promoted this development. Certainly a group like the Cohelmec Ensemble is an example of creative French music from a composite basis, but this ensemble is not the norm. Only a handful of French ensembles have been able to sustain or attract the attention of the French music community. There are probably many other worthwhile collectives of note which have not had an opportunity to have their activity experienced on a "real" level. Because to deal with the reality particulars underlying what French collectives are up against is to understand the natural competition factors that surround a scene like Paris. In a given week, there could be any number of concerts throughout the city—and as a result of this diversity, the audience support factor is necessarily selective. This is not only the case in Paris, but every large city has this problem. But if that city has the dynamics of Paris—and the artistic intensity as well—then the seriousness of this phenomenon is compounded. I have not meant to imply that any given French collective must somehow be less dynamic than any other attraction presented in its same time slot—this is not my point at all. Rather, the social-reality realness of France does not move to necessarily give the native French musician—and/or collective—the same regard that is generally acknowledged in other areas of its greater cultural creativity. It is this "non-expectation" which characterizes the dilemma French musicians are dealing with in this cycle. For while it is clear that the progressional spread of the music has actualized from outside of France, it is also clear that without high expectations, and public support, the social reality of French musicians will remain difficult.

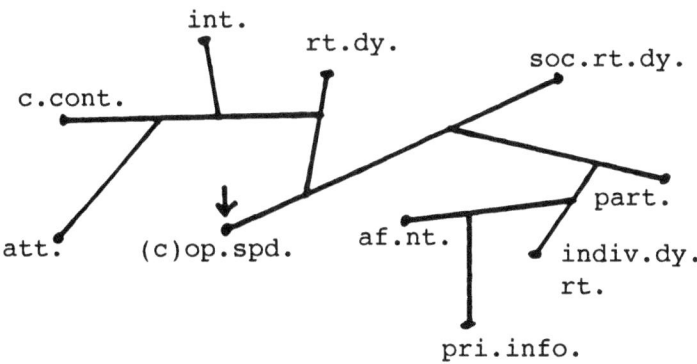

There are many factors related to the creative music scene in France. For to deal with the reality of creative music is to understand the composite considerations which determine how given individuals participate in every aspect of affinity postulation. If we are to view the creative French musician and understand the present physical universe particulars of his (her) position, then we must first understand the many other factors dictating the reality specifics of this subject. The fact is, if there is one factor related to the sparsity of French creative musicians, that factor would have to do with present-day French music education. The music education system in France can be viewed as quite possibly the worst of its kind—especially if we are focusing on creative improvisation as opposed to traditional classical music. The real reality and pedagogy of creative music is passed on separately from the educational institutions—from individual to individual. This has always been the case with creative music (even in America)—yet the situation in France cannot be viewed without understanding its special vibrational particulars. Many of the schools in France are even more oppressive than the schools in America. And the phenomenon of cultural programming in these institutions is also much more intensive in many respects. France has always prided herself on the spectrum of her informational and vibrational dynamics. In actual terms, the historical realness of this culture has long assumed accented importance—and with that context in mind, this pride is understandable. This is a country full of history, and every day one is reminded of this—even by walking down the street. On one hand, this ability to maintain history is applaudable—for the historical progressions of a given cultural group are important to the life potential of that culture—yet, on the other hand, the challenge of this cycle calls for a non-isolationist awareness—and multi-composite information. The dynamics of the creative French musician must be viewed with respect to what all of these complexities mean in actual and vibrational terms, and this is most certainly true for the option-spread dynamics of collective functionalism.

(R)TR.INFO.   -----ACC.DY.

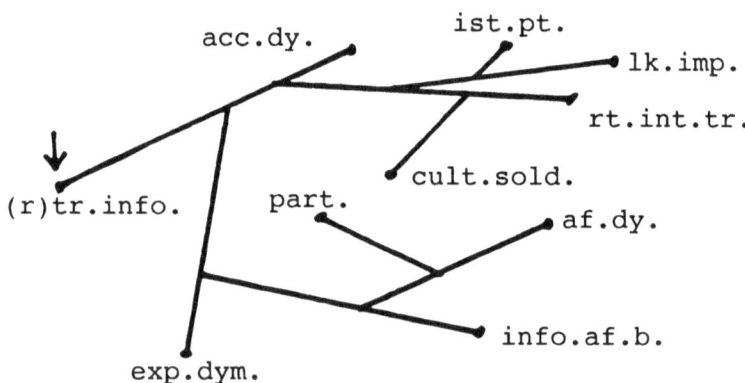

By commenting on the dynamic reality complexities of post-war France, I have not meant to imply that no important creativity has developed through French culture—because only a light examination of this subject would show otherwise. France has long been involved in creative music throughout its history. It was in France that the activity of Django Reinhardt was to solidify—which is to say, France is the home of several very important musicians who have contributed to the music.

In this time zone, one can view Stéphane Grappelli as one of the most dynamic musicians in this time cycle. His creative activity has generated interest throughout the world and he has also sustained a very high level of craftsmanship and creative invention—for many generations. In fact, the emergence of Reinhardt's and Grappelli's activity can be viewed with respect for its composite implications concerning creative collectivism. Both of these great musicians were shaped through their work in a collective musicians' community in France (yet Reinhardt's development cannot be exclusively viewed as developed and shaped in any one planet sector). This phenomenon must be viewed for what it signifies about the progressional spread of French creativity.

The present cycle in French creativity can be viewed with respect to the dynamics of individuals, rather than collectives (yet it is important that I state that my observations are necessarily limited in this regard—which is to say, I am basing this section from my own experiences and observations—and there is the real possibility that there are at least four hundred collectives functioning in France that I am ignorant of—and this must be stated), and there are many brilliant musicians whose activity can be viewed in these terms. The projectional realness of French creativity must also be viewed with respect to the dynamic spread of its individuals, for the reality spread of French musicians is no different from the rest of humanity. It is possible to view musicians who are contributing to the traditional thrust of the music as well as those who function in what are now called "non-traditional forms," and this is true of social-reality particulars as well. To experience a musician like Eddy Louiss performing organ with Stan Getz—using either traditional standards or original compositions—is to understand the dynamics and beauty offered through creative French musicians to the composite whole of the music—and this is not an isolated example.

The transition cycle that occurred in the sixties would see the emergence of several important French musicians, and the importance of this, their creativity, would have multi-dimensional implications. In this cycle, musicians like François Tusques would begin making his influence felt, and the cross-sectional dynamics of his activity would extend into many different areas of creativity. This is also true of musicians like Daniel Humair, who, while being of Swiss extraction, settled in Paris in the middle sixties. Humair has demonstrated his activity in many different contexts—working with such diverse musicians as Phil Woods, Michel Portal, and Joachim Kühn. In each of these contexts, he has shown himself to be an extremely talented and creative musician, and the thrust of his activity has been a positive impetus for the composite creative scene in Paris. Siegfried Kessler must also be mentioned for the work that he has done in both his own trios as well as his work with musicians like Archie Shepp. And finally—to view the realness of creative music in Paris would be meaningless if the activity of Georges Arvanitas were not mentioned, for the work that he has done has contributed greatly to the composite scene in Paris—both in its own right, and also in its contribution to guest musicians. Many musicians have long used Arvanitas's trio as a support group when performing in Paris. His ensemble has functioned as a pivotal factor in French creative music.

The progressional development of creative French music must be viewed on many different levels, for the composite spectrum of its contributing musicians is extremely diverse. This is especially true if one is to deal with the realness of a musician like J. F. Jenny-Clark—whose music reality transcends singular focuses. Jenny-Clark's works represent the state of the art of bass playing—and this is true on any level (which is to say, I am not saying that the brilliance of his activity is only real in French culture —rather, this musician's creativity can be viewed for what it implies on a composite world level). The diversificational spread of Jenny-Clark's activity can be experienced in both its western art music context—he has functioned as a member of various notated ensembles—and his improvisational work (e.g., with musicians like Gato Barbieri or Keith Jarrett). In every medium, he has greatly contributed to the music. The music of Michel Portal has also helped to bridge the gap between notated and improvised music. His various ensembles—as well as his work with Vinko Globokar—have helped to make him very influential in his own right. All of these musicians have solidified the reality of creative music in France (and, of course, there are many others as well).

The creative notated classical community is another development that must be understood if one is to view the reality dynamics of present-day French creativity. The realness of this sector must be viewed in still separate terms from the improvisational community—and there are many reasons for this. For if the actualness of non-collectivism characterized the composite social-reality tendencies of the improvising community, then the opposite is true for the classical contemporary community. The composite solidification of French contemporary music can be viewed as both highly organized and focused. I do not mean to imply that there are no differences in the classical community whatsoever, because obviously people always differ on something—nor have I meant to ignore the fact that there are several "so-called" opposing movements, which cannot work together. But the greater majority of musicians in French contemporary music function from a composite unified stance, and even the opposing groups are organized—on some level. The end result of this organizing is that many government-sponsored forms of assistance have been secured for their objectives—both in the form of grants and in the construction of buildings and relevant technology. Without doubt, the central figure most responsible for this phenomenon is Pierre Boulez. It was Boulez who organized the now defunct Domaine Musical (an organization which produced contemporary concerts throughout the whole of the year). Domaine Musical gave performances of many different composers, not only French but also German and American. This group also sponsored concerts by composers like Karlheinz Stockhausen or Luciano Berio, and gave European premieres of works from Elliott Carter or Robert Crumb. The effect of this organizing would create a very special momentum for creative notated music in France, and this phenomenon would also play an important role in the projectional spread of the music as well. Moreover, the realness of sophisticated organization would help advance the work of contemporary composers to the greater public. For it must be understood that the performing outlet realness of the contemporary music scene was not limited only to outlets in Paris but extended throughout the whole of France. The dynamic organization of these performing outlets would extend their influence into every aspect of French culture—and as a result of these efforts, France today is a very healthy country with regard to its exposure of contemporary music. The later collapse of Domaine Musical would lead to the forming of IRCAM, which now functions as a potentially important factor in music research and/or performance. (The real effectiveness of this development remains to be seen. For it must be understood that one of the most basic problems surrounding the contemporary scene in Paris is its inability to open to what it perceives as being "outside" or "outsiders," which seems to be nine-tenths of the world's creative community.) Nevertheless, the facilities this organization has secured must be viewed as potentially positive.

The diversity of present-day French contemporary music organizations has moved to create a healthy vibrational state throughout the country. For if the facilities of IRCAM are not available to many sectors of the creative community, the end result of this exclusion has brought many positive effects. The spectrum of creative communities existing now in Paris can be viewed as very exciting. For while there is IRCAM on one end, representing the established wing of the contemporary music community, there are also individual efforts by composers like Iannis Xenakis to establish alternative organizations and/or outlets. Xenakis has constructed his own electronic studio for creative music, and the solidification of this center has created even more opportunities for the creative musician. Add to this the many open studios which have been developing in the last seven to ten years and one might have some idea about the dynamic state of contemporary music in France. The reality of composite creativity in France is not separate from the particulars of its social reality—which is to say, the dynamic spread of creativity in France during this cycle gives some insight into the role France will have in the future. Obviously the few particulars I have cited do not sum up the whole of French creativity. One can only speculate about the composite state of so vast a subject. I do believe, however, that the state of creative music in France is positive. In this country, one can view many dynamic continuums of activity affecting every avenue of creativity. The realness of this diversity promises to help define the next cycle in earth creativity—which is to say, the work taking place in France in this period will have much to offer humanity. The state of creativity in France is indeed healthy.

Italy

The reality dynamics of creative music in Italy must be viewed in very different terms from France. For to understand the events which have transpired in Italy since the middle sixties—on the social and physical universe levels—is to become aware of the nature of its current progression in the seventies. At present, Italy is dealing with realness of change on several levels (i.e., vibrational and actual), and the cosmic implications of this phenomenon are also directly related to what has taken place in its affinity relationship with creativity. Yet I have not meant to imply that composite Italian creativity can only be viewed in limited terms, because creativity—regardless of planet sector—functions with respect to its own laws—and as such, is not limited to one given stratum. But there can be no denying the special dynamics underlying the present cycle this country is now going through—which is to say, there is no way Italian creativity could avoid the composite implications related to this cycle and still be real. The particulars of this time zone are of great importance to the progressional continuance of Italy for future generations. Because the present changes reshaping this country will have much to do with both its political and economic response to future change. To be in Italy during this cycle is to experience another level of excitement and political awareness—for at present there are many questions in the air. Moreover, the progressional continuance of this cycle has brought a pronounced intensity in the search for alternative viewpoints. The realness of cultural focus in this context must be taken very seriously, because the changing social and physical universe reality of Italy seems to forecast profound insight about the composite change dynamics of western culture. It is not just a question of over-generalization (e.g., "as Italy goes, so goes Europe")—but rather, the changing physical universe situation happening now in Italy should not be lightly viewed if we desire composite understanding. At present, the vibrational desire for change in this country is manifested on many different levels, and the alternative functionalism actualized from those desires will give insight into the nature of the next cycle of world progressionalism. Yet I have not meant to give the impression that the "tone level" of Italy can be viewed as mono-dynamic—that being, of limited scope or focused only on matters of political interest—because while many factors are being re-examined, the life realness of Italian society is just as diverse and dynamic as ever. The creativity taking place in this cycle affirms this diversity, and any attempt to view the changing creative transition now taking place in Europe would most certainly involve what has happened (and is happening) in Italy.

In many ways, the vibrational dynamics of Italian culture can be viewed in extreme terms, and this is especially true in creativity. For if the post-Ayler creative movement had practically no effect in Italy during the earlier sixties (even though many musicians from both America and Europe had performed throughout the country in that decade), by the middle seventies the music had become the primary focus of many different alternative-functioning groups. Even more interesting is the fact that the gradual acceptance of post-Ayler creativity by those groups would move to discredit the composite music because of the nature underlying their perception of extended dynamics. For creative music, and in particular creative black music from the post-Ayler junction, would come to be viewed by these groups as directly relevant to the social-reality tenets of Italian culture in the context of spectacle—like in America. This phenomenon was inevitable. For the post-Ayler projectional thrust did represent a dynamic and revolutionary extension of creativity (not to mention, the dynamics of this thrust were also embraced by alternative-functioning groups in America). The adoption and gradual awareness of post-Ayler forms in the seventies would have considerable impact in Italian "perceived" revolutionism, and between 1972 and 1977 one could find many American musicians performing their music in Italy. For while the music was associated with the underground—in terms of what it posed with regard to alternative ideology and functionalism—on the other hand, the sophistication of alternative cultural movements in Italy would create better performance possibilities than the political establishment. The performing possibilities that developed in Italy during this period extended throughout the whole country—from north to south, east to west.

There were many other factors related to the transition cycle that occurred in the early seventies in Italy. Certainly one cannot overlook the power of the music itself—especially if some of the musicians are mentioned. For musicians like Don Cherry would have a profound impact and effect on the Italian music scene, and his work would be extremely important for how it contributed to the overall awareness of the scene. Later, groups like the Art Ensemble of Chicago would have an important effect as well. This would be the first AACM group to really tour throughout the country. It cannot be over-emphasized that because of the progressional controlling factors of the sixties (i.e., performing outlets and recording), the work of individual ensembles took on added importance. For the success of those groups in the early seventies is directly responsible for the activity that would follow. Up until the seventies time cycle, the most performances anyone could expect in Italy was one or two concerts a year (e.g., come into a given city, from maybe a thousand miles, and perform maybe one concert and leave the country). The impact that would result from these new performances must be viewed with the work musicians like Steve Lacy contributed in the middle to late sixties. For Lacy was an important catalyst in opening up Italy to alternative creativity (through his performances as well as teaching). Lacy would also become an important catalyst for cross-sectional activity—involving the composite improvisational community in Italy. His activity within this area would have a profound impact on Italian creative music, and creative music in general.

To understand transitional Italy at the beginning of the seventies would be to deal with the nature underlying how given aspects of the scene were politically controlled—and this is particularly true with creativity. One reason alternative creativity proceeded at a snail's pace in Italy during the sixties is that the established performing outlets were reserved for only the most traditional forms of creativity. As such, Italy could be viewed as extremely conducive for bebop performances but not for extended projections. The time zone of the late sixties would thus see the optimum performance outlets utilized only for established musicians of that genre, and while much great music would ensue, the progressional realness of this situation necessitated alternative attempts to establish separate outlets for post-Ayler creativity. In a time zone of only two years—from 1974 to 1976—one could see many changes in the Italian creative scene as a result of those attempts, and by the middle seventies, the music scene in Italy would see a reversal of its creative information focus. Yet if the sixties represented the time zone where the collective forces of Italian culture would focus entirely on bebop, the mid-seventies would move to focus entirely on post-Ayler projections to the same extent—which is to say this new interest would move to distort the composite significance of the music in the same sense as the sixties. The end result of this phenomenon would promote separating the total music—with the misunderstanding being that only post-Ayler creativity is viewed as relevant to transformation. Because of this development, Italy can be viewed as similar to America—especially America during the time zone of the sixties (because this same phenomenon took place in America as well). Yet I do not mean to imply that the reality of Italian creative music (and its related information) is the same as in America on every level—because it isn't. Unlike America, Italy has long been a country open to creative music—regardless of form—and the awareness tone level of the culture has always been more conducive to alternative creativity than America. In other words, even in its most difficult cycle, Italy must be viewed as a country that has long had interest in creative improvised music. For this reason, one has always been able to find many musicians—from all planet sectors (regardless of style or medium)—practicing their craft in Italy—even with an audience.

The composite realness of alternative creativity in Italy must be viewed from a broad perspective, because this subject is not limited only to those developments we associate with America. The transition of Italy in the seventies would also encompass the creativity that had been solidifying throughout Europe. Musicians like Evan Parker and Derek Bailey would have an important impact on the developments surrounding Italy as well, and in a given time zone many other musicians from all over Europe would come to perform in Italy. The collective impact of this activity would be an important factor in the vibrational transition of Italian creative music, and the composite realness of the music would be of monumental importance for what it signified about alternative functionalism. For it must be understood that open-improvisational approaches in Italy during this time period were viewed with respect to both the actual music as well as what it implied for alternative functionalism (i.e., politics). In this cycle, one could observe the utilization of creativity as a center impetus for both the forming of new magazines and intellectual dialogue. The sudden awareness of alternative music would also bring forth a whole new generation of writers and organizers. Publications like *Jazz Magazine* and the now defunct *Gong* would suddenly become the spearhead of "new interpretations." By 1978, a complete transition had taken place in creative music consciousness in Italy, and this phenomenon could be viewed as a primary motivational factor (yet to view the music without also recognizing the composite spectrum of creativity—dance, painting, etc.—would of course be a distortion) that would underlie Italian information dynamics.

The work which took place in Italy's contemporary classical community must also be recognized for its contributions to transition. For by the early sixties, composers like Luciano Berio and Luigi Nono would have a dynamic impact on the progressional development of Italian creativity. The realness of this sector of the creative community would underlie the emergence of many different groups of creative musicians—groups whose activity also presented alternatives to the post-Webern serial school. It was in Italy that Musica Elettronica Viva solidified, and this ensemble would come to be important for the breakthroughs it initiated in live electronic music. The ensemble would also be one of the first of the Euro-classical groups to function from a composite aesthetic. Musica Elettronica Viva opened its participation to creative musicians from every sector of the music, working with such diverse people as Steve Lacy and Evan Parker. The nucleus of Viva, Frederic Rzewski, Alvin Curran, and Richard Teitelbaum, have since individually developed to expand this approach on a composite world level. The collective dynamics of all of these musicians must be viewed as a positive asset to the creative music community in Italy. Yet I have not meant to neglect the creative improvising musicians who developed in Italy both during and after the transitional cycle of the sixties. For it is clear that a musician like Enrico Rava has greatly contributed to the scene as well. Rava has worked with a dynamic cross-section of both Italian and American musicians, and the progressional spread of his activity through the sixties and seventies would involve his work with musicians like Lee Konitz and Roswell Rudd—nor is he alone in this context. For the thrust continuum of Italian creativity has also seen the rise of many talented musicians from many conceptual slants. Musicians like Andrea Centazzo can be viewed for the realness of his contributions, and the musician/composer Giorgio Gaslini has also had a profound impact on the scene. At present, Italy is very favorable for creative music in the sense that many different sectors are functioning for the music. This is not to say that there are no problems as well, for my personal scan is necessarily limited and I do not pretend to really know all of the many different variables surrounding what is happening in Italy—on a particular level. My point is only that Italy can be viewed as an extremely interesting country in this time period for what is happening with its composite information dynamics. From what I can tell, the present cycle seems to suggest that the future will be even more exciting.

Northern Europe

The reality dynamics of northern Europe can be viewed quite separately from those of central Europe—and this is true on many levels. Somehow the vibrational continuum of this sector has moved to block the normal feed of cross-sectional information exchange from composite Europe, and in doing so, has accented instead the uniqueness of its own regional affinity dynamics. Sweden and Denmark are very different from Germany and/or the Netherlands—not to mention Italy—and this difference is profoundly reflected in the creativity. It is unfortunate that so little music from this region is distributed on a composite level. Few Americans are even aware of this region's existence (with the exception of the music lately recorded for ECM Records—which is available in America and Japan). To write that many people would be surprised by the activity of this sector is an understatement, for the composite realness of northern Europe is very involved with dynamic creativity regardless of form. This is not to say that my awareness of this subject extends throughout all of northern Europe—because it doesn't. My basic awareness of northern Europe has been shaped by my experiences in Sweden, Denmark, and Norway. At present, I have had no opportunity to learn about—or see—Finland or Greenland. Nevertheless, the dynamic implications of Sweden, Denmark, and Norway clearly signify that something is happening in northern Europe—and it is important to make some effort to understand what this means. For the progressional realness of northern Europe has not just become involved in extended functionalism and alternative creativity—as a recent discovery or new event—but has instead been a dynamic factor in every period of creative music—yet somehow these contributions are not usually recognized. Without doubt, our ignorance of this region is connected to the nature of present-day information dissemination—especially concerning international creativity. This is so because the most basic cross-sectional information that determines present-day western idea formation has to do with information transference (and as such, focus) between countries like America and Germany—America and France—America and Britain—Britain and Germany—America and Italy (however, this affinity relationship has not permeated the composite lining of America's vibrational identity)—Germany and France—Britain and France—and, finally, Germany and Britain. The whole of the composite western vibrational hierarchy in this time zone can be viewed with respect to some aspect of one of these relationships—and this is especially true of America. For by viewing a country like Germany, it is possible to see where the base affinity attitude of many areas of American "participation" have come from (e.g., architecture or technology), and French and British influence can also be seen in this same context. The end result of this phenomenon is that a progressional lack of notice has somehow crept into America's awareness of northern Europe—and this must be changed.

Of course it would be an overstatement to say that America has no relationship to northern Europe, for there have always been Swedish and Danish Americans functioning throughout the whole of this time period (from the very beginning of America as a source-transfer "culture" solidification). Yet the realness of that effect has never been a matter of intense focus or chest-beating, and quite possibly this is the real reason so little is written about the northern European sensibility. For if there is one consideration that characterizes my understanding of northern Europe, that consideration would involve the subtlety of this area—as a region that does not "push" in the way we have come to view things. It is for this reason that so little is written about the accomplishments of American immigrants from northern Europe, and it is also because of this natural unaggressiveness that so little is written about northern Europe's creativity. Hopefully not only will the next cycle focus on this most important subject, but while doing so also adopt some of the dynamics of their attitude.

Sweden

The reality particulars of Sweden are very different from those of any region I have seen in central Europe. Many Americans would undoubtedly be surprised at the wealth of talent this one country has. There is creativity in every sector of this country—whether we are focusing on the dynamics of its large cities or small towns. Moreover, the spectrum of its creative projections is not limited to any one aspect, for in Sweden there has long been both a so-called classical and so-called jazz community, since the emergence of Louis Armstrong's early music. The vibrational realness of this sector has also managed to receive contemporary projections without moving to isolate its particulars from the tradition of the composite music. In other words, I found more receptivity to the whole of dynamic creativity in areas like Sweden than anywhere else in Europe (or America, for that matter). Young musicians are schooled in both the tradition of the music and also taught to respect its extensions—and the thrust of this attitude has helped to create another continuum of relevant musicians in Sweden. Many of the musicians I encountered were among the most capable in Europe: that being, well-rounded and not hemmed in by limited considerations concerning what is music. Sweden alone can boast of being one of the few countries that has encouraged the composite growth of creative music organizations throughout the whole of its territories. This country probably has more creative orchestras than any other country comparable to its size. Hopefully it will be possible for more people to experience the actualness of Swedish creative music as we move towards the next cycle. There can be no doubt as to the dynamic quality underlying the creativity coming from this region—regardless of form (or focus).

Without doubt, one of the most basic factors that characterizes the reality continuum of Swedish creativity is the dictates underlying what socialism implies as a functional philosophy. For the expanded implications of socialism have moved to shape every aspect of Swedish life—and this is true regardless of area. The reality of music performance in this country is regulated on a level that is very different from other countries in Europe—not to mention America. On my last visit to Sweden, for instance, there was only one club for so-called jazz that was backed (or funded) by the government—and I found this situation in accordance with the whole of Swedish functionalism. In other words, the reality of regulation in Sweden has created a situation that has affected individual initiative—as this concept is viewed in central European countries (as well as America), and it is important that this difference is understood. For the net effect of Swedish functionalism has moved to make individual postulation very difficult, in that the reality of present-day bureaucracy discourages "doing"—in a dynamic sense. The resulting effect of this phenomenon has greatly changed the dynamic effectiveness of alternative functionalism in this region. Because the city which had only one club for possible performances that I referred to earlier was Stockholm—and this is not a small city by any means.

Hopefully the next cycle of Swedish progressionalism will see more and more musicians playing outside the country. Many people will be quite surprised at the level and dynamics of the music from this region. Musicians like Palle Danielsson and the Norwegian Arild Andersen are greatly respected throughout the whole of Europe, and rightly so, because they represent some of the finest musicians playing creative music. I have no doubt that if more of these musicians were to receive proper exposure, a transformation would solidify in the composite dynamics of the greater world music scene. This is so because the only thing missing in Swedish creative music due to its isolation is non-participation in the greater dynamics of world cross-sectionalism. At present, very few non-Swedish musicians are allowed in the country—for any time—and the net effect of this policy has been a kind of insulation between Sweden and central Europe. The realness of present-day Sweden is very different from the reality continuum that produced the Golden Circle period. The net effect of present-day isolation has been the gradual suppression of composite information dynamics—coupled with a gradual non-support of alternative functionalism on the part of the public. Nevertheless, the present reality position of this region is subject to change—as in every region—and as such, there is reason to be optimistic for the future. As long as there are individuals like Bengt Nordström functioning in alternative dynamics, then Swedish progressionalism must be closely watched. There is a great deal of creativity in this country that we have yet to experience.

Denmark

Denmark has long been viewed as one of the "meccas" in so-called jazz, even though its image has necessarily been inflated for many years. There have been many stories floating throughout the American musicians' community for years about this one country—especially after musicians like Dexter Gordon and Kenny Drew settled in Copenhagen. Nevertheless, this region has always been a wonderful area for creative music—and, for once, the myth is not too separate from reality. Certainly times have changed—not only for Denmark but for every country—and the reality of improvised music has seen a universal lack of support and interest throughout the planet. Many of the clubs in Copenhagen that once catered only to improvised music in the sixties are now rock clubs (or so-called jazz clubs one or two nights a week). Even the famous Montmartre has suffered periodic closures—and during several cycles did not exist at all. Yet there has always been a sustained interest in creative music in this area (or at least, there has always been a group of people interested in the reality of alternative functionalism)—and somehow, the basic scene in Copenhagen survives.

The normal focus of creative music interest in Copenhagen has long been basically concerned with the form we call bebop—as opposed to the more extended forms—and as such, more interest is culturally directed to this area of creativity. This is true even though there was real interest in the post-Coleman developments in the early sixties—in places like Copenhagen. Both Cecil Taylor and Archie Shepp worked extensively in this area during that period. Nevertheless, by the late sixties, attention would be refocused on bebop, and work possibilities in this region have been somewhat limited ever since. However, this region has developed many extremely talented and important musicians—for, first and foremost, this is the region which brought us Niels-Henning Ørsted Pedersen—who must be considered one of the greatest bass players on this planet—and this is also the region that brought us John Tchicai, whose activity was among the first of the post-Coleman transition (and also among the most dynamic). But the composite specifics of this region go outside what I can comment on, because I have no real perspective to formulate a viewpoint.

Both Sweden and Denmark (and probably Norway too, but on this I am not sure) make extensive use of their radio stations—on every level. Practically all of the musicians involved in creative music in these regions are connected to given national radio stations as a means to make a living. In this context, the radio stations in northern Europe can be viewed as a kind of major power center, and this makes for a very interesting phenomenon (something like the situation on the west coast of America—the California studio scene). For the most basic reality alignment that comes from this development is the problem of playing music as a job for eight hours a day and later functioning as a creative musician at night. Yet I do not mention this phenomenon as a means to negatively comment on the musicians in this region—because the reality of a given situation is as it is. There is also the realness that if no job opportunities exist on a regular basis then the existence of governmental radio does provide a positive function. Obviously there must be something in this notion, for the desirability of these jobs transcends the dynamics of the region—many musicians from both central Europe as well as America have regularly competed for these same jobs. As such it would probably not be correct to only view the existence of these stations as necessarily in the same zone as the west coast studio syndrome. One thing is certain, the last fifteen to twenty years have seen the emergence of very sophisticated big band musicians in northern Europe. As we move into the eighties, this phenomenon will also play some role in this region's progressional continuance. Musicians like Thad Jones have recently made the decision to base their activity in Copenhagen, and I have read several articles where he spoke excitedly about northern Europe's inherent creative particulars. Many of his viewpoints corresponded with my experiences in this area as well. There is something happening in northern Europe that has yet to make itself felt internationally. It is unfortunate that so few outside musicians have had the opportunity to visit or live in this sector of the planet, because to experience northern Europe is to be made aware of "other considerations." Hopefully by the time I approach Writings 4, I will have had more opportunities to visit this sector myself—(not to mention, I have hardly even mentioned Norway—for I know next to nothing about this region). One thing is clear: the composite continuum of alternative functionalism in this sector has its own affinity dynamics. Hopefully the next cycle of composite progressionalism will see this region's creativity as a valuable addition for real world change. Many of us will be extremely surprised at the work taking place in this region. Creativity is alive and well in every sector of this planet.

Japan
At this point I have not had the privilege to really visit the far east and/or far west with the exception of Japan—and I am hopeful to one day learn more about these regions. If Japan is any example of its planet sector, then I can only wait with anxiety for an occasion to visit. For the composite developments shaping creativity in Japan during this cycle must be viewed as very inspiring—to say the least. Many of us have heard about developments in Japan—either concerning music or technology. But there is really no way to understand this phenomenon until one is able to experience it live. The fact is, Japan represents one of the most exciting sectors of the planet—and this is especially true for creativity. The most impressive factor that struck me about this country was the level of its awareness about composite creativity and multi-information. This is true for the spectrum of creative improvised

music, whether we are referring to the traditional projections, popular projections, or so-called radical projections. Quite possibly there are more relevant record stores in Tokyo than in any comparable city of its size, and as a result, more people seem to support the music—whether pertaining to records or live performance. In fact, there are many records of creative music that one can purchase only in Japan—and this is true for both American and European creative music. It is somewhat difficult to write about the reality of creative music in this country, because there is nothing to compare Japan with. Certainly I do not mean to imply that everything in this country is perfect—because of course it isn't—rather, the collective forces which control Japanese reality have not moved to suppress creativity on the same level as in the western countries. The composite spectrum of creativity can be experienced in this country on a level not available to any country that I have ever seen.

The progressional development of alternative Japanese extended creativity can be viewed as early as the middle sixties—and the composite solidification of this movement could be seen forming by the early seventies. And while the music functioned in the underground of the culture—as it did in every culture—one of the factors that distinguished the creativity of this sector was the unification it inspired. After reading about organizations like the AACM in Chicago and Instant Composers Pool in Holland, the musicians in Japan quickly understood the significance of alternative functionalism. By the middle seventies, the realness of collectivism would solidify several alternative performing outlets for creative Japanese musicians—and this is also true for their recording attempts. It is unfortunate that the social-political factors affecting information dissemination during this time cycle have produced a situation where few of the musicians associated with this movement are known in America and Europe. For the composite realness of their activity would surprise many people—especially Americans. Many Japanese musicians have even come to America or Europe to learn about so-called western creativity—on a world composite level. As such, the solidification of present-day Japanese alternative creativity is of composite relevance for what insight it can contribute back to the entire world group.

There are also many other factors related to the uniqueness of Japan's position in the music—one of which undoubtedly is the uniqueness of its planet position. The intensity of the research which developed in Japan was necessitated by the fact that many musicians from the west were simply not able to come to perform their music in Japan as they might in either America or Europe—thus Japan's distance became an economic as well as information question. The only American musicians who are able to perform in Japan are those who have been invited (and, of course, there are many musicians who have not been invited to perform in Japan). The reality of the Japanese musician is greatly affected by the implications of this situation as well—for if a given individual has not been invited, then the only way to learn about his (or her) activity is by purchasing records—or traveling abroad.

Of the handful of Japanese musicians whose work has become available internationally, one can find an extremely high level of creativity. The realness of what this creativity implies about the composite dynamics of the total scene should not be ignored. This is not to say that every recording of Japanese creative music can be viewed with respect to the significance of restructuralism, for the Japanese are no different from any other composite group. To experience a cross-section of creative Japanese music is to experience a broad creative continuum—some of which (on the surface) can be viewed as more original than others—just like in America. The composite offerings of this region must be viewed as significant because they give another necessary viewpoint about earth, life, and creativity.

To understand the realness of Japanese music is to focus on those individuals whose work has surfaced on the international scene. Compared to composite Japanese music, the records available in the west represent only a small segment of the total creative involvement shaping the music. Yet it is possible for one to get some idea from these records about the vibrational nature of present-day Japanese creativity. For the records which have surfaced on the international scene are by musicians whose activity is very important to the composite reality platform of Japanese creative music. Which is to say, many of the artists whose records are distributed on a worldwide basis represent what is best about Japanese creative music. To experience their activity is to gain insight into the composite reality of present-day Japan.

It is unfortunate for everyone that the separation factor between western and Japanese creativity has created a one-way culture gap. For it must be understood that every area of information about creative music—whether from America or Europe—is received in Japan. The realness of this phenomenon must be viewed in its progressional context, for the present developments surrounding the creative music scene can be traced to the principal exposure of the music in Japan after the Second World War. All of the developments that would affect cross-transfer progressionalism in alternative Japanese activity solidified vibrationally in this cycle. The progressional development and spread of Japanese creative music is directly related to what this thrust-transfer response would mean—with respect to either its vibrational consequences and/or language implications—in actual terms. Because of this, many westerners have come to view the activity in Japan as not necessarily representing another viewpoint, but rather only imitative. Yet the same progressional factors—and cycle—that Japan is going through can also be viewed in Europe—which is to say, how is Europe capable of creative "relevant" music and not Japan? There, of course, will be many answers to this question (and most of these answers will probably be racist).

Nevertheless, the present reality of Japanese creativity is not available for international scrutiny, and as such, this separation cannot be viewed as positive on any level. Until this problem is rectified, there will be many extra problems in the progressional forming of a composite world culture vibrational stance. This is not only true for Japan, but there are many other sectors of the planet that exist outside of the western information-focus continuum. The realness of this separation can be viewed as counter-productive to the challenge of this time cycle. Even more threatening is the realness that the implications of narrow information interpretations (and focuses) will assume even greater vibrationaltory consequences if not checked in the future. To understand this dilemma is to understand what progressional continuance really means.

CRTF.D.------ALT.F.

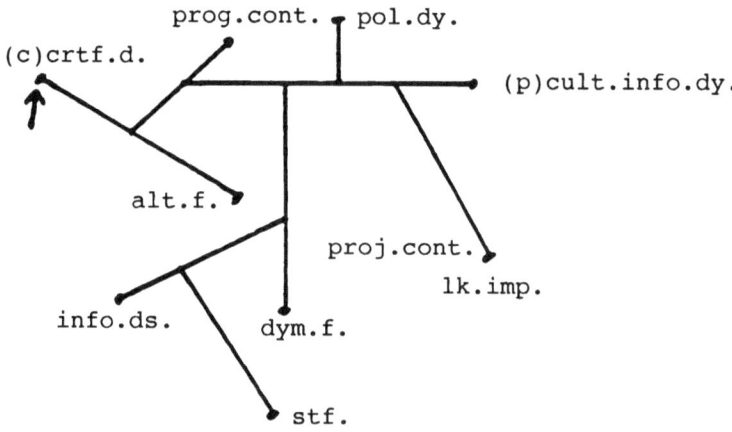

(R)EXP.INFO.B. -----LANG.DY.

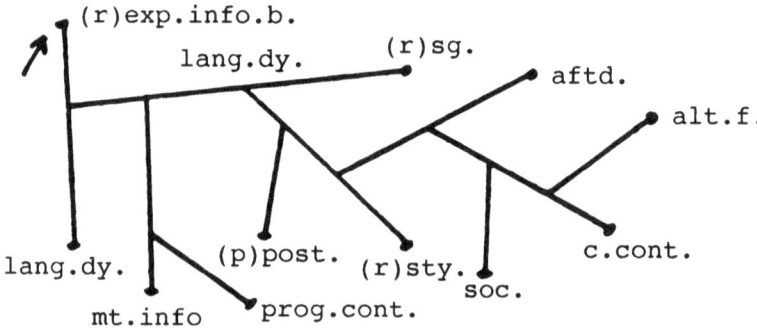

To view the dynamic realness of Japanese creative music, one has only to experience some of the available records. This is especially true on an individual level, for at present there are many records available of "particular" Japanese artists. Certainly the work of a musician-composer like Toshiko Akiyoshi can give one insight into the brilliance of Japanese creativity. The spectrum of this artist's viewpoint must also be viewed with respect to its progressional dynamics—from the early ensembles with musicians like Charlie Mariano on through to the work she is presently doing with the creative orchestra. In all of these contexts, Akiyoshi's activity can be viewed as an important and dynamic contribution to creative music. This is a musician who has studied both in Japan as well as America, and the thrust spectrum of her activity has international significance. Only in this time zone (the late seventies) has there been any composite focus on her work, and she has finally come to gain some of the recognition she so richly deserves (this is especially true for her composing and arranging abilities). The realness of her position in this cycle promises to add a significant viewpoint for creative music in the next cycle. Her work must be viewed in its own terms as well as for what it signifies about the composite world implications of Japanese creative music. For if there are more musicians of her caliber in Japan—and obviously there are—then one can only hope that these musicians will one day have their activity available on a world level. This is what is needed. The brilliance of Akiyoshi's activity will hopefully promote more record companies to make other Japanese musicians' work available (yet I do not mean to sound naive—because it is clear Ms. Akiyoshi's activity did not simply become available because some record company decided to be nice guys or something—rather, the realness of her present situation was brought about because of much work on her part alone), because in the final analysis, her work must be viewed for what it signifies about the composite vibrational viewpoint of this region.

Another musician whose activity can be found outside Japan is the saxophonist-composer Sadao Watanabe. This musician, who is very popular throughout his country, can also be viewed as an example of the musical level that has been attained in Japan. For Watanabe is an accomplished instrumentalist whose proficiency in both the mechanics and dynamics of his craft is substantial on any level—which is to say, he is not just a good Japanese saxophonist as compared to the composite scene. Watanabe has been leading various ensembles in Japan for at least a decade (actually it has been much longer, but on this I have no basis to properly speculate), and the progressional realness of his activity has found him participating in many different aspects of the music—from bebop to jazz-rock forms. From time to time, one can view Watanabe outside Japan—especially in Europe (I recall seeing him and his ensemble performing at the Montreux festival in Switzerland), but he does not seem to travel as much as a musician like Akiyoshi—or at least I have not heard anything about him traveling in America of late (with the possible exception of a Newport performance that I am not sure about). Watanabe, like Akiyoshi, can be viewed as representing the first wave of post-bebop Japanese creative musicians—or at least their activity was among the first recordings that would have an expanded market.

Both musicians spent time in America, and Watanabe—like Akiyoshi—also studied at the Berklee School of Music in Boston. The progressional realness of their activity would have a profound impact on the next generation of creative musicians in Japan, for much of their activity has long been available for the greater Japanese public to experience and learn from. It is unfortunate that Watanabe's work is not documented in this country (America), because in him, the Japanese have an extremely gifted and versatile musician that everyone could benefit from.

The physical universe position of Japan—as a country situated very far away from the west—must be viewed as a factor in its information nature and creative-function options. In other words, the particulars of Japan's physical universe position are not separate from the dynamics of its creative investigation. This is especially true if one is to understand the reality options of Japanese creative musicians. For the separateness of Japan limits the work possibilities and collaborations of their artists—and while this is not necessarily bad (and not necessarily true either, because Japan, while not being close to the west, is close to the east—China in particular), the composite cross-transfer shift of creative improvised music is situated in the west, and its related information dynamics must be viewed with respect to what this distance means—which is to say, the essence factor of the music and its resultant vibrational community are important if one is to seriously participate in the music. What this means is that the reality option spread of Japanese creative music must be viewed with respect to its inability to have expanded contacts with the world community. For the great majority of Japanese creative musicians do not perform outside their own country—not to mention that any one place can have only so many performing outlets. The social reality of Japanese creative music must be viewed with this consideration in mind, for the dynamics of this situation are very different from what is taking place in the west. It is because of the realness of this phenomenon that many musicians have made the decision to travel abroad—as a means to gain a composite world viewpoint, and as a means to develop an international audience. Yet I have not meant to imply that Japan—or any one country—is "not enough" on its own, but rather, if the dynamic implications of transformation forecast the resolidification of world creativity, then this resolidification implies some degree of social and vibrational interaction from earth people. The realness of what this resolidification means will also include the creative contributions of Japanese invention.

To understand the world implications of creativity is to understand what routes given individuals have pursued as a means to have their activity expand. The realness of what this phenomenon means can help one to understand why brilliant musicians like Terumasa Hino can be found in places like New York City, where he has worked with such diverse musicians as Jackie McLean and Gil Evans. For the only reality options creative Japanese musicians have in this cycle are to either travel or run the risk of not developing in accordance with the composite dictates of transformation (if this be the desired alignment of a given individual). This is not to say that no important work is being done in Japan during this cycle, because there is always much important activity—regardless of region or focus. The work done in places like the Shinjuku Bunka Center during the early seventies was both important and dynamic in every context—nor was this an isolated phenomenon. Rather, the composite realness of this period calls for a multi-informational spread—not only concerning Japanese musicians, but rather all musicians. The degree to which this state is practiced and attained is directly related to what can transpire on the social and physical universe levels in the future. To view the composite realness of Japanese creativity in this cycle is to understand that Japan is undergoing a change of profound importance (and, of course, this change is not limited to creativity, but concerns the whole of its affinity dynamics). The realness of what this change means will be a factor of great importance to the composite world community. It is unfortunate for us that the creativity related to this change is not universally available, for there is much of worth for the world community from the Japanese people. The progressional realness of Japanese creative music can be viewed as extremely intense on many different levels—with greater promises for the future. At present, all we can do is experience the handful of individuals whose activity is available on the international scene and be grateful that at least something is available.

OF COURSE THERE ARE MANY OTHER SECTORS of the planet that I have not included in this section. For I am limited by my own experiences (and hopefully the next series of books will have more additions about this subject). The fact is, every section of this planet is engaged in some aspect of "necessary" creativity, and as such, there is something essential for us to learn in every creative music or participation—regardless of planet region. I have included this section only as an attempt to provide a world focus for viewing creativity—and of course, I have much more to learn about this subject. The omission of Africa and the Middle East (as well as the Caribbean Islands and South America) was necessary since I have not had the opportunity to visit these sectors. I am looking forward to my own next cycle in this regard, for the study of world culture has long been one of my primary concerns. The basic thrust of this section is only that the multi-implications of creative music are not separate from the nature underlying how given continuums have affected composite earth culture—as well as how those "effects" have shaped the present vibrational, social, and political realities we now exist in. This viewpoint can be separated into two basic aspects: those being the projectional significance of creative music and its dynamic spread, and the vibrational significance and the implications of creative black music as a germ transformation factor for world culture. To view the realness of this present cycle is to see both viewpoints. It is not just a question of over-postulating the significance of creativity in this time zone, rather it is a question of understanding the nature underlying both progressional spread and projectional spread. For if the subject is creative music, and if the focus is on the dynamic forms which have come to utilize improvisation and composition, then it is important to not isolate what this phenomenon means in a composite context.

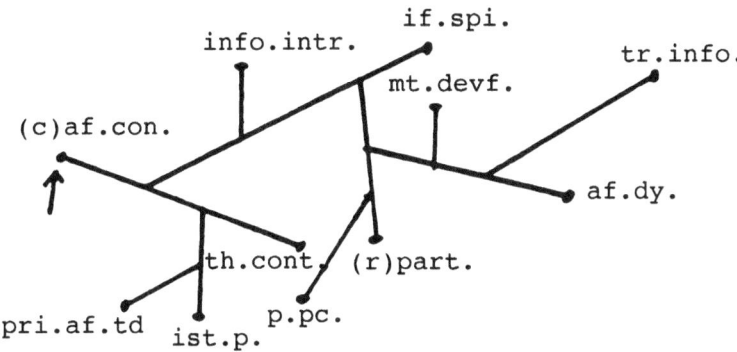

The progressional spread of creative music must also be viewed with respect to the many musicians who have traveled and sometimes lived outside of their given physical universe sector and/or cultural sector. The significance of what this phenomenon poses is important. For the spread of creativity is not only relegated to records. To view a creative musician like Tony Scott is to become aware of the composite impact of his activity over a very wide physical universe space. His travels have included practically every region of the planet, and no one can honestly calculate the positive impact of what so great a performance space has meant to the spread of the music. Nor is Mr. Scott an isolated case, for the individual spread of creative music by given musicians might surprise many people. All of these factors have brought us to the present state we are now in—which is to say, the dynamic spread of creative music has forecasted the real possibility of positive transformation. It is important that the reality focus of this subject opens to include what transformation means in actual terms. Because in this time cycle, many of us view only western culture as "real"—and this attitude is directly related to how composite information dissemination has been practiced—on a world level.

CMOA(II)–40

I have come to have a very special admiration for those creative individuals whose life thrust helped them function on a composite world level (and spectrum). For individual communication and information exchange in the final analysis will be more important than any one culture's records or books. The real dynamics of world transformation will be directly proportioned to how individuals deal with the challenge of actual reality expansion—both theoretically and actually. For this reason, the world implications of creative music must be viewed as related to the composite future of transformational postulation.

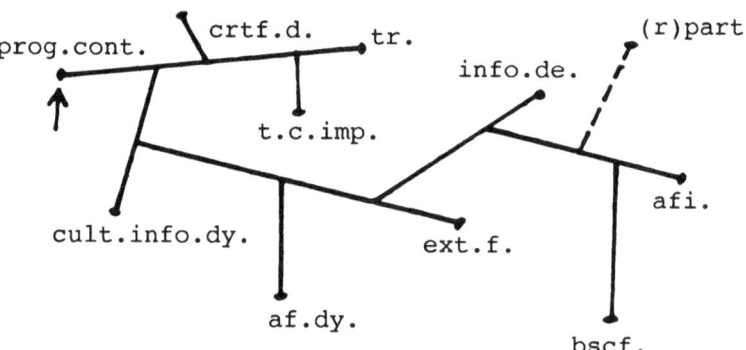

To view the composite spread of creative music, and how that spread affected the particulars of given planet sectors, is both interesting and complex. For no one factor is responsible for the present dynamic reality of the music. It is possible to hear creative music—from the Coltrane language continuum—in many places around the globe—even in places normally not associated with the music. I can still recall the amazement I felt when experiencing bebop in Seoul, Korea—because somehow I had not realized the extent of present-day information dissemination. Nor have I meant to imply that post-Coltrane language techniques represent the "latest" information postulates in world culture, for the composite dynamics of creative music in all of its multi-forms can be experienced on a global level. It is important that this dissemination be recognized—because it does mean something. If nothing else, it attests to the commonality of human beings on the planet, because there is no projection style which is not practiced on a composite world level. In other words, every vibrational intention is meaningful on a composite world level—and the reverse is also true. For if the vibrational and actual reality of creative music from the black aesthetic has meaning for the composite realness of world culture, so too do the dynamic offerings of world creativity have meaning for western culture. The only factor that has retarded the total unification of composite information in this time period is the narrowness underlying how western people (and western culture) have come to view themselves (as a result of suppressed information focuses). It is important to understand that without a better awareness of Chinese or African creativity, we cannot know that part of ourselves—not to mention that the thrust dynamics surrounding what those forms really are are lost to us. The move towards world consciousness is a move towards actual consciousness—the two are not separable. For while it is clear that western culture in this time cycle is in its strong cycle, there is still much of value that we can learn from our neighbors. A proper vibrational composite focus would have a profound positive impact on everyone. The present interest the world community attaches to the creativity (and technology) of western culture implies that on some level the world community is already aware of this viewpoint. It is important to understand that whether or not we meet this challenge, the world community will continue to learn about "what is most real" in composite information dynamics. In the final analysis, the progressional continuum of world culture will absorb both our creativity as well as its own creativity—and this absorption will be positive for what information results from its use—and also for what it will signal about positive alternatives. It remains to be seen whether or not the west will meet this same challenge—for the present signs are very positive—and very negative.

ON AN INDIVIDUAL LEVEL, it is possible to view the progressional spread of creative music as a dynamic continuum. Musicians like Johnny Griffith and Art Farmer are only a few who made the decision to move outside of America to continue their activity. The particulars underlying why so many musicians have had to leave America are of course vast, but the most basic factor would most certainly be that working opportunities in America are always decreasing. The particulars of the physical universe reality situation in America vary according to what time cycle is being discussed—which is to say, the planet-region particulars and the social-reality-dynamic particulars of a given cycle do vary—but in the final analysis, the reality cycles of American culture have long been too difficult to sustain alternative functionalism—especially alternative creative functionalism. This is not to say impossible—obviously many musicians have persevered—but only that the realness of American vibrational dynamics has long necessitated that creative musicians could not simply survive from their music without some other source of income. For most musicians, survival has meant occasionally leaving the country, and for others it meant either permanently leaving or leaving for greater stretches.

The net effect of this phenomenon has ironically been beneficial for the composite spread of creative music. For after a given time zone, one can view a dynamic spread of creative musicians relocating in many different sections of the planet. Nor has this spread included only Europe, for musicians like Randy Weston would travel and settle in places like Africa—and later directly participate in creating music schools in that region. The end result of this phenomenon is that the dynamic realness of creative music can be experienced throughout the planet. And as Leo Smith so accurately pointed out, the progressional spread of creative music was not brought about from the realness of war—and/or conquering land. Rather, the present situation of composite earth can be viewed with respect to how the music was conceptually, vibrationally, socially, and politically desired by every sector of the planet (even including the so-called communist countries). In every case, creative music from the black aesthetic has served as a positive dynamic factor for its host country, and while doing so, also functioned as an important liberating factor for both the vibrational tone level of the country and the continuum implications of dynamicism (as related to the affinity-insight principle). In other words, creative music from the black aesthetic has functioned as a profound regenerating factor for world culture—and in particular Europe, Japan, and the Americas. This is not to say none of these regions in themselves have contributed nothing of their own, nor have I stated this viewpoint as a means to have one perceive any given region as "less." I have tried to emphasize throughout the whole of this book that every sector of the planet has contributed something of worth for all of us to experience. I have also tried to comment on the dynamic particulars surrounding the implications of source transfer on a composite world level. But if one is to understand the present factors which have most generated the composite world continuum (with respect to creative postulation) in the three planet areas I have mentioned (Europe—Japan—America) as far as principal creative projective dynamics—restructured creative alternative functionalism—new use of both improvisation and process (and their resultant language particulars and forms)—new information focuses with their resultant instruments—as well as new particular dynamic extensions, then one has to view the realness of what has been offered through the progressional continuum of creative music from the black aesthetic. It is not simply a question of viewing the composite particulars of these regions as a means to view what is really happening in the music. Nor has the spread of creative music been offered as a means to claim some false notion of superiority; rather, the expansion of creative music has come about because of the basic responses of the composite planet. In other words, the progressional spread of creative music was not the result of a theoretical design, but the result of natural affinities which transcend national boundaries. Not only has the music been viewed as relevant by the world group, but its adoption would signal new (or particular) continuums in world creativity—affecting the progressional realness of both popular music and art music, and this is true regardless of region—whether we are discussing the creative continuum of northern Europe (e.g., Norway or Sweden) or Australia. So real has this expansion been, and so real have these forms been offered on a global level, that one would probably think some real level of appreciation must be felt by the world community for the musicians and people who have made all of this possible (or at least for the musicians who have helped to design the actual projectional strains which have made this phenomenon possible), and of course this appreciation is happening—on some levels. But there are several factors related to the complexities of observation dynamics that directly shed light on present-day progressional continuity—and particular continuity (as well as the seriousness of racism)—that are also related to this phenomenon and cannot be ignored. For if my observations about the spread and dynamics of creativity from the black aesthetic are correct, then what occurrence could possibly take away from what this expansion has undoubtedly meant for all humanity?

In the beginning of this section I wrote on how the dynamic spread of creative music is related to the multi-dimensional implications of transition and transformation, and I also stated that this phenomenon has social and political consequences. For related to every period of expansion and restructuralism are particular social responses—and this is true regardless of period or focus. My point is that there is a continuance pattern that can be observed concerning the principle-exposure cycle of creative music—to the social cycle of creative music—to the transfer-shift cycle of creative music—to the redocumentation cycle of creative music—and finally to the suppression cycle of creative music. I call this sequence the "trans-response-shift pattern"—and this concept can be viewed as a progressional phenomenon connected to every spread sequence of creative music from the black aesthetic. To view the progressional spread of creative music without also dealing with the repercussions of this same phenomenon would be a serious mistake. For the present situation of creative music is not separate from the cross-factors which substantiated how events are interpreted—with respect to either the historical realness of a given period, or the conceptual implications concerning what a given projection posed in its source-initiation context. To view the phenomenon of creative music outside the United States is to view how the trans-response-shift pattern is utilized as an integral factor to respond to what this phenomenon poses. And it is important to understand that I am not simply writing about the progressional particulars of a given cycle. Because the realness of the trans-response-shift-pattern concept must be viewed as related to the multi-dimensional use of applied gradualism—in that this response is directly connected to what factors are utilized in the cross-sectional redocumentation of composite information dynamics (or in this case, creative music). Quite possibly the best way to explain this concept is to break down its components.

By "principle-exposure cycle of creative music" I am commenting on the time cycle which characterizes how new initiations of creative projections are received in a given new country—or new environment. This is the period where the vitality of the music functions as a dynamic lifeline consideration, and this is also the period where the reception of the music by that new country can be viewed as "interesting." For in the beginning, a new projection is intercepted by the controlling forces of its given culture group and "microscoped"—even before the musicians have arrived in the new country. The best example of this phenomenon can be viewed by understanding the information-focus implications of present-day media.

Suddenly the music is something to be "written on" and "talked about" (with the tone-vibrational implications being that "I know about something that you don't")—which is to say, the early arrival of a "new" creative projection is used by the media as a measuring tool from which given groups of controllers (or definers) can wedge positions between themselves. This is also the cycle where ambitious young (or old) critics will have the greatest possibility to make names for themselves (should the form they champion take hold with the greater public). Add to this phenomenon the romantic notions surrounding the music—many of the artists who champion new forms are usually either young or not in the established power structure reality—which is to say, many of these people are poor and struggling. Thus, this reality position can also be used by many people (e.g., individuals who might desire to start a record company—or two—are always interested in the possibilities of recording an artist whose work might later be claimed as significant but who can presently be paid very little). All of these factors come into play if one is to really understand the "principle-exposure cycle of creative music." There is also the nature underlying how competition is viewed between musicians themselves (and what this viewpoint in its most distorted state proposes). Nevertheless, after a given time cycle, the realness that a new form has developed—and does exist—is viewed as a positive diversion for applied information focus (manipulation)—and in this cycle, many musicians even come to believe what they read about themselves in the press. The intensity of this phenomenon is very important if one is to properly view how given thrust alignments are received into a given society. For it must be understood that the "principle-exposure cycle for creative music" determines the dynamics of the next ten to fifteen years—and some—of the creativity. Moreover, the nature underlying how a given thrust is principally exposed also determines what progressional sequences are to follow on the spectacle curve of its given time cycle. The sequences surrounding a given thrust exposure must be viewed for what part it has in the total progressional spread of the music, because the definitions related to this phenomenon will stay with a form throughout its life (unless a progressional move is instigated to change those definitions), and that could take many years—considering if it is possible. Actually, the definition implication of principle exposure seems to stay with a form throughout the solidification of the transition—or transformation cycle—it occurred in. In actual terms, it is important to understand that there is no real difference between the concept of "principle exposure" in America (or country of origin) and its subsequent routes (or in Europe and/or Japan—Canada)—or the nature of its progressional spread. In other words, the progressional spread of a given thrust alignment is not only relegated to its actual particulars (music), but rather this phenomenon includes many different factors. In fact, it is possible that the music itself only plays a minor role in the composite factors related to its "principle exposure." For creativity in this context is utilized as an active agent to stimulate the composite continuum of its host culture group. This is true for the early forms of creative music from the black aesthetic, and this is true for the present. Thus, by the time a given projection completes its "principle exposure" cycle, there are many other dynamic factors at work—many of which have nothing to do with the music (as far as the meta-reality implications of thrust alignment implies)—and some of which are directly the inverse of what the music poses as a positive transformational and vibrational tool.

PRI.INFO.------AF.DY.

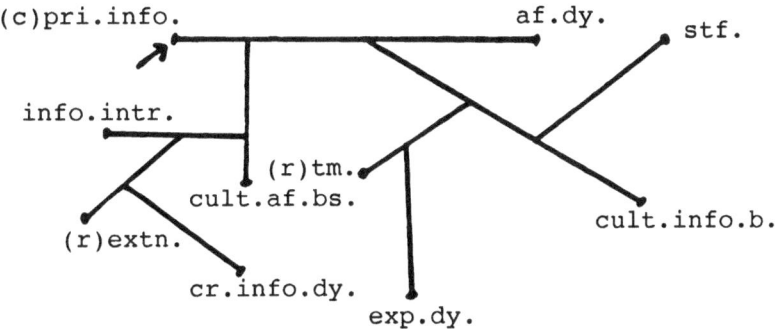

INFO.DS. -----C.CONT.

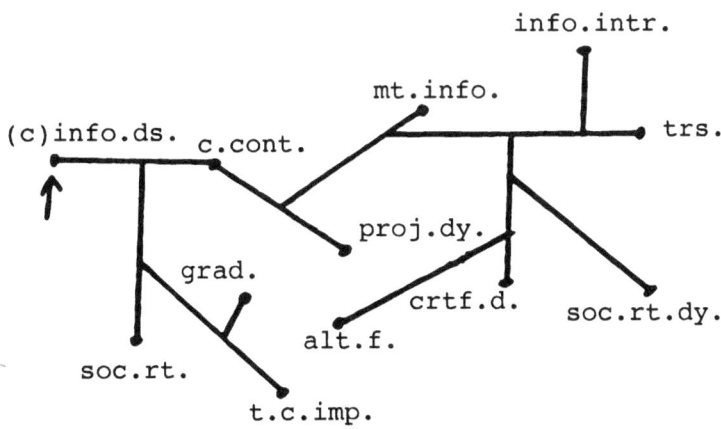

CMOA(II)–48

The "adaptation cycle of creative music" can be viewed as the second sequence of progressional spread. It is in this cycle where the existence of a given thrust alignment becomes apparent, and it is also in this cycle where the influence of that given thrust is felt—with respect to the community or sector it inhabits. In other words, after the arrival of a given alignment, slowly but surely the greater community comes to deal with the realness of its existence. Moreover, the first community sector to respond to this change phenomenon are the musicians of the new host country (or region). It is in this cycle where regional musicians will begin to play the music (for it is important to understand that when a foreign creative projection arrives in a given new country, the musicians are the first to know of it—and should be). The reality of the adaptation-cycle phenomenon can thus be viewed for its effects on given musicians' communities (or sectors), and to understand this phenomenon is to also understand that every given performance of the music is immediately checked by all concerned. As such, this is the cycle where regional musicians become familiar with the music, and after a given time zone, those same musicians will later be seen performing the music with the principal musicians who created the extension (projection). This phenomenon can be viewed in the same context of progressional osmosis—which is a regular physical universe occurrence. (The concept of the session is another example of progressional osmosis, the stages of which are (1) exposure—(2) imitation—(3) stylism—and, if possible, (4) restructuralism.) Thus, the end result of the adaptation-cycle phenomenon is that a new composite society of the music is developed, and the composite acceptance of the music by the greater public is not far behind. Because at this point, the greater sector of the society (or community) also begins to take a real interest in the music.

PRI.AF.TD.------C.CONT.

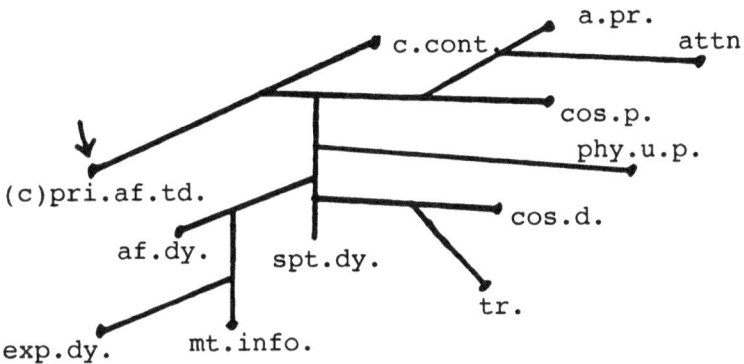

The social cycle of creative music has to do with the nature underlying how a phenomenon is substantiated. This is the cycle where substantial momentum has insured the realness of the music—as a thrust of lasting importance (and acceptance—by the greater culture). It is also in this cycle where suddenly every musician has many friends—and all that goes with "friendship." Quite possibly, this cycle might be viewed as the "happy cycle," for with the "social solidification of creative music" come many parties and much press attention. There are also many cult-like groups that can be seen floating in and out of music—and musicians' communities. And let us not forget what the social realness of this cycle implies for meeting nice people who are "interested" in the music—for it must be understood that by the time the music gets to this cycle, many of the musicians have become "heroes" of a sort. Not only are there parties, but everyone is treated like a king. Much attention is centered on given individuals with respect to their (and usually we are talking of men rather than women) idiosyncrasies, and so-called hip dynamics. All of this activity eventually helps to feed the images that have been erected around the music—as well as around black people and culture. For it is clear that in the minds of most people, the "world of jazz" is really a "far-out" world having to do with all sorts of far-out fantasies and strange people. Last but not least, it is in the social-emergence cycle of creative music where one can view how success eventually affects the actual musicians themselves. For it must be said that when a situation is perceived as optimum—even on a primitive level—many musicians do not seem to be able to handle it. This is the cycle where crimes against humanity are committed—crimes which will have a lasting value—only to come and haunt the aggressor for years on end; having to do with taking advantage of people; assuming more power than one really has, arrogance and greed, and assuming that something is "real" when it isn't. Nevertheless, the social emergence of creative music must be viewed as a "ball"—a good time for all—and "drinks on the house."

The transfer-shift cycle of creative music can be understood by viewing the progressional factors related to the adaptation sequence. For this cycle is a direct outgrowth of the change of position that occurs when "one does not know about something" then suddenly "one does know about something." In particular, this cycle has to do with the progressional ability of the host country (or sector) to successfully practice the music without the need of primary musicians—or innovators. In other words, when the laws (or disciplines) of a given reality are understood, then it is possible to function from those laws—without the need of a guide (or aide). When this position is secured, the transfer-shift cycle goes into effect—yet I have not meant to imply that this change is quick; rather, the transfer-shift realness of creative music is an "apparently slow" process (occurring within the time zone of, say, five to seven years after a principle exposure—sometimes earlier, but it depends on many different outside factors). Nor does the transfer cycle only have to do with the musicians. For the collective forces of its particular region also related to this same phenomenon. It is in this cycle when suddenly one might read an article whereby the student of a given principal musician is suddenly viewed as more significant than his teacher (and of course, these things do happen—no one stands still—but the interesting feature of these types of articles is that in most cases the student has not advanced the nature of the actual music, but has rather found his own voice—which usually consists of language implications that were formed by his teacher). In the beginning of this phenomenon, there are only one or two of these types of articles, but later this shift in press coverage will come to be the norm. In other words, after a gradual amount of time, the transfer-shift realness of information shift will move to redefine both the nature of the music and the images connected with who is playing the music. Invariably, after a given cycle, the basic focus of the music will be reshaped and perceived in accordance with another set of criteria. In all cases, the black musicians—who brought the form into being—will be viewed as "less" when compared. Yet I have not tried to over-simplify this most complex subject, for there are many other factors related to this development as well. One of those factors would be the progressional move to separate the musicians—as a means to make one a "star" and, as such, drop all the rest (and what is amazing is that this strategy always works). Nevertheless, the visiting musicians suddenly can't find a good party—and this is just the beginning. For the transfer-cycle realness of creative music in this context is also related to work possibilities as well. Which is to say, the composite realness of performance possibilities is related to the total reality underlying how events—and particulars—are viewed. This is not to say there are not work possibilities—rather, the realness of this cycle will determine the reality-option spread of the music, with respect to how far it will be allowed to penetrate into the culture or sector—and for how much money.

```
RT.DY.------POL.SIGN.
```

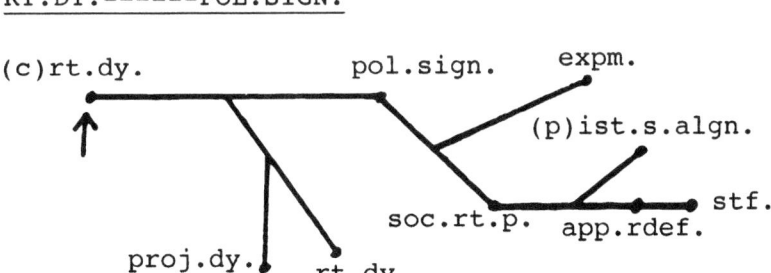

The redocumentation cycle is the time zone where all of the operating factors are in motion, and this is also the period that sets the final vibrational tone progression of the music. It is in this period when suddenly the composite viewpoint of the music is totally separated from the actual musicians. For by now there are many extended schools of thought which have strung from the original initiation of the music. But if, in the beginning, the arrival of creative music from the black aesthetic was viewed in positive terms—as a form with new dynamic potential—by this cycle, the music is viewed as an obstruction to the scene. The basic vibration of this phenomenon can be understood by the concept of "what are you doing in this sector?" (country). For the most basic notion that has formed in this cycle is the concept that "the music you do is not as advanced as ours," which is to say that suddenly many people have begun to notice flaws in the primary musicians who originally brought the music. Suddenly, cries can be heard that the original music is "primitive" when compared to the "sophisticated" music of the community. Not to mention, one can sometimes hear "we had this music anyway—long before you came." And suddenly, in a given conversation, it is possible to hear about "host" musicians who were playing this music back in 1237, long before any of the American blacks even thought of it—and even present "proof." "Not to mention, none of these musicians have good technique anyway." After a given time period, this viewpoint becomes the vibrational sentiment underlying the total scene. It is usually followed by a re-evaluation of the composite thrust, and suddenly records that were greatly appreciated only five years before will get one and a half stars. "Now I can see that such-and-such was really not quite as advanced as 'John Doe,' who had a much more profound approach to the music—as long as three thousand years ago." When these statements happen, you can be sure that you are witnessing a redocumentation cycle.

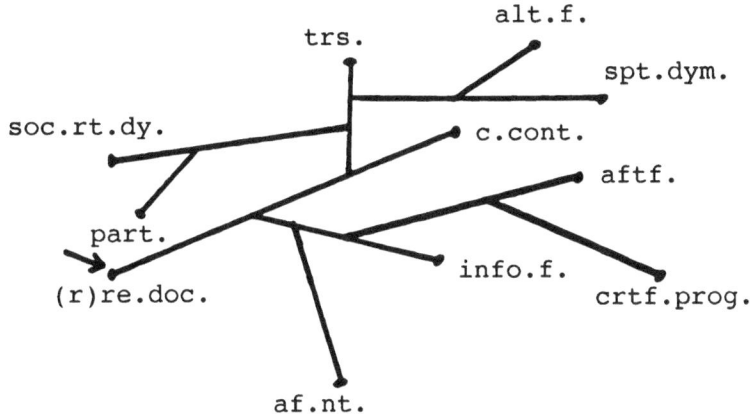

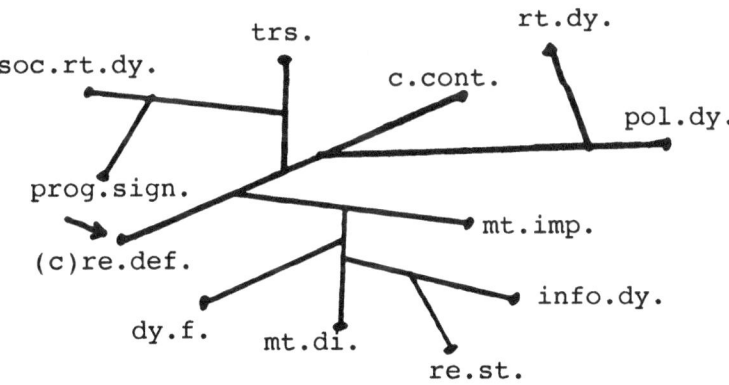

The suppression cycle speaks for itself—which is to say, this is the period where one asks the question "whatever happened to ole Joe?" From a dynamic beginning, where a given thrust alignment served as basis for both new projectional forms and vitality, and in doing so provided the vibrational uplift for composite world culture, to a suppressed scattering of surprised musicians (who probably are still fighting each other)—this is what I mean by "trans-response-shift pattern." And while I have described this cycle in narrow terms—because certainly there is much more to be said—in actual terms, this is really the essence of what has happened and is happening with the music. Where once one would see many people showing up at a given concert—suddenly, there is no one. It is really that simple. Nor have I meant to poke fun at any particular aspect of this progression because—even though on the surface there is much humor attached to the working of the culture (and planet)—in the final analysis, this cycle is not conducive to the musicians or the music. The only humor I can find in this cycle is the realness that very few musicians tend to learn from collective past mistakes—and as such, this phenomenon is repeated over and over. Yet I have not meant to imply that the progressive spread of the music is not important—obviously it is. But to research the historical realness of expansion dynamics is to see what has transpired from this phenomenon in actual terms.

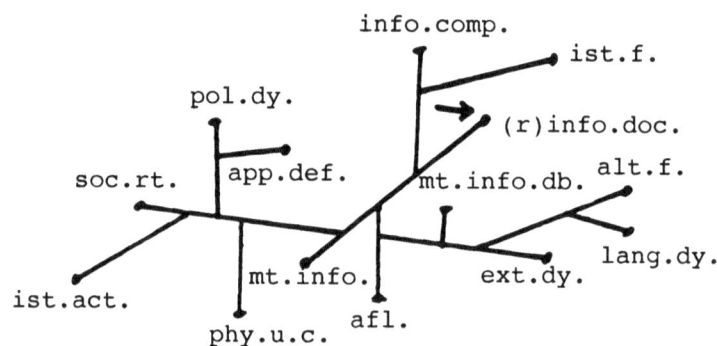

By viewing the dynamics of progressional spread in creative music, I have not meant to distort the realness of source transfer. Obviously people learn from one another, and moreover, there are many sectors on the planet which offer dynamic viewpoints on creative music. The diversity of this phenomenon must be viewed as a positive achievement for earth creativity—and later, hopefully, world solidification. To understand this is to understand extended creative music, for the significance of this subject has yet to be really examined for what it tells about the future. I believe we are on the verge of a new cycle in creative music, having to do with the cross-transfer composite realness of early creativity—regardless of mixture. Moreover, the promise of the next cycle has a good chance to solidify a composite meta-reality base. Hopefully, the significance of creative music from the black aesthetic will also be viewed for its role in helping this change to happen.

(Level Three)

1. Why do you support European creative music?

The whole point I have been trying to make in this book—and this series of books—is that the composite wonder of creativity is too significant to be confused with narrow physical universe particulars. My support of European creativity is related to my support of black creativity, Asian creativity, etc.—because in the final analysis, we are really commenting on earth creativity. I do not accept any viewpoint that seeks to isolate humanity to the degree where we cannot see ourselves in each other. We are all necessarily related to every aspect of everything—whether the focus is creativity, science, and/or information dynamics. To not embrace the positive achievements of Europe is to be "less" in that area of achievement—which is to say, to be separate from "what is." I do not believe individuals should be separated from what the composite reality of information dynamics implies—unless that individual chooses to be separated. I support, and indeed am grateful for, all of the wonderful creativity that has solidified—or actualized—on this planet, from the dynamics of the American Indian, to the dynamics of Asian creativity and, yes, the composite continuum of European creativity.

2. There has been much talk in the seventies in Europe, especially among the promoters, that black musicians in America tend to view Europe as Mecca— and in doing so, have somewhat over-extended their individual importance as well as price. What is your viewpoint?

It is true that many young musicians (black and white) in America tend to view Europe as more positive than it is, and it is also true that many musicians—even young musicians—tend to over-estimate their importance after a given exposure in Europe. But I view this phenomenon as directly related to what European promoters and the press obviously seem to want. For every promoter I have talked to in Europe is always concerned about "what is new" in America, or American jazz. The reality of decisions at practically every festival in Europe is always directed towards springing a new musician from America—as a means to claim that "they (the promoters) knew about a given musician before anyone else." This is also true of the so-called jazz magazines—everyone is looking for what they think is "new" or the "next thing." In the final analysis, the black musician is used as a pawn in this game, for the total spectacle of this phenomenon is built on a modern version of the slave trade. This is especially true for the young black musician. Because young musicians are encouraged to come to Europe and then exploited on twelve thousand different levels—from concert or club fees to recording contracts. Later, after a period of one or two years, that same musician can't find a gig. Moreover, if that musician should somehow come to view his work as valuable—and as such, wants to be better paid—then he (or she) is viewed as both arrogant and egotistical. In other words, NO, I do not agree with this viewpoint at all.

3. How do you view the emergence of the European-only jazz festivals?

I view this phenomenon as positive for European musicians and listeners (on whatever continent). Hopefully in the eighties there will be more work possibilities for creative American musicians in America, for it is clear that the new European festival is a signal about the coming changes in European social reality. I do not believe the general public will ever totally block performance possibilities for American musicians in Europe, but the future of European dynamics will profoundly alter the present situations—concerning every area of the music business. The existence of European-only festivals can also be viewed as another option for dynamic presentation, as well as another step in European alternative functionalism. It is hard to know what this development will mean in the next cycle—in terms of its real implications. Hopefully this phenomenon will be connected to the solidification of dynamic functionalism in other areas as well. For the emergence of an all-European festival context is a significant move that promises to change and expand the option-spread possibilities of European creative musicians.

4. Do you feel that Americans, on the whole, are open to European improvised music?

I would say of the Americans who are interested in improvisation—which is a very small group to begin with—I doubt if the country a person comes from would make much, if any, difference as to whether or not his (or her) music can be successful or accepted in America. This is not to say there are no special interest groups and listeners in America—because America is no different than any other country (in that context). I believe the majority of people interested in improvised music would support a given person based on the actualness of the music, and not the origin of the person playing. Obviously this is true—witness the success of European popular musicians in America, from Tom Jones to the Beatles (who have probably made more money than any group in the history of popular music). Nor have European jazz-rock musicians had any problems being received in America. For the emergence of groups like Weather Report or Urszula Dudziak and Michał Urbaniak have been very well received. On many levels, the composite dynamics of European creativity are profoundly desired in America—even more than American black people in many respects. For the spectrum of the European creative person involves initiations which solidified in Europe (e.g., western art music—traditional opera—Russian dance—art films) as well as performers who have based their functionalism entirely on black music (where in some particular ensembles or individuals, there is no discernible difference between their creativity and black creativity)—but, in every case, I believe the American public would prefer to support the European musician than the black musician.

5. How do you view the idea that the bulk of a person's activity can be effective only if that person is functioning from his or her tradition?

I would agree to some aspects of this statement, but there are many factors which must be qualified. It seems to me that the realness of a person's activity is most meaningful when it affirms whatever each individual desires it to affirm. In other words, a person should be able to function from whatever context or vibrational alignment is most real to that person—because while there is such a thing as tradition, there is also no such thing as tradition. It seems to me that when the concept of tradition is used in this context, the reality intention is to inhibit the dynamics of the individual rather than to better understand the reality implications of a given "postulation." To really examine the particulars of any tradition is to see some relationship to every area of information dynamics and participation. To state that a given person's effectiveness is related to whether or not that person observes the particulars of his or her tradition is simply another way of saying that there can be imposed criteria, outside of the actual music, that can determine whether or not a given offering is valid—imposed criteria that challenge the right of a person to both grow and learn. In most cases, this way of perceiving moves to totally ignore the actual music.

6. To what extent do you view the European state-owned radio and television system as related to the option dynamics of European creativity?

I believe the use of state-owned media has profoundly affected the reality of European creative possibilities, and I see this phenomenon as superior to what is happening in America—in every sense. To understand this is to view the dynamic possibilities that exist for the European creative persons as compared to Americans. Every country in Europe gives creative people more possibilities in the media—this is true for radio and television. There are more programs on the spectrum of the music, and the radio on given occasions will even hire musicians. Every radio station in Europe also has an orchestra, and a creative orchestra—which is to say a composer has a much better chance to get a performance, as well as to become more familiar with the orchestra technically. The state radio in this context becomes a cultural arm of the country—providing both exposure for creative artists as well as facilities. To really view how Europeans utilize their information dynamics is to see how barbaric America really is. For even though America is without doubt one of the richest countries in the world, no real provisions have been made to further its creativity—either in education or exposure. I believe that the emergence of the dynamic media center is a positive step in the right direction. To erect cultural institutions in this manner is to view the realness of creativity as being just as important as building a tank. I believe creativity is more important in the long—and short—run.

7. What is the reality position of extended creative music in the Middle East?
Difficult question, for at this period of my life I know very little about this particular area's relationship to western creativity. I can't recall even reading about any musicians or ensembles that have made tours to this planet sector—yet it would be strange if this is true. In the late fifties, Dave Brubeck did tour the Middle East, and the State Department of the U.S. certainly followed this tour with something. But at this point in time, I have had no information about the particular reality of the Middle Eastern creative musician. In countries like Israel I have heard there are many different possibilities for contemporary musicians and composers. For the cultural community of this country is very much interested in contemporary music—yet, to my knowledge, this interest is directed towards contemporary western art music as an exclusive thrust. Musicians who are interested in improvisation, or black creativity (from the juncture of post-bebop and beyond) must necessarily travel outside of the region. Hopefully the next cycle of my life (i.e., the next ten years) will involve traveling to these regions, and more effort on my part to find relevant literature about this subject.

8. How do you view Ayatollah Khomeini's decision to ban western music in Iran?
I view this decision as one of the profoundest decisions made in this time period—especially for what it could signify for third world progressionalism. It is important to understand that the spread of imperialism is brought about from several sectors—involving both politics and information dynamics. Khomeini's decision to ban western music was important because in making that decision, Khomeini recognized the value and power of creativity—as well as its potential for greatest harm. The fact is, the reality of transformational unification does not imply that only one route of fusion is real, because the weight of a given encounter depends on the composite state it takes place in. The thrust of the last two

hundred years has seen the use of source-transfer convergence as a means to solidify the present hold western culture now has on the composite planet. This is so because source transfer is practiced and solidified with the western affinity interpretation in the dominant position—and this can no longer be tolerated. World culture must be very careful about how it deals with western music (i.e., from the western art aesthetic or the extended functionalism sector of black music), because the essence criterion that determines western invention is aspiritual—or even worse, "not understood." To simply allow western creativity to permeate one's culture is to take more than a great risk, because there is nothing worse than a continuum that doesn't know what "it" is (both "its").

9. What relationship does cultural imperialism play in the suppression, and later succession, of world creativity?

The thrust of cultural imperialism moves to lessen the reality position of a given culture's center—and in doing so, functions as a dynamic negative factor for the life of that culture's identity. There is no one area of cultural imperialism that can be separated as a means to exemplify the composite dictates of this phenomenon, because the realness of this concept is not one-dimensional. One thing is clear: the reality of a given imperial implication moves to (1) mis-document the realness of its host culture's greatness (and in doing so, moves to make the inhabitants of that culture feel inferior to those who have so-called conquered them), (2) cultural imperialism moves to affect the information affinity dynamics of its target culture (and in doing so, moves to direct everyone's affinities to the dictates of alien sensitivities), and (3) cultural imperialism moves to economically aid the nature of this adaptation (that is, supports the dynamics of source transfer initiations and the manipulation of "images"). To understand this phenomenon is to begin to understand the struggles now taking place in Africa or South America. For the people in these sectors are determined to regain control of their destinies. Cultural imperialism is directly related to how human beings have historically dealt with each other. For the most basic tenet that accompanies a given territorial violation is the notion that "what you do is not as good as what we do and therefore you must be changed"—in other words, inherent in this concept is the notion that "someone thinks they are better than someone else."

10. Why has the spread of black creativity penetrated so deeply into European culture?

The progressional expansion of black creativity has penetrated deeply into Europe because the realness of what it poses—as a creative music with its own dynamics as well as the implications of its functionalism—is directly relevant to composite western continuance. The realness of this phenomenon should not be too narrowly viewed, for the methodological dynamics of black creativity (i.e., improvisation and the introduction of alternative functionalism) are only one aspect of something much, much greater. It seems to me that the realness of black creativity is compositely viewed as a balancing factor to all of western culture—and that in this period in time anyway, a balancing is needed throughout the whole of western culture. In other words, the penetration of black creativity is related to the fact that people really want the music—either to simply experience, or to scientifically use as a basis for changing their music and related information continuum. I view this penetration as positive on most levels, for the thrust of black creativity is now in the position of possibly helping to accelerate the composite nature of the next change cycle. The problem, as I am able to understand it, is to help educate people about what black creativity is—in its own terms. The significance of black creativity in composite western culture is related to how successfully it transports us to a new world music. Either this is accomplished or this period in time will come to be viewed only in "spectacle" terms.

11. What is the reality of creative music in places like Africa?

My research in this area is much the same as in the Middle East. There does seem to be much extended creative music in Africa—in fact, based only on the conversations I have had with African musicians, there seems to be much interest in every area of creativity in Africa. I have focused this section of the book on western Europe because in the last ten years and some, I have traveled throughout the whole of Europe. It is my intention in this period (of my life) to now discover Africa—and the Middle East—as well as South America and China. Hopefully, I will be able to include more material about this area of world creativity in Writings 4 and 5—obviously it is needed. Nevertheless, if the musicians I have already met are indicative of the African music scene, then Africa is indeed playing an important role in composite transformation (outside of the three-fourths "generating" I had already suspected). I look forward to the next ten and twenty years for what I will learn—about creativity and about living. From what I have studied so far, it seems that Africa has played a significant role in bringing us to this point in time, and it also seems that Africa will continue to be relevant as we move towards the future.

12. What is the most basic disadvantage that black musicians living in Europe face?

It depends on the individual—and it depends on what each person is looking for in his or her music (and life). There are, of course, advantages and disadvantages to being in any context, and this is also true for the expatriate black musician. Certainly the realness of being in a different community makes its own problems—not to mention that prolonged exposure in Europe moves to separate one from his or her roots—if that concept is valid (and for some, it might not be). The problem with this question is that somehow it vibrationally obscures the composite picture of expatriatism. For instance, most black musicians in this time zone go to Europe because "whatever can happen" is perceived as better than "what was happening." In other words, most musicians are attracted to Europe because of the reality of their home situation. As such, I am not sure if the nature of this question is phrased correctly, because whatever advantages or disadvantages Europe offers the American black musician, the simple fact that Europe offers an alternative must be viewed as positive. This is not to say there are no problems in Europe—because there are always problems—but I am not sure it is proper to view those problems in the context of "what is the most basic disadvantage," because somehow vibrationally it doesn't sound correct. Nor by viewing this question have I meant to imply that Europe owes nothing to the world group—because history would not agree with this viewpoint either. Many of the people who have been forced to migrate to given European countries were related to some aspect of European colonialism (e.g., the Africans in Great Britain, the Algerians in France, and the Spanish in Switzerland), and I believe these people are entitled to have more than just a "guest attitude" about European particulars.

13. Have the European collectives in Holland and Germany taken the next step in dynamic collectivism from organizations like the AACM?

In many ways, I believe they have. For the collected realness of European creative organizations have helped totally reshape the dynamic participation of all European musicians. The thrust of their organizations has helped to open new performance possibilities in every country in Europe, and I believe the dynamic implications of this phenomenon have only just begun. This is not to say European collectives have necessarily achieved every breakthrough attained by organizations like the AACM—because each of the European collectives are very different from one another. To my knowledge, there has been no effort towards erecting a school of music, nor have the European collectives necessarily been conceived with respect to better community relations—ideas which were important for the AACM. Instead, the thrust of the European collectives has been directed towards the music, and towards surviving from the music—and in this context, they have been very successful. For instance, the solidification of alternative recording—a concept that was theoretical in the AACM—has helped to change the reality position of extended European creativity. Companies like Incus and FMP (Free Music Production) are very sophisticated compared to the reality of alternative recording in America. The Europeans in this context are showing that alternative recording can work—and this is extremely important. Secondly, the actual longevity of many of the sixties' collectives are significant because they have shown that unification can work. The realness of this phenomenon is related to the success of the Globe Unity Orchestra, as well as the development of alternative festivals—like the one held opposite the Berlin Jazz Festival in November. I believe the realness of this unification is indicative of the next cycle of dynamic alternative functionalism, and as such represents the next extension of collectivism.

14. How influential has the European free jazz continuum been in affecting the reality of American creativity?

I believe the composite continuum of European free jazz has most certainly had some effect on American creativity—but to what extent I cannot say because it is still in progress. It seems to me that we have now entered a time period where, because of contemporary communications, it is possible to experience and learn from many different kinds of music—and this is exactly what is happening. The last five years—and probably even earlier—have seen the emergence of several American schools (or movements) of music that seem to be directly inspired from European free jazz. There is now a movement in San Francisco centering around people like Henry Kuntz and Henry Kaiser, and there are also movements in cities like New York—and even in Canada. It is too early to make a real judgment about the nature of this influence—certainly the thrust of functionalism developing in areas like London seeks to solidify a totally improvised music—with its own vibrational feeling, separate from what is happening in America, or American black creativity. But there can be no denying that European extended creativity is making a profound imprint on American creativity. What this influence will mean in the long run is impossible to say at this point in time.

15. What role have institutes like the Goethe Institute played in affecting the option dynamics of the European musician?

I am not sure of the composite realness of this question, because certainly the reality of support for creative music differs from place to place—or country to country. But if the Goethe Institute is any example of what is happening throughout the whole of Europe, then the European musicians can be viewed as extremely fortunate—especially when compared to America. The Goethe Institute in Germany has helped to provide a world forum for German creativity. Musicians are given the opportunity to perform all over the world—from India to South America, from Canada to Australia—and this is true for every form of German music (from western art music to the so-called avant garde). At this point in time, I cannot attempt to compare this institute with any other governmental context involving creativity because I don't have sufficient information. Even in America there is the realness of the State Department and its related functionalism. But I can say I am completely impressed by the Goethe Institute. Many musicians—some of whom I am close with—have in the last seven years had the opportunity to travel on several Goethe Institute tours—tours which paid very well, and tours that involved countries one might normally not have the possibility to see. I view this phenomenon as positive.

16. Is the reality of the music business in Europe necessarily on a higher level than in America?

The present reality of business in western culture can be viewed as consistent—regardless of what sector one is in. In other words, there is no way to really deal with this question because, in the final analysis, the reality of business depends on the reality of the people doing the business—and there are no universals that can be superimposed on this context. In other words, I have found that "people are people" and one is as apt to get a good or bad deal in Europe as in America. Europe does have extra problems for many Americans because of the language problems—as well as the present state of world economics. Many individuals have also experienced unfortunate business transactions because a given business agreement was written in a language they did not understand. To really begin to understand the dynamics of world business it is necessary to not approach a given transaction with the misunderstanding that "everybody feels the same way about everything"—because this concept has helped to make many musicians unhappy. I have found for myself that the dynamics of business in Europe are definitely different from the "particulars" in America, but it is also different from country to country—but definitely not on what could be called a higher level—I would say European business is "different—but not different."

17. What are the main barriers that European musicians deal with in Europe and in America?

    I believe European musicians are dealing with the same basic problems that all musicians performing extended creativity are dealing with, those being: (1) survival, and (2) acceptance. Along with these problems, many European musicians are also fighting against misconceptions which have surrounded either the white improvisor or non-American musician's right to participate in the music—what this means vibrationally and economically. However, it would not be correct to say all European musicians are dealing with these problems, because obviously Europeans participating in commercial creativity do not feel non-accepted or financially suppressed. For the most part, I feel all non-commercial musicians—European or otherwise—are really struggling to solidify greater public interest in non-commercial creativity. For connected to the present state of things is the realness of dynamic misinformation—and this is the main barrier. As far as what barrier the European faces in America, the answer is clear—no exposure, and little interest. But again, this is not only true for the European musician, for the problem of non-support in America is dynamically manifested throughout the whole of the culture. It is for this reason that so many American musicians are forced to leave.

18. Is the European festival a political tool—on some level?

    Everything can be viewed with respect to what it poses politically—even a festival of music. For that reason, the choice of musicians on a given festival program is not an affirmation that has no multi-consequence, but a decision that ultimately affects the vibrational state of things. It is for this reason that the composite spectrum of earth creativity should be exposed to the greater public—because creativity does affect things, more than we realize. Yet the political implications of a music festival should not be used to distort what positive attributes this phenomenon poses as well. For I have always viewed the festival context as a positive forum for creative music. What we need is more festivals, not fewer. Hopefully the future continuance of this phenomenon will see more diversification in festival funding. For the success of a given festival depends not only on the so-called caliber of the music, but also extends into the dynamics of its funding and financial backing. In Europe during this time zone, the reality of festival funding is related to either the government or the vast network of radio and television funding (most of which is, again, from the government). I believe Americans can learn much from the functionalism that supports the diversity of festivals in Europe.

19. *How do you view the concept that European musicians are technically inferior to American musicians?*

This is a somewhat difficult question, for on the surface I would say clearly America has the best so-called jazz education possibilities, but since I believe three-fourths of what is being taught about so-called jazz is not true, the complexity sets in. It seems to me that the most basic tenet that gives real insight into realness of the music is exposure, and only after that exposure can one really begin to understand the reality of the music. If that is true, then I believe the composite vibrational arena of Europe seems to offer a more healthy environment to learn about the music, in this time period, than America. This is not to say European music schools are necessarily more aware about given teaching techniques—or even the dynamics of creative music functionalism—than American institutions, because this does not seem to be the case. But if the spirit foundation of a given reality is important, if one is to become proficient in that reality, then I believe that in many ways Europe in this period is much more healthy than normally thought of. Education is not only limited to the particulars of a given functionalism—rather, the dynamics of this phenomenon are related to the composite realness of what it purports to teach.

20. *Has the spread to extended improvisation led to any cross-projects input involving European musicians and composers?*

Yes. There have been many such collaborations between European musicians and composers—even including American musicians. In the late sixties, musicians like Don Cherry have done projects with composers like Penderecki, and collaborations of this sort are not as rare as one might think. I have heard that composers like Hans Werner Henze have participated in collective projects with musicians like Gunter Hampel and others. I believe the progressional continuum of post-Ayler creativity has stimulated much interest in improvisation—even affecting the western art music community (more than they would like to admit). Certainly, the work of composers like Karlheinz Stockhausen can be viewed as related to the dynamics of extended improvisation. Stockhausen has even worked with so-called jazz musicians on given occasions, and one would be quite naive to believe he has not, on occasion, been inspired by post-Ayler inventions. Many European composers are presently studying the post-Ayler continuum very seriously as a means to understand what new instrumental dynamics are possible (in terms of sonority or language), as well as what new functionalism can be brought about through improvisation.

21. Why do you feel creative western music is not supported in the Middle East?

At this point in time, I cannot with any authority state that this is the case or not—because I have never been to the Middle East and my information about this area is necessarily limited. From what I have been able to understand, the vibrational nature that permeates the Middle East has to do with the dynamics of this sector's all-consuming relationship with its tradition and spiritualism. For the most part, to comment on this area is to be commenting on a region that is primarily Muslim, and primarily concerned with things Muslim. This is not to say that no western concepts have been able to penetrate the Muslim world, but I do somehow get the feeling that most Muslims would prefer as little penetration as possible. At this point in time, I cannot agree with the notion that western creative music is or is not supported in the Middle East because (1) I really have no idea about whether or not it is true, and (2) I do not know if enough interchange has taken place between westerners and Middle Easterners to be able to gauge whether western creativity is viewed as attractive or not. I do feel that, in the present state of things, the dictates and dynamics of western music can be very dangerous for any culture that has a tradition—and wants to keep its tradition. Because the reality of western creativity (and western information dynamics in general) moves as a phenomenon to challenge any and all things—holding nothing sacred, because it has no center of its own (but instead only curiosity). There are other reasons why the Middle East might find western creativity difficult. For the texture and dynamics of western music might also be viewed as foreign—in a negative sense—to the vibrational dictates of middle eastern creativity—but then again, this is not necessarily true either.

22. How do you view the present reality of currency exchange between America and Europe as this consideration involves performance fees?

The present reality of world currency is very unstable—to say the least—and the realness of this phenomenon profoundly affects the business nature of creative music transactions. The changes in the dollar rate alone have dynamically affected the reality of concert performance in Europe and have also undermined the composite state of world culture transactions (and this has not happened by accident). What this means is that the old concept of measuring income by the dollar must come to an end, and in its place, one should maybe think about the German mark or Swiss franc. At present, I see the currency exchange business as one of the biggest rip-offs of this time period—because (1) everyone gives a different rate, and (2) to sell money is always less than to buy money. In other words, every time one changes money he or she loses. For myself I am looking forward to the hopeful development of a world currency, and the next ten years might well see this concept begin to take shape. Hopefully, the Euro-dollar will be a reality by the end of this decade. I see this development as only the first step in realigning the present complexities surrounding money.

23. What is the present reality of customs laws—as this subject concerns musicians?

The last five years have seen an increase in enforcing strict customs laws, and this is especially true in countries like France. Many creative musicians find entry into France very difficult at particular borders—or on the train. Most customs officials at these points will and can make many problems for musicians whose instruments are not officially documented. I would advise every traveling musician to get papers on his or her instrument before leaving the country—but even this cannot guarantee an easy entry.

CMOA(III)–16

In the final analysis, a smooth entry by car through a given country has more to do with luck than anything else. The most basic argument I have heard about customs rules has to do with insuring that individuals are not allowed to enter a country and sell musical instruments without a permit. For this reason, one must purchase a carnet that lists all instruments and possessions—and there is also a time stipulation. To my knowledge, this procedure is the most efficient way of insuring no hassle—but nothing can be guaranteed. The present reality of customs laws makes it very difficult for creative musicians, who have little money anyway, to travel from country to country. Yet, by the same token, no country can be faulted for trying to protect what it feels is in the best interest of its citizens. I would, however, suggest that one should always fly into France when possible—or Canada, too, for that matter. Nothing is more annoying than to be held in customs for a whole day—and still not gain entry.

REALITY ASPECT OF CREATIVE MUSIC

(Level One)

THE TRANSITION IN CREATIVE MUSIC that led to the forms we now refer to as bebop is generally considered to be the point of separation between extended creative functionalism (and/or alternative functionalism—having to do with the solidification of not only new language lines, but extending to the meta-reality implications of what those lines really signified) and public acceptance—and/or interest. The emergence of bebop would have a devastating effect on the composite reality of creative music from the black aesthetic on every level. It is important that some effort is made to understand just what this expansion has meant, because the meta-reality implications of the form we call bebop have underlined and altered every subsequent projection of contemporary creativity—in other words, the music we call bebop has helped to shape the reality and vibrational particulars we are now dealing with today. To understand the realness of this phenomenon is to begin examining what transpired in the source-initiation collision between extended functionalism (from the post-Parker continuum) and the imposed definitions of the collective forces of western culture. My point is this: the composite information that characterized western journalism in the forties can be viewed with respect to the nature of its transitional alignment with post-existential interpretations, as well as the dynamic acceleration of new technology. Further—the realness of this phenomenon would also determine the vibrational nature underlying which affinity interpretations would attach themselves to the forming projectional continuum of alternative functionalism. As such, the solidification of transitional commentary in the late forties would establish a particular affinity attitude in interpreting the "particulars" about black creativity. For it must be understood that the "so-called" intellectual community surrounding alternative creativity (both in America and in Europe) mistakenly viewed the projectional continuum we now call bebop as an extension that functioned with the same meta-reality dynamics as western creativity. The resulting interpretations that have solidified about this period of creative music can be viewed as directly related to the use of "cross-transfer" definitions and the intensive use of gradualism as a means to "have something to know about." This is so because the nature of the journalism that took place in the early period of bebop transcended the particulars of a given focus (or opinion), but instead moved to suppress the reality position (and/or affinity dynamics) underlying what a given "creative participation" really meant (in its vibrational and cosmic sense).

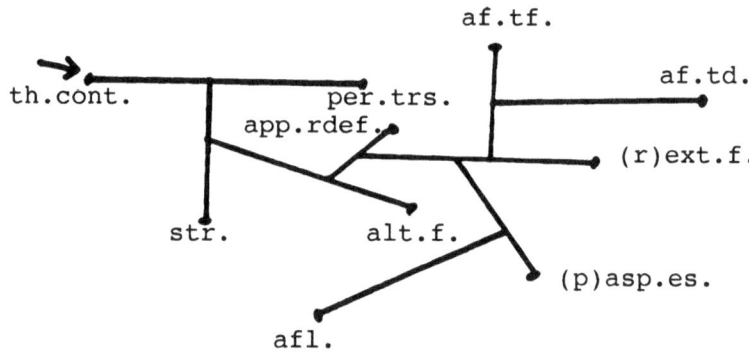

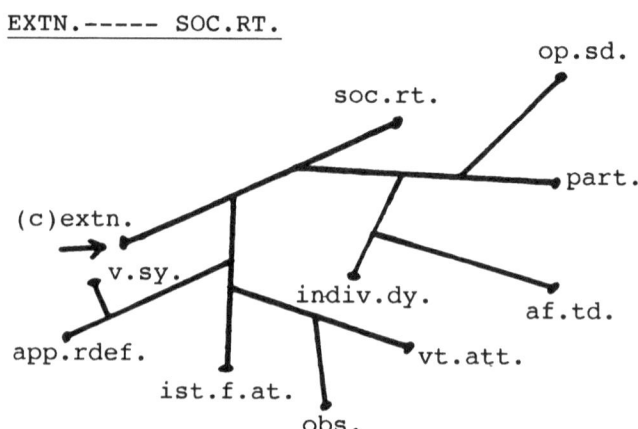

The emergence of bebop would supply new fuel for the critical and defining communities' real belief (and hope) that the progressional thrust of alternative creativity from the black community had indeed exhausted itself (the dialectics for this argument were of course borrowed from the same people who proclaimed that extended creativity from the post-Webern juncture represented the end of western art music—the "Schoenberg is dead, long live Aaron Copland" group). As such, the collective forces of western culture (and information regulation) moved to view bebop as a form that did not properly conform to what they had already defined as the correct zone for black creativity—and the seriousness of this discontent would permeate the reality of post-bebop information, from the forties until today. The resulting commentary that characterized so-called jazz journalism would amplify the dissatisfaction of the western definers' community on several levels: (1) with respect to the particulars of a given performance, and (2) with respect to the meta-reality particulars of a given viewpoint; and the two most basic positions that jazz journalism would take were: (1) bebop is no different from what already took place in western art music—which is to say, classical commentary is valid because "this form is understood," and (2) the solidification of this form (bebop) implies a profound separation from the composite continuum of black creative music (in other words, two viewpoints which were united only in that both positions were wrong).

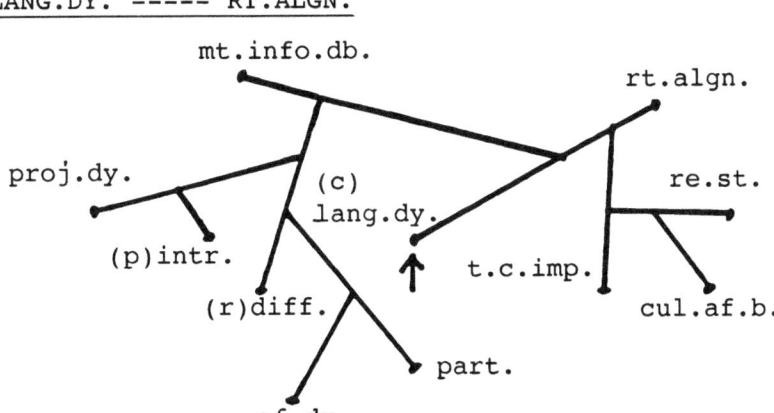

R(AS) CM(I)–4

It is important that attempts are made to view the reality of present-day information lines—and this is especially true if we desire to really understand alternative creativity. The nature of a given information focus is serious because it represents an "input" in a region of profound importance. Moreover, the present reality of alternative functionalism in this time period is compounded by the lack of real opportunities to challenge the existing state of things—whether the state has to do with misdefinitions or the challenge of supplying new viewpoints. A given opinion from the collective forces of western culture is presented as the total reality of a particular phenomenon—rather than simply another opinion. The dominance of western information interpretation in this time period is important for how it has affected cultural affinity dynamics—and also affinity options. For the nature of a given commentary (or exposure) has a profound effect on the greater public's initial vibrational receptiveness to new viewpoints or initiations. In the end, western information interpretation moves to regulate the terms underlying how a given phenomenon is to be introduced to the greater society, and this is part of the problem. That the collective forces of western culture perceived bebop as a destructive form of creativity is in itself not surprising. The dilemma of this perception has to do with what the monopoly of contemporary information lines means to the greater public. We are slowly entering a cycle where certain factors must be re-examined if alternative functionalism is to play a role in shaping the next period of earth life. There is now a need to make clear the separation between the actual reality of alternative functionalism (and the implications of what that reality poses for the greater community) and the reality of the commentary that ensues from the "so-called" experts in present-day media dissemination.

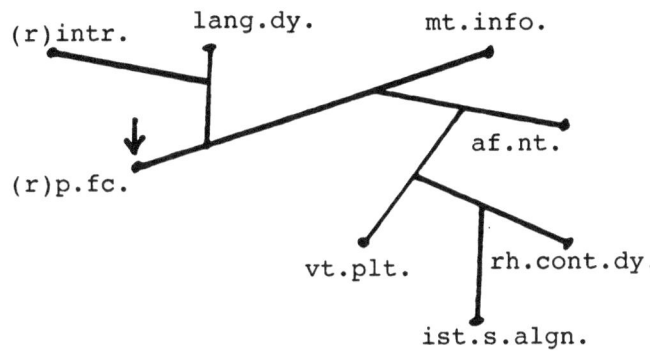

To comment on the present reality of creative music and the role of collective manipulation in shaping public opinion is both important and necessary if we are to understand the dynamics of interpretations that have solidified in the last thirty years. Because the sophistication of contemporary media lies at the heart of our understanding or misunderstanding of everything we know about creative music and/or alternative functionalism. This is not to say that everything written about creative music from the forties until this period is necessarily wrong—or even consciously designed to be wrong—because nothing is either completely this or that. Rather, the progressional applications of interpretations from the collective forces of western culture must be viewed with respect to the basic tenor of America's vibrational lineage—because this has been consistent. To examine the opinions that have permeated so-called jazz criticism and jazz journalism is to begin understanding the workings of information manipulation—and this is only the beginning. To really view the workings of what I have termed the "reality aspect of creative music" is to focus on the composite spectrum of factors surrounding the music, involving not only the press but extending into every area of information dissemination.

Quite possibly the best way to begin examining the reality aspect of creative music is to review the factors responsible for the present position of extended creativity in western culture. For the most basic understanding handed to us concerning this subject is the idea that creative music is not embraced by the greater public because the actual music itself is unattractive or deemed not worthy of support. Thus the reality position of alternative creativity in this time zone is viewed as separate from the composite pulse of the actual culture—which is to say, creative music (or art music) is somehow viewed as not necessarily relevant to the real life force of the culture. The progressional realness of this viewpoint has moved the greater culture to somehow dismiss all of the creative projections that have solidified since the forties as not necessarily aligned with the real events that make up social reality (or vibrational reality) and, as such, as nothing more than esoteric gymnastics. The end result of this vibrational sentiment is that present-day alternative functionalism can be viewed as isolated from the greater society—and this isolation is serious for what it implies about the dynamic implications for future change to both western and world culture. To view the realness of creative music is to make some attempt to understand what this phenomenon really means.

Certainly it is clear that the reality of extended functionalism implies that given "affinity adjustments" must be made on the part of the musicians as well as the listeners. In that context, it is also clear that given sectors of a particular community would find the demands of alternative creativity to be outside their established relationship to listening. But I do not believe that the composite reality position of creative music in this time zone can be solely reduced to the vibrational dynamics of a "given encounter" (or "series of encounters"), because there are other factors related to this most important phenomenon. To really view the realness of composite creative music in western culture (and in particular, American culture), then, one is forced to examine the extended implications of information manipulation, especially with respect to the acceleration of contemporary media. In the final analysis, I believe that the present reality of creative music can be directly related to lack of exposure given the music by the composite spectrum of western media, and, in the case of creative music from the black aesthetic, I believe the suppression of alternative functionalism is coupled with the composite distortion of all information of relevance to possible transformation. Moreover, I also believe that the reality of western information dissemination is so infested with both racist-sexist—and nationalistic—redefinitions that it represents the most important bastion of disruption in this time zone.

POL.DYM.------SOC.RT.

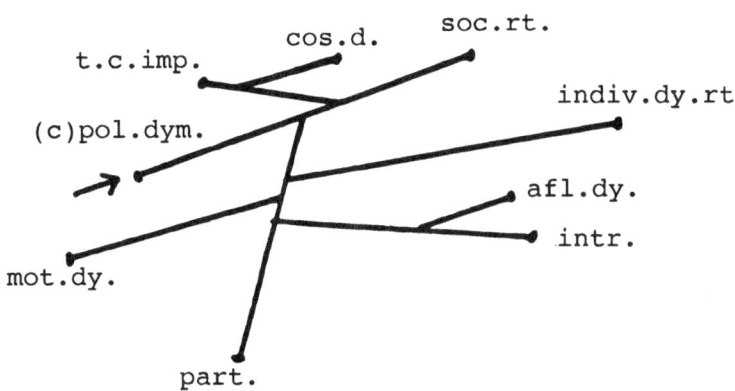

Before this section attempts to review the particulars of information manipulation—as it involves either creativity or alternative functionalism—it is important that some effort is made to clarify the reality options of extended functionalism. That is, the particulars of social reality in this time zone have produced only two most basic options for progressional continuance—and this is true for every thrust of alternative creativity (whether we are commenting on the future extension of so-called black or white creative projections). There are only two possibilities: either (1) alternative creativity will lend itself as a positive tool for transformation and, as such, move to instigate change while clarifying the next level of functionalism; or (2) alternative creativity will continue to be utilized as a diversion factor by pseudo-intellectual groups and definers as a means to continue the present "state of things" (and as a means to exoticize alternative functionalism with many of the concepts of "hipness" that surround the music). In this context, alternative functionalism can derive significance only from its ability to provide useful diversions for given sectors of the society—while forfeiting its dynamic implications in the process (that being, its potential for changing the world). It is important that both of these options are understood—and soon, because "decision time" is already upon us.

Without doubt, the reality of alternative functionalism will not change on its own accord. Unless some consolidated efforts are brought together, the progressional realness of extended functionalism will continually be reduced to "something to write and talk about" in certain intellectual circles, as opposed to a living and breathing affirmation of creativity with transformational potential. As such, the reality aspect of creative music today must be viewed to understand what steps must be taken tomorrow. For unless the dynamics of western information lines are held accountable for the position creative music has in present-day social reality, nothing will change. In the final analysis, there is no way that creative music can function as a positive factor for society—let alone transformation—unless people can actually hear the music.

The dynamic manipulation of contemporary information lines is a subject that transcends any one focus—which is to say, the reality of the mis-information that has personified western media is not limited to creative music but encompasses everything we think we know. Yet it is also clear that there are no other options available for the dissemination of information in this time period. The total domination big business enjoys over the media must be viewed as extremely important in that a relatively small sector of the greater society controls the total output of all information regulation. This is true whether the area of information pertains to either world events or conceptualization. As such, the seriousness of this situation implies that somehow inroads must be solidified in the next cycle for alternative information-interpretation outlets—this is true whether we are focusing on music journalism or American television. The success of the next thrust of creative progressionalism is directly related to whether or not the gains of this cycle are properly digested and/or understood. Thus, the reality of the next immediate time period must involve the gradual infiltration of alternative information in every media focus. Contemporary music must find a way to appear on television and/or radio—in every sector of the greater community—nothing less will do (yet I have not meant to only focus on music in this regard, for the dynamics of alternative dance must also be exposed to the greater public—the changes reshaping sculpture—painting—all of these extensions are necessarily relevant and connected to the composite well-being and hope of any intelligent—or that wants to be intelligent—culture).

I have not meant to imply that to utilize contemporary media lines—as they exist in this cycle—is necessarily all positive—or without risk—because it isn't. The fact is, distortion is an integral factor that is not separate from how western media views information—which is to say, even with more exposure, creative music (or alternative creativity) will undoubtedly suffer in terms of its meta-reality implications. Yet it is also clear that the advantages of media far outweigh their disadvantages—for whatever misconceptions are transmitted, the most basic problem that has plagued alternative creativity is the realness of no exposure at all. Hopefully, even a distorted exposure of a given creative thrust can inspire the greater public to research the actual reality of the music for themselves. This is probably all one can ask from the media—in this cycle (yet it would be somewhat arrogant and unfair to suggest that there are no individuals in media who are—or might be—concerned about the state of creativity—which is to say, there is always the possibility of an intelligently presented program sooner or later—or every now and then).

In a sense, the reality particulars of the creative transformation that occurred in the sixties and seventies mirror the particulars of the forties. Because while the transformation that created bebop and the post-Webern thrust was forming, the composite culture was preoccupied with the greater realness of economic intensity and (in some cases) world disorder—or war. The transition that created bebop and post-serialism was balanced by a recession that vibrationally moved to accent other areas of both information and creativity. The actual changes in the music thus occurred in the wee hours of the morning—or in the shadows of much greater factors—and the recorded documentation that was left only scratched the surface of what really happened (this is true even though there were—and are—many important recordings of the music). There are several factors related to this phenomenon, for whenever the socio-economic factors of the greater culture are intense—whether the situation is labeled a recession or depression—the creativity of that culture is usually the first area to experience its naked economic implications. It also follows that if creativity is to be among the first areas to suffer the pangs of economic decline, then the music we refer to as either jazz or extended creativity (the avant-garde) will in all probability experience the greatest neglect (whether that neglect has to do with either performance or recording possibilities—or being paid from performing or recording). As we move into the eighties, it is now possible to view the sixties and seventies in the same light. For the dynamics of the post-Ayler and -Cage continuum have yet to be documented properly. Only in the middle seventies have some of the smaller companies begun recording the music (and the post-Cage movement has yet to experience even that much). At present, there are only a handful of books on the music (and three-fourths of those books are nonsense) and, in general, there have been no real efforts by the media to educate the greater public as to the significance of the many changes reshaping creativity. Yet many of the so-called established critics controlling information on the music would have us believe that the lack of public support for alternative creativity is indicative of the insignificance of the music—as opposed to the failure of contemporary media to properly educate and expose relevant information. A comparison between the activity which revolutionized creativity at places like Minton's—and the fact we have so few recordings of that period (as well as how that activity was—and is—viewed by the musicians who actually participated in that change)—and the dynamic continuum that solidified the AACM is most certainly justified for what it reveals about present-day information dissemination (especially with respect to the implications of extended functionalism after the Second World War). It is important that some efforts are made to view what these similarities really mean.

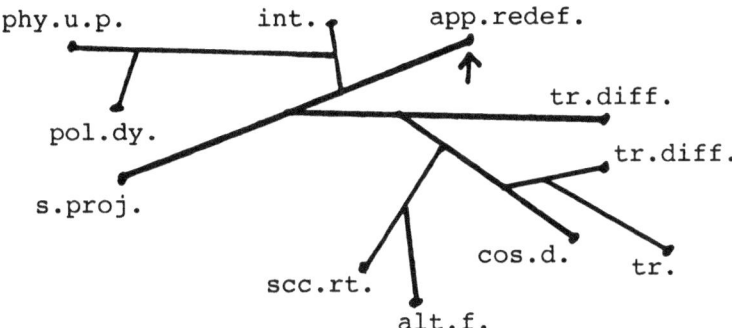

At the heart of this essay is my belief that the reality dynamics of information interpretation in this cycle have determined more than just a "principal attitude" towards creative postulation or extended functionalism—instead, the nature of the commentary surrounding the music moves to give insight about much more important matters. In other words, the realness of western culture's affinity position with extended functionalism is only one surface symptom of a much greater area of concern. This phenomenon is also related to a composite progressional pattern that has regulated extended functionalism—from the forties to the present. For the most basic factor that has dictated commentary on extended functionalism since bebop has been the use of "time lag" definitions as a means to stagnate the source-initiated definitions of extended creativity—while also providing a wedge for the gradual forming of source-transfer redefinitions. In other words, the reality of contemporary information manipulation has created a situation that blocks any given definition (source initiation) until that definition can be made to conform with "how its culture group sees itself" (source transfer). The seriousness of this phenomenon must be understood if we are to view the progressionalism of the last thirty years. For the use of "time lag" re-interpretation—as a factor that functions with respect to the realness of cross-transfer definitions exclusively (as opposed to "source-initiated interpretations," which actualized from the actual music—that being, "how the musicians, in this case, saw what they did")—is directly related to how alternative functionalism is suppressed and—in the end—rechanneled to correspond with "the desired reality perspective of western information." The challenge of alternative functionalism is directly related to whether or not this phenomenon is checked. By now, it should be clear that the collective forces of western information dissemination are not about to change their relationship with information on its own (and it is important to understand that in many cases the "re-adjustments" done by western information regulation are because "many of these people only understand source-transfer definitions"—which is to say, in many cases it would not be correct to simply imply that information distortion is what western culture is interested in—rather, in many cases, the realness of alternative definitions is simply outside of western culture's affinity relationship with information). As such, it is important that the stifling of information is not taken "personally," but seen as only one factor that must be eliminated, whether it is intended to be negative or not (even though everyone knows it is). My point here is only that the seriousness of correct information will be important for what it will mean for the next cycle. As such, it is time to make the media account for the position they have over the greater society. The phenomenon of "time lag" re-interpretation cannot be allowed to continue unchecked because we all suffer from "incomplete information."

ALT.D.------SOC.RT.

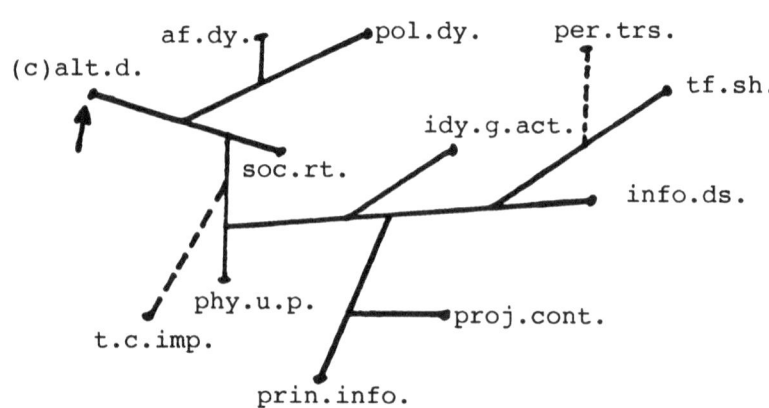

The reality of "time lag" definitions can best be understood as a logical consequence of media suppression. In other words, the emergence of redefinitions—in, say, music journalism—can be traced to denying source-initiated interpretations access to the basic channels of cultural information output and machinery. The end result of this denial is that given initiations must wait until the controlling wing of western continuance decides to comment about the "reality" of their existence. Moreover, commentary in this regard is always realigned to correspond with "what these people feel they already know" or to "what these people have decided to know." Add to this phenomenon the realness of present-day social reality, as well as the ingredient of racism and/or "special interest," and one can imagine the looseness of present-day-sanctioned definitions. In other words, there is no information on the established information lines that is not in some way reshaped to correspond with the "sanctioned viewpoint" that the greater "powers that be" would like us to believe. This is not to sound paranoid—nor am I attempting to McCarthyize the reality of creative music. My point is only that the dynamics of present-day available information are as they are because they don't threaten the "basic order of things"—and this is important to understand. The real "meta-reality" of creative music—as well as the dynamic implications of principal information—cannot be viewed unless one's reality of perception transcends the present notions we now have—of country, race, science, spirituality, etc., etc. The use of redefinitions must be viewed from this same context—that being, with respect to what it raises for "continuing the present state of things." All of these considerations can be better understood by examining the relationship of media to creativity—and in particular, alternative creativity—because the implications of information suppression are not one-dimensional. To examine the particulars of information dissemination in this time period is to begin seeing what has really happened in western culture. As such, the thrust of this section will attempt to focus on the reality aspect of creative music as it pertains to given areas of information dissemination.

R(AS) CM(I)–14

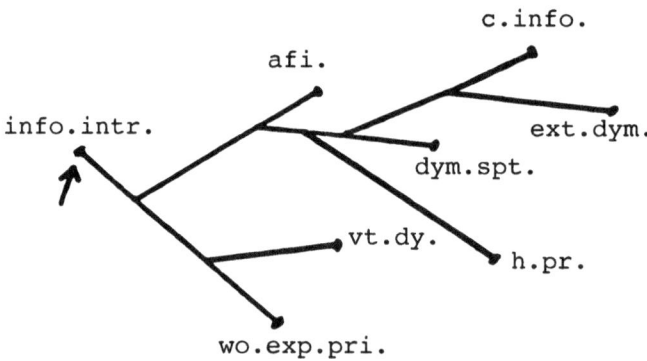

Rather than deal with the specifics of contemporary media as representing only one entity—and risk the possibility of over-generalizing the most important subject—the main thrust of this section will attempt to comment on the particulars of each area of information dissemination. An approach of this kind is necessary if we are to really understand—and hopefully correct—the reality continuum that surrounds creative music. Certainly there are many areas of relevant information related to the dynamics of contemporary information dissemination—and this is true on every level. But the reality of a given creative projection is directly related to how the media utilizes it—that is, the dynamic and effective implications of a given phenomenon are not separate from whether or not it is exposed—nor is that phenomenon separate from "how" it is exposed. To investigate the realness of contemporary media is to begin understanding the composite factors that shape the greater society. It is important to understand the real position of creativity in western culture—as opposed to the one-dimensional notions we have been handed in the past one hundred years. The dynamic realness of this subject cannot be relegated to only certain sectors of the greater society, because creativity is not about a "brick." Instead, the reality underlying this subject sheds light on—and indeed affirms—the composite lining of its base culture group. The realness of a given projection (or information focus) should concern everyone.

THE MEDIA

Television

However one chooses to view the dynamics of contemporary media, it is clear that the medium of television has profoundly affected the total realness of western culture (and this is particularly true of American culture). In a time period of thirty years (and some), television has become the most dynamic vehicle for information dissemination—and this one medium has totally eclipsed every other channel of transference. It also goes without saying that the potential of this one medium is staggering—whether that potential is directed towards world change or composite consciousness—or whether that potential involves manipulation (towards lower levels of existence and/or focuses). So influential is this one medium that any attempt to really view the realness of western culture would necessitate that some effort is directed towards understanding its special implications. To really deal with this subject would take twenty-seven point five years—and even then, there would be other areas to comment on. As such, I am forced to limit my inquiry about this subject to only those focuses related to creative music.

I have already commented on the use of television in Europe for creative music, and I have already commented on the resulting effects of this difference. It is ironic that a musician of the stature of John Coltrane was given exposure on American television only once, to my knowledge—and that was when he was a member of the Miles Davis Quintet (sometime in the fifties). For musicians like Cecil Taylor or, for that matter, any of the individuals who have gained prominence in the early sixties through what was then considered the avant-garde, there has been no exposure on national television at all (in the last couple of months, both Ornette Coleman and Sun Ra have had their television debut—for ten minutes, maybe a little more or less—on the *Saturday Night Live* television show). The realness of what this means is so incredible that it boggles the mind, for it must be understood that the reality of improvisational music can never be recaptured—that is, the dynamic realness of what, say, a musician like Cecil Taylor is doing in this period (the late seventies) cannot be duplicated in the eighties or nineties—not to mention, the realness of a given individual's health and/or life is not guaranteed either. The fact that no exposure or visual documentation is being done on individuals of this magnitude by American television is simply frightening. Moreover, even the two musicians I named as having appeared on American television didn't really have their craft presented on the level it deserves. What is needed are intellectually presented programs about the realness of their music—as opposed to a ten-minute slice of a given performance. The failure of American television to responsibly present creative music will one day be seen as one of the great tragedies of this time period—for it must be understood that the neglect of artists like Charles Mingus is more than a simple oversight: what we could have learned from visual documentation of his work cannot be replaced.

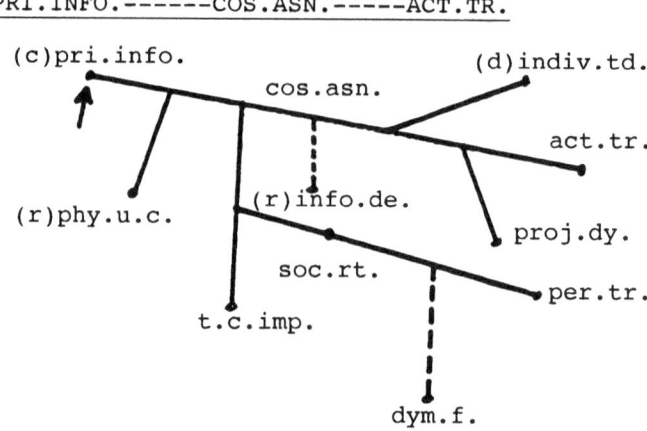

The seriousness of television has long been understood by the creative community, and there have been many attempts by musicians themselves to change the existing situation. In 1968, Roland Kirk, along with a group of black musicians, did take over *The Tonight Show* by storming the stage— and after the pandemonium, obtained three or four performances (that being, three or four ten-minute allocations for a given exposure). But to propose fighting every television show in America in order to get three or four performances would be ridiculous. There have also been some gains in educational television for creative music—at least when compared to network television. Yet exposure for post-Ayler or -Cage creativity is kept at the bare minimum (for instance, a half-hour allocated to the World Saxophone Quartet or to Philip Glass), but this is better than nothing. (I have also been told that education television did broadcast a program on the work of John Cage—but as of this time zone, I cannot say if this is true or not.) My point, however, is that the inclusion of one or two programs a year on contemporary music means very little. What is needed is normal exposure—that being, the appearance of the music in the media as if it really existed (and did not die with the dinosaur).

I recall experiencing creative music on several independent stations throughout America in given time periods, but none of these shows have resulted in long-term exposure. Even public television cannot be viewed as having lived up to its expectations. There have never been attempts to really change the situation of alternative creativity. Instead, the few inclusions of creative music are approached as "specials"—that being, outside of the normal programming diet (which is to say, not regularly programmed). To even experience alternative creativity once a month—or two months, even—would be revolutionary. Television's neglect of contemporary music is a reflection of the total vibrational alignment of western culture. This is true with respect to the manipulation that has solidified the principal vibrational tone of the culture, and this is also true with respect to which zones the collective forces of western culture seem to be moving towards. The progressional continuance of this time period has moved to solidify alternative functionalism as totally separate from the most basic focus of the society—that is, by denying alternative functionalism access to the medium of television, the collective forces of western culture somehow create the impression that new music is "less real" than everything else. It is possible to count on one hand the number of programs devoted to contemporary music on American television in a year.

The information suppression surrounding creativity in this time period is not relegated to only creative music from the black aesthetic, but extends to cover western art music as well. For the most part, there have been no attempts to educate the greater public as to the dynamics of post-Webern (let alone post-Cage) extensions. Even worse, when finally a given program does materialize, it is always about the works of a European composer—rather than an American composer. This is not to underrate the work of European composers—and certainly the public should have the opportunity to experience every region of earth culture—but one would think that the work of contemporary American composers merits some attention as well—but this has not been the case. I can recall seeing programs of Boulez discussing Varèse's music sometime in the early seventies, but this is not the norm by any means. However, when these rarities do occur, it is usually on a much higher level than so-called jazz programming. Usually a television production of contemporary western art music has two performances of a given work separated by commentary about the reality and background of both the work and the composer. A production of this type can be very educational as well as effective. To my knowledge, Boulez did several programs of this type, and I believe the hope of constructive television lies in this direction. However, I have yet to see any programs on American television about the music of Morton Feldman or Earle Brown (and why hasn't some station done a program on the work of Harry Partch by now?). There is much room for improvement in every area of American television—regardless of region of information focus.

The basic focus of American television's relationship to western art music has been on orchestras like the New York Philharmonic. Many of these programs are in fact quite good. There have been programs scanning the spectrum of western art music from the early forms up to Stravinsky. In the last couple of years, public television has even begun to broadcast operas, and this decision has probably been the best thing to have happened in American television. There have been many live broadcasts—even from places like the Metropolitan Opera—of operas like *Othello* or *Carmen*. Hopefully this area of television will continue, because opera is especially suited for television—and the composite culture can begin to experience this most glamorous and—until now—closed form of creativity. To experience television in this context is to understand the real role this medium could play in helping to educate and elevate the composite society.

The last three or four years have seen some changes in American television's relationship to traditional creative music from the black aesthetic—especially in so-called popular music (although most of the programs that would qualify as shows on black music—rhythm and blues, rock, etc.—are done by white performers, in which case, there is usually a "token" guest or two to show there are no bad feelings). The situation in American television as we move into the eighties is nowhere as bad as it was in the fifties (because in this period, I can only remember seeing Lennie Tristano on *Look Up and Live* and Dave Brubeck on the same program, and also as a guest on *Playboy* magazine's television show, and Duke Ellington and Count Basie as guests on given shows—usually this involved backing up the star, who in most cases was a singer, like maybe Frank Sinatra—and later having the opportunity to play a number of their own as well). Let us not also forget to pay homage to the great "session" shows that appear every now and then to celebrate "De good ole jazz days, you all." Public television, even in this time period, seems quite fond of these kinds of situations. Can anyone imagine how interesting it would be if a program would present the New York Philharmonic for a five-to-ten-minute piece, followed by the Chicago Symphony for a ten-minute piece (and of course we would have to throw in Dave Brubeck for the third or fourth set—"because, you know, Dave always takes part in these kinds of things"), followed by Martha Graham—a real salute to all those talented white people and America. But, of course, this will never happen, because western culture would never put itself in this position. This is not to knock the concept of the jam session—but by now one would think that maybe Count Basie has been around long enough to merit a program devoted to his music alone. Maybe it would be really educational to compile films and tapes of Duke Ellington for an extended program on just his contributions to creativity. I realize, however, that given sectors of American culture would say that my charges are unfair—and I understand what they mean.

There is another aspect of television that greatly affects the music, and that aspect is how the medium sees itself—in short, the "show business" mentality of television functions as a distortion element for creative music.

R(AS) CM(I)–20

Television is directly connected to the emergence of the "is it jazz or not" syndrome. Of the handful of performers who have gained access to this medium, very few have been able to keep the integrity of their activity intact. This is so because before any performer can gain access to the medium of television, there must be a certain amount of flexibility on his or her part. This is how the medium is designed (the need to attract decent ratings, and the actual position of television as a tool for maintaining anti-culture). I do not mean to imply that every creative musician who has been on television has sold out, because to state such would be ridiculous—there have been many isolated programs where musicians have been able to perform their actual music. But I do mean to imply that extensive use of this medium is directly proportionate to one's ability to function within the sanctioned vibrationaltory context of present-day information transference. For it is clear that television is a tool that maintains the established defining forces' ability to dictate information dynamics—and/or focus. In this context, it is not surprising to find musicians of the caliber of Aretha Franklin singing pop songs, or Count Basie backing up Frank Sinatra, etc. Television is a principal tool for solidifying "gradualism" (as a source-transfer factor). Flexibility in this case has to do with one's ability to bend and fit within the sanctioned reality of the defining forces shaping America's composite vibrational position—"what is to be acceptable and what is not." This is so because television is oriented towards what is functional—functional in this context means what will make money.

As for the handful of programs that somehow do get televised, there is another dilemma that cannot be ignored. For many of the people who host these shows are the same people who have helped to misdocument the music. I recall turning on the television to see a given musician and, "lo and behold," the master of ceremonies was the same person whose writings have helped to discredit the very person he was presenting. This is quite common, in fact, but I am still always shocked when it happens. For the masters of ceremonies in most of these situations are the people who have been designated as the "experts" on the music. It goes without saying that if these people are put into positions of influence, then the distortions which solidify their writings (and reviews) are transmitted to an even greater audience. In other words, the prevailing attitudes and misconceptions that surround the music are broadcast to thousands of people. We can talk of this phenomenon as representing a negative throwback for the music—and of course, it does, but in the final analysis, the reality dynamics of television in this cycle present no other possibilities. Rather, it becomes a choice of "bad against worse." For the reality position of alternative creativity has little choice but to accept whatever exposure it can get (even if that exposure is out of context with the real reality of the music, and even if that exposure puts more emphasis on misinformation as opposed to the actual music). It is better to have some outlet for hopefully stimulating public interest than no outlet at all.

Radio

The reality of creative music in the medium of radio is somewhat different from that of television. It is possible to experience alternative creativity on a more regular basis through this medium—regardless of focus—as opposed to the television "special" mentality. Yet in no way has radio measured up to the responsibility of its position. But the past ten years (and some) have seen a great many changes occur in this medium, and it is now possible that every major city in America has at least one station devoted to alternative creativity (or what is now called "the jazz station"). In many cases, the concept these stations have of jazz involves Chuck Mangione or what is now called jazz-rock—which is to say, to state that the actual dynamics of alternative creativity can be experienced in radio is somewhat of an over-statement. I do not mean that the utilization of these forms is not positive—because it is. It serves no purpose to compare the exposure popular music receives to that of creative music in this time period—obviously, in every case, alternative creativity receives much less. More stations will always program commercial music to a much greater degree than "art" music, and no one can really expect this to change—as long as the culture is as it is. The fact is, the reality of media programming is not separate from the economic decisions which have solidified the whole of this time period. Moreover, it is also clear that the greater public is simply more interested in popular and commercial forms of creativity (and how could anyone not be when all of these alignments are programmed by some of the most sophisticated mechanisms in this time zone). The present programming of rock and popular music on radio must be seen as normal within what has been established for the composite society.

There is, however, a growing trend in radio towards a more democratic approach to programming—and the implications of this trend could have profound importance for the future. I have, in my travels throughout the country (America), noticed a resurgence of stations attempting to devote some of their programming to focuses other than commercial creativity. This is not to say real change is on the immediate horizon, but to not acknowledge this phenomenon would in itself be unfair. Radio has always had the potential to function more flexibly than television, and the future of this medium does look somewhat brighter.

In the past fifteen years, there has been a significant change in FM radio programming all over the country. For in the early fifties, FM stations were basically outlets for classical music, news, and a small amount of popular music (e.g., Glenn Miller or Henry Mancini), but by the end of the sixties this pattern was altered considerably. The most basic factor that changed the policies of FM stations had to do with economics as well as the realness that the majority of people in the country wanted to hear rock. If the sixties represented the period whereby business would completely embrace rock music, it could also be said that the net effect of that decision left FM radio little choice but to move in the same direction, and that is exactly what happened. The situation for FM radio today is very similar in one regard to the early sixties and late fifties—for if, in the beginning, FM functioned as a tool for classical music exclusively, today rock music has that same position (and now there are only a few FM stations in a given city that program classical music—let alone creative music).

It is important to understand that the spectacle of rock did not just come from nowhere—rather, this phenomenon became an integral part of composite America because of its utilization in the media. People finally had to "is" the fact that it existed whether or not they liked it. With the dissemination of the music through the media, it was inevitable that the public would relate to it—at some point it was also clear that no one had any choice. The reality of this phenomenon seems to be that once a person has a chance to be exposed to a given particular, within a given time frame, he or she is apt to find some aspect of its focus that can be positively experienced. It was through the medium of radio that rock music attracted new listeners, and today, not only has rock been assimilated into the culture—where the positive aspects of the music have been experienced—but this activity (rock music) has also contributed to the present curiosity about creative improvised music.

(R)PRI.INFO. -----SG.------PROJ.DY.

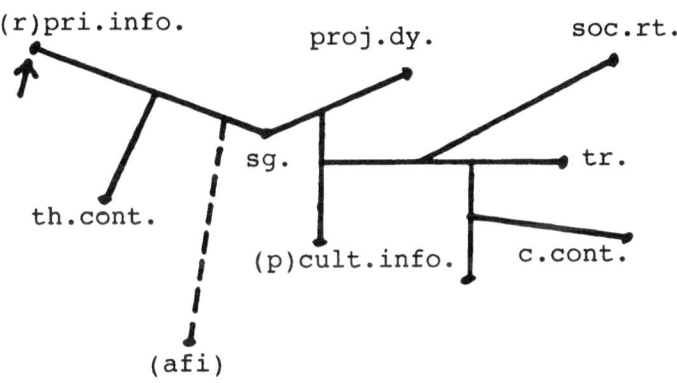

To view the totalness of the situation dictating radio in this country, it is important to acknowledge all the variables underlying its actual practice—in short, we must be aware of the real factors that dictate policy for western information dynamics, and what this phenomenon means on the physical universe level. In doing so, we have no choice but to "is" the realness of radio and big business. For although this medium certainly provides a useful function with regard to its scientific and dissemination potential in providing these services, radio also increases its own potential to make money for big business. My point is this: creative music in this time period has been neglected not because of the music—or the fact that the stations fear no one really wants to hear the music—but because the medium has yet to find a way to align this phenomenon with the factors that control the vibrational lining of American culture (and in this context, big business cannot make money).

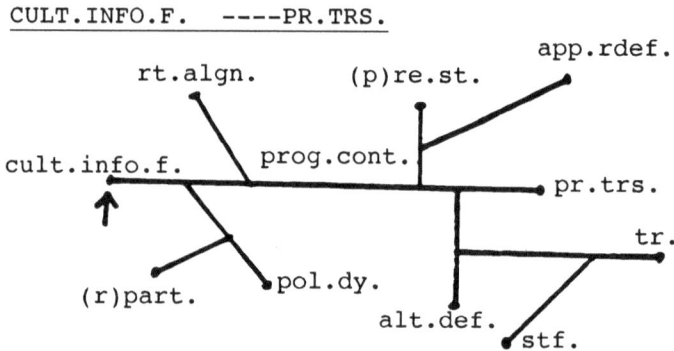

In the final analysis, the consideration of economics really dictates whether or not a given "factor" is made available for the general public. Certainly, if some kind of marked increase developed for alternative creativity, companies like RCA and CBS would respond accordingly. It would not be a question of corporate consciousness—or of new-found responsibility and/or concern for the greater society—rather, the large companies that produce consumer products will respond to any consideration that carries the promise of "greater profits." This is what America is all about (that being, profits and products which can be molded "in accordance with the basic fabric of American life"—in other words, "throw some words on them and keep moving"). There are many ways that given corporations could lightly test the waters for possible profits—for if a company like CBS is not inclined to record new music, it could instead release some of the creative music it already has—either way, this effort could serve the music. It is important to understand that a company like CBS has much valuable music in its vaults—music that should be made available to the greater public. And this is especially true for creative music from the black aesthetic in its early forms, as well as western art music. For instance, I have been told that CBS has more tapes of Miles Davis (in all of his different periods) which have never been released.

Assuming that Mr. Davis would give his consent, this music should be made available to the public (and of course if Mr. Davis does not want this music out, then it should be destroyed—but not left to rot away in the vaults of CBS or any of the large companies). RCA has a great deal of music by Fats Waller that has never been released in America—not to mention, the early records of Duke Ellington should have been made available in America long ago. The greater public must be educated and exposed to its creativity—this should be one of the main challenges of contemporary media (involving composite creativity, and from every area of the planet—nothing less will do).

There is also another aspect of radio that must be commented on— for the realness of this medium has profoundly opened new alternatives for present-day information transference. The aspect I am referring to is the emergence of college radio stations throughout the country. For the broadcasting done in this sector of radio has shown much more flexibility than the commercial stations, in every area—concerning both creativity and public affairs programs. Undoubtedly this flexibility has resulted from the lack of restrictions placed on their daily operation—for college radio does not have to make money in the same sense as commercial radio. To view the realness of this phenomenon is to have real hope about the future of this medium (radio)—for the work reshaping radio programming in this period has really actualized from various campuses throughout the country.

It is possible to view a kind of transition in radio broadcasting during this period. For the progressional realness of this time period has seen the solidification of several effective stations all around the country. Stations like WMAQ in Chicago, WKCR in New York, KSAM in San Francisco, etc. These stations are among the new wave in media programming, and hopefully the example they are setting will provide stimulus for even greater change in radio programming. All of these stations vibrate to some form of balanced programming and are making attempts to be involved in the community from which they broadcast. Nor by balanced programming am I referring only to how a given station utilizes creative music from the black aesthetic—rather, balanced programming encompasses the reality dynamics of every kind of music and poetry: from western art music to reggae—in other words, world creativity. Only by experiencing the realness of composite earth creativity will we—as a collective people—be able to understand the realness of what being on earth really is—and could be. Certainly I have not meant to imply that the composite state of radio "has arrived," because it hasn't. There remains much work to be done in every area—but it is important to acknowledge the work college radio is doing in this time zone, because few independent stations have had as much overall success (not to mention, none of the large networks have shown any interest in anything except making more and more money).

There is still another factor in radio that promises to be a factor in transitional programming. For the acceleration of black-owned radio stations in the sixties and seventies has many creative possibilities. Within the next five or six years, I believe black-owned radio stations will become an important alternative to traditional programming. Hopefully, these stations will begin to take up the challenge of broadcasting composite creative music—from the early forms to the present. At present, however, the basic focus of these stations is directed only towards the commercial market—and while it is understandable, it is still no less regrettable. In many cases, the so-called black-owned radio stations are among the narrowest stations in this time cycle—but this phenomenon cannot really be viewed separately from the composite fabric of American society—or American progressionalism. For the emergence of non-white radio ownership must be coupled with the composite economic factors pertaining to the whole of American business—involving understanding what must be done to first survive and later compete. The realness of this phenomenon can better explain what has happened and is happening in black-owned radio outlets. Probably the dictates of social reality will make change extremely difficult in the very near future—and as such, black radio will undoubtedly function from what is clearly the most attractive product it has—that being black popular music (and in fact, this is their right as well, since everyone else is making money from this same commodity). For the dynamic implications of this phenomenon transcend any one use of creativity. Hopefully the next cycle will see composite programming of black creativity in all of its dynamic forms (not to mention the eventual hope of broadcasting every kind of music without respect for the supposed origin of a given form). This is not to ignore the need for programming black creativity on radio, nor by focusing on world music have I meant to imply a lack of respect for any particular area of creativity. Rather, the challenge for black (or non-white) radio stations in the next cycle will have to do with their ability to transcend their "supposed" zone and instead function from whatever perspective they desire. This is true for non-white radio stations, and this is true for non-white people in general. It is important that the next cycle of media transference moves to solidify a more expanded position for alternative functionalism. Because no one sector of the greater community can afford to remain relegated to a "prescribed bag"—each of us should have a choice. The mere fact that America has black and white radio stations broadcasting only aspects of its composite creativity gives insight into this cycle in time. Hopefully a developed understanding of earth creativity could bring about a situation that transcends present-day categories (but this "state of being" can only come about if the composite culture is made to understand it is also in their positive interest). Actually, as this book is being written, more emphasis is placed on black creative music by white radio stations and/or university-owned stations than by black-owned stations. Most of this emphasis has been brought about through the collective work of young students—and every region of the country has benefited from their efforts. The neglect of composite black creativity by black radio stations is simply a phenomenon that seems to be in accord with the social factors which have dictated events—as it concerns the composite reality of black progressionalism—since the Civil War.

Yet I do not intend to excuse irresponsibility, because the challenge of planet transformation is not only the work of young or old white people—let alone students. It is past time for the black community to take up the full challenge of alternative functionalism—and this is especially true for those black people who have become successful—whatever zone or area. Certainly the dynamic realness of western culture has made the possibility of social change difficult—and this cannot be over-emphasized. For the nature of western racism has profoundly determined the basic vibrationaltory state of American society (and this phenomenon has never been conducive to examining or re-examining the nature of basic progressionalism—as it exists in this period)—but in the final analysis, we are all responsible for our own destiny; which is to say, the black community cannot wait for any other sector of humanity to do what we can do for ourselves.

Ornette Coleman, in an interview in *Downbeat* magazine, once raised an interesting point. He said, "Why is Aretha Franklin more important to black people than, say, Frank Sinatra, and why is Frank Sinatra more important to white people than Aretha Franklin?" Certainly these factors will not change overnight—nor have I meant to imply that radio should seek on the first level to make Frank Sinatra more important to black people. Rather, only by having the composite realness of earth creativity available can the greater society begin to understand their total relationship with what is actually happening in their country. I believe that cultural unification—and/or composite vibrational solidification—can come about only by first becoming aware of the diversity and richness of multi-information (whether that information affirms a given form of creativity or methodology). The realness of contemporary media must be viewed with respect to what it poses for this challenge. There is a responsibility related to the advances which have reshaped contemporary media—and it is time for steps to be taken towards some kind of accountability.

Record Companies

It was in the early sixties when the established recording industry began to understand the dynamic potential of rock music as a valuable money-making venture. The whole of the sixties and seventies can now be viewed as the most profitable period in the entire history of record making. However one chooses to now view this phenomenon, it is clear that the decisions made in that cycle have revolutionized composite western culture, and this is true on every level. For the utilization of rock music did not stop at only recording the music, but instead involved the total implications of new marketing techniques. The recording industry in this period would thus record the music and also control its related progressionalism—to insure the success of its product. As such, a given company would record the music, distribute the music, and insure its exposure on radio. The dynamic continuum of this phenomenon would also be responsible for the concept of the "top forty" syndrome, and while this concept might on the surface sound humorous, the fact is, the world of producing and selling is extremely serious. The concept of the "top forty" (which is connected to the same mentality that brought us the "Jazz Poll") is utilized because it has proven itself to be a successful marketing tool.

    I have not mentioned the manipulation of big business in this section to comment only on the dynamics of contemporary functionalism—obviously, the recording industry is serious about the business of selling records and will do whatever has to be done to achieve this goal. Rather, I have mentioned this phenomenon as a means to put a real perspective on the decision-making that surrounds the music industry. For while the decisions of the sixties moved to solidify rock music as the most dynamic commercial music of this time zone, those same decisions collectively moved to isolate and suppress alternative creativity even farther away from the greater public than it already was (and it was bad enough before rock). The situation of alternative creative music in the sixties can be viewed as flowing in opposition, in a sense—to the gains that took place in rock music. By the end of the sixties, very few musicians in alternative creativity were able to get any kind of gig—and that was only the beginning.

    To really understand what has resulted from the composite acceleration of new business dynamics in recording is to view the actual economic continuum that surrounds alternative creativity. Very rarely could a creative musician receive any real money for recording his (or her) music—and this is especially true for the small independent labels that sprang up in the sixties and early seventies. The most basic going price for recording with large companies was about one thousand dollars (that being, one thousand dollars but all of the musicians' fees are to come from that one figure)—"Lord help the fool who only hears orchestra music"—yet there were exceptions. For the persistent musician, five percent royalties are supposed to exist somewhere—but if I am any example of this concept, it is indeed a "concept." Not to mention that totally improvised music cannot be copyrighted unless it is notated after the fact (which cannot always be done). The realness of these examples is only a slice of what is happening in the contemporary music business—and I have only commented on the nice aspect of what is now currently accepted as normal business practices in the industry (which is to say, there are other aspects even farther out). There is obviously a need for changes to take place in this area. As the situation now stands, it is practically impossible for alternative creativity to attract the kind of audiences it should have, and it is also impossible for the greater society to learn about the composite realness of its own creativity (and it goes without saying that alternative creativity in this cycle will never be able to compete with rock music in record sales—which is doubly unfortunate for the music, because record sales is the most basic factor that decides who records and who doesn't). The most basic condition put on any form of music in this time period—by the large companies—is that its sales must be at least in the hundred thousand (units) range to be financially feasible.

But the reality particulars of creative music are much more involved than any one context—for while it is clear that the machinery surrounding producing and distributing music necessitates huge sums of money to even break even, there are also other factors that must be considered. This is so because the commercial implications of western art music are in the same position as so-called jazz—that being, compared to rock, classical music also sells very little. Yet the sixties and seventies have been very productive periods for this area of creativity—and what this phenomenon means is very interesting. For it is understood that the financial spectrum of recording, say, a symphony orchestra transcends the one-thousand-dollar zone—yet there have been no appreciable attempts to cut down on this kind of activity (nor have I meant to imply that there should be—for I believe the activity taking place in this area of creativity is of necessary importance for the composite society—just as the composite spectrum of all creative music is). My point in mentioning this phenomenon is only to point out the complexities surrounding the music business, as well as the inconsistencies one must constantly deal with in attempting to comment about the "special treatment" creative music has long endured—and this is especially true for so-called jazz. Because if the sales of classical music do not turn a profit (which is what the collective solidification of western business has also said about so-called jazz), then why are large projects of this type allowed to continue? (no kiddin').

The real reason classical music continues to get such support from the established recording industry and business communities throughout America is because white people are aware of the significance of culture—as it relates to "white" culture. For if creativity does function as an important factor to retain the vibrational identity and essence of a given cultural group (as well as what its functionalism implies for both vibrational and progressional continuance), then any attempt to negate that factor would threaten the composite "balance of things" (or basic order of the culture—and/or information and information dynamics related to the culture)—and in doing so, risk that culture's longevity. As such, if classical music is not the most basic vibrational thrust that the greater public listens to in this time zone, it is not because the music isn't available, or that situations have not been constructed to teach the music to the public. Rather, the reality particulars of classical music—as the most basic cultural creative focus—are directly connected to the composite transformation western culture is presently going through—having to do with many other factors (and ultimately moving to clarify the particulars of either the "next order" or the "next clarification" of continuance). The political position of western art music, however, has not diminished very much—if any. For in the final analysis, the composite reality of western art music serves as a factor to preserve "what is viewed" as "that which is most 'pure Aryan'" (having to do with the preservation of western civilization as the last bastion of white power). The economic and political support of this creativity is not separate from what this phenomenon means as well.

PROG.CONT.-------(P)DOC.

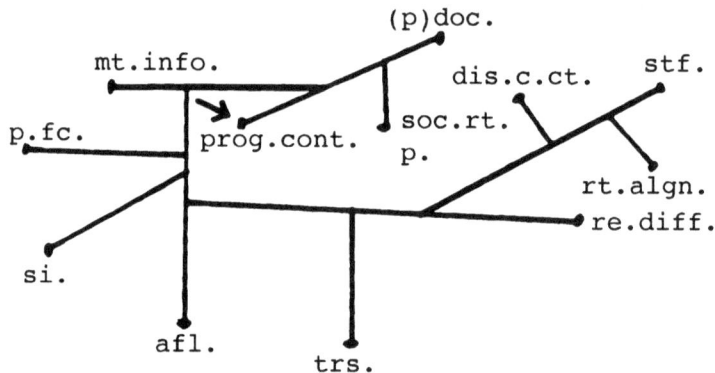

The complexity of the contemporary music business is also related to the emergence of alternative recording by the musicians themselves. For by the middle of the sixties, it was clear that no assistance would be coming from the established recording companies, and it was also clear that the natural expansion of creativity could not wait for these companies to change their minds. The intensity this situation promoted would supply the final initiative for given individuals or groups to begin assuming total responsibility for their creativity. The present reality of independent recording has moved to affect the composite dictates of music recording—and the future promises to see this development assume even greater importance. For the actualness of this phenomenon has created a "bypass" situation for greater public exposure. Yet the thrust of this movement is not without its own problems as well. As such, it is important that some attempt is made to comment on this most recent development—for the progressional realness of alternative recording will be a major part of the next cycle. It is important that the greater public is made aware of the seriousness this phenomenon poses.

Actually, the realness of alternative recording is not a new development. Composers like Harry Partch made their own records in the forties, and Sun Ra did many of his own records in the fifties. There have also been many isolated developments from the post-Parker cycle of the music—among those being the recordings by Charles Mingus (of his orchestral concert in California) and Max Roach (*Freedom Now Suite*). But the major factor that characterized alternative recording in the sixties was the number of musicians who decided to participate at once—and there have been many successes. Certainly the work of the Jazz Composer's Orchestra must be considered a major success for how it altered traditional business functionalism, and this is also true for the work of Strata East records. The implication of this phenomenon is directly related to the realness of decentralization (that being, the possibility of breaking the dominance that certain sectors of the planet now enjoy over the composite planet with respect to both information exposure as well as economics).

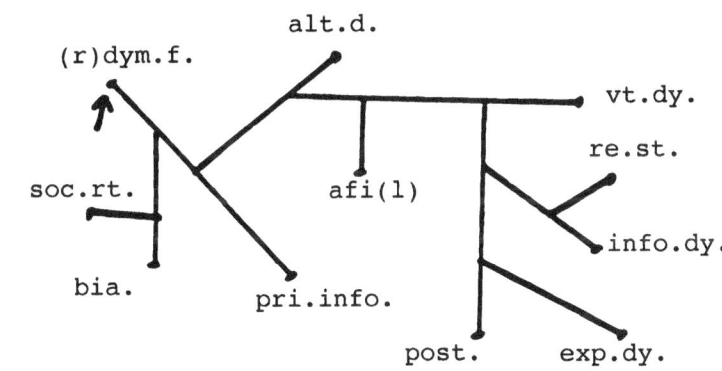

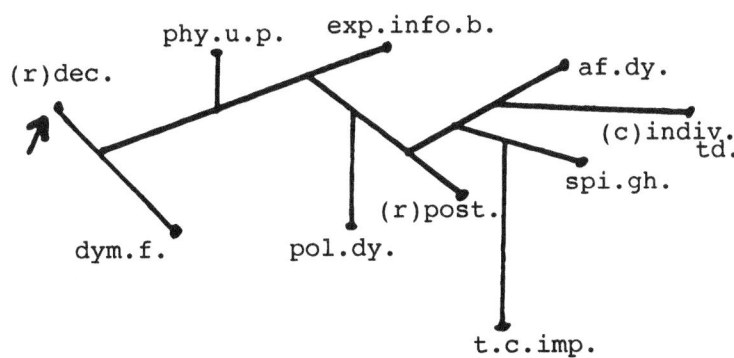

The dynamic implications of alternative recordings have also helped clarify the next continuum of business preparation and consciousness. Before this phenomenon very few creative musicians had any idea of the real business reality surrounding their profession. Instead, the most basic attitude that shaped the creative musicians' community in the late fifties (on through the sixties) was the "separate from normal life" artist nonsense that western culture has long initiated. Somehow the world of business and the dynamics of negotiations (and contracts) had come to be viewed as foreign to what "artists" were supposed to think about—and the business implications of this viewpoint were reflected in the resulting physical universe position of alternative creativity—in real-life terms. The emergence of independent recording has moved to re-examine the composite role of the so-called artist, and this re-examination can only be viewed in positive terms.

Yet the decision to participate in alternative recordings should not be approached in light terms, because the realness of this phenomenon demands more work than is generally acknowledged. For the most basic factor that consumes this area of involvement is the sheer amount of time needed to run a business properly. Nevertheless, as this phenomenon continues to grow, there will be many positive changes in the overall reality of the music business. For instance, one of the problems alternative recording experienced in the early fifties was the realness of distribution—because there were no outlets for independent records, and the established distribution lines were either not interested in their products or needed more volume (records) than was possible to produce. But by the end of the seventies, the reality of independent recording companies could boast of several distribution lines created especially for their music. This is not to say that everything is now perfect for alternative record companies as we enter the eighties—rather, there have been many improvements since the early sixties to make it somewhat easier. Certainly the basic thrust of alternative recordings will not run CBS or RCA out of business—at least in this time cycle—but I do believe the progressional continuance of this phenomenon will have profound implications for the next cycle (involving the composite reality of the music business). Because the solidification of alternative recording is only the first step towards creative people assuming charge of their total reality.

Hopefully the time zone of the eighties will see artists starting their own magazines and books.

WORK CONDITIONS

Clubs

Black creativity has long been associated with the reality of nightclubs as a means to survive and/or expand. This one outlet has played an important role throughout the composite history of black creative music from the very early periods until today, and there are many reasons for this phenomenon. Because the emergence of the nightclub context is not separate from social reality—which is to say, to really understand the relationship of creative music to its performance outlets, it is important to understand the particulars of social dynamics in black culture (as well as the option particulars resulting from imposed dynamics). The reality of the club situation has long been conducive to the music for what it posed to natural continuance and projectional exploration. For creative improvised music—more than any other form—is not only a theoretical postulation, but instead a living and breathing discipline that requires establishing a particular relationship with one's instrument (and ideas)—as well as audience—to continue. The reality of the "club" situation has long provided an arena for this relationship to continue—and every period of black creativity has experienced part of its solidification through this context. It is unfortunate that present-day social reality has moved to undervalue the significance of this performing outlet. For the club performing context has long been viewed by the upper echelon of western culture as proof that black creativity has no extended dynamics and is instead only a minor popular music at best. This has been the viewpoint of the classical music community, and this has also been the viewpoint of the established defining community that disseminates composite information (on the established communication lines) for western culture. The realness of this viewpoint is interesting in that it seeks to deny the actual reality of American culture—and in its place superimpose alien concepts of "high culture" that have nothing to do with black creativity and/or black people (or non-white people). Nevertheless, the reality of the nightclub is directly related to the reality aspect of creative music. Any attempt to view the realness of this subject must involve coming to terms with the special reality particulars of its performance past, as well as what these particulars have meant to the actual music.

The last ten years have seen many different viewpoints about the use of clubs for creative music. The two most basic arguments about this subject are: (1) the reality continuum of the club context is still necessarily relevant for the music, and (2) the club, as a positive tool for alternative functionalism, has now become an obstacle to the continuance of the music. Both of these arguments have meaning and should be examined. The argument of "necessary relevance" has validity because the club medium is one of the few areas of real access to the music—for both the musicians and the public. The fact is, the dynamic realness of American culture has never intended to include black creativity in its composite performance outlets—and without the existence of the clubs, there would hardly be any work possibilities at all. There is also the realness that this outlet is just as important now as it was a hundred years ago for the actual music. For the club context represents one of the few performing outlets where creative musicians can work on their craft consistently and learn from playing every day. The atmosphere of most clubs is informal enough so that given sets (or performances) can transcend the constricted nature of concert performances (e.g., the music can be longer than a forty-five-minute concert half—and sometimes something as seemingly unimportant as time length can be very important to one's development). Finally, the reality of club performances can provide a perfect platform for musicians to learn their craft.

But there are other factors related to this subject that must also be looked at if we are to fully understand its particulars—especially with regard to the composite music. The area that undoubtedly causes the greatest concern is the economic dynamics of this context—especially the economic consideration with regard to the overall pattern that has been established in the past twenty years. This is so because it is practically impossible to listen to creative music in the club context without being hassled by a number of distracting factors. Nor have I meant to ignore the realness of any club owner's situation either—for to operate a club is to deal with many different economic factors just to break even. But in the final analysis, the practical aspect of one coming to hear the music must take precedence over all matters (for the concept of a performing space is about people having the opportunity to experience the creativity), and if that is true, then many changes are needed before this context—the club—can function as a truly positive factor for creative music.

The fact is, the reality of club performances has become quite expensive. One could go hear the Metropolitan Opera for the same amount of money it now takes to hear one set in the average club. Not only that, but the listener must also contend with the hassling that surrounds the selling of drinks—all of which interferes with hearing the music and limits, to some degree, what areas of exploration can be attempted. For the most part, the club situation is still used as a factor for entertainment (with the music providing only half the focus) and, as such, an average engagement finds the musicians having to compete with the audience "for the floor." In the final analysis, it becomes a question of weighing the difference and each person making his (her) choice.

The situation in Europe is not much different. Clubs like Le Chat Qui Pêche in Paris—where Eric Dolphy played his last Paris performance two weeks before his death—would surprise many people. This club has long been famous throughout Europe, and a list of the musicians who have performed at this one place would read like a "who's who" of black creativity: including such figures as Ben Webster, Dexter Gordon, Coleman Hawkins, Archie Shepp, etc. But the actual reality of Le Chat Qui Pêche was only a small dive that was uncomfortable to both the musicians and the public. Very few people were able to attend a given performance, since the space was so small, and consequently no one was able to really be paid for their music (there is more, but I think my point is clear). The reality dynamics of this situation must be understood because Le Chat Qui Pêche was not an anomaly by any means. Rather, this outlet is one example among thousands (yet I have not meant to imply that every club has the same exact problems—but I have meant to imply that the reality of most of these outlets is dismal).

The late sixties and seventies would also see another phenomenon related to the reality of the club situation—that being the emergence of musician-owned clubs. Artists like Sam Rivers would play an important role in accelerating composite functionalism—and his Studio Rivbea became a major outlet for creative music in this most important time period. Rashied Ali's club Ali's Alley also played a decisive role in helping to provide outlets for alternative creativity, and for a while it seemed as if this phenomenon would be the next extension focus for alternative functionalism. In the end, however, all of these outlets would come to a close before the beginning of the eighties. Quite possibly, the strain of trying to function as both artist and business person (on an everyday basis) was simply too much. Whatever, the close of these two major independent clubs moved to lessen the attractiveness of this challenge. It is credit to both Sam Rivers and Rashied Ali that they were able to function as long as they did. Both clubs, to my knowledge, functioned for about a decade (give or take a few years). Hopefully, the decline of this phenomenon is only momentary—but there can be no denying that club ownership responsibilities are no easy task, especially when one's time is equally divided between running its particulars and continuing as a musician.

Other Sources

In the early fifties, Dave Brubeck moved to establish the reality potential of the college circuit as a valuable outlet for creative music. Brubeck actually helped to pioneer this area for alternative functionalism (and as such must be given credit for establishing an important new area of functionalism). The last fifteen years have seen this phenomenon increase to where the university is slowly moving to accept its responsibility—as a dynamic information center as well as cultural outlet.

The business particulars of the college circuit have also changed radically from Brubeck's early encounters, for the last seven years have seen the rise of student groups (or clubs) organized for the sole purpose of organizing concerts. There is even now a national network of college performing outlets that programs an entire season of given schools (involving the structure of a given tour, as well as which groups are to have the opportunity). For the most part, the sophistication of these new organizations has been directed towards only a limited sector of the composite creative community—i.e., very few contemporary creative people have had access to the national college performing circuit—and very few, if any, black creative musicians from the post-Ayler junction have been invited to participate. For the most part, the college situation has been interested in either rock or folk music—or, at least, the committees who make up their concert schedules have only employed this type of music. Nevertheless, I believe the future of this outlet will be important to all creative musics.

Finally, no attempt to view the reality aspect of creative music would be complete unless some mention is made of the many independent people who have long worked to both provide performing outlets for alternative creativity as well as creative input into their communities. Fortunately, there have always been individuals or groups who have cared about creativity—and the music could not have survived without these people. For instance, groups like the Left Bank Jazz Society in Baltimore, Maryland, have been instrumental in providing outlets for creative music for years—and there are many other such groups throughout America (and the planet). The work of this area of functionalism must be viewed as extremely important on every level—and the creative community owes a debt to these independents that can never be overstated. Hopefully both the creativity and this kind of functionalism will move to uplift the composite "state of things" for the total planet. The realness of the composite functionalism taking place in this time cycle will determine the vibrationaltory implications for the future.

(Level Two)

It has now been twenty years since Ornette Coleman and Cecil Taylor first began reshaping creative music. Many of the records that were completed in this cycle have gone on to become classics—totally affecting the realness of both American and world culture. The implications of what their early music signified must still be dealt with today—for the work done in that time zone was extremely rich and profound—and I consider that activity required listening for any serious music listener or for musicians, as well as universities. Many of us have come to already view the post–Coleman and Taylor junction of the music as having happened only recently, and the extreme opposite of this viewpoint is also true, that being: many of us have come to view the Coleman/Taylor junction of the music as a thrust projection that represents the far and distant past (having little to do with the realness of this time cycle—the late seventies). There are many reasons for these varied viewpoints, for the activity of artists like Ornette Coleman and Cecil Taylor has never really been made known in this culture—western culture (and in particular American)—on a level comparable to the significance of their contributions. This is not to say nothing positive has ever happened to these musicians, for surely many positive things have happened—and it is also true that they have carved a place for themselves in the annals of creative music history—by anyone's definition. But the reception of their work has always been extremely interesting if one would consider the actualness of life in America. For it must be understood that there are other sectors of the society that can be viewed to substantiate the comparative option particulars that musicians like Coleman and Taylor have to either their peers or to the opportunity options of other segments of the society. Nor am I comparing the realness of musicians like Coleman and Taylor to the opportunity options of groups like Grand Funk Railroad or Kiss—both of whom have gone on to put their stamp on every strata of American society—for if this was done, I am sure there would be many cries of unfair comparison (which is not really true, but there is a distinct difference between the option-spread implications of "art" creativity as compared to "popular" creativity—yet all of these differences are not natural differences but rather manufactured. For it must be understood that everyone needs creativity, and not only one thrust alignment—which is to say, to compare the present state of creative music from the affinity insight (1) principle to that of creative music of the affinity insight (2) principle is really a valid approach—but what is the relationship of Coleman's and Taylor's position to their so-called peers in the respectable community of western art music? In other words, if the option-spread implication of the music has only to do with what principle is utilized (whether a thrust is perceived as art as opposed to commercial), then what does this tell us about the reality of musicians like Ornette Coleman and Cecil Taylor—especially when viewed with respect to their peers? For if my earlier point is true (that being, both of these musicians have undoubtedly contributed a definite viewpoint with regard to the progressional continuance of world creativity—which will be perceived as either black creativity or American creativity—and as such have attained a "particular" position in the culture as a result of those contributions), then there can be no doubt as to the realness of their creative offerings with respect to all of the great people who have realized something of beauty for the composite well-being of the greater people and culture. To view this phenomenon is to deal with the reality aspect of creative music, and the answer to these questions can give real insight about what has happened and is happening in this cycle. For by focusing on musicians like Coleman and Taylor, it is possible to really view the dynamic factors which surround how creative music is dealt with on a composite level—and this information can help everyone.

I also realize there is a danger in attempting to compare anything—especially if we are dealing with actual people. For certainly the option-spread dynamics of a given individual are not separate from the "person" of that individual—which is to say, there are many different factors that determine how far a given individual can travel in a particular culture—or planet region. Yet if we are to really understand the reality implications of creative music, we have no choice but to acknowledge the dynamics of what this viewpoint raises—either it is discussed or we run the risk of obscuring the truth about this subject. For the dynamic reality options of musicians like Ornette Coleman and Cecil Taylor must be viewed for what they pose on an individual and cultural level—and this cannot exclude what we "really" know about the culture. Because if Cecil Taylor is viewed as one of the most important pianists to have emerged in this time continuum, then what does this mean with respect to the concept of reality options when compared to a pianist—who is also great—like Vladimir Horowitz? And if Ornette Coleman is considered a genius in his activity (having to do with his profound understanding of multi-instrumentalism and composition), then what does this mean when compared to a creative musician like Leonard Bernstein? To really view the dynamic implications of reality options is to understand on some level what these comparisons tell us about this time cycle (late seventies). Because neither creative music nor the musicians I have mentioned live in a box. All of these considerations are related to the—if I can use the phrase—"real world," and all of these considerations are also reflective of the composite reality of creative music—especially creative music from the black aesthetic. It is not just a question of trying to portray anyone in an unfavorable light, and I should also state very clearly that I am, like most of us, a great admirer of Messrs. Horowitz and Bernstein on every level. But to view the progressional realness of western culture—understanding that, as I stated earlier, the post-Coleman/Taylor junction is now twenty years old—is to begin understanding (and sensing) the particulars which surround the reality of creative music—especially for the black musician. To view the realness of these particulars can be important for establishing a basis for the coming decade. For if in comparison we are able to understand something about reality dynamic options, then it is important to do so. I believe something of positive value can come from many different investigative approaches. I have always believed this.

R(AS) CM(II)–4

(R)INDIV.TD.------COS.P.

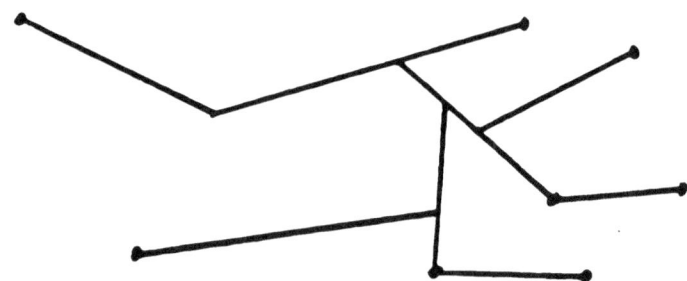

The most basic factor that differentiates the reality of creative musicians like Ornette Coleman and Cecil Taylor from creative musicians like Vladimir Horowitz and Leonard Bernstein is that the former are black and the latter are white—and the reality dynamic option implications related to what this difference means. But I realize that the time continuum of the sixties and seventies have made us numb to the subject of racism—and as such, no one wants to hear any more about this subject (it has gone out of fashion, in a way), so rather than press on this sore issue, I prefer instead to elaborate on reality dynamic options in concrete terms (which will bring about the same vibrational position anyway). The fact is, the concept of reality dynamic options has to do with how far a given individual is allowed to pursue or advance his or her information and affinity dynamics, and this concept also has to do with how the culture perceives given aspects of that same pursuit. For it must be understood that the dynamic impact of a given area of creativity is directly proportional to whether it is allowed to become "ised" into the greater public sector. In other words, the effect ratio of a given projection (style) is not separate from the nature underlying its endorsement and/or access to the collective channels of its given culture's information spread (i.e., the media and additional support). To view the reality options of musicians of this level can tell us something about what is really happening on the social, political, and vibrational planes of American society.

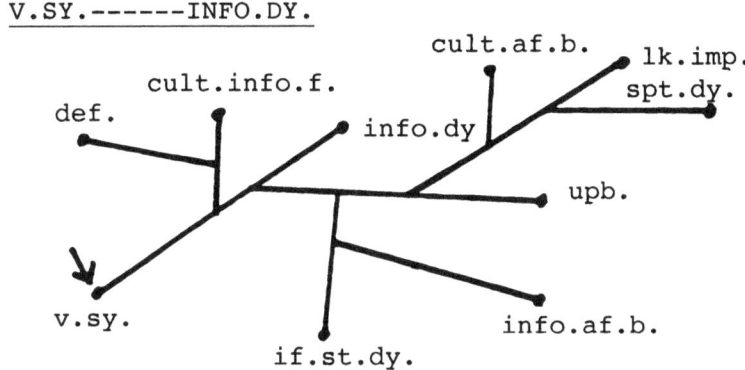

The sad truth is that the option-spread dynamics of Ornette Coleman and Cecil Taylor are not even in the same league as those of Vladimir Horowitz and Leonard Bernstein. For by option spread I am commenting on what degree an established individual is allowed to really shape his or her destiny with regard to the progressional spread of the work or the progressional route surrounding how that work is to be disseminated. This is not to say Messrs. Coleman and Taylor cannot develop their craft, nor have I meant that performance opportunities aren't available for these musicians. Rather, my point is that the reality options of western culture are very different for black people—and in general for all people of color—as opposed to white people, regardless of region. In other words, "a black person can only go so far in western culture"—and this is particularly true if that black person is functioning with respect to "source initiation" (as opposed to functioning from a position that is viewed—rightly or wrongly—as affirming a "western vibrational or methodological alignment"). And it is important to understand that if this is true for artists like Ornette Coleman and Cecil Taylor—whose contributions cannot be challenged (plus they have survived as well)—then the average person of color must be viewed in even harsher terms. Why is it that there have been no programs on television devoted to the realness of Cecil Taylor's work—while he is alive? Why is it that Ornette Coleman has had only one performance of his ambitious work *Skies of America* in America? To understand this is to understand that I am not simply being paranoid when I write of the concept of reality options—and reality dynamic options. Why is it that there have been no special courses developed in American universities to teach about the work of these two great musicians? (And understand, even though I am aware that many of our so-called institutions have little real focus on anything—of those schools that do offer extended courses in creative music, one can find a class or two on twelve-tone music technique and its resultant period, and special courses on Schoenberg on through to Cage—and if in this context Coleman and Taylor are viewed as too young to have a class on their music, then what about Duke Ellington—is his work also "too young"?). Why haven't these two great musicians had the opportunity to discuss and perform their work (and not as a free lecture) in most of the great universities existing in America—and what about an opportunity to present special works in places like the Kennedy Center and/or Lincoln Center (which are two of the great theatres this country has erected for music)? Bernstein has had this opportunity, and so has Horowitz (and please don't misunderstand me, for I am not writing of Horowitz and Bernstein as if they have had one performance in these great halls—my point, rather, is that these opportunities exist for the Horowitzs and Bernsteins—musicians such as Horowitz and Bernstein perform in these situations all the time, like Thad Jones and Mel Lewis perform at the Village Gate. In itself, the use of Lincoln Center, Kennedy Center, etc., represents nothing new to artists like Bernstein and Horowitz—and because they are great artists, they should have the use of what is best about this country). My point is that Coleman and Taylor are equally great for what they have accomplished, but the reality options available to them are necessarily limited because of their blackness.

By making these comparisons I have not meant to sound paranoiac nor have I meant to underrate any of the artists who have the benefits of cultural and political support. But if we are to really view the realness of the reality aspect of creative music, then we must focus on the composite implication of this subject—regardless of context. For by citing Lincoln and Kennedy Centers, I have not meant to imply that every performance of any musician should be at a great hall, but only that the dynamic option spread of creative musicians should not be excluded from what is "most real"—concerning the best western culture has to offer. And this is especially true when artists of the stature of Ornette Coleman and Cecil Taylor are viewed.

THE REALITY ASPECT OF CREATIVE MUSIC is directly related to the challenge of positive transformation. The realness of this subject is not separate from what insight it sheds on cultural information dynamics. Many of the problems we are dealing with in this time zone are directly related to the affinity and actual position of information dynamics (as this phenomenon is perceived in exclusive western information terms). But with a proper (correct) perspective, the realness of this subject could be an important factor to help shape both individual and collective consciousness. Creativity in this context could function as a positive life alignment and spiritual factor—affecting the thrust continuum of composite humanity. But the present use of information dynamics in western culture is directed towards narrowing vibrational dynamics as opposed to expansion—and the realness of this difference has profoundly disturbed world information dynamics (as well as their related creativity). The applied interpretations now permeating world creativity are not separate from the interpretation structure that underlies present-day social reality—and the realness of this phenomenon has multi-complexual implications if not corrected.

Nor have I meant to over-emphasize the realness of this phenomenon in a particular sense—because, on some level, every thrust alignment (projection) has suffered from the applied use of narrow information dynamics. The reality aspect of creative music must be viewed in all of these various contexts—if we desire positive transformation. For the corrections which must be made cannot be done in only one community, but involve the total culture (and planet). The realness of this phenomenon is related to education—how and what we are taught—and extends into every focus of social reality to the degree that overnight solutions cannot succeed. The importance of restructuralism should not be lightly viewed or we run the risk of complacency—and time is an important consideration. For the reality aspects of creative and positive living are not separate from basic physical universe change cycles—which is to say, the realness of transformation will not wait until we are neatly prepared for its challenge. Change simply takes place—on its own, or in accordance to cosmic cycles which have nothing to do with us—on an individual or cultural level (or so it seems or doesn't seem).

The aim of transformation (with respect to reality options) is not about fancy theoretical positions, nor does it have anything to do with isolated information focuses, because I am not writing of a selected viewpoint. Rather, reality transformation has to do with making available what is available. In other words, as far as creativity is concerned, the reality-aspect implications of transformation would only have to do with making the dynamic creativity of a culture available so that people can experience it. Moreover, the solidification of this development would also imply that people are taught about the realness of all their creative dynamics and that given initiations are able to utilize its relevant information lines. In other words, I am not talking about a subject whose only relevance pertains to Mars, space travel, ocean life, or rocks—rather, the concept of reality transformation directly relates to what is happening in our actual lives. Viewed correctly, the move to expose composite creativity is a move to positively reshape society—for all people—and this must be the goal of positive transformation.

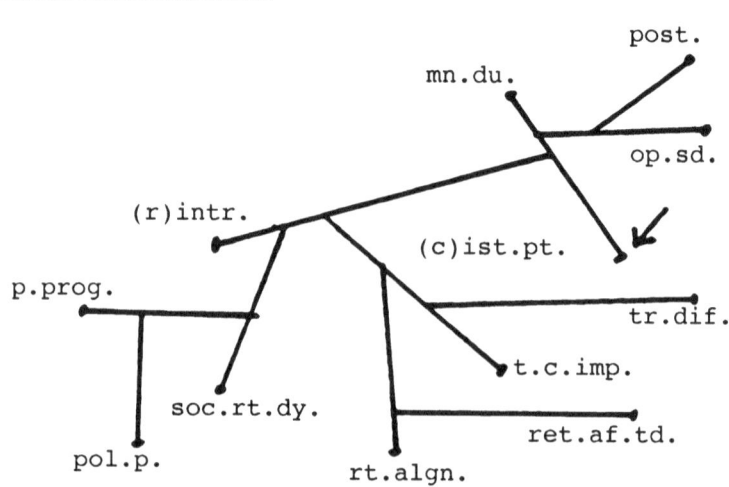

To view the composite reality of creative music—with respect to the reality implications of this time cycle—it is necessary to continue along the lines of the previous section—that being, individual focus. An approach of this type is necessary if we are to better understand the particulars of present-day western culture (i.e., how the "scene" developed). Not to mention, observation in this context can better give one perspective about future functionalism. For to view the reality aspect of creative music— with respect to its particular focuses—should also differentiate how each of us can help bring about positive change. Because the magnitude of this subject transcends the scope of any given individual. To examine present-day social reality can help us to understand the real situation of western culture information dynamics. Many of us come to view (even in vibrational terms) this cycle in creativity as the natural result of what people want, rather than the natural result of other factors. It is important that this idea is challenged—because the present situation we are now living in has not simply come from nowhere.

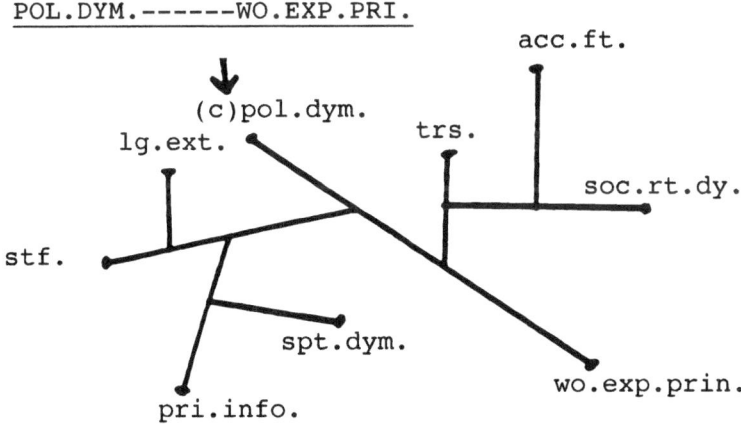

To understand the present reality of creative music is to understand the reality of cultural information focus—regardless of context—for the actual position of creativity is related to many factors, and this is particularly true of creative music. The fact is, the impact and success of any creative form depends on whether or not that form is allowed proper exposure, or at least given use of the facilities that govern information spread (dissemination). For while it is clear that certain individuals will always be aware of their culture's creativity, this is not true for society as a whole. The seriousness of cultural information sources should not be taken lightly—because the collective realness of information spread does affect people. It is through these sources that we come to base many (or all) of our ideas—involving both focus as well as participation. Thus, the reality implications of information spread must be viewed as vital to transformation; for without some attempt to make all cultural information sources "of relevance," there can be no hope of re-establishing composite unification (based on the respect that real information promotes—respect concerning how people view each other, and respect concerning alternative functionalism). In other words, people function from the dynamic alignment implications related to what information is made available to them—and this is true for all people. The distortions we are now dealing with in present-day information must be viewed for their role in maintaining the spectacle-diversion syndrome of information regulation—which is to say, for the success it has had in solidifying the focus dictates of multi-information. Because my most basic point in this chapter is that the reality of cultural information we have been receiving—especially if I would focus on the last thirty years—is "something less than what really is"; and this "something" has helped to advance western culture in a "particular" way (having to do with the use of information to promote certain images and interpretations—as well as information as a tool to suppress world culture affinity dynamics). The end result of this "focus" has brought us to the juncture we now find ourselves in—and, of course, many people view this time cycle as extremely positive (it all depends on what aspect one chooses to look at—for to be white in America and be the recipient of the thrust continuum of western culture can move one to interpret events on one level, and to be non-white (or Asian) is to be in another position—it just depends on the many thousands of factors related to what makes what what). My point, however, is that the dynamics of different opinions are related to how people are, as well as what these differences mean when viewed with respect to information dynamics: that is, because of the composite realness of "being," a given information source will perceive particular events in completely different terms from another source—and in this I have no quarrel (how could I, since the phenomenon seems to be "what's happening" on the physical universe level). My point, however, is that the collected realness of information dynamics has—in the last three hundred years—moved to distort the world implications of progressionalism to the degree that many people no longer know who they are and what they are and what they could be. The use of information dynamics in this context exceeds any notion of mere subjectivism, but clearly functions instead as a distortive redefining agent. In other words, by commenting on this phenomenon, I am writing of a thrust continuum that consciously manipulates events as a means to secure particular vibrational positions. The reality-aspect realness of creative music is not separate from what has come about from this manipulation—nor is the reality realness of physical universe life separate from what this re-ordering has meant either. Unless some means is taken to correct the distortions which surround present-day information sources, the probability of positive transformation will lessen. It is not just a question of an "opinion"—because all of us have opinions—but rather, the challenge of real information involves its ability to bring about higher and wider affinity ranges for viewing both particular and composite ideas. Real information should benefit all humanity, and real information should serve to strengthen the composite vibrationaltory lining of its culture as well—if it vibrates to the composite continuum of world culture (including western culture). It is important that this is understood, for I am not implying that to write of murder will bring everyone together, nor am I saying that an article on wallpaper will benefit humanity. I am commenting on information that is indigenous to the reality of particular "focus" rather than "actual information"—which is to say I am using the word *information* as knowledge related to what happened to make "this" (life) real, or how "it" happened—or knowledge that affirms some aspect of cosmic and galactic law (or laws), or knowledge related to understanding the mystical and vibrationally related laws, and/or focus—or focuses—underlying what this experience (living) is—that is, knowledge related to the teachings of composite world information and its resulting spread, etc.

R(AS) CM(II)–12

MT.INFO.------T.C.IMP.------INF.AFB.

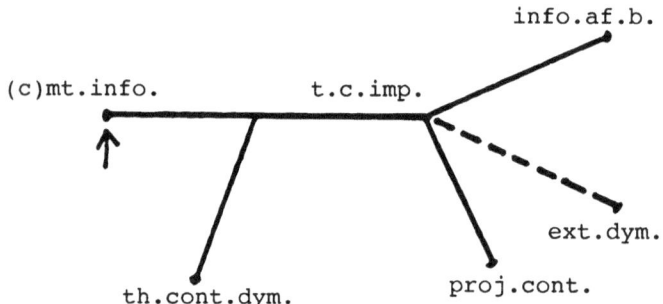

PER.VT.U.FUND.------PROG.CONT.

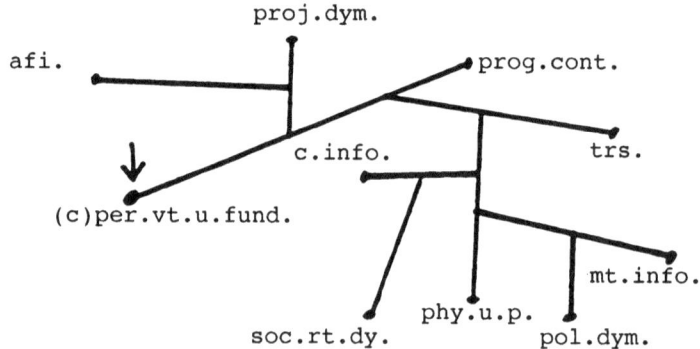

SCI.DYM.------PRI.INFO.

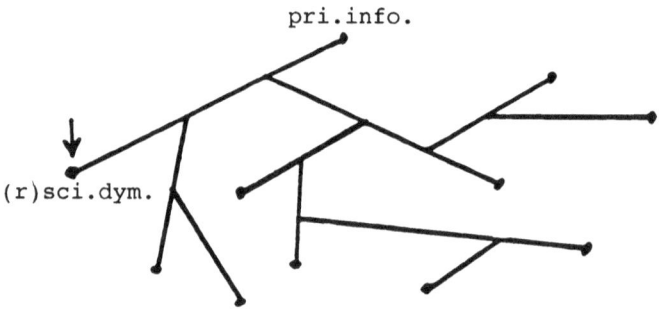

There are two ways to view the composite information spread of this time cycle—(1) the use of information in accordance to the spectacle-diversion affinity alignment, or (2) the spread of information within the aspect-essence focus. However, neither of these two examples can promote real understanding, because without a composite center factor there can be no basis for real observation. To view the present dynamic of western information sources is to be involved with "the use of words" as a means to advance particular vibrational stances—rather than to substantiate real information. The end result of this phenomenon is that information in this time period is a joke—having to do with the use of particulars as a means to give the illusion of momentum (cultural life). Yet while this viewpoint is true on one level, on another level the present realness of western information sources can be viewed with respect to its "intention consideration"—or "primary intention." Because in the final analysis, this culture has come to the junction where whether or not a given area of information is true is beside the point. Because however given idea routes are perceived in their affinity sense, in the final analysis, present-day interpretations are utilized for what vibrational and functional results can be attained from their use—as opposed to what effect they could positively generate. We call this syndrome "freedom of the press." To view the present realness of western culture as we move into the eighties is to see the most dynamic use of information spread in this time cycle, and to view the effect of this same phenomenon is to see less real information than in any other documented civilization. Which is to say, one would normally view an extended information platform as a positive factor that could serve humanity—because of its ability to positively and creatively transmit necessary information. But this has not been the case—or at least, while one can always cite a particular positive and meaningful use of applied information, this has not been the reality of present-day information dynamics. Yet I have not meant to over-generalize this most important subject, and indeed there is no need to. For the realness of present-day information dissemination would show my writings to be, if anything, much too mild. It is not just a question of citing the dynamic misdeeds of present-day information sources in creative music. Because in the total context of things, the music is secondary. Rather, the composite realness of western information dynamics must be viewed for its effect on the total culture—and from that context, everything—including creativity—can be viewed in its proper context. For the particulars of this time cycle have totally reshaped the reality of perception dynamics on many different levels, having to do with every sector of our lives—nothing has been left untouched. Moreover, we are the end result of this phenomenon—for the dynamic sophistication of present-day information and manipulation is with us from the first time we turn on the radio—all the way through school, in libraries, on television, in newspapers, etc. The dynamics of present-day western information regulation are related to what articles we purchase in stores, what images we vibrate to, what clothes we wear, what food we eat, how we view the world, what religion we belong to, who we choose as our friends, where we travel for vacations, etc., etc., and also what creativity we are able to relate to (as well as what creativity we come in contact with). To deal with the realness of present-day information dissemination is to understand the position it has in our lives—from birth to death. There is no one not affected by this phenomenon—and this is especially true in the west, where technological sophistication is so pronounced. That there are any people open to alternative information at all is amazing—because the "normal" reality of present-day education is very different from what this phenomenon (alternative functionalism) postulates. If anything, the realness of alternative information shows the dynamic flexibility of human beings to adopt and adjust to whatever is perceived to be real (of course, this same flexibility can also be interpreted as falling within the spectacle-diversion recycling sequence—it depends on what factors are operative).

To view the particulars of present-day information dynamics with respect to their relationship with spectacle diversion is to have some basis for understanding what has happened (and is happening) in this time cycle. For the cross-continuum of western information dynamics is directly related to the very fabric of our culture. In actual terms, this phenomenon can be viewed by looking at how particular information focuses are manipulated as a means to interpret given time cycles—from one day to a year or more. This use of information manipulation is not separate from the advertising done on television—the only difference being the "product" in this case is our collective lives. It is possible to view many different aspects of present-day social reality with respect to this phenomenon—whether we are commenting on the sudden tax revolt mentality (all of a sudden the public recognizes that their tax dollars are being misused—when in fact this has always been the case, and everyone knows it) or the use of particular images on television as a means to realign affinity dynamics. Because in the final analysis, the information tools we have created—"we" being the greater public—have made us the object of its focus, rather than the other way around. This phenomenon is connected to the understanding we now have of free information and free information use, for the First Amendment has long been one of this culture's greatest prides (as it should be . . . ?), but the actual situation we have in "real cultural life" in western culture is that only certain sectors of the society are in positions to qualify definitions. The present multi-problems people are dealing with in this time period are not separate from who—and what factors—are defining cultural terms. Because if the free press in this cycle can be viewed with respect to its "right to write anything" (since this is what's happening), then what has that freedom meant to the forming of present-day social reality? Certainly the world group recognizes this problem as well, and many moves are now being taken to sanction the ability of the western press to subvert composite information. To understand this growing awareness is to understand that the progressional continuum of western information has produced a situation where the focus of a given route of knowledge is secondary to the real intentions underlying what is really communicated. In other words, "people say what they want to say" (or people write what they want to write) and the total reality of a given information interpretation in this context is shaped by one's "intention"—rather than the reverse. It is because of this "reverse alignment" that the multi-information continuum of western culture must be viewed seriously, for this development is related to the composite reality of earth. As such, the realness of western information dynamics must be viewed with respect to its position to function both positively and negatively—and, for this essay, "especially negatively" (because the basic focus of this section is concerned with what has transpired in creativity as a result of western information politics).

The reality of present-day interpretation must be viewed with respect to the aspect-essence information dictates—as this phenomenon involves focus particulars. This is necessary because the realness of this phenomenon can be viewed in every area of information—from scientific investigation to social reality. This is not to say any given area of western information is wrong in itself; rather, the nature of this phenomenon has moved to isolate the multi-implications of world culture interpretations—and this is the problem. The best example of this phenomenon can be viewed in western journalism—as this subject relates to creative music and observation. So many distortions have crept into the meta-realness of world creativity that the greater public has become totally confused about creativity. Because the vibrational nature of the collective forces of western culture have moved to isolate the progressional and projectional dynamics of world creativity in the same context and spirit that it views its own dynamics, and the challenge of positive transformation must view these applied techniques as serious violations. Not only has the effectiveness of a given creative projection in world creativity (i.e., trans-African music) been narrowed—as far as its potential ability to function as a positive factor on the physical and vibrational universe level—but the sophistication of western reinterpretation has created a situation where no one even knows about the music—in a real sense. The progressional application of aspect-essence information techniques can be viewed throughout the entire continuum of creative music from the black aesthetic—on the initiations developed in America, as well as the initiations developed in Africa. This has been done by redefining every aspect of the music—from its aesthetical base to its particular methodology—outside of its principle-affinity reality (as a means to apply gradualism or proclaim inferiority). The use of alien definitions has also been a major factor in "jazz criticism" as well, and so profound has this use been that it will take many years to rectify. To understand the reality aspect of creative music is to begin surveying what has happened to creativity on a composite level—because the present reality of this subject is both complex and varied. It is important to understand that the primary factor underlying western culture is the sophistication of its perception techniques—as well as how it's practiced. Yet there is no reason to suspect that "that which has been distorted cannot be restored"—which is to say, if the meta-reality dynamics of information serve as the most basic factor to substantiate how this cycle has come about, then there is no reason to assume that the restoration of composite affinity dynamics cannot restore a more humane and developed society. The composite implications of this challenge must include every aspect and focus of world culture if we are serious about transformation. To understand the present reality of creative music is to focus on those "particulars" that have solidified present-day social reality . . . and this is my intention.

Newspapers

The reality implications of the newspaper medium can be viewed in every sector of the country, and have played a great role in spreading information on a daily basis. For many people, this medium represents the only information focus that is utilized on a continuance level. The relationship of newspapers to creativity has of course been established long ago—that being: the paper serves as a continual forum that advertises and reviews concerts, records, etc. Usually once a week (e.g., Sunday), most newspapers will also print interviews with given musicians—and other articles on the music (in their "art" section). This information continuum plays such a large part in most of our lives that many of us now take it for granted. For the most part, the greater public only utilizes other focus interpretations if their given paper goes on strike, like the *New York Times* has on occasion. The two major news services that we depend on for our daily news (Associated Press and United Press International) have connections all over the planet, and as such provide a given route for information to be disseminated on a composite level—not just in the United States, but everywhere. Thus to lightly examine the relationship of newspapers to creative music is a valid approach—if we are really interested in the reality aspects of creative music. For the realness of this medium affects the total reality tone level of the culture.

Without doubt, the "business dynamics" and multi-implications of present-day western newspapers can really shed light on the reality implications of alternative creativity. Nowhere can the seriousness of the media be better viewed, for if the most basic idea we are dealing with in this time zone is the concept that alternative creativity of the affinity-insight principle has had its chance to be exposed and was rejected by the public, then what does this argument mean when viewed in a composite sense, especially within the context of present-day advertising? To better understand my point, all one has to do is to buy the Sunday *New York Times*. For the money that now goes into advertising—and everything else—is incredible, including full-page ads on what we call commercial music. Nor is dynamic advertising of this type found only in newspapers, for this is the case in every area of journalism. But my point in mentioning all of this is that the sophistication of advertising is rarely dealt with when the subject is creative music. Because alternative activity is expected to compete with the progressional-thrust span of the most successful advertising blitz in this country's history without any of the tools of present-day marketing. We have been led to believe that the non-awareness of and limited participation of the greater public in alternative music is the fault of the music when, at the same time, the progressional sophistication of western advertising now programs information on an unprecedented level. Not only is this true, but even in this time cycle—the late seventies—there is no creative artist whose activity has received the same thrust leverage as even the most unsuccessful commercial artist. This is not to deny that given artists do have their activity available on the world market, but if the reality of advertising can be viewed with respect to what has happened to rock music, then how can one view having an isolated creative record available to the machinery that surrounds a group like the Rolling Stones—giant billboards all over the country, t-shirts, television, radio, particular focus—movies—magazines—posters—dolls—toys—cassettes—international tours—fan clubs. I mention this not to downgrade popular music, because this is beside the point; rather, with this kind of machinery in operation, what music wouldn't be successful? I could make Paul Zabinsky's great-grandson's uncle a star with this kind of treatment. In other words, the reality realness of present-day information spread is related to many different factors—which is to say, to view the present situation of creative music, the seriousness and effectiveness of advertising cannot be overlooked. For after a given record of commercial music is made, many factors go into operation—sometimes the budget for a given project is less then the advertising for that same project. As far as newspapers are concerned, one can view a given music section and see the realness of what advertising is—and how it is used. I find it amazing that there is an audience for classical and creative (let alone "world") music at all—not that there isn't any advertising for alternative forms to some degree, but the composite thrust of present-day machinery for popular music is almost overwhelming. The seriousness of what this phenomenon means is not separate from the reality realness of creative music.

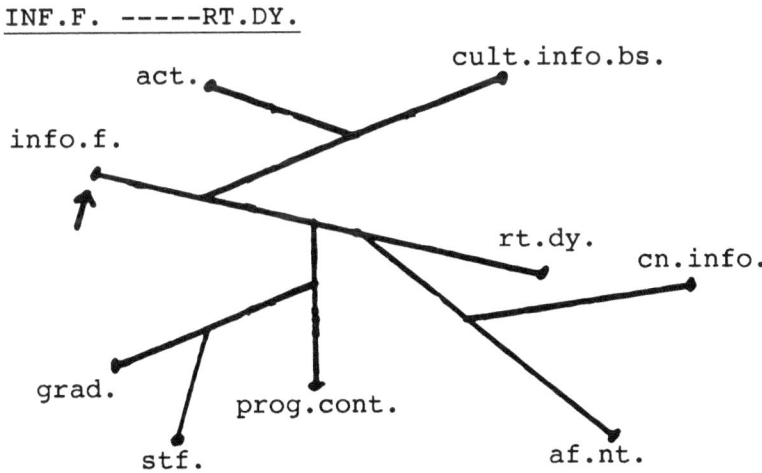

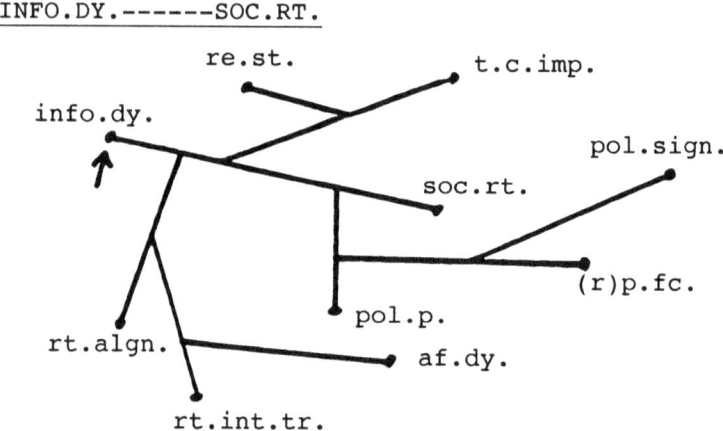

I mentioned the *New York Times* earlier because of the position this paper has in American society—for this information source is generally considered to represent what is best about American newspapers. As such, the information associated with this paper is significant for what it tells about American culture and also for how it affects the composite information focus of American culture. The realness of the *New York Times* is also important for what it tells us about the reality aspect of creative music, for the vibrational reality tone of the paper functions as a device for the established east coast defining collective. Certainly one of the more interesting features of the *Times* is how it deals with creative music, for in its arts-and-leisure section "all the news that's fit to print" concerning creativity is dealt with every week. There are always many interesting articles on western art music focusing on the implications of Schubert's songs, the implications of Beethoven's string quartets, something on opera, etc.—but rarely is the main focus of its music section on contemporary music (yet I have not meant to make a blanket accusation, because every now and then one can find an article of this type). However, nowhere will one find in this section a serious focus on the dynamics of creative music from the black aesthetic. Black music and world creativity are virtually relegated to its back pages (when included at all). The question then becomes, what does this mean? For if the *Times* can give real focus to the activity of a composer like Elliott Carter (who most certainly deserves the attention—for he has never really been given cultural focus comparable to the effect he has had in American culture), then what about someone like Cecil Taylor? Nor do I mean to pick on the *Times*—but the question I'm raising is "why have musicians like Taylor and Coleman not been the recipients of this most basic cultural information focus, comparable to what their contributions have been?" Why have there been no articles on the significance of Duke Ellington's activity—or Fletcher Henderson—or James P. Johnston, Fats Waller, Thelonious Monk, etc.—in the headline focus of the arts-and-leisure section, not only of the *Times*, but in newspapers across the nation? It is possible that the reader might view this example as too extreme—or out of context. Yet if the present reality of creative music has to do with how it is being dealt with in respect of the collective forces of western culture, then by focusing on isolated areas of information dissemination, the realness of present reality can better be understood. Certainly I have not meant to imply that there have been no articles on creative music, or creative music from the black aesthetic, in the *New York Times*—or any of the thousands of newspapers that exist—because there have been many articles. Instead, I have tried to focus on how the composite music is portrayed as a means to view creative music's treatment with respect to other forms. Maybe in itself this approach is extreme, but when added to the total reality picture of the music, a certain pattern can be discerned. In other words, when I wrote that the present position of creative music is the result of many factors, I was referring to the complexities of the present time cycle we are in. For it is not a question of whether given articles on the music can be found in newspapers around the country, nor can it be said that every now and then creative music can't even be found on television—because of course it can. My concern (and point) has more to do with how these focuses are portrayed, because no serious efforts have been made to really inform the public about the realness of the music. For instance, it is clear that the so-called jazz community is aware of most of the developments occurring on the creative music scene—just as most of the classical followers are aware of what is taking place in classical music—but how is one to really learn about the music if he or she is outside of the mainstream of its information? This is what I am referring to when I focus on the collective forces of western culture, because to understand this is to understand how the society can positively influence and teach about creativity—and this is exactly what is happening—in classical music. For the uninitiated listener can turn on the television set and receive programs that teach about classical music—the famous young people's concerts—regular broadcasts of classical music—courses (serious courses) in the universities—and of course focused articles in papers like the *New York Times*. Only with this type of positive media involvement can anyone expect to really increase awareness of alternative creativity.

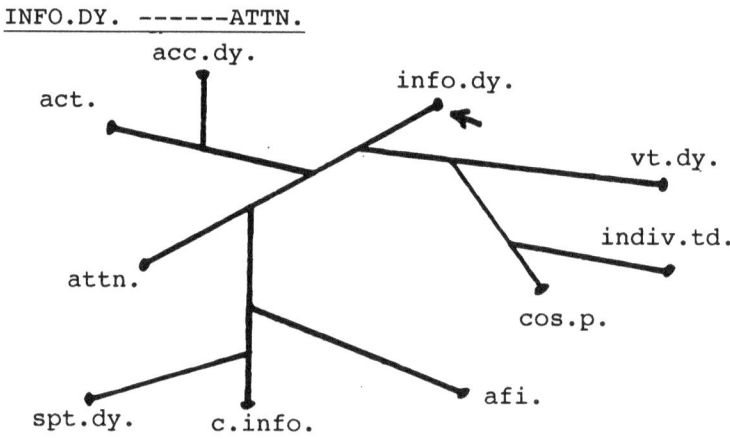

The reality of the newspaper medium does not stop with only given articles on the music—there is also the consideration of weekly and daily reviews. Every day, one can pick up a paper and read several reviews of the previous night's performances. This is not only true of music but theatre, dance, and movies. So real has this practice become that many of us have come to see it as normal (having something to really do with music—or performance). Certainly this type of activity does play a potential positive role in the sense that if the review is positive—and if the performance is programmed to continue for more than one day—there is a chance it will attract more people to a concert than might normally attend on their own. As such, the realness of this activity must be viewed as serious—for the difference between a good and a bad review can affect the total life of a given performance (and this is particularly true for Broadway shows, whose very existence hinges on a given word or two from the right information source). I can only hope that the methods of reporting found in creative music are not the same used in Broadway shows, for very rare is the reviewer who stays to experience a total performance. Reviewers for creative music (jazz) will normally come to a given concert and stay—at the most—for half of the first half of the concert, then leave to write their review. Thus the review is of only part of the concert—and this is "normal," or the "normal way" it is done. Certainly I can understand that the review has little or nothing to do with the concert. Moreover, I am not only commenting on one or two newspapers in a given planet sector —rather, this procedure is common to newspapers all over the planet. Not to mention that the normal review is about one or two paragraphs long—which is to say, "Your concert is worth one or two paragraphs"—that's it. Invariably the approach of a given review can take two poses—(1) to write descriptively on the concert without elaboration on what it meant or what it suggested vibrationally, or (2) the review will simply put up or down the particular concert (using bits and pieces of the concert as proof). Nowhere is there space to really do anything else—not to mention that the composite continuum of western culture has never really tried to view the music with respect to what a given projection really is—or means—anyway. Thus, the reality of creative music when viewed with respect to the collective newspapers can better be understood—for this medium has yet to live up to the challenge and responsibility of its position in society. Instead, the news media are concerned with information flow—regardless of content, regardless of consequence, regardless of positive insight, it is a question of "keep it moving."

Performance Structure

The reality of performance and work possibilities for creative music is also a factor that must be looked at if we are to understand this time cycle. For if the effectiveness of a given creative projection is directly related to whether or not it can be experienced, then the reality implications of the "business" dynamics of creative music are important. The realness of post-Ayler creativity especially must be viewed from this context, for as I have already mentioned, this projectional thrust is now at least twenty years old—in other words, by viewing the post-Ayler continuum, we are not focusing on a thrust alignment that started yesterday. The present reality cycle in creative music must be viewed for how the effectiveness of the music has been allowed exposure to the composite reality of American culture, and whatever we can learn from this can directly shed insight on what is really happening with creative music. To view this consideration is to begin having some real understanding of the "actual" position of alternative creativity in this period, for by creative music, I am not only referring to one segment of the post-Ayler continuum, but rather all of the projections that have solidified from that thrust initiation (not to mention the composite particulars for post-Ayler creativity are not that different from the total picture of alternative creativity in America—including so-called contemporary music—or contemporary music from the western art music continuum—yet there are some differences (and this will be commented on).

Quite possibly the first area of interest that gives insight into present-day creative music business practices would be the dynamics of performing possibilities. For clearly this area can give real insight about the most basic factor that all creative musicians are dealing with. Moreover, this information can also tell us about the economic implication of being involved in creative music, for it is understood that without work there can be no income—and this is true for everyone. The reality of creative music must be viewed with respect to what performance options are available to creative people and for what those options imply about the total culture. For to view the composite continuum of American culture is to see there are performance patterns—and outlet centers—in every sector of the country. Which is to say, every major city has a major performing outlet—and this is true whether we are discussing Omaha, Nebraska, or Greenville, Mississippi. Moreover, all of these performing centers can be viewed as functioning within the context of a network information line. This is not to say that a given performance of the Chicago Symphony will find them in Kansas at the performing center in that city—rather, all of the major performance spaces throughout the country can be viewed by their relationship to "culture function." In other words, all of these performing spaces are conceived with respect to the perpetuation of what is considered "culture" or "cultural." Thus, it comes as no surprise that composers like Bach and Beethoven can be experienced in every sector in America, because even though their activity is not perceived as commercial or popular music, it is perceived as being "of culture." In more than a few cases, these spaces are even donated to particular orchestras as well, for the realness of a major performing space gains its significance by its relation to "cultural and serious" music. Thus, the performance of classical music is not about economics as such—because whatever has to be done to keep the music will be done. And as such, one can find major outlets throughout the whole of this country, outlets that were created especially for "culture" or "cultural events." The reality of any form of creative music is related to whether or not that form can have the possibility of performance—and the focus realness of creative music must also be viewed with this in mind.

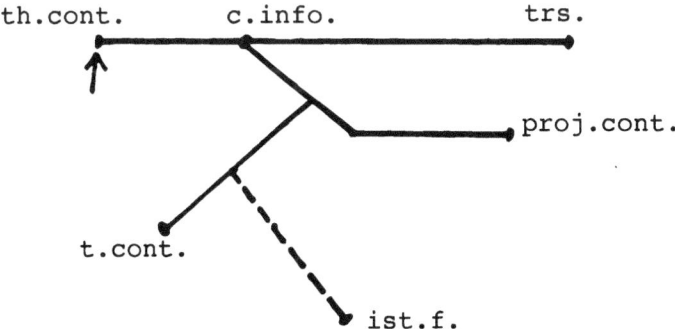

The location outlet significance of creative music must be viewed in isolated terms, for the performance sector range of the music has only been made available in particular regions of the country. For instance, it is not possible to talk of a real performance reality in most of the southern areas of America, and this is also true in the lower eastern states as well. Nor has there been any real effort to bring creative music in much of the western parts of America—there are isolated sections in places like Boulder, Colorado, but this is not the norm. In other words, the performance spread of creative music can only be viewed as really existing in the upper sections of America—with isolated outlets in the midwest. This is not to say given performances have not occurred in other regions of the country—because they have—rather, there has been no continuous outlet for sustained exposure. Yet to view a progressional time sequence, one can observe particular developments that have solidified and disbanded—like the activity which developed in St. Louis (and the collective movement it forecasted). Nor are there any continuous creative music outlets in the western southern region of America—in states like Texas, Idaho, Oklahoma, etc. To understand this is to really view the reality position of creative music—and the situation for contemporary classical music is not much better (and sometimes even worse—depending on what factors and region are focused on). The basic reality of creative music can be viewed through its relationship with mostly large cities—in particular, I am referring to New York City, Boston, Washington, D.C., Chicago, Detroit, San Francisco, Los Angeles, and that's about it. There are, of course, other cities, none of which sustain the composite flow of the music on a regular basis (not to mention, of the cities I have mentioned, in a given cycle an outlet might suddenly disappear). The realness of what this means is related to the actual reality position of creative music today, because to view the option particulars of performance possibilities is to understand that there are no real composite outlets for alternative music—but quite possibly this can be viewed in both negative and positive terms (positive in the sense that the music has the potential to help develop another whole reality context for American and world society—involving both new and concerned people who are prepared to deal with the challenge of transformation; and negative in the sense that nothing can happen unless the music is first exposed).

(R)POL.CON.-----PHY.U.P.

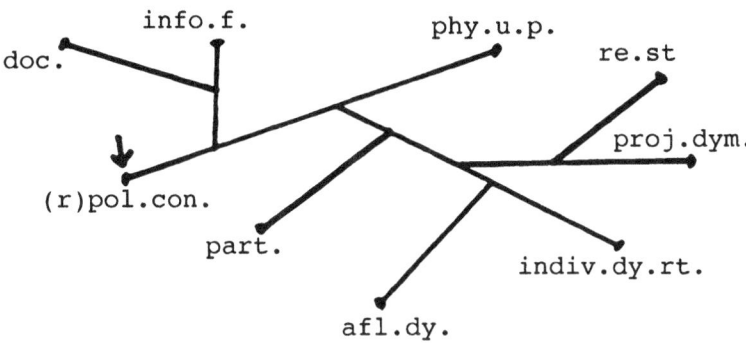

The present situation in creative music must be viewed as a kind of closed-society continuum as a result of little exposure. This is true both of the musicians who practice the music as well as the people who are instrumental in helping to create performance outlets for the music. For clearly the option range of the music makes it unattractive for younger musicians—because if most of the principal musicians who have created the music are not really working, then it is clear that a younger musician would have an even greater struggle. It is because of this situation that many would-be creative musicians are forced to move towards more commercial forms (although it must be said that each individual in the final analysis is responsible for his or her life decisions—but certainly the realness of limited work possibly is a significant factor). The most basic reality focus that most creative musicians have come to accept is that work will always be a non-continuance factor—and as such, many musicians try to function from the broadest possible base—having to do with travels outside of the country when possible. Moreover, there is nothing happening in this cycle that seems to suggest this phenomenon will change—on a composite level (yet I have not meant to imply that everything related to participation in creative music is gloomy, because it isn't). The realness of the present scene can be understood by looking at how the creative community has adapted to the present reality of events—which is to say, the closed-society continuum of the creative music sector is directly related to the physical universe intensity of this time period—and this is true for promoters as well. In other words, up until this point in time, the reality of creative music is not separate from the reality particulars of a handful of people who are functioning and have been functioning with the music. The implications of this development are significant for what they tell about the future of the music, for unless new people can be attracted to alternative creativity and alternative functionalism, the progressional continuance of the music will continue to exist underground, and be severely limited as a real transformation tool. The music has to move to the greater culture or remain a pseudo-diversion for spectacle diversion. This is true for creative music from the black aesthetic, and this is true for creative music from the white aesthetic, and this is true for creative music from the Asian aesthetic, creative music from the feminine projection dynamic continuum—and even opera. At present, the reality of the music can be viewed as a kind of club for people with different viewpoints, but the potential of cultural growth is directly related to what "different viewpoints" are all about. For this reason the challenge of creative music is no different than the challenge of the culture—I am only writing about the need for positive change.

Universities

The reality situation of creative music can also be viewed by what is happening in most of the universities throughout the country, for there is the mistaken belief in this period that much positive activity can be found on the campus communities—but this is not necessarily the case. The fact is, only a handful of schools have tried to deal with the seriousness of creative music performance in their curriculum. The great majority of our so-called higher institutions know nothing about the music's existence—this is true even for so-called music or fine arts schools. The most basic school performance curriculum has to do with the support of rock and other forms of popular music, and in itself no one should really be surprised. For the present-day school curriculum is not separate from the composite culture in the sense that most concert schedules reflect the sanctioned information focus of their culture's information dynamics—having also to do with the students themselves deciding what artist or artists to support. Out of two hundred colleges in a given year, it would be difficult to find from one to three performances of creative music (and I am being very generous with these numbers—"one" would be closer). Thus the reality gap between the music and the public gets wider and wider, for without performances no one can experience the music—which is to say, without some awareness of the music no one is apt to consider supporting it. Unless something is done to change social reality, the music will continue to have less contact with the composite society. The realness of this dilemma is not isolated in any one sector of the culture—or university. For there has been no composite attempt to deal with the reality performance possibilities of creative music by any sector of the greater culture—or cultural university complex. I write this not as a means to put anyone or any group down, but only to comment on what is now happening in creative music. Certainly there are particular groups who have tried to do something about this problem—groups like the one at the University at Buffalo who put together a festival of creative music that included all aspects of the music, or the organization at the University of Michigan in Ann Arbor. But the fact is, all of these groups are separate from what is really happening in present-day composite America. One would think that the average university would want to hire particular musicians to function in residence for a given time period—and not simply theoreticians, but instead real practicing musicians, for the insight they could get about actual and living creativity. One would think that musicians like Ornette Coleman and Cecil Taylor would be a great asset to any university—in whatever capacity (yet I do not mean to only mention these two great musicians, because there are many others as well—what about the services of musicians like Gerry Mulligan or Dexter Gordon?). This is not to say every creative musician even wants this opportunity—because everyone is different—but I am sure there are some who would be interested (when I think of musicians like Pepper Adams or Jimmy Heath, I realize how many great musicians we have in this country—people who, if utilized, could greatly contribute to every sector of our culture—or world culture). The inability of our universities to recognize or deal with this fact is depressing to say the least. For the isolation of creative music, and its resultant community, helps no one—and stagnates the possibility of positive growth.

R(AS) CM(II)–30

Agents

To understand the progressional spread of the music is to also focus on the dynamics of the music business, for it is understood that the role of the agent is intertwined with the success of the music. The best example of what this means can be seen in what has happened with rock music. For a given tour of a successful rock group involves many factors—and all of these factors involve more than one person can accomplish on his or her own. I am referring to the contracting of possible performing spaces, the handling of transportation, the routing of a tour, etc. The end result of this work is directly related to the success of the tour, and as such, many of the important music booking companies are very successful. At present, the realness of these booking agencies can be viewed as related to the progressional continuum of rock music, classical music, country and western music, every kind of music one can name. But name one artist of the post-Coleman juncture of the music who has any real machinery connected to him or her. In other words, there are none, and what this means cannot be ignored—because when Johnny Cash and June Carter's daughter decided to really make it, she was able to get a big booking agent to handle her, when Tiny Tim first made his decision to be involved with creativity, he got a booking agent, and this was also true for the Olympic star Bruce Jenner—but what about the master musician Bill Dixon, or again, Cecil Taylor? All of the artists who function in creative music are relegated to function from a more difficult position. This is not to say no creative artists work with agents of some kind, but only to point out that the established agents have never had any use for the music—and this rejection is related to the composite reality of alternative creativity music.

C.CULT.AT. -----RT.DY.

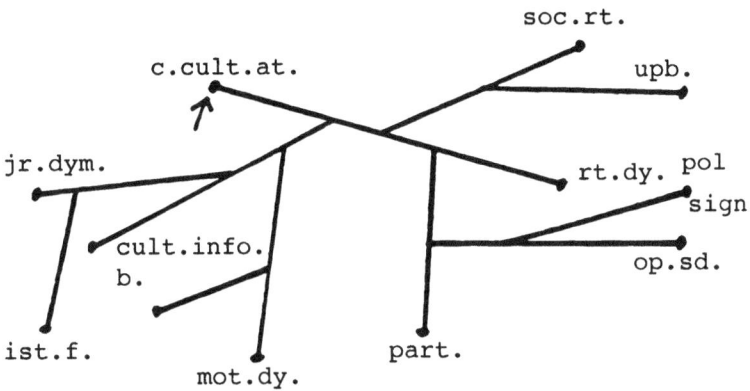

CULT.AF.BS. ------INFO.DY.

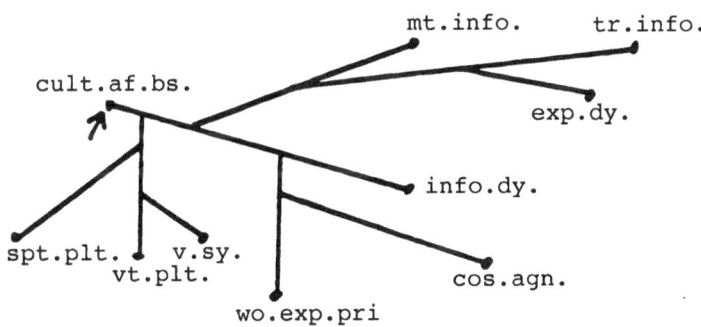

Rather than utilize the established performing agencies, most creative musicians work with one of the two or three jazz booking agencies available, or work independently. This is understandable, since the jazz agencies can handle only so many musicians. Artists like McCoy Tyner and Art Blakey work with people like Jack Whitmore, who is one of the few successful established jazz agents (about as high as any creative musician can expect). But the Jack Whitmores are few in between, and the actual reality of most creative musicians is to function as both musician and agent. Obviously this is not the optimum situation, for to function in music on its own is hard enough without also having to contract work. In the last three or four years, there has been another development as well—that being, the rise of the individual agent and promoter for creative music, and at this point in time it is too early to comment as to whether this has been a positive or negative emergence. For clearly the functional range of the individual agent is limited, especially when compared to the grant agencies which have sprung up in the last fifteen years—yet at the same time, to have one person helping is better than nothing. The last three years have seen many aspiring agents come into the music—and, after one year, get out just as quickly. Many of these people have come and gone so quickly that it is hard to realize they were ever really there. The effectiveness of running an agency is directly related to the establishment of multi-information lines—that being, having composite communication with as many sectors of the country as possible. One of the great problems many post-Coleman musicians are experiencing is the inability of potential promoters to be able to contact or even locate them (or their agents). A given promoter in Texas might really desire the activity of Oliver Lake, but without a relevant communication line, will instead hire someone else—and this is understandable. To function in creative music without an agent is even harder, and it must be understood that even in the time period of 1974–75, three-fourths of the creative musicians' community functioned by themselves—because no one was interested enough in their activity to come forth and help. No wonder so few musicians were able to sustain themselves from isolated performances in that time period, because the composite scene itself was very confused (no one knew how to contact anyone and no one knew what to charge for a concert fee, etc.). To a great extent the situation has improved somewhat—for the situation had to change somehow, and many musicians now work through some of the newly formed agencies which have grown up with the musicians. As we move towards the eighties, hopefully these newly formed agencies will be viewed as the new alternative business structures they are, for it must be understood that all of these new organizations have had to build from nothing. It is important to understand that even though there are no performances in the southeastern sector of America, it does not mean there is necessarily no interest in the music in that section—this phenomenon is the result of many factors (one of which being that no information lines have developed). The challenge of developing an increased reality spread for creative music will be the main function for alternative-functioning agencies as we move to the next cycle, and hopefully the realness of these new information lines will lead to actual performances—not by creative musicians of any one persuasion, but by all creative musicians. The very survival of the music is related to whether or not its borders are extended—and this is particularly true of the generation of musicians who solidified in the sixties. For by 1980, all of these people will be in their middle thirties to late forties—which is to say the reality of securing the music is no light matter. It is one thing to half-exist when one is in his or her early to late twenties, but by the time that person approaches forty, the nature of what can be successfully tolerated for survival changes considerably. In other words, it would not be practical to assume that given individuals can continually live in intense environments—where the whole of his or her existence is threatened at every moment—without having adverse effects on some level. However, I do not mean to paint the wrong picture of this phenomenon, for by citing the need for booking agencies and agents, I am not talking of a situation where, when completed, each musician and agent will immediately become a millionaire or in "who's who" listings—rather, the solidification of alternative business outlets will hopefully produce a situation where musicians can at least live on a human level. It is because of only practical physical universe considerations that this section is even included.

There has been another important development in the last ten years of music business that has revolutionized the reality of particular musicians. That development is the move many record companies have taken to form their own booking companies or agent groups. The end result of this maneuver has been that tour promotion and record releases are coordinated with advertising—as to make a maximum effective impact—and it works. Hopefully this trend will eventually include creative music as well, for the support of a record company is viewed as an encouraging factor by concert promoters. Many record companies will now buy advertising time when one of their artists is performing in a given city. The importance of this move cannot be over-generalized, for many concert promoters are directly spared expenses in situations like this—which is to say, artists who have this kind of backing have a distinct advantage over artists who haven't. The net effect of expanded record company involvement can be understood by the impact this involvement has on record sales and in general popularity. For it must be understood that without becoming "known" on some level, there can be no real involvement in either the music—as a composite thrust—or the individual making the music. Thus, the consideration of "popularity" is directly proportionate to how far that individual will be allowed to expand his or her activity—and this is particularly true when the question of project budget is brought into focus. No wonder the world of creative music is full of solos, duos, trios, quartets, and quintets—the fact is, these formations—while being wonderful—are also cheaper to produce. Which is to say, the dynamic implications of creative music cannot be totally achieved unless given musicians can have the opportunity to function in the composite spectrum of their activity—because duos, quartets, orchestra music, etc., can move to give an expanded realness of what is really happening in creative music.

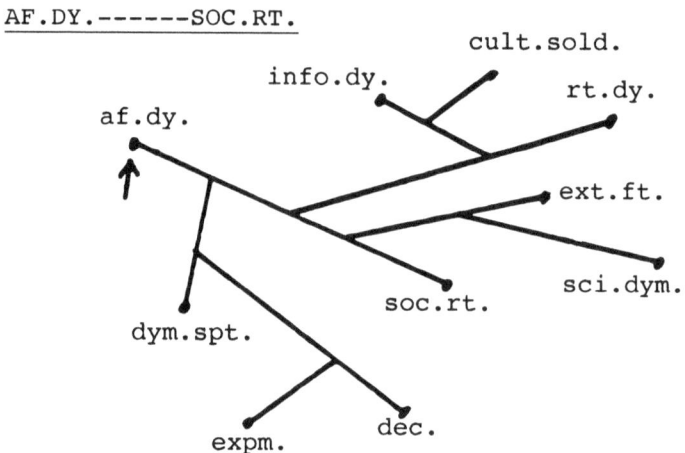

Hopefully, as more record companies become involved with creative music, the reality of its "tour" possibilities will increase. For if the particulars of rock tours have to do with from twenty to forty or more concerts that are precisely organized—so as to achieve minimum effort—this planning is very different than the reality of touring creative musicians. It is very rare indeed for a creative musician to have a string of ten concerts—in a human sequence (where the physical universe route of each concert can be viewed in some sort of linear development). The normal tour usually consists of about four to seven concerts—one in Chicago, one in Texas, one in New Jersey, one in San Francisco, one in Washington, D.C. (of course, I have exaggerated some, but I could not resist this opportunity)—and afterwards, everyone is totally fatigued (and usually broke). But the possibility of having a smoother tour cannot be attained until there are more information lines or agents. And while many people (in fact, most people) view the reality of touring as an extended vacation, I have no doubt that after participating in one or two of these ventures that this viewpoint would radically change. For the reality of touring is hard work—having to do with long hours in either a car—or airplane—hotels (some of which are good, but when they're not—"oh my")—train stations—flat tires, and sometimes little sleep (yet it can't be all that bad, I mean there must be something positive about the reality of performing music or no one would be doing it). Nevertheless, the move by record companies to support their music (and musicians) is a positive sign—and hopefully a similar commitment will be made for creative music. For as long as the music is treated as second-class activity, the public will continue to relate to it as such. The basic mentality surrounding alternative creativity will have to change—and this is particularly true of record companies. Because the most basic idea underlining the recording industry is the notion "why support creative music, because it will never sell." This attitude is self-serving—because without support it is surely true that the music won't sell, nor by support am I referring to one week of ads in *The Village Voice*—because limited support will change nothing. What is needed is a long-term commitment to the music and to developing an audience for the music. And underlining that commitment must be an awareness of responsibility for both the music and the needs of society. For the state of a given culture has to do with the composite particulars of its information and vibrational dynamics. Without exposure and education about alternative creativity, there can be no real hope of positive change.

Alternative Functionalism

If there has been any one positive factor that has emerged in this time cycle, with respect to the reality aspect of creative music, that factor would be the emergence of alternative functionalism. For if the realness of the present scene is as I have stated, then it is clear that the composite option spread of creative music has reached critical levels. Nor am I alone in thinking this, for the new developments taking place in creative music can be viewed as a direct response to the present reality that has solidified in cultural dynamics—especially in America (although the problem is really a world problem—or western world problem, to be more exact). Quite possibly in the long run, the present reality of creative music will be viewed as positive for what it has necessitated in physical universe action. Because the reality crisis of creative music in this cycle has sowed the seeds for alternative functionalism—and this is true on many levels, not only the music. (For example, the emergence of home videotape recorders and cable TV can be viewed as a positive response to the level of television programming, and this is only one example among many.) The realness of alternative functionalism in this context will be important for both the end result of a given sector and the vibrational-tone-level implications underlying what that result will mean for the culture. For many of us have come to accept the present reality of things as being unchangeable. But the work taking place in this cycle shows very clearly that change can be brought about because of individual initiative. It is not a question of trying to compete with the large established companies which control both multi-information and products, for obviously no one can really compete with this sector of society; rather, the emergence of alternative functionalism can be viewed as an attempt to make other options available, with the eventual hope that given segments of the population—relevant to the affinity dynamics particulars of its focus—can have the opportunity to have composite information if they so desire. From one or two individuals in the sixties to hundreds of functioning sectors, the realness of alternative functionalism threatens to change the composite reality of this period. By alternative functionalism in this context, I am referring to the rise of independent recording companies, books, publishing companies, as well as booking agencies and festivals. All of these factors will eventually change the state of creative music and society, for the emergence of alternative functionalism functions as the most dynamic factor for world change.

Record Companies

There have always been individuals involved in alternative recording. One can cite the work of Harry Partch as an example of a musician with awareness of alternative functionalism, and this is also true of someone like Sun Ra—who, on his own Saturn Records, documented much of the work he did in the fifties and sixties. Without the awareness of both of these musicians, we might never have had the opportunity to really experience their activity—and this is particularly true of Sun Ra, for the realness of his work is directly related to "present time" because he functions with improvisation (actually it would have been wonderful if both of these musicians could have had video recorders in the fifties—and forties—because both work with theatre). But the time zone of the sixties would represent the first real composite move to alternative recording and record companies. Probably this was due to the nature of the total suppression that creative music would endure in America during this same time cycle. For where in the fifties given musicians were usually able to find some company to record their music (even though they wouldn't necessarily be paid any real money), by the middle sixties even this area would close. Without doubt, the emergence of post-Ayler activity would be related to how this phenomenon came about, for if bebop's arrival was tinged in bitterness, it was nothing compared to how post-Ayler activity was greeted. The composite effect of this thrust would help disintegrate an already dismal scene, and the net result of that disintegration would be conducive for the solidification of jazz-rock and the transfer focus of media. Left by themselves, the musicians had no choice but to either produce their own product or starve—or leave the country (and I believe everyone participated in one or all three options). For a time, the early recording scene was somewhat confused—and this would be the cycle when everyone began learning just what the reality of alternative recording meant in actual terms: learning about business, keeping records of business, the problems of distribution, etc. But by the late sixties, many positive gains could be seen, and some of the companies that emerged in this cycle have gone on to become quite successful. The realness of what this sector has contributed to the total community is very important. Their survival has meant the beginning of a whole new period—and thrust continuum—for earth culture.

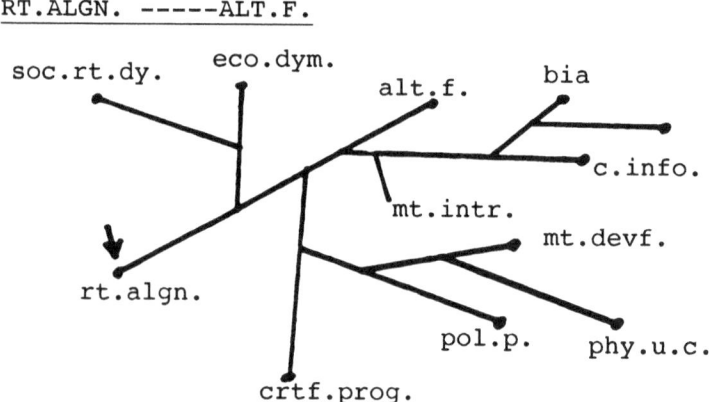

The emergence of alternative recording dynamically altered the composite implications of progressional functionalism, and its development would suddenly make available the realness of creative music on an unprecedented level. The implications of what this move signaled could be seen forming in the middle sixties—encompassing not only creative music from the black aesthetic but the composite spectrum of creative music. To understand what this emergence would mean is to view the many dynamic recordings which surfaced by the end of the sixties, for the move to alternative recording would help establish many musicians whose activity might have taken many more years to surface through conventional channels—if it would happen at all. Moreover, the solidification of alternative recording would also be accompanied by a move to develop alternative distribution lines as well. Which is to say, by the end of the sixties, several important distribution lines had solidified—and these lines were open to any individual who desired their use. The work of the Jazz Composer's Orchestra would be important for how it participated in establishing awareness about alternative functionalism, and this same organization would also be in the vanguard of those working to create alternative distribution. By the early seventies, the reality of alternative recording would be "real"—and as such, a valuable functional tool for creative musicians. The realness of this solidification can be viewed as bypassing the established system, and the progressional thrust of this movement forecasts a revolutionary and dynamic re-involvement with creativity. It is not a question of competing with the large and established record companies, for obviously no one has the money and systems to compete with multi-national power structures—rather, the solidification of alternative recording is the first step towards re-establishing the composite realness of creative music—and there is more. For the progressional move to alternative recording must also be viewed as a necessary step towards changing the composite defining and controlling reality of creative music. This is so because no one tells the musicians (or composers) what to play, or how to play a given area of music. The people who utilize alternative recordings are free to do what they do—or what they want to do—or what they can do—and this is the optimum state for any creative person. In other words, the solidification of alternative recording can be viewed as an important progressional step in the re-establishment of creativity—as defined by the people who are creating. Moreover, the defining aspect of alternative recording is not the only factor of importance, for the realness of this aspect—alternative recording—must also be viewed for what it poses for alternative control (because this is as important as the consideration of definition). Nowhere can a given individual better move towards understanding the reality particulars of the zone he or she functions in than by actually having to "deal" with the particulars of that zone—in actual terms. The solidification of alternative recording has helped to bring about reality awareness about the total dynamics of creativity. It is in this sector where creative musicians are forced to become involved in the music business—as something real, rather than a joke. It is in this sector where creative musicians can be found playing records and learning about shopping, learning about how much given considerations really cost (e.g., record pressing and covers)—learning about distribution and distribution lines—and all of this information brings a new awareness of the "actual" reality aspect of creative music. Thus, the realness of alternative recording must be viewed as an important consideration that is related to the move towards real awareness—have to do with taking complete control of one's reality.

The progressional spread of alternative recording is not limited to any one sector, but can be found throughout the country—from the west to the east coast. There are many records detailing the dynamics of present-day creative music, and we can now experience some of the creativity from the midwest and far west, and many people are surprised at the freshness and insight of much of the activity developing throughout the country. The establishment of alternative recording can be viewed as signaling the heartbeat of creativity in this time cycle, and where it seems to be going. There are independents in regions like Minnesota who are functioning, and this is also true for regions like Los Angeles. Hopefully by the middle eighties, the phenomenon of alternative recording will come to be perceived in other terms—not an "alternative" but instead as a necessary and stimulating addition to the culture. In fact, this already seems to be happening—and hopefully the next cycle will see the completion of a total distribution network throughout the country, because if there is any one area of alternative recording that still needs more improvement, it would surely be that of expanded distribution—but these things do take time.

```
T.C.IMP. ------RT.DY.
```

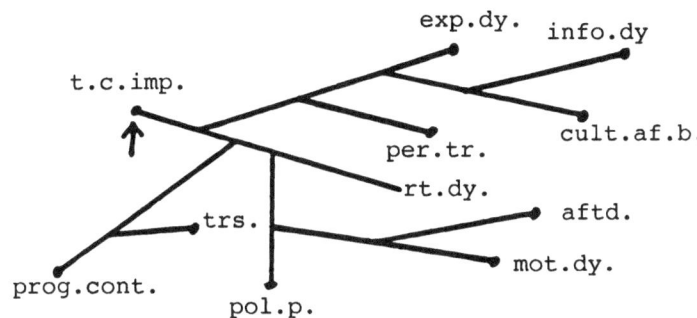

It is possible to view the middle sixties as a primary time junction that dictated how the spread of alternative recording could be utilized and made successful. For this was the period which saw the solidification of companies like Strata East and the Jazz Composer's Orchestra. Both of these companies, which started out as small alternative companies, have gone on to make important gains for alternative recording. The momentum created by these two independents has helped many musicians to consider this route. Nor are these two companies isolated examples, for musicians like Rashied Ali and Gunter Hampel can also be cited for the contribution their viewpoints have made on this phenomenon. At present, there are many areas of the country (USA) where alternative companies are making a real impact on the composite level—and this is particularly true of New York City, Boston, and Chicago. Even the Art Ensemble of Chicago has established its own label, and I feel this is only the beginning. The progressional continuance of alternative recording offers the best hope for composite exposure for creative music—and this is true for the total musicians' community. Even musicians who have access to major record companies now participate in alternative recording, for the establishment of an independent company insures a continuous output (and later total ownership will mean a lifetime of receiving complete royalties and publishing rights).

To understand the reality of alternative recording one must understand what has traditionally happened to creative musicians in their dealings with established recording companies. This is so because rare is the musician who has received all of his (or her) royalty statements and/or publishing. There are thousands of musicians from the time zone of the fifties who recorded twenty or more records who have not received one penny of royalties from those companies. This is not to say every recording company is crooked—for obviously there are companies that are completely honest (?)—but the progressional realness of creative music has seen more than its share of dishonesty. The move towards alternative recording must be viewed as a major step towards each musician handling his or her own business, as well as creative universe. The success of this venture is directly related to how involved each individual becomes in his or her own reality. For while it is clear that alternative records won't necessarily make one a millionaire, it is also clear that most musicians can make back the investment money put into their own product. The fact is, most recording ventures are successful, and the realness of the future seems to suggest that this area will continue to be important—and supported by the public. The success of this area must be viewed as related to the success—and continuance—of the music itself. There can be no question that recording for a large company directly helps a given individual increase public awareness about his or her activity, and there can also be no question that as individuals advance in their independent projects, established companies will begin to seek them out—because this is how business works. But the realness of alternative recording is not separate from the progressional continuance of the music—for without this most important area, the reality of the music will revert back to the fifties.

The dynamics of alternative recording can also be viewed outside of America, because no one sector of the planet has monopolized this most important transformational tool. In many ways, Europe can be viewed as more advanced in this regard than America, for the sophistication that surrounds alternative recording in Europe is much more advanced as a viable alternative than in any other planet sector I have visited. It is possible to look at the work of Willem Breuker as an example of what is best about alternative recording. Here is a musician who both creates and distributes his activity—throughout all of Europe. Breuker's activity vibrates to every definition of success and at present shows no sign of stopping. This is also true of Incus Records in England, where musicians like Evan Parker and Derek Bailey have worked together to create a dynamic alternative recording base. There is really nothing in America to compare with these companies, for both Breuker and Incus are light-years ahead of what I have seen in America. This is not to negate the positive work being done in America during this cycle—for obviously there is much positive work being done—but rather, if we are to view the realness of alternative recording, then we must allow ourselves to learn from those who have helped to advance positive areas of creative functionalism. Both Breuker and Incus, as well as the Free Music Production company (which used to be a collective but is now owned by given individual musicians), have made great inroads towards establishing alternative functionalism for creative music. The work being done by these companies has helped to produce a situation in Europe where practically every environment has some awareness of their product (some of the records are now finding their way to America as well). There are only a handful of American companies who have done as well, and to not learn from the work—and resulting information—of those who have successfully expanded this area would be foolish.

The dynamics of alternative recording must be viewed as one step in the overall move towards creative functionalism—rather than an isolated move by individuals. For the progressional implications of alternative recording are related to the much larger question of composite functionalism.

What is needed is the development of a total alternative creative stance—having to do with alternative recording—books—performance outlets, etc. By itself, alternative recording represents only one aspect of a much greater change cycle—and should be viewed as such. The reality dynamics of creative music can only be realized if all of the reality functional options are utilized and positively channeled for transformation. This is especially true if creative music is to function as a real transformation factor. There is at present a real need for books by creative musicians on the music to correct many of the misconceptions surrounding the music. It is not a question of every musician having the same kinds of ideas as every other musician—since life does not seem to be this way—and, obviously, even musicians will disagree with each other about the aesthetics of music. But the value realness of creative music can only benefit positively from the writings of creative musicians, because only a person involved with the actual music can really communicate with authority about what his or her participation really means. The move by creative musicians to become involved with writing must be viewed as beneficial to the music—because this is what is needed. For this reason, the work of musicians like Leo Smith or Derek Bailey must be viewed as extra important, for their activity might hopefully inspire others to come forth with more written literature on the music. Already the percussionist Arthur Taylor and Babs Gonzales have completed their books, and by the end of this decade there will probably be other offerings as well. The writings which have solidified the post-Webern continuum can be viewed as related to how that continuum is now viewed—and how given individuals would prefer it to be viewed. At present, practically every European composer of note has a book on his or her music which can be bought in many of the music stores—or at concerts of the individual composer. I view this achievement as extremely positive—for the reality dynamics of a given projection are not separate from how each individual perceives of his or her work. This is true for contemporary classical music and this is also true for creative world music. The challenge of the next cycle will hopefully move to expand the reality and dynamic functionalism underlying how alternative creativity is perceived—and hopefully the realness of the music will be perceived as related to the composite challenge of creative functionalism—rather than an end in itself. The fact is, we are living in a very difficult and dynamic period in creative music—and in actual life as well—and the challenge of this period implies that all creative musicians move towards dynamic functionalism—either this or watch the gap between the public and the music widen.

ALT.FT. -----PRI.INFO.

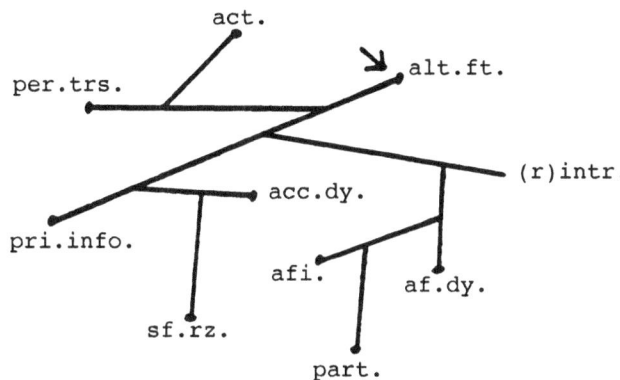

Quite possibly the factors that most distinguish dynamic functionalism in America from that of Europe would be the nature of how unification is perceived—or not perceived. In America at present, it is very difficult to have the same degree of unification that can be seen in Europe. The end result of this situation can be understood in the phrase "every man for himself" (or "every woman for herself"). The dynamics of this kind of separation can be viewed as positive on some levels and negative on most levels. Positive in the sense that either the individuals become very strong or perish (which is to say, the survivors can become very strong and committed people). Negative in the sense that there can only be a few survivors of this kind, as the dynamics of the physical universe involve many different factors . . . and things. Whatever, the present situation concerning creative music in America has to do with isolated individuals—some of whom are functioning, and most not. The success of real transformation implies that somehow this situation is corrected on some level—yet this sounds easier on paper. The truth is, it is difficult enough to function as an individual—but to have to deal with people who are not as sincerely committed (or who, because of their physical universe situation, can't be as committed) to the same level of functioning in the music is, in many cases, simply too much. What is needed is some real awareness of dynamic functionalism—for there are many areas which need to be dealt with, and no single person can do it alone. Whatever, as long as the physical and vibrational universe of America is as it is, individual musicians will have little choice but to function independently as a means to advance their own activity—rather than collectively. Quite possibly, there is some value in this approach as well (what can I say since this does seem to be what's happening) and hopefully we will learn from the "actual" functioning of particular creative artists (people in creative music are no different from people in general—which is to say, many of us can only learn by "example" rather than by communication). In Europe there seems to be more possibilities for unification on various levels—yet I do not mean to imply no differences exist between various individuals or groups (because there are always differences between people on various levels)—but in general, the basic environment in Europe does seem more conducive for unification than in America.

    The dynamics of creative functionalism must also include the move to establish alternative programming outlets. For the realness of recording and writing represents only one aspect of exposing the music. Many musicians in the sixties began to understand the significance of alternative performing spaces, and by the early seventies one could view the forming of new performing spaces in a variety of contexts. Musicians like Rashied Ali would open their own clubs as well, and the seventies would see the forming of alternative collectives to deal with the challenge of creating new outlets. By the middle of the seventies, there would be so many alternative spaces that the media would refer to the change as "the development of the loft period." In this kind of atmosphere, the composite realness of the music benefited greatly—for the development of the music is directly related to whether or not it can be performed. The establishment of alternative performing spaces must be viewed as directly related to the positive spread of the music. Many of the spaces would be opened to a wide sector of the creative community, and as such performed a service to the total creative community. One example of such a performing space would be Sam Rivers's Studio Rivbea. This performing space has been instrumental in the progressional thrust of the composite creative music scene in New

York City. Many artists have had their first New York performance in this space, and Rivers has also used it as a center for teaching as well—involving both performing and theory. Studio Rivbea has also been instrumental in the development of alternative festivals for creative music, and several times helped to participate in alternative festivals (which resulted from the Newport Jazz Festival's inability to promote contemporary alternative projects). Also, the work of Studio We must be acknowledged as a positive alternative-functioning collective. This collective (I believe it is a collective, but on this I might be wrong) has functioned for as long as Studio Rivbea and has been an important performing space for creative music of all types. The number of performing spaces of these types would be too great for me to list (not to mention that there are undoubtedly many more I am unaware of)—certainly the work of Joe Lee Wilson should also be mentioned—and I am told saxophonist Charles Tyler has also opened up a new space. In the final analysis, all of these spaces have helped create positive momentum for the music, and as such this phenomenon must be viewed as positive on every level. In some cases, the move to create alternative performing spaces can be viewed as directly instrumental in helping to create more conducive spaces for musicians and listeners alike. For without spaces for "sessions" and "jamming," younger musicians have no places to experiment and play. The new alternative performing outlets that solidified in the middle seventies now provide such a space, and the results of this phenomenon can be experienced by hearing the music. In most cases, the solidification of alternative performing spaces has been conducive to a healthier interchange between both the musicians and the audiences. This is so because many of the new spaces vibrate to a more relaxed environment—more conducive to communication of all kinds.

    The move to establish alternative performing spaces must also extend to include other areas of the society. More than ever before, there is now a need for healthy interaction between the music and the community. The work of the AACM has made very important contributions along these lines, and hopefully an increased involvement of this type will continue. For too long, the community has come to view alternative creativity as having little to do with their lives—especially in "actual" terms. The challenge of the next cycle must include more involvement between all segments of the creative arts and the greater public—and this is true regardless of sector. The idea of the musician being separate from the community must be replaced by new moves towards total transformation. The reality aspect of creative music must give insight as to how this desired composite alignment can be brought about—between all sectors of a given community (from the composite community extending to the composite planet). Nor am I engaging in wishful thinking when I write of unification on this level. Rather, to deal with the realness of what is really possible in this cycle is to postulate nothing less than composite planet unification. Not only is composite transformation possible, but anything less will keep us on the same basic course that has brought us to this juncture.

The move towards more community involvement must also extend into the reality of education for both young and old—including the musicians. More than ever before, the seriousness of what is happening in the education system must be re-examined. There is now a need to even consider forming alternative educational systems or replacement schools. Young people from every persuasion must be given new impetus for receiving ideas—of all kinds—and new teaching methods must come into being. The seriousness of transformation calls for action on this level—and more. To view the educational system in present-day America is to confront what could only be called an alarming situation—and this is particularly true of the poorer communities, in whatever region. Unless a new sentiment can be established, this country will continue to turn out too many young people not prepared for positive participation in society—let alone contributing. I do not cite this area of focus (i.e., schools and the general educational process in America) as a means to point a finger at any one group—because obviously the reality of this phenomenon is multi-dimensional, and there is also the realness that little money is allotted to education by both state and federal levels. But the very future of earth society depends on how successfully information can be transferred. That the present educational crisis seems to be increasing rather than decreasing is alarming to say the least. What is needed now more than ever are outside attempts to restore order, as well as new sentiment by every sector of the community to move towards positive change. For creative musicians, positive functionalism could involve establishing new courses to help people become involved with creativity. Yet I realize this is no easy task—but by examining the progressional work which solidified in the sixties, one can view many different approaches to this challenge. In particular, the work done by the AACM could serve as a foundation or model for beginning functionalism, and the black artists' collective in New York is also a good example of isolated but positive functionalism. All of this is necessary, because the reality aspect of present-day education is in seriously bad shape. Unless moves are now made to deal with this problem, the future promises to be extremely severe—on many different levels. It is not just a question of the greater public being unaware of the music, nor is it a question of a given sector of the community suffering because of no attention by politicians and/or established functioning agencies—rather, the reality realness of this cycle must be viewed in composite terms. The fact is, the real problems dictating this time cycle are much more profound than only education or music. It is important to understand that there are many people, both in this country and on the planet in general, who are barely able to exist. Moreover, the progressional continuance of this cycle seems to suggest that the collective forces of western culture can be viewed as being directly responsible for how this condition has come about. I am not implying that every individual who functions within the system—regardless of level—has consciously made the decision to tamper with the projectional and vibrational potential of composite humanity, but I am writing that the progressional continuance of western culture in its most natural progression has moved to create the reality particulars we are presently dealing with. It is for this reason that I have come to view the realness of alternative functionalism as the most important transformational—and transitional—tool that could have positive impact and meaning. Because unless something is done and done soon, nothing will change—unless it gets worse. The challenge of bringing about positive change is not separate from the move to have more creative people become involved in total social reality.

For this reason, the relationship between creative musicians and their community must be viewed as important.

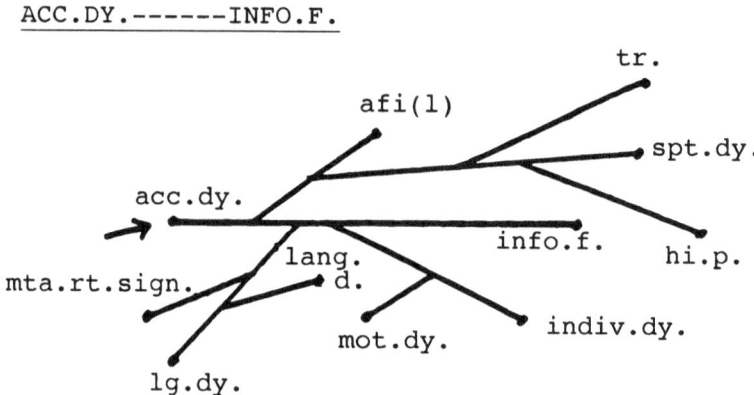

Decentralization

The realness of alternative functionalism is also related to the concept of decentralization. For to view the dynamics of the affinity spectrum is to understand that the present situation we are in is not conducive to optimum expansion. In actual terms, the challenge of the next cycle in creative music implies that creativity will not be isolated to only given sectors of the community, but instead spread throughout the planet and dynamic regional sectors. This is not to negatively comment on New York or any of the large cities which now serve as creative centers, but only to look at the composite significance of our present situation from a world perspective. Not to mention that at any given time the basic thrust continuum of the music has always involved many different people who were not born or raised in New York anyway, but were instead forced to migrate as a means to make a living. To understand this phenomenon is to also understand that many communities all over the country (and planet) are without some of their strongest creative forces.

The move to establish decentralization must be viewed for what it implies about the dynamic spectrum of creativity, and for what it poses for regional dynamics. This is not to imply that given individuals should stay away from New York City or any other city—rather, the realness of decentralization would move to re-channel the composite creative communities' relationship with how these large cities are now utilized. The best example of a functioning ensemble that understands the significance of decentralization would be the Crusaders creative ensemble—originally from Texas, but now residing in Los Angeles. Long ago, this ensemble made the decision simply not to move to New York but instead to only use the city—as another performing outlet—in their performing schedule. In making that decision, the Crusaders showed a profound awareness of regional dynamics, for it is clear that the dynamics of a given creative thrust are not separate from the actual "life space" of its participants. The concept of decentralization must be viewed as a positive cultural and functional necessity. For while it is clear that New York now functions as the center of media and cross-information, at the same time it is also true that any given region promotes its own regional dynamics. Many musicians have come into New York with dynamic viewpoints only to be swallowed up after a given time zone—and later losing their own special affinity nature (eventually sounding like every other musician). But this is not the only reason that decentralization is important, for the very lifeblood of the culture is directly related to how its dynamics are situated. The move to re-establish decentralization must be viewed as an attempt to utilize the composite lifeblood of the culture—in its own vibrational terms. The fact that this is not being done in this cycle can be viewed as directly related to the present dictates of social and vibrational reality: that being, nine-tenths of the creative community is situated in particular sectors of the country, and the greater culture is basically unaware of their existence. The creative community in this context can only become a "hip" club—or secret society, rather than a dynamic functioning entity.

The realness of decentralization does not only comment on the regional dynamics of a given country, but also involves the composite planet. In fact, the emergence of creative music outside America must be viewed as directly related to the dynamics of this phenomenon. In many ways, Europe can be viewed as more conducive to the dynamics of decentralization than America. For by viewing the various activities taking place in given sectors of Europe, one can see a healthier interaction between different countries, as well as a respect for regional and affinity dynamics. For this reason and more, I am very excited about the progressional thrust underlining what will happen in Europe during the next cycle (say, the next ten years, even). Because with respect and European unification all options are available, and creativity in this context can only expand. It is my hope that the coming cycle will involve more cross-sectional information, while at the same time more respect for regional dynamics (and affinity dynamics). This is definitely what is most needed. For the cross-sectional planet creativity already happening in this cycle is much more dynamic than is generally recognized—and this is especially true in America (which places very little emphasis on trying to understand the world group reality—or any "outside" initiation).

Finally, the concept of decentralization can be viewed with respect to actual functionalism. For the solidification and acknowledgment of decentralization is related to the possible forming of alternative performing networks—having to do with the creation of alternative performing spaces for creativity on a regional, country, or planet level. In the final analysis, the creative community can look at no one to do this for them. The realness of decentralization is directly related to alternative functionalism—having to do with respecting all that is here, and also having to do with functional moves to help bring that about by a revolutionary awareness of earth creativity. The first step towards realizing real change is to examine the present reality aspect of creative music. Our desire must be to create a better world for all humanity and composite earth. There is much work to be done.

(Level 3)

1. Do you have any basis for writing that the political and economic sector of western culture has consciously shaped our present understanding and relationship to creativity?

Yes. The reality position of a given culture's information dynamics is directly tied to how that culture functions politically and economically. All of these matters are directly related to the well-being and affinity position of a culture—or even "regulated society." Politics is not only about how given individuals are elected—instead, this consideration is related to the very fabric of what a culture is. My basis for writing about this phenomenon can be substantiated by merely viewing what I call the collective forces of western culture—that is, the agencies responsible for what information the greater public is exposed to, what interpretations are to be adopted, what funds are to be supplied for whatever purposes, what documentation is to be supplied (concerning both planet history and particular history), what regions of information are to be given use of the media—and in what way—what sector is to be rewarded or awarded, and for what achievement. All of these considerations are political and profoundly related to economics. Because in the final analysis, even the basis from which a given factor is made "of value" must be viewed as the result of political decisions. Either this is true or I can simply proclaim the dirt in my backyard is worth four or five billion (not to mention the printing of money and/or the elevation of gold was not pre-ordained by the cosmics, but instituted instead from politics and political decisions). Finally, the reality of creativity must be viewed for what it ultimately is—that being, the most powerful accelerator for vibrational informational transference. In other words, the reality implications of a given continuum of music affects its listener on more levels than what is generally talked about. Music can ultimately influence: what zone of information a person can understand, the composite reality of healing, the dynamics of spiritualism, the nature of social relationships, the dynamics of style, the spirit of investigation, etc. As such, the move to control cultural creativity must be viewed as a move to profoundly manipulate sensibilities—and this is why and how we have arrived at the juncture of the eighties.

2. *What is the significance of decentralization?*

The concept of decentralization is really related to the realness of planet restoration. For the collected manipulation and misinformation of the western controlling and defining community has created a situation that is basically unhealthy—because by accenting only the particular creativity of certain regions, and ignoring the composite state of things, the reality continuance of creativity is put off balance—and this is serious. The present state of western reality dynamics is that "artists" must necessarily move from their environment if they are to be viewed as "successful." The effect of this misconception is that given regions are drained of their creative people, and "local" artists are not respected on the level their work deserves. But this is only the beginning. For the present centralization of creativity has made "spectaclization" very easy in that, by having all artists in a given region, the media is able to control and affect the state of "creative reality." The concept of decentralization really has to do with encouraging creative people to find their own individual solutions about their creativity—in the area of their choice. Only by having this kind of participation can we ever hope to bring about positive transformation.

3. *Does the concept of decentralization clash with the idea of world culture?*

No. Decentralization is a concept that involves alternative functionalism as a means to broaden and clarify affinity dynamics. In no way does this clash with the concept of world culture. The most basic factor that underlines the realness of world culture is what this concept—world culture—poses for the possible solidification of a new spiritualism and/or attitude. Not to mention, even after the solidification of world culture is achieved, people will still be living in different parts of the planet—different parts with different creative dynamics and affinity balance. Decentralization is only a concept to hopefully advance what this diversity can bring about. There is no incompatibility between these concepts at all.

4. *What is your view on independent recording?*

I feel the emergence of independent recording represents one of the major breakthroughs in this time zone. Sooner or later, the momentum of this area of functionalism promises to radically change the music business. This is so because independent recording only accelerates the composite implications of alternative functionalism. Hopefully we have now entered the time zone (the eighties) where the next phase of this phenomenon can be solidified—that is, alternative distribution. The thrust of independent recording has made it possible for many musicians to release records who normally might never have had the opportunity—or would have had to wait much longer to be asked by the large companies. I view all of this as extremely positive as well as important. For the previous reality of music recording has always functioned as a political bloc of sorts, and a musician had necessarily to be connected with the right political group before his or her career could be advanced. The emergence of present-day independent recording has changed this syndrome somewhat, but, more important, the extended solidification of this phenomenon promises to dynamically alter the composite reality of the recording business. Because of this alone, independent recording must be viewed as positive.

5. *How do you view government assistance in the form of grants for creativity?*

I believe the dynamic implications of creativity must be viewed as related to composite cultural life and continuance, and as such should be supported by every level of its culture. This is especially true for creative availability programs—like music in grammar and high school. Because every young person should have the opportunity to be involved in the creative outlet of his or her choice. I also believe some form of funding should be made available for creative projects by established artists—yet this phenomenon is very dangerous. For the last fifteen years have seen an over-reliance on federal assistance—for projects that could have been completed without outside help. It seems to me that special funding should be made available to particular sectors that represent dynamic creative functionalism—for the betterment of the composite culture. At present, the National Endowment for the Arts supports European art music more than it does American creativity—and this cannot be viewed as positive on any level. Yet, by the same token, I am not advocating that no assistance be given to any particular sector—just more fairly distributed. It seems to me that the "first" step to be taken in positive federal functionalism is the creation of projected programs for teaching the greater public about creativity. This is necessary because something must be done to offset the collective manipulation of contemporary media (which, of course, has also been aided by the federal government). It is important to understand that the vibrational reality of creativity affects the composite culture's relationship with information—regardless of what area and/or focus. Which is to say, the distortion surrounding this subject has permeated the progressional lining of American continuance. If we are to postulate what is most positive for future generations then something must be done to re-establish (or let's just say establish) a more positive basis for understanding creativity as well as erecting a cultural creative attitude.

6. If the media is not able to change its relationship with black creativity, what can be done?

In all honesty, I do not believe that black people—or non-white people—will ever have positive and/or correct interpretations of black or world creativity in the western media. This is not to say there are no positive individuals functioning in the western media, because obviously there are many ... (?) My point is only that the reality of black creativity in America is the same as the reality of black people in America, and I believe as long as America is America there will never be fair treatment of non-white people, because America is about "something else." The real challenge for black people in the coming decades is to create their own outlets—alternative outlets—and this is true for every sector of disenfranchised peoples. There is now a need for alternative books, radio, television, etc. To wait for a real change in the vibrational and physical reality of America is to be waiting for a long time. As long as the collective forces that make up America remain, there can be no hope of real human unification.

7. What do you think about the idea that universities should employ creative musicians to teach creative music, as opposed to traditional music teachers?

I feel that the future relevance of extended education is directly related to whether or not the university can provide a broader spectrum of information interpretation—and this is especially true for world creative music. As such, I see the inclusion of the creative musician as a positive factor for practical information transference. However, in the final analysis, the transformational teacher must necessarily be able to teach more than only one information interpretation in any given region of creativity. It will probably be years before this kind of teacher can be developed en masse, because only a few institutions are even interested in world culture—and its related information dynamics. As such, the use of the "artist in residence" concept can be important for providing alternative viewpoints—and this is also true for the "master class." What is needed is for more creative musicians to collate their creative universe as a means to have a "program" to teach.

8. Do you consider the media basically irresponsible?

The reality of western media is both dynamic and complex. I do not view this phenomenon as necessarily irresponsible—instead, it is a question of responsible to whom? I believe the dynamic implications of western composite information transference involves the realness of a multitude of factors—having to do with the so-called natural diversity of a so-called democracy as well as the use of interpretation directives from the upper echelon of the western controlling and defining community. In the final analysis, the natural dynamics of western media will move to undermine the continuance of western culture, because the reality of information and/or information transference from this so-called observation platform is based on the dismantling of its own information identity: that is, western media is perceived as an instrument to "comment on" and, in doing so, naturally challenge the reality of its "living criteria" (or essence identity). The thrust of this consideration (media) will inevitably aid cultural disintegration, because the result of a given interpretation must necessarily accelerate both divisiveness and particular motivation.

9. Do you feel that black creativity should be taught separately from western art music in the university?

I feel that courses in black creativity—its correct history, methodology, and aesthetics—should be included in the composite curriculum of every public and private educational system. I believe there are many contexts where both black creativity and western art music can be taught together, and I also believe there are regions of both musics which must be approached separately. But this approach should be no problem because it is in keeping with how education is in fact practiced. There are already separate courses on music history, harmony, etc., and black creativity in this context represents simply another subject area to be taught. Yet the dynamic inclusion of world creativity in the western educational system will pose different problems. Because the reality of established information interpretation and/or transference in western education does not necessarily lend itself to providing the kind of insight that must be achieved from the study of world music—and/or black creativity—and herein lies the real problem. Probably the only way black and world music can be taught accurately in western institutions is for new alternative forums to be established, but this will, of course, take time. I have very little faith in the traditional community of western education—in fact, I am in disagreement with how this sector teaches western art music, let alone black music.

10. Is economics the primary factor behind the inability of record companies in America to promote creative music?

I believe the consideration of economics can most certainly be viewed as a factor related to the reality of the music recording business and its rejection of creative music—but I do not believe that economics is the sole basis for that rejection. This is so because the American businessman has clearly shown that anything can be sold—quality, especially, is not even a factor to be considered. The present rejection of creative music is related to the dynamic implications of alternative functionalism and mis-education. This is so because the essence realness of extended creative music carries profound consequences for the composite reality of this time period—

with respect to informational and vibrational transference. I believe the inability of recording companies in America to deal with creative music is an affirmation of what has taken place throughout the composite sector of the western defining and controlling community. For the rejection of extended creative music—especially extended black creativity—is related to the overall suppression of alternative functionalism (as this concept is viewed in both cultural and progressional terms) throughout the total culture. To really understand what this means is to examine the nature of both information transference and political dynamics in western culture—because the rejection of creative music is not just an isolated rejection but rather a definite political decision that has been prepared for on a number of levels. There is no real appreciation of any kind of creativity not viewed as commercial (or that can't be made commercial)—and this is true whether the form is traditional or modern. The realness of this "unappreciation" is directly related to the fact that only certain areas of creativity can be "used" in this time zone (used in the sense of being made to conform with the "appearance of things" and the "intent" of the collective forces of western culture). Finally, the rejection of creative music and alternative functionalism by the western recording companies is a decision shaped through dynamic mis-education. Because any real understanding of culture and cultural continuance would clearly reveal the significance of "life creativity" and cultural art. The rejection of creative music and alternative functionalism in present-day western culture is consistent with its composite rejection of both common sense and social responsibility.

11. Have the independent recording companies which emerged in the sixties affected the economic reality of established recording companies' relationship with creative musicians?

The functional information surrounding what independent recording companies had to learn to solidify their business has had a profound effect on the total musicians' community. This is so because the thrust of this phenomenon has helped uncover the reality of recording costs for record productions. The rush in the sixties to establish independent recording would also shed light on the margin-of-profit possibilities—and in doing so clarify the real economics of the record business. It is important to understand that few independent companies have actually lost their money by going independent—for the actual fact is that a sale of around one thousand records will guarantee that the company will break even on basic production expenses. Certainly there are no independents capable of printing records on the level of the large companies—and at this point in time, alternative distribution has yet to solidify on the level one would have hoped for—but all of this takes time. Nevertheless, from the efforts of early independents, it is now possible to understand the real reality of the record business, and it is also possible to begin trying to change the record business. Many large companies have long maintained that it is impossible to make a profit from creative music—but this viewpoint does not correspond to the successes of independent recording. For the music can be sold, and a market can be cultivated—it is really a question of dedication and patience.

12. Have you implied in this book that the music unions serve no positive purpose for creative music? Does this apply to all musicians?

I believe the solidification of the musicians' union is a positive step for all musicians, and this is especially true for musicians who are able to work on a regular basis (i.e., in the studios or on television shows). The union helps to protect musicians' jobs and functions as a positive force for pay raises and overall fair play from the established companies. But for the most part, very few creative musicians are able to work regularly, and herein lies the problem. The average creative musician, especially in his or her early period, might not make enough money in a year to pay dues—let alone live. But the union has never functioned as a force to help find jobs for these people—or at least the reality of union procedure is really not set up for alternative creative music or musicians. Yet I do not mean to be unfair. Certainly any union musician, so-called avant-garde or polka, is protected once a given performance space signs a contract concerning performance—and maybe this should be enough. I admit to being somewhat anti-union in my youth and slowly I am questioning the validity of that position. I believe the reality of unions in this time period is not geared to deal with the particulars of alternative creativity—but I believe this less and less. I really don't like my argument on this question. Because while my point is real, somehow in the final analysis, I am not convinced that separating from the union is necessarily better. I have the feeling I am wrong.

13. Are you opposed to the concept of the jazz festival as it exists in America in this time period?

    Not really. Probably, if I were able to affect the greater functionalism of western culture—and in particular America—I would move to create as many festivals as possible. I would try to stimulate the composite culture to create festivals that utilized world creativity as well as festivals that only dealt with particular musics. There is nothing wrong with the concept of a jazz festival, and this is true for festivals in Europe or America. It is very fashionable to be down on the Newport Jazz Festival because the music is not what a given person might desire—and I have also heard many arguments about the Monterey Jazz Festival which complained about the lack of new music. But I completely disagree. My point of view is this: both George Wein and Jimmy Lyons should have the right to run their festivals any way they want—as long as they respect the laws of honest business. If a given person disagrees with their viewpoint, let him or her start another festival—this is what is needed anyway. By writing this I have not meant to overlook the composite reality of western functionalism, because certainly everyone is not in the position of starting their own festival. But in the final analysis, no one can be faulted for what area of creativity they are attracted to. It seems to me that too many people in America have come to rely on other people to do what they could do themselves (if effort was applied). For me, if I were in charge of a festival—or moving in that direction—I would provide a platform for the broadest possible spectrum of creativity. Still, I would also have a couple of all-Beethoven festivals—maybe an all–Duke Ellington Festival—or a Stockhausen Week or Basie Month. All of these possibilities are creative, and all of these possibilities are culturally life-giving.

14. What effect have developments in the communication media had on the creative artist today?

    The dynamics of contemporary communications technology are directly related to the awareness and influence of world culture. For the realness of this phenomenon has moved to bring the composite planet together. It is now impossible to not be aware of events taking place on any part of this planet—this is true for politics as well as creativity. The progressional continuance of contemporary communications has helped break down many of the misconceptions we have about other people, and, in its place, is currently helping to solidify a more honest foundation for building world unification. To really comment on the significance of dynamic communication is practically impossible in this time period, because the effects of new communications have been so great and so diverse that it is impossible to separate this phenomenon from the composite reality of this time period. This is true on every level and in every context—having to do with both positive and negative implications. The future continuance of dynamic communication technology promises to have even greater implications for life on this planet—ultimately this consideration will help to solidify world culture.

15. What adjustments does a musician have to make in dealing with the recording medium—in terms of attempting to document one's creativity to its best advantage?

    The answer for a question like this differs from musician to musician, and probably the criteria underlining this question also change from project to project and from time period to time period. It really depends on where each individual is at in his or her life. For myself, I found that in the recording studio the consideration of editing is very important. In my early period, I approached each solo as if it were the last moment of my life—super-duper technique and intensity and twelve million notes (where one note would have sufficed). I remember the first opportunity I had in the studio very clearly because after attempting to blow the walls down, the replay had very little to do with what I thought I had played. It was at this point that I began understanding there were other considerations related to recording—as well as performing in general—that I was not dealing with. For the problem—as I am able to understand it—is to have people hear what you are playing as clearly as possible. But I was guilty of poor editing and this was indeed a problem. I came to eventually learn that a given passage requires a certain amount of space if a certain degree of intention is to be communicated. As a woodwind player, I also found that certain adjustments must also be made to get the sound I wanted from my instruments: that being, reed adjustments and timbre adjustments. There is also the consideration of dynamics; because the natural softs are too soft and the natural louds are too loud in the studio. My point here is only that the reality of studio recording is very different from live performance—and as such, adjustments must be made. How much adjustment, however, depends on each individual.

16. What are the advantages of the recording medium, and how is this phenomenon different from live performance with respect to purpose?

The recording medium gives the creative or uncreative musician a chance to document some aspect of his work. Unlike the concert situation, which is conceived as an outlet where the greater public can experience a given person's creativity, the recording medium must be viewed as a documentation and economic consideration. This medium offers the musician a chance to have a given "moment" distributed throughout the composite culture, and in doing so affects that musician's chance of gaining greater work possibilities and establishing one's "name." The sophisticated use of the recording medium can help secure one's ability to continue his or her creativity, for music is not about "the closet" but involves instead having someone to play for. To approach recording is to move towards having one's work experienced by the composite planet—almost—and is also the first step towards establishing one's life relationship with the business of music.

17. How do you view the medium of recording with respect to the use of notation?

In many ways, the recording medium is an extension of notation. Because the reality of notation has only to do with the time freeze of some aspect of a given participation and/or functionalism. A recording of Charlie Parker playing "Now's the Time" can be viewed as fixed as a Mozart string quartet score—of course there are differences, but my point is that both disciplines can be used to "re-actualize" something which did not exist, or something that did exist but doesn't anymore (something that "happened"). The difference between notation and recording has to do with what the dynamic implication of a given methodology means with respect to its reality function. In other words, notation, in its most real sense, is a discipline interconnected with what it proposes to codify—and as such, this discipline is spiritual (even though in this time zone we are no longer aware of the meta-reality position of a given function). The recording medium, on the other hand—to my knowledge, anyway—is not a spiritual function but instead a means to freeze sound for reproduction. Possibly after the transformation, this medium will be "zoned" for its real position in dynamic spiritualism—this is possible because I believe every functionalism has a meta-reality position in the hierarchy of world information.

18. What effects have the economic dynamics of the music business had on young practicing musicians of the seventies generation?

The dynamics of the music business in the seventies have profoundly affected the composite reality of the seventies generation of practicing musicians. For the thrust of this period has seen the institution of music business elevated past the institution of music. Young musicians today are more aware of the business than ever before, and hopefully they will not make the mistakes of previous generations. However, the nature of present-day business dynamics has helped to obscure the reality dynamics of individual intention, and this must be viewed as the most dangerous signal yet about progressional continuance. More than ever before, musicians are encouraged to make whatever adjustments are necessary to be successful. The present reality of competition in commercial and so-called avant-garde music is both dangerous and distasteful. The thrust of this time period moves to make musicians conform to what is commercially effective as opposed to what is most creative—or real.

Many of the younger musicians are now growing up without the necessary perspective to make accurate decisions about "the reality" of their creative course. Both the music business as well as the media are to blame for this situation. The realness of western culture is slowly bringing the dynamics of creativity down to its lowest possible level because of limited economic interest and gain. I write this not because of a lack of respect for popular music—because I can and do respect every form of earth creativity—but because of the shabby way we have let creativity be used and distorted. The present reality of the music business has helped to isolate the creative musician from his or her option dynamics, and in its place has put a formula mentality.

19. What are the advantages and disadvantages of functioning as a local musician in either one city or one area?

The advantages of functioning as a local musician are that one has the possibility to develop a particular audience as well as work outlets—and this is important if one is to survive from his or her music. The local musician also has the advantage of not being too far away from his or her family—for the realness of extended travel can be very hard on a family (not to mention the special particulars involving the raising of children). The realness of local performing is also conducive to extended research or even extra schooling—and practice. This is so because it is impossible to continue the level of research that one might desire on the road (at least this is true for me anyway). In short, I believe the so-called local musician has the best chance to participate in creativity and, while doing so, also have a normal life. The disadvantages of being a local musician involve not being able to command the kind of money that national or international musicians can ask for—this is so because people are more likely to support a musician who doesn't perform often in their community as opposed to someone they can hear on a regular basis. Another disadvantage is that no matter how good or creative a local musician might be, he or she is never respected on the same level as a national musician—because people find it difficult to accept their neighbors—and this lack of appreciation can be hard on one's feelings and ego.

20. How important is it for musicians to learn about the music business?

The business of music must be viewed as another part of one's music pedagogy, and this is especially true in this time period. I believe all musicians should be deeply involved in the composite spectrum of their creativity—of which business is part. It is important to learn about the reality of contracts and percentage points because the proper organization of one's business is directly related to whether or not survival is possible. Practically all of the established big-name musicians are also expert business people. One of the greatest misconceptions that must be discarded is the notion of the artist who is too much above petty economic matters to even care about his or her business. Yet by the same token, the reality of economics should not be viewed as more important than who you are either. Many of the decisions which have shaped this time zone seem to suggest that too much attention on the music business might be just as harmful as too little attention. In the final analysis, I guess the reality of one's business should be an affirmation of what one is about—if possible. Whatever, musicians can no longer afford the luxury of not caring about their business. Nobody is too good to not be concerned about their own affairs.

21. Has the emergence of the post-Ayler continuum since the late seventies seen any collective response from black agents and/or business people?

To my knowledge, there has been no collective response from the black business community for post-Ayler creativity—or any continuum of black creativity for that matter. It seems to me that the black business community's disregard for the music is typical of middle-class black America's commitment to dynamic change—in other words, there is practically no commitment. This is not to say no individuals are concerned about black creativity—nor can I write that no given organization has ever contributed to alternative functional movements. But the fact is, there is a black middle class that has more influence (money) than we normally acknowledge, and this sector has never really been politically involved on the level one would have hoped. The only consistent involvement I can comment on has come from individuals and small collectives, and hopefully the future will see more composite concern about the seriousness of creativity. By the same token, it is important to recognize the dynamic effectiveness of those special individuals who have long worked to upgrade the composite reality of both black culture—and its related information awareness—and world culture. Individuals like Kunle Mwanga deserve special mention for the positive work he has been doing for over a decade, and my hope is that his efforts will inspire more involvement by all people concerned about creativity, in the next cycle.

22. *Why have you not mentioned public radio's efforts to program creative music?*
To be honest, my neglect of public radio was simply a mistake (and with the entry of this question, I have an opportunity to correct this error—somewhat). Public radio has indeed been functioning to expose people to creative music and alternative composite creativity, and it is important that its work is acknowledged. In many sectors of the country this is the only platform for intelligent information dissemination. In this time period, public radio has initiated an important effort to broadcast live performances of creative music—usually in conjunction with a given festival (e.g., the Newport or Kool Jazz festivals) or performances from college concerts. I view this phenomenon as positive—and it will be even more positive when the musicians are paid for these broadcasts. (I know, I know—the musicians are supposed to be paid . . . but somehow the money never arrives—but then again, maybe I'm asking too much; after all, I've only waited for my broadcast money for the short period of five years. I need to realize that these matters take time . . . huh!)

MUSIC AND POLITICS

(Level One)

THE REALITY OF CREATIVITY AND POLITICS is a subject that transcends any one context and moves to comment on the totalness of life itself. In other words, the dynamics of this most important subject is manifested on so many different levels that it is difficult to know where to begin isolated inquiry. Because the actualness of creativity and politics is really about the reality of "doing"—as it applies to both individual and cultural participation. Moreover, the most basic factor that determines both of these considerations has to do with what "doing" raises about composite spirituality—in other words, the concept of politics is not isolated to only "how something is done," but instead must include the total position of that "something" in terms of what it signifies about the vibrational identity of its composite culture—and this is also true for creativity. As such, if we are to really understand the realness of progressional continuance, as this phenomenon applies to creativity and politics, then it is important to view the "particulars" of a given progressionalism as well as its "nature"—and this is especially true if we are to understand the transition of the sixties. The thrust of this section will attempt to define both the reality of politics, as this consideration is viewed in world culture—and possible transformation (terms)—and also the cross-sectional implications of information dynamics (i.e., creativity and alternative functionalism—activism) as a factor to determine progressionalism. An approach of this type is necessary if we are to understand the nature of progressionalism that has determined this cycle, for the dynamic functionalism of the sixties has yet to be digested into the mainstream of present-day information continuance. To really understand the reality of cross-information dynamics is to have a basis for viewing the relationship between creativity and politics, because this relationship is not outside the composite laws of information dynamics—and this is what interests me.

MP(1)–2

There was, of course, much talk in the sixties about politics, and the thrust of this period is generally considered to be important for the nature underlying how alternative functionalism was practiced. The realness of this cycle would see the emergence of many areas of alternative activism—and this is true regardless of "focus-objective." There would be the activity against the war, the activity against political parties—against the draft—etc., etc. This would also be the period that would solidify the second transitional functionalism continuance of black America—having to do with the activism necessary to implement what the *Brown* decision in 1954 implied, and also having to do with the necessary vibrational adjustments that this cycle in time would dictate. The composite realness of activism in this period would move to affect every aspect of American society and it is important that some attempt is made to view the implications of this momentum—for if we are to really understand the realness of creativity and politics, then that understanding must be based on something "real" (something that has occurred), or we run the risk of over-theorizing. As such, the dynamic realness of sixties functionalism offers us a perfect point of departure for examination (and this is especially true if we are to understand the reality position of both creative dynamics and alternative functionalism—as manifested in what we now call politics).

Certainly, the time period of the sixties was significant in what it implied for social reality—especially in the black community—involving both the solidification of alternative activism and vibrational realignment as well as expansion and information dynamics. The scope of these changes would move many people to view black functionalism as a social revolution—and indeed in many ways it was. The realness of this phenomenon could be understood by reviewing the multiplicity of factors that would come into play as black people began to challenge the composite factors underlining American society—and certainly the emergence of functional political consciousness in itself was and remains one of the most important gains to have come from this period. Thus, if we are to understand the realness of progressional continuance, as this concept involves the sixties, there can be no denying the profound implications of transitional functionalism in the black community. Yet it is also important that the whole of these events is viewed within a proper context. For while the sixties most certainly did inspire many dynamic areas of information and functional transference, many of the interpretations documenting this cycle have moved to violate the actual reality position concerning "how these changes came about." In other words, even though many changes did occur in the sixties—especially in the black community—it would not be correct to view the functionalism in this period as "a successful revolution" by any means. Instead, the real significance of this period might lie in what this junction means for black people as we enter the eighties—that being, the nature of how sixties functionalism has helped to set the stage for transitional functionalism of the second degree (as this consideration will apply to extended multi-functionalism in the coming periods). To really view the reality dynamics of sixties functionalism will undoubtedly necessitate more time, but it is clear that the composite continuum of alternative activism did profoundly alter the basic route of American progressionalism. Clearly the emergence of new ideologies from the black community was one of the most basic factors to affect the route of functionalism which ensued in this cycle—and as such, the emergence of radical political activism can be singled out as a major consideration that affected the composite imprint of the sixties, both with respect to its vibrational identity as well as the multi-dynamic routes of functionalism that would be opened for scrutiny in this period. It was this phenomenon that dictated many of the events that underlined our understanding of the sixties (having to do with the dynamic implication of multi-functionalism and political involvement), and however we look back at this phenomenon now, at the time it did seem as if radical activism carried the seeds for dynamic transformation and world change.

MP(I)–4

(R)SG.------TR.

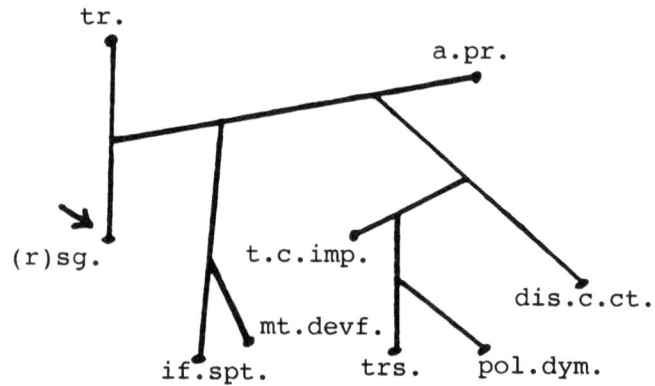

STF.------POL.DY.

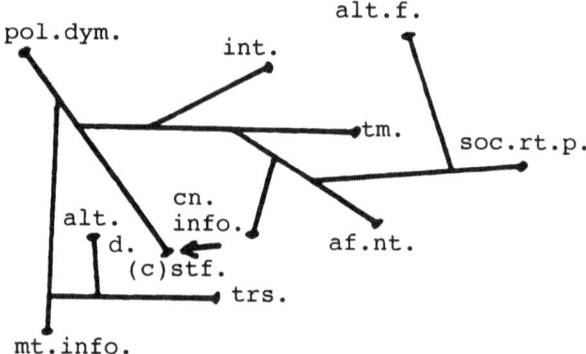

It is not the purpose of this book to review the particulars of individual activism or the collected realness of radical functionalism—as this subject relates to either alternative functionalism and/or political dynamics. Nor am I necessarily interested in commenting on the ideals of a given so-called revolutionary leader, because to do so would not necessarily move to shed light on the basic information focus of this book. Rather, I am interested in viewing the reality position of sixties functionalism as a means to better understand the state of progressional continuance in this period (the early eighties). My point is this: It is possible to view the functionalism of the sixties as directly related to the present vibrational state of American society—having to do with the use of dynamic functionalism as a positive tool for helping to establish world change on the one hand, as well as the consequence for what this same phenomenon has posed on the other hand. In actual terms, we can view the solidification of dynamic activism as a factor that aided—and advanced—the composite goals of black people, as we move into the next cycle; and we can also view the emergence of political activism as a phenomenon that, because of its inability to foresee the consequences of certain vibrational and functional positions, carried profound negative implications as well. To investigate the reality of sixties functionalism within these contexts is necessary because there are many misconceptions surrounding the whole of activism in composite America that are still with us today. There is now the need to clarify the reality and vibrational implications of sixties functionalism as this subject relates to both political activism and vibrational dynamics. Because in the final analysis, if we are to ever solidify a transformational viewpoint for extended functionalism, then the particulars of this most important period must necessarily be re-examined on every level. For the composite thrust of sixties functionalism supplied the first response to the vibrational dictates of this transition cycle—and the nature of that response was never one-dimensional.

TF.SH. ------POL.DY.

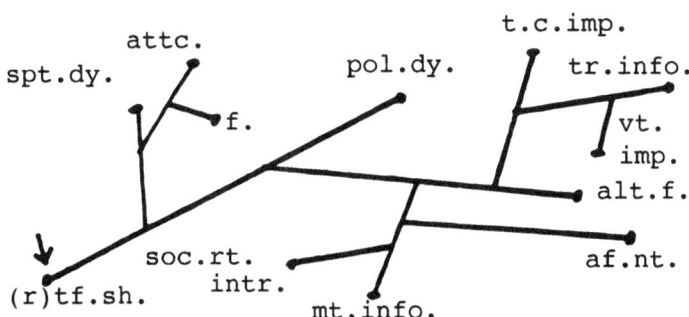

MP(1)–6

The progressional continuance of sixties activism would color the composite dynamics of western alternative functionalism—regardless of level—and it is important that some attempt is made to clarify the nature of this phenomenon. Because the emergence of alternative activism would come to be perceived as necessarily related to the affinity-reality tone of the post-Coleman creative continuum—and of course to some degree this was true. But the dynamic implications of extended creativity and alternative functionalism were not an affirmation of any one particular postulation—which is to say, there is still a need to clarify the relationship between what was being posed in the creativity and what was being posed in composite activism. This is not to say there was no connection between the music and political movements, but rather that the connection was never as simple as the articles written in the sixties seemed to imply. For instance, Frank Kofsky, in his book *Black Nationalism and the Revolution in Music*, tried to impose a viewpoint that implied the relationship between black creativity and political activism necessarily pointed to the appearance of Marxist sympathies. The thrust of his writings would move to investigate the reality of John Coltrane's music within the spectrum of that belief, and in doing so, not only did he defeat the purpose of his book (not to mention the real reality of the music) but again he perpetrated the misnotion that black creativity in that cycle was no more than a beacon for the particular activism that characterized the sixties. As such, if we are to ever understand the vibrational realness of alternative functionalism—as this concept relates to the dynamic implications of creative music—then the whole of this phenomenon must be re-examined on every level. This is not to say that Kofsky's book was necessarily wrong on every level, nor have I meant to imply that every viewpoint about sixties progressionalism has no relationship to the music—because nothing is either all or nothing (and the truth of a given phenomenon is not one-dimensional). Rather, the seriousness of this subject cannot be understood from only one context—let alone with one set of intentions—because the reality of postulation permeates the entire realness of "doing"—regardless of level—and moves to give insight into the "real state" of a given phenomenon. In other words, accurate commentary about a given creative projection involves many different factors, because the reality of postulation is about the reality of a people's vibrational identity and/or destiny. In other words, to really comment on the reality position of projectional continuance is to tamper with something very serious—and real. To write that the thrust realness of extended functionalism in the black community carried the seeds of Marxism is to not understand the vibrational identity and/or alignment of black people, but to instead elevate the concept of Marxism at the expense of the subject.

The theatre of events in the sixties saw the emergence of many different areas of functionalism—this is true regardless of what sector of the community one chooses to view—and as such there were most certainly given groups in the black community that advocated some form of Marxism. (If I remember correctly, Marxism, as a concept, had become the new toy for both liberals and so-called radicals, especially in political conversations and/or campus lectures.) But the progressional continuance of alternative functionalism did not start in the sixties, let alone because of a mono-vibrational focus. To really understand the dynamic continuance of alternative creativity is to view the subject from the proper perspective— with respect to what it really poses for transformation and world change. As such, the meta- and vibrational implications—and position—of creative music in that cycle must be reviewed, as a basis to really come to terms with this phenomenon. It is important to understand that people like Eldridge Cleaver were not necessarily aware of the changes reshaping alternative creative postulation when they were formulating their own political philosophies. And the reality of events that transpired in that cycle only accents that fact.

There is no documentation that links any of the prominent leaders of radical activism with alternative creativity—and this is true for the whole time period of the sixties. Furthermore, the thrust of the documentation that does exist on this subject seems to draw more connections between sixties radical activism and west coast rock than any other form of music (which might surprise many people, for, on the surface, one would probably presume that black activism would have been more inspired from rhythm and blues or what we call jazz). This is not to say no individuals in radical activism were aware of creative music, because there have always been individuals whose information scan was multi-directional. In the early sixties, an activist like Amiri Baraka would even write liner notes for a John Coltrane record—and undoubtedly this interest was not an isolated event from the whole of sixties functionalism. Nevertheless, there is no evidence that the composite reality of radical activism was necessarily connected to the progressional continuum of alternative creativity—this does not seem to be the case vibrationally, and this does not seem to be the case functionally (or at least, this does not seem to be the case with respect to the reality position and/or objective alignment of either persuasion), and however one chooses to view the whole of this period, it is important that the distinctions between these two areas of continuance are noted, and on some level understood. Yet I have not meant to imply there were no similarities whatsoever between both continuums either—because there were many in this regard as well. It is important that some attempt is made to clarify the dynamics of sixties continuance—especially as this subject relates to creativity and politics—because as this book is being written, there are only a handful of alternative viewpoints about this period. Somehow the collective forces of western culture have moved to simply "wrap up" how this period is to be documented, without any outside interpretations—and this cannot be to anyone's advantage. The scope of these applied interpretations has misdocumented every region of alternative functionalism—especially as this phenomenon applies to black people and/or "things not perceived as pure caucasian." As we enter the eighties, the importance of real documentation about this time period will take on added significance. The thrust of this section of the book is thus an attempt—admittedly incomplete—to give a more balanced understanding of the factors underlining sixties functionalism—especially as this subject concerns creative music.

ALT.FT.-----POL.DY.

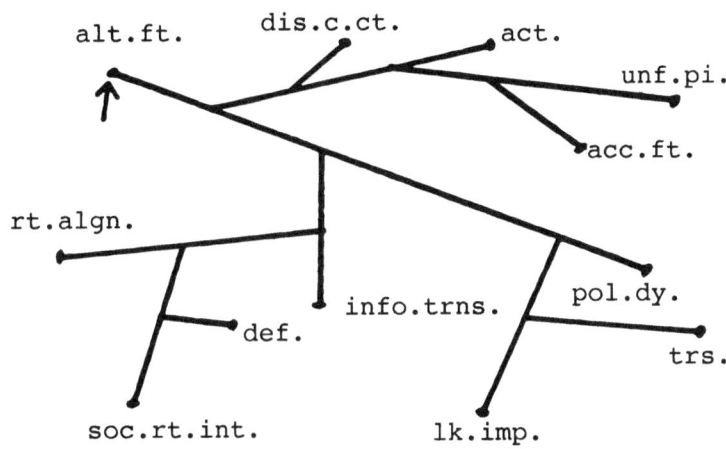

There was, of course, a relationship between alternative creativity and the emergence of political consciousness in the sixties. For the realness of this period in time would establish a particular vibrational state that permeated the composite spectrum of "doing." It is this state that dictated the vibrational and reality positions of both alternative creativity and functionalism (i.e., political activism). Therefore, the progressional nature of the sixties must be viewed with respect to what it raises about cosmic particulars—that is, the actuality of this state can be viewed as an important link in shaping the total continuance of this period in time (having to do with the route western culture has since taken—and the positive and negative implications of that route—and also the cross-interaction implications of this phenomenon as it relates to extended matters—and particulars). In other words, the real significance of sixties progressionalism must be viewed in the total context of earth progressionalism and cosmic change. The realness of this "state" involves everything—including creativity and politics. Yet the dynamics of this subject involve many different factors—because on the physical universe level there are also many inter-related aspects between creativity and politics. The fact is, many musicians have long been aware of and involved in alternative functionalism—as this consideration relates to politics—and it is clearly documented that many musicians were also actively involved in helping to shape the path of alternative activism. But this does not mean that the majority of creative people were necessarily supportive of every area of political activism in the sixties—especially the so-called revolutionary activism that would solidify in the middle of the decade. There is a difference between being interested in transformational functionalism—as this consideration relates to world change—and being a participant in the political activism of the sixties—involving what came to be known as the black revolution. If we are to understand the relationship of alternative creativity—as a term that comments on the composite realness of positive change and world unification—to sixties activism, then it is important that this difference is understood. Because the thrust realness of sixties activism would comment on many different regions of both cosmic and vibrational focuses, and the implications of this phenomenon would move to clarify both the nature of progressional continuance—in terms of available directions for activism—and the extent to which a given postulation could be viewed as "necessarily in accordance with what is most spiritual." By the end of the sixties, the accelerated continuum of political activism would solidify its own dynamics—and the realness of that phenomenon is not separate from the whole of alternative functionalism (as a signal about the complexities of the coming time cycle). The thrust of both of these phenomena—creativity and politics—has determined the composite reality position of this time period, as well as the next cycle.

PART.------HI.P.

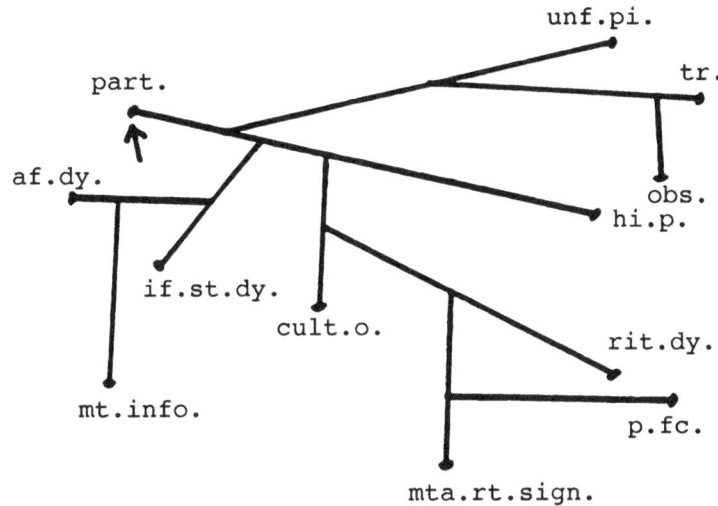

PART. -----ALT.F.

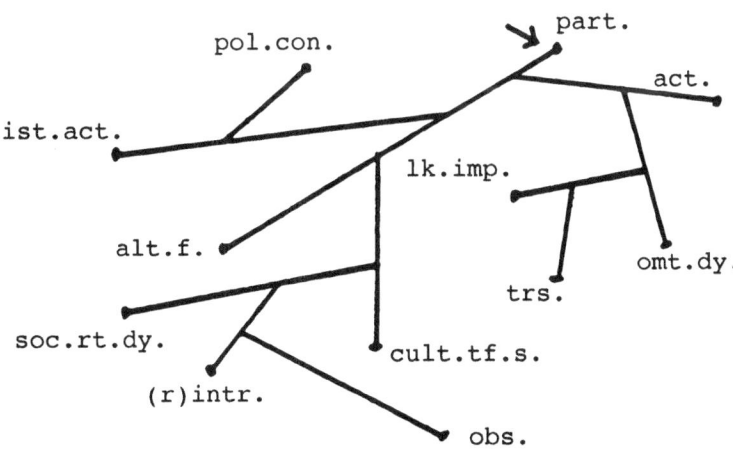

MP(I)–12

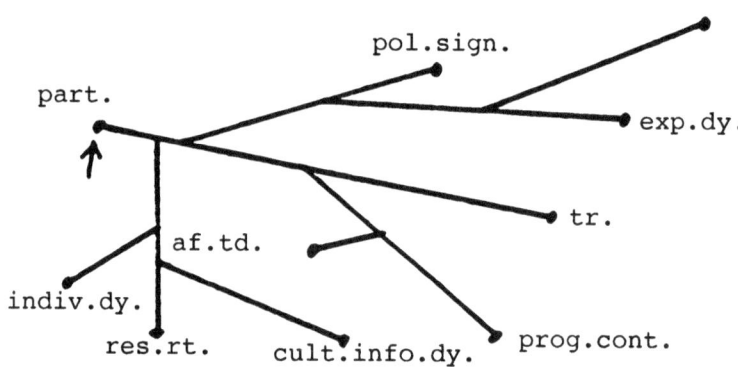

On the physical universe level, the separate continuum of alternative creativity and radical activism can be viewed with respect to the decisions and intentions that have long surrounded the black community in America. For the accelerated division between black creativity of the affinity insight (1) principle and the black community could be seen forming after the emergence of bebop—having to do with the misinformation that would accompany this continuum. The fact is, the emergence of bebop was significant for what it implied about both dynamic and vibrational continuance for black people as well as world change. The essence lining of this projection would comment on the affinity insight (1) principle reality state of alternative functionalism—in every degree. But the dynamic realness of this phenomenon would be completely misinterpreted by every sector—that is, the white press as well as the general actualness of black American society—and as such, bebop would come to be viewed as "something hip" in the white liberal community (and for young musicians—black or white—the projection represented "the latest thing" to learn about), while in the black community the realness of this phenomenon would come to be viewed in negative terms—that being, a projection of creativity that had less and less relevance to the interests and aspirations of composite black people. The realness of this viewpoint would not be immediately apparent, but would instead solidify as a gradual response to the collective factors surrounding the music; for in the beginning, the emergence of bebop was embraced in the black community as a logical/unlogical (since logical on this level has nothing to do with the vibrational realness of experiencing a music—let alone accepting what one is experiencing) extension of black creative music. The gradual disavowal of bebop in the black community would come as a result of both the redefinitions attached to its essence lining by the western press, and the reality-continuum decisions that would accelerate the spread of bebop to the greater world community. This is not to say any given sector of the black community was necessarily opposed to the expansion dynamics of bebop; rather, the resulting separation of this continuum from the black community would involve the nature underlying how that split came about. The resulting split between bebop—which really represented creative extensions as solidified through the affinity insight (1) principle continuance zone—and the black community could be broken into three categories: (1) the emergence of Europeans supporting the music would strengthen the mis-idea that bebop was actually an intellectual projection conceived in the same spirit of western art postulation—and as such, the appearance of this phenomenon would move the black community to perceive bebop as a form that did not address itself to the vibrational and reality needs of the black community (source-transfer continuance); (2) the realness that the composite continuum of bebop—in terms of its meta-reality implications—had been profoundly misinterpreted and as such altered by the collective forces of western information regulation; and (3) the composite reality of performing outlets for the music would gradually be moved from the black community to either the white community or some kind of "neutral zone"—that being, a region that provided equal accessibility to experience the music. All of these considerations are related to the separation of the affinity insight (1) principle from the greater black community. This is true even though obviously there have always been given sectors of the black community that stayed with the music—since black creativity comes from the black community (people)—but even this phenomenon cannot be stated without qualification. For the rejection of bebop by the greater black community really has to do with the "vibrational identity and desire" of the black middle-class sector (which has always identified with certain areas of "what it perceived to be what is most white about white people"). If we are to really understand the reality position of extended functionalism—and creative postulation—then it is important that the nature of this phenomenon be understood. Because when I wrote that the rejection of bebop is related to the "social desires" of the black middle class, I was really stating that the emergence of bebop is the projection whose affinity-dynamic implications were directly perceived in accordance to what the black middle class should have been looking for—but wasn't. This is so because the projectional solidification of bebop was formed as a continuance that would postulate learning and growing as related to those areas of information that pose "a total re-examination of the state of things" as made real from its zone. As such, this then would be an art music whose meta-reality implications would call for the same—if not greater—vibrational attitude (and its related research) as any continuum of art music. But the challenge of this emergence would not be acknowledged by the black middle class because the people who were possibly qualified to assimilate and multi-translate this phenomenon were instead listening only to Bach. The gradual split that would develop between black creative music of the affinity insight (1) postulation and the composite black community would begin at this point—yet this is only the beginning. Because the rejection of extended black creativity by the black middle class would mean there would be no alternative challenges to the interpretations of the so-called liberal white community, and the unchallenged misinformation from this sector would be related directly to the accelerated interest in bebop as a dynamic stimulant for composite extended functionalism in western information-dynamic terms. The realness of this phenomenon—and the constant state of western economics—would move the music both vibrationally and physically away from the black community (or at least, this is how forties and fifties progressionalism would come to be perceived). By the time the sixties radicalism began to surface, the effects of this phenomenon were clear, because very few of these people were even aware of the composite continuum of black creativity—let alone its meta-reality significance—and who could blame them? The end result of this situation would be that the progressional continuance of creative music from the affinity insight (1) principle (and understand, many more changes would reshape the music after the forties, and as such, the reality dynamics of this projection would have gone through what is now called "hard bop," on through to Ornette Coleman and John Coltrane) would come to be perceived as either in the underground, or in the underground "and let it stay there." Because the dynamics of its existence had long since been dismissed, and in this context rejection was understandable—yet serious problems have resulted from this separation, problems which, to this day, have not been resolved. Nevertheless, while there are books documenting that individuals like Malcolm X were aware of extended black creativity, this is more the exception than the rule. For example, Huey Newton—who grew up in Oakland, California—attached himself to the rock music of the sixties, and there are numerous articles in print where he discusses the relationship of his activism to west coast rock—and Newton was not alone in this regard.

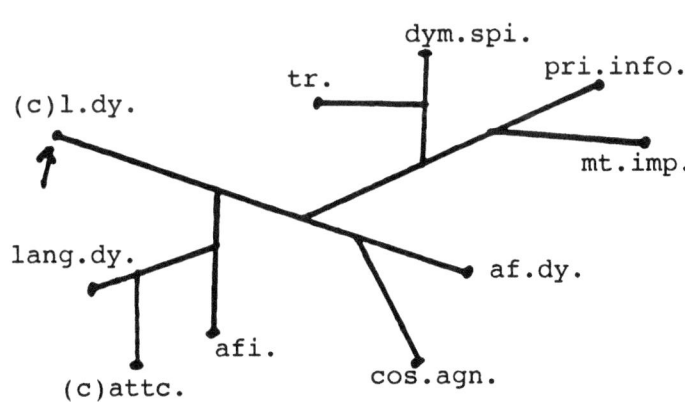

It is important to understand the complexities surrounding extended creative postulation and political functionalism in the black community—regardless of context and/or focus. Because the seriousness of this relationship cannot simply be confined to any one focus. For while the collected forces of western culture—along with the black middle class—can be viewed as obstructing the dynamic realness of alternative composite progressionalism, this obstruction was not the only reality position of black creativity. There are also many other factors related to this most important subject. For to view the activity of a musician like John Coltrane is to see a body of music whose thrust realness has always expanded with respect to every aspect of alternative functionalism—as perceived in the black community or the world community. To view compositions like "Reverend King" is an obvious acknowledgment of the work of Dr. Martin Luther King, Jr.—and there are many other examples of this kind (throughout the whole of black creativity and alternative functionalism). But the seeds underlying the composite dynamics of both of these individuals—Dr. King and John Coltrane—are much more complex than the obvious. For the realness of John Coltrane's activity can be viewed as directly related—and indeed, affirming—the same thrust alignment that Dr. King's activity vibrated to. In other words, the affinity-alignment implication of John Coltrane's activity functioned as a related continuum to the cosmic and/or vibrational purpose of activists like Dr. Martin Luther King—and the realness of this phenomenon is directly related to the real relationship of composite alternative functionalism to transformational world change.

In actual terms, there are two most basic routes of continuance to bring about real change—and the dynamics related to either route carry their own implications (or "things to deal with"). The realness of this phenomenon is compositely manifested in both vibrational and functional terms—which is to say, the nature of progressional continuance can be viewed with respect to what it raises about this concept—because everything that changes is related to the laws governing what change really is. As such, it is important to translate this concept in physical universe terms—that is, if the reality continuance of sixties progressionalism is to be understood. My point is this: if Martin Luther King, Jr., can be viewed as a person whose activity was directed to dynamic change as this consideration applies to the black community as well as the world community—then the realness of this position can be viewed as an example of "one" route of applied functionalism. The reality of this route involves "change with respect to what this consideration poses to both its particular and expanded applications" (as well as change with respect to what this consideration cosmically poses). The solidification of this route of functionalism also characterizes the composite work of John Coltrane. For the thrust of Coltrane's activity had to do with "change," as this consideration involves the particulars of given physical universe focuses as well as its cosmic (or spiritual) implications. In other words, the realness of John Coltrane's activity and Dr. Martin Luther King's activity solidified the same vibrational position with respect to what it posed for alternative functionalism. The realness of this agreement represents the most basic "center platform" for creativity and functionalism (having to do with the "spirit" of a given participation). It is also possible to draw many different analogies between the work of these two great people. For on the physical universe level, we can view Dr. King as a great orator whose message functioned as a force to bring about social change for all of humanity, and the work of John Coltrane would employ the same message vibrationally: having to do with creativity as a vehicle to bring about expanded consciousness (and this consciousness would, of course, bring a better understanding of Dr. King's mission). In other words, there is a natural complementary factor between alternative functionalisms, as this consideration relates to the dictates of its "given vibrational route assignment"—and the realness of this phenomenon is not one-dimensional, because the reality position of alternative functionalism is not dependent on the order of a given sequence. Frank Kofsky was right when he cited the activity of Max Roach in the fifties as an early example of the multi-relationship between creativity and politics. For the progressional realness of this phenomenon has never actualized in only one context. That is, the composite thrust of alternative creativity has long functioned as a directional beacon for the political and vibrational continuum of its culture. If we are to really understand the realness of creativity—and its relationship to politics—then the dynamic implication of this phenomenon must be both acknowledged and—on some level—understood.

MP(I)–18

(R)MTH. ------RE.ST.

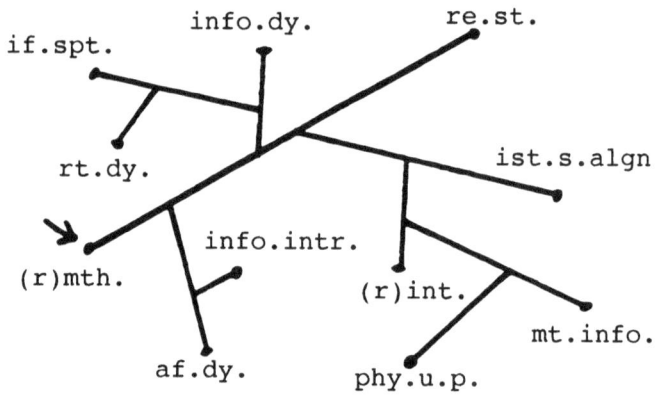

TH.CONT.----- PROJ.DY------ AFL.

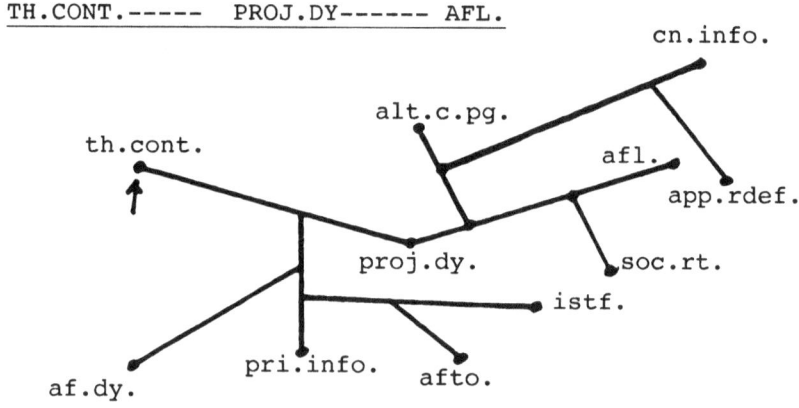

I have written on the vibrational-reality position of alternative functionalism—with respect to what I have called "one of its routes"—and I have also written about the inter-relationship of what this phenomenon poses for creativity and physical universe activism. But there is another route just as important, and the realness it implies has also affected the composite reality of things. If we are to understand the nature and/or reality position of alternative functionalism to transformational change, then it is important that this "route" is viewed—especially if we are to understand sixties functionalism. Because the early deaths of both John Coltrane and Dr. Martin Luther King would have a profound impact on the nature of progressional continuance—as this consideration applied to both creativity as well as activism. The realness of this tragedy would, in my opinion, establish the path nature of progressional continuance—leading up until the eighties (and, as this book is being written, has yet to really be "resolved" as such)—and in doing so, color the composite realness of alternative functionalism—regardless of focus. Because the most basic reaction that solidified as a result of the deaths of these two great people was the realness of separation: that is, dynamic separation and the emergence of the "two routes" (one of which I have written on already). The dynamic implications of this tragedy would thus alter the composite state of alternative functionalism. Thus, the first movement that solidified after Dr. King's death was the movement that sought to continue progressionalism as it related to the same policies and vibrational continuum as Dr. King's original intentions (whose vibrational dynamics have already been discussed). The other continuum to emerge from this same period was "the continuum that focused on the particulars of social reality dynamics" and, in doing so, necessarily moved to isolate itself from the world group—as a means to alleviate "the intensity of the struggle taking place in that period." The emergence of these two routes of functionalism after Dr. King's and John Coltrane's deaths would totally alter the reality dynamics of extended functionalism.

To understand the particulars of the second route of alternative functionalism, it is necessary to view the nature of sixties functionalism. For the aftermath of King's death would destroy the vibrational balance between composite information received and learned by a generation of black activists and the impending information and emotional dynamics as experienced by another generation of black activists. In actual terms, the realness of this phenomenon can be understood by viewing the "state of things" in western culture by the middle of the sixties. The emergence of radical activism, in its early period, had to do with the dynamics of sixties emotionalism as the composite lining of western culture moved into transition. This was the period where young leaders would move to solidify functional responses to the many different levels of injustices surrounding non-white and poor America. The fact that most of these new leaders were young people would only increase the intensity of their "viewpoints"—that is (even though very few young people would want to agree with what I am going to write), the very "state" of youth does not lend itself to be in accordance with understanding the multi-implications of a given act, but instead moves to solidify quick solutions. Many of the young leaders who came into power during the sixties would necessarily "have all the answers" for dynamic social change (even though, in reality, very few of these people even had the "right questions"—let alone answers). The thrust of the sixties would thus see the emergence of much rhetoric—as well as functionalism: having to do with every conceivable route for dynamic change—or as radical activists would say, "revolution." The nature of this area of political functionalism would play an important role in shaping sixties dynamics—and this is true on many different levels, both positively and negatively—especially negatively. In other words, the intensity generated by this sector would call the attention of the greater public (and world group) to the situation of non-white and poor people in America, and at the same time, the composite functionalism of this same sector would isolate the reality implications of alternative functionalism even further. For the vibrational consequences of much of the so-called new activism would carry profound consequences for the state of progressional dynamics as the seventies came in. The effect of King's and Coltrane's deaths would see children assuming positions that required vision and experience (as opposed to limited experience and passion). However, by citing the deaths of Dr. Martin Luther King and John Coltrane, I have not meant to imply that there were only two black leaders whose activity carried multi-dimensional implications. Obviously this is not true. Nor have I meant to imply there were no qualified leaders whose vision could have molded the composite thrust of alternative functionalism—as this consideration involves both social reality and/or spiritual consciousness—because there were many. But the fact is, the trauma of both of these deaths—added to the composite dynamics of sixties progressionalism (i.e., the assassinations of President Kennedy and, later, Malcolm X and Bobby Kennedy, as well as the unjust war in Vietnam)—would provide the final stimulus for dynamic separation and action by young people—as separate from their elders. It is possible to view the whole of sixties progressionalism with this understanding in mind, for the composite dynamic of sixties activism would move to challenge every information focus, every philosophical focus, every functional objective that came into view. The realness of this phenomenon would see children coming into power—this is true, even though many positive attributes were also related to the work done by this sector. But the negative implications of this phenomenon would dynamically alter the route of composite progressionalism. For the thrust of sixties functionalism would see a separation of its information nature as well as a division in social-reality tendencies. The realness of this phenomenon would serve as the basis from which the new "is it black, or is it not black" arguments would come, and the extended significance of this phenomenon would establish the "accented focus on blackness," at the expense of the composite realness of all humanity—as well as what this isolation means with respect to available composite information. Even worse, the solidification of this period would color the progressional path and nature of three-fourths of the activists' community—where, after a period of from ten to fifteen years, it was no longer a question of "children having wrong ideas"—but instead "what is it that these people haven't looked at?" The dynamic solidification of sixties misinformation would as such establish the next level of seventies indecision—and this most certainly has been the greatest letdown of this time cycle.

AF.POST.------SPT.DYM.

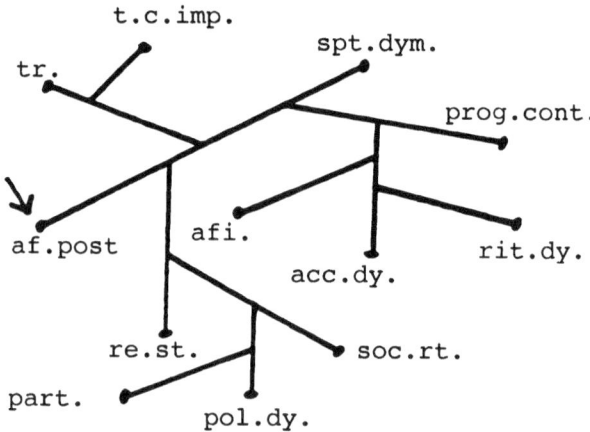

The late sixties was thus the period that would see the emergence of dynamic separation in the black community—as well as the greater country. The realness of this phenomenon would directly aid the dynamics of "particular" investigation, while on the other hand retarding the possibility for transformational unification. Because of this phenomenon, the work of activists like Jesse Jackson would take somewhere around five years before becoming a composite consideration for the black community to build on—and the possibilities for new coalitions would also meet much resistance in this same period. There were many reasons for this. For the accelerated division between alternative functionalism and isolated focus would create an atmosphere that did not lend itself to any aspect of moderation. Instead, the vibrational dynamics of this period would move to have individuals align themselves with one given philosophical or vibrational position—one that was inherently opposed to any other position.

The seriousness of this phenomenon would thus separate every level of alternative functionalism throughout the country—for the dynamics of this split transcended black and white people and instead encompassed the total spirit of America's vibrational lining. The major difference in what this split posed, however, did have special repercussions for black people—because black people could not, in the sixties or any other time, afford the dynamics of separation. The effect, then, of this condition would have a profound impact on progressional continuance for the whole of extended functionalism in the seventies. The dynamics of the split in composite functionalism that occurred in the late sixties would even move to isolate alternative creative movements in the black community, and many of the new movements would operate necessarily separate from each other. In many cases, given organizations that existed only miles apart would have no contact—let alone collective projects. The result of this isolation would see the extended advancement of every area of creative focus (e.g., dance, music, philosophy, painting), but no attempt to solidify a composite meta-reality position. Instead of tapping the composite implications of transitional dynamics and alternative information, the black community in the sixties would fragment itself to the point of suppressing its own dynamics. In other words, by not examining the inherent implications of composite dynamics—as this consideration relates to the progressional continuum of solidified information from and through black culture (from Egypt to the present) as well as western and Asian culture—the composite position of black functionalism in the late sixties would place itself at a real disadvantage—a serious disadvantage. Because the inability to solidify a composite viewpoint would promote an over-reliance on western ideologies as the most attractive tool for bringing about world change. The effect of this over-reliance is what we are still dealing with as we move into the seventies.

MP(I)–24

INFO.DY.------ALT.FT.

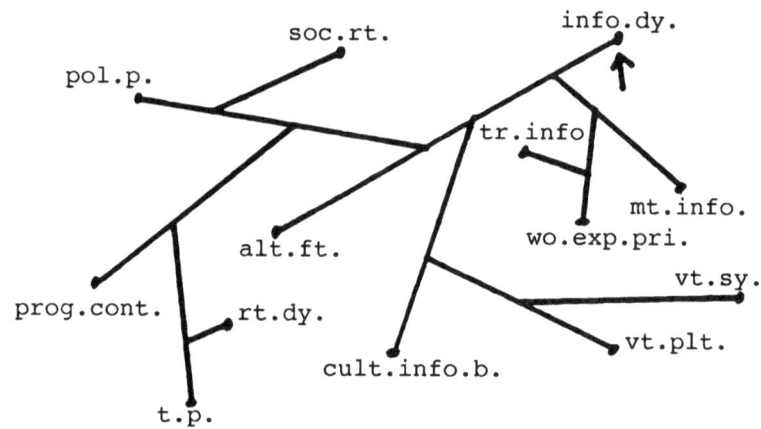

DYM.FT.------C.FO.ACT.

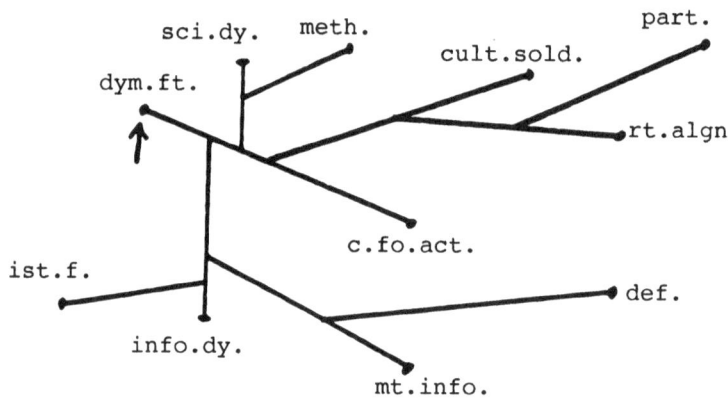

I recall talking to Cecil Taylor in the late sixties about the relationship between the new black political awareness and contemporary black music, and I remember him saying something to the effect that many of the black political activists had practically no knowledge of who they were (in terms of their relationship to both black history and the black vibrational thrust)—let alone their relationship to black creative music. Cecil was commenting on what the social factors had produced in the sixties—for the situation of the black activist groups was directly related to distortions which invariably arise when the "center factor" of a given phenomenon is not understood. Taylor's comments were most certainly true, for if I recall correctly, there were many developments forming which went directly contrary to what the creativity was implying—and what black history seemed to suggest as well. Much of the rhetoric I had been hearing from the activist groups in the sixties was a combination of Marxism and other "ised" western philosophies—and to a great extent, much of this thrust is still with us today. But when I stated that the divisiveness of the sixties was detrimental to understanding what was implied in the composite alternative thrust of black culture, it would be best to expand on what I actually mean—and in what sense. For it is in looking at the different aspects of life in the black community (i.e., the creativity, the political activity, and their relationship in center) that we can better understand what was really actually happening in the sixties. Because when I write that much of the sixties political activity was distinct from the potential implied in the creativity in that same period, I am only commenting on the consequences of division as a detrimental factor for establishing a composite thrust.

To better understand the significance of alternative functionalism—as this consideration concerns the realness of creativity and politics—it is necessary to establish the broadest possible context for investigation. Because if we are to really understand what this phenomenon poses for transformation, then it is important that some attempt is made to view the essence basis that determines what creativity and politics really celebrate—with respect to its position (or information lineage) in regard to essence (and/or route of procedure). The seriousness of an investigation of this nature would also clarify the reality position of sixties functionalism (activism) and its relationship to what was being posed in the music, because as I have already stated, the seeds underlying alternative functionalism (as practiced through the creativity) were not necessarily affirming the composite state of sixties radical activism by any means. Instead, there were many other factors related to this most dynamic phenomenon—factors which directly shed light on the nature of what I perceive to be "what is most different" between sixties creativity and functionalism. To understand this viewpoint, however, it is necessary to first establish a basis from which a larger context can be erected to deal with the seriousness of what this inquiry necessitates—because the subject of creativity and political activism is not about creativity and politics, but instead what creativity and politics "really is." As such, to begin the thrust of this viewpoint it is necessary to first state: there is no philosophy coming from any so-called western sensibility that, in its normal flow, takes into account the natural collective regions of affinity dynamics of non-western people as a means for sustaining a center (and/or culture)—and by saying this, I am addressing the whole of existing western philosophies (as well as the information lines, and/or positions, related to their collective identity), be they Marxism, socialism, capitalism, or whatever "isms" one chooses to attach. This is not to say I have no respect for things western, nor by commenting on the limitations of western philosophy in this context have I meant to discredit the whole of what we now call western culture. Rather, the realness of my viewpoint is connected with what the dynamic solidification of western affinity dynamics—and postulation—has really created in this time zone—and if we are to understand the meta-reality implications of alternative creativity (which is really the re-emergence of information as solidified in world culture terms), then it is here where we must start. For to view the reality basis of creative music from the black aesthetic is to establish a basis for viewing the essence lining of both black and world culture, and to do so is to begin shedding light on the real vibrational implication surrounding sixties activism—that being, the realness that many areas of sixties activism not only did not vibrate to the precepts of world culture, but overly relied on the information continuance of western culture. Because sixties activism was a western phenomenon, as opposed to the challenge of dynamic transformation, which is a composite world group phenomenon—moreover, the reality implications of alternative creativity were solidified in composite world culture terms as well—but I do not mean to jump ahead of myself.

WO.EXP.PRI.   ----INFO.DY.

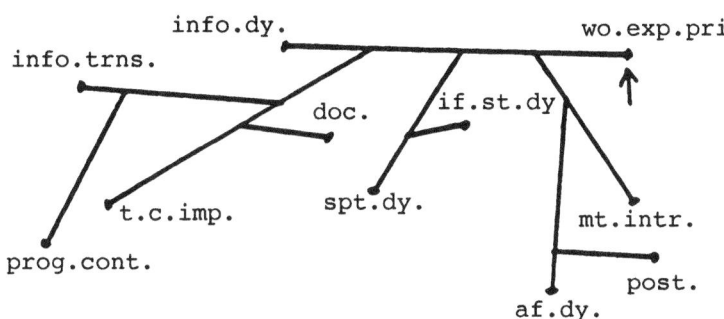

Any real look at the political continuance of sixties radical activism—no matter how one might feel about any given area of focus—would have to deal with the state of where this continuum is today (the end of the seventies), and the realness of this state cannot be simply dismissed as irrelevant if we are to understand either the path nature of sixties progressionalism, or the cosmic purpose underlying how given areas of activism came to see themselves. This is especially so if we are to understand the state of this phenomenon as we enter the eighties, for all of the factors that emerged in the sixties—involving the so-called revolutionary movement—have long since given way to a reliance on western functionalism to bail out the remains of "what was thought to be the tenets of the new black revolution." The reliance in this context has taken the form of moving to embrace both western ideologies and heroes as the only possibility to bring about real world change—and by the end of the sixties, everyone had rediscovered Marx (which later would lead to scientific socialism, as a term that "implied not a complete surrender" to western ideology). The realness of this phenomenon cannot be ignored if we are to understand the profound difference underlying alternative functionalism as actualized in the post-Ayler projectional continuum and sixties political activism. Because the gradual adaptation of western informational dynamics by the so-called black revolutionaries cannot be simply dismissed as normal within the multi-informational state of things (source transfer), because not only would the black radical activists adopt western philosophies, and include western interpretation to "clarify" their viewpoint of continuance, but all of these adaptations would move to solidify western information dynamics in a dominant position, with respect to the affinity-alignment make-up of sixties functionalism (and related so-called philosophies). The dynamics of sixties radicalism, then, can be viewed as a reaction to "the state of things" and later moving to solidify a functional strategy from "that same state." The end result of this dilemma would see the thrust continuum of alternative functionalism in the black community in even worse shape in the seventies than in the sixties. It is possible from this point to better understand the difference between alternative creative music—as a continuum that generated particular areas of information dynamics as well as functionalism—and sixties political activism (or in this case, black political activism). This is so because the meta-reality of alternative creativity has, regardless of its route, maintained its constant alignment with the basic tenets of transformational information dynamics. For while I am not in disagreement with the vibrational alignment of western culture, it is clear that the progressional application of western affinity dynamics serves to re-enforce the exclusive position of only western culture, and this position cannot be viewed as "revolutionary" on any level.

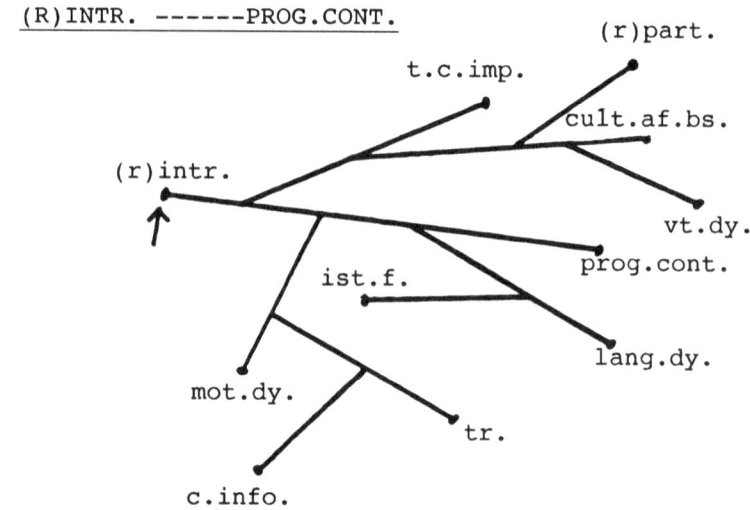

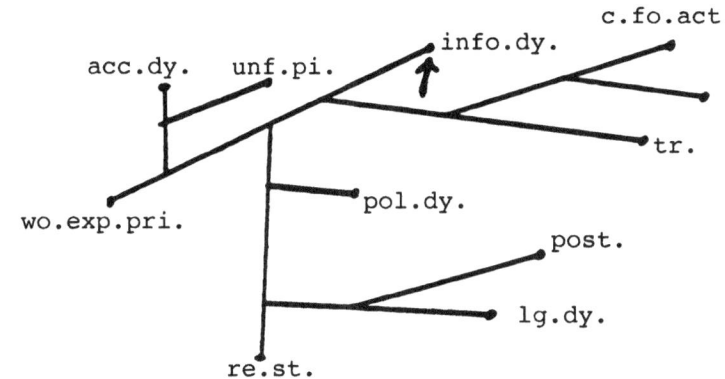

It is only in black creativity where black people can still experience source initiation—that is, activity not only derived from source initiation—mirroring the essence-factor thrust of the black methodological and vibrational pull, and applying that pull for whatever moment, but also for what that essence means in itself. In other words, the seeds underlying black creativity also influence the functional physical universe situation as it affects the political arenas as well. The fact that many of the activist groups in the twelfth hour had no choice but to embrace Marxism shows only too clearly that many of these people had no real fundamental understanding of what trans-African philosophical and expansion dictates really implied. The conceptual and vibrational implications of black creativity show only too clearly the proper alignment for relevant culture in regard to both black people and the forming world group. Any rush to the existing western ideologies must take into account what that move would imply on a practical and spiritual level. I am saying that Marxism—like capitalism—is the affirmation of European and Euro-American methodological perception dynamics, having to do with functional-equal (as opposed to equal-equal), and the net result of this phenomenon is directly in accordance with the western thrust alignment for anti-culture (which is what we now have). Moreso, the adaptation of Marxism—as it would apply to the entire world group after transformation—is also a move that would secure the position of western culture, at the expense of the world group. My point is that the seeds underlying black creativity show there are other ways to establish culture—and those ways are directly in accordance to what has been lost in Africa during the transformation of Egypt. Before any activist movement can really function as a positive alternative factor (especially in regard to black and non-white people), there must first be a serious re-examination of black information dynamics concerning their position on spiritual and functional tenets as this subject relates to the forming and maintaining of composite dynamic culture. Nor by commenting on the dynamic implications of black creativity (and/or transformational functionalism) have I meant to negate the realness of western culture—and/or its related information continuum (continuums)—because to do so would serve no positive purpose and would instead be a divisive factor. Obviously there is much positive about western culture, and the dynamics of this continuum will have a profound effect on the whole of composite continuance in the next cycle. I have commented on the particulars of transformational functionalism and black creativity as a means to understand the special position of alternative information in this time period (and also as a means to clarify the real position of black creativity—and its related information continuum—to world culture, and composite transformation). To understand the nature of this relationship (black creativity/culture to world culture/information) is to understand my belief that the seeds underlying black creativity are related to composite change, while the seeds underlying western information dynamics are related to the "preservation of the present state we are now living in."

This is not to say the path of a given information route won't necessarily draw on—and hence, learn from—the dynamics of information solidified through western investigation, because undoubtedly it will (i.e., the whole concept of "fusion development" is related to the very nature of how cross-information continuance is solidified in this period—and every period). Rather, my concern is directed towards understanding which "persuasion" will dictate (or correlate) the basis of transformational interpretation. My point here being that "there can be no positive transformational solidification" with the western information affinity basis in the defining position (that being the most basic factor interpreting the nature and "reason to be" of world information—as it relates to "real" change). The fact that, in the twelfth hour, the composite-reality position of black political activism would have to adopt the vibrational and actual tenets of western ideology cannot be viewed lightly. Because the realness of this adaptation would clarify the real "reality" position of this phenomenon—and this is true on every level.

PRI.VT.TD.------PROG.CONT.

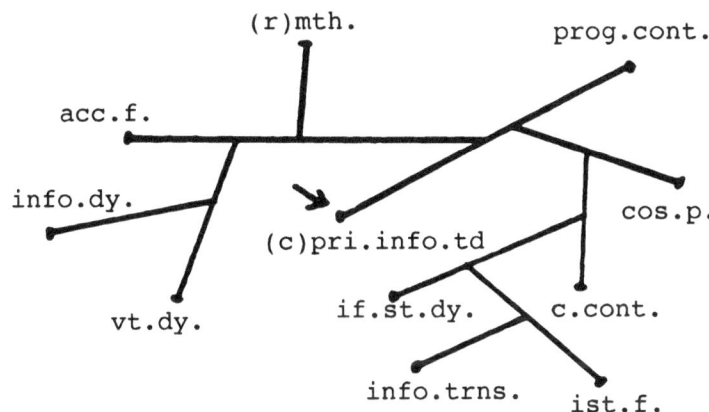

To view the composite continuum of black creativity—and its related information continuum (that being, real alternative viewpoints about the spectrum of information focuses—involving history, science, philosophy, etc.)—is to deal with the first-degree encounter of world transformation, because the seeds underlying this phenomenon are "of and from the world group." Moreover, by commenting on creativity in this context, I have not meant to imply that only music alone is of relevance but, rather, the composite spectrum of creative dynamics: dance, painting, literature, sculpture, science, spiritualism, etc. I believe that the first junction of dynamic activism can only come about if there is some awareness of what this phenomenon compositely means. Because the reality implications of that which we call creativity are not simply about "What's on channel four, Dad?" but rather, the seeds underlying this phenomenon are related to the complete restoration of "all that was lost," "all that was not lost,"

and "all." Any information continuum that moves as a basis for dynamic separation cannot possibly function in accordance with what the dictates of alternative functionalism imply—and this is true regardless of time period. That is, the seeds underlying positive world change can only be based in a profound love of "all that is"—and as such, world change involves the hope of a better "state of being" for all peoples—and "things" (because "it" is not necessarily about people either).

Yet if I am implying that the real problem of the activist groups in the sixties was their separation from the composite arena (as a means to create a composite thrust), then it is also possible to discredit the creative community as well. For unless more creative people lend themselves to working within functional movements for change, there can never be a united alternative viewpoint. Without doubt, one of the main problems the creative community has to overcome is the definitions which have been used to separate different segments of the culture. The actual dilemma of the creative person in this time zone is that few creative people feel as if they are an integral part of the actual culture, but instead, privileged members of some elite group of specialists who have very little relationship to the problems of the actual community. In short, many of these people have accepted the present-day notion of "artist" as it has come to be defined in the annals of the western position. As the developments in the sixties began to accelerate—leading to the forming of serious activism—only a handful of black musicians were even aware of what was happening—for by the end of the fifties, every sector of the black community was separated on some level. Nevertheless, groups like the AACM were not the norm, for the reality of the sixties was a period which saw the phenomenon of separation increase—not decrease. There are, of course, exceptions, but it would be totally unfair to put down the political activist movement without also putting down the creative community. Any attempt to deal with the real relationship of creativity and politics would imply that some effort be made to clarify the concept of "artist," and what it really means in itself and in relationship to the political arena—especially in this period.

There have been many attempts to deal with the relationship of the artist's position to his culture. Many of these attempts, depending on what philosophy is being employed, seek to find a proper balance between how art is to be dealt with as a factor in itself, and what the proper relationship is between any particular area of art and the greater culture. The understanding of the artist's situation varies depending upon what vibrational slant is taken. Nevertheless, we find that in some instances the artist is perceived as a communication link of the people: expressing ideas which are in accordance with the vibrational lining of the culture, and affirming the general reality of its environment. Or the artist can be looked at as being different from the general environment; and in this case, one's creativity is looked at as a natural affirmation of that individual's separate life in an existential sense. There is also the concept of the artist that strengthened after the industrial period: that being, the idea of the artist as scientist and visionary, etc., etc.

In my opinion, all of these ideas are valid on one level or another, but there are still other factors related to this subject that cannot be ignored—especially when applying the concept of "artist" to creative music "ised" through the black aesthetic. It is important to understand the relationship of black music to the vibrational reality of composite American culture and what that relationship implies in terms of source transfer and source progression. Because if the vibrational-thrust flow—nature—were the same in all people, this consideration might not necessarily be a factor to consider: that is to say, if the vibrational-thrust flow were the same in every racial and social life strain, there would be no reason to consider the implications of source transfer as a political tool, but that is not the case, because these surface differences (between people) are real—and have to be considered. For the truth is that different sensibilities manifest themselves as affirming different realities to the degree that unless some effort is made to distinguish the significance of black culture—as a real and separate factor to be considered for transformation—the process of gradualism will subvert what this difference implies about source-transfer progressionalism. That is, the concept of the artist has to be re-evaluated in terms of what Europeans and Euro-Americans mean when they use the word, and what this concept could mean—and does mean, for the world group. For however we choose to understand the implications of creativity as a functional tool for promoting positive transformation, we are first forced to also realize that black creativity has only been used in this time period (the last two hundred years) as a tool to stimulate (western) white culture and disrupt the possibility of world unification. In other words, black people cannot afford the luxury of "artist" if that concept moves contrary to transformation—and indeed it does.

PROJ.------PRI.INFO.

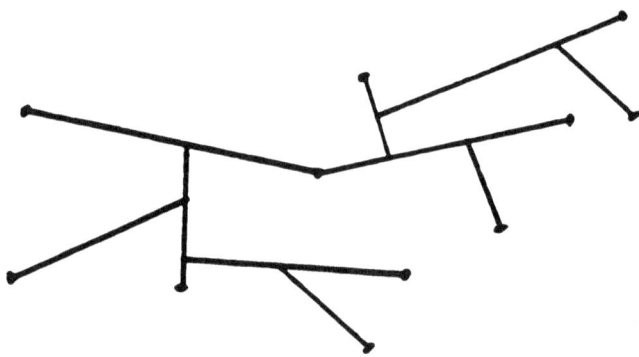

When I wrote that I know of no western philosophy that has anything to do with the most basic vibrationaltory-source flow of non-white people, that is not to invalidate these vibrational and political considerations for whom they were designed. For it is common knowledge that western philosophy addressed itself to the needs of trans-Europeans, as it was designed by white people for white people. My point is that the situation black people are in in America is basically an alien situation that functions contrary to what is really implied in the basic essence lining of trans-African vibrational and spiritual laws. Because of this, the definitions that are used to lock black people in are important, and for this reason the concept of the artist does indeed matter. Because to deal with creativity in the west during this time zone, it is important to understand the actual significance of black creativity as a major consideration to be used for transformation. It is my opinion that black creativity not only poses the strongest alternative for stimulating and lifting consciousness, but black creativity also serves as the most dynamic center factor for re-establishing what was lost during the decline of black civilization for non-white people, as well as the world group. The realness of what this restoration means on a political level will only come about when black people re-establish their ability to define who and what we are—and what we intend to do with who we are. This understanding of transformational definitions must also be reflected in the political and creative arena as well; but my point is that the activism that occurred in the sixties never secured what was implied in the actual creativity (not just the music), because of the inability of black people to overcome the dynamic forces related to disunification. For however any group chooses to understand communism, socialism, etc., these viewpoints are still philosophies which, however utilized, seek to secure the white sensibility in a dominant position, and this can no longer be tolerated on any level.

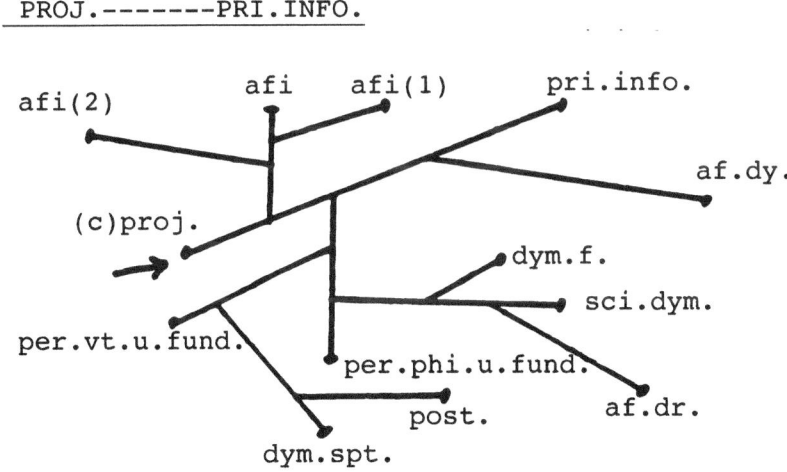

I personally do not believe that the concept of the artist is a necessary function that needs to be preserved. In fact, the present view of the artist in western civilization is disfunctional in regard to transformation. Because the basic understanding that surrounds this concept is "separation" as a means to accent the contribution of individuals rather than the group. The idea of the artist is directly related to words—rather than what is really happening in actual life. This is not to negate the creativity happening in any given period or culture group, but only to put that creativity in its proper perspective. Certainly there are individuals who are born into zones that have more to do with participating in creativity—of a particular thrust—than other people, and I recognize this. Even in Africa, there is the concept of Master Musician, and this is true for every vibrational thrust. But the concept of the artist is not separated from the basic thrust of the actual culture—yet this is the situation we are now dealing with in the west. My point is that however the consideration of artist is understood, black people cannot afford the luxury of not making distinctions between how their work is understood and that of the white artist (who in reality has the option to align his/her work with whatever suits its needs at any given moment).

It is in looking at the political consideration—and its relationship to creativity—that we are finally forced to move towards a composite functional stance (in regard to laying a basis for transformation). I recall a saying in the sixties, mostly in the universities, which stated that everything you do is politics. At the time I did not agree with that statement, and even now I feel that in itself it is not necessarily true. But the present situation that poor and non-white people are in will not be changed unless attempts are made to recognize the political implications underlining how present western reality is maintained; and if that is true, then everything can be viewed in relationship to the political factors which define it. Certainly, as I have tried to express in this book, the implications of black creativity have been greatly affected by the political forces that dictate western culture—this has been the case with every period of the music, from the early slave songs to the present. The distortions that surround the meta-reality of black creativity are directly related to the potential of the music to serve as a factor for transformation. It is precisely because of the potential of creativity to change "given stated particulars" that the collective forces of western culture have put so much effort into controlling its information dynamics. This is so because it is not to the advantage of western culture to have poor and non-white people cognizant of alternative options for establishing both functional and vibrational change. It is for this reason that few people are aware of source initiation—in regard to music or alternative ideas—for the controlling factors inherent in this culture have long since developed ways of both preventing and discrediting outside or unwanted initiations. The sophistication of the western political position in this time period remains unchallenged, because the great majority of the citizens have not been able to get through the many different obstacles that have been constructed to distort comprehension about social and political reality. The utilization of source transfer—gradualism—words (or their use in outlets like western criticism)—misdocumentation—and outright lies are only a few of what I call the available procedures that have been established in the west as factors to regulate culture. It is for this reason that alternative creativity must first come through the spectacle-diversion cycle of information regulation before the public can actually be exposed to its particulars; that is, where the creativity is exposed in the media or given assistance by the many foundations, etc.

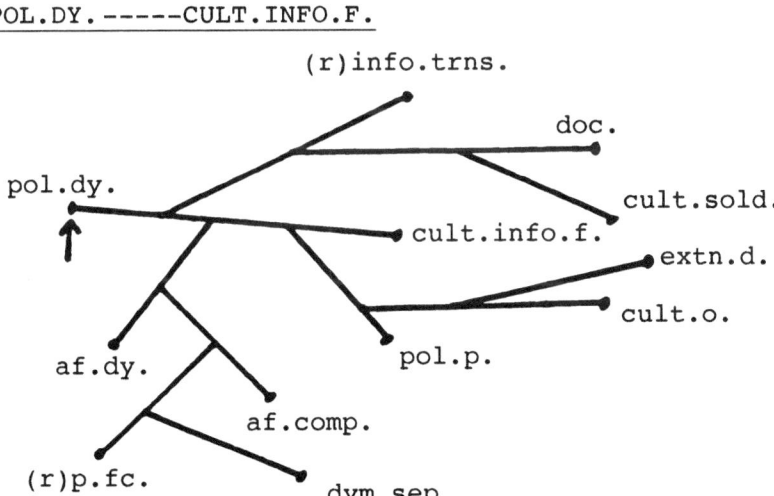

Black creativity today appears to be moving into another transition cycle, and slowly the considerations outlining this change are becoming clear—especially in regard to what challenges must be met. Undoubtedly, the most pressing of these challenges will have to do with the role of the creative person and his relationship to the political and functional demands that this change necessitates. It is from this context that the concept of "the artist" must be dealt with—in other words: can the musician or creative person be talked of as being in a special group as opposed to the masses—or will the challenge of transformation imply a unification of people functioning without regard to surface interest or individual specialties. It is my opinion that the latter will prove to be more in accordance with the implications of world change (transformation). Nor do I mean to imply that musicians and creative people will necessarily have to drop their activity and instead function as guerrilla fighters. Rather, the creative community in this time zone should strive to connect to the composite arena of black culture—or world culture—and function in accordance with what this position really implies. This is really what the transition in the sixties seemed to be saying as well. In this period (sixties), we were fortunate to have musicians like Archie Shepp to expand on political consciousness. Shepp proved to be one of the most eloquent voices in the black creative movement in regard to the challenge of political dynamics and how they relate to music. Shepp understood not only the political implications surrounding his creativity, but also what his work implied as an alternative factor for transformation. For to understand the present reality dictates of western culture, one must first become not only aware of the political consideration (and what creativity implies on a physical universe level), but this awareness must also encompass both alternative-composite ideological realities and alternative functional realities as well.

It is not the purpose of this section to detail the different political realities of all of the countries on the planet. I have included this subject because however one chooses to understand earth life (and composite progressionalism), we can no longer afford to not be aware of the realness of the political arena, and we can no longer view creativity as separate from total events on the planet. If the magnitude of the next transformation promises to affect every aspect of the physical universe situation we live in—whether or not one chooses to participate in making that transformation—then it would be to our advantage to help shape what this transformation will alternately mean—both with regard to creativity and composite life. Either we meet the responsibility of the next cycle or be prepared to become the effects of dynamic change. The political implications of creativity can no longer be controlled by white people exclusively—especially the political implications of creative music from the black aesthetic. The realness of the changing political reality—and its relationship to creativity—proposes a great deal of research and responsibility—and more than that, implies actual functioning on the physical universe level. And no one is excluded, not even the people who call themselves "artists."

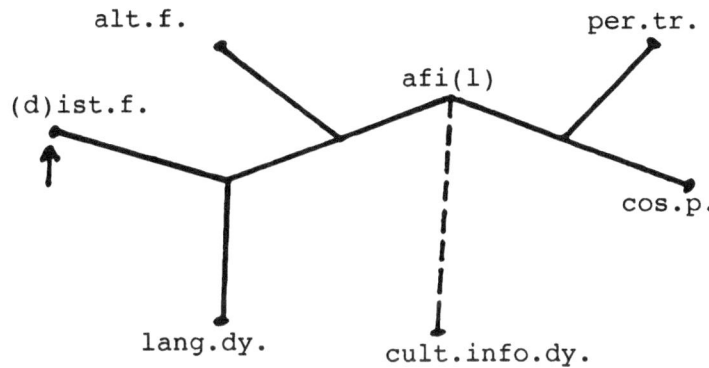

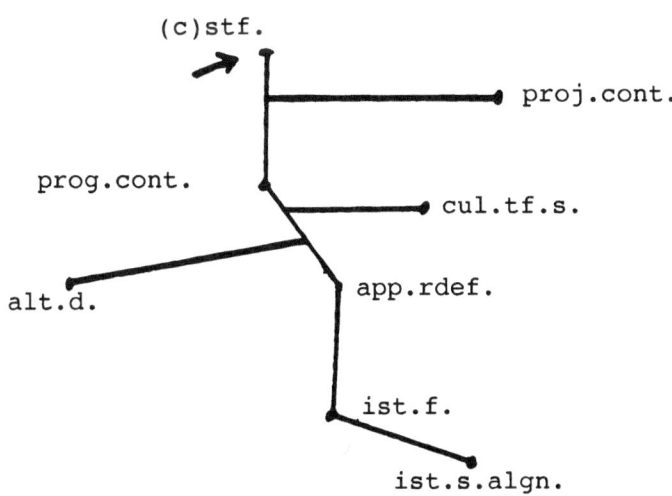

The disintegration of the composite arena of alternative activism in the mid-sixties was without doubt the single most important factor related to the political dilemma black people are now in today. Today, when we talk of the so-called left we are actually talking of fragmentary groups rather than a unified alternative thrust. Very few of these groups have been able to accomplish much more than rhetoric and pointless revolutionary jargon. The effects of the spectacle-diversion cycle can be seen very clearly here—for not only has the system successfully diverted the potential of alternative activism as a life-giving factor, but the scares of the sixties will make it that much more difficult to actually help matters in this country—and planet as well. For when I talk of transformation I do not mean to imply that everything depends on our whims—whether we should come and work for change or not, as a united earth community—instead, my understanding of transformation leans more towards "ready or not, here I come!" In other words, the disintegration of the alternative activist movements as a possible positive factor in transformation was a serious loss. Yet the rebuilding of a composite alternative movement might still be the greatest challenge in this time period, and hopefully we have learned something from the example of the sixties. At any rate, it is clear that the factors which dictated the need for alternative functionalism have not changed very much either—except for the worse. Unless something is done, we should not expect the established defining community to change by itself—for that would be simply wishful thinking. Because of the inability of the alternative activist movements to understand the multi-dimensional and cosmic consequences of transformation, the establishment has successfully weathered the time period of the sixties and seventies. But if the sixties represented the first cycle of what functional transition could really be, then maybe we are only at the beginning of this struggle.

Political Reality—Western Art Music

The present reality of western art music and the political forces surrounding it is directly related to the option dynamics and dilemma of the modern composer. Very few composers are able to have their compositions performed unless they are connected to established power centers. This is why there are so few performances of contemporary notated compositions created from individualists' viewpoints. The established power centers I refer to can best be understood by separating present-day creative notated music with respect to its planet region. For the most part, in America the established power centers are educational institutions—in particular the universities—while in Europe the basic outlet that regulates creativity is government-subsidized: for example, in France one outlet would be the ORTF. All of these power centers are constructed so as to make it practically impossible to bypass their influence—this is so because of the nature of their position, and the fact that these outlets have facilities creative musicians need. The needs I speak of in this case have to do with either orchestras or money to complete projects—an electronic studio, etc. The fact is, very few people can afford the types of facilities that large institutions have. My reason for mentioning this subject has to do with the political connections related to this phenomenon, as well as what this development implies with regard to the actual creativity—because in the final analysis, this must be of concern.

The more successful composers from the post-Webern era are individuals who have amassed substantial power. Thus it follows that any discussion of composers like Boulez and Stockhausen is a discussion of individuals who have not only amassed a great deal of wealth but also influence as to the total state of western culture political dynamics—as this consideration relates to both performance and assistance. In other words, the influence of a composer like Boulez extends well beyond his ability to effect the reality of his own works—and this is important. The dynamic implications of present-day post-Webern politics can be viewed as extremely interesting and complex.

For the continuance of this thrust has moved to secure the composite spectrum of both funding and performance space. A given project, with the right connections, could involve anything—from federal or governmental funding (involving more money than most so-called jazz musicians will ever see in a lifetime for one project) to having that performance "in the right place." The realness of political dynamics in western art music touches on many areas that one might not necessarily believe. For the thrust continuance of western art music is viewed—and rightfully viewed—as the progressional continuation of "what is most western" about the west, and as such is the beneficiary of all that is available from its culture base. The realness of this availability is related to the institutions which have been designed to perpetuate the exclusivity of western culture—as well as its information dynamics—and this phenomenon is also not separate from the "reality" of performing outlets that are available for western art music.

For example, in 1979 Krzysztof Penderecki premiered his composition *Paradise Lost* in Chicago as a piece for the bicentennial celebration. The reality dynamics surrounding why this man was chosen must be viewed in political terms—but this is not my point. The fact of this premiere must be seen in its greater political context, for the sum of money that went into this project would boggle the mind of the so-called jazz musician. Not only that, but the performance of *Paradise Lost* in Chicago was, in fact, only the first performance in a series of performances—which is to say, either someone paid for the Chicago Symphony to travel with this piece, or political machinery had set up different orchestras for this purpose—nevertheless, we are talking about a lot of money. (I recall seeing the piece advertised in Milan, Italy, at La Scala.)

To view the reality dynamics of western art music politics is to focus on the "real reality" of decision-making and economics in the west. For the financial spectrum of this sector's "option span" can be traced to the reality of budgets, as it involves from solo music to projects larger than anything one can imagine. In this sector of cultural politics, everything is possible—nor have I meant to discredit Penderecki or his project, because he should have the right to make whatever business deals he can make (this is just how it is). Not to mention his production of *Paradise Lost* is not the grandest documented project, but instead simply another project. The fact is, projects like *Paradise Lost* are always happening in the western art music world. The reality continuum of opera sees projects "on a scale that would boggle the mind" every year. My point in mentioning all of this is only to comment on the reality options of western art music, and to relate this phenomenon to politics (because these considerations are political). For the person who felt Ornette Coleman's composition *Skies of America* had a financial super-budget, it is important that these concepts are put in the right perspective. Because no other form of music in this time zone enjoys the political and financial support that western art music takes for granted—witness the completion of Berg's opera *Lulu* (can anyone even imagine what the whole of this production cost?). Not to mention that the reality underlying what we call "making a profit" doesn't even enter the picture—if one is to really view the option dynamics of western art music. The money is simply there—there for the purpose of advancing the arts, there for the purpose of necessary research, there for the purpose of "having a balanced performing season," there because "that composer looks promising," there because "it's time to try something different." It's there if the persons there are white and "not in disfavor" with the powers that be.

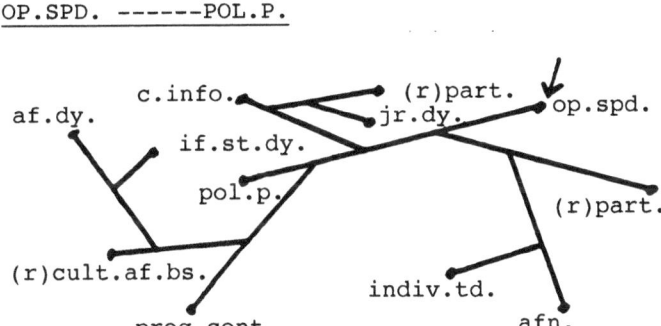

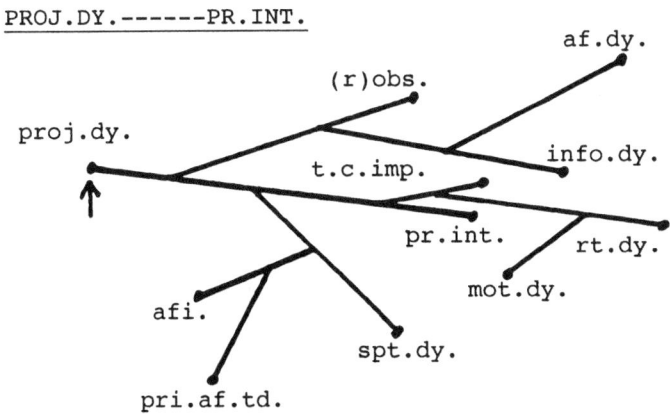

MP(1)–44

To understand the political dynamics surrounding the reality of western art music, it is necessary to view the realness of its performance spectrum. For the thrust continuum of many of the most beautiful theatres and spaces has long been reserved for western art music—even worse, in most cases (in every case, actually) the dynamics of a given theatre were built for the exclusive performance of western art music. Believe me, there is no black music in the Metropolitan, and even worse (now that we are still experiencing the last gasps of the 1954 liberal cycle), when black creativity is performed at these "centers of culture" there are always acoustic problems (because the halls were never designed for the use of any projections but western art music). The solidification of this phenomenon can only be understood in political terms—but there is more. The information reality that sustains western art music—whether in America or Europe—is completely isolated from the greater public's view. Instead, the greater public's only involvement with this sector's existence is to see the notice of a given exposure (or performance) in the *New York Times*. How is it that "Patricia Von Dupotstein" (a name I made up) is given a performance in Alice Tully Hall—when I know NO ONE KNOWS WHO THE HELL SHE IS, let alone where she came from. My point is that all of these matters are political.

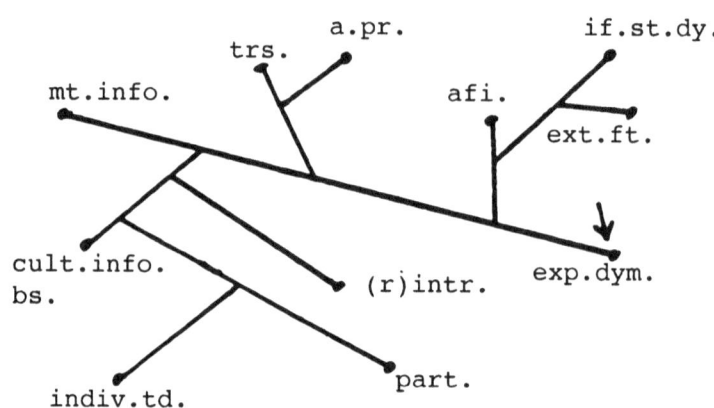

Nor is the performance option spread of western art music only limited to certain sectors of the country—or planet, because the concept of the festival is also a phenomenon that is directly related to "dynamic funding." Nine-tenths of the festivals that solidify in a given year are connected to politically established networks—and the benefits of this phenomenon are carefully screened onto those individuals whose work will function within the composite quilt of western continuance. Very few composers can afford not to deal with these agencies if they are to be successful, for the realness of this phenomenon is not one-dimensional, but instead permeates the composite lining of western culture (and its dynamic influence). But there is another phenomenon related to this area of information which must be looked at. Because what of those individuals "who have not behaved"? That is, what is the reality of those composers whose activity has somehow not been accepted into the composite reality dynamics of western culture? Many so-called jazz musicians might be surprised to find out that the "particulars" of this sector are as difficult—and in some cases, even more difficult—than the "life of the jazz man." This has been the case for the post-Cage continuum in the fifties (although by now much of its work has been accepted into the mainstream of western dynamics—or at least, some of it has been accepted). But in the early fifties this was not the case. Nor have the west coast advances of the post-Partch continuum yet to be made beneficiary of the "big money" that this sector has. My point is that all of these matters are political.

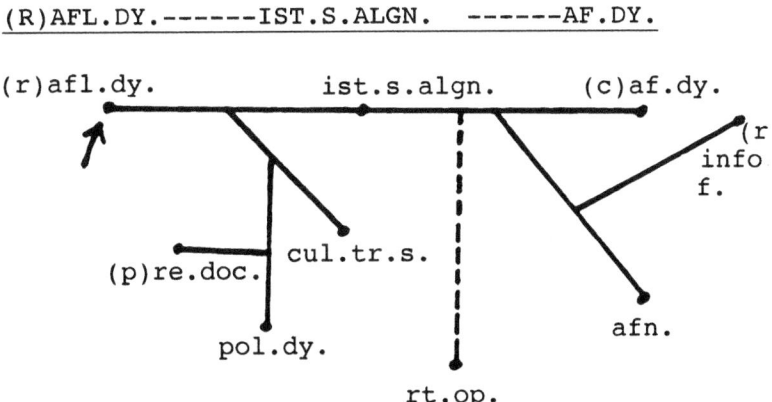

As such, if we are to understand the dynamic particulars of western functionalism, then it is important that the composite generalizations surrounding this subject be torn down. Because there are as many different regions of "respectability" in this continuum as in any other (the only difference being, "if you are accepted in the upper echelons of this continuum, you are then attached to the real power structure"). It might come as a surprise to the so-called jazz community (which basically makes no distinction at all in viewing the "classical" community), but in reality, there is no real unity in this region either—and there has been no unity in this region since the emergence of Beethoven (not to mention the post-Webern continuum). What this means in actual terms is that given individuals are put into zone fields that are programmed for instant success, and other individuals are likewise programmed for "being on the outside, looking on the inside." This is true. And the seriousness of transformation must be viewed as a phenomenon that must also address itself to correcting this sad state of affairs. Because everyone should have a chance to make himself/herself into what is "most" about what he/she wants to be.

Without doubt, one of the grossest distortions surrounding creative music is the notion of the poor jazz musician and the rich young composer. For the thrust of this viewpoint moves to paint a totally unrealistic picture of creative functionalism. The fact is, the reality continuum of the contemporary so-called classical composer is filled with the same frustrations that are found in every area of alternative functionalism. In some way, the reality conditions for the contemporary classical composer are even worse than for the so-called jazz musician, because no real market has been developed for "new" classical music. As such, the average composer in this continuum has a very difficult time finding possibilities for both performance and development—and this is especially true if that person is not connected with a university of some type. And the situation for recording contemporary classical music is even more impossible than for so-called jazz. There are only a handful of labels interested in documenting contemporary classical music—this is true in both Europe and America. The seriousness of this dilemma is not helped by the many levels of separation that have long plagued western art music—even its so-called contemporary extensions. For the social and political reality of the east coast composers bloc is very separate from the west coast, nor do the post-serial schools have any real contact with the post-Cage movement (not to mention, both of these groups have long tried to pretend that Harry Partch's music never existed). The end result of these separations has made an already grim situation even worse, because the mis-unification that this phenomenon has promoted has helped to secure the "strange" hold that European art music has long enjoyed on American creative notated music.

The political reality, then, of contemporary creative musicians/composers from this continuum has had to rely on the social dynamics related to their status as white people in a "privileged society"—and in doing so, this reliance has helped to isolate their work from the mainstream of American society even further. The thrust of this continuum would move to establish dynamic new "performance and information lines" in the middle sixties—and in reality, these performance spaces could be viewed as the solidification of an "all-white" performing network for alternative creativity from the western art music continuum. The dynamics of this phenomenon would move to create new performing spaces (e.g., the emergence of the art gallery as promoter and/or financier) as well as a "new identity and vibrational position." Underneath the surface of its exterior, however, the realness of this phenomenon could be viewed as the first response by the collective forces of western culture—and in particular the western art intellectual community—to actively begin championing the exclusive dynamics of the white avant-garde (the only problem with this sector, however, is that, in their need to be above the "commoners," they have mistakenly embraced exclusively at the expense of real exposure). Because the "unpretty" fact is, the actual dictates of this sector have never desired composite awareness—let alone support for their activity—be that activity art, sculpture, or music. And this is a problem (or could be a problem). It is past time for alliances between this sector and the greater community of world music—and alternative functionalism—but this can never come about unless there is mutual respect between so-called classical musicians and so-called jazz musicians. (What is even more interesting is the fact that, aesthetically, there is no real difference between any creative music, whatever its so-called designation, and world creativity. All of these forms are inter-connected because they are "from each other.")

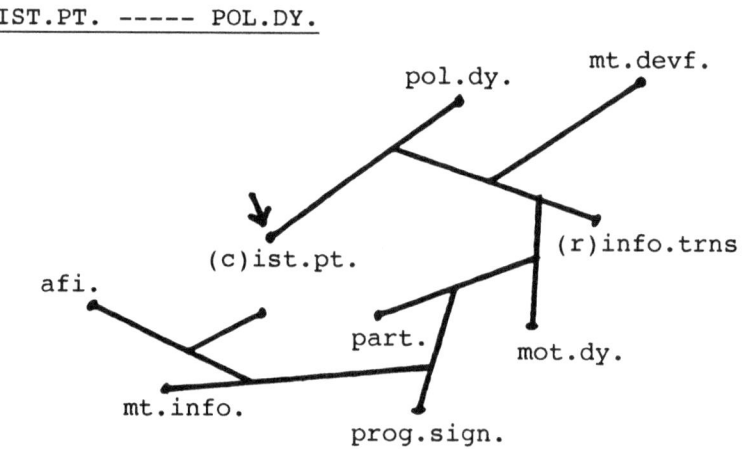

To view the present reality of contemporary western art music is to be forced to examine its political nature—and what this has posed for social reality. Because the thrust continuance of western art music has deliberately chosen to become an elitist music—as opposed to a dynamic thrust whose composers are fighting to both teach people about their work as well as fighting for performance possibilities—rather than a living and breathing continuum. Contemporary western art music has become an esoteric extension shielded by the protective cloud of static intellectualism and "highbrow" social reality (with correct adjectives spoken in the most correct English—as only educated gentlemen would understand). This is true even though there have always been many courageous people who have fought to advance their music against the system. Certainly Charles Ives did not fear the social lining of western political traditionalism, and because of his "in-touchness" was able to contribute to the real spirit continuum of the music—this is true for practically all of the great contributors to western art music.

For the present social and political state of western art music is composed of the same people who could not hear Bach's larger works, or could not hear Beethoven while he was actually composing—but could instead only embrace their works a hundred years later. Nevertheless, the dynamic implications of this phenomenon will remain as is until real collective efforts are made to change it. It is not enough to think that only one segment of the collective community can really change the composite state of things—because the realness of this time period transcends the functionalism of one group. Yet that is just the position black creativity is in, for the reality dictates of contemporary western art music seem to only be interested in risk-free alliances—because, unlike the position of black creativity, in time, any disenfranchised movement of western art music can hope to possibly resolidify with the whole of composite western culture (and in doing so, enjoy all the benefits it brings). It is for this reason that "proper distance" is maintained between these movements (because there will always be an area in social dynamics that must necessarily exclude non-white participation—and everyone knows this as well)—and there is more. In actual fact, it is not necessarily true that the contemporary art music community would like to be viewed separately from Europe. Three-fourths of the American composers have stated their preference to be viewed only in terms of their relationship to the European tradition—as opposed to the world group. The American composers' continuum has created its own aristocracy of a sort in America—and the basic thrust of this movement prefers to remain as an exclusive reality separate even from the mainstream of American culture. It is because of the separation of the creative community—and the reluctance of the creative composer to step outside of his pseudo-universe—that relations between the classical music community and the creative music community are so poor. Needless to say, the realness of racism is also involved in this dilemma—and I do not mean to imply that the creative music community is saintly either. The separation of the creative composing tradition and creative black music is fed by both groups, but the major difference is that the classical music community enjoys the benefits of its position in western culture, while the creative musician is alone and without any kind of power. There are even more divisions within the contemporary classical music community itself. One has to understand that the same facilities would not necessarily be available to a composer like John Cage as compared to a composer like Aaron Copland—or even Charles Wuorinen. This is simply because contemporary music has never had the acceptance that classical music enjoys—or the same establishment backing with regard to economics—and this is also a reflection of the political influence of the educational institutions in America. For the most part, only the composers and musicians who function directly in accordance with the classical European music reality can expect to have real financial backing—and for those who do (if he or she is perceived as talented), there is unlimited support. Nevertheless, my point is that the facilities available to contemporary classical music are still distinctive enough from those available to the creative black musician that they cannot be talked of as being in the same political reality. And it is important to understand that the collective forces of western functionalism intend to keep this situation as is.

There has been no composite effort by the classical community to eradicate the present situation as it is in America. From this I can only deduce that the predicament of the creative black or non-white musician does not bother the classical community. The present relationship between these two groups begins to take on the undertones of a class power struggle—and in the end, we all lose. For while a considered amount of energy will have to be directed to deal with this situation, in the final analysis only a small handful of people support either music. The separation between the contemporary notated community and the contemporary creative community is also a factor that serves to retard the potential for composite alternative functionalism, and that is unfortunate. Because the composite vibrational arena of creative music has never been more conducive to positive interchange than now. Yet no matter how flexible one would like to be, in the end we are forced to deal with the fact that there have been no efforts on the part of the contemporary classical community to even indicate that it is conscious of the present situation. In fact, the opposite seems to be true, and in this period of time the contemporary music community functions as a factor to enforce the present physical universe and political reality situation of western functionalism. Any look at the closed contemporary music societies all over America only reinforces this view.

Rock Music

Many of us have come to think of rock music as a creative form that functions in accordance with the forces working to establish alternative realities in this time zone. And in this context, rock music is generally thought of as being "anti-establishment" or political. But in actual fact, commercial and rock music has long been utilized by the collective forces of western culture to stifle alternative functionalism (and positive change). Rock music, more than any other form of creativity, is used by the collective forces of western culture factors as a controlling agent to direct affinity dynamics. The time zone of the sixties can be pinpointed as the juncture which dictated how this phenomenon would function with regard to the potential transitional factors of that period. In other words, controlled creativity was directly related to the dissemination of composite functionalism. The adaptation of rock music is directly connected with the spectacle-diversion factors that eventually distorted and finally destroyed sixties alternative functionalism. To understand the political implications of this phenomenon, one would only need to consider the position popular music now occupies in this time period—and how that position affects both the total affinity relationship that people have been taught to have with creativity as well as the economic reality lining of the culture itself. Any look at the political implications surrounding commercial music would immediately show that this form—by definition—was to be the most economically attractive factor for sustaining the controlling forces now dictating western information dynamics. This control would extend into the creative potential of affinity insight (2) postulation as well as its economic implications. Both considerations were not only attached to the emergence of rock music as a political factor, but in helping to shape information and social focus, the designing forces responsible for the present veneer of culture have actually become stronger because of its use (rock music as a controlling source). I have already written on the distinction between rock music as a source-transfer vehicle and creative black music, in regard to what position these musics occupy in the cosmic and vibrational hierarchy of white and black culture—yet it is necessary to again emphasize that these musics are in fact not the same. The major difference between these two musics basically reflects how the spectacle-diversion cycle works in American culture (and this difference also extends into the political implications underlying what we are now dealing with in this time zone). It is in understanding how creativity is utilized in the west that we can better view its political implications. For if, in the beginning, the concept of politics had to do with how people could deal with existing together within a given space, we have now arrived at the junction where the political arena has affected how a given space can deal with people. In other words, not only has this consideration become distorted in terms of its use in this period, but unless we meet the challenge of the next cycle, the political implications inherent in the western position threaten to increase their ability to thwart real existence. Nor do I mean to imply that only creativity—whatever principle thrust—is in this dilemma, because the political sophistication which dictates the western political hold on the world in this present period has equally affected every level of the planet. There is no activity happening on the planet level that is not affected by political consideration—even a person working at a steel mill can be looked at in terms of what effects he or she will have in securing particular political positions. Yet the nature of a given particular implies that its consequences will also affect us on a variety of levels—on an individual level this viewpoint can be understood, and on a composite level it is just as true. The most basic factors we are dealing with in this time zone in regard to the existing political arena are: political activity as a controlling factor on the physical universe level, and political activity as a factor to dictate the vibrationaltory lining of a given space. The manipulation of creative music—from the affinity insight (2) principle)—is directly related to this phenomenon, and that is why it must be understood if we are to change it.

It would, of course, be a gross distortion of real information to simply reduce all popular music to activity that functions to sustain the status quo, and I do not mean to make this mistake. Yet there is no way to ignore the real relationship between rock music and the political considerations underlying its availability (as well as the information interpretations that have solidified as a result of this relationship). The position popular music now has in this period is directly related to the political factors which control western culture, and this is my point. It is also clear that the utilization of rock music was found to be attractive because the meta-reality of the form was not in disagreement with the vibrational arena of the controlling community—in short, the forces controlling events in the west utilize rock to the extent they do because there is no separation between what that form is and who they are—and the controlling forces dictating policy in the American functional establishment are not revolutionary. Rock music was found to be an attractive commodity because of its ability to fall within the sanctioned reality of American culture—that is: the idea of rock having anything to do with revolution was an idea probably thought up at Columbia Records. (If it was about revolution, why didn't the controlling forces deal with people attached to the real revolution; and if the establishment was so concerned about the revolution, why didn't it record and distribute records by Malcolm X?)

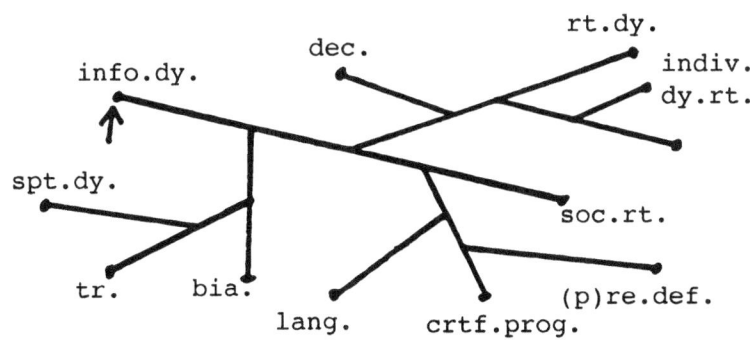

MP(I)–54

To understand creativity in this time zone would require many different considerations, for it is clear that nothing exists as a separate factor in itself, and it is also clear that any person wanting to deal with this subject must recognize the multi-complexual consequences related to what this phenomenon poses as a life commitment. Any area of creativity has to be viewed in terms of its relationship to the economic dynamics of its base culture (what is implied in the relationship between creativity and business as a cultural controlling tool). We can also say that by the time creativity is given access to the general communications media, so much has been lost from its basic and original thrust particulars that, in most cases, the music is completely transformed from its source initiation. Nor have I meant to limit this phenomenon either. My point is only that the collective forces of western culture function to maintain basic vibrationaltory arena dictates—and as such, this phenomenon has designed a situation that affects creativity in a multi-complexual sense. When I wrote that by the time a given initiation is available to the public that in most cases the form has undergone source transfer, I am referring to a spectrum of factors related to the music. The most important of these factors sheds light on the present arena of creativity with regard to its political position. Because by the time a person is able to experience a given creative manifestation, that creativity has had to go through criticism, publicity, radio or television, and, most harmful of all, words. All of these considerations are directly connected to establishing a particular vibrationaltory stance—and we are more affected by this phenomenon than it might seem. In attempting to understand this situation—and its relationship to the present physical universe situation—we can hopefully have a better basis for establishing real alternatives in the future. Yet it is also clear that the optimum state of creativity is to not be in the position of having to make it a commodity. In this time period, the phenomenon of creativity mirrors the same overbalance taking place on the physical universe level: the fact that certain people can make a living from being creative as opposed to others who have to make their money and spend it to experience other people being creative has nothing to do with the real potential of creativity. The net result of our present situation serves as an obstacle to transformation—moreso, the result of this overbalance has nothing to do with a person's inherent potential for being creative as well as one's inherent desire to experience another person's creativity—without having to pay or be made aware of the separation between those who do and those who do not realize that they can do.

The questions that any creative person has to face concern both the reality of one's creativity as well as the reality of the business that surrounds that creativity. In other words, the realness of one's relationship to his or her activity is not the only fact that must be understood if the seriousness of a given career decision is to be based on "what is really happening out here in the world." Because the challenge of functioning in creativity is also related to the dynamics of one's "flexibility" in physical universe matters. The reality of what creativity and politics really means determines how we have come to view the concept of success—regardless of context. "Flexibility" in this case, then, is the degree to which one can be molded in accordance with the dictates of a given position (i.e., the political particulars related to how far one might be able to penetrate the "accessibility of things"), and also flexibility as a consideration related to whether or not one is socially perceived as "from the right zone." Every creative person is affected by the dynamics of this phenomenon. Because in the final analysis, one's ability to realize certain projects is a result of many factors that normally have no relationship to creativity (e.g., contacts and personality, dress, or the right teachers, wife, husband, money—of course—club, etc.). No wonder there are so few individuals who are able to survive the creative life with their "original intentions." Because the need to have things like food, clothes, and shelter is a consideration that compels many different levels of adjustment. Nor have I meant to negate the composite realness of "how life seems to be." For it is clear that life seems to carry, what I will call here anyway, "good and bad" cycles (or "easy and difficult" cycles) for everyone, and I have not meant to disrespect this phenomenon either. But the realness of present-day continuance in western culture cannot be simply dismissed as being "business as usual," because the dynamics of modern-day living seem to point clearly to what can only be called "the artificial construction of space games." In other

MP(I)–56

words, we cannot say that the present reality surrounding the recording industry is the planet's fault—as designed by the planet—which everyone experiences on some level; rather, it is related to what we have created, as opposed to the planet "picking on us." The challenge of transformational politics is to change those problems that can be changed.

(Level Two)

I HAVE TRIED IN THE FIRST HALF OF THIS SECTION to comment on the dynamic implications of creativity and politics as this subject concerns the reality particulars of western culture and alternative functionalism. But the realness of this subject cannot be understood by only focusing on western continuance, because creativity and politics have to do with composite life in this region—or area of space—involving all of us, regardless of country or so-called nationality.

In other words, the dynamic implications of both creativity and politics concerns the whole of this planet, because the reality implications underlying how these considerations (creativity and politics) are viewed have multi-complexual significance for the whole of humanity—and it is important that this is understood. Many of us in the west have come to view ourselves as the center of the universe—but this is definitely not the case. The fact is, the political decisions being made in this time period are the same decisions that will affect the composite agenda of the next cycle. That is, not only does the world group have to deal with the specifics of a given decision coming from the west in this time zone, but the realness of transformation implies that the west be held accountable for the end result those decisions bring about—or call into being. As such, it is important to understand the nature of what "forces are at work" in this period—because "the reality of collected decisions" is not as simple as many of us would like to believe. My point is this: the solidification of a culture has to do with its collective vibrational state and cosmic identity. Everyone in that culture is necessarily connected with what this phenomenon means, and everyone in that culture is affected by the vibrational lining that permeates their living state. Because of this relationship, it is important to begin viewing the dynamic implications of world decision-making, because the course of a given decision has multi-implications as well as consequences (probably this was what Rod Serling was referring to when he commented about "Maple Street," in its last calm and reflective moments—"before the monsters came"). The dynamic realness of cultural decision-making is related to the cosmic destiny of a culture.

Obviously, the realness of creativity is a phenomenon equally manifested throughout the whole of this planet (and sector of space)—which is to say, the realness of this subject is not separate from the vibrational nature and collective imprint of world culture. For the solidification of a given affinity state directly sheds light on the information continuum of its culture group as well as the route dynamics of its path. For this reason, creativity has long been utilized as a cross-vibrational factor for establishing both communication and affinity adjustments between so-called different peoples and/or different nations. The use of creativity in this context has proven very significant in determining what option routes are available for both alliances (on an individual and/or culture level) and information dynamics (or possibilities). As such, the actualness of this subject cannot be ignored as a profound political tool—because the spectrum ratio of a given creative projection transcends any one focus—this is true for this period as well as the past. If we are to understand the dynamic reality implications of the next cycle, then some effort must be made to view this subject with respect to what it poses about world progressionalism. For the future as well as the present nature of events is not separate from what particulars are "at work" in this cycle. It is important to understand how creativity is being used in present-day politics, and how it has been used in the past. For the present "reality of events" has not simply solidified without our taking part—and we are not the victim of unbridled continuance; rather, the present vibrational area of this planet is the direct result of how humanity has approached living—and dying. It is important that this phenomenon (creativity and politics) is understood—on whatever level.

The dynamic realness of creativity has long functioned as a vibrational transfer factor by the collected forces of western culture—and this is true for world culture as well (regardless of time period). In this context, creativity has often been utilized as a tool for bridging cultural differences, with the understanding being that art transcends particular boundaries—and as such can be shared. In this cycle, we can view the Chinese and Egyptian exhibition tours as an example of modern-day cultural interchange. For exhibits like the Tutankhamen showing have attracted great support all over the country, and these exhibits have also helped to teach about the realness of world creativity. Many of these exhibits have enriched our lives on several levels, and the progressional continuance of world art exposure has indeed served as a positive transitional factor—which is to say, we can only be grateful to those individuals who have made world exhibits possible. Hopefully the next cycle will bring forth more exhibits of this kind—because this certainly is needed. Yet the realness of present-day dynamics must also include some awareness of the extended context which determines creativity and creative world art exhibitions. The fact is, many of the decisions related to whether or not a given exhibit is to be shown—in what ever country—are based on political and economic realities as much as artistic significance. And while this might not necessarily mean anything when viewed on specific focuses, the composite inter-relationship between creativity, economics and politics can begin to take on more complexity when viewed on a planet level. Moreover, I am not only referring to the dynamics of creativity when I cite the expanded implications of this relationship, because the composite reality of creativity and politics has very little to do with creativity as such. Rather, creativity in this context can be viewed as another available tool for political manipulation—but I do not mean to over-generalize this most complex relationship. One thing is sure: the realness of creativity has always functioned as a stimulating factor for world politics, and this interest shows no sign of abatement in this cycle.

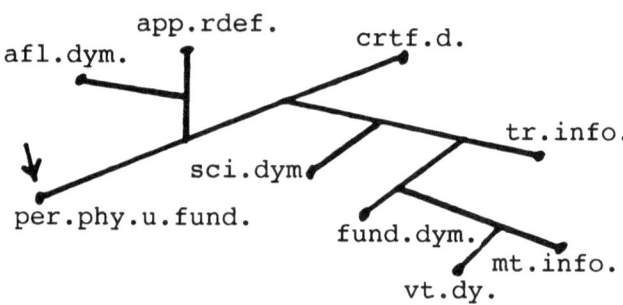

To view the progressional dynamics between creativity and politics is to become aware of the total dynamics of transfer shifts—as a natural and forced consideration. For the acquisition of world creativity is coupled to the spread of humanity as well as the realness of solidification and destruction. The whole concept of the musician is related to what this expansion has meant, for it must be understood that the economics surrounding creativity in this cycle have taken on new proportions from what was happening in the past. The best example of this phenomenon can be viewed by understanding what took place in the plundering of Africa. For the end result of the many wars which brought about that region's transformation was accompanied by a ravaging of its creativity as well. Many different nations simply came into Egypt and took what they wanted—later placing alien economic consideration on the creativity—to give it "value" (or to make that value real for the people who took it). All of these matters must be viewed as political, and the progressional use of this phenomenon is directly related to what we are now dealing with in this time cycle. I have mentioned this aspect of transfer cycles only to place the consideration of creativity in its most basic context. For the historical acquisition of world culture bounty was not separate from the realness of war and devastation—and the later economic considerations related to this phenomenon were imposed rather than copied. Before the onslaught of this time cycle, creativity in world culture had always derived significance from its position in the composite spiritual hierarchy of its base culture group—and in that context was not about "selling" or economics. To view the historical realness of transfer cycles can better help us understand what is happening in this cycle, for it is popular to now view creativity—and works of art—in a somewhat highbrow and elite fashion (using the same analytical and affinity balance that western culture uses to define its own creativity—even though world creativity has never had anything to do with one type of affinity dynamics). The use of transfer cycles would play a great role in helping to establish creativity as a political tool, and the particulars of this phenomenon are directly related to what cycle we choose to focus on. This is not to say that no relationship existed between creativity and politics in world culture information terms, because, in its most basic sense, politics has only to do with how given societies function—in actual terms. Which is to say, the creativity of any region is related to the composite reality of that region (including its physical universe particulars).

PER.PHY.U.FUND.------SPT.DYM.

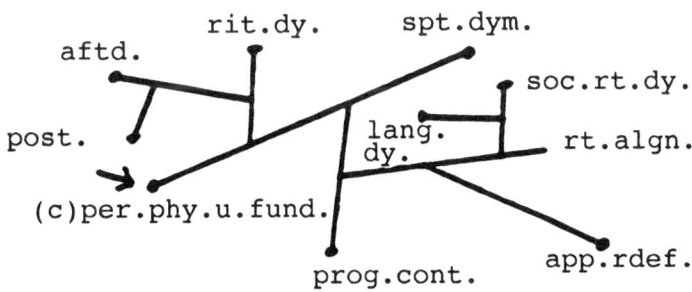

MP(II)–6

(R)PER.VT.U.FUND. -----MT.INFO.

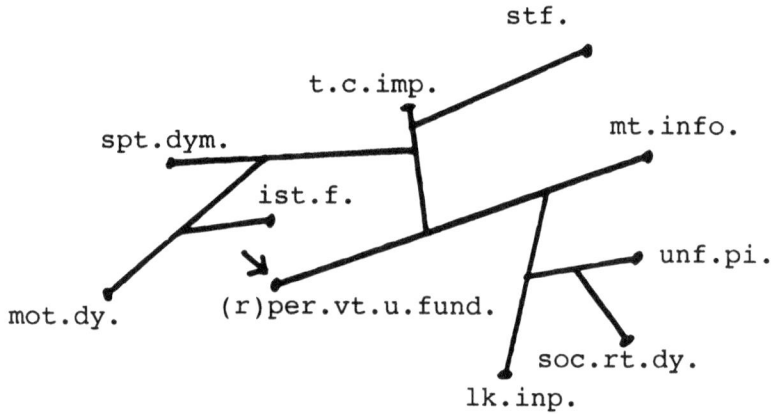

The emergence of international exhibits is not a recent development, nor is this the only use of creativity by the collected forces of world culture. Creative music has long functioned as a political consideration for both social dynamics and extended dynamics, and any attempt to deal with the realness of this inter-relationship would imply observing many different factors. To view the progressional spread of creative music is to see the political implications related to how particular information is utilized (i.e., affinity-transfer manipulation). The State Department has long recognized the realness of this phenomenon, and creative music has functioned as an accelerated political factor—and tool—since the middle forties (after the Second World War).

To understand why creative music has been utilized by the State Department of the United States is to recognize how the music has long been viewed by the composite world community. For creative music—from the black aesthetic especially—is generally recognized as the most dynamic projection to have solidified from America (in many cases, creativity from this sector is viewed as the only art projection that has come from America). This has been the basic view since Europe was exposed to the very early projections of the music. The State Department's use of creative music must be viewed as a response to that interest, and the music has greatly affected the vibrational dynamics of every culture group that has experienced it. Frank Kofsky was one of the first writers to really examine the political implications of creative music in this context, as well as how it came to be utilized in this cycle (and in particular, the present use of creative music by the State Department). It is interesting that America would finance the use of creative music for foreign countries while at the same time not deal with the music within its own borders, but that seems to have been the case. The use of creative music in this context had to do with vibrationally affecting so-called communist countries through regular broadcast on the radio. Many of these stations (e.g., Radio Free Europe) have utilized creative music as a factor related to "what capitalism is about" (and, of course, this relationship has been imposed, for the progressional thrust of creative music from the black aesthetic has nothing to do with the reality particulars of capitalism. In many ways, creative music exists in spite of all of these "isms")—and the use of the music in this context would serve as a factor to vibrationally participate in disintegrating the composite center factor of its targeted countries. To understand this use of creative music is to understand that the political realities of this cycle are not concerned about the actualness of creativity, but only to what degree it can be utilized as a positive manipulative tool. It is the lack of concern for the music in its own right that best characterizes the relationship between the American government and its use of functional strategies. Creative music, in their view, can only be useful as long as it can effectively function—as a tool—in the ideological and vibrational political arena. This is how the music was viewed in every progressional stage of its development, and there is nothing to suggest that anything has changed in this cycle. It should also be stated that the use of creativity as a political tool has brought about the desired results—which is to say, the overall use of functional creativity has been very successful, and there are many reasons for this. First and foremost, the realness of creativity is about affecting the vibrational dynamics of the environment it happens in. It is important to understand that creativity is not just a word, or a given set of activities, but rather "particular" activity that functions with a complex and dynamic multi-effect—for anyone experiencing it. This is true for every form of creativity, whether its meta-reality consequences are understood or not. The State Department's use of creative music must be viewed as a real factor for political persuasion, yet it must also be understood that at no point has this agency ever had any real understanding of what it was broadcasting. In other words, the vibrational tone level of American and western culture has never examined the meta-reality realness of its own creativity—especially creativity from the black aesthetic. To the degree that the music has had an effect on communist countries, it has also had the same effect in America (in those regions where the music is exposed)—but at no point can we assume that the collected forces of western culture have ever understood the real implications of this use (and what they have really created).

STF.------MTH.

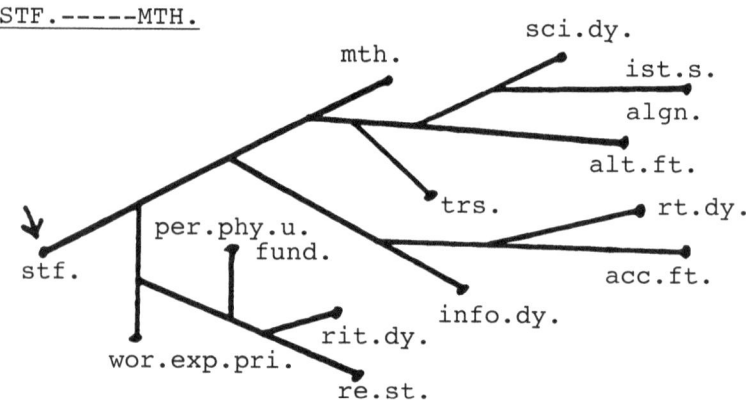

SCI.DYM.------PROJ.DY.

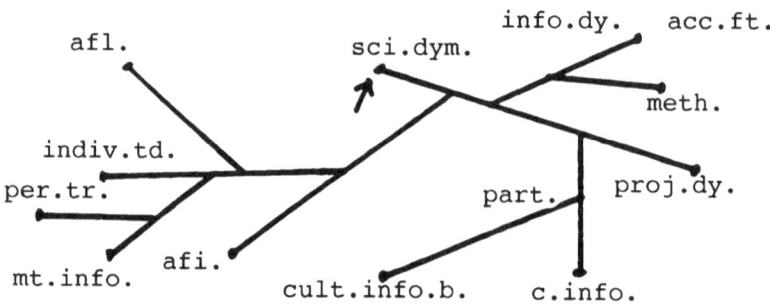

To really view the composite implications of creativity and politics is to have some understanding of what is taking place on the physical universe level. In other words, if we are to view the realness of creativity in this cycle, then the dynamics of world politics must be observed on some level. This is so because we are living in what can only be called "a very interesting period." So interesting that the progressional implications of geo-political realities seem to suggest the present cycle is now undergoing profound changes—on many different levels. The seriousness of these changes will most certainly affect the reality implications of creativity— but even more important, our actual lives will not be separate from this same phenomenon. This is not to imply that my writings can clearly detail the composite planet political situation in every context, because no one is qualified to make claims on that level, but even a limited approach to geo-political progressionalism can give insight about transition and transformation—and its effects on creativity. One thing is clear: the reality implications of creativity are not separate from the actual political reality of its culture group—or focus. The realness of geo-politics must be viewed for what it has activated in both creativity and affinity dynamics. And this information is important if we are to solidify the necessary perspective for viewing the present. From this context we can hopefully learn about the nature of transformation as well as how to better prepare for future world change. And there are many more questions about this subject that must be first established. It is important to clearly understand the relationship between the progressional spread of information and affinity dynamics (in this case, creativity, but this is not the only related focus) and political reality, and the inter-relationship of source transfer and political reality. The seriousness of politics must be viewed as a multi-dynamic factor that touches on every aspect of life—regardless of community or planet sector.

CN.INFO. ------AF.DY.

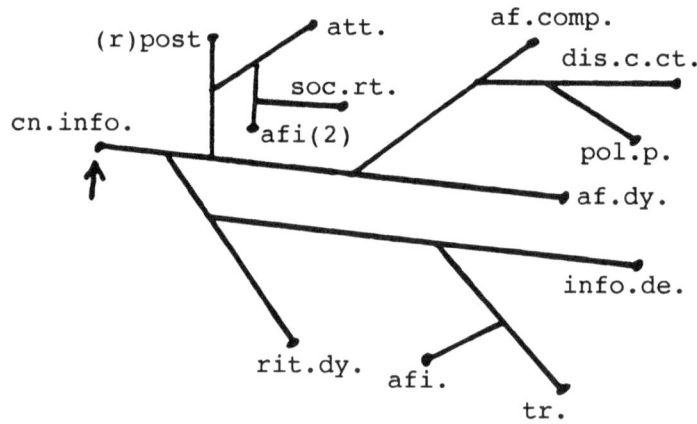

MT.INFO. ------CRTF.PROG.

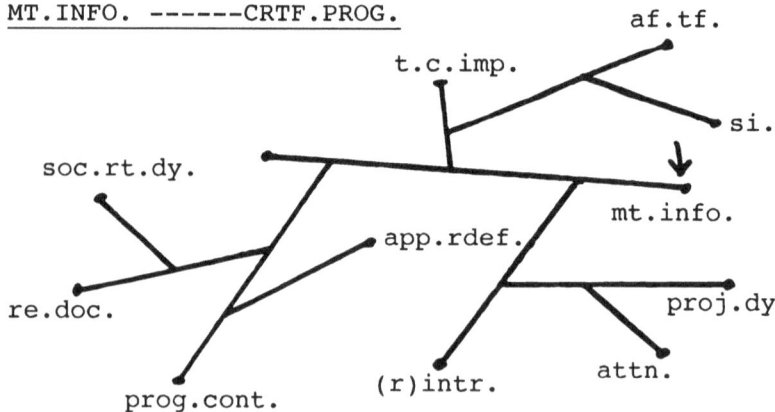

VT.DY. ----- DIS.C.CT.

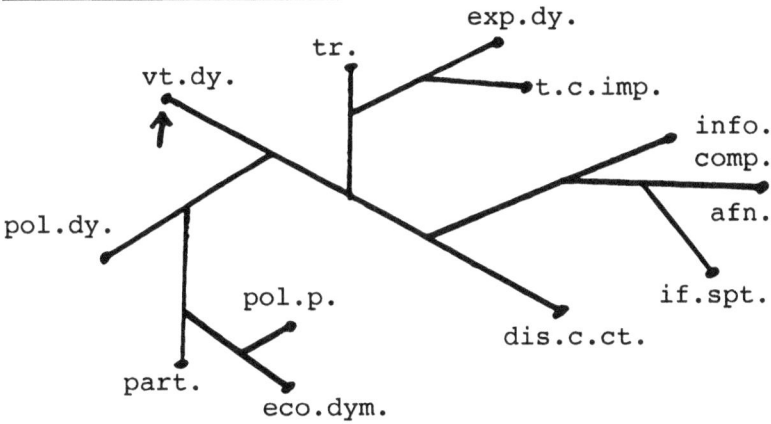

IF.ST.DY.------PART.

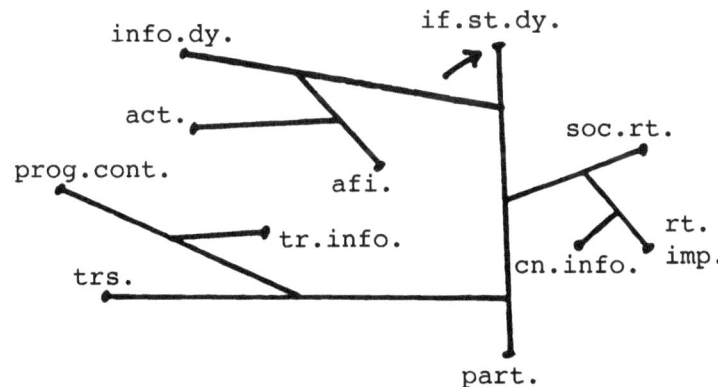

MP(II)-12
Changing Political World Situation

Without doubt, the best way to approach the composite complexities of politics is to view this subject with respect to what is taking place in this time cycle on a total level. This approach is especially necessary if we are to understand the reality particulars of this time period. Many forces are now active on the physical universe level—and it is important to view what factors are shaping the nature of progressional continuance (hopefully towards positive transformation—but not necessarily positive). In many ways, we are fortunate to live, witness, and be a part of the dynamics of this time zone, for the composite realness of world politics has come to an important junction in time. There is no area on the planet not dealing with "real" change, and we can all view the forming political-reality implications of the next cycle—or future. At the same time, it can also be said that living in such a complex cycle is most certainly not a blessing—for the dynamic realness of complexity has moved to unsolidify many of our primary notions about reality and life. So many of our basic concepts—as a nation and community—have been successfully challenged, that it is increasingly difficult to hold on to any of the ideas we have grown up with, and this is particularly true for people over forty. Every concept has been challenged—from religion, and its role in society, to political reality—race, and society. The time zone of the sixties would have a great effect on the rapidity of this phenomenon, and in doing so, actualized the nature of the transition we are now dealing with. Nor have I meant to imply that only particular sectors of the culture have been affected by the progressional complexities of physical and vibrational universe change, for the dynamics of this phenomenon transcend particular territories and communities. Every sector of the planet is feeling the implications—vibrationally and socially—of present-time progressionalism, whether we are referring to white people, black or Asian people—men and women—rich or poor. For the composite realness of this phenomenon seems to forecast something more than a mild realignment but, rather, real transition—with the possibility of even transformation. The progressional and projectional realness of creativity is not separate from what this phenomenon means either—and as such, the political dynamics of this cycle must be viewed as directly related to necessary information. For this reason, it is important to examine aspects of world culture with emphasis on progressional continuance and political reality—and political transition.

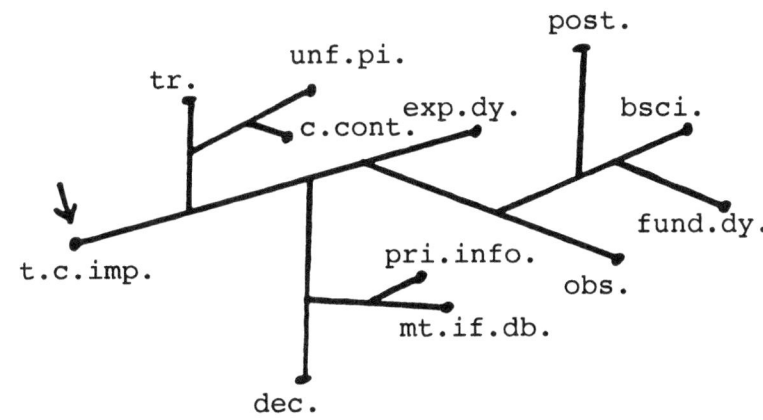

U.S.A.

The most basic factor many Americans have had to come to terms with is the changing position of the United States as a world power. This is not to say the United States is without power, nor have I meant to underrate America's achievements in any way, but if we are to really understand the complexities of present-day geo-politics, then the nature of America's political dynamics and vision must be recognized. The most relevant context which has determined the particulars of this subject can best be viewed from the period after the Second World War to the present. For until that cycle, America was perceived as the bulwark for so-called free nations—and protector of composite western democracy. Under this banner, America's political policies had to do with its ability to successfully control and manipulate political and economic reality for the world group. In this relationship, Europe would look to America for both military and economic support, and also for vibrational identity. The progressional continuance of this phenomenon would see America's involvement in Korea, Africa and the Caribbean, and later the east. This involvement had to do with how America viewed herself in extended terms—as the only nation capable of defending against so-called communism—and as such, the last thirty years would see the use of "whatever was deemed to be appropriate for political continuance." Of course there is much more to this phenomenon and I do not mean to isolate American functionalism from world politics, because it is no different from any other western country in this cycle (the only difference would be its economic position and technological sophistication). My point in mentioning any of this is only to clarify America's planet position until the sixties. For until this cycle, the planet was viewed in unrealistically narrow terms—having to do with America, the Soviet Union, and China—with the understanding being that all other nations were background players. In this context, America would come to view herself in such extended terms that many people would really believe "God was on their side." But by the end of the sixties, the realness of planet reality would begin to slowly take hold and America would be forced to re-assess its own reality focus. Because the most basic factor that determines political reality is the realness of economics—alliances and flexibility—and this is not only true for America but for the composite world group. In fact, to view the realness of politics in this time cycle is to view what can only be called an extremely sensitive and changing subject. This is so because the vibrational and actual realness of earth dynamics is changing on many levels. The realness of transition dynamics must also be viewed for what it means when applied to economics, alliances or transfer dynamics. To understand this is to understand the nature of present-day progressionalism—because "it is not about the forties anymore." Which is to say, the reality of political functionalism America pursued in the forties has greatly changed—in terms of particulars—even if its ultimate objectives haven't. Even more interesting is the realness that present planet developments seem to imply there will be more changes coming in the future. For the most basic factor that has changed the present particulars of political functionalism—and as such, political theory and reality—is the position of world culture (i.e., the Middle East, Japan, Europe) in this time cycle (and the realness of the future will see this reality context change even more, because the dynamics of transition will also include many more participants—e.g., Africa, China, the Caribbean). America in this cycle can now be viewed as functioning from a wider observation context, yet I am not endorsing any particular aspect of western foreign policy.

To really understand the political reality of America in this cycle is to understand what this country has meant to world culture. This is especially important if we are to understand what has and is happening to non-white people on a planet level. It cannot be ignored that the political situation in South Africa, for instance, has had the support of the American government, and that the economic dynamics of world culture has had to bear the weight for so-called advantages Americans take for granted. The fact is, the progressional expansion of western culture is directly responsible—and thoroughly involved in—what has transpired in world culture. If we are to view the political realness of western culture—and, in particular, America (in this cycle)—then we are forced to recognize what this phenomenon really means. And while I have stated that the particulars underlying present-day political functionalism have not changed since the forties, it is important to also state that the actual functionalism which has resulted from this phenomenon has not really changed either. It is because of this consistency that America is viewed in such negative terms by world culture. Many westerners are somewhat surprised to hear of the realness of anti-Americanism, for somehow the basic reality of western culture views itself as being separate from what is happening to the world community. But in fact this has never been the case. America has long been involved in the total particulars of world politics. It should come as no surprise that few countries of the third world view America (or the Soviet Union) in positive terms. The realness of composite politics can be viewed with respect to what areas the so-called super powers have helped to shape—or mis-shape (as is usually the case), and the consequences of these policies will be a major factor in the present transition we are going through.

MP(II)–16

```
(R)PHY.U.FUND.  ------DYM.F.
            if.st.dy.
                            dym.f.
     lang.dy.

                       intr.
(r)phy.u.fund.                      mt.info.
            ist.s.algn.
                            vt.dy.
              c.cont.
```

    The progressional thrust of world politics seems to suggest that America can now be viewed in isolationist terms—whose influence and power is on the wane—and this is true in many different areas of the planet. To understand this is to view the balance of western political philosophies in this time zone, for the so-called democratic countries are a definite minority when compared to socialist or communist countries. Which is to say, the political dynamics of capitalism is not universally viewed as a positive political philosophy. Moreover, it is important that the collective move away from America is viewed seriously, for while this phenomenon might not seem to affect the reality particulars of this time period in actual terms, the future suggests otherwise. Very few Americans seem to be aware of the forces that are now forming on a planet level. Many of us have come to see the planet in nationalistic and racial terms—the understanding being, "we got ours, so you should get yours." But the progressional spread and functional manipulation of western culture has made it extremely difficult for many of the poorer nations "to get theirs." In fact, the forming transition seems to suggest that the world community has come to a critical juncture for survival. Any movement that hopes to really re-establish itself must necessarily view both America and the Soviet Union as a negative factor—and this is exactly what is happening in Iran. For the collective forces of western culture (and in particular, in this context, America and the Soviet Union) must be viewed as affecting the composite reality of every cultural and planet sector it comes in contact with. I am writing about the nature of business considerations, the use of de-naturalizing the environment (and, in some cases, the over-consumption of oil), the use of land for military bases, the use of unethical medical research and practice, and the dis-unification of cultural affinity dynamics. To view the realness of political reality in American foreign policy is to see all of these different factors and more. This is so because politics is about "how a given sector lives," and in this case, the "how" involves the exploitation of world culture. Moreover, the next cycle will see the dynamics of political functionalism in many other contexts, for clearly the present situation cannot stay the same. For instance, the reality of fuel consumption will, within our lifetime, see the drying up of regions like Saudi Arabia—not to mention, what will this region do if plans for moderation are not complete when its oil is used up. However one deals with questions of this nature, my point is that the reality of world progressionalism is not an isolated phenomenon but involves many different factors (not to mention, what will happen to America's foreign policy toward the Middle East if oil prices continue to rise?). To view the realness of present-day political reality is to look at all of these questions and many more. My point, however, is that the political reality of America is not separate from what is transpiring on a composite world level—and as such, if this context is understood, then America must be viewed with respect to the role she has played in creating the present geo-political junction we have arrived at. But this is only the beginning.

Africa

To view the realness of geo-politics is to also become aware of the changing physical universe developments occurring throughout the planet. Of these changes, none has more importance than what is now transpiring in Africa—and developments in that sector will have a profound effect on the composite world group in the near future. For over three thousand years, Africa has played a pivotal role in world politics, and this cycle is no different. The future of all black people is related to the transitions now occurring in Africa, for the particulars underlying this subject are directly related to the resolidification of composite black culture. What role Africa will play in this time cycle is unclear, for the present reality platform of this region is directed towards liberating its various sectors. Hopefully this cycle will see Africans regaining control of their land, but this will be no easy task. Until that goal is achieved, the next immediate cycle in African progressionalism will see much struggle and war. It will probably be some time before Africa can again rise up and become an important force in the world community.

To really understand what has happened in present-day African reality dynamics, one must view the progressional implications of the last three to four hundred years. This is so because the present reality Africans are now dealing with has its root in world history. Quite possibly no other continent has experienced as many dynamic transitions as Africa in the last two thousand years (and some). The nature of these transitions have colored the basic vibrationaltory tone of its space—and the present time zone seems to suggest that Africa has not yet finished dealing with the consequences of multi-transition (and transformation). History shows very clearly that many people have dominated the basic vibrational focus of Africa—as both host and invaders. Nothing is more fascinating than the transformation cycle which saw the final decline of black Africa—and the significance of what this transformation really implies has yet to be dealt with by the west (or by anybody outside of an emerging group of new black scholars—whose activity promises to be of major importance for future transformation)—and the emergence of what we now call western culture. The restoration of black Africa can only be seriously attained when the composite whole of Africa has liberated herself from colonialist manipulation. So real is this challenge that the political dynamics of Africa cannot be viewed as separate from the future hope of composite humanity (that being, the opportunity to live healthy and productive lives for all people). To understand this viewpoint is to understand that without the transformation of Africa there will be no real forum—or platform—for non-white people to really explore the essence implications related to what perception (and perception dynamics) can mean with respect to the dynamics of alternative affinity alignments (or world affinity alignment as "ised" from that region). The dynamics of the next transition in Africa will be very interesting for what its liberation will means to alternative functionalism. Because the seriousness of colonial manipulation has created a necessarily complex situation for information dynamics and expansion dictates.

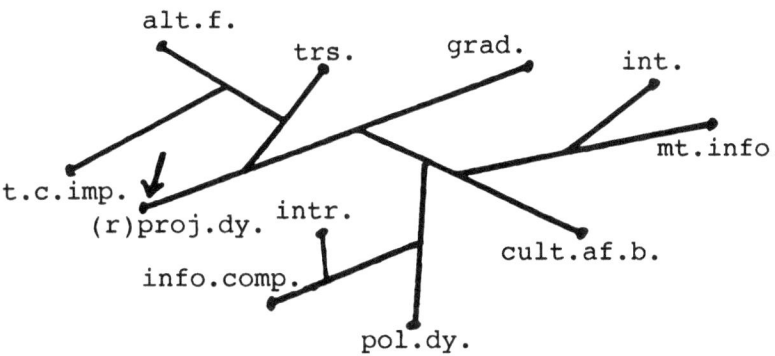

The progressional struggles now taking place in Africa have much importance to the total world group—and this is especially true for black people. This is not to slight the functionalism taking place in other parts of the globe—for obviously there are many other situations (and planet areas) that are of profound importance. But the functionalism taking place in Africa must be viewed with respect to what it signals about dynamic transformation—rather than isolated change. Because no matter how given areas of the planet are perceived—as far as the particulars related to how given political groups deal with various factors of the world community (especially western nations and their relationship with non-white people)—there is no other area of the planet that has as much relevance for reshaping composite transformation. No other sector of the planet has any interest in establishing multi-dynamic civilizations not based on notions of racial or national superiority. The nature underlying how this change can be brought about will have a profound impact on the world community, and this is especially true for black people—yet I do not mean to conjure up false pretenses about what Africa will ultimately be like, because I cannot possibly know. Yet the political dynamics of this cycle has placed a particular burden on Africa—and her role in composite functionalism. Nowhere will black people have any real chance to re-establish cultural and affinity ties but in Africa. Nowhere can one sight any possibility of potential dynamic alternative functionalism—as related to the present balance of world powers and their progressional continuum—but in Africa. This is not to say Africa is now ready to reshape the present world power balance—because obviously it isn't. Nor am I saying that the realness of Africa will necessarily move to disagree with every aspect of western culture—because this does not seem to be the case either (especially since many of the areas we normally associate with the west have their origin in—and from—Africa—thus, to reject these aspects would be to reject "yourself")—but the restoration of Africa can be viewed as the first real step in a series of progressions that will have a profound effect on the reality—and reality potential dynamics—of black people, and also the dynamics of political transformation for the composite humanity. It is, of course, impossible to forecast how a particular move toward transition will actualize, for by transition, in this context, I am commenting on the actions and motives of individual people. For this reason, it would not be to my advantage to comment on the particulars of present-day African progressionalism. One thing is clear—the present reality of Africa seems to imply there will be many more struggles in the coming cycle—ten to twenty years (and probably longer). Moreover, if the optimum reality tone vibration for Africa has to do with how greater unification can be brought about, then quite possibly the time period to transformation must be extended to an even longer period. For it must be understood that the previous transformation achieved in Africa brought about a profound separation between various groups of people—regardless of sector. The progressional continuum of those separations have made present-day Africa all the more difficult to unify—and this is true for several other sectors of the planet as well. The realness of these divisions must be viewed as the result of how transformation was carried out in Africa (in actual terms). To view Africa in this time cycle is to look at how the dynamics of transformation have affected the composite region—and this effect is not separate from the reality position of black people all over the planet. It is because of this total phenomenon that Africa occupies such an important position for all black people. The resolidification of this region will have far-reaching consequences for the world community—affecting both the nature of information dynamics (investigation) as well as the move to construct alternative functionalism.

China

The reality and political dynamics of China must also be viewed as directly related to the composite realness of transformation. For not only does this area of the planet house almost a third of the world's people, but the progressional continuum of Chinese culture has offered much to the composite world group—and promises even more. The realness of what this means will become especially clear in the next cycle, for at present, many factors seem to be changing China's relationship to the composite world community. The nature of what this change will mean in actual terms will greatly affect the forming of the next transformation—because China is in an excellent position for affecting dynamic functionalism in this time cycle. So real is the position of China in this period that any attempt to deal with changing political functionalism in the late seventies and eighties would imply understanding the special role of Chinese functionalism. What this will mean in the future is, of course, impossible to speculate; but one thing is clear—the realness of Chinese functionalism is not separate from what the collective world community will be dealing with in the next cycle. China will have much to offer the composite world community, and the nature of how this cycle proceeds will have a profound effect on world politics for quite some time. The immediate future can be viewed as extremely interesting on many different levels—because already the progressional continuum of world political events has witnessed a surprise from this great country. There can be no doubt that the nature of events taking place in this period will unfold into many new areas of information dynamics.

MP(II)–22

The last forty years have seen many changes come and go in the political reality of Chinese culture, and all of these changes are important for what it signifies about alternative functionalism. This is so because the progressional continuance of Chinese—and Japanese too, for that matter—politics can be viewed with respect to what it poses to source transfer—and affinity dynamics. China has shown itself to be extremely sophisticated in its ability to transfer given systems and philosophies into its system without necessarily losing its primary essence—and cultural base. Even more amazing is China's ability to make dynamic changes throughout its total culture in relatively short time cycles—and make it work. Many of us in the west have not understood the sophistication underlying what these changes really mean, for the last forty years—and some—has shown China to be a great and vibrant culture. This is not to say that every particular aspect in China can be viewed as necessarily positive—but where on this planet can the composite factors which make up what we call reality be viewed as all positive—but rather, the progressional continuance of Chinese culture has shown itself to be an important factor related to the dynamics of world culture. The flexibility China has shown in the past forty years must be viewed as a strong signal about the vitality of its total culture group—as well as its spirit. China has shown that various elements of western culture can be adopted without necessarily having to sacrifice "the move towards transformational culture." This ability to understand trans-information is not separate from China's ability to use particular political and functional theories of the west as models for the establishment of new approaches to its own functionalism. The move towards Marxism can be viewed in this same context, and this also seems to be the case with China's recent overtures to the west (American and Europe). It is clear that the next cycle of world functionalism—politics—will see China continuing to play an active and important role. At present, China can be viewed with respect to the special position that both the Soviet Union and America have—that being, the third entry of a super power state. The realness of this country plays an important role in balancing the functionalism of both America and the Soviet Union—and this role is important. Moreover, it cannot be ignored that China also has another role in geo-political existence. For China is the only major power that cannot be perceived as western and is not defined and controlled by European or Euro-American caucasians. To understand this is to be aware of the special position non-caucasian people are in during this cycle. The fact that China is Asian does not necessarily mean anything in itself—but if we are to understand what has happened in this cycle to the composite world group, then we are forced to deal with what the exclusion of non-white people has come to mean in both vibrational and actual terms. It would be extremely difficult to comment on what the realness of Chinese political policy will signify—with respect to its indigenous Asian postulation particulars—for the composite actualness of this phenomenon is vibrationally multi-dimensional, but if the concept of affinity dynamics does indeed have relevance—as an idea that comments on the relationship of both doing and perception with respect to how particular peoples (or groups of people) perceive of phenomena—then most certainly the present position of China is necessarily important—for what it signifies about the balance of power—and affinities—in this period.

The recent establishment of normal relations between China and the United States will be interesting for what it poses for geo-political strategies. The realness of this relationship threatens to affect the composite platform of political events in the late seventies—and eighties. Hopefully this new relationship will make it possible for cross-sectional information to develop in both countries—involving every segment of information dynamics—as opposed to only politicians. There are many areas of important information that can be interchanged between different cultures—regardless of focus. It would be extremely useful if creative people could somehow find ways to meet and communicate about alternative possibilities for world culture. There are many people in both America and China who would be interested in exchanging countries to study the other's creativity (and culture)—but this is only the beginning. The political dynamics surrounding what is now taking place in this cycle between China and the western world must be viewed as extremely important for how it can affect the future. One thing is certain: China will continue to function as an important factor in the next transformation.

MP(II)–24
Middle East

The dynamics surrounding developments in the Middle East must be viewed as extremely relevant for transitional and transformational politics. Many of the developments reshaping this sector of the planet will have important implications for future continuance of world peace and transformation. At the present, there are many dynamic problems concerning both the political and vibrational state of many sectors—and regions—of the Middle East, but there is also the hope that the functionalism taking place in the cycle might lay the groundwork for a real peace. Certainly, the developments shaping this cycle will have far-reaching consequences for the future. The intensity of the forces functioning in this cycle have created a serious situation that will call for sensitive understanding and trust. Yet to really view the composite picture of the Middle East is to see that there is also reason to have hope for positive change. It is my belief that the near future will see the emergence of composite and universal unification throughout the whole of this region. Yet if I have written that it will be some time before Africa can finally assume its rightful position in world functionalism, so too must I state that the present reality particulars of the Middle East seem to imply a longer time cycle to really solve its composite situation.

The actual world position of the Middle East is extremely interesting for what it implies about alternative functionalism. For over half of the world's known oil supplies come from this region—which is to say—every sector of the planet has an interest in the Middle East. The realness of this planet region has totally affected the composite worlds' economic system, and at present no one has really found a way to get around what this effect has posed. The progressional continuance of this phenomenon is directly related to what planet options the Middle East has in actual terms. That being, the present reality of events is directly related to how Middle Eastern functionalism is perceived. The use of petro dollars as a means to change the composite dynamics of culture is the most basic factor that will dictate how many countries in this sector can proceed rebuilding.

The nature underlying how western functionalism is adopted will be of utmost importance and, as such, the progressional development of the Middle East can be viewed in much the same context as China. That being, the use of western functionalism—and technology—as a means to rebuild and "modernize" while avoiding the related reality posture of American anti-culture. The eventual unification of this sector of the planet promises to have a profound effect on world developments—for this sector of the planet has always been spiritually rich and dynamic.

But the dynamics of the Middle East are not limited to any one focus, for the realness of this region has much to offer the composite world group. The creativity that has solidified in this region must be viewed as a dynamic addition to world culture because of its overwhelming diversity. One can only imagine what this planet sector will contribute to future creative developments. To view the progressional continuum of creative music offered from the people in this region is to be reminded of the uniqueness of the Middle East. This is true for Jewish and Arab cultures, Christians and Muslims, notated or improvisational functionalism, or folk or secular musics. All of the various people in this region have profoundly contributed to earth creativity—and this is true regardless of time zone. The whole of the Middle East must be viewed for what its progressional continuance promises in the next cycle. Very few Americans have any idea about the creativity from this region (because the collective forces of western culture have isolated world perception dynamics to the degree that few Americans are even aware that other focuses are happening), and hopefully the forming of the next cycle will see this dilemma change. There will be much for us to learn about—from the progressional realness of this sector's creativity to the dynamics of its extended spiritual music (and dance). Undoubtedly, the political realities of this time cycle will dictate how and when communications can be developed between this region and the world group. There have been many hopeful signs that hint of positive movement towards peace and unification in the Middle East—and hopefully a composite peace can be attained in the near future for all of its various countries.

South America

For South America to be as close to the United States as it is, one would probably presume there are many similarities between both regions—but this is not the case. The United States has never had any real interest in South America and her various cultures (and dynamics). In fact, it is amazing how little communication has developed—or not developed—between these neighboring regions. The only relationships the United States has developed in South America are for business and political interests. Any attempt to understand the present political cycle of South America would involve the degree to which this relationship is corrected. This is not to say the United States is the only factor that has dictated the reality options of South America—because obviously there are many other factors—but the dynamics of the U.S.'s political involvement in South America cannot be viewed as positive on any level. The present time zone in South America can be viewed as extremely difficult for what it signifies in actual terms. At present, there seems to be much turmoil in this region of the planet and, as such, the immediate future of South America seems to forecast struggle on many levels. The reality situation of Chile can be viewed as only one example of what many of our South American neighbors are dealing with. Yet I do not mean to only paint a picture of despair about this region, for what we seem to be witnessing in South America is the beginning of new alliances—that being, the seeds of positive alternative functionalism are now being planted.

It is somewhat difficult to comment on the particulars of composite South America, because there are no sources other than the western press to draw from. But the impression I have in general is that there seems to be a progressional move by the general public to change their existing political situation as well as the political alliances related to how those situations developed. The picture that has emerged in this time zone seems to suggest that many underground movements have materialized as a means to become involved in actual functionalism. The western news media has in many cases labeled these groups subversive, and most certainly the functionalism resulting from some of the policies I have read about are indeed not "spiritual" either. This is not to say I endorse the composite spectrum of alternative functionalism as practiced in South America or the U.S.—but rather, the seriousness of what is now taking place in this region cannot be simply changed by playing badminton. The challenge of the next cycle of South American progressionalism is not separate from whether or not alternative functionalism is successful.

The creativity from this region can be viewed as both dynamic and necessarily relevant for world transformation. There has long been a continuum of diversified creativity from South America—extending from both its folk music to "contemporary" forms. Even the popular and commercial creativity from this region functions with a more meaningful relationship to composite culture than in the United States. Music has always been an important factor in the actual life imprint of this region—and in many ways, South America's cultural affinity use of creativity resembles Africa. Hopefully the next transition cycle will see the discovery of South America creativity by the world group. The progressional realness of creativity from this sector will be important for what it teaches us about affinity dynamics—as well as cultural and life (living) dynamics. For no matter the particular medium, to view the creativity actualized from South America is to see a diversified multi-thrust that doesn't function as a cultural spectacle factor, but rather as a cultural life sustainer. The discovery of this region's creativity can hopefully serve as basis for realigning the total realness of this planet sector (the Americas, and later the planet). For the actualness of creativity is not separated from the vibrational affinity alignment of culture—which is to say, a better understanding—and exposure—of South American culture could hopefully serve as a positive basis for re-examining the reality of political functionalism—and this is what is needed. Hopefully the next cycle will see the acceleration of South America as a power in its own right, and in becoming so, this acceleration will not be separate from whether or not its alternative functionalism can be practiced. The progressional continuance of South America can be viewed as directly related to transformation—and real world unification. One thing is certain: the neglect this continent has suffered cannot go on indefinitely—sooner or later, the world group will have to deal with this region of the planet. The major difference next time will be that South

Americans will be defining their own reality terms—as an equal to any region on the planet. In doing so, the total nature of geo-politics will be greatly changed.

Cuba

It has now been twenty years and some since Cuba declared her independence, and any attempt to deal with the realness of progressional geo-politics would imply that the revolution which transformed this region is dealt with and understood on some level. This is especially true if we are to observe the progressional forces related to how this time continuum seems to be unfolding. The realness of Cuba signifies what is most real about change-possibilities, and even more important, the reality of this change has not been one-dimensional but has involved its composite information dynamics. Cuba can now be viewed as one of the most exciting countries in this sector. Here is a culture developing at an incredible pace on a number of levels—especially with respect to cultural affinity postulation. The seeds underlying the solidification of this phenomenon are not separate from the progressional route of world culture change. Because Cuba, and its experience during the last twenty years, must be viewed as being in the vanguard of those countries who are establishing alternative realities—which is to say, there is much world culture can learn from this one country.

Many Americans in this cycle have been given the impression that Cuba has suffered greatly from her decision to form a transformational government. But to view the last twenty years of this country is to reconsider that impression. This is not to say every Cuban has a color television set, or that the culture vibrates to the U.S.'s relationship to technology, because this does not seem to be the case. Cuba cannot be viewed as a "rich" country in the sense we see the U.S.—that being, economically rich. Rather, the richness that is Cuba has to do with the spirit of its culture—having to do with the establishment of functional politics that sustain and develop real culture, and real progressional change. This is not to say everything related to present-day Cuba is perfect—because Cuba is no different from composite humanity—but the achievement of the Cuban people must be respected. There is much emphasis on learning—about the country's history, about creativity, as well as other areas of information (e.g., science, etc.). As such, Cuba must be viewed for both what has happened in the last twenty years and for how that same period has shaped its future progressionalism. The progressional implications of this phenomenon should not be taken lightly. For many of us in the U.S. have come to have a non-functional understanding of time progressions. Twenty years is a very short period of time in the life of a country—let alone the life of a vibrational time period. The nature underlying how countries like Cuba have utilized the last time cycle should not be taken lightly—rather, the great changes which have occurred must be viewed with respect for what they tell us about the people and their future. I have long been impressed at the emphasis Cubans have put on both creativity and athletics—as well as education and future extension. Obviously the people did not intend to build an alternative political reality without a cultural foundation. The realness of what is happening in Cuba is an important lesson for world culture.

Changing Reality of World Politics

The changing reality of world politics cannot be viewed in narrow terms, because many different factors are related to how given periods are "ised." But if we are to really understand the realness of creativity—and what this subject means in actual terms—then it is important to attempt viewing what factors seem to be of special importance—with respect to change, or potential change. One thing is certain: this period in time—like all periods—is subject to change, and if there is any one factor that seems to be consistent with how the universe functions, that factor would be that change is inevitable. As such, the realness of this time zone is not outside of the natural or unnatural dynamic of cosmic law. If we are to understand the progressional potential of creativity as a life-giving factor then we are forced to view this subject with respect to how given progressions seem to be transforming. In other words, we must look at the reality of creativity with respect to what factors seem to be forming in the next cycle. The realness of this viewpoint can better help us understand what political functionalism means as well, for the meta-reality implications of creativity are connected to—and gain their significance from—its principle essence formation (having to do with both principle vibrationaltory center factors—attitudes—and their spiritual and mystical implications). In other words, every creative projection has insight as to the actualness of political functionalism. To view the nature underlying the coming change cycle is to view what factors are forming in both actual and vibrational (dynamic) terms, as well as how those factors relate to actual policy.

VT.U.PT.-----POST.

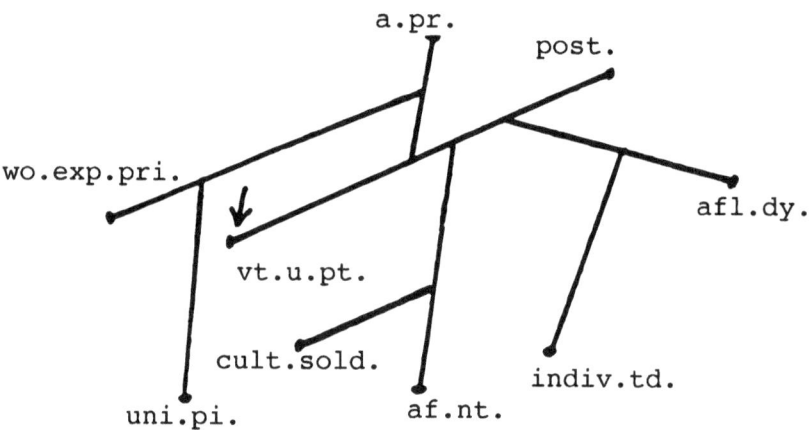

PRI.INFO. ------LK.IMP.

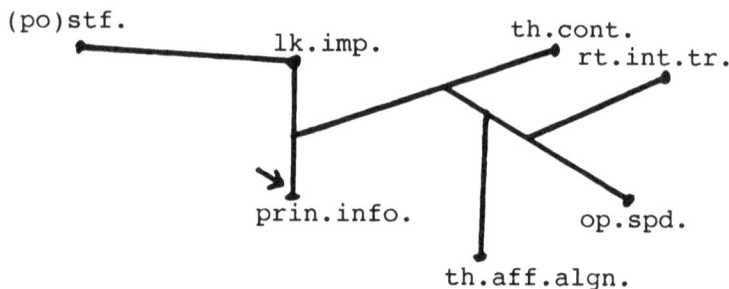

Without doubt, one of the most basic factors that signals how a given political reality is to survive is the question of power source—or in this case, energy. To view the present reality of events in this cycle is to see the nature underlying how functionalism is utilized—and this is especially true in politics. Because the realness of energy is not confined only to one area or focus—for this consideration permeates the total fabric of contemporary politics. No wonder the dynamics of the Middle East have assumed such importance. Many people in the west have somehow come to believe that the natural order of events on the physical universe level will remain constant—and in believing this, few people are aware of the crisis that looms on the horizon. If the oil shortage of the sixties proved anything, it showed very clearly how fragile western culture is with respect to the realness of energy. Yet somehow people still seem to believe that the basic laws of the universe do not apply to western culture—and that somehow the dynamics of energy consumption is not as serious as it seems to be. Unless real awareness is solidified in the near future, there will be many areas of the west totally unprepared for the next twenty to thirty years. The factors related to this phenomenon are indeed political, for the average American stakes his assumption of everlasting energy from the belief that American politics is designed to properly deal with reality decisions. And there are many reasons for this faith (none of which are valid).

But the energy crisis is not simply a political ploy, or at least, the dynamics of the next time cycle are not about politics as usual. The realness of our situation can simply be reduced to numbers—that being, there is only so much oil and coal on a planet, and unless used wisely, this source of energy will naturally deplete (even if used wisely, this source will naturally deplete). I am not writing that the reality of energy threatens to dry up tomorrow, because this does not seem to be the case either, but the seriousness of our present relationship to energy seems to suggest problems for the future. The political implications of this dilemma are obvious. For the reality of political functionalism is not separate from what alliances are made—as well as what policies are initiated. One would have to be extremely naive to not know that the situation in Iran (at the end of the seventies) is not separate from the tampering of western powers—and in particular the United States. This can be made especially real if one considers the question of world information—and in particular, the crisis of the American dollar—or by examining the dynamics of political relationships (e.g., the use of installing puppet governments as a means to influence the political reality of a given planet or cultural sector). Any attempt to deal with the dynamics of world politics at the close of the seventies must take into account all of these factors and more. It is not simply a question of the policies of one given country—nor have I meant to single out only the United States at the expense of the whole planet (and the present power alignments of this time cycle)—rather, it is a question of viewing how political functionalism has helped to expand the material and geographical reality of western culture, while progressively crushing the life options of composite world culture. The nature underlying how these various progressions have actualized is indeed related to the realness of politics, and this concerns the whole of humanity.

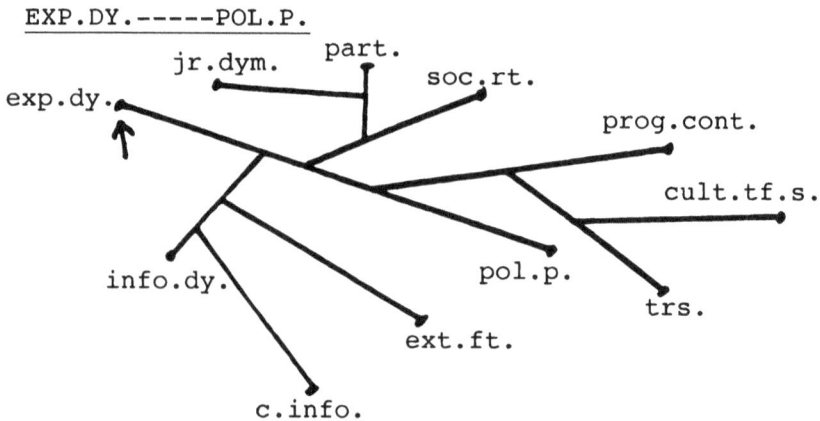

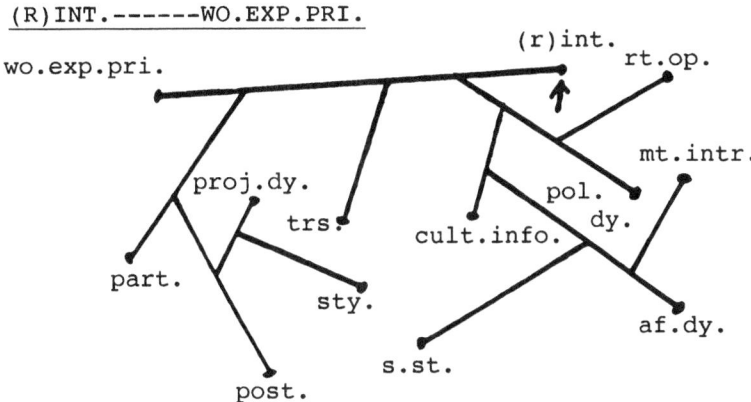

If the reality of energy is a factor that has special importance in this cycle, then the resultant effects generated from this subject must be isolated and understood. For the energy question is not separate from the functionalism it has necessitated in actual terms. Thus if we are to understand what has happened to our environment, then we are forced to view the composite implications of politics. The fact is, the basic policies western culture is pursuing in this cycle are directly related to what is happening to our environment. It is not just a question of exhausting the planet's natural resources—obviously we are doing just that—rather, the ecological implications of political functionalism must be viewed as directly related to the coming dilemma we are leaving our children to face. In this light, we must ask the questions— "What is happening to our air?"—"What is happening to the beautiful rivers and lakes of this planet?"—"What will become of this planet unless serious changes are made?" The reality of ecology in this period is the biggest joke of the year. For most people, this subject is not even relevant as a side issue of minor importance. The last fifteen years and some only echo this dilemma, for ecology, like civil rights, was the subject of the hour in the middle sixties—and as such, many political decisions were made to supposedly deal with dynamic change. But as we enter the eighties, it is clear little has been done— with respect to either education or actual functional policy. By the time western culture makes the decision to really deal with the realness of ecological dynamics, we will be living on an asteroid.

It is important to understand that the progressional realness of distorted politics is responsible for the forces now gathering in the next cycle. The fact that western politics have yet to deal with the challenge of ecology—as a real area of legitimate concern—cannot be overlooked, because in bypassing this subject, western politics have failed in their responsibility to the culture. The seriousness of this failure will have a lasting effect on life potential, for the nature of its related effects will profoundly affect future progressionalism. The dynamics of responsible politics must extend to every area of cultural welfare. This subject is not separate from the construction of nuclear reactors without considering its long-term implications to the region, country or planet. It is one thing to make a mistake in an automobile accident, or to fall on your head—but it's quite another thing to build a nuclear reactor and discover a given design was not correct (or safe) after the reactor destroys a total community in a single blast. Not to mention, no one has really solved the problem of nuclear waste materials in a rational way either. All of these particulars are not separate from the dynamics of responsible politics—and all of these particulars are not separate from what the total world group will have to deal with in the next cycle. It is for this reason that politics cannot be simply overlooked and unquestioned, for the composite realness of this subject touches all of our lives—on every level.

The progressional continuum of world politics has seen many changes in the last fifty years—and as such, to write on this subject is to write of a diversity of cross-relationships. Certainly the inter-relationship of politics to big business is as old as the subject itself—for this phenomenon can be viewed throughout the whole of cultural history. The fact is, politics is a direct outgrowth of the business of the culture it represents—and in itself, the reality of this relationship is not separate from what—or how—a given culture "is." But the nature of this inter-relationship has changed in the last thirty years (and some), and if we are to understand the present realness of contemporary politics then this difference must be commented on. For the last thirty years has seen the rise of extended functionalism in the western business community (regardless of context or focus), and this change has directly affected the nature underlying how business is now perceived and practiced. With the solidification of multi-national corporations, the dynamic continuum of geo-politics has moved to a new level. So real has this change been that any attempt to understand the particulars of present-day political functionalism implies that the emergence of multi-national corporations is focused on—and the complexity of this phenomenon can be understood by viewing the nature of its expansion in even the last thirty years. This is so because to view a corporation like International Telephone & Telegraph or General Motors is to see another level of both diversification and activism. The solidification of multi-national business functionalism must be viewed for how it has affected the political decisions of this time continuum, as well as for what those decisions mean for world culture. This is particularly true if we are to understand the position world culture is presently in— with regard to economics and/or development. The rise of multi-national business structures can be viewed as a progressional factor related to how western culture has expanded. The solidification of this phenomenon can also tell us something about the reality options of third world alternative functionalism. For the most basic viewpoint one can have about this subject is that by solidifying accelerated functionalism in this context, western culture has moved to secure its hold on the total planet. The rise of multi-national corporations is only the fastest development of a much greater progressional phenomenon.

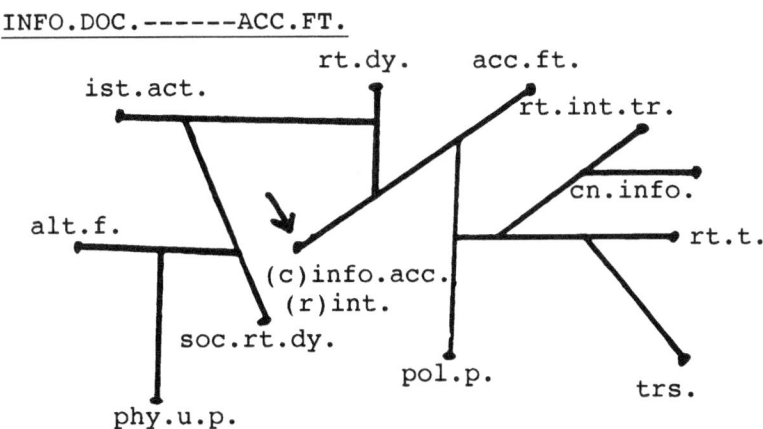

The development of multi-national corporations also accents the much deeper question of whether the composite political machinery of a culture is a tool for the decision-making responsibility of its culture group or whether that machinery is the functional arm of a given country's functionalism—or business. Certainly this might not necessarily be true, but it is questionable if the decisions affecting governmental policy can function in the long run without respect to the greater dynamics of its multi-business complex. Obviously this is true. Because in practically every case, the people who are elevated to serve in important political contexts are the same people who have much to lose if their multi-national investments are damaged. The policies resulting from this relationship are obvious—and if we are to really view the last twenty years with this relationship in mind, then quite possibly one can better interpret the dynamics of western political functionalism—whether or not it is morally uplifting. This is not to say every political decision in the past cycle has been based on multi-national interest, but this is to say the realness of multi-national power politics has completely permeated the composite fabric of western politics—and its resultant functionalism. Moreover, no political decision of consequence can be viewed as separate from the composite area of controlling factors related to what a multi-national company really is. Because among other things, politics is about power—and economics.

(R)PHY.U.FUND.------POL.DYM.

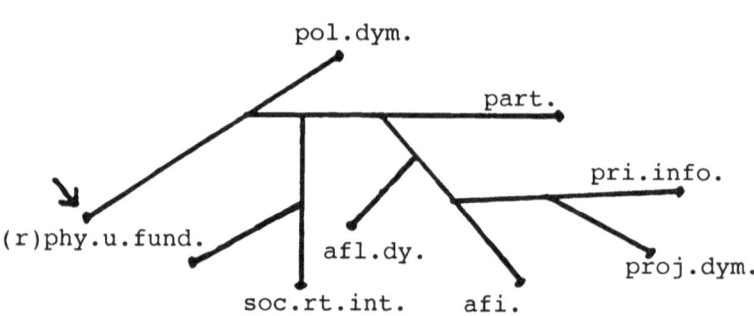

MP(II)–37

The changing reality of world politics is directly related to the transition western culture—and in particular, America—is now undergoing. For if the realness of power politics and the rise of multi-national control are indicative of what has transpired in the last time cycle, then the effect of this phenomenon has also solidified a particular response from the world community. This is not to say the world's community has solidified a response (or policy) to this phenomenon—because it hasn't. Rather, the progressional continuance of this time cycle has moved to create a definite vibrational response from the world community—having to do with its perception of western culture—and the three so-called super-powers. And while most Americans continue to view the planet with respect to what is most beneficial to them, slowly but surely, the world community is moving to change its position. It is this change which interests me, for the realness of transition is not mono-dimensional; moreover, the west is not the only sector that can utilize dynamic change—because everyone and everything vibrates to this phenomenon. While it is too early to draw definite conclusions about what the nature of the next transfer cycle will be, it is clear that the world community is slowly moving to deal with alternative functionalism—as a means to change their position.

The reality dynamics of world culture can be viewed by looking at what is happening in the United Nations. The vibrational atmosphere of this forum has changed very radically in the last twenty years, and a definite political pattern has slowly emerged. This is not to say every collective position taken by the world community is for humanity or necessarily correct, but rather, the fact that smaller countries are no longer intimidated by the superpowers is in itself a positive development. One thing is clear: a marked separation has developed between the composite interest of world culture and the so-called superpowers. Whether or not this schism is as significant as I perceive it to be, the nature of present-day political functionalism is changing—and I believe this is just the beginning. The hope of transformation is directly related to whether the move towards world unification can be realized. Nor am I implying that world culture can afford to or should (whether it can afford to or not) exclude any particular segment of humanity—including the west; rather, the forming alliances now taking place must be viewed as a progressional tool for composite change. Clearly the west cannot be counted on to change the imbalance it has benefited from (not to mention it helped to create). The challenge of the next cycle must fall on those countries which have been affected most by this cycle—and which, in the final analysis, have no choice but to become activists. Unless the pattern of progressional continuance in this period is checked, world culture will continue to pay for the advantages western culture enjoys, and this cannot go on indefinitely without extinction. Before the next level of composite functionalism emerges, there will be many different levels of struggle in the near future. However, the fact is, these struggles have already been taking place—for a much longer time than most of us are aware of. The particulars underlying present-day earth dynamics involve many different factors—having to do with hundreds of years (that being, the composite progressional factors related to geo-politics). For this reason, the reality actualness of politics must be viewed as necessarily related to not only the state of given creative projections, but must include the future of the planet itself. To be involved in creativity (and creative postulation) is to be involved in positive functionalism—and as such, the consideration of politics is not separate from what this involvement means in actual physical universe terms.

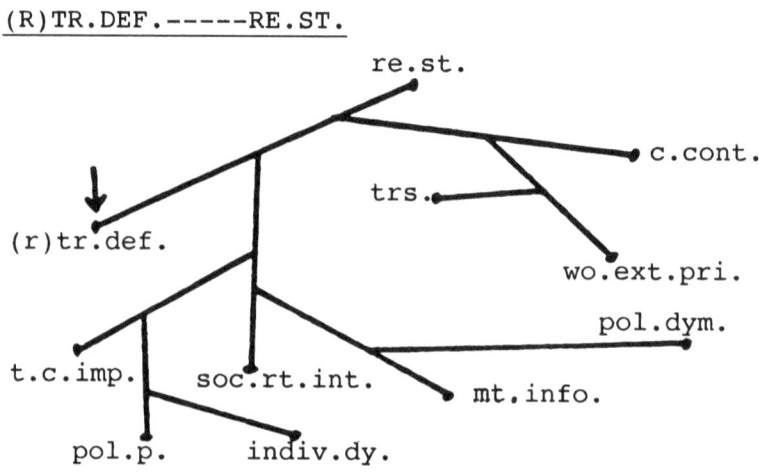

The Effects of Western Expansionism

If we are to view earth with respect to how given change cycles seem to be manifested, then our observation must also take into account the nature of perceived expansionism—regardless of focus or region (because every time period has witnessed the dynamics of this phenomenon). This is true for the progressional solidification of Egyptian culture as well as the progressional growth of the Roman Empire. The nature of this phenomenon in all cases is directly accompanied by the realness of both re-documentation and cross-transfer progressionalism. To view the realness of this time period seems to also indicate that very little has changed since Rome, for the reality particulars of super-power nations is very different from the reality particulars underlying life in the third-world countries. Certainly the clearest example of this difference can be understood by examining what takes place in actual confrontation (or war), because in every case, small countries (even if not involved in the actual conflict that led to the war) are ravaged simply because they are small and without defense. This phenomenon is not separate from what expansionism really poses for smaller countries—because there are no defenses against the forces large countries now have. But as horrible as outright invasion is, there are also many other factors related to this phenomenon—and the end result of what those factors bring about are in many cases equally as horrible as confrontational destruction. To view the realness of geo-politics in this cycle is to deal with the multi-dimensional implications of expansionism.

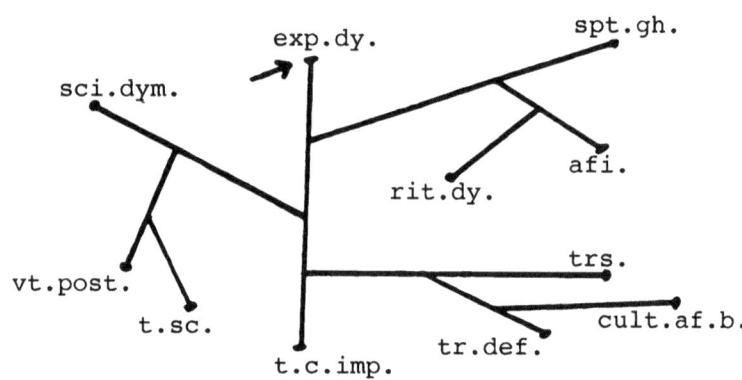

The progressional continuance of this time cycle can be viewed with respect to what western expansion particulars have solidified in the last three hundred years. For when I wrote that the present cycle can be viewed as dynamically beneficial to western culture exclusively, I did not mean this lightly. It is not simply a question of examining the material wealth of the planet, for the particulars of this subject go much deeper than the surface reality surrounding one-dimensional functionalism. The effects of western expansionalism have permanently altered the basic continuance of every sector of this planet. This phenomenon is not limited to the unequal distribution of material wealth but extends into the sophistication that surrounds re-information and applied definitions. To view the realness of western expansionalism is to view the multi-complexual implications underlying what control has meant to: (1) the redocumentation of a given culture's meta-sensibility, (2) the disintegration of a given culture center, (3) the overwhelming influence of media programming, and (4) the move to drain a given culture's natural resources. To understand the realness of political expansionalism is to deal with all of these variables, and this is just the beginning.

By "redocumentation of a given culture's meta-sensibility," I am referring to the second level of progressional transition. For the seriousness of this phenomenon has a much more profound impact on a given culture's longevity than naked aggression. The realness of this type of expansionalism directly affects the heartbeat of what a given group or culture group is all about. "Meta-sensibility transfer" is my phrase for the progressional functionalism that seeks to gradually reorient a given people or culture to foreign affinity alignments. The use of this technique can be understood as the first level of security against resurrection—that being, cultural resurrection against a given invader. The realness of meta-sensibility transfer can be viewed in the same basic context as "affinity transfer"—but the most basic difference would be that one is forced and the other isn't.

The use of sensibility transfer can better be understood if the sophistication of modern-day colonialism is examined. For this phenomenon functions as the first safeguard against the possibility of cultural-rebound. That being, the use of meta-sensibility transfer serves as a dynamic programming vehicle for brainwashing. Yet I have not meant to imply that the use of this technique can be brought about in a relatively short time zone—because it can't. The use of sensibility transfer must be viewed for how its use over a given time period progressively moves to dampen—and later suppress—a given culture's view of itself. It is because of the use of this technique that colonial powers have had such success—especially in this time period. For the use of sensibility transfer moves to reorient a given culture's affinity dynamics to the degree where that culture can no longer relate to what it was—or how it was. Yet I am not commenting on the use of source-transfer progressional techniques as such, for the realness of sensibility transfer does not necessitate that a given cultural group's physical and social universe situation has the actual opportunity to practice re-orientation. In other words, the use of sensibility transfer can be viewed as a phenomenon related to the dynamics of source transfer (or simply transfer shifts), but the actual result of its use doesn't give the possibility for objects of its focus to actually participate from its criteria. The end result of forced imposition is that the people of the culture are suddenly without base—without real control of their homeland or use of their homeland, vibrating to information dynamics of an alien culture, and even worse—unable to really practice (or live) what this re-orientation affirms. Because in order to vibrate to the dynamics of western culture values, one has to first have the means—and in those cases where the colonialists are not western, there is still the problem of "transfer values"—which is to say, no matter who the aggressor is, the use of sensibility transfer cannot be viewed as positive. Thus the redocumentation of a culture's meta-sensibility has to do with how the affinity dynamics of a given culture is reshaped by colonial powers—to the degree that the total reality of that culture group is affected. The progressional use of this technique can be viewed for how it eventually moves to re-evaluate that culture's perception of itself—which is to say, after a given time zone, the use of sensibility transfer moves to make a given culture group see itself as "less." The success of a given colonial expansion is directly related to whether or not its use of sensibility transfer is effective. For the successful use of this technique can ensure years of relatively easy exploitation—and of course this is exactly what has been happening. There are many countries from the world community that are only now starting to recover from the use of this technique. The progressionalism and dynamics surrounding "recovering from colonialism" is what we are witnessing in this time zone, and this phenomenon is important if we are to understand what is now happening in forums like the United Nations.

The "disintegration of a culture's center" is the juncture where actual expansionism can take hold—and as such become real. The dynamics of this phenomenon are directly related to sensibility transfer in the sense that both can be viewed in sequential terms. Disintegration in this context can be viewed as the second sequence of expansionism (of a successful expansionism)—for the arrival of this juncture has already signified the success of its first degree (that being sensibility transfer). Disintegration as a second degree of expansionism speaks for itself—that being, this is the zone where a given culture has successfully been co-opted as such—and while there is always the possibility of recovery, it is not easy. This then is the cycle where actual source transfer can be applied—and after a given time zone, a given culture's perception of itself is suppressed. The actualness of disintegration has occurred many times on this planet—in other words, the progressional continuity of world history seems to suggest that many cultures have come and gone—some by natural tragedy—most by disintegration. The dynamics of this phenomenon have to do with how, after a given time cycle, the indigenous people of a given culture can no longer relate to what they once were, or in many cases can't remember what they once were. After a given time cycle, people who have had everything taken from them eventually move towards being ashamed of either what they were—or how they were. Yet I do not mean this in light terms, for surely the dynamics of disintegration is not one-dimensional by any means. But if we are to really understand expansionalism, then it is important to view this phenomenon with respect to what it really signifies in the lives of actual people. For the changing reality of world politics is based on the nature underlying how transitions occur—having to do with more factors than many of us would like to admit. This has been the case for the whole of recorded history and nothing has changed in this period.

The realness of expansionalism has to do with many factors—all of which are political. If we would view the progressional continuance of Africa through the last five hundred years, we could begin to understand what political functionalism really means. For if sensibility transfer represents the first most basic principal to establish colonialism—and as such, the first necessary juncture to secure expansionalism—leading to disintegration as the completion of source transfer, then the realness of this phenomenon must be viewed for what it implies about the dynamics of political objective. The fact is, the success of a given expansionalism is directly related to how a given culture group has come to perceive survival—that being, the nature underlying how expansionalsim is practiced on earth has to do with a profound sense of separation. As such, the realness of this phenomenon is in opposition to the dynamics of world transformation. For if the concept of transformation has to do with unification as a means for human beings to deal with existence on this planet—having to do with sharing the natural resources of the planet as a means to collectively experience this sector in space, then expansionalism has to do with moves to functionally secure a given area of the planet as a means to—in most cases—exploit what is best (or "most") about that environment for the people of the aggressive culture only. The use of this type of expansionalism can be viewed as being in accordance to the basic vibrationaltory flaws we have come to accept as being natural—or "what life is all about." The nature of political expansionalism in this cycle can be viewed as not separate from the basic flaws permeating this time cycle—that being, "planet isolation" and "despirituality." Yet the progressional realness of physical universe law necessitates that if this planet is to ever gain a composite change of consciousness (to a higher level), then the present reality tone level must first be dealt with. In other words, it would not necessarily be effective to talk of brother- or sisterhood with a person setting your house on fire. The first necessary juncture to address in this context is to stop that person from burning your house down. The challenge of political functionalism in the next cycle can be viewed in the same terms. That being, the nature of the next level of positive functionalism will have to do with the utilization of progressional politics as a means to first deal with what is most immediate about "particular areas of disagreement," and to later move towards creating a platform that contains some kind of positive integration of affinity particulars. Until this is accomplished, we will continue to deal with the rise and fall of negative transformation. For this reason, the dynamics of political functionalism must be viewed as necessarily important—especially in this cycle. The spectrum particulars of this time zone seem to forecast only two real possibilities for the future of this planet. For with the discovery of nuclear principles and the development of new science, we have slowly come to the juncture where the next transformation will have serious repercussions for the total "isness" of this planet. This is not to say I have joined the doomsday group because I haven't. But if the collected forces of this planet really engaged in an all-out nuclear war, the nature of the next transformation cannot be viewed as an attractive alternative. Undoubtedly there will be survivors—or maybe there won't be—but life as we know it will probably be very different.

In actual terms, the realness of expansionalism can be viewed as a progressional tool of "source transfer," having to do with both the acquisition of land and the reshaping of affinity dynamics. Thus, if we are to really view the realness of political dynamics in this time zone, we are forced to observe the nature of what affinities are now being developed. It is because of the importance of alliances that new initiatives must be taken to move towards rebalancing the distribution of wealth. Poor countries can no longer be exploited to feed the superpowers if this planet is to have a positive future. The success of the next period will be directly related to whether or not the right alliances are made—and whether those alliances are undertaken with respect for what is spiritually and morally right. The use of source transfer in this regard must be understood as well. For if the concept of affinity dynamics comments on the "natural" attraction that particular groups, cultures and individuals have towards given information routes, then it is important that the progressional continuum of world politics not move to exploit this phenomenon. Obviously every country is impressed with the progressional particulars underlying how life is experienced in the west. This feeling is understandable. On the surface, western culture seems to have all of the benefits one could offer—and certainly western culture has many things to offer the world group. On the other hand, there are many things we can also learn from our neighbors—having to do with what we have lost on the road to modernizing (i.e., life). The nature underlying how cross-transfer affinities are approached in the next cycle will be of utmost importance, and the challenge of positive functionalism is not separate from whether sharing is utilized on a composite level. Because this has clearly not been the case up until this point.

The progressional continuance of expansionalism in this cycle can only be viewed with respect to how given areas of manipulation have been practiced. As such, we can look at how the sophistication of media has been utilized for affinity suppression. This is true for its use on the composite world front as well as at home. But in the case of world culture, the media has shown itself to be almost as successful as religion in helping to totally disenfranchise the center factor of given cultures. To understand this is to understand the seriousness of cultural breakage. For the most basic factor that has resulted from the use of sensibility transfer is the loss of cultural identity. This dilemma is accomplished by the use of mis-education, books, and, in this cycle, radio and television. The composite world group has yet to really recover from what this sensitivity manipulation has caused. Nor have I meant to only comment on the position of the west as opposed to many other sectors of the planet. The fact is, no one group is responsible for the present state of the planet, just as no one "particular" has dictated the composite reality of political functionalism. Moreover, the challenge of transformation cannot be the job of any one sector either. For the seriousness of the next cycle will call for nothing less than a world commitment to positive change. It is for this reason that as concerned citizens we must all become involved and aware of politics and political change. The realness of transformation implies that creative people must become aware of the composite dynamics of world culture—regardless of region. Only when this is done can we as people begin to reshape earth in accordance to what is "most" about all of us. The consideration we call politics is profoundly important.

(Level 3)

1. What is the political significance of western art music?

I am not exactly sure what is meant by this question. The political significance of western art music is undoubtedly connected to the position it enjoys as the recipient of the accented nature of composite western culture. This is true on several levels—having to do with both perception and support. For the reality position of western culture in this time zone has political control of the composite planet. The decisions of this one sector determine the particulars of composite economics, as well as distribution of wealth (and basic materials). As such, the realness of this phenomenon is directly related to the whole of how western culture has now moved to completely dominate the planet. The dynamics of this conquest are manifested on many different levels—for given interpretations by the world group will move to view western expansionism as a signal of its so-called superiority, and other viewpoints will view this same expansion as negative—but the most basic fact is, no one can ignore the realness of accented western culture. In this context, western art music is viewed as an affirmation of what western culture is—and there can be no doubt that it is a great music. As such, the present reality of composite earth moves to view western art, and all things western, as either somewhat superior to the rest of humanity or a testament to western greatness. Western art music has also benefited from its position in western political reality in its economic support. For the thrust of this music has been advanced through the spread and continuance of western success (i.e., the winning of war and its related expansion implications—or the achievements in western science—and the acquisition of material wealth—by whatever means) as well as the accented interpretation of western education (and affinity dynamic transference). The political significance of western art music would have to do with the fact that it (the music) can be used—like anything—to advance the interests of western culture, either vibrationally or actually. In itself this does not have to be negative (because there are as many intentions as there are people).

2. Can black people in America separate their destiny from black people outside the U.S.? Does Africa still play an important role for composite non-white people?

I do not believe that American black people—or any sector of black people for that matter—can afford to separate themselves from each other, and from Africa in particular. This is not to ignore the seriousness of isolated concerns and regional purposes, because everything is important. But the particulars of any one sector of black people must be viewed in both its separate and composite sense, because the nature of a given focus has its own reality dynamics, and the arena responsible for the composite state of non-white people is not separate. I believe the future of Africa will be extremely important to all people, both black and white, and I also believe a rebalancing of world power will be as important for white people as black people. The composite realness of all black people must be concerned about recovering everything that was lost—or taken—in Africa—because Africa is our home, and more important, our future. I believe that whatever our destiny is—as black people—it cannot be separated—which is to say, I do not believe black people can afford to (nor should they want to) view themselves as independent from the composite destiny of each other and of Africa. It is important to understand that the western cultural continuum has been designed for—and is about—white people, and I do not think this will ever change (as long as western culture is western culture). Still, I am not saying that black people should exclusively view themselves as Africans—but I am saying that black people should view themselves as Africans.

3. Would you say that the creative music that emerged in the sixties was a politically conscious music—or politically motivated?

I believe the creativity that emerged in the sixties certainly flowed with respect to politics, but I do not believe that the basic thrust underlying what the music was, was "about politics." Nor do I view this phenomenon as necessarily any different from the whole of black creativity and progressionalism (in the last two hundred years—and I would even guess, the last two thousand years). To understand my point is to broaden the context of this question. Because when I stated that black creativity in the sixties was no different than before, I was referring to the meta-reality dynamics and purpose of black creativity and its relationship to alternative functionalism. To write that the sixties creativity was politically aware is to not understand that every projectional continuum before the sixties was just as politically aware (and real)—even further (and this is what must be understood), the vibrational basis that determines any form of black creativity is not a one-dimensional criterion concerning "what is political" but instead a thrust continuance conceived with respect to "what is spiritual" and "what is to be done?" In other words, every form of black creativity has manifested some awareness of political consciousness, but the music is not about politics. Finally, the thrust continuance of black creativity in the last two thousand years must also be viewed for what it has transferred with respect to imprintation (in terms of what has transpired for humanity in general). The lining of this thrust continuum is much more profound than the one-dimensional concept of "politically motivated," because in actual fact the dynamic intent of all earth creativity flows "with a concern for humanity and what is most" about all of us.

4. On the physical universe plane, would you say the creative music that emerged in the sixties was politically motivated?

I do believe the dynamics of extended functionalism in the sixties were conceived with respect to "changing the reality nature" of this time zone, and as such the basic motivation of each succeeding projection (forms) in the last thirty years has been to restore the dynamic implications of the individual as well as the aesthetic. This intention can be interpreted as politically motivated. Political in the sense that a new order was needed to restore positive functionalism in the music—and in a greater sense, this motivation cannot be separated from what "solidification" (intention and science) poses to the physical universe aspect of this phenomenon. Because creativity is about the people who are creating—which is to say, the reality position of a given thrust alignment is not separate from the reality position of its base culture. But even in this context, I have not meant to imply that given individuals are necessarily thinking about politics—as we view the term in this time period. Because I do not believe this is how progressional continuance works, or—for that matter—creative people. Rather, the nature of politically motivated functionalism (and intentions) in this context has to do with the multi-relationship that permeates the reality dynamics of "creative participation": that being, the dynamic implications of "doing" and the dynamic implications of "wanting to do something positive." In the end, the cosmic arena really determines the nature of a participation.

5. Is western intellectualism a tool for sustaining the political arena of present-day western culture, and if so, what does this tell us about the reality of affinity insight (1) and affinity insight (2) principle continuance?

Western intellectualism can most certainly be viewed with respect to what it poses, or doesn't pose, for dynamic change. This is so because the core of this phenomenon is not really about solving or understanding in any real sense, but instead is more a tool for sustaining "interesting" at the expense of culture. As such, the reality of western intellectualism is interconnected with the basic continuance of western culture, because it supplies the discussion that substantiates each "diversion." Western intellectualism can also be viewed for what has happened in western progressional continuance—concerning the route of its creativity and the affinity-alignment implications of that creativity's state. The spectrum of divisions between its information dynamics is the first juncture directly related to what this phenomenon has established (i.e., affirmation of intellectualism). For the move towards total separation has underlined the emergence of the affinity insight (1) principle and the affinity insight (2) principle, and the composite reality of western cultural dynamics has been the loser in the final analysis. Because dynamic separation is not conducive for a composite spiritual society and/or "real" high culture. The accented separation of the affinity insight (1) and affinity insight (2) principle is consistent with the implications of this same phenomenon.

6. Is the present state of religion an obstacle to the dynamic implication of world transformation?

The reality of religion in this period—no matter how diverse—attempts to instill some link to the greater forces that dictate "what is," and this can only be viewed as positive. Yet I believe the future must see more tolerance from this sector for the right of different people to have different beliefs and religions. For the basic reality position of present-day world churches is that "either you see it my way or else," and while I can understand (to a point) the need for real doctrine, still, the changes reshaping our lives in this time period are much more profound than this sector seems to realize. I believe we are slowly moving towards a new spiritual state that will incorporate tenets from many different viewpoints. It is important for the church to take the lead in this new challenge, as opposed to being afraid of change (or pretending it doesn't exist). I write this because change will come whether or not this sector becomes involved—change will come whether anyone is involved (because change is not about "involved"). I cannot say the present state of religion is an obstacle to transformation (because there is much more to the realness of this question than I can properly deal with in this period of my life—I am not much in agreement with the religious particulars of the last two thousand, five hundred years, but on this I need more research and living time), but I cannot say that the present state of religion is conducive to transformation either.

7. Do you feel that the alternative organizations which emerged in the sixties represented the best approach to establishing a political base for creative music?

I believe any attempt to solidify a movement concerned about the composite state of transformation functionalism must be viewed as positive. Many of the collectives that emerged in the sixties represented a new beginning—of involvement—and this alone is important. Certainly there are many areas of improvement that must be brought about, and I have not mean to imply that sixties functionalism was without problems, because there were many. But the realness of organization must be viewed as a positive step towards dynamic functionalism, because the implications of involvement move from the particulars of individual dynamics to the particulars of the greater society (or at least this is how it should be). Organizations like the Jazz Composers Guild represented the first attempt towards this objective, and collectives like the AACM and Free Life Communication represented the second degree of involvement. Hopefully, the next degree of alternative functionalism will advance involvement to even greater heights.

8. Has racism been the major obstacle to dynamic collectivism?

I believe racism permeates the composite lining of western culture, involving every area of participation and focus—and any attempt to view the realness of western functionalism must necessarily come to terms with what this means. Yet, by the same token, I do not believe only one consideration can be viewed as the principal obstacle to the composite state of any criteria. Racism, as bad as it is, is only one consideration among many other considerations that must be dealt with. To say that racism is the major obstacle to dynamic collectivism is to deny the realness of what sexism has posed—to say that racism is the major obstacle to dynamic collectivism is to ignore the separation happening between black people and black people, and finally to say racism is the major obstacle to dynamic collectivism is to not deal with the flaws that caused the unsuccess of many multi-racial collectives. It seems to me that if there is any one factor that can be singled out as directly related to the "present state of things" (and even in this case, one cannot be too dogmatic), that consideration would be misinformation or unspirituality.

9. Will the emergence of third world countries affect the acceleration of world music dominance?

I believe the acceleration of world creativity is directly linked to the nature of the particular cycle we are now entering in this time period. For as we enter the eighties, the source-transfer convergence of world creativity is profoundly affecting the reality of creative options—which is to say, the basis for this acceleration has already been put in place. The present changes now taking place in the Middle East, for example, promise to profoundly affect the west in the next cycle—on more levels than we have come to expect. I believe that the dynamics of these events will move to accelerate not only the dictates of western creativity but composite western information. I believe this even though the realness of this phenomenon also promises to potentially bring about dynamic reaction—or inwards pull (resulting in a period of information negation towards world interpretation, and in reliance on "what is perceived as most western"). But in the end, it is inevitable that the impetus of third world functionalism will accelerate the solidification of composite transformation.

10. Do the so-called left political groups in America have a different understanding of the significance or role of creativity than the so-called establishment?

I really don't know. Not to mention, there are as many philosophies as there are political bases. I found in my own experiences that many of the so-called revolutionaries of the sixties had little or no understanding of the role of creativity in composite functionalism. The thrust of available viewpoints in this period covered Marxist interpretations, to the generalized "music is fun and life is fun" viewpoint, to the "music is revolution" wing, and finally, the "everything is everything" sector. This is not to say no practical functionalism was brought about from people or groups connected with so-called left sensibilities or philosophies, because in fact many people from all persuasions have functioned for positive change. Certainly the inner-city activism that resulted in the solidification of day-care centers and creative music programs must be viewed as important—and these changes were brought about through the efforts of politically motivated groups (and it is also important to state that this kind of activism could be indicative of what has been happening throughout the country—which, as such, does signal something about the nature of political involvement and/or motivation—but as to whether or not this phenomenon is related to the so-called left- or right-wing viewpoint is another question), but I still cannot say that any of these groups have necessarily developed any viewpoint on the reality position of creativity in philosophical or spiritual terms. In actual fact—at this point in time—I really don't know what's happening with this subject. I think this is my real answer.

11. If the time zone of the late seventies can be characterized as a period of American contraction—in response to the defeat of Vietnam (and social reality particulars)—then what has this introspection posed to the vibrational nature of its cultural identity (and taste)?

There can be no doubt that the events in Vietnam have profoundly affected composite life in America—on every level. Moreover, the realness of this tragedy has moved many Americans to question every aspect of their lives—and this is not necessarily negative at all. But the composite dynamics of this phenomenon are multi-complexual. Because the net effect of this phenomenon has moved the composite culture into a time warp whose collective affinity posture is attracted only to the past (as a means to sort out cultural identify and/or pride). But on the other hand, the disintegration of composite American precepts has helped stimulate interests in new forms and expanded world creativity in the so-called artistic community; and the dynamics of this research have moved to clarify and inspire the realness of spiritualism as well as world consciousness. As such, there is a very interesting opposition that has developed in American culture—or so-called culture—because on one hand the greater public has moved to withdraw into that which is perceived as being "most American," while on the other hand the dynamics of its creative community are moving towards world culture. I believe the eighties will clarify what this opposition means in real terms; because the nature of this phenomenon is also connected to the overall ineffectiveness of alternative functionalism (or alternative creative functionalism in this case). It is for this reason (among others) that extended creative music has such difficulty in amassing real support in America.

12. Can the new music in Europe be separated from the reality continuum of political dynamics in this region?

I believe it is imperative to view the vibrational emergence of European new music as a factor not separate from the composite theatre of present-day European continuance. I believe this because the nature of any phenomenon is not separate from the bases responsible for its beingness—or the particulars of a given phenomenon are necessarily intertwined with the composite dictates of its reality base. This is true for European creative music and any other form of music. I believe that the emergence of alternative functionalism in Europe has only just begun, and I also believe that the acceleration of affinity dynamic participation has only just revealed the tip of its iceberg—in terms of its ultimate meaning. We are slowly entering a period of dynamic change, involving the totalness of earth existence, and no region will be exempt from what this change will entail. The new music emerging in Europe must be viewed for what it implies about the whole of this phenomenon—having to do with its relationship to European particular dynamics as well as world culture. In other words, it will become increasingly difficult to view a given phenomenon with respect to only the particulars of its region—because the isolation of the past no longer applies to what is now happening. The thrust of European creativity must be viewed from a composite spectrum of focuses—because there is no such thing as one kind of European, any more than there is one kind of American.

13. Are the dynamics of black creativity better received in particular regions in Europe, or is the music more or less viewed in the same vibrational context?

It is really difficult to say, for in many ways all of the countries in Europe are very different from one another; and in another way, there is what could be called a composite European vibration. It seems to me that France could be singled out as one country that is especially conducive to black creativity—yet on this I am not sure whether it is simply because France seems to be more concerned about composite creativity anyway. Whatever, there is a long history between France and black creativity—with African or so-called African-American—and France seems to have always had more affinity and involvement in composite black creativity than any other country in Europe. At this point, I have not been able to really understand the nature of this involvement—which is to say, there is something happening here that I am not familiar with (or something I should know about). At present, Germany can also be cited as conducive for black creativity—in terms of performance possibilities—but not in the same sense as France. And for the most part, the whole of southern

MP(III)–10

Europe (Italy, Spain, Yugoslavia, Austria, etc.) seems to really be open to black creativity. This is not to say that black creativity is not received in northern Europe, because it is—but the vibrational response and support of black creativity is manifested in different ways in northern European countries like Sweden and Norway. I find this question especially difficult, because even though I feel that the composite dynamics of black creativity are better received in some sectors of Europe than others, I still can't seem to put my finger on what is really happening with this total phenomenon. I'm not even happy with this answer either. Probably the best response I could make would be "insufficient data" (return card).

14. Do the reality particulars surrounding creative music improve during difficult economic periods—as far as performance possibilities?

It seems this might be the case—certainly something is happening with this question. Probably intense economic periods, more than any other kinds of period, promote the need for individuals to seek some form of entertainment as a means to put the physical universe particulars out of mind. Certainly the depression did not stifle social reality, nor did this period close up the dynamics of performance possibilities. Even in this time zone, this same phenomenon can be viewed. For as the inflation index continues to rise, one might think that the composite culture would see a significant drop in creative support or outlets—but this has not been the case. There is much more to be said about this phenomenon, and hopefully with more research we might be able to understand something else about what creative support really means to cultural continuance. My personal feeling is that the very life and hope of a culture is related to whether or not its creative dynamics are supported by its people. But what this means in particular terms would require a separate book of its own.

15. Can America be talked of as a multi-racial country in regard to the "melting pot" concept?

It is a fact that America is a multi-racial country, but I do not believe the melting pot concept has any real validity—in terms of its present-day vibrational slant. This is not to ignore that there have been, and still are, many different levels of synthesis between so-called different people, nor have I meant to discredit the dynamic information conversion that has solidified as a result of this synthesis. Even with its many problems, there are few countries, if any, that have embraced so many different (or so-called different) peoples within its reality and composite identity, and I view this aspect of America as positive. My reason for rejecting the melting pot concept has to do with the dictates of progressionalism in American culture, involving both social reality and information reality. From the very beginning of America, there has only been one defining position—and that position concerns "information as made real through European and/or Euro-American definitions." In other words, no matter the nature of cross-information, only white people are in a position to define terms for the greater society—and this position has been used to only benefit white people (and western culture). I am saying that in the final analysis, the composite nature of America's surface culture is misleading, because the actual position of non-white people is one of "background" figures, rather than a people who equally participate in shaping the culture. If the melting pot concept has any relevance, it would undoubtedly be that the cross-sectional people who now live and work in America can be viewed from this kind of context, but the real question (and the real problem as well) is not whether this phenomenon constitutes a melting pot—because obviously it does. Rather, the question is "whose melting pot?" We can say that America is Mr. Smith's melting pot, France is Mr. Jones's melting pot, Brazil is Mr. Rothman's melting pot. But all of the misters are white men (or are controlled by white men or cultures).

16. Can each continuum of creative music be viewed with respect to the particulars of given political cycles? For example, can the continuum of creative music be viewed as related to the composite dictates of a people's history, and historical progression?

The answer to this question must be yes. If this were not the case, it would imply that creativity serves no real purpose (and in doing so, reduce this most serious area of participation to the "art for art's sake" zone). The progressional continuum of black creativity in America runs parallel to the composite continuum of America's own development. It is possible to view the reality dynamics and specifics of black Americans by studying the reality of each strain of black creativity—regardless of time zone. This is true from the early slaves' songs to the present, because all of these forms vibrationally manifest some aspect of the collective route that black people have traveled in America. Nor do I mean this in only one context. There have been many books that attempted to view the continuum of black creativity from a sociological context in this time period, but I have not seen any books that dealt with the philosophical implications related to what each projection posed—for both black people (in or out of America) and for the reality of composite black aesthetic—for America and for the planet. In terms of political implications, there is more than a casual relationship between the political and social progressional cycle that stretched from the cold war period (in the fifties) to Vietnam, and the reality continuum of creative music from the post-Parker continuum to Albert Ayler. The dictates of political dynamics are not separate from the composite arena of vibrational constants.

17. How have America, China, and the Soviet Union utilized creativity as a political tool (in cultural exchange programs) as a means to perpetuate culture?

The cultural exchange programs now utilized in this time zone are designed to showcase the realness of an actualization as a separate entity from its political reality. In this context, creativity is used as a basis for competition and/or a focal point for cultural achievement. Yet in many cases, the utilization of a given focus is only one aspect of the greater sophistication of cultural image-making. For instance, America has sent many so-called jazz ensembles on tour, even though the music has long been disrespected at home—by the people as well as the government. Jazz, to the American government, since the late forties, was useful because Europeans viewed it as our (America's) only original art form. Thus, even though Americans or the American government didn't really like the music, it could still be effectively used as propaganda. Every country uses creativity in this manner—but most countries also support the product they use to influence others. Nevertheless, all of these programs are highly influential—even more than what is generally assumed, and I have the feeling that this "cross-transfer of cultural bravado" will have a profound impact on everyone involved (who can deny the beauty of the Russian ballet or Chinese ballet, who can deny the beauty of a dancer like Mikhail Baryshnikov or the Japanese theatre—or Oscar Peterson in Russia for that matter?)—but not necessarily in the way intended.

18. Do you see any real difference between communism and capitalism as far as the actual political reality in this time zone?

There are most certainly differences in the functional space each country moves in—that being, the dynamics surrounding how living is approached. For the west undoubtedly offers an environment that gives more freedom to the individual (supposedly). But there is little difference in the essence center of either culture, for the realness of both America and the Soviet Union can be viewed as an affirmation of empirical functionalism, as opposed to spiritual and vibrational composite functionalism. In other words, both cultures utilize one-dimensional functionalism without regard for the dynamic implications related to what transformation or composite functionalism could really mean—as practiced in world culture. But there are other areas of similarities as well. Both the United States and the Soviet Union are continuums that are conceived with respect to furthering their own interests, rather than the composite well-being of all humanity. This is true as far as the nature of its decisions in terms of economic and political functionalism, as well as its reality position with respect to information transference. Both countries perpetrate the same dynamic flaws in their aesthetic (or vibrational) center, and the success of either country, in the final analysis, must be viewed as non-positive for the continuance of world culture—and especially non-white people. In other words, regardless of the present nature of surface physical universe dynamics, in the final analysis, there is little difference between the Soviet Union and the United States—as far as what each country poses for transformational change.

19. What does the move towards communism in Europe mean for creative music? How has Euro-communism dealt with creative music—at least in the seventies?

It is difficult to say what Euro-communism will mean for creative music over a sustained period because I have no way of knowing. It is important to not confuse the present dictates of European communism with that of the Soviet Union—because both continuums are very different from each other, at least at this point in time. If Euro-communism would solidify in the same way as the Soviet Union, then quite possibly the reality of its creativity could be viewed from the same context. Which is to say, the reality of creativity in Europe would be similar to what is taking place in the Soviet Union. But this is not the case at all in Europe at present. Moreover, if Italy is an example of what Euro-communism poses for creative music, then I would most certainly endorse it as positive. For the emergence of Euro-communism has helped bring about many new possibilities for creativity—in terms of dynamics as well as performance outlets. In this period (the beginning of the eighties) there are also many new festivals of music throughout the whole of Italy—festivals of so-called new music, popular music, and traditional music, and I view this as positive. It would, of course, be somewhat naive to view these developments as necessarily indicative of what communism would mean in Europe on a long-term basis, but it would also be somewhat presumptuous to dismiss this phenomenon as necessarily negative. In the end, people should have the right to choose whatever government they feel is best for them.

20. Does the composite continuance of art creativity pose a more vital alignment to understanding the present nature of progressional continuance than popular creativity?

I would say any form of creativity that is not "under the focus" of western manipulation stands a better chance of retaining its real identity and purpose. Obviously this is true, because to view the present reality of popular music is to view a reality that has been shaped as much by business people as by the musicians. This is not to say every particular participation in commercial creativity is necessarily irrelevant, because nothing is totally anything. But the dynamics of western manipulation in commercial creativity permeate every aspect of its reality base—and we would be quite naive if we chose to ignore what this manipulation means. Clearly Madison Avenue is not the place where dynamic alternative functionalism will solidify, for this is exactly the place one must have an alternative to. Yet I do not mean to imply that any form of commercial music is necessarily unrevolutionary—because this does not seem to be the case either. I believe any participation that can retain its true intentions is important, whether or not that participation is commercial or esoteric, because the realness of creativity (and people's lives) transcends narrow definitions on this level. But there can be no denying the awesomeness of western big business and information manipulation. To view the reality of what is now called commercial music is to view a continuum that is necessarily related to how this manipulation works. Very few people have been able to enter this area of commercialism and leave completely intact—with respect to their original intentions—and this does mean something.

21. Can the fact that there are no powerful black nations in this time period be related to the misinformation surrounding black creativity?

Yes. I believe that as long as the present political reality is sustained, black people can depend on more racism and suppression—in every area. For the reality of a given phenomenon in this time period is not separate from whether or not it has a political base to make it stick. In other words, many of the information positions we now accept and take for granted wouldn't necessarily have a chance in another context—outside of western culture. Positions in this context would include our present historical interpretations about western culture, our understanding of the Bible, and the western information designation of reality. All of these focuses are related to the present position of western culture and white people in general. The dissolution of black civilization can be viewed as the most basic factor that has determined the present misinformation surrounding the whole of black culture and/or black people. The resulting misdocumentation has moved to paint black people as somewhat "less" when compared to white people, and this effort has been successful because there is no one to challenge it. This is not to say there is only one factor related to the present position of black people—for there are misconceptions about many areas of humanity, involving not only black people but also Asian and white people—but the fact that black people have no dynamic political influence (as compared to western culture) in the greater context of present-day functionalism, cannot be underestimated. The whole of black invention and dynamics has been made to suffer because of this present predicament. And nothing will change unless it is made to—or unless "it" changes (or "as" it changes).

22. What did the concept of conservative mean in the seventies?

Conservative in the seventies can be viewed as the viewpoint that sought to maintain the status quo of America's traditional solidification with social reality—both vibrationally and with respect to economics and economic programs. There are many different interpretations of what this concept means with respect to particulars—for the dynamics of conservative philosophy differ from politician to politician. But in some areas, the realness of this concept is perfectly clear, for the reality implications of seventies conservatism have a direct message for both non-white and poor people. Conservatism can be viewed as the rallying philosophy for those who have come to desire some retardation in the programs initiated in the sixties to uplift the reality of poor and non-white people. The understanding of this sector has also gradually developed a viewpoint to validate their intentions, that being: (1) there is a need for less federal government, because whenever any assistance is given, the government powers increase, and (2) America was founded in a manner for every person to make it on his or her own ("if I did it then they can do it"—before that, the justification was "black people should not be entitled to equal treatment because they are not human beings, let alone equal!"). But what is really happening with this viewpoint is that if conservatism is successful, then most of the people who will suffer from its implementation are the same people that most conservatives happen to not like anyway—what a coincidence! Whatever, conservatism—which is a loose term to begin with—is a vibrational idea/feeling, that can be understood as the ideology of contraction (especially "their" contraction) as well as the political functionalism that moves to slow down the so-called advances of non-white and poor people—both economically and vibrationally.

23. *What is the political significance of black creativity?*

The political implications of black creativity are interconnected with the vibrational significance of composite alternative functionalism—that being, exposure to a given participation or specific functionalism will set certain vibrational particulars in motion. This is not only true for black creativity, but involves every focus—in other words, creativity is not only about "having a good time," but instead the realness of a given projection has a profound effect on whoever experiences it (whether or not the experience was perceived as positive). As such, the political significance of black creativity would have to do with what affinities it transports to its listeners—and also whether or not those affinities are conducive to the political context of the moment. There is, of course, much more to this question, for the present continuum of western dynamic manipulation has moved to utilize black creativity throughout the whole of western culture—without necessarily weakening the greater culture's identity alignment either. But regardless of the reality of source-transfer continuance, every thrust alignment does carry its own vibrational implications. The realness of a given alignment—that being, the source-initiation state of a continuance—will definitely make itself felt on some level or another. Which is to say, it is impossible to totally suppress the dynamic implications of thrust continuance—in either its source-transfer or source-initiation route. It is because of this phenomenon that creativity is political—regardless of form or time period. Because the reality of creativity is related to the reality of information in general—that is, the vibrational dictates of a given affinity position are necessarily intertwined with composite information (i.e., science, religion, style—as well as politics and/or desired political state).

24. Is art a political tool or intellectual tool?

It depends on the basis from which we are viewing the concept. For the present idea we have of art involves the relationship of participation to dynamic intellectualism, because there is no real composite spiritual basis in western culture. But the dictates of world creativity view creativity as a spiritual affirmation of "what is"—as well as "doing," and this viewpoint is not intellectual in the way western culture views the word. As far as whether or not art is political, it is difficult to say. Because anything that affirms something's "state of being" can be called political, because it functions as a factor to sustain a point of view (or involvement). Which is to say, art can be viewed as political by nature. But the realness of "life creativity" really transcends how we have come to view affirmation. Which is to say, the dictates of creativity have nothing to do with whether one is a Democrat or Republican or Asian or black, or western or Chinese, but instead has to do with "affirmation" as a means to move into the light of the greater forces. This use of postulation transcends our limited understanding of politics.

25. There are two very arrogant positions that can be discerned in geo-political perceptions from so-called liberal western intellectuals concerning the reality of world culture movements. What are those positions?

The two areas of misinformation concerning world culture, and world culture movement, that have historically characterized western culture perception dictates have to do with the game liberal western intellectuals have long been playing—as far as their world viewpoint, and use of particulars for spectacle diversion. In the sixties, the liberal intellectuals came to view world culture—or non-western culture—in necessarily over-idealistic terms as a means to balance the reality of what was happening in America (i.e., the war, and general intensity of the sixties)—and in doing so, moved to put unrealistic demands on the reality nature of composite functionalism. For example, in the sixties the liberal sector worshipped Mao Tse-tung as if China could be viewed as the perfect example of real civilization. But my point is that China—the real China—never had anything to do with the spectacle notions of the sixties. China was instead involved in its own dynamic continuance—which is to say, it was never perfect in the way liberal intellectuals portrayed it, because no country can be viewed in that context. By the same token, the disappointments now voiced by this same liberal contingency are arrogant (and inconsistent) because these same people now assume they know more about China than the Chinese. To me, this arrogance is related to the general nature of American racism. Because at the heart of sixties and seventies radicalism (or flirtation with alternative politics) can be found a kind of deep-seated paternalism—that being, (1) the unnatural elevation of world culture as a means to justify endorsing it, and (2) the idea that the west "knows better about what is best for a particular country than the people in that country." To me, this phenomenon is only another symptom of the arrogance of western culture.

GLOSSARY

Accelerated Dynamics: (1) a time period that experiences an increased rate of dynamic particulars; (2) the phenomenon of increased motion and information awareness or exchange; (3) information or dynamic particulars which are occurring at a faster rate than the concept of "progressional continuance" (which is my phrase for the "normal" pulse flow of information and/or affinity dynamics); (4) the phenomenon of moving faster towards affinity insight—or self-realization—than what is otherwise viewed as normal.

Accelerated Functionalism: (1) a "particular" that advances the nature or effectiveness of a given discipline; (2) the phenomenon of a given discipline expanding at what is perceived to be faster or greater than normal.

Activism: (1) the act of participating in a given discipline; (2) the act of participating in a given moment or collective with the intent to making a "particular" result solidify.

Actual Terms: (1) my phrase for "concrete terms"; (2) in the physical universe sense of a given phenomenon act; (3) a term used to bring in a physical universe or "solid" example of a given concept or statement; (4) a term for either clarifying or simplifying the concept being dealt with.

Actual Transformation: (1) the state of "total change" in both the physical and vibrational universe; (2) the arrival of transformation whether or not it was intended; (3) the phenomenon of transformation solidified because the precepts of the phenomenon (or focus) under review adhered to the dictates of what transformation is; (4) the phenomenon of total physical and vibrational universe change.

Affinity Alignment: (1) the way of one's vibrational nature or sensibility; (2) how a given nature is manifested in both doing or perceiving—in terms of its vibrational and actual slant.

Affinity Compression: (1) a move to lessen an individual's vibrational make-up; (2) the reality of isolating affinity dynamics for the purpose of limiting a given individual's vibrational or spiritual realness; (3) the phenomenon of stagnating a culture or individual's ability to gain self-realization or affinity-insight awareness about their lives—or life purpose; (4) the phenomenon of suppressing affinity dynamics.

Affinity Convergence: (1) the phenomenon of different vibrational sensibilities coming together; (2) the solidification of different so-called affinity tendencies; (3) vibrational unification or point of.

Affinity Dictates: (1) the reality of information as it applies to the particulars of a given sensibility; (2) the realness of information or observation tenets as it involves the laws which govern fundamentals and affinity postulation, and what this means for a given vibrational observation or participation; (3) that being, the laws which support a given reality of information and/or information affinity basis; (4) in other words, whatever one does there are fundamental laws that are related to whether or not a given focus can be successfully utilized—this is also true for the nature, or vibrational realness, of those fundamentals.

Affinity Dynamics: (1) vibrational diversity or the spectrum of possibilities related to a given vibrational position; (2) the related vibrational spectrum of a given phenomenon—that being, areas that are related to the vibrational particulars of a given phenomenon; (3) the scope of a person's life options, as related to vibrational attraction and what this phenomenon means with respect to that person's vibrational make-up.

Affinity Insight: (1) the uncovering of necessary information through self-realization; (2) the phenomenon of spiritual awareness as uncovered by an individual tapping his or her "life experiences" and vibrational make-up; (3) the secrets of a given information continuum as made real by affinity dynamic awareness.

Affinity Insight (1): (1) the realization of spiritual and necessary information about the whole of a given route of participation or culture, or cultural group, by or through self-realization; (2) self-realization as a basis to understand the reality of a given phenomenon as that phenomenon pertains to the greater culture or space; (3) the uncovering of spiritual information as to the "composite state of things."

Affinity Insight (2): (1) the use of self-realization as a basis to connect to one's own "life realness"; (2) the phenomenon of individual awareness as developed by the individual to better understand how to live; (3) taking one's spirit and beingness into one's self as a basis to connect with "the IT" as a means to better understand one's life or life purpose—or desired purpose.

Affinity Nature: (1) the reality of a person's feeling and vibrational make-up; (2) the reality of a phenomenon's inherent tendencies; (3) the reality of a given individual's basic feeling and vibrational tendencies.

Affinity Negation: (1) the move to not acknowledge the "way" of a person's vibrational nature; (2) the realness of isolating the reality interpretation of a given phenomenon in a way that doesn't correspond to the composite platform of affinity dynamics; (3) the isolated vibrational focus of a given area of information as a basis to undermine that same information's composite value.

Affinity Postulation: (1) the phenomenon of "reaching" for "understanding" without the information tenets that are accepted as true, but instead "reaching" with respect to what one feels and senses; (2) postulation with respect to affinity dynamics and affinity insight; (3) learning with respect to one's basic nature (or way of doing "things") and/or feeling.

Affinity Tendencies: (1) the nature of principle information that a given individual normally vibrates (or draws) from; (2) a concept which observes that given individuals over a period of time in "normal situations" are attracted to particular aspects of principle information rather than composite information interpretation; (3) the nature of a continuous "attraction" to a particular vibrational focus.

Affinity Transfer: (1) the phenomenon of changing vibrational continuum interpretations; (2) the refocus and interpretation of principle information with respect to its affinity nature—usually taking an extended time period to become solidified; (3) the natural exchange of principle information with respect to its focus particulars and vibrational dynamics.

Agreement: (1) vibrationally conducive to; (2) in accordance with; (3) a phenomenon whose vibrational properties and "way of being"—with respect to interpretation of the reality of procedure—are within the accepted nature and reality position of those individuals or "things" that are dealing with it.

All-Purpose: (1) a term to emphasize that the actual realness of a given phenomenon has to do with cosmic or spiritual matters; (2) a term to stress that even though I have observed a given information line or observation route to the best of my ability, I am also aware that its real "reason to be" goes much further than its surface; (3) a term used to comment on the destiny implications, or greater spiritual purpose, of a given phenomenon.

Alternative Activism: (1) participation that is outside of what is perceived to be in accordance to the "accepted" reality of things; (2) participation that is not viewed as politically conducive to sustaining the "vibrational" or physical universe reality of things; (3) participation that utilized different information tenets or vibrational tenets from what is perceived to be the "accepted" reality of procedure.

Alternative Composite Progressionalism: (1) my term for the time continuum changes which are taking place, involving total information tenets (that being spiritual and empirical)—as those tenets relate to given cultures or movements or vibrational phenomena—that are separate from the cultural manipulated version of "sanctioned progressionalism"—or its interpretation; (2) a term to comment on the dynamics of progressionalism, as a given focus is accented to the degree that it becomes necessary to include the fact that other movements (or focuses) were also happening as well (and the thrusts of some of those focuses were and are in opposition to the dictates of the accented focus mentioned).

Alternative Definitions: (1) definitions that are equally as real but not accepted or realized; (2) definitions that are related to other regions of affinity dynamics; (3) definitions that are related to other areas of its principle information reality and in some cases give a completely opposite interpretation from its other alternative type.

Alternative Functionalism: (1) disciplines that are perceived as not being in alignment to what is accepted as "correct" or "culturally sustaining"; (2) disciplines that are the outgrowth of alternative information and/or affinity positions; (3) disciplines whose "participation intentions" are not perceived or practiced as a means to affirm what is generally believed to be true for only one region of information, but instead participation that is directed towards uncovering other aspects of principle information and information dynamics.

Application Dictates: (1) a term used in the integration schematics to denote the reality of application for its given concept mixture; (2) a term in the integration schematics to clarify that the reality of a given set of ingredients must be calibrated into actual use (as opposed to simply using in any manner or order).

Applied Redefinitions: (1) the move to reinterpret what a given area of information means; (2) the point underlying when a given information interpretation is changed—and for what reason; (3) the move to focus on another aspect of a given definition's vibrational dynamics; (4) the conscious move to change what a given area or focus of information means—or could mean.

Aspect Essence: (1) the phenomenon of focusing on one part of a given area of principle information as a means to proclaim a universal interpretation; (2) a phenomenon that accents the particulars of a given focus on principle information to the degree where it moves to distort what that principle information really means—or could mean; (3) a phenomenon related to information manipulation in the west involving how given areas—and interpretations—of information are kept in perpetual motion as a means to sustain what is considered to be "interesting" at the expense of what is "most spiritual."

Attachment: (1) to be aligned with or the act of aligning with; (2) to be in agreement with and in being so, to come together with; (3) to not be in agreement with but to come together anyway.

Attitude: (1) vibrational persuasion or way of being; (2) having to do with the vibrational state underlying how a given person or composite culture approaches "phenomenon."

Attraction: (1) to be drawn towards a given focus; (2) to naturally be moving towards a given phenomenon because of either interest or not interest or vibrational interest; (3) the coming together of different phenomena because those phenomena were supposed to come together because of cosmic matters.

Basic Science: (1) in this context involves the use of this term in present-day western culture—that being, extended empirical investigation without respect for (or awareness of) spiritual dynamics; (2) extended functionalism that moves to investigate "the reality of things" as that "thing" works but not as that "thing" is.

Bi-aitional: (1) my term for viewing the reality of principle information with respect to the realness of two basic vibrational continuums, that being the masculine and feminine vibrational principle.

Circular Information Dynamics: (1) the phenomenon of changing the focus of a given principle information interpretation to the detriment to its real reality; (2) the phenomenon of continually refocusing on principle information as a basis to accelerate information dynamics.

Collected Forces of Western Culture: (1) by this term I am referring to all of the agencies that have been constructed to perpetuate the reality of western culture—whatever that perpetuation involves. In other words, the western media, and its educators, the so-called right and left wing (and new left), the western scientific community, western politics, western information interpretation and regulation, etc.

Composite Activism: (1) participation that functions with respect to humanity and composite information; (2) participation with respect to physical universe objectives and spiritual dynamics; (3) the realness of different so-called sectors of humanity working towards the same objective; (4) participation with respect to composite information dynamics—thereby having positive relevance to the composite community.

Composite Affinity Alignment: (1) a vibrational relationship to principle information that attempts to respect and reflect the greater dynamics of composite humanity; (2) a vibrational relationship to information that brings together empirical information dictates with spiritual intent or insight; (3) a vibrational relationship to information that seeks to better understand and include composite humanity within the tenets of its particular focus; (4) the bringing together of composite humanity by establishing an all-encompassing information basis for information and information transference.

Composite Continuance: (1) repeated involvement with respect to both composite information and composite humanity; (2) the reality of time progressionalism as it involves composite humanity; (3) the nature of time changes as it involves composite information.

Composite Culture Attitude: (1) the reality of a culture's vibrational sensibility as it concerns all of the different vibrational persuasions in that culture; (2) the state of a given culture's composite vibrational nature and way of being.

Composite Focused Activism: (1) participation directed at a "particular" that also seeks to reflect the composite concerns of humanity; (2) participation by different kinds of people—both vibrationally and socially—on a particular area of interest; (3) composite participation on a given focus as a means to interpret that focus for the greater good of composite society. Composite participation and/or interest in a given area of information or physical universe particulars.

Composite Humanity: (1) all humanity—men, women, and children, regardless of planet sector; (2) with respect to all humanity.

Composite Information: (1) information that gives insight into the physical universe principle reality of a given phenomenon and also its accompanied vibrational or spiritual universe particulars; (2)

information that respects and reveals the multi-dynamic realness of a given phenomenon.

Composite Research: (1) research with respect to the past and present; (2) research with respect to composite information and interpretation; (3) investigation with respect to composite perception dynamics.

Controlled Information: (1) interpretations that have been sanctioned for the greater public to assimilate and believe; (2) interpretations which have consciously been manipulated as a means to suppress affinity dynamics and/or alternative definitions.

Cosmic Assignment: (1) a term to acknowledge that the "particulars" of a given phenomenon really have to do with "the greater forces" or quite simply "GOD," rather than something that can be only "talked about" or "written on"; (2) a term to acknowledge that some phenomena and/or focuses are indicative of the intent of forces that are greater than humanity or "what humanity can do."

Cosmic Dictates: (1) a term to acknowledge that the fundamentals or particulars underlying a given focus transcend the "intentions" of humanity and instead involve "the greater forces" or "GOD"; (2) a term to acknowledge that the reality of a given set of dictates is related to increased "understanding—or not understanding" of the cosmic realness of everything.

Cosmic Particulars: (1) that being, the reality of a given focus has nothing to do with our information dynamics but instead has to do with spiritual matters; (2) the point of a given interpretation or focus that transcends words and moves into the "real."

Criticism: (1) the phenomenon of commenting as to the reality particulars and/or dynamics of another person's participation; (2) the move to isolate a person's participation as a basis to apply value judgments—even if those judgments are outside the actual reality of that person's affinity participation; (3) an existential observation tool that moves to isolate a given phenomenon's "way of being—or participation" as a means to determine the success of that "beingness or participation"; (4) a unique tool of western information dynamics that involves the imposition of observation criteria (without spiritual dictates) as a means to isolate whether or not a given postulation is in accordance to its dictates.

Cross-Transfer Definitions: (1) interpretations which are solidified and applied when a given continuum of information moves into its change (or affinity refocus) cycle; (2) interpretations that are made "real" as a given continuum of information changes its vibrational or physical universe perceived focus; (3) definitions that had no or little meaning (or different meaning) in a given information continuum that are suddenly elevated into prominence because of the change of that information's use (on the physical universe level or political level).

Cross-Transfer Progressionalism: (1) the reality of continuums coming together and moving apart (and while doing so, taking or exchanging information dynamics in the process); (2) the reality of alternative continuums and the point of interchange between their reality or vibrational ingredients.

Cultural Transfer Shift(s): (1) those cycles in time which underline the phenomenon of different cultures changing or exchanging information and/or information dynamics; (2) the phenomenon of a given culture coming to an end while at the same moment another culture is emerging based on the same information or information dynamics—and what this inter-relationship means.

Culture Affinity Basis: (1) the reality of a culture vibrational and postulation make-up and what this phenomenon means for the establishment of that culture's "way of doing things"; (2) the vibrational particulars which underlie a given culture's reality and vibrational way of living.

Culture Information Basis: (1) the reality of a given culture's idea nature and its accompanied dynamics; (2) the affinity dynamic nature of a culture's intellectual "way of being."

Culture Information Dynamics: (1) the natural and unnatural possibilities that are related to a given culture's idea alignment in terms of "participation spectrum" and "vibrational postulation spectrum"; (2) the variety of focuses or "things" that are related to a culture's information reality—or position; (3) the spectrum of "focuses" or "things" that are related to—and the result of—a culture's relationship with its information.

Culture Information Focus: (1) the agreed-upon interpretation of a particular area of information by those individuals responsible for establishing cultural information; (2) the reality of how a given focus of information reflects the dynamic solidification of its culture's idea nature.

Culture Order: (1) the establishment of whatever devices are necessary to insure that a given culture can function in whatever way that culture desires to function; (2) the move to functionally insure that a culture can "work" the way its founders intended; (3) the reality of those devices which have been designed to solidify "how a culture works" with respect to that culture's political reality and/or dynamics.

Culture Solidification: (1) the establishment of the physical universe situation for a way that affirms the collective intent and desire of those individuals in that space, for the purpose of living in accordance to what is perceived to be "most real."

Decentralization: (1) the move to open up the reality dynamics of a given phenomenon as a means to have the greater spectrum of its forces able to equally have both input and relevance; (2) the move to spread the resources of a given phenomenon to all areas of its principle space, and in doing so, opening up the greater dynamics of the composite space.

Definition: (1) meaning of; (2) the reality of.

Despiritualization: (1) the phenomenon of having something viewed in less spiritual or vibrational terms; (2) the move to solidify the reality of a given spiritual phenomenon in terms that adhere to what is now called rational or logical—that being, the reality of "how something is" as opposed to "how something really is"; (3) the move to take away or not acknowledge—or not even be aware of—the magic or spiritual realness of a given focus.

Disintegration of a Culture's Center: (1) the phenomenon of a culture's vibrational and informational tenets moving to complete destruction; (2) the realness of a culture's idea and affinity support structure being overthrown.

Documentation: (1) the recording of information and particulars as a means to have that information available for future study or use.

Dynamic Functionalism: (1) a discipline that is pursued with respect to its number dynamics as well as spiritual dynamics; (2) a discipline that can bring about a spectrum of information awareness because of its ability to tap the system's particulars of a given phenomenon as well as vibrational dynamics related to that same phenomenon; (3) disciplines that are pursued because they are related to advancing the state of composite humanity; (4) disciplines that are pursued because their tenets are from—and moving towards—composite humanity (that is, disciplines that are about positive transformation).

Dynamic Separation: (1) the isolation of information to the degree that its particulars are viewed without respect for the whole of its principle platform and the creation of a dynamic functionalism from those separate focuses; (2) the intense focus of particulars as a means to view its fundamental law as a means to solidify that procedure for "spectrum participation and investigation"—all of this being done separately or not separately from its spiritualism.

Dynamic Spiritualism: (1) a spiritualism that is all-purpose—involving every aspect of one's life and living; (2) a spiritualism that moves to solidify living in accordance to the secrets and intentions of the greater forces; (3) a spiritualism or mystery system that serves to help humanity to come together for positive acts; (4) a spiritualism that moves to "ritualize" the reality of participation.

Economic Dynamics: (1) the reality and multi-particulars that involve how "contractual dynamics" are solidified and in what form.

Establishing High Order: (1) solidifying composite all spiritual and dynamic functional context, in accordance to transformational precepts; (2) solidifying the spiritual and information dynamics of a given state (and its related pedagogy all system); (3) solidifying the "most" spiritual and vibrational platform with the co-ordinates of the "moment" (or integration mix).

Existential Definition: (1) a definition that views the realness of a given phenomenon with respect to what happened on the physical universe level; (2) an observational phenomenon that views the nature of an occurrence from outside of that occurrence based on how that occurrence is perceived to have happened.

Existential Observation: (1) observation with respect to "how" something seems to be—as separate from the spiritual context of that something; (2) observation with respect to what appears to be happening (in terms of the physicality of that something—and how it "is"—in terms of its "movement" or "low system"), but not in terms of the composite all spiritual nature of that "something."

Existentialism: (1) the phenomenon and state of being that arises when spiritualism is subjected to logical analysis without respect for its proper affinity adjustments, which results in despiritualism and emphasis instead on the "particulars" of a physical universe occurrence—with the understanding being that "something that happens is really what has happened" as opposed to "something that happens is an expression of . . . greater forces."

Expansion Condition: (1) a concept that has to do with how change is solidified in cultural terms; (2) having to do with the reality of intentions surrounding how change is perceived and moved towards.

Expansion Condition (1): the reality and concept of expansion as it relates to composite focus (that being humanity and all spiritualism).

Expansion Condition (2): the reality and dynamics of expansion as it relates to the individual desiring that expansion.

Expansion Dictates: (1) the reality of procedure as it involves expansion; (2) the infra-structure particulars—in their correct order—underlying expansion dynamics (in a given context).

Expansion Dynamics: (1) a term that has to do with the conceptual or vibrational factors that are related to a particular point or kind of expansion. In other words, a given approach or area of expansionism carries its own vibrational or actual implications.

Expansion Information Basis: (1) the phenomenon of increasing the idea spectrum of a given information line as a means to better understand the multi-complexual realness of principle information; (2) the attempt of increasing the affinity dynamic postulates related to what a given information line really means or could mean; (3) the solidification of an idea platform that has relevance to all of the people in its culture, and in doing so, having the dynamics related to what this phenomenon poses to information dictates.

Expansionism: (1) the phenomenon of growing in a given period of time, or the inherent additives that result from a "solidification" in a given time; (2) the move to encompass more territories and/or information without regard for whether or not the inhabitants of those said territories are in agreement with that encompassing; (3) the conscious move to increase the territories or "stuff" of a given culture as a means to "grow"—or support a "growth" that has already occurred.

Extended Dynamics: (1) the uncovering of more information or vibrational possibilities as that phenomenon relates to the reality of investigation; (2) the solidification of more insight about the reality of participation and/or living as that insight relates to a given discipline's meta-secrets or methodological possibilities.

Extended Functionalism: (1) a discipline that provides more insight as to the spiritual and actual particulars underlying what is normally perceived to be "real"; (2) a discipline whose infra-structure and/or particulars are related to, and gives insight into, the dynamics of positive transformation; (3) a discipline whose utilization can provide greater affinity insight as well as composite positive assistance for bringing about positive insight and change; (4) the act of advancing a given discipline to where its meta-reality can begin to provide some of these attributes.

Extension: (1) to move deeper into or towards; (2) coming into, closer to.

Form: (1) how something is; (2) the structure concerning how something seems to be or how something happens; (3) the context, and its related laws, that house a given phenomenon; (4) the spiritual platform that houses a given phenomenon; (5) the physical universe materialization of a vibrational ritual—that being, the context of a participation as well as what that participation means.

Fundamental Dynamics: (1) the focus particulars related to what a given discipline is, or could be in its optimum state; (2) the spiritual and "actual" possibilities that are related to a given "law," or discipline's reality.

Fundamental Particulars: (1) a principle focus or aspect of a given discipline's dictates; (2) the reality of a given discipline's separate parts.

Gradualism: (1) the phenomenon of re-defining information and/or particulars to have that information be viewed in accordance to the intent of its re-definers; (2) the phenomenon of changing information or contributions by groups or nations as a means to have that information or achievement perceived (or re-documented) as coming from the culture of those who changed the information; (3) the act of claiming ownership of concepts and/or achievements done by others as a means either to claim superiority or to claim historical "right of" or "linkage to."

High Purpose: (1) participation with respect to what is most positive for humanity; (2) participation with respect to what is perceived to be "most positive" for humanity; (3) spiritual participation that is done for what is most real for the greater forces; (4) cosmic phenomena that are about cosmic phenomena.

Improvisation: (1) a discipline that involves the science of creative postulation as it unfolds in "actual" time; (2) a discipline that utilizes the dynamics of moment postulation in both the context of individual postulation and its related affinity dynamics, as well as cultural vibrational transference; (3) the science and multi-discipline of existing—having to do with the appearance of "moments" and making life choices (either with respect to "particulars" or spiritual growth) and the gradual awareness of how best to proceed with that information in "rapid-moment-decision contexts."

Individual Dynamic Reality: (1) that being those "particulars" of the greatest positive attributes in a given individual's physical universe reality; (2) a concept that accents the realness of the individual and what that individual's vibrational spectrum could be in its most positive sense, as related to the particulars of his or her physical universe reality.

Individual Dynamics: that being, the "natural" or "particular" vibrational properties that each individual has—and is born with (or can acquire, depending on the situation)—having to do with the areas that individual is attracted to, the areas that individual can excel at, the information that individual can relate to (and later contribute to as well). Having to do with "what is most" or "can be most" about a given individual in his or her most positive state.

Individual Tendencies: (1) having to do with what region of principle information a given individual is continually drawn to, and functions from (in his or her natural feeling and "postulation" nature); (2) a concept which observes that given individuals vibrate to different areas of the same information because every information continuum is related to its particular "nature spectrum"—and this phenomenon also corresponds to the different types (or so-called types) of people.

Information Affinity Basis: (1) that being, the vibrational particulars which determine what a given idea structure is to really mean. My viewpoint is that the dynamics of vibrational postulates come before the actual idea or concept interpretation; (2) the affinity or vibrational nature that determines what aspect is to be affirmed of a given principle information line.

Information Alignment: the reality of a given idea or concept as it connects to principle information, and also the reality of a given interpretation as it affirms its vibrational basis.

Information Compression: (1) same as affinity compression but also involves the physical universe removal (or put-down) of given areas of information which are not in the interest of those who choose to do the compression; (2) the blockage of information.

Information Convergence: (1) the coming together of different continuums of information—either involving principle information dynamics or particulars; (2) the phenomenon of information expansion and/or affinity linkage.

Information Degrees: my term for information tenets. I have chosen this term because it moves to involve the reality of spiritualism more than the word "tenet." By "degree" I am saying that each aspect of a given information line moves to both substantiate the reality of its principle focus as well as its spiritual designation. I view the term "tenet" as more related to intellectual dynamics—having to do with the dynamics which support a given focus's particulars but not its affinity basis.

Information Dissemination: (1) the phenomenon concerning how given ideas and concepts are spread on the physical universe level; (2) the phenomenon that underlines how given practices are transmitted to the greater culture or through a sustained time cycle; (3) the spread of information.

Information Documentation: (1) the recording of knowledge—whatever the context or focus—as a means to have it taught or later re-examined; (2) having to do with the reality of recorded concepts and ideas and how it is passed on through different time cycles.

Information Focus: (1) the particular emphasis on a given aspect of principle information; (2) the point of a given intention as manifested in actual terms; (3) the reality underlying how a given principle information line is perceived in actual terms (that being, the reality concerning what factors and affinities underlie how a given information line is repeatedly perceived and practiced).

Information Focus Distortion: (1) that being, the particular point in a given information tenet structure that is consciously or not consciously distorted as a means to have an understanding that corresponds to what one wants to believe, rather than what that information seems to be saying; (2) the point in a given information complex that is misused or not understood, or not viewed correctly.

Information Forum: (1) the reality of what information is available in a given context; (2) the solidification of what information is to be made available in a given context—and in what terms; (3) a platform for information—or given information—that can or cannot be experienced by the greater public.

Information Integration: (1) solidifying given areas of information—regardless of thrust alignment or affinity nature; (2) bringing given continuums of information together.

Information Interpretation: the reality of attempting to deduce what a given idea or concept means—with respect to both that concept's principle information greater context, as well as its particular degrees.

Information Order: (1) the reality structure that underlies a given area of information; (2) the focus ingredient that establishes a given area of information; (3) "how" a given type of information is, and "how" it should be in its most correct alignment.

Information Projection: (1) this term refers to the actualness of a given viewpoint and what that viewpoint poses for its greater information multi-complex. In other words, a projection in this context is indicative of "one particular" manifestation of a given principle information complex; (2) that being, an actual example or particular of a principle information multi-complex.

Information Reality: (1) viewing the actualness of a given information concept with respect to its physical universe realness; (2) an informational example in concrete physical universe terms; (3) that being, "how a given information is" in the physical universe context of its existence.

Information Solidification: (1) bringing all aspects of a given focus (or set) of information particulars together; (2) completing the infrastructure of a given information continuum as a means to make it (the information) real—or correct; (3) the same as information integration (but in a more progressional sense).

Information Transference: the changing of information—either from person to person (whether vibrational or actual) or culture to culture.

Infra-Spirituality: (1) that being, the reality of spirituality as it involves the particulars of a given discipline; (2) how a given part of a particular discipline also has spiritual connotations; (3) finding the "god" of a given discipline or point of activism.

Infra-Structure Dynamics: (1) that being, the possibilities related to the particulars of a given system in terms of what the procedure of that discipline implies for other focus spectrums; (2) having to do with the ritual implications of a given participation—that being, every aspect of a given structure carries a physical universe and vibrational multi-implication.

Intellectualism: (1) having to do with the reality of ideas and the dynamics of inter-relationship seeded by the vibrational concern (or attraction) to what is perceived to be "interesting" or logically true, as opposed to what is spiritually true; (2) the reality of ideas without regard for its spiritual context; (3) the dynamics of concepts and isolated information focus with the intent to understand as separate from spiritual insight.

Intention: having to do with the reality of a given motive.

Interpretation: (1) having to do with extracting the meaning of a given phenomenon or information line; (2) the reality of providing the context and tools to receive insight into the state of a given phenomenon; (3) having to do with viewing what a given principle information line means or could mean for the beings in a given affinity focus—or spectrum; (4) having to do with providing insight into how a given spiritual and vibrational actualness can be solidified—and understood—on the physical universe level, and practiced.

Investigation Dictates: (1) the reality of correct observation as it relates to a particular focus; (2) the reality of perception dynamics as this concept involves establishing correct criteria for examination; (3) investigation with respect to the tenets of what is being investigated; (4) the reality of proper investigation as it involves procedure.

Isolated Activism: (1) participation with respect to the particulars of a given focus; (2) participation with respect to one or "whatever is defined" area of interest or focus, for the purpose of achieving a desired result; (3) participation that is practiced without respect for the composite physical or vibrational universe situation but instead is directed to deal with the immediacy of a particular (or particular set of) focus or focuses.

Isolated Focus: (1) that being, to view the "particulars" of a given phenomenon rather than the composite picture; (2) to focus on only certain aspects of a given phenomenon as a means to deal or not deal with that aspect.

Isolated Focus Activism: (1) that being, participation with respect to the interest of particular sectors or people, rather than the composite sector; (2) participation that is undertaken from the reality of a particular focus rather than a composite focus.

Isolated Focus Dictates: (1) the pedagogical structure underlying a given focus; (2) the reality of fundamental information that supports a given focus; (3) taking into account—in the perception of a given focus—its underlying information tenets; (4) the reality underlying how a given focus must be observed with respect to its fundamental support systems.

Isolated Particulars: (1) having to do with separating a given idea or focus from its principle information multi-focus as a basis to only deal with a given independent idea; (2) that being, a particular focus that is separated and viewed with respect to whatever the intentions of the viewer are.

Isolated Systematic Alignment: (1) that being, the independent logic systems which are solidified as a basis to view the particulars of a given focus—as opposed to an all-encompassing logic system; (2) the reality of linkage as it involves different isolated idea focuses (as made or viewed separately from its vibrational foundation).

Journalism Dynamics: the possibilities inherent in the reality of present-day journalism—involving its interpretation dynamics, its focus (or not focus) dynamics, its semantical dynamics, and its ability to profoundly affect the greater culture (both positively and negatively—especially negatively).

Language: (1) the reality of symbols as a basis to codify particulars; (2) the reality of symbols as a basis to transmit intention; (3) the reality of procedure as a basis to convey information.

Language Dynamics: (1) that being, the inherent possibilities that are related to the particulars of a given functionalism (or set of symbols) in terms of what can be successfully communicated through its particular use; (2) having to do with what the use of a given language poses for dynamic postulation as well as spiritual insight; (3) having to do with how a given communication discipline can also affect and determine the option-spread possibilities of the person or culture utilizing the discipline.

Linkage Implications: (1) the possibilities related to the coupling or inter-relationship of two phenomena and/or focuses; (2) the reality of possibilities as it relates to the coupling and/or inter-relationship of two different phenomena and/or focuses.

Logical Dissolution: (1) that being, the rational result of; (2) that being, the rational consequences of—as a result of using a particular technique and/or discipline or act; (3) in accordance to the context that has been defined—or dissolution in accordance to the context that has been defined.

Manipulation: (1) having to do with controlling the meaning of—or use of—how a given phenomenon is viewed or utilized; (2) having to do with the intention to utilize a given phenomenon in a way to achieve a desired result that is not necessarily related to what that same phenomenon would achieve if utilized differently; (3) the conscious use of materials and things as a means to solidify and/or establish a given result or results.

Media Dynamics: (1) the reality and vibrational dynamics related to how the media works; (2) how the media is, and how it can be; (3) the inherent possibilities related to the reality of accelerated information transference and its established institutions.

Meta-Implications: (1) vibrational related possibilities or consequences; (2) cosmic or vibrational relationships (and possibilities).

Meta-Reality: (1) the vibrational or cosmic "living" or "being" context of a given phenomenon; (2) a term that injects cosmic or spiritual being matters as a consideration not separate from what is being discussed; (3) having to do with the spiritual or vibrational weight of a given idea or focus.

Meta-Reality Significance: (1) the vibrational or spiritual meaning of a given postulation or focus; (2) having to do with what a given function or focus will ultimately mean in vibrational or spiritual terms.

Methodology: (1) the reality particulars of a given function or discipline; (2) the science of a given discipline and how to execute a given function; (3) how something is done and the discipline to make it happen again; (4) the spiritual and vibrational procedures necessary to gain insight into the "all motion" realness of the physical and vibrational universe; (5) the reality of doing in its most highest context with the establishment of ritual as the most correct or effective procedure to make a particular "thing" happen.

Mono-Dimensional: (1) the reality of one context or one observation plane; (2) a concept that has to do with viewing a given phenomenon in only one affinity and/or actual context; (3) the reality of a given phenomenon as it is viewed in only one or two (or a limited amount of) contexts—and in doing so moves to limit that phenomenon's affinity and/or actual life options and/or "being" options.

Motivation Dynamics: (1) the reality of intention as it applies to a participation; (2) the spectrum of intentions related to a given participation.

Multi-Dimensional: (1) many dimensions on many different levels; (2) dynamically complex and related to many different factors and/or contexts; (3) means more than only one interpretation and extends into many other areas, and things.

Multi-Information: (1) information that is not only about one particular focus but instead is relevant and meaningful on many different levels; (2) information—ideas and concepts—that have relevance on many different levels and/or focuses.

Multi-Informational Degree Basis: (1) a western information phenomenon that utilizes dynamic information in a way that enables a given word or statement to be utilized and interpreted in as many ways as is necessary for the real purpose to be actualized; (2) a phenomenon that helps to keep the reality of western information dynamics in constant motion.

Multi-Transfer Shift Activity: a concept that observes the different dynamic contexts which dictate the reality of a given discipline's effectiveness.

Multiple Diversification: (1) a term that comments as to the many different possibilities related to a given phenomenon; (2) a term that comments on a given phenomenon's dynamic possibilities as well as the realness that those possibilities are not limited to any one particular level.

Multiple Interpretation: (1) to decipher meaning on several different levels; (2) a term that comments on how a given focus is interpreted and on how many different levels.

Observation: (1) to view something; (2) the reality of viewing a phenomenon as a means to understand it (or some aspect of it).

Option Spread: (1) the opportunities available for a given person on the physical universe level; (2) the life pursuance possibilities of a given individual in terms of his ability to achieve either information, economic gain, cultural recognition, and/or cultural participation.

Participation: (1) the reality of "doing something"; (2) to be a part of and actively functioning; (3) the act of doing something.

Particular Focus: (1) a particular subject; (2) an isolated subject that is being viewed for whatever reason.

Particular Progressionalism: (1) an isolated continuum; (2) having to do with the reality of a given continuum of either information or people (culture) or vibrational "way of doing things."

Perceived Physical Universe Fundamental: that being the perception of a given discipline or focus as indicative of a fundamental or primary law that underlies how the all-motion dynamics of earth—and/or the heavens—are made "real" (or work).

Perception Dynamics: (1) the reality of observation with respect to the variables—and spectrum of possibilities—underlying a given way of looking at "things"; (2) the vibrational and "actual" factors that underlie a given observation context (or platform).

Physical Universe Context: (1) having to do with viewing a given phenomenon with respect to what that phenomenon reveals as it is made real in actual concrete terms; (2) in concrete terms or in "actual" context.

Physical Universe Fundamental: (1) a law that seems to be dynamically and cosmically related to how the actualness of this experience (living and the appearance of things as they seem to be and the realness of vibrations as it seems to be) is made real; (2) a law or discipline that expresses some aspect of how the physical universe is able to be as it is.

Physical Universe Particular: (1) that being, a focus or particular that can be viewed in concrete terms as a basis to participate in that context; (2) a given focus that is concrete with respect to the dimension we refer to as the physical universe.

Political Consciousness: (1) awareness of what is taking place in the reality of politics; (2) the awareness of what politics means—or could mean as an expression of dynamic spiritualism; (3) the awareness of politics and how given realities are solidified and/or maintained.

Political Dynamics: (1) the inherent possibilities that are related to the political context of a given physical universe space; (2) the related possibilities of a given political system as it concerns cultural option dynamics—spiritual dynamics, social dynamics, and particular focus dynamics.

Political Order: (1) the securing of a given political philosophy and reality posture and its actualization on the physical universe level; (2) establishing a given reality context in accordance to a given political system (or philosophy).

Political Policies: (1) involves the reality of what laws are established in a given political state; (2) involves the particulars of a given political system as it relates to what is viewed as correct, positive and beneficial, as opposed to what is labeled negative, not correct and "against the state."

Political Significance: (1) has to do with what a given action poses to the reality of the political arena it takes place in; (2) has to do with what a given postulation poses to the reality of its given political space; (3) has to do with the reality of "meaning" as it relates to political tenets and/or dynamics.

Political State: that being the reality of politics as it shapes the particulars of its culture's actual living.

Postulation: (1) the act of bringing something forth as in expressing an idea or a feeling; (2) the reality of what one aspires to and works towards—that being the creation of an objective and/or focus that did not exist before; (3) the phenomenon of vibrationally expressing the actualness of a given phenomenon from one's own affinity particulars (or culture affinity particulars); (4) the expression of a cosmic and/or vibrational dictate that is manifested and/or made real through dynamic existence—as in "doing" or "movement."

Primary Affinity Tendencies: (1) a concept that views the reality of vibrational postulation with respect to (a) what is called traditionalism, (b) stylism, and (c) restructuralism.

Primary Intention: (1) the basic motivation of; (2) what a given phenomenon really makes happen when utilized and the purpose behind who decides whether it is to be utilized (or explored) or not.

Progressional Continuance: (1) a term that views physical universe reality changes and/or events with respect to sequential time blocks and/or parameters (and/or time cycles); (2) looking at given time periods with respect to blocks of tendencies (and/or variables) as a basis to view the world expansion principle.

Progressional Extended Functionalism: (1) the phenomenon of viewing a given discipline and/or science and how it moves into greater areas of its dynamics; (2) the reality continuance of advanced discipline in its own right (that is, how a given advanced discipline has continued its existence as separate from the composite arena of a given continuum and/or discipline).

Progressional Significance: (1) the meaning and/or value of a given phenomenon as that phenomenon advances different time periods; (2) the reality of change and the reality of a given phenomenon's significance as it advances through change cycles and/or time periods.

Progressional Transfer Cycles: a concept that refers to those periods in time which are conducive to or "about" the interchange of composite information and/or information dynamics.

Projection: (1) a term that is used to comment on information off-shoots as it involves ideas and concept lines from a principle information continuum; (2) a style or isolated information focus continuum; (3) in music, "projection" is my word for style or music type.

Projectional Continuance: (1) the continuation of a given style of idea type focus throughout a given time period or periods; (2) the use or realness of a given projection in the larger context of time or time changes.

Projectional Dynamics: (1) the diversity or possibilities related and/or based from the reality of a given projection; (2) the possibilities connected to a given projection; (3) a term to comment on the spiritual dictates related to the particulars of a given discipline, and what those dictates translate into as actual and/or vibrational terms.

Race: (1) the compilation of a people in a given physical universe space for an extended period in time to the degree that their physical traits and affinity spectrum traits move to affirm a particular identity; (2) the vibrational attraction phenomenon that underlies a given group of people with respect to their affinity dynamic dictates and destiny; (3) an applied precept concerning the reality of isolated particulars as this concept involves the family of humanity and existence; (4) the dynamic realization and/or actualization of affinity dynamics—as made real in human beings and/or all living things (and non-so-called living things) that expresses some or all aspects of the cosmic realness of "it" and/or "is" and/or "this."

Reality Alignment: (1) the physical universe application or view of; (2) the physical universe context and use of; (3) viewing a given phenomenon with respect to what that phenomenon would mean on the physical universe level—if utilized, or as a context to view from.

Reality Dynamics: (1) the possibilities or diverse particulars of a given physical universe situation; (2) the related possibilities of a given physical universe context.

Reality Implications: (1) the related information and/or phenomenon possibilities to a given physical universe situation; (2) what a given physical universe situation poses for extended circumstances.

Reality Initiative Traits: (1) what is most common to the reality of postulation as it concerns a particular physical universe space; (2) the "way of doing things" in a given physical universe space and/or culture.

Reality Options: (1) that being, the opportunities or avenues of participation in a given physical universe space and/or culture; (2) having to do with what living opportunities are available for a person or persons in a given physical universe context.

Recontinuance: (1) the continuance of a given phenomenon that seemingly was not there before; (2) the re-appearance of a given "way of doing things" or "viewpoint"—"law system"—that seemingly was not there before; (3) a cosmic phenomenon that underlies how given areas of information (or "things") are brought into and out of being in accordance to factors that have nothing to do with what we know about.

Redefinitions: (1) giving a definition and new definition; (2) changing the meaning of a given definition and/or focus.

Redocumentation: (1) changing what is documented; (2) either rewriting or correcting what has been documented.

Related Procedure: (1) a term used in the integration schematics to denote that a given combination of terms should be utilized at that point in its solidification; (2) a term to denote the usage of a given set of variables in the information schematic.

Relevant Application: (1) the reality of what is "most real" to a given application; (2) application with respect to the cosmic dictates of positive utilization; (3) application with respect to what is most effective.

Relevant Technology: (1) technology that is solidified in accordance to spiritual and dynamic dictates; (2) the use of technology with respect to what is "most" (for humanity) about that technology; (3) technology that is related to what one professes to be about—or would like to be about (both dynamically and spiritually).

Restructuralism: (1) the reality of realigning how a given system or structure works; (2) changing the surface particulars of a given structure but keeping the fundamentals that gave that structure its laws; (3) changing the particulars of a system as well as its dictates.

Responsibility Ratio: having to do with what extent and/or degree a given person or culture is to be held accountable for the reality and/or particulars of a given focus and/or discipline and/or reality; (2) the spectrum of an individual's responsibility in a given context.

Retrograde Affinity Tendencies: that being, those vibrational urges which, if allowed, would pursue their particulars in focuses that are considered in the past.

Ritual Dynamics: (1) the possibilities and diverse particulars related to the use of a given ritual; (2) the dynamic possibilities that underlie what a given ritual is or does or makes happen.

Scientific Dynamics: (1) the possibilities and/or particular discoveries that are related to a given use or reality of science; (2) the particulars related to a given type of area or science.

Self-Realization: (1) having to do with the individual becoming aware of who he or she really is—as made real through both physical universe particulars and spiritual insight; (2) spiritual discovery.

Social Programs: (1) organizations established to help uplift given aspects of social reality; (2) organizations for bringing about positive changes—and participation—in social reality.

Social Reality: (1) the particulars related to events on the physical universe level; (2) the "way of life" on the physical universe level as it involves living and functioning in a given space.

Social Reality Development: (1) the reality of bringing about positive reforms in social reality; (2) positive participation—or effect—for a given social reality context (or sector).

Social Reality Dynamics: (1) the possibilities and particulars related to a given social reality context and/or physical universe context; (2) the particulars related to what and how a given social reality space is—as far as achievement possibilities and/or postulation possibilities.

Social Reality Interpretation: (1) "meanings" that have solidified in a given social reality context (that have been accepted) for the greater culture; (2) the meanings that are to be accepted in a given social reality context.

Social Reality Particular(s): (1) the actualness of a given focus or focuses that is related to—or draws its ability to be from—its social reality context; (2) that being, the reality of a given focus as that focus is made real from its social reality basis.

Source Initiation: (1) the point and/or reality from which a given initiation solidifies; (2) the reality concerning when a given particular solidifies.

Source Projection: (1) a style or language that has solidified from its historical continuum; (2) an information line that has come into being from its greater information basis; (3) a term that views a given style or focus with respect to its greater continuum position (as related to either principle information or historical point of solidification).

Source Shift: (1) the phenomenon of a given continuum (that being "reality or way of doing things") suddenly realigning its path or "surface nature"; (2) the phenomenon of a projection changing its path and taking the attributes of another continuum; (3) having to do with the phenomenon of two or more continuums entering into a "time or cosmic" cycle whereby either one or all of the continuums will attach it or their self to the "particulars" of the other, and proceed from that point.

Source Transfer: (1) the phenomenon of a given continuum—or documented continuum which is more accurate—adopting tenets and/or particulars from another continuum; (2) the point of a continuum change of information and/or particulars; (3) the phenomenon of a continuum adopting or simply taking the attributes (and way of being) of other continuums.

Spectacle Diversion: (1) a concept involving the rotation of a culture's information dynamics and/or forces as a means to have "people involved" but not involved in "something"; (2) rotating "information dynamics" as a phenomenon to give the impression of either "high culture" or "real involvement."

Spiritual Awareness: (1) the act of having some insight as to the reality of spiritualness and/or spiritual dynamics; (2) understanding something about spiritualism, and what is real "for the person" understanding.

Spiritual Dynamics: (1) the reality of possibilities and/or "things" that are related to or brought about from spiritualism; (2) having to do with what can happen through spirituality.

Spiritual Growth: "becoming" as made real through learning about and "being in" a spiritual state or trying to be in a spiritual state—or "becoming" because of one's relationship to spiritualism.

Spiritual Unification: (1) the bringing together of concrete and abstract information and affinity dynamics as a means to "be" in accordance to "greater forces"—or as a means to solidify the proper platform for real "insight"; (2) the bringing together of all religions as a means to establish a composite "all religion."

Style: (1) the appearance of a projection or "way to be"; (2) the reality of a particular interpretation line as that line is actualized into physicality; (3) the manifestation of a particular information dynamic focus into concrete terms; (4) the reality of "ways to be" as it involves actualizing the particulars of a proven information and/or vibrational continuum.

Technological (or Technology) Dynamics: (1) the reality of possibilities—or variables—related to a given functionalism (or related to composite technology); (2) the vibrational and "actual" dynamics related to a given technology (or to composite technology—with respect to its composite position in "all information").

Terminology: (1) the reality of a definition; (2) the reality of how a given language is made real and for what reason; (3) the reality of a given definition as it is made real from its vibrational and/or spiritual base.

Theoretical Science: (1) the reality of ideas as a focus to dynamic methodology for extended functionalism and/or scientific discipline.

Thrust Affinity Alignment: (1) that being, the reality of a given continuum (vibrational and physical universe) way of being; (2) the dynamics of a particular continuum and how it is constructed.

Thrust Continuance: (1) the time advancement or advancing reality of a composite continuum or vibrational and empirical continuum; (2) the reality of a continuum as it advances through time.

Thrust Continuance Dynamics: (1) the dynamic possibilities related to a given continuum as it moves through time—in terms of that continuum's information order and/or vibrational alignment.

Time Continuance Implications: (1) having to do with what results to a given phenomenon in the course of a particular time cycle and/or progression; (2) the possibilities related to a given phenomenon in a given period of time.

Time Lag: (1) the phenomenon of a given particular and/or focus as viewed past the interpretation dynamics of its allotted or designated time period; (2) the reality of a given phenomenon when viewed after the time cycle that made it real; (3) the effects of a given phenomenon and/or focus when viewed and/or perceived past its actual time parameter.

Time Presence: (1) the phenomenon of participation with respect to and awareness of the reality of "actualness" and what that means with regards to events in time and moment awareness; (2) "doing" with respect to (and awareness of) the vibrational realness of the moments in that "doing"—as that "doing" relates to what we call time and what we call motion; (3) the spiritualness of "doing" and also the related vibrational dynamics of "all motion" (or "actual motion").

Trans-Definition: (1) an interpretation that carries over different time periods and/or so-called culture groups; (2) an interpretation that actualizes cosmic significances and as such cannot be simply ignored or stopped because of physical universe particulars or information dynamics.

Transformation: (1) a concept that involves total physical and vibrational universe change; (2) the close of a given or particular physical and vibrational universe cycle and the beginning of the next.

Trans-Information: (1) information that spans physical universe territories, having to do with the laws of this "state" and the experiencing of this "state"; (2) information that is universal and "all real"—regardless of time or culture; (3) information that is not about a given culture and/or focus but instead is cosmically directed because it is "real."

Transition: (1) the change of a given and/or particular state in terms of its surface information and/or focus dynamics—but not its total "beingness"; (2) the change of some aspects of a given physical universe and/or vibrational universe state.

Underlying Philosophical Basis: (1) the reality of a given phenomenon's idea and focus bases—having to do with viewing the factors which support what a given information interpretation means, or is supposed to mean.

Unification: (1) the affinity solidification of humanity as a means to live in accordance to the dictates of dynamic spiritualism; (2) the actual and/or vibrational bringing together of a given phenomenon; (3) a state of composite intentions.

Utilization: (1) the use of a given terminology mix in the information schematics; (2) in other words, the point in the schematics where the given terms should be utilized.

Value System: (1) the ethical and spiritual weight of a particular focus or participation; (2) the reality of a given focus with respect to whether its implementation advances the particulars of spiritual well-being and positive composite well-being, or not; (3) the reality of a given "state of being" and/or phenomenon as evaluated with respect to its assignment and/or desired assignment.

Vibrational Affinity and/or Attitude: (1) the reality of a vibrational state with respect for how a given attitude colors what can or can't be achieved or completed; (2) the reality of given feelings and what those feelings mean in actual terms—as far as whether or not a given objective can be achieved or understood.

Vibrational Attitude: (1) that being, the real attitude before the "words," or before the particular focus that the attitude is directed on; (2) the "way" of a particular vibrational way of being.

Vibrational Dynamics: (1) the possibilities and diverse focuses related to a given vibrational "way of being" (or way of "not" being).

Vibrational Implications: (1) the related possibilities and "things" connected to a given vibrational state and/or position that aren't necessarily connected to the basic focus or reality "stuff" of what that vibration really is—when viewed in its separate state and/or basic reality tone—but can be activated if that vibrational state is utilized or not utilized correctly.

Vibrational Platform: (1) having to do with utilizing the reality of a particular vibrational position as a basis from which to mount either a participation or a focus; (2) the reality of basing an assumption and/or action from a particular vibrational focus—or focuses.

Vibrational Postulation: (1) the same as affinity postulation but not as "deep"; (2) the same as affinity postulation but semantically having less to do with an individual's vibrational and affinity nature and more to do with the act of postulation as this phenomenon happens with respect to other factors (e.g., like the greater culture).

Vibrational Science: (1) that being, the reality of mystical or high spiritual or vibrational (e.g., music or what is called art) discipline with respect to its law position or moving to understand its law position—as made real through multi-information dynamics and high spiritualism; (2) observation and participation in vibrational discipline as that discipline unfolds some aspect of the dynamic functionalism and/or order of the universe (or what we call the universe); (3) vibrationally doing as a means to cosmically grow and love.

Vibrational Tendencies: (1) the reality of possibilities—or attractions—as related to vibrational dynamics; having to do with postulation or "vibrational reception"; (2) the reality of vibrational tendencies as related to the individual (i.e., see individual vibrational tendencies) or environment—or focus dictates.

Vibrational Universe Particulars: (1) the reality of a given focus that is seeded in vibrational terms; (2) the reality of a given focus as it unfolds some aspect of its vibrational universe dynamics.

World Change: (1) the re-alignment of earth in terms of how people live and how people perceive of living—and the reality of postulation and participation.

World Expansion Principle: (1) the reality of change as it affirms the dynamic particulars underlying composite physical universe change.

World Methodology: (1) the reality of a given procedure when viewed in its greater context; (2) a term to underline that a given focus or particular cannot be viewed as the result of one or two countries but, instead, is the property of or related to composite humanity.

World Unification: (1) bringing people and "things" together—harmony with what the "experience of living could mean" in its most positive state.

www.ingramcontent.com/pod-product-compliance
Lightning Source LLC
Chambersburg PA
CBHW071849290426
44110CB00013B/1082